EU Data Privacy Law and Serious Crime

OXFORD DATA PROTECTION AND PRIVACY LAW

Series Editors
Christopher Kuner, Affiliated Professor of Law, University of Copenhagen
Graham Greenleaf AM, Honorary Professor, Macquarie University, Sydney, and Senior Researcher, AustLII

The aim of this series is to publish important and original books on legal issues of data protection and privacy. This includes many different areas of law, including comparative law, EU law, human rights law, international law, privacy on the Internet, and others. Prospective authors are welcome to submit proposals for the series, as outlined on the series website: global.oup.com/academic/content/series/o/oxford-data-protection-and-privacy-law-odppl/

RECENT TITLES IN THE SERIES

Standardizing Personal Data Protection
Irene Kamara

Data Privacy and Competition Law in the Age of Big Data
Unpacking the Interface Through Complexity Science
Samson Y. Esayas

Data Protection Law and Emotion
Damian Clifford

Governing Cross-Border Data Flows
Reconciling EU Data Protection and International Trade Law
Svetlana Yakovleva

Coherence between Data Protection and Competition Law in Digital Markets
Klaudia Majcher

Vulnerability and Data Protection Law
Gianclaudio Malgieri

EU Data Privacy Law and Serious Crime

Data Retention and Policymaking

NORA NI LOIDEAIN
Institute of Advanced Legal Studies, School of Advanced Study, University of London

OXFORD
UNIVERSITY PRESS

OXFORD
UNIVERSITY PRESS

Great Clarendon Street, Oxford, OX2 6DP,
United Kingdom

Oxford University Press is a department of the University of Oxford.
It furthers the University's objective of excellence in research, scholarship,
and education by publishing worldwide. Oxford is a registered trade mark of
Oxford University Press in the UK and in certain other countries.

Published in the United States of America by Oxford University Press
198 Madison Avenue, New York, NY 10016, United States of America.

British Library Cataloguing in Publication Data
Data available

Library of Congress Control Number: 2025938667

ISBN 978–0–19–883716–9

DOI: 10.1093/oso/9780198837169.001.0001

Printed and bound by
CPI Group (UK) Ltd., Croydon, CR0 4YY

MIX
Paper | Supporting
responsible forestry
FSC® C013604

The manufacturer's authorised representative in the EU for product safety is
Oxford University Press España S.A. of El Parque Empresarial San Fernando de Henares,
Avenida de Castilla, 2 – 28830 Madrid (www.oup.es/en or
product.safety@oup.com). OUP España S.A. also acts as importer into Spain
of products made by the manufacturer.

Acknowledgements

This book began with my PhD thesis at the University of Cambridge: a feat that would not have been possible without the invaluable advice and feedback from my supervisor Professor David Feldman. I am also grateful to my viva examiners Professor Kenneth Armstrong and Professor Andrew Ashworth for their helpful advice on transitioning the thesis into a book. In addition, I must thank the reviewers who gave the green light to a book proposal that sought to marry the importance of civil liberties within EU data protection law at a time when such links were being contested by some policymakers before the enactment of the GDPR and the LED. It is hard to overstate just how much this area of law within the EU and ECHR legal systems then changed in the eventful years that followed. There was also a global pandemic which added some unexpected delays to the completion of this updated work and the other small matter of a series of (ongoing) landmark judgments by both the Court of Justice of the EU and the European Court of Human Rights. As a result, what lies before you, dear reader, is a very different, and much stockier, book to the one that was wrapped up just after the Data Retention Directive was struck from legal existence in *Digital Rights Ireland*.

I have been fortunate over the course of this project to have received some invaluable feedback and insightful suggestions on various chapters in this book from friends and colleagues in academia, policymaking, and practice. I am very grateful to Christopher Kuner, Damian Clifford, and Graham Smith who read and provided early feedback on chapters that informed critical revisions to the overall book. Many thanks to all of those who attended my workshop session and provided feedback on my paper at the Privacy Law Scholars Conference 2023 (University of Colorado) and special thanks to Margot Kaminsky, Philip Hacker, and Orla Lynskey for their suggestions. Huge thanks to Professor Martin Schenin and Professor Robert Spano, former President of the ECtHR, and to everyone who reviewed and commented on my paper at the British Academy Workshop, 'Addressing the Digital Realm through the Grammar of Human Rights Law 2023' (University of Oxford). From 2020 to 2024, I was privileged to be part of some excellent conference panels on EU data protection law, European human rights law, and cross-border data transfers. The rich discussion and debate that followed with my fellow panellists always further developed my understanding of the complexities and broader policy implications of this rapidly evolving legal area within and beyond the EU. I must also thank them for their patience and understanding for those times when I may have run ever so slightly over time during my own interventions: Anna Buchta, Theodore Christakis, Christopher Docksey, Laura

Drechsler, Vanessa Franssen, Hielke Hijmans, Herke Kranenborg, Christian Svanberg, and Peter Swire.

There have also been invaluable discussions and debates with friends and colleagues that informed the insights and recommendations in this book. I am grateful to my colleagues at IALS for all their support and particularly to Hester, Ben, and Dalia at the IALS Law Library for their much appreciated help with all those book and journal requests. Special thanks also to former colleagues at the Director of Public Prosecutions Office of Ireland (especially Barry Donoghue and Tricia Harkin), University of Cambridge (David Erdos, Lionel Bently, David Runciman, John Naughton, and Julian Huppert), and King's College London (Perry Keller). I would be remiss if I did not mention the most fantastic community of scholars and practitioners that I have the privilege to know from being part of the CPDP community that gathers every year in Brussels to discuss and debate all things related to data protection law, privacy, and now 'AI': Jef Ausloos, Julia Ballasc, Felix Bieker, Franziska Boehm, Ian Brown, Fanny Coudert, Lorenzo Dalla Corte, Daniel Drewer, Helen Dixon, Lilian Edwards, Jan Ellerman, N. Fatou van den Hoff, Gloria González Fuster, Seda Guerses, Paul de Hert, Joris van Hoboken, Edina Harbinja, Irene Kamara, Eleni Kosta, Ronald Leenes, Gianclaudio Malgieri, TJ McIntyre, Jan-Jaap Oerlemans, Teresa Quintel, Charles Raab, Juraj Sajfert, Bethany Shiner, Lachlan Urquhart, Michael Veale, Sandra Wachter, Gabriela Zanfir-Fortuna, and Frederik Zuiderveen Borgesius. Many thanks must also be given to Kezia Johnson, Peter Daniell, and all the editorial team at Oxford University Press whose support, understanding, and patience made getting this book done a reality.

I am so grateful to all my close friends and family who provided endless encouragement and inspiring pep talks throughout this project and were always there when needed. None of this, of course, would ever have been possible without the love and support of my parents, Tom and Bridie, even if I was the one making the tea during those writing retreats in Connemara. Finally, but most importantly, thanks to James. There are times when finishing a project like this seem impossible but you always knew exactly how to be there and what to say during the highs and lows. And it's not because you always stepped up to take care of dinner, or walk Waffle, or arrange sanity-saving cinema trips, but through it all you still decided to marry Sally Albright.

Nora Ni Loideain
Saffron Walden, United Kingdom

Contents

Abbreviations

ACHPR	African Commission on Human and Peoples' Rights
AFSJ	area of freedom, security, and justice
AI	artificial intelligence
API	advance passenger information
CCDH	Steering Committee for Human Rights
CFI	Court of First Instance
CFR	Charter of Fundamental Rights of the EU
CFSP	Common Foreign and Security Policy
CJEU	Court of Justice of the European Union (Luxembourg Court)
COE	Council of Europe
COE 108	Convention of 28 January 1981 for the Protection of Individuals with regard to Automatic Processing of Personal Data (ETS No 108)
COE 108+	Modernised Convention 108, adopted by Committee of Ministers in 2018
CSAM	child sexual abuse material
CSP	communication service provider
DAA	Draft Accession Agreement
DPA	Data Protection Authority
DPO	Data Protection Officer
EC	European Community
ECHR	European Convention on Human Rights
ECJ	European Court of Justice
ECtHR	European Court of Human Rights (Strasbourg Court)
EDPB	European Data Protection Board, established under Article 68 of the GDPR (EU) 2016/679, replacing the Article 29 Working Party
EDPS	European Data Protection Supervisor
EEC	European Economic Community
EESC	European Economic and Social Committee
EION	European Intelligence Oversight Network
FISA	Foreign Intelligence Surveillance Act (US)
FRA	EU Agency for Fundamental Rights
GC	Grand Chamber
GCHQ	Government Communications Headquarters, UK Intelligence Service
GDPR	General Data Protection Regulation (EU) 2016/679
ICCPR	International Covenant on Civil and Political Rights
ICR	Internet Connection Records
IoT	Internet of things
IP	Internet protocol
IPCO	Investigatory Powers Commissioner's Office (UK)
ISDN	Integrated Services Digital Network

ISP	Internet service provider
JHA	justice and home affairs
LED	Law Enforcement Directive (EU) 2016/680
LIBE	Committee on Civil Liberties, Justice and Home Affairs of the European Parliament
MEP	Member of the European Parliament
ML	machine learning
MLAT	Mutual Legal Assistance Treaty
NGO	non-governmental organization
NSA	National Security Agency, US Intelligence Service
OAS	Organization of American States
OECD	Organisation for Economic Co-operation and Development
OSCE	Organization for Security and Co-operation in Europe
OSINT	open-source intelligence
OTT	over-the-top
PIU	Passenger Information Unit
PNR	passenger name record
RIPA	Regulation of Investigatory Powers Act 2000 (UK)
SIGINT	signals intelligence
SIM	subscriber identification module
SIS	Schengen Information System
SOCMINT	social media intelligence
TEU	Treaty on European Union
TFEU	Treaty on the Functioning of the European Union
UDHR	Universal Declaration of Human Rights
VIS	Visa Information System
WP29	Article 29 Working Party, established under Article 29 of the Data Protection Directive 95/46/EC

1

An Introduction

Article 8 ECHR and Communications Data in the Global Data Privacy Framework

We kill people based on metadata.

General Michael Hayden
Former Director of the United States
National Security Agency (2014)[1]

A. Introduction

The retention and surveillance of digital communications is one of the most dynamic and technically complex areas of privacy and data protection law within EU law and European human rights law. This book examines the data privacy standards of Article 8 of the European Convention on Human Rights (ECHR) within the context of data retention and surveillance by public authorities and the instrumental role Article 8 ECHR has played in shaping EU data retention law and policymaking. In particular, the book focuses on the evolving dialogue between the EU and ECHR legal systems in matters of data privacy, serious crime, and national security and offers a complete picture of the EU's approach to Article 8 ECHR regarding EU data retention law, including the dialogue between the Court of Justice of the EU (CJEU) and the European Court of Human Rights (ECtHR).[2] This doctrinal and comparative analysis examines the influence of the right to respect for private life on data retention within EU law, with a particular focus on the use

[1] Michael Hayden, 'The price of privacy: Re-evaluating the NSA' (John Hopkins Foreign Affairs Symposium, 2014) <youtube.com/watch?v=kV2HDM86XgI>. Judge Louis-Edmond Pettiti prophetically observed the power of modern data processing based on artificial intelligence (AI)-based systems and profiling for surveillance purposes decades earlier: 'The amateurish tapping effected by police officers … now exists only as a memory of pre-war novels … computer processing make it possible for interceptions to be multiplied a hundredfold and … Through use of the "mosaic" technique, a complete picture can be assembled of the life-style of even the "model" citizen.' See *Malone v United Kingdom* [1984] ECHR 10 (concurring opinion). All URLs for this chapter were last accessed on 22 April 2024.

[2] Before 2009, the CJEU was known as the European Court of Justice (ECJ). The ECJ was formally renamed the Court of Justice under the Lisbon Treaty. Under Art 19(1) of the Treaty on European Union (TEU), the CJEU is also the collective term for the three separate courts of the EU—the upper tier of the Court of Justice and lower tier of the General Court (formerly the Court of First Instance) and the Civil Service Tribunal. For ease of reference and consistency, this book refers to the Luxembourg Court throughout as the CJEU.

EU Data Privacy Law and Serious Crime. Nora Ni Loideain, Oxford University Press. © Nora Ni Loideain 2025.
DOI: 10.1093/oso/9780198837169.003.0001

of communications data and passenger travel for the purpose of countering serious crime.

Secondly, this analysis casts a broader spotlight on the real and actual extent of the weight being given to the 'mainstreaming' of fundamental rights within the EU policymaking process, providing a more complete picture of the role and impact of human rights on this specific area of law and policymaking.[3] The analysis includes detailed analysis of the European Commission's *ex post* evaluations of related EU laws: the Data Retention Directive 2006/24/EC, the Advance Passenger Information Directive 2004/82/EC, and the Passenger Name Record Directive (EU) 2016/681. Thirdly, the book critically examines the diverging approaches, standards, and impact of the tensions and dialogue between the EU and ECHR legal systems within the surveillance and data retention case law of both courts for the right to private life and EU data protection law. This analysis also highlights standards from these leading landmark judgments on Article 8 ECHR and Articles 7 and 8 of the EU Charter of Fundamental Rights relevant to data-driven measures for countering serious crime in existing and future EU legislation, including the EU AI Act and the Advance Passenger Information (API) Regulations. Recommendations are provided in the relevant chapters on how some of the complex issues identified within the ECHR and EU legal orders which threaten the mainstreaming and protection of the right to private life could be addressed.

Chapter 1 begins with setting the legal and technological scene and explaining and providing an in-depth analysis of the evolving concept of 'communications data', with a special focus on data retention measures for countering serious crime and the increasingly significant role of the private sector in providing public authorities access to this information. The discussion explores how and why the significance of communications data has become such an essential part of the investigatory and intelligence toolkit. This is followed by an examination of the importance of the right to private life, as enshrined in Article 8 ECHR, within this area of law and policymaking and the machinery of protection underpinning Article 8 ECHR and its enforcement. The relationship between Article 8 ECHR with related data privacy regimes concerning data processing for law enforcement purposes within the legal systems of the EU and Council of Europe and other relevant international frameworks is then explored. In conclusion, an overview is provided of the topics analysed in later chapters.

[3] European Commission, 'Strategy to strengthen the application of the Charter of Fundamental Rights in the EU', COM(2020) 711 final, 15–16; Council of the EU, 'EU Action Plan on Human Rights and Democracy 2020–2024', 18 November 2020, <https://consilium.europa.eu/media/46838/st12848-en20.pdf>. Mainstreaming is essentially an attempt by policymakers to ensure that the 'rights review' of law happens across the cycle of a legislative framework. By ensuring this scrutiny occurs across the law's drafting, implementation, evaluation, it is not then solely a matter for the courts to review. See Chapter 6.

B. Data Privacy and Communications Data

1. What is communications data?

The term 'communications data' used throughout this book refers to the information processed, and generated, when a communication is transmitted, namely all data except for the content. It is an evolving concept without international consensus and is defined differently in the laws of various jurisdictions that cover different types of information related to the making/receiving of a communication.[4] Adding to this complexity, the concept of communications data is also referred to differently, and sometimes interchangeably, in many legal instruments in Europe and worldwide. It is often referred to as 'metadata', 'traffic data', 'location data', 'subscriber data', and 'call associated data'.[5] Some consistency and clarity was achieved within the EU when the Data Retention Directive 2006/24/EC was adopted and communications data became a term used more consistently by courts, policymakers,[6] and academics.[7] Before its invalidation by the CJEU in 2014, the scope of retention provided for by Directive 2006/24/EC concerned traffic data, location data, and 'related data necessary to identify the subscriber or user'.[8]

EU law had nevertheless already provided a broad definition for 'traffic data' under the e-Privacy Directive 2002/58. This states that 'any data processed for the purpose of the conveyance of a communication on an electronic communications

[4] Jason M Young, 'Surfing While Muslim: Privacy, Freedom of Expression and the Unintended Consequences of Cybercrime Legislation' (2004) 7 Yale Journal of Law and Technology 346, 372–73; Nora Ni Loideain, 'Surveillance of Communications Data and Article 8 ECHR' in Serge Gutwirth, Ronald Leenes, and Paul de Hert (eds), *Reloading Data Protection* (Springer 2014) 185; Darragh Murray and Pete Fussey, 'Bulk Surveillance in the Digital Age' (2019) 52 Israel Law Review 31, 34.

[5] See Council of the EU, 'Availability of data and issues related to data retention—elements relevant in the context of e-Privacy', WK 11127/2017, 10 October 2017.

[6] Regulation of Investigatory Powers (Communications Data) Order 2003, SI 2003/3127 (UK); Communication (Retention of Data) Act 2010 (Ireland); European Commission, 'Evaluation of the Directive of the European Parliament and of the Council on the retention of data processed in connection with the provision of public electronic communication services and amending Directive 2002/58/EC', COM(2011) 225 final, 4 April 2011; UN Human Rights Council, 'Report of the Special Rapporteur on the promotion and protection of the right to freedom of opinion and expression', A/HRC/23/40, 17 April 2013; Joined Cases C-203/15 and C-698/15 *Tele2 and Watson*, judgment of 21 December 2016 (ECLI:EU:C:2016:970) (GC); *Big Brother Watch v United Kingdom* [2018] ECHR 722; *Wieder and Guarneiri v United Kingdom* [2023] ECHR 668.

[7] Ian Brown and Dorff Korff, 'Terrorism and the Proportionality of Internet Surveillance' (2009) 6 European Journal of Criminology 119, 124; Marie-Helen Maras, 'The Economic Costs and Consequences of Mass Communications Data Retention?' [2012] European Journal of Law and Economics 447; Eleni Kosta, 'The Retention of Communications Data in Europe and the UK' in Lilian Edwards (ed), *Law, Policy and the Internet* (2nd edn, Hart 2018); Omer Tene, 'Systematic Government Access to Private-Sector Data in Israel' in Fred H Cate and James X Dempsey (eds), *Bulk Collection: Systematic Government Access to Private-Sector Data* (OUP 2017) 100–03.

[8] European Parliament and Council Directive 2006/24/EC of 15 March 2006 on the retention of data generated or processed in connection with the provision of publicly available electronic communications services or of public communications networks and amending Directive 2002/58/EC [2006] OJ L105/54, Arts 2(a) and 5 (Data Retention Directive). See further Chapters 5 to 8.

network or for the billing thereof'.[9] This wide scope encompasses many types of data about a communication, including the subscriber/user, how it was accessed (phone network or Internet), which service provider was involved, location data for billing purposes, and the SIM (subscriber identification module) card number used on a particular mobile phone that identifies the SIM card owner. Compared to accessing the content of a communication, the CJEU, ECtHR, and long-established international legal frameworks treat the information revealed from access to communications data as a less intrusive interference with the right to privacy, particularly subscriber data,[10] arguing that the latter should not be subject to the same level of legal safeguards that apply to the retention and use of other communications data for countering serious crime.[11]

Communications data has also been framed in more simplified terms under EU law as data that will not reveal the 'content' of a communication.[12] As discussed further later, however, changes in modern technology have drastically changed the amount of private life information that may now be revealed from access to communications data. There are now far greater volumes of communications data concerning an individual relative to content data. For every piece of content data, such as the content of an email, there are multiple pieces of associated communications data, including the sender and recipient(s), time, date, location of transmission, and email priority status.[13] Communications data is also generated even if no content is ultimately communicated, such as mobile networks which log the cell location to which a mobile phone is connected even if no call is made or received.[14] Thus, as many scholars and practitioners point out, having access to even basic communications data may often reveal the same or considerably more than the content.[15]

[9] European Parliament and Council Directive 2002/58/EC of 12 July 2002 concerning the processing of personal data and the protection of privacy in the electronic communications sector [2002] OJ L201/37, amended by Art 2 of Directive 2009/136/EC (e-Privacy Directive 2002/58/EC), Arts 2 and 6.

[10] Ian Walden, 'Accessing Data in the Cloud' in Christopher Millard (ed), *Cloud Computing Law* (OUP 2021) 441–76.

[11] Council of the EU, 'Council Conclusions on improving retention of data for the purpose of fighting crime effectively', 7833/19, 27 March 2019; *Big Brother Watch v United Kingdom* [2021] ECHR 439 [302] (GC); Joined Cases C-793/19 and C-794/19 *SpaceNet AG and Telekom Deutschland GmbH*, judgment of 20 September 2022 (ECLI:EU:C:2022:702) [32].

[12] Data Retention Directive 2006/24/EC, Art 5(2); Council of the EU (n 5).

[13] Royal United Services Institute, *A Democratic Licence to Operate* (RUSI 2015) 18.

[14] ibid.

[15] Alberto Escudero-Pascale and Gus Hosein, 'Questioning Lawful Access to Traffic Data' (2004) 47 Communications of the ACM 77, 78; Marie-Pierre Granger and Kristina Irion, 'The Court of Justice and the Data Retention Directive in *Digital Rights Ireland*' (2014) 39 European Law Review 835, 847; EU Agency for Fundamental Rights (FRA), *Surveillance by Intelligence Services* (FRA 2015) 56; Jonathan Mayer, Patrick Mutchler, and John C Mitchell, 'Evaluating the Privacy Properties of Telephone Metadata' (2016) 113 PNAS 5536; Xavier Tracol, 'Ministerio Fiscal: Access of Public Authorities to Personal Data Retained by Providers of Electronic Communications Services' (2019) 5 European Data Protection Law Review 127, 133; Maja Brkan, 'The Essence of the Fundamental Rights to Privacy and Data Protection' (2019) 20 German Law Journal 864, 872.

Even if this problematic premise of content interception being the most intrusive of all monitoring were to be accepted, communications data from just one communication still reveals the context of a communication. Contrast this with the content of a single message from a busy friend or colleague which may often just contain a one-word response. This content effectively reveals nothing without knowing more about the overall conversation. Criminal gangs or terrorists may also use such shorthand or even coded language, or actions in an online game, to communicate which may render access to the content of a communication effectively moot.[16] The communications data concerning one such single interaction by these individuals may reveal far more detailed and thus valuable information for public authorities. This may include who was contacting whom; how many parties were involved; the date, time, and location of everyone involved; what communication devices were used; and the duration of the conversation.

Indeed, the European Commission acknowledged the value of communications data in playing a potentially critical role in the tracing and combating of the Covid-19 pandemic.[17] Acquiring communications data, in other words, will always have value for law enforcement and intelligence agencies, whereas content data by itself may reveal little or nothing about a communication or individual. Relatedly, the UK's oversight body for bulk surveillance has reported that access to communications data is 'the most widely used investigated power' by police and intelligence agencies.[18]

2. Communications data and content: an increasingly questionable distinction

A key issue that policymakers in Europe and worldwide continue to grapple with is the increasingly blurred line between what constitutes 'content' and communications data. UK law, for instance, effectively treats a website address up to the first slash as only communications data, thereby falling within the scope of 'Internet Connection Records' and not content.[19] However, a record over six months of these specific web addresses where an individual goes when browsing online may

[16] David Anderson, *A Question of Trust* (HM Stationery Office 2015) 54.

[17] European Commission, 'Commission Recommendation on a Common Union Toolbox for the Use of Technology and Data to Combat and Exit from the COVID-19 Crisis', COM(2020) 2296 final.

[18] 'Annual Report of the Investigatory Powers Commissioner 2021' (2023) [2.11].

[19] Investigatory Powers Act 2016, s 62(7); Anderson Report (n 16) [6.6]; UK Home Office, *Code of Practice: Communications Data* (31 August 2021) [2.75]; Graham Smith, *Internet Law and Regulation* (Sweet & Maxwell 2019) 897. Communications data requests are mainly directed to telecommunications providers or Internet Service Providers. This book collectively refers to both as 'Communication Service Providers' (CSPs). The updated Code of Practice now states that what constitutes Internet Connection Records (ICR) data depends on the context of the 'service' accessed and the relevant CSP. On proposed UK law reform in this area, see David Anderson, *Independent Review of the Investigatory Powers Act 2016* (Home Office June 2023).

reveal a considerable amount about personal concerns, political opinions, and interests. Thus, having access to what is effectively an individual's online stream of consciousness would show, for instance, what news source or any health-related, financial, religious, or political websites a person reads frequently or apps that they use daily. These could include 'www.cancerresearchuk.org' or 'www.theguardian.com'. There are also many datasets which can be used directly or indirectly to identify the services, or sites, accessed by an individual.[20]

One approach that could contribute to providing some much-needed legal clarity to this complex distinction would be to treat communications data and content equally. This would require providing that the retention and use of both types of information be subject to the same level of legal rules and safeguards.[21] This reform would serve three important aims. First, it would abandon the now outdated fallacy that access to communications data will always reveal less about an individual's (or a group of individuals') privacy than access to content data.[22] Secondly, it would address the questionable current hierarchy of often overlapping and unclear definitions being applied to different types of communications data, such as Internet Connection Records. Thirdly, this reform would deal with the reality that the level of intrusiveness to private life and data protection posed by the retention, and access to, of communications data or content by public authorities will always be context-dependent. These circumstances vary and may include the nature of the relevant criminal investigation or national security issue, the public authorities involved, the means and scope of the retention (targeted or bulk), types of analysis (use of AI-based or other powerful algorithmic systems), and the use/purpose of the collected information.

Both the CJEU and the ECtHR have held that certain subscriber data (most notably an individual's mobile phone number) reveal little about an individual's private life and thus are less privacy-intrusive types of communications data.[23] This is based on the reasoning that acquiring this specific type of communications data will not allow public authorities to draw 'precise conclusions' about an individual's private life.[24] A body or individual authorizing retention and/or giving access to this data should, however, take into account the specific aim, scale, and context for acquiring that data. This assessment should include, for instance, whether the relevant legal framework permits various types of communications data once obtained to then be subject to automated analysis and cross-referenced with other databases. This is often done by public authorities to speed up investigations or is

[20] Smith (n 19) 897.

[21] A fundamental rights-based approach that the CJEU (sitting as the Grand Chamber) seems to endorse in Case C-673/17 *Planet49 GmbH*, judgment of 1 October 2019 (ECLI:EU:C:2019:801) [70].

[22] As has arisen in key case law of the ECtHR. See Chapter 3.

[23] *Breyer v Germany* [2020] ECHR 95; Joined Cases C-511/18, C-512/18 and C-520/8, *La Quadrature du Net and Others*, judgment of 6 October 2020 (ECLI:EU:C:2020:791). See further Chapters 3 and 5.

[24] Case C-207/16 *Ministerio Fiscal*, judgment of 2 October 2018 (ECLI:EU:C:2018:788) [60].

used for urgent investigations, such as kidnapping or a terrorist threat.[25] Indeed, the ECtHR has highlighted that subscriber data may be used as a 'key to (sensitive) telecommunications data' enabling a person to be linked to a phone number or a phone number to be connected to a person.[26]

3. Communications data surveillance in a data-driven society

In the last century, the power to retain and access more precise and sensitive personal information from communications data expanded dramatically. This was a direct result of the shift from analogue processing to the digitization of data which began in the 1960s, a seismic technological change that has triggered ongoing privacy concerns.[27] As US privacy law scholar Alan Westin predicted decades ago about the significant implications for privacy posed by the digital age, '[a]lmost inevitably, transferring information from a manual file to a computer triggers a threat to civil liberties, to privacy ... because access is so simple'.[28] Three further major technical developments have expanded the amount of private data that may be revealed by retaining and accessing communications data: (1) the mobility of communication devices; (2) the ubiquitous use of Internet services and the pervasive collection and analysis of information; and (3) the convergence of the two previous developments through the creation of 'Internet-enabled' (or 'smart') mobile devices.[29] Thus, the amount of information that can be derived from a landline telephone is much more limited when compared to a mobile phone. For instance, location data revealed by a landline phone is clearly much more limited when compared to a mobile phone, given that the former is fixed to the same location, such as the caller's residence. Communications data from mobile phones today reveal unprecedented amounts about an individual's private life.

It is also becoming, as highlighted by the ECtHR, a far more important source of evidence for law enforcement given that encryption methods for digital communications have become more mainstream, thereby making content difficult to access.[30] The contextual information provided by access to communications data

[25] David Lyon, 'Surveillance, Snowden, and Big Data' (2014) 1 Big Data And Society 1, 6–7; Iain Cameron, 'Balancing Data Protection and Law Enforcement Needs' (2017) 54 Common Market Law Review 1467, 1469.

[26] Dissenting Opinion of Judge Ranzoni in *Breyer* (n 23). See further Chapter 3.

[27] Alan Westin, *Privacy and Freedom* (Atheneum 1967) 3; Daniel J Solove, *Understanding Privacy* (HUP 2008) 4; Lee A Bygrave, *Data Privacy Law* (OUP 2014) 9–10.

[28] Lacey Fosburgh, '23 to Study Computer "Threat"' *New York Times* (12 March 1970).

[29] Stephen Wicker, *Cellular Convergence and the Death of Privacy* (OUP 2013) 8.

[30] *Big Brother Watch* (n 6) [353]; *Big Brother Watch* (n 11) [342]. Future technologies, like quantum computing, could be used to counter encryption techniques (once such quantum computers are of a size and capacity to do so). See Chris Jay Hoofnagle and Simon L Garfinkel, *Law and Policy for the Quantum Age* (CUP 2022); Ot van Daalen, 'The Right to Encryption' (2023) 49 Computer Law & Security Review. On the importance of strong encryption for the exercise of the rights to private life and data protection, see European Data Protection Board and European Data Protection Supervisor, Joint

is particularly useful for constructing evidence trails and verifying the alibis of suspects.[31] The CJEU has relatedly held that law enforcement authorities in the EU should be allowed to access SIM card personal data (number, name, address of SIM card owner) from the private sector in order to reveal the users of a stolen mobile phone and thereby identify the perpetrators of the theft.[32] Additionally, location data from a perpetrator's use of their mobile phone can prove instrumental in identifying false alibis in more serious criminal cases. For instance, a murder conviction in a high-profile case in Ireland relied heavily on communications data to track and identify the mobile phones bought by the perpetrator for himself and his victim. The same phone was used by the perpetrator in his workplace and for arranging the location of the murder.[33]

Communications data today may therefore reveal the 'who' (parties involved), the 'when', the 'how long and how often' (time, duration, and frequency), the 'what' (type of communication—phone call, message, email), the 'how' (the communication device used—smartphone), and the 'where' (location of devices used) of every communication. Moreover, as recognized by both the ECtHR and the CJEU, the long-term retention, aggregation, and analysis of modern communications data can provide 'very precise conclusions' to be drawn from an individual's private life, including their daily movements, activities, behaviour, and relationships.[34] Furthermore, where bulk acquisition of communications data is involved,[35] the 'degree of intrusion is magnified [and] ... could be capable of painting an intimate picture of a person through the mapping of social networks, location tracking, Internet browsing tracking, mapping of communication patterns, and insight into who a person interacted with'.[36] The rate at which devices which are *not* connected to the Internet are now utilized (eg landline telephones) has also declined to such an extent that monitoring the communications data generated by their use is increasingly of little benefit for public authorities.

Opinion 4/2022 on the Proposal for a Regulation of the European Parliament and of the Council laying down rules to prevent and combat child sexual abuse (EDPB & EDPS, 28 July 2022) [96]–[102].

[31] European Commission (n 6) 23.

[32] *Ministerio Fiscal* (n 24).

[33] *Dwyer v Commissioner of An Garda Síochána* [2020] IESC 4. This case resulted from a legal challenge concerning the lack of a domestic legal basis for use of the communications data following the CJEU ruling in Joined Cases C-293/12 and C-594/12 *Digital Rights Ireland Ltd and Seitlinger*, judgment of 8 April 2014 (ECLI:EU:C:2014:238). This landmark judgment resulted in the striking down of Directive 2006/24/EC due to its incompatibility with the EU Charter of Fundamental Rights. The Irish Supreme Court will review the case again in 2024 as part of a separate appeal concerning the murder conviction.

[34] See Chapters 3 to 5.

[35] On bulk surveillance in the EU and its legal oversight, see EU FRA, *Surveillance by Intelligence Services*, Vol II (FRA 2017); FRA, *Surveillance by Intelligence Services* (updated report, 2023).

[36] *Big Brother Watch* (n 6) [356]. This major judgment concerned legal challenges to various bulk surveillance programmes following the Snowden revelations and was referred to the Grand Chamber in 2019. On both judgments, see Chapters 2 and 3.

In the era of AI digital assistants, smart cities, cars, and homes, the use of Internet-enabled communication devices, and the communications data that they generate, has become ubiquitous. These are all particularly significant developments that enhance and expand the monitoring capacity already provided through daily use of online apps that readily identify and use location in real time. Such location data is being collected by data brokers and commercial firms (not just communication service providers (CSPs)) and subsequently sold to governments which then use that data for immigration and border control enforcement without first obtaining a court order.[37] Thus, having access to mobile phone location data is essentially 'akin to virtual tracking' of an individual.[38] Moreover, access to this location data alone can identify an individual due to the vast amounts of data our phone use generates daily and what this reveals about our regular routines.[39] It also dispenses with the need for public authorities to deploy more onerous surveillance methods, such as installing transmitters/GPS receivers on a suspect's vehicle.[40]

4. Data retention and 'data power'

The vast scope of information concerning an individual's private life that can now be revealed through the daily surveillance of communications and other Internet-based devices has advanced in tandem with dramatic technological, social, and economic developments. For instance, the 'Internet of Things' (IoT) is already operating within many households and offices due to several factors. These include the increasingly low costs involved in computing power, the ease of access to cheap cloud storage, existing Internet connectivity, and the interest of governments and industry in extracting information from the masses of personal data (and other data) ubiquitously collected from all smart systems and devices. One such IoT device is the AI-operated virtual personal assistant. These collect communications data, content, and even emotion data from live web browsing searchers made by its users on devices like smart televisions and smartphones, such as Amazon's 'Alexa' and Apple's 'Siri'.[41] From 8.4 billion IoT devices worldwide in 2017 to a predicted roll-out of 41 billion by 2025, the IoT is very much an established and rapidly expanding feature of many people's daily lives.[42] This includes

[37] Editorial, 'The Government Uses "Near Perfect Surveillance" Data on Americans' *New York Times* (7 February 2020).

[38] Lorna Woods, 'Automated Number Plate Recognition: Data Retention and the Protection of Privacy in Public Places' (2017) 2 Journal of Information Rights, Policy and Practice 1, 10.

[39] Luca Rossi, James Walker, and Mirco Musolesi, 'Spatio-Temporal Techniques for User Identification by Means of GPS Mobility Data' (2015) 4 EPJ Data Science.

[40] See *Uzun v Germany* (2012) 54 EHRR 121.

[41] Nora Ni Loideain and Rachel Adams, 'From Alexa to Siri and the GDPR' (2020) 36 Computer Law & Security Review. See generally Damian Clifford, *Data Protection Law and Emotion* (OUP 2024).

[42] European Commission, 'The next generation of Internet of Things' <https://digital-strategy.ec.europa.eu/en/policies/next-generation-internet-things>.

regular use of Internet-enabled 'wearables' that enhance the traditional functions of accessories: from smartwatches to track and log fitness, to sharing photos and videos on social media using sunglasses equipped with AI-powered cameras and microphones.[43]

Devices for the 'quantified self' are often worn constantly in order for individuals to record, and then measure, their daily activities, such as sleep trackers.[44] Insurance companies have responded to the increasing shift by the public towards 'life-logging' their lifestyles and exercise habits by developing policies that incentivize customers to be tracked by monitoring the amount of exercise they undertake daily in return for lower premiums.[45] Unsurprisingly, the constant collection and generation of data, now via items with unseen recording capacity (smart sunglasses), and the growing reach of governments and industry for monitoring individuals in this ever-connected environment, has sparked major debates on the legal and ethical implications for modern democratic societies. The constant trail of communications data left behind from the ceaseless use of so-called smart devices, and the increasing smart environments of homes, offices, cars, and cities, facilitates the collection of unprecedented amounts of data and presents unique privacy challenges.[46]

With the added ease of collecting, retaining, using, and sharing this data, a level of monitoring of an individual's every communication and movement is possible like never before. The risk of an individual's personal data being processed unlawfully, or without their consent, in this increasingly data-driven world of AI and other emerging technologies has also increased dramatically.[47] Despite location services being switched off, for instance, a person's smartphone can still be found through use of cell towers, wireless networks, and even satellite data.[48] Malte Spitz, a German Green Party politician, demonstrated the scope of this monitoring in a

[43] Nora Ni Loideain, 'A Port in the Data-Sharing Storm: The GDPR and the Internet of Things' (2019) 4 Journal of Cyber Policy 178, 180; Brian X Chen, 'How Meta's New Face Camera Heralds a New Age of Surveillance' *New York Times* (13 December 2023).

[44] Information Commissioner's Office, *Big Data, AI, Machine Learning and Data Protection* (ICO 2017) 66.

[45] European Network and Information Security Agency, *Risks and Benefits of Emerging Lifelogging Applications* (ENISA 2011). See eg Vitality Insurance: <https://vitality.co.uk/support/vitality-programme/how-points-work/>.

[46] See generally Kevin Werbach (ed), *After the Digital Tornado* (CUP 2020); Jiahong Chen and others, 'Who is Responsible for Data Processing in Smart Homes?' (2020) 10 International Data Privacy Law 279; Kashmir Hill, 'Your car is tracking you. Abusive Partners May Be, Too' *New York Times* (31 December 2023); Nellies Bowles, 'Thermostats, Locks and Lights: Digital Tools of Domestic Abuse' *New York Times* (23 June 2018).

[47] The term 'processing' used throughout this book follows the broad definition provided under EU data protection law. This encompasses the many actions that personal data may be subject to, including collection, retention, access, analysis, sharing, deletion. See Regulation (EU) 2016/679 of the European Parliament and of the Council of 27 April 2016 on the protection of natural persons with regard to the processing of personal data and on the free movement of such data and repealing Directive 95/46/EC (General Data Protection Regulation, GDPR) [2016] OJ L119/1, Art 4(2).

[48] Tommy Cooke and others, 'Satellite Data: The other type of smartphone data you may not know about' *The Conversation* (20 February 2023).

request to his mobile phone provider over a decade ago. His access request sought a record of the communications data collected and retained from the use of his mobile phone. Over the course of six months, the communications data tracked his location and mobile phone usage more than 35,000 times. This built a rich and clear account of his movements and his communications, thus highlighting the importance of the right to access under EU data protection law.[49] Consequently, these developments have led commentators to note that now is the era of omnipresent data mining, 'dataveillance', 'surveillance capitalism', and even a 'Golden Age of Surveillance'—where the personal data of every individual is systematically stored and monitored in vast databases by a host of public and private sector bodies.[50]

Data privacy concerns have also been raised about the expanding reach of the State into the private sector (and vice versa). These range from the large-scale retention and transfer of personal data in response to law enforcement and national security requests, data localization initiatives, and more systematically through private cloud storage, and 'public private partnerships' projects like smart cities.[51] Both 'Big Data' and dataveillance directly contribute to the creation of rich digital dossiers of private information concerning an individual's past and future conduct which could be misused by bad actors within the public or private sectors. These dossiers are the result of several privacy harms posed by 'aggregation', one of the key advances in information processing techniques during the twentieth century. It could be argued that aggregation is merely information gathering about a person. Its overall effect, however, contributes to a growing power imbalance between the individual, the State, and industry; particularly when the combining of seemingly innocuous pieces of information reveal to the State and industry 'new facts' about an individual that could not be expected to be revealed when the data was first collected in isolation from the individual.[52]

Further concerns have been raised about the increasing imbalance of 'data power' between the individual and the private sector especially in light of major mergers and acquisitions by global data-driven CSPs, such as Alphabet and Meta, the parent companies of Google and Facebook.[53] Power asymmetries between the

[49] ibid; Malte Spitz, 'Your Phone Company is Watching You' TED Talk Global (Edinburgh, June 2012).

[50] Roger A Clarke, 'Information and Technology and Dataveillance' (1988) 31 Communications of the ACM 498, 499; Solove (n 27); Shoshana Zuboff, *Surveillance Capitalism* (Profile Books 2019); Carissa Véliz, *Privacy is Power* (Penguin 2020).

[51] See Nora Ni Loideain, 'Cape Town as a Smart and Safe City' (2017) 4 International Data Privacy Law 314; Nadezhda Purtova, 'Between the GDPR and the Police Directive' (2018) 8 International Data Privacy Law 52; Orla Lynskey, 'Criminal Justice Profiling and EU Data Protection Law' (2019) 15 International Journal of Law in Context 162; Sarah Brayne, *Predict and Surveil* (OUP 2020); Litska Strikwerda, 'Predictive Policing' (2020) 94 The Police Journal 259; Helen Warrell and Nic Fildes, 'Amazon strikes deal with UK spy agencies to host top secret material' *Financial Times* (25 October 2021); Stanisław Tosza, 'Internet Service Providers as Law Enforcers and Adjudicators' (2021) 43 Computer Law & Security Review; Anu Bradford, *Digital Empires* (OUP 2023); FRA (2023) (n 35) 7.

[52] Solove (n 27) 118.

[53] See generally Orla Lynskey, 'Grappling with "Data Power"' (2019) 20 Theoretical Inquiries in Law 189; Uta Kohl and Jacob Eisler (eds), *Data-Driven Personalisation in Markets, Politics and the Law*

individual, industry, and the State are being exacerbated by the retention of and access to vast quantities of data and powerful 'profiling' techniques used to identify a person's personal and professional relationships, their racial or ethnic origin, political opinions, religious or philosophical beliefs, trade union membership, or data concerning health or sex life.[54] If illegally accessed by third parties through lax data security or hacks, this communications data could also be used to cause additional harms, including unlawful surveillance, fraud, identity theft, corporate espionage, and blackmail.[55] Other significant potential harms posed by the profiling of this data include the creation, or reinforcement, of unequal treatment of the most vulnerable groups in society.[56] Most profiling today is done using increasingly sophisticated and complex types of AI and modelling techniques, particularly 'machine learning' (ML). This involves a 'set of techniques and tools that allow computers to think by creating mathematical algorithms based on accumulated data' which is broadly separated into two types of learning, supervised and unsupervised.[57] Whichever type is used, it is the ability of the algorithms to change their results based on their 'learned' experience that gives ML its power.[58]

Scholars and regulators have consistently raised concerns about the considerable and often insidious threats of unfair bias and manipulation that may arise from the use of certain ML systems.[59] Major algorithmic harms may also arise from

(CUP 2021). Of course, concerns on the imbalances of data power between individuals and the private and public sectors are far from novel. See eg Westin (n 27); Kerstin Anér, *Datamakt* (Gummesson 1975).

[54] GDPR, Art 4(4) broadly defines profiling as: 'any form of automated processing of personal data consisting of the use of personal data to evaluate certain personal aspects relating to a natural person, in particular to analyse or predict aspects concerning that natural person's performance at work, economic situation, health, personal preferences, interests, reliability, behaviour, location or movements'.

[55] European Data Protection Supervisor (EDPS), 'Opinion 4/2020 on the European Commission's White Paper on Artificial Intelligence', 21–22. On profiling concerns, see Mirelle Hildebrandt and Serge Gutwirth (eds), *Profiling the EU Citizen* (Springer 2008); Karen Yeung, 'Five Fears About Mass Predictive Personalization in an Age of Surveillance Capitalism' (2018) 8 International Data Privacy Law 258; Oscar H Gandy, *The Panopticon Sort* (2nd edn, OUP 2021).

[56] ibid.

[57] ICO (n 44) 7–8.

[58] ibid.

[59] Literature on this topic is extensive. See eg Solon Barocas and Andrew D Selbst, 'Big Data's Disparate Impact' (2014) 104 California Law Review 671; Frank Pasquale and Danielle Keats Citron, 'Promoting Innovation While Preventing Discrimination: Policy Goals for the Scored Society' (2014) 89 Washington Law Review 1413; EDPS, 'Opinion 7/2015: Meeting the challenges of big data'; Sandra Wachter, Brent Mittelstadt, and Luciano Floridi, 'Why a Right to Explanation of Automated Decision-Making Does Not Exist in the GDPR' (2017) 7 International Data Privacy Law 76; Andrew Selbst and Julia Powles, 'Meaningful Information and the Right to Explanation' (2017) 7 International Data Privacy Law 233; Lilian Edwards and Michael Veale, 'Slave to the Algorithm? Why a Right to an Explanation is Probably Not the Remedy You Are Looking For' (2017) 16 Duke Law & Technology Review 18; Kate Crawford, *Atlas of AI* (Yale UP 2021); Jeremias Adams-Prassl, Reuben Binns, and Aislinn Kelly-Lyth, 'Directly Discriminatory Algorithms' (2023) 86 Modern Law Review 144; Nora Ni Loideain, 'Lawfulness and Police Use of Facial Recognition in the UK' in Rita Matulionyte and Monika Zalnieriute (eds), *Facial Recognition in the Modern State* (CUP 2024).

how such tools classify or stigmatize groups.[60] Risks of indirect discrimination are particularly problematic here with respect to those affected being unaware of the harms caused, and thus unable to legally challenge them and seek redress.[61] As these decisions are often based on information retained and collected from them obliquely, groups are less likely to be aware of their status as victims of categorical profiling.[62] They are consequently less likely to organize as an aggrieved group in order to challenge any unfair or inaccurate targeting unless a problem with a particular system used to profile becomes publicly known.[63] Furthermore, to the extent that an individual (via group profiling or otherwise) is reduced to 'inferences' about their machine-readable behaviour and is targeted based on such inferences, their liberty from unreasonable constraints to construct their identity with dignity may be violated.[64]

Hence, as demonstrated by the Cambridge Analytica scandal in which it was alleged that millions of profiles of Facebook users were illegally collected to 'microtarget' individuals with political messages in order to sway voter behaviour, data-driven profiling also has major implications for other important rights that the protection of privacy enables.[65] This includes freedom of expression, particularly the capability of each and every individual to impart and receive diverse and pluralistic information that is essential to a functioning democracy.[66] These wider societal risks grow alongside the increasing use of data-driven profiling that may also perpetuate such discrimination in data processing unless the risks to 'society as a whole', not just individuals, posed by unfair processing are addressed by the relevant regulatory framework.[67] As discussed later, similar concerns have been expressed regarding predictive policing systems which also rely on the combination of unrelated and massive datasets that may produce aggregated data with existing discriminatory stereotypes.[68]

[60] Edwards and Veale (n 59) 24–25.

[61] On ML systems and EU anti-discrimination law, see Philipp Hacker, 'Teaching Fairness to Artificial Intelligence' (2018) 55 Common Market Law Review 1143; Janneke Gerards and Raphaële Xenidis, *Algorithmic Discrimination in Europe* (Publications Office of the EU 2021).

[62] Biometrics and 'emotion recognition' are increasingly used as sources of data for profiling individuals. See EU FRA, *Bias in Algorithms* (FRA Report 2022); Clifford (n 41).

[63] Lawrence Lessig, *Code and Other Law of Cyberspace* (Basic Books 1999) 153–54; Oscar H Gandy, 'Data Mining and Surveillance Post 9/11' in Kirstie Ball and Frank Webster (eds), *Intensification of Surveillance* (Pluto 2003) 26–41; Edwards and Veale (n 59) 69.

[64] Mirelle Hildebrandt, 'Learning as a Machine' (2017) 4 Journal of Learning Analytics 6 ; Sandra Wachter and Brent Mittelstadt, 'A Right to Reasonable Inferences' (2019) 2 Columbia Business Law Review 494.

[65] Karen Yeung (Rapporteur), *Responsibility and AI*, Council of Europe Study (DGI 2019) 5, 29.

[66] See Susie Alegre, *Freedom to Think: Protecting a Fundamental Human Right in the Digital Age* (Atlantic Books 2022).

[67] EDPS, 'Opinion 4/2020' (n 55) 23.

[68] ibid 9.

5. Communications data: a valuable tool for policing and national security

The increasing datafication of our communications, lifestyles, and environments means that there is an ever-increasing amount of data held by private companies that may subsequently be accessed by public authorities. Thus, the dramatic change from the prevailing use of a fixed household device (a landline phone) to the use of multiple smart mobile devices has significant implications for enhancing the value of communications data for public authorities in the twenty-first century. This data-driven environment facilitates an increasingly rich and targeted digital tracking ecosystem as 'mobile devices are typically personal to an individual, almost always on, and with the user'.[69] Law enforcement authorities now have the capacity to access from the private sector an increasingly rich narrative data of a person's private life generated automatically by their frequent use of mobile phones and other personal smart devices. AI digital assistants and health-tracking wearables, for instance, are now used to track movements and investigate alibis for investigating serious crimes.[70] Concerns surrounding large-scale surveillance programmes, especially systematic access to private sector data concerning the public's communications, travel, and Internet usage, are far from novel but were heightened following the 'Snowden revelations' in 2013.

Edward Snowden is a US. citizen who currently has temporary residence in Russia. A former computer analyst for the CIA, he was subsequently employed as a defence consultant with Booz Allen Hamilton, a private management and technology consulting company contracted by the National Security Agency (NSA), which is the US Intelligence Service. In June 2013, in Hong Kong, Snowden released thousands of US government records collected in his capacity at Booz Allen Hamilton. These revealed details of programmes involving the mass surveillance of communications belonging to individuals within and outside the US to a select group of journalists in the UK and US news media, mainly *The Guardian* and *Washington Post*.[71] Journalists in Europe and worldwide also raised concerns regarding the legality of the US national security authorities sharing personal data obtained from these large-scale monitoring regimes with governments outside the US.[72] Among the many secret surveillance regimes that became public knowledge,

[69] US Federal Trade Commission, *Mobile Privacy Disclosures* (FTC 2013) 2. See generally Gina Neff and Dawn Nafus, *Self-Tracking* (MIT Press 2016).

[70] See Christine Hauser, 'Police Use Fitbit Data to Charge 90-Year-Old Man in Stepdaughter's Killing' *The New York Times* (3 October 2018); Conor Gallagher, 'Privacy fears over possible Garda use of Alexa to collect evidence' *Irish Times* (18 April 2022). These sweeping technological developments also enable the risk of misuse by law enforcement of 'dragnet-style' searches of communications data via Internet and mobile phone usage: see Kashmir Hill, 'Deleting Your Period Tracker Won't Protect You' *New York Times* (22 June 2023).

[71] Glenn Greenwald, *No Place to Hide* (Picador 2014); Ewen MacAskill, '"No regrets", says Edward Snowden, after 10 years in exile' *The Guardian* (8 June 2023).

[72] Article 29 Data Protection Working Party, 'Opinion 04/2014 on surveillance of electronic communications for intelligence and national security purposes' (WP 215).

one particular programme had been in operation for over seven years. The programme, like the Data Retention Directive 2006/24/EC, involved the mass retention of and access to communications from the use of mobile phones for national security and law enforcement purposes. Following a court order issued under the Foreign Intelligence Surveillance Act (FISA) 1978 framework, the Foreign Intelligence Surveillance Court required Verizon, one of the major CSPs in the US, to provide the NSA, on a daily basis, with millions of phone records concerning its US customers, including the communications data of both US and non-US citizens.[73] Although the duration of the FISA order was only for three months, the order had been renewed for seven years. The revelations of this controversial programme and others have prompted ongoing global debate concerning the increasing sophistication and use of bulk surveillance powers and their impacts on an individual's right to privacy.[74]

Despite various legal reforms in the EU, across Europe, and globally since the Snowden revelations and the line of landmark CJEU judgments thereafter, including *Digital Rights Ireland* and *Schrems II*, there is an increased demand by law enforcement and intelligence services for access to communications data stored by the private sector. Note, for instance, efforts at the EU level to address the increasing trade in unregulated spyware technology.[75] For those companies in the private sector whose business models do not involve data processing for law enforcement or national security purposes, they may still be legally required to become a key supplier of the architecture and data that enable State surveillance. Some companies provide annual transparency reports on the access requests they receive from law enforcement authorities. Note that due care should be taken when

[73] 'Verizon forced to hand over telephone data—full court ruling' *The Guardian* (6 June 2013). On the bulk collection of US citizens' phone records and related reform recommendations which contributed to the subsequent enactment of the US Freedom Act in 2015, see the President's Review Group on Intelligence and Communications Technologies, *The NSA Report* (Princeton UP 2014); Privacy & Civil Liberties Oversight Board, 'Report on Telephone Records Program Conducted Under Section 215 of the USA Patriot Act', 24 January 2014.

[74] Christopher Kuner and others, 'PRISM and Privacy: Will This Change Everything?' (2013) 3 International Data Privacy Law 217; Maria Helen Murphy, 'The Pendulum Effect: Comparisons between the Snowden Revelations and the Church Committee' (2014) 23 Information and Communications Technology Law 192; Orin Kerr, 'A Rule of Lenity for National Security Surveillance Law' (2014) 100 Virginia Law Review 1513; Jemima Stratford and Tim Johnston, 'The Snowden "Revelations": Is GCHQ Breaking the Law?' [2014] European Human Rights Law Review 129; MIT and Institute of Law, University of Amsterdam, *Privacy Bridges Report: EU and US Privacy Experts in Search of Privacy Solutions* (Amsterdam UP 2015); Nóra Ni Loideain, 'EU Law and Mass Internet Metadata Surveillance in the Post-Snowden Era' (2015) 3 Media and Communication 53; Peter Squire, 'The USA Freedom Act, the President's Review Group and the Biggest Intelligence Reform in 40 Years' *IAPP* (8 June 2015); Félix Tréguer, 'Intelligence Reform and the Snowden Paradox: The Case of France' (2017) 5 Media and Communication 17; Nora Ni Loideain and others, 'An Unstoppable Force and an Immoveable Object? EU Data Protection Law and National Security' (2018) 8 International Data Privacy Law 1; Agustín Rossi, 'How the Snowden Revelations Saved the EU GDPR' (2018) 53 The International Spectator 95, 104–07; Clifford (n 41) 27–28.

[75] Tamar Kaldani and Zeev Prokopets, *Pegasus Spyware and its Impact of Human Rights* (Council of Europe 2022). On reforms in the EU after Snowden and the Pegasus revelations, see FRA (2023) (n 35).

comparing statistics provided in such reports as the types of data, level of detail, and scope of information provided by each company concerning law enforcement requests can vary hugely.[76] Obligations on the private sector to provide public authorities with data access to their customers' communications and movements may also go beyond such requests. These more demanding obligations from States can take the form of significant measures like 'data localization' that involves mandatory local retention of data within a country's borders and are often claimed to enhance privacy.[77] Measures to regulate or block completely the transborder flow of data, however, may also stem from other government interests such as censorship and political control.[78]

All these technological and political developments have dramatically altered the scope of private information that the processing of communications data can now capture for law enforcement purposes in two fundamental ways. First, the scale and detail of information that can be acquired from the long-term retention (and subsequent correlation) of traffic and location data make the nature of communications data immeasurably more intrusive than access to the content of a single letter, email, or telephone call. Whilst monitoring by the State of an individual's communications is by no means novel, the difference in the threat posed by modern telecommunications technologies is their efficiency and power. Previously, technology was mainly administered by humans and, in terms of monitoring, only what was different was noticed.[79] In complete contrast, especially in the post-Snowden era, digitized data processing today collects and analyses everything and does so using more automated techniques. Thus, the increasing 'ready availability' of data acquired from the private sector for law enforcement purposes and national security interests has inevitably altered how these public authorities now operate surveillance programmes, particularly the scale and reach of such monitoring to see into an individual's private life.[80]

The ease and scale of retained information that can now be accessed by law enforcement authorities, originally stored by companies for commercial purposes, has major implications for the scope of personal data that may now be acquired by the State from the private sector. These developments have made it just as feasible to issue a warrant for data solely to identify the location of a specific individual from the tracking of their mobile phone in order to verify their involvement in a

[76] Eleni Kosta and Magdalena Brewczynska, 'Government Access to User Data: Towards More Meaningful Transparency Reports' in Rosa Maria Ballardini and others (eds), *Regulating Industrial Internet through IPR, Data Protection and Competition Law* (Kluwer 2019).

[77] Christopher Kuner, *Transborder Data Flows and Data Privacy Law* (OUP 2013) 31; Christopher Kuner and others, 'Internet Balkanization Gathers Pace: Is Privacy the Real Driver?' (2015) 5 International Data Privacy Law 1.

[78] The 'Great Firewall' of China being a well-known example. See Philip N Howard, *Pax Technica: How the Internet of Things May Set Us Free or Lock Us Up* (Yale UP 2015).

[79] Lessig (n 63) 151.

[80] Julie Cohen, *Between Truth and Power* (OUP 2019) 242.

crime scene (or an area of interest for national security reasons) as it would be to obtain the mobile phone location data of anyone who would have been nearby at the time.[81] This dramatically magnifies the number of private lives interfered with as the mobile phone location data of thousands of innocent people may be swept up by a broadly framed warrant.[82] Consequently, as already well established in the Article 8 ECHR case law of the ECtHR, safeguarding against the risk of dragnet-like collections of communications data demands independent and robust oversight. This is essential to ensure that the laws in place are being meaningfully adhered to. They 'cannot be drafted in such vague terms as to leave room for speculation and assumptions with regard to its content' and should only be authorized when shown to be necessary and proportionate.[83]

The increasing practice of direct reuse of raw private sector communications data for law enforcement purposes also carries some significant risks. CSPs retain and collect mobile phone communications data primarily for business purposes, not for the investigation of serious crime.[84] Thus, algorithmic profiling based on errors from private entities serves to compromise the effectiveness of police and border management work due to incorrect correlations and data distortions.[85] Data of varying quality being collected in bulk for one purpose (commercial use), but which is then reused for the different purpose of law enforcement, requires a higher standard of evidential quality. For instance, after questions arose about the reliability of phone location data obtained from the private sector in Denmark, authorities released thirty-two prisoners after a review of 10,700 criminal cases in 2019. Nearly forty new cases were also postponed under a two-month moratorium on the use of mobile phone records in court after police found multiple glitches in the software that converted raw data from phone masts into usable evidence.[86] Denmark has since established an Independent Inspectorate of Evidence to ensure that any technical evidence processing that the police and the prosecution perform undergoes appropriate prior assessment and oversight.[87] Of course, serious risks to a person's privacy and liberty posed by inaccuracies embedded in the re-purposing of such datasets are not unique to communications data and have also

[81] Jennifer Valentino-De Vries, 'Tracking Phones, Google is a Dragnet for the Police' *New York Times* (13 April 2019).

[82] See Kate Allen, 'Thousands of bystanders caught in Toronto police sweep of cellphone data' *The Toronto Star* (24 March 2019).

[83] *Niemietz v Germany* (1992) 16 EHRR 97. See further Chapter 2.

[84] The Federal Trade Commission in the US has expressed concerns that the country's six largest Internet Service Providers are retaining their customers' communications data, particularly subscriber data ('demographic data') and web browsing history, beyond what is reasonable for business purposes. See FTC Staff Report, *A Look at What ISPs Know About You* (FTC 2021) 31–38.

[85] Costica Dumbrava, *AI at EU Borders* (European Parliamentary Research Service 2021) 26.

[86] Jon Henley, 'Denmark frees 32 inmates over flaws in phone geolocation evidence' *The Guardian* (12 September 2019). Similar police errors have arisen elsewhere: Olivia Solon, 'Kansas family sues mapping company for years of "digital hell"' *The Guardian* (9 August 2016).

[87] The EU FRA has commended this reform, describing it as a 'promising practice': FRA, Annual Report 2023 (June 2023) 187.

arisen in thebulk retention and analysis of passenger name record (PNR) data for countering terrorism and serious crime.[88]

Technological developments now make it possible to reveal details from an individual's public and private life that may predict their future conduct. Months before the Snowden revelations, a multinational defence security company had already acknowledged sharing this type of technology with the US government and CSPs as part of a joint research and development effort to help build a national security system capable of analysing 'trillions of entities' from the Internet.[89] This shift towards more predictive and proactive policing with an increased focus on strategic intelligence and analysis, all of which necessarily entail extending the breath and duration of the data collected and retained by the public and private sectors, has also moved from the national security context to that of criminal justice. This has prompted concerns of 'weakened legal safeguards' due to the increasingly blurred lines between what data retention and surveillance programmes are being undertaken for the purposes of criminal justice as opposed to national security.[90] A lack of clarity, if left without adequate regulation and oversight, may enable an increasingly wide range of public authorities to use mass surveillance tools and treat every individual as a suspect.

Relatedly, predictive policing has become a norm for many US law enforcement authorities and is making inroads in Europe and elsewhere.[91] Disconcertingly, however, findings from the few but gradually increasing number of independent reviews on the use of such systems worldwide cast doubt on whether these predictions are sufficiently accurate to justify their use in potentially life-changing decisions, such as bail or sentencing.[92] Further concerns have been raised that these tools reinforce current biases within the criminal justice system and are equally, if not more, opaque. Indeed, it has been demonstrated that they often derive decisions from inferences which in fact serve as proxies for sensitive data such as gender or race and that they rely on the questionable use of datasets derived from social media sources. Less sophisticated data-driven police systems have already

[88] See Chapter 9.

[89] Ryan Gallagher, 'Software that tracks people on social media created by defense firm' *The Guardian* (10 February 2013).

[90] European Parliament, Resolution of 12 March 2014 on the US NSA Surveillance Programmes, surveillance bodies in various Member States and their impact of EU citizens' fundamental rights and on transatlantic cooperation in Justice and Home Affairs, 2013/2188(INI) [12].

[91] See generally Andrew Guthrie Ferguson, *The Rise of Big Data Policing* (NYU Press 2017); Ni Loideain (n 59); Kate Crawford and Jason Schultz, 'AI Systems as State Actors' (2020) 119 Columbia Law Review 1914; Marion Oswald and Alexander Babuta, 'Machine Learning Predictive Algorithms and the Policing of Future Crimes' in John Daniels and Ken Pease (eds), *Policing and AI* (Routledge 2020).

[92] See eg Priscilla Hunt, Jessica Saunders and John S Hollywood, *Evaluation of the Shreveport Predictive Policing Experiment* (RAND Report, 2014) 49–52; Lyria Bennett Moses and Janet Chan, 'Algorithmic Prediction in Policing' [2016] Policing and Society 1; Julia Dressel and Hany Farid, 'The Accuracy, Fairness, and Limits of Predicting Recidivism' (2018) 4 Science Advances; Songul Tolan and others, 'Why Machine Learning May Lead to Unfairness' [2019] *Proceedings of the 17th International Conference on AI and Law* 83–92.

resulted in disparate impacts on minorities and disproportionate over-policing of vulnerable groups in society.[93]

Certain types of communications data, such as IP addresses (every device connected to the Internet has an IP address, providing location data), or subscriber data (a postal address), could prejudice individuals from those areas if a particular address is associated with a high number of individuals who have a history of prior arrests. Relying on this proxy may increase the risk of innocent individuals being far more likely to be arrested for an offence due to being deemed guilty by association.[94] The accuracy and necessity, and hence fairness, of such systems is often also rendered impossible for independent researchers to verify, given the proprietary algorithms used in their design by the private sector.[95] These issues raise significant questions regarding the compatibility of using such opaque data-driven systems with an individual's rights to private life and data protection. Put simply, unless evidence of effective operational use that respects human rights can be provided through some means of independent oversight, the legality and proportionality of such data-driven systems for countering serious crime and safeguarding national security is suspect. This means that the compatibility of such profiling systems with Article 8 ECHR and EU fundamental rights law is highly questionable.[96] Policymakers and regulators in Europe thus continue to acknowledge the regulatory challenges posed by Big Data approaches and predictive analytics in law enforcement and national security contexts where increasingly powerful but often untested ML and other AI-based systems are involved.[97]

C. Article 8 ECHR and Data Privacy Law

Article 8 guarantees the 'right to respect for private life' and forms part of the European Convention which protects numerous human rights and

[93] See Cathy O'Neil, *Weapons of Math Destruction* (Penguin 2017); Vikram Dodd, 'Met removes hundreds from gangs matrix after breaking data laws' *The Guardian* (15 February 2020); Brayne (n 51); Fionnuala Ní Aoláin, 'Report of the UN Special Rapporteur on the promotion and protection of human rights and fundamental freedoms while countering terrorism', A/HRC/46/36, 22 January 2021, 6.

[94] House of Lords, 'Technology Rules? The advent of new technologies in the criminal justice system' (2022) 17–18; FRA, *Bias in algorithms—AI and Discrimination* (FRA Report 2022) 24.

[95] Sam Corbett-Davies and others, 'A computer program used for bail and sentencing decisions was labelled biased against blacks. It's actually not that clear' *The Washington Post* (17 October 2016); Article 29 Working Party, 'Opinion on some key issues of the Law Enforcement Directive (EU 2016/680)', WP 258, 2017, 13; FRA ibid.

[96] Rosamunde van Brakel, 'Pre-Emptive Big Data Surveillance and its (Dis)Empowering Consequences' in Bart van der Sloot, Dennis Broeders, and Erik Schrijvers (eds), *Exploring the Boundaries of Big Data* (Amsterdam UP 2016) 132; Ni Loideain (n 59) 317; Lynskey (n 53) 175.

[97] House of Lords (n 94) 75–78; European Commission, *Report on the State of the Digital Decade* (2023) 30–31; EDPS, 'Opinion 4/2023 on the Proposal for Artificial Intelligence Act in the light of legislative developments'.

freedoms.[98] The ECtHR has interpreted the scope of the protected interest of 'private life' broadly under Article 8(1) ECHR with the aim of keeping up to date with emerging technologies and surveillance practices. Thus, the ECtHR has held that the mere retention, regardless of any subsequent use, of personal data for law enforcement or national security reasons concerning an individual's communications or movements offline or online constitutes an interference with the right to respect for private life.[99] Like certain other rights under the ECHR, Article 8(2) ECHR clearly shows that the right to respect for private life is not absolute. The ECtHR is consequently required to balance this qualified right alongside other competing rights and interests, including the prevention of serious crime and safeguarding national security.

Article 8 ECHR provides:

1. Everyone has the right to respect for his private and family life, his home and his correspondence.
2. There shall be no interference by a public authority with the exercise of this right except such as is in accordance with the law and is necessary in a democratic society in the interests of national security, public safety or the economic well-being of the country, for the prevention of disorder or crime, for the protection of health or morals, or for the protection of the rights and freedoms of others.

1. The ECHR and its 'machinery of protection'

The ECHR is an international human rights law treaty of the Council of Europe (COE) that has been signed by all forty-six Contracting States, including all EU Member States. The COE also shares close links with other non-European countries, such as the US which was granted observer status in 1997. This status gives those countries the opportunity to cooperate with the COE, accept its guiding principles, and to send observers to various expert committees and conferences.[100] Recently, for instance, the US has been represented at the COE Committee on AI which is tasked with drafting what could be the world's first international treaty on AI, the COE Convention on AI.[101] The COE is a separate organization to the EU and has been the most important human body for promoting human rights and the rule of law in Europe for over seventy years. Like the European Coal and Steel

[98] Council of Europe, Convention for the Protection of Human Rights and Fundamental Freedoms, ETS No 005, 04.XI.1950, <www.coe.int/en/web/conventions/full-list/-/conventions/treaty/005> (ECHR).

[99] See Chapters 2 and 3.

[100] COE Resolution 95(37), adopted by Committee of Ministers on 7 December 1995.

[101] COE, Committee on AI (CAI), Extract from CM(2021)131-addfinal.

Community (the EU as it was in 1951), the COE was established after the atrocities of the Second World War to ensure greater cooperation and unity between countries in a fractured and divided Europe. The EU originally pursued this aim through economic measures. Although the drafters of the EEC Treaty envisaged a role for human rights protection within the EU legal system in the 1950s, human rights would not be recognized as part of EU law until 1969.[102]

The COE, in contrast, was unequivocally set up to achieve unity across Europe in the postwar era through enhancing the rule of law, democracy, and human rights standards.[103] Its key mission was thus to act as 'an early warning system to combat the first signs of totalitarianism'. It was signed shortly after in 1951, entering into force in 1953 after the required number of signatures from ten Contracting States.[104] The wide ratification of the modern ECHR legal system makes its reach more extensive in some respects than that of the EU, thereby enabling its human rights standards to be relevant to 700 million individuals.[105] Accordingly, this means that the UK's exit from the EU did not affect its ratification of the ECHR or other COE instruments.[106] Once a Contracting State signs and ratifies the ECHR, it is then bound in international law to the enforcement and 'machinery of protection' of the ECHR. A system of enforcement, as held by the ECtHR, that would be 'materially weakened' if individuals did not have access to the ECHR system.[107]

Protocol No 11 to the ECHR amended the original procedural rules of the ECHR significantly when it came into operation in 1998. Two part-time bodies were created in the 1950s—the European Commission of Human Rights and the Court—to ensure the observance of States that had ratified the ECHR. Both were replaced with a new permanent court following amendments under Protocol No 11.[108] When negotiating this treaty, all Contracting States which were parties to the ECHR agreed that States should all permanently accept the jurisdiction of the

[102] Case 29/69 *Stauder v City of Ulm* [1969] ECR 419.

[103] On the complex dialogue between the legal systems of the ECHR and the EU, see Chapter 4.

[104] Síofra O'Leary, 'Why the European Convention on Human Rights Still Matters' [2024] Cambridge Yearbook of European Legal Studies 1, 3. On the origins of the ECHR and its major reforms, see further Ed Bates, *The Evolution of the European Convention on Human Rights* (OUP 2010); Alastair Mowbray, *Cases, Materials, and Commentary on the European Convention on Human Rights* (3rd edn, OUP 2012) 14–63.

[105] Since the entry into force of the ECHR, the Court has delivered over 26,000 judgments and reviewed over 1 million applications: Council of Europe, *Annual Report: European Court of Human Rights 2023* (COE 2024) 82, <https://echr.coe.int/documents/d/echr/annual-report-2023-eng>.

[106] On the impact of Brexit for EU–UK law enforcement and data protection, see Nora Ni Loideain, 'Brexit' in Eleni Kosta and Franziska Boehm (eds), *The EU Law Enforcement Directive* (OUP 2024).

[107] See *Szabó and Vissy v Hungary* [2016] ECHR 579 [33]; that said, there has been a shift in recent cases concerning Art 8 ECHR and national security where the ECtHR has stressed that 'a fundamental feature' of this machinery is that it is 'subsidiary to the national systems safeguarding human rights': *Wieder and Guarneiri* (n 6) [63]. See further Chapter 2.

[108] Council of Europe, Protocol No 11 to the Convention for the Protection of Human Rights and Fundamental Freedoms, restructuring the control machinery established thereby ETS No 155, 11.V.1994, <https://coe.int/en/web/conventions/full-list/-/conventions/treaty/155>. Bates (n 104) 213–21.

ECtHR over cases brought against them by individuals. Previously, the Committee of Ministers had a role in determining the merits of cases but now its function is restricted to ensuring that States comply with the ECtHR's judgments.[109] By virtue of signing and ratifying Protocol No 11, the Contracting Parties accepted what became Article 34 ECHR. This provides that the ECtHR may receive applications (without States hindering in any way the effectiveness of this right) 'from any person, non-governmental organisation or group of individuals claiming to be the victim of a violation by one of the High Contracting Parties' of the rights set out under the ECHR or its protocols. Article 34 ECHR requires Contracting States to undertake to secure these rights and freedoms to everyone within their jurisdiction.

Further major reforms to the ECtHR then needed to be made to address the rising caseload of the Court from 1999 and the overall efficiency of its enforcement. Following the eventual ratification by Russia of Protocol No 14 to the ECHR, these much-needed reforms became operational in June 2010.[110] As a High Contracting Parties to the ECHR, the States accepted what is now Article 44 ECHR. This provides that a judgment of a Chamber of the ECtHR (comprised of seven judges) becomes final after three months or earlier if the respondent State indicates that it will not refer the case. Another significant reform for the ECHR was the entry into force of Protocol No 16 in 2018.[111] Articles 1 and 5 of which provide that the highest courts of the Contracting Parties may now request the ECtHR to give non-binding 'advisory opinions' on questions of principle relating to the interpretation or application of rights within the ECHR concerning cases pending before the requesting court.[112] Protocol No 16 was adopted in 2013 in response to calls for improving dialogue between the ECtHR and the national courts, reducing case overload, and in preparation for the EU's accession to the ECHR.[113] The ECtHR has stressed that this advisory mechanism should not restrict the right to individual application under Article 34 ECHR 'which is at the core' of the ECHR.[114]

Critics of Protocol No 16 have notably included the CJEU. In *Opinion 2/13*, the CJEU warned that this extended advisory capacity could render the ECHR system less efficient, greatly delay the caseload of the ECtHR, and threaten the autonomy

[109] The ECtHR and the Committee of Ministers are among the COE's key institutions which also include the Parliamentary Assembly, the Secretariat, and the European Commissioner for Human Rights: Steven Greer, Janneke Gerards, and Rose Slowe, *Human Rights in the Council of Europe and the European Union* (CUP 2018) 60–70.

[110] See further Mowbray (n 104).

[111] Síofra O'Leary, 'Advisory Opinions and Judicial Dialogue Strasbourg Style' (2022) 59 Common Market Law Review 87.

[112] ibid 91–92.

[113] ibid 90. On the most recent opinions issued by the Strasbourg Court, see European Court of Human Rights, *Annual Report 2023* (COE 2024) 73: <https://echr.coe.int/documents/d/echr/annual-report-2023-eng>.

[114] ECtHR, 'Reflection Paper on the Proposal to Extend the Court's Advisory Jurisdiction', 2013: <https://echr.coe.int/Documents/2013_Courts_advisory_jurisdiction_ENG.pdf> [45].

of the EU legal order, thereby hindering the much-delayed EU accession to the ECHR.[115] EU law already requires Member States courts of last instance to refer questions concerning fundamental rights primarily to the CJEU and to respect those decisions insofar as they are called upon to determine a dispute within the scope of EU law.[116] In contrast, some commentators have highlighted the potential benefits of Protocol No 16,[117] noting that advisory opinions by international courts are a commonly used instrument adopted to ensure that the overall system of oversight operates more efficiently in general[118] and that the mechanism may have the benefit of helping to clarify existing ECtHR jurisprudence in certain areas or even to develop the case law.[119] It may also serve to strengthen human rights protection by improving dialogue between the ECtHR and the national courts.[120] Moreover, the caseload of the ECtHR could be reduced and applicants could avoid a potentially lengthy wait for redress if an advisory opinion concerning one case submitted by a national court using Protocol No 16 could be immediately applied in similar later cases.[121] At the time of writing, the ECtHR has delivered numerous such opinions but none have concerned questions of EU law.[122]

Other significant reforms took effect in 2022. Pursuant to Protocol No 15, the time limit for applying to the ECtHR was shortened to four months from the date of the final domestic decision. The new time limit applies only to applications where the final domestic decision was taken from 1 February 2022.[123] It is important to note that the ECtHR also deals with interstate petitions but most of its caseload (the extensive backlog of which is now less of a serious concern for the effective functioning of the ECtHR) concerns applications from individuals against the Contracting States.[124] Finally, rarely and sometimes controversially, judgments may be referred to the Grand Chamber of the ECtHR for a rehearing (comprising seventeen members).[125] These judgments, if the Grand Chamber panel decides that the application should be reheard, are hugely significant in guiding future judgments and have no appeal.[126] Two such landmark judgments were delivered

[115] Opinion 2/13, Draft Agreement on Accession of the EU to the ECHR, opinion of 18 December 2014 (ECLI:EU:C:2014:2454) [196]–[200]. See further Chapter 4.

[116] See Chapter 7.

[117] Ada Paprocka and Michał Ziółkowski, 'Advisory Opinions under Protocol No. 16 to the European Convention on Human Rights' (2015) 11 European Constitutional Law Review 274; Thomas Voland and Britta Schiebel, 'Advisory Opinions of the European Court of Human Rights' (2017) 17 Human Rights Law Review 73.

[118] Voland and Schiebel (n 117) 91.

[119] Paprocka and Ziółkowski (n 117) 292.

[120] Koen Lemmens, 'Protocol No 16 to the ECHR' (2019) 15 European Constitutional Law Review 691.

[121] ibid 712–13.

[122] Council of Europe (n 113) 10.

[123] ibid.

[124] ibid 8–9. Greer, Gerards, and Slowe (n 109) 93.

[125] Mowbray (n 104) 57–61.

[126] Article 46(1) ECHR provides: 'The High Contracting Parties undertake to abide by the final judgment of the Court in any case to which they are parties.'

in 2021 dealing with bulk surveillance and communications data retention for countering serious crime and safeguarding national security.[127]

2. Achievements and criticism of the European Court of Human Rights

The ECtHR has been lauded as the 'ultimate guardian' of human rights law in Europe and the COE's 'main achievement' among its 200 other treaties due to it being one of the world's most influential and important human rights documents. It is a trusted international institution in the protection of human rights and receives about 60,000 applications a year.[128] Nevertheless, the ECHR is not without its critics and challenges. Given its extensive membership and reach, both the extent of this criticism and the impact of the ECHR have been found to vary depending on the relevant Contracting State.[129] That said, there has long been a consistent consensus that Article 8 ECHR has been 'an important driving force'[130] in the scrutiny of domestic laws governing communications surveillance by public authorities and for ratcheting up data privacy standards across Europe and within EU law.[131] There is, of course, a deft balancing act to be struck by the ECtHR in ensuring the adoption of its supranational standards and also in recognizing its limits as an international court. Thus, as Gerards points out, the ECtHR must always carefully take the latter into account when casting judgement on sovereign States with 'very different constitutional systems and ... which may harbour significantly different values and opinions on contested fundamental rights'.[132] Given this difficult position, and being a court of last resort, the COE Committee of Ministers'

[127] *Big Brother Watch* (n 11); *Centrum för Rättvisa v Sweden* [2021] ECHR 440 (GC). See Chapters 2 and 3.

[128] Iris Canor, '*Primus Inter Pares*. Who is the Ultimate Guardian of Fundamental Rights in Europe' (2000) 25 European Law Review 3, 21; Julian Go, 'Modeling the State: Postcolonial Constitutions in Africa and Asia' (2002) 39 Southeast Asian Studies 558, 578–79; Helen Keller and Alec Stone Sweet (eds), *A Europe of Rights* (OUP 2008) 3; Janneke Gerards, *General Principles of the European Convention on Human Rights* (2nd edn, CUP 2023) 1–34.

[129] See generally Patricia Popelier, Sarah Lambrecht, and Koen Lemmens (eds), *Criticism of the European Court of Human Rights* (Intersentia 2016).

[130] David Feldman, 'Secrecy, Dignity or Autonomy? Views of Privacy as a Civil Liberty' [1994] Public Law 41.

[131] John Spencer, 'Telephone-Tap Evidence and Administrative Detention in the UK' in Marianne Wade and Almir Maljevic (eds), *A War on Terror?* (Springer 2010); Bygrave (n 27) 86; Marko Milanovic, 'Human Rights Treaties and Foreign Surveillance: Privacy in the Digital Age' (2015) 56 Harvard International Law Journal 101; Mary Arden, *Human Rights and European Law* (OUP 2015) 144; Kirsty Hughes, 'Mass Surveillance and the European Court of Human Rights' [2018] European Human Rights Law 589, 597; Nora Ni Loideain, 'A Bridge Too Far? The Investigatory Powers Act and Human Rights' in Edwards (n 7) 168. Scholars have raised concerns, however, about recent developments in this previously lauded Art 8 ECHR jurisprudence. See further Chapters 2 and 3.

[132] Janneke Gerards, *General Principles of the European Convention on Human Rights* (CUP 2019) 3.

supervisory task of enforcement and implementation of the ECtHR's judgments may sometimes be challenging and take several years.

Indeed, some States have sidestepped, disagreed, or rejected outright the ECtHR's judgments. One such example is Russia, no longer part of the COE following its invasion of Ukraine in 2022.[133] Prior to its swift expulsion, the COE's largest Member State had adopted legislation allowing its Constitutional Court to declare a Grand Chamber decision finding a violation of Article 8 ECHR unenforceable if it conflicted with Russian constitutional law.[134] This followed a judgment by the ECtHR where it held that the regime in Russia governing warrantless law enforcement access to private mobile network data violated the right to respect for private life under Article 8 ECHR.[135] Despite the closer alignment overall between Strasbourg and the UK courts on the application of the ECHR, another example of conflict with Strasbourg was the lengthy dialogue that took place with the UK concerning its refusal to recognize the case law of the ECtHR that prohibits a blanket ban on prisoner voting.[136] Although reforms were eventually adopted regarding the latter, there have been new concerns following the post-Brexit government proposals to replace the UK legal framework governing its implementation of ECHR rights (the Human Rights Act 1998) with a 'Modern Bill of Rights'. The proposal has attracted much criticism especially following an independent report, commissioned by the UK government, which found 'no evidence' supporting such reforms.[137]

It is perhaps worth noting here the findings from a comprehensive study of fifteen Contracting States which showed Russia and the UK to be among the more critical States of the ECHR largely on the basis of the sovereignty argument and

[133] Russia was a comparatively recent newcomer to the ECHR legal system having ratified the ECHR in 1998. Weeks after invading Ukraine, the Committee of Ministers decided to expel Russia from the COE: Council of Europe (n 105) 7–8. See generally Lauri Mälksoo and Wolfgang Benedek (eds), *Russia and the European Court of Human Rights* (CUP 2017).

[134] President of Russia, 'Amendments to Law of Constitutional Court', 15 December 2015, <http://en.kremlin.ru/acts/news/50935>. Despite ceasing to be a High Contracting Party to the ECHR, the Committee of Ministers continues to supervise the execution of relevant judgments and friendly settlements and the Russian Federation is obliged to implement them. See eg the facial recognition judgment of *Glukhin v Russia* [2023] ECHR 540.

[135] *Zakharov v Russia* (2016) 63 EHRR 17 (GC).

[136] *Hirst (No 2) v United Kingdom* (2006) 42 EHRR 41; *Millbank and Others v United Kingdom* (App No 44473/14) (unreported) 30 June 2016; *The Independent Human Rights Act Review*, CP 586 (HM Stationery Office 2021) 153–59. The UK was among the first ten states to ratify the ECHR in 1953. Its delay in executing the ECtHR's case law on prisoners' rights was highly controversial It was described by former CJEU AG Francis G Jacob as 'deplorable': Vasiliki Kosta, Nikos Skoutaris, and Vassilis Tzevelekos (eds), *The EU Accession to the ECHR* (Hart 2014) vii. On the impact of these reforms, see Robert Jones and Gregory Davies, 'Prisoner Voting in the UK' (2023) 86 Modern Law Review 900. On the alignment between Strasbourg and the UK courts regarding ECHR rights, and the reduction in cases from the UK being brought before Strasbourg, see O'Leary (n 104).

[137] *The Independent Human Rights Act Review* (n 136) 30. See further Ni Loideain (n 106). On previous proposals to replace the Human Rights Act 1998, see generally Conor Gearty, *On Fantasy Island: Britain, Europe, and Human Rights* (OUP 2016).

the ECHR as a 'living instrument'.[138] The latter doctrine is the view adopted by the ECtHR, developed in its jurisprudence that the ECHR is capable of fundamental change. This requires the ECHR to be interpreted in light of new and emerging technologies and applied in a manner that renders its safeguards practical and effective.[139] Recognizing again the limits posed by its legal status as an international court, the ECtHR has rightly made clear that it is not its role to substitute the assessment of the national authorities of what might be 'best policy' in the field of State surveillance;[140] the latter having the role of determining questions of fact and interpreting domestic law. This approach is more likely to be taken by the ECtHR where it considers that the national authorities 'are better placed' to assess the necessity to restrict a right and where there is no consensus on the matter among the Contracting States.[141] This may happen, for instance, where the domestic law under review is complex or the relevant State is not at liberty to disclose relevant information to the ECtHR due to national security reasons.[142]

Nevertheless, since the 1970s, the ECtHR has consistently maintained that Contracting States do not enjoy unlimited discretion to subject individuals to secret surveillance. As the ECtHR has consistently held, this 'European supervision' is necessary given the risk that a system of secret surveillance set up to protect national security may 'undermine or even destroy democracy under the cloak of defending it'.[143] As discussed in Chapter 2, States are then required to show that adequate and effective safeguards are in place to prevent abuse of these powers. When reviewing these safeguards, the ECtHR will employ the use of its 'margin of appreciation' doctrine in determining how far it is 'right' to defer to a Contracting State's interpretation of the situations it faces in permitting a limitation on the right to respect for private life.[144]

3. Article 8 ECHR and data protection: a late arrival of 'fundamental importance'

It is now well established in ECtHR case law that the protection of personal data holds the status of being of 'fundamental importance' to an individual's right to

[138] See Roger Mastermann, 'The United Kingdom: From Strasbourg Surrogacy Towards a British Bill of Rights?' and Aaron Matta and Armen Mazmanyan, 'Russia: In Quest for a European Identity' in Popelier, Lambrecht, and Lemmens (n 129).

[139] *Airey v Ireland* (1979–80) 2 EHRR 305 [24].

[140] *Klass v Germany* (1978) 2 EHRR 214 [49]; *Leander v Sweden* (1987) 9 EHRR 433 [51]; *Weber and Saravia v Germany* [2006] ECHR 1173 [94]; *Big Brother Watch* (n 11) [256].

[141] Arden (n 131) 58.

[142] *Big Brother Watch* (n 11) [256].

[143] *Klass* (n 140) [49]; *Weber and Saravia* (n 140) [106]; *Szabó and Vissy* (n 107) [57]; *Zakharov* (n 135) [232]; *Big Brother Watch* (n 11) [308].

[144] Dean Spielmann, 'Allowing the Right Margin' (2012) 14 Cambridge Yearbook of European Legal Studies 381. See further Chapter 2.

respect for private life as guaranteed under Article 8 ECHR.[145] This contrasts with its early jurisprudence when the informational aspects of the protected interest of a 'private life' were not considered to fall within the ambit of Article 8 ECHR.[146] The ECtHR has since, however, clearly departed from this initial approach. Adopting a broader interpretation of the scope of the right to respect for private life in relation to personal information, it has gradually approached the protection of personal data as a sub-right or an aspect of privacy protection in its application of Article 8 ECHR. In 1987, the ECtHR recognized that the retention of data on a secret police register concerning an individual's private life for national security purposes amounted to an interference with the right to respect for private life.[147] A decade later, the ECtHR recognized that 'the protection of personal data, not least medical data, is of fundamental importance to an individual's enjoyment of their right to respect for private life as guaranteed under Article 8 ECHR'.[148] The ECtHR incorporated provisions from the 1981 COE Data Protection Convention (Convention 108) to mandate stronger safeguards for the processing of sensitive data[149] into its requirements that States must satisfy in order for disclosures of medical data to be justified under Article 8 ECHR.[150] Yet, it was not until 2000 that the ECtHR explicitly established that the purpose of Convention 108 corresponded with the broad interpretation of the right to respect for private life as protected under Article 8(1) ECHR, the purpose of which is 'to secure in the territory of each Party for every individual ... respect for his rights and fundamental freedoms, and in particular his right to privacy, with regard to automatic processing of personal data relating to him'.[151]

The ECtHR established, and has held consistently since, that Article 8 ECHR aligns with the main aim of Convention 108 to ensure that every Contracting Party to the ECHR provides every individual with their right to privacy regarding any automatic processing of personal data relating to them. Such personal data being defined as 'any information relating to an identified or identifiable individual'.[152] Like EU law, the definition of what constitutes 'personal data' under Convention 108 is considerably broad. It is important to note, however, that this concept has been approached and developed very differently by the ECtHR and the CJEU. The ECtHR has in certain cases, for instance, approached this aspect of Article 8 ECHR with the qualification that in order to fall within the application of Article 8

[145] *S and Marper v United Kingdom* (2009) 48 EHRR 50 [103] (GC). See further Chapter 3.

[146] David Feldman, 'Information and Privacy' in Jack Beatson and Yvonne Cripps (eds), *Freedom of Expression and Freedom of Information* (OUP 2000) 306–08.

[147] *Leander* (n 140) [48].

[148] *Z v Finland* (1998) 25 EHRR 371 [95].

[149] Council of Europe, Convention of 28 January 1981 for the Protection of Individuals with regard to Automatic Processing of Personal Data, ETS No 108 (Convention 108). Convention 108 entered into force from 1 October 1985.

[150] *Z* (n 148) [95], [96].

[151] *Amann v Switzerland* [2000] ECHR 87 [65] (GC).

[152] *Breyer v Germany* [2020] ECHR 95 [76]–[78].

ECHR, the relevant information must concern the applicant's private life.[153] Thus requiring 'an additional element of privacy' in order for personal information to be included within the scope of private life. In contrast, the CJEU has adopted a far more expansive and normative interpretation of what constitutes personal data.[154]

Nevertheless, recognition of the importance of data protection law being effective in order to ensure that data processing by law enforcement is consistent with Article 8 ECHR reflects the ECtHR's view of the ECHR as an evolving and 'living instrument' capable of being applied in a way that renders its safeguards practical and effective.[155] This is demonstrated in the well-established Article 8 ECHR requirement regarding 'the need for such safeguards [being] all the greater where the protection of personal data undergoing automatic processing is concerned, not least when such data are used for police purposes'.[156] The application of this requirement is evident in *M.K. v France* where the applicant was charged, but not convicted, of book theft. His fingerprints were subject to retention on a database by the public authorities for twenty-five years despite the case being discontinued. Having regard to its finding that the applicant's chance of his deletion request being successful were 'at best hypothetical', the ECtHR considered this twenty-five-year time limit 'in practice tantamount to indefinite retention'. It held that reliance solely on individual requests to ensure the proportionate removal of fingerprints from a national database, likely to be rejected by the public authorities, was a 'theoretical and illusory' safeguard. The ECtHR also flatly rejected the argument that the public prosecutor's refusal to delete the fingerprints was motivated by the need to protect the applicant by ruling out his involvement should someone attempt to steal his identity. Indeed, the Strasbourg Court noted that accepting the argument based on an alleged guarantee of protection against potential identity theft 'would in practice be tantamount to justifying the storage of information on the whole population of France, which would most definitely be excessive and irrelevant'.[157]

D. EU Law and Related Frameworks

This section provides an overview of related data privacy frameworks and their relationship with Article 8 ECHR in Europe and internationally. Particular

[153] See further Chapter 3.

[154] Juliane Kokott and Christoph Sobotta, 'The Distinction Between Privacy and Data Protection in the Jurisprudence of the CJEU and the ECtHR' (2013) 3 International Data Privacy Law 222, 224; Lee A Bygrave and Luca Tosoni, 'Article 4(1) Personal Data' in Christopher Kuner and others (eds), *The EU General Data Protection Regulation (GDPR): A Commentary* (OUP 2020) 103–15.

[155] See further Chapters 2 and 3.

[156] *S and Marper* (n 145) [103]. The CJEU has followed this Art 8 ECHR standard in its data retention case law. See Chapter 5.

[157] *M.K. v France* [2013] ECHR 341 [40]–[44].

attention is given to instruments concerning data retention for countering crime and terrorism.

1. Council of Europe

By the 1970s, the Committee of Ministers had adopted various resolutions on personal data protection which referred to Article 8 ECHR.[158] Work on these resolutions was prompted by a perception at the time that the high-level principles of the ECHR did not provide sufficiently detailed protection for individuals' privacy in the face of major advances in computer processing and mass data retention.[159] Convention 108 was intended to help fill the gaps in this area of legislation by stimulating the adoption of national laws within the COE Contracting States.[160] The resulting key instrument, based on several COE resolutions and recommendations from the 1960s and 1970s, was Convention 108 enacted in 1981. It remains the only legally binding instrument within international law governing data privacy.[161] Article 8 ECHR has also been shaped more by Convention 108 than any other COE treaty within the context of State surveillance and data retention measures. An additional amendment to the Convention was made in 2001 requiring the establishment of supervisory authorities and new requirements concerning transborder data transfers.[162] Between 2011 and 2018, Convention 108 was also the subject of modernization proposals.[163] This modernized framework is otherwise known as 'Convention 108+'. Subject to the amending Protocol being ratified by thirty-eight Parties to Convention 108 after 11 October 2023, it will enter into force.

Like the globally influential but non-binding Organisation for Economic Co-operation and Development (OECD) Privacy Guidelines of 1980, updated in

[158] See Council of Europe, Committee of Ministers (1973), Resolution (73) 22 on the protection of the privacy of individuals vis-à-vis electronic data banks in the private sector, 26 September 1973; Council of Europe, Committee of Ministers (1974), Resolution (74) 29 on the protection of the privacy of individuals vis-à-vis electronic data banks in the public sector, 20 September 1974.

[159] Peter Carey and Bridget Tracy, *Data Protection* (4th edn, OUP 2015) 1.

[160] Bygrave (n 27) 34–43.

[161] EU law is *sui generis* and thus the GDPR does not have the legal status of international law: Opinion 2/13 (n 115) [170]–[176].

[162] Additional Protocol to the Convention 108 for the Protection of Individuals with regard to Automated Processing of Personal Data regarding supervisory authorities and transborder data flows, ETS No 181. Entered into force 1 July 2004.

[163] Modernised Convention for the Protection of Individuals with regard to the Processing of Personal Data (consolidated text), adopted by the 128th Session of the Committee of Ministers, 17–18 May 2018; CETS No 223, Protocol amending the Convention for the Protection of Individuals with regard to Automated Processing of Data, 10 October 2018, Art 37. At the time of writing, there were thirty-one ratifications. See further Paul de Hert and Vagelis Papakonstantinou, 'Framing Big Data in the Council of Europe and EU Data Protection Law Systems' (2021) 40 Computer Law & Security Review.

2013,[164] Convention 108+ requires the public and private sectors to comply with a broadly similar set of key principles for data processing. Much to the surprise of commentators, both core instruments on data protection by the COE and OECD have remained effectively unchanged despite major technological changes that have taken place since their drafting decades earlier.[165] Convention 108+ retains its key principles. First, that personal data shall be processed lawfully and fairly (lawful and fair principle). Secondly, personal data must be collected for explicit, specified, and legitimate purposes and not processed in a way incompatible with those purposes (purpose limitation principle). Thirdly, processing must be adequate, relevant, and not excessive in relation to the purposes for which the data are processed (data minimization principle). Fourthly, processing must ensure that the personal data is accurate and kept up to date where necessary (data accuracy). Fifthly, personal data must be maintained in a form which permits identification of data subjects for no longer than is necessary for the relevant purposes of processing (storage limitation). The more recent significant reforms of Convention 108 mainly reflect reforms under EU data protection law (primarily the GDPR). These include the recognition of data protection as an autonomous right, that controllers ensure greater transparency of processing through more detailed private notices, and further procedural rights for individuals.[166] That said, some key technological developments concerning privacy and data protection, cross-border transfers, government data access, and profiling, such as Big Data and AI-based systems (facial recognition), have since been addressed elsewhere by the COE and OECD in guidelines, recommendations, and declarations.[167]

As demonstrated by its ratification by several COE non-Member States, there has been growing interest in Convention 108 in Africa and Latin America thereby indicating its continuing influence beyond Europe.[168] Its general impact globally notwithstanding, it is also likely that non-European countries will view their ratification of Convention 108 as a key stepping stone towards the recognition of adequacy for data transfers with the EU. As part of its lengthy list of

164 OECD, Guidelines Governing the Protection of Privacy and Transborder Flows of Privacy Data, C(80)58/FINAL, as amended on 11 July 2013 by C(2013)79, <https://oecd.org/sti/ieconomy/oecd_privacy_framework.pdf>.

165 The GDPR has been similarly criticized: Bert-Jaap Koops, 'The Trouble with European Data Protection Law' (2014) 4 International Data Privacy Law 250; Tal Zarsky, 'Incompatible: GDPR in the Age of Big Data' (2017) 47 Seton Hall Law Review 995. For more optimistic views, see Mirelle Hildebrandt, *Smart Technologies and the End(s) of Law* (Elgar 2015); De Hert and Papakonstantinou (n 163).

166 Convention 108+ (n 163) Arts 3(1), 8, and 9.

167 See eg COE, Guidelines on the protection of individuals with regard to the processing of data in a world of Big Data, T-PD(2017)1; COE, Guidelines on AI and Data Protection, T-PD(2019)01; COE, Guidelines on Facial Recognition, T-PD(2020)03; OECD, Declaration on Government Access to Personal Data Held by Private Sector Entities, DSTI/CDEP(2022)22, OECD/LEGAL/0487.

168 Graham Greenleaf, 'The Influence of European Data Privacy Standards Outside Europe' (2012) 2 International Data Privacy Law 68; Lee A Bygrave, 'The "Strasbourg Effect" on Data Protection in Light of the "Brussels Effect"' (2021) 40 Computer Law & Security Review.

criteria for adequacy, the preamble of the GDPR explicitly states that ratification of Convention 108 will be taken into account by the European Commission in its assessment of whether the data privacy standards of a non-EU country (a 'third country') are 'essentially equivalent' to that of the EU.[169] Thus, UK data protection law (enacted following the Brexit referendum in 2016) governing the processing of personal data for national security purposes explicitly states that it is subject to Convention 108.[170]

Although Convention 108 does not explicitly reference Article 8 ECHR, its protected interests and safeguards are found throughout Convention 108. In one of many convergences with ECtHR jurisprudence, the aim of Convention 108 to protect every individual with respect to the processing of their personal data 'and in particular the right to privacy' clearly corresponds with the right to respect for private life under Article 8 ECHR.[171] Again, like Article 8 ECHR, the protection of personal data under Convention 108 is not absolute and must be balanced alongside other legitimate interests.[172] The scope of Convention 108's principles and safeguards also applies to the automated processing of personal data by both the public and private sectors and was 'commended' by the former UN Rapporteur for Privacy for extending to both law enforcement and national security purposes.[173] In order for an interference with private life to be justified under Article 8 ECHR, the processing of personal data must meet the following three tests. It must be in accordance with law, be undertaken for a legitimate aim (such as countering serious crime), and be necessary in a democratic society.

These three key conditions underpin the principles required for legitimate processing under Convention 108, especially the requirements to process data lawfully, fairly, transparently, and proportionately. Indeed, paragraph 55 of the Explanatory Report for Convention 108 explicitly confirms the influence of Article 8 ECHR by specifically stating that Article 9 on exceptions and restrictions for data protection 'are modelled' on Article 8(2) ECHR. A crucial divergence between both regimes is that Convention 108 lacks any equivalent to Article 8 ECHR's machinery of protection, especially the jurisprudence of the ECtHR.[174] That being said, although Convention 108 is not subject to the judicial supervision of the ECtHR, it has been taken into consideration in the case law of the ECtHR within the context of Article 8 ECHR.[175]

In addition to Convention 108, other more sectoral instruments and standards with 'a more practical bite' have been intended to help fill the gaps in areas

[169] GDPR, Art 45(2)(c); recital 105.
[170] Data Protection Act 2018 (UK), Part 7, s 183(2)(c).
[171] Convention 108+ (n 163) Art 1. See further Chapter 3.
[172] ibid Arts 5(1) and 11(1).
[173] ibid Art 3(1); Joseph Cannataci, Report of the Special Rapporteur on the right to privacy, UN General Assembly, A/HRC/40/63, 27 February 2019 [27].
[174] Graham Greenleaf, *Data Privacy Laws in Asia* (OUP 2014) 13.
[175] FRA and COE, *Handbook on European Data Protection Law* (FRA and COE 2018) 25.

involving State surveillance by stimulating the adoption of national laws within COE Contracting States.[176] These have included measures on the retention and use of personal data within the criminal justice system.[177] Others focus on the regulation of special investigative techniques in relation to serious crimes, terrorism, and cybercrime and have been cited by the ECtHR in some cases dealing with Article 8 ECHR and State surveillance.[178] Further COE standards and reports followed in the wake of the 9/11 terrorist attacks in the US in 2001.[179] Calls for reform urged States to provide greater regulatory safeguards and independent oversight of the increasing retention of Internet usage data and mobile phone location data and the growing role of the private sector in national security activities.[180] The COE institutions also stressed the need to retain data in order to keep records to monitor unlawful police activities, such as racial profiling, and to have 'paper trails' of data sharing between intelligence agencies, thereby fostering accountability and informing future policymaking.[181] This highlights a dual function of data-driven policing measures. First, it may serve as an important monitoring power for the State for countering serious crime both through real-time access requests and through general obligations on the private sector for longer term data retention (or 'historical data'). Secondly, records of such requests and obligations could be further used as an important oversight mechanism for intelligibility. The latter is an essential safeguard for accountability in practice as it enables effective audits and impact assessments of otherwise often impenetrable and opaque surveillance systems which increasingly operate across both the public and private sectors.[182]

Following the Snowden revelations in 2013, several COE institutions produced investigative reports and instruments responding to renewed privacy concerns

[176] Bygrave (n 27) 42.

[177] See eg COE, Recommendation No R (87) 15 of the Committee of Ministers regulating the use of personal data in the police sector (adopted on 17 September 1987) and Recommendation No R (92) 1 of the Committee of Ministers on the use of analysis of deoxyribonucleic acid (DNA) within the framework of the criminal justice system (adopted on 10 February 1992); COE, Recommendation No R (95) 4 on the protection of personal data in the area of telecommunication services (adopted on 7 February 1995); COE, Criminal Law Convention on Corruption of 27 January 1999, ETS No 173 (entered into force on 1 July 2002).

[178] See notably COE, Convention on Cybercrime ETS No 185, 23.XI.2001 (entered into force on 1 July 2004) (Budapest Convention). Cited in *Big Brother Watch* (n 6) [209]. Adopted in 2021, its Second Additional Protocol established new provisions to enhance cooperation and disclosure in specific criminal investigations and proceedings related to cybercrime and digital evidence.

[179] COE, European Commission Against Racism (ECRI) General Policy Recommendation No 11 on combating racism and racial discrimination in profiling in policing (adopted on 29 June 2007); COE Venice Commission, Report on the Democratic Oversight of the Security Services (adopted 1 June 2007) CDL-AD(2007)016 [260] (Venice Commission Report 2007).

[180] Venice Commission Report 2007 (n 179) 13–14.

[181] ECRI Recommendation No 11 (n 179) Explanatory Memorandum [41]; Venice Commission Report 2007 (n 179) [260].

[182] Frank Pasquale, *The Black Box Society* (HUP 2015) 156–59. The ECtHR Grand Chamber has stressed the importance of logging for ensuring effective surveillance oversight: *Zakharov* (n 135). See further Chapter 2.

raised by the large-scale surveillance activities of national security agencies.[183] Particular attention was given in these initiatives to the significant risks posed to privacy by bulk surveillance powers and communications data retention. Most policy recommendations focused on compliance with long-established Article 8 ECHR standards, especially the requirement for governments to ensure independent and effective oversight regimes of any bulk surveillance measures.[184] On democratic oversight of national security surveillance activities specifically, the COE Venice Commission has been active in producing a series of comprehensive investigative reports with recommendations for governments.[185] The Venice Commission is an advisory body to the COE whose reports in this area since 1998 draw on the expertise of highly qualified members, including senior civil servants. Like the COE, its aims are broad and concern promoting the rule of law and democracy and strengthening the understanding and harmonization of the laws of COE Member States.[186] In recent judgments concerning bulk data retention and bulk interception regimes before the ECtHR, findings and recommendations from two highly relevant Venice Commission reports (2007 and 2015) have played a clear role in shaping the submissions of both governments and applicants. Furthermore, the ECtHR has acknowledged such findings from these influential reports in its reasoning and conclusions.[187]

While other COE instruments have been cited by the ECtHR,[188] Convention 108 has been the most influential COE instrument in the case law dealing with Article 8 ECHR, State surveillance, and data retention measures. When other COE instruments are mentioned, they are usually as additional supporting authority for the relevant provision of Convention 108 or to further bolster the relationship between Convention 108 and Article 8 ECHR. The ECtHR in *Marper*, for instance, openly referred to the provisions of both Convention 108 and the COE recommendations on data processing for law enforcement purposes within the context of finding indiscriminate data retention to be incompatible with Article 8 ECHR.[189]

[183] COE Commissioner for Human Rights, *Democratic and effective oversight of national security services: Issue Paper* (2015).

[184] ibid 11–15.

[185] COE Venice Commission, 'Internal security services in Europe', 7 March 1998, CDL-INF (98) 6; COE Venice Commission Report 2007 (n 179); COE Venice Commission, Report on counter terrorism measures and human rights, 4 June 2010, CDL-AD (2010) 022; COE Venice Commission, Update of the 2007 Report on the democratic oversight of the security services and report on the democratic oversight of signals intelligence agencies, CDL-AD (2015) 006, 20–21 March 2015.

[186] Resolution RES (2002) 3 Adopting the Revised Statute of the European Commission for Democracy through Law, 22 February 2002, CDL (2002) 27. See generally Paul Craig, 'Transnational Constitution Making: The Contribution of the Venice Commission on Law and Democracy' (2017) 2 UC Irvine Journal of International, Transnational, and Comparative Law 57.

[187] See *Centrum för Rättvisa* (n 127) [86]–[91], [244], [264]; *Big Brother Watch* (n 11) [197], [330], [350].

[188] *Dragojević v Croatia* [2015] ECHR 28 [62]–[65]; *Benedik v Slovenia* [2018] ECHR 363 [126]; *Centrum för Rättvisa* (n 127) [85].

[189] *S and Marper* (n 145).

The ECtHR proceeded to highlight the importance of the data protection principle of data minimization and the resulting requirement for retention periods to be more proportionate and tailored to the relevant criminal offence or particular circumstances.[190]

2. EU legislation

Despite the EU not yet acceding to the ECHR, EU fundamental rights law and the ECHR have long been closely intertwined, with the CJEU's first reference to Article 8 ECHR taking place in 1975.[191] Article 52(3) of the EU Charter also provides that all measures within the scope of EU law that interfere with fundamental rights must meet, as a minimum, the standards mandated by the corresponding ECHR rights under ECtHR case law. Hence, the GDPR—the EU's cornerstone secondary legislation on data protection—explicitly recognizes in its recitals that any restrictions to data privacy must comply with the EU Charter and the requirements of the ECHR, thereby including Article 8 ECHR standards.[192] In addition to its key legislation governing data protection under the GDPR and data protection becoming an autonomous fundamental right under primary EU law since 2009,[193] the EU has enacted four key legal regimes governing data protection, privacy, and retention within the criminal justice context.[194] The most relevant of these was the Data Retention Directive 2006/24/EC which was struck down by the CJEU in the landmark judgment of *Digital Rights Ireland* for its incompatibility with the rights to respect for private life and data protection.[195] Following this annulment of Directive 2006/24/EC in 2014, Article 15 of the e-Privacy Directive 2002/58/EC is the EU legislation that currently authorizes the requirement of data retention obligations on communication service providers for law enforcement purposes.[196] The influence of Article 8 ECHR on the drafting, implementation, and post-legislative scrutiny of

190 ibid [103]–[110].

191 See further Chapters 4 and 5.

192 GDPR, recital 73.

193 In addition to the right to private life guaranteed under Art 7 CFR, Art 8 CFR also provides a distinct and separate right to the protection of personal data under EU law. See further Chapter 4.

194 e-Privacy Directive 2002/58/EC; European Parliament and Council Directive 2006/24/EC of 15 March 2006 on the retention of data generated or processed in connection with the provision of publicly available electronic communications services or of public communications networks and amending Directive 2002/58/EC [2006] OJ L105/54; Directive (EU) 2016/680 of the European Parliament and Council of 27 April 2016 on the protection of natural persons with regard to the processing of personal data by competent authorities for the purposes of the prevention, investigation, detection or prosecution of criminal offences or the execution of criminal penalties [2016] OJ L119/89 (LED); Directive (EU) 2016/681 of the European Parliament and Council of 27 April 2016 on the use of passenger name record data (PNR) data for the prevention, detection, investigation and prosecution of terrorist offences and serious crime [2016] OJ L119/132 (PNR Directive).

195 See Chapters 5 and 8.

196 See further Chapter 7.

the impugned Data Retention Directive, particularly the standards established in *Digital Rights Ireland*, are discussed in other chapters. Chapter 9 also deals with the same matters with respect to the EU Directive on the bulk retention of passenger name record (PNR) data for countering terrorism and other serious crime.

Other EU instruments concerning data retention and criminal justice include the 2005 Prüm Convention on cross-border cooperation, particularly in combating terrorism, and the (since repealed) 2008/977/JHA Council Framework Decision on data protection and data sharing in criminal matters.[197] The Prüm Convention, and its related framework and amendments,[198] set out rules for the sharing and exchange of fingerprinting, other DNA material, and vehicle registration data between law enforcement authorities in EU Member States. It also requires that any such data sharing be subject to the requirements of Article 8 ECHR and COE Convention 108 and that data be deleted once the established data retention period had been met.[199] Concerns, however, have been raised regarding the Prüm Convention's legal basis and legitimacy in light of its development by just seven signatories and the compliance of its vague and imprecise language and general lack of safeguards.[200] In order to provide some legal certainty around the oversight and transparency of DNA data exchanges between law enforcement, for instance, the European Data Protection Supervisor warned that the Prüm Convention should not have been adopted until after the entry into force of the 2008/977/JHA Council Framework Decision.[201] Despite these concerns, regular data exchanges continue between law enforcement authorities of the EU Member States (and the UK) under the Prüm framework.[202] The European Commission published legislative proposals in 2021 ('Prüm II') to update and reform the existing framework which may in future include the exchange of facial images for biometric matching.[203]

[197] Council of the EU, Prüm Convention on the stepping up of cross-border cooperation, particularly in combating terrorism, cross-border crime and illegal migration (signed by seven Member States on 27 May 2005) 7 July 2005, 10900/05 LIMITE; Council Framework Decision 2008/977/JHA of 27 November 2008 on the protection of personal data processed in the framework of police and judicial cooperation in criminal matters [2008] OJ L350/60.

[198] See amending Council Decisions 2008/615/JHA and 2008/616/JHA and Regulations (EU) 2018/1726, 2019/817, and 2019/818.

[199] Prüm Convention, Arts 34 and 37.

[200] House of Lords EU Committee, 'Prüm: an effective weapon against terrorism and crime' (18th Report of Session 2006–07, HL Paper 90) [22]–[24], Elsbeth Guild, Written Evidence, 21 March 2007.

[201] Council of the EU, Opinion of European Data Protection Supervisor on the draft Council Decision on the implementation of Decision 2007/ … /JHA on the stepping up of cross-border cooperation, particularly in combating terrorism and cross border crime, 5056/08, CRIMORG 6, 8 January 2008.

[202] Since 2020, eg, public authorities in the UK and Germany have been exchanging DNA and fingerprints daily via Prüm. See further Ni Loideain (n 106).

[203] European Commission, Impact Assessment Report accompanying Proposal for a Regulation of the European Parliament and of the Council on automated data exchange for police cooperation (Prüm II), SWD(2021) 378 final.

In 2018, Framework Decision 2008/977/JHA was repealed by a much more comprehensive legal framework for data protection under the Law Enforcement Directive (EU) 2016/679 (LED). The LED carries on the practice of allowing law enforcement authorities to adopt either an explicit time limit or the less strict safeguard of undertaking a periodic review to verify the ongoing need for a particular data retention measure.[204] Unlike Article 8 ECHR, and Convention 108+, EU law (Art 4(2) TEU) provides that any national security matters are solely the responsibility of the EU Member States. However, in a series of landmark cases since 2015, the CJEU Grand Chamber has established that EU law does in fact apply to surveillance and bulk retention programmes adopted for countering crime and safeguarding national security of non-EU countries and EU Member States. NGOs have welcomed this landmark data retention case law. National courts and some scholars, however, have raised concerns regarding how a number of these strict standards may serve to hinder, rather than enhance, the protection of EU fundamental rights in practice.[205]

3. Future reforms in EU law: communications data and CSAM

Acknowledging rightly that the e-Privacy Directive 2002/58 needs to keep 'pace with the evolution of technological and market reality', the Commission in 2017 proposed an e-Privacy Regulation. These proposed reforms included providing greater clarification around the concept of communications data.[206] A new definition of 'electronic communications metadata' was put forward covering any 'data processed in an electronic communications network for the purposes of transmitting, distributing or exchanging electronic communications content'.[207]

These long-awaited new e-privacy rules, however, have been subject to lengthy delay. In 2021, the Council of the EU adopted a new draft text and Member States agreed on a mandate for negotiations with the European Parliament resulting in the beginning of the 'trilogue' process.[208] Despite recent calls for 'intensified efforts' by

[204] Note that these requirements are subject to the higher standards set by the CJEU in its case law.
[205] See further Chapter 5.
[206] European Commission, Proposal for a Regulation of the European Parliament and of the Council concerning the respect for private life and the protection of personal data in electronic communications and repealing Directive 2002/58/EC (Regulation on Privacy and Electronic Communications), COM (2017) 10 final, recitals 6–9. Note that the e-Privacy Directive 2002/58 was subject to some amendments under Directive 2009/136/EC concerning online tracking. On EU regulatory reforms concerning the extension of EU telecoms regulation to 'over-the-top' (OTT) communications services generally, see Directive (EU) 2018/1972 establishing the European Electronic Communications Code (EECC) and Case C-142/18 *Skype Communications Sàrl*, judgment of 5 June 2019 (ECLI:EU:C:2019:460). OTTs provide their services in the form of applications running over the Internet access service (hence 'over-the-top'). Examples of OTTs include Google, LinkedIn, Meta, Microsoft, X (formerly Twitter).
[207] ibid Art 4(3)(c).
[208] See European Parliament, Legislative Train Schedule: Proposal for a regulation on privacy and electronic communications, <https://europarl.europa.eu/legislative-train/theme-connected-digital-single-market/file-jd-e-privacy-reform>.

the Commission and Members of the European Parliament (MEPs) to adopt the Regulation, this has yet to be followed by any concrete developments at the time of writing.[209] Regulators and scholars have also raised concerns regarding the compatibility of any proposed data retention provisions in the e-Privacy Regulation with the case law of the CJEU.[210] In June 2023, the European Commission established another High-Level Expert Group on challenges to law enforcement access to digital information, especially encryption and data retention. To quote one Member State: 'Data retention is the basis of this whole topic. Simply put: if there is no data retained, there is no point in talking about access to data.'[211] Given these intractable tensions between the EU institutions and the rapidly evolving data retention standards of the CJEU, swift progress on the e-Privacy Regulation seems unlikely without some change in the current status quo.[212]

Moreover, recent EU legislative developments dealing with the confidentiality of communications, the retention of traffic data, and public safety have been criticized for their questionable compatibility with the fundamental rights and data protection standards set out in the case law of the CJEU. These include Regulation (EU) 2021/1232 which was adopted on a temporary basis in 2021 and allows for derogations from several provisions of the e-Privacy Directive 2002/58.[213] Subject to the requirements of what has been referred to as the 'Interim Regulation', the framework does so by enabling CSPs on a voluntary basis to put in place specific measures to detect online child sexual abuse material (CSAM) on their services (eg images, videos, etc) or the solicitation of children (grooming). Articles 5(1) and 6(1) of the e-Privacy Directive 2002/58 do not then apply when service

[209] Luca Bertuzzi, 'Leading MEP enraged by Swedish Presidency's neglect of e-Privacy Regulation' EURACTIV (8 March 2023); European Parliament, 'Answer given by Mr Breton on behalf of the European Commission', P-000742/2023(ASW).

[210] EDPB, 'Statement 3/2021 on the e-Privacy Regulation', 9 March 2021; Valsamis Mitsilegas and others, 'Data Retention and the Future of Large-Scale Surveillance' (2023) 29 European Law Journal 176, 198–202. On updated guidance on the e-Privacy Directive 2002/58 and new tracking methods using 'similar technologies' to cookies, see EDPB, Guidelines 2/2023 on Technical Scope of Art. 5(3) of e-Privacy Directive (adopted 14 November 2023).

[211] Council of the EU, 'Proposal to establish a High-Level Expert Group on Access to Data' 7184/23, 20 March 2023, <https://statewatch.org/media/3855/eu-council-access-to-data-expert-group-7184-23.pdf> (comments made by Estonia). See European Commission, 'High Level Group (HLG) on access to data for effective law enforcement', <https://home-affairs.ec.europa.eu/networks/high-level-group-hlg-access-data-effective-law-enforcement_en>.

[212] Some commentators suggest that parts of the jurisprudence of the CJEU could be 'channeled' into new EU data retention legislation: Adam Juszczak and Elisa Sason, 'Recalibrating Data Retention in the EU' (2021) 4 EUCRIM 238, 262. On the relevant case law and reasons for the CJEU to adopt a less quasi-policymaking approach in its data retention case law, see Chapters 5 and 9.

[213] Regulation (EU) 2021/1232 of the European Parliament and of the Council of 14 July 2021 on a temporary derogation from certain provisions of Directive 2002/58/EC as regards the use of technologies by providers of number-independent interpersonal communications services for the processing of personal and other data for the purpose of combating online child sexual abuse [2021] OJ L274/41. At the time of writing, this temporary derogation had been extended to April 2026: see European Parliament, 'Child sexual abuse online' Press Release, 10 April 2024, <https://europarl.europa.eu/news/en/press-room/20240408IPR20311/child-sexual-abuse-online-current-rules-extended-until-april-2026>.

providers store and report (or undertaken other types of processing on behalf of law enforcement) any relevant content and traffic data generated when 'suspected online child sexual abuse has been identified'. Article 10 of the notably succinct Interim Regulation provided that it would cease to be in operation by 3 August 2024. Hence, the EU legislature published in 2022 a permanent CSAM Regulation to detect and combat CSAM that, if adopted, would impose mandatory requirements on service providers for online CSAM detection activities.[214] At the time of writing, however, the highly controversial draft CSAM Regulation was still far from being finalized. The proposal had reached the trilogue stage pending further pre-legislative scrutiny by the European Parliament and Council with many technical and legal issues still to be resolved.

While there should be no question about the risks and threats children may encounter online, it is hard to overstate just how strongly various stakeholders have expressed their concerns regarding the actual effectiveness and compatibility with EU law of both the Interim Regulation and the proposed CSAM Regulation. Academics, regulators, civil society, the European Parliament, and the Legal Service to the European Council have all questioned how such far-reaching intrusive bulk scanning can be assessed as compatible with the safeguards enshrined in Articles 7 and 8 of the EU Charter.[215] Particularly serious concerns persist over the proportionality of indiscriminately scanning the communications of millions of Internet users. There are also false positive risks inherent in the use of (probability-based) automated detection systems which could falsely identify and link innocent individuals with CSAM-related crimes.[216] Other major concerns include the adverse effects on encryption which is essential for protecting privacy and other human rights online. This is part of a broader problem in this area of policymaking as there have long been calls from law enforcement in Europe (and beyond) about the challenges posed by encryption for accessing digital communications. Addressing this challenge, however, remains a Gordian knot. As Walden and others point out, the debate between law enforcement and privacy remains highly polarized and further frustrated by an ongoing lack of sufficient evidence from public authorities showing 'the true extent' of the 'Going Dark' problem.[217]

[214] See European Parliament, 'Legislative Train Schedule: New Legislation to Fight Child Sexual Abuse Online', <https://europarl.europa.eu/legislative-train/spotlight-JD22/file-combating-child-sexual-abuse-online>.

[215] See EDPB-EDPS Joint Opinion 4/2022 on the Proposal for a Regulation of the European Parliament and of the Council laying down rules to prevent and combat child sexual abuse, adopted on 28 July 2022; Teresa Quintel, 'Renewed Concerns About Compliance of the Proposed "Regulation to Prevent and Combat Sexual Abuse"' (2023) 9 European Data Protection Law Review 173; European Parliament, Draft LIBE Report, 14 November 2023; EDPS, Summary Report of EDPS Seminar on the CSAM Proposal: 'The Point of No Return?', 10 November 2023, https://edps.europa.eu/system/files/2023-11/23-11-10_report_from_edps_seminar_on_csam_en.pdf.

[216] ibid. See Kashmir Hill, 'A Dad Took Photos of his Naked Toddler for the Doctor: Google Flagged Him as a Criminal' *New York Times* (21 June 2023).

[217] Ian Walden, 'The Sky is Falling!—Responses to the "Going Dark" Problem' (2018) 34 Computer Law & Security Review 901. On the US policy debate, see Peter Swire, Testimony to Senate Judiciary

Findings from a patchy report on the Interim Regulation's implementation published by the European Commission in December 2023 also failed to address the above concerns. Shortcomings in the report included a lack of comparative statistics from OTTs on the number of false positives made by their systems, insufficient detailed comparative statistics from Member States, and no statistics from Member States on how many reports led to actionable cases.[218] The Commission further stated in the report that the lack of sufficient data prevented 'definitive conclusions' from being drawn regarding the 'central question', namely the necessity and proportionality of the Interim Regulation. In other words, the report could not confirm whether the framework had balanced protecting the fundamental rights of children (including their online safety) and safeguarding the rights of affected users (privacy, data protection, freedom of expression, effective remedy).[219]

4. UN and other international initiatives

Article 12 of the UN Universal Declaration of Human Rights of 1948 (UDHR) provides for the right of protection against any 'arbitrary interference' with privacy, home, family or correspondence. Article 17 of the International Covenant on Civil and Political Rights of 1966 (ICCPR) closely follows the wording of Article 12 UDHR. Few countries internationally have implemented the Optional Protocol to the ICCPR to allow it to be enforced through the UN human rights system, which lacks any equivalent to the enforcement mechanism of the ECtHR.[220] Neither of these international instruments explicitly refer to the protection of personal data. The text of Article 8 ECHR also departs from the structure of these instruments and takes the opposite approach with respect to its substantive elements. Unlike the UDHR and ICCPR, the starting point of Article 8 ECHR guarantees the right to private life whereas its second section deals with the matter of what may justify an interference with that right. Consequently, like Article 8 ECHR, the UDHR and the ICCPR both provide that while the right to privacy is not absolute, any interferences with the right must be subject to the requirements of legality, necessity, and proportionality.

Committee Hearing, 'Going Dark: Encryption, Technology and the Balance Between Public Safety and Privacy', 8 July 2015, <https://fpf.org/wp-content/uploads/2015/07/SwireCrypto070715.pdf>; Tripp Mickle, 'Apple Details Plans to Beef Up Encryption of Data in its iCloud' *New York Times* (7 December 2022).

[218] European Commission, Implementation report on the e-Privacy Directive temporary derogation, 19 December 2023, 9–15, 31–33, https://home-affairs.ec.europa.eu/implementation-report-e-privacy-directive-temporary-derogation_en.

[219] ibid 33.

[220] At the time of writing, the UK had not yet implemented the ICCPR Optional Protocol: see Murray Hunter and others, *The Making of Bills of Rights: An Analysis of the United Kingdom's Obligations, Bonavero Report 1/2023* (University of Oxford 2023).

Prompted by privacy concerns raised by the Snowden revelations, a special rapporteur on the right to privacy was appointed in 2015 following the adoption of the UN Resolution on the 'Right the Privacy in the Digital Age' 28/16 in 2013.[221] In addition to the critical observations made in the often cited Resolution 28/16,[222] on the threats to data privacy posed by mass retention and communications surveillance, UN rapporteurs on freedom of expression also published detailed reports on the human rights implications posed by mass communications surveillance and bulk data collection regimes in various countries worldwide. Indeed, a prescient report was published by the then UN Special Rapporteur for Freedom of Expression, Frank La Rue, just months before the first Snowden revelations in 2013,[223] which called for mandatory communications data retention regimes to only be required of the private sector when shown to be proportionate and with independent oversight of government access.[224] The report noted the importance of strengthening existing data privacy standards, including Article 8 ECHR and highlighted the need for governments to update safeguards in their relevant legislation given the significant technological developments that have shaped current communications surveillance.[225] These included the need for independent judicial oversight and the right to *ex post* notification (once there is no longer a threat of jeopardizing ongoing investigations) if an individual's communications or communications data has been accessed by the State.[226] Forecasting key developments in later CJEU case law,[227] the report also stressed the interlinked and mutually dependent relationship of the rights to privacy and freedom of expression by highlighting that an infringement of either right through communications surveillance 'can both be the cause and consequence of an infringement upon the other'.[228]

Related recommendations also featured in other international initiatives, including a joint statement made by five European oversight authorities on international intelligence exchange in 2018 (Belgium, Denmark, Norway, Netherlands, Switzerland). The statement urged governments to adopt a more oversight-by-design approach where the need to strengthen the resources of oversight bodies is taken in account when intelligence services implement new surveillance

[221] UN Human Rights Office of the High Commissioner, 'Biography of Joseph Cannataci, Special Rapporteur on the right to privacy', <www.ohchr.org/EN/Issues/Privacy/SR/Pages/JoeCannataci.aspx>.

[222] *Zakharov* (n 135) [139]; *Centrum för Rättvisa* (n 127) [65]; *Big Brother Watch* (n 11) [202].

[223] Frank La Rue, 'Report of the Special Rapporteur on the promotion and protection of the right to freedom of opinion and expression, UN General Assembly', A/HRC/23/40, 17 April 2013.

[224] On the rise of communications data specifically by governments worldwide for law enforcement and national security purposes, see ibid [39], [65]–[67], [85].

[225] ibid [78].

[226] ibid [81]–[82].

[227] *Tele2* (n 6) [101], [107] held that communications data retention interfered with the rights to respect for private life, data protection, and freedom of expression.

[228] La Rue (n 223) [79].

systems.[229] The joint statement also recommended that a forum be established to exchange information with other oversight bodies on methods and best practice and international challenges in order to limit the risk of an oversight gap in international data exchange between intelligence and security services.[230] This call for closer cooperation between European oversight bodies aligns with collaborative policy initiatives adopted by public authorities in the common law jurisdictions of Australia, Canada, New Zealand, the US, and the UK. Otherwise known as the 'Five Eyes' community, the group is comprised of an intelligence-sharing network between the security and intelligence agencies within that group of countries. Five Eyes is arguably the most powerful surveillance network in the world and has its origins in agreements between the UK and the US made in the early Cold War era of the 1940s.[231] The Five Eyes community established the 'Five Eyes Intelligence Oversight and Review Council' in 2016. This closed forum of the Council shares information and best practice in oversight and meets annually in person and quarterly by secure electronic communication.[232] In parallel to the Council, the former UN Special Rapporteur for Privacy has established an annual conference attended by oversight bodies and regulators to discuss matters of intelligence oversight.[233]

Other international initiatives in this area put forward by civil society have drawn significantly from the standards and safeguards of Article 8 ECHR, include the 2013 'Global Principles on National Security and the Right to Information'.[234] The Principles are also referred to as the 'Tshwane Principles' and were drafted in South Africa by twenty-two international organizations and academic centres in consultation with more than 500 experts from over seventy countries at fourteen meetings held worldwide. Four UN special rapporteurs on freedom of expression and the special rapporteur on counter-terrorism and human rights, the African Commission on Human and Peoples' Rights (ACHPR), the Organization of American States (OAS), and the Organization for Security and Co-operation in Europe (OSCE) were also involved. These principles and recommendations focus particularly on public accessibility to oversight mechanisms and remedies. The Tshwane Principles have been cited in reports by the Council of Europe on State surveillance and oversight and have been endorsed by the COE Parliamentary

229 Joint Statement: Strengthening Intelligence Oversight Cooperation, 14 November 2018, 10, <https://english.ctivd.nl/documents/publications/2018/11/14/index>.

230 ibid.

231 For the declassified documents, see NSA, 'UKUSA Agreement Release': <https://nsa.gov/Helpful-Links/NSA-FOIA/Declassification-Transparency-Initiatives/Historical-Releases/UKUSA/>. Snowden described the UK as having the 'biggest internet access' of the Five Eyes community due to the mass transit of Internet traffic in the region: Anderson (n 16) [4.41].

232 Joanna Dawson and Samantha Godec, 'Oversight of the Intelligence Agencies: a comparison of the "Five Eyes" nations', Briefing Paper No 7921 (House of Commons Library 2017) 9.

233 Otherwise known as the 'International Intelligence Oversight Forum' (IIOF). The fifth IIOF was held in France in 2022.

234 ICJ, 'New global principles on the right to information launched', 12 June 2013, <www.icj.org/new-global-principles-on-the-right-to-information-launched/>.

Assembly in resolutions and recommendations, noted in proceedings before the ECtHR, and cited by regulators in other jurisdictions on matters dealing with oversight of law enforcement and intelligence agencies.[235] In 2018, the German-based NGO 'interface' (formerly Stiftung Neue Verantwortung) created the European Intelligence Oversight Network (EION). EION has brought together various European intelligence oversight officials and civil society experts on a regular basis and has contributed to policy reports on the challenges to the regulation and adequate oversight of national security. Findings and recommendations therein often draw on the standards of the ECtHR dealing with Article 8 ECHR and secret surveillance.[236]

E. Conclusions and Overview

The ECtHR has over decades developed an influential set of principles and minimum safeguards governing the secret surveillance of communications by public authorities under its Article 8 ECHR case law. These requirements have played a major role in shaping similar data privacy standards within EU law, the Council of Europe, and other legal systems across Europe and beyond.[237] Chapter 2 examines in detail the Strasbourg Court's development of this influential jurisprudence within the area of communications interception (including its controversial changes in recent case law). This critical analysis continues in Chapter 3 and turns to how the ECtHR has applied these requirements specifically to the retention and acquisition of communications data for law enforcement and national security purposes. In Chapter 4, the highly complex dialogue and relationship between the ECtHR and the CJEU on the right to private life is considered, with a focus on the case law of both courts concerning the right to private life, surveillance, and data retention. Here particular consideration is given to the impact and importance of the Lisbon Treaty reforms, especially the constitutional requirement for the EU to accede to the ECHR, and the elevation of the Charter to EU primary law.

[235] ENNHRI, Third Party Submission to ECtHR in *Big Brother Watch*, 5 February 2016, <https://ennhri.org/wp-content/uploads/2019/11/Big-Brother-Watch-and-Others-v-The-United-Kingdom_Written-Observations-of-ENNHRI.pdf>. Australian Human Rights Commission to Parliamentary Joint Committee on Intelligence and Security, 'Inquiry into the impact on the exercise of law enforcement and intelligence powers on freedom of the press', 25 July 2019.

[236] See eg Thorsten Wetzling and Charlotte Dietrich, *Disproportionate Use of Commercially and Publicly Available Data: Europe's Next Frontier for Intelligence Reform?* (SNV 2022) 44–45. Oversight bodies that have contributed to EION to date include representatives from Belgium, Denmark, Germany, the Netherlands, Norway, UK, Serbia, and Switzerland.

[237] Note the significant role played by Art 8 ECHR in the South African High Court judgment of *amaBhungane Centre for Investigative Journalism v Minister of Justice and Correctional Services* [2019] ZAGPPHC 384 where it was held inter alia that the law permitting secret bulk surveillance of international communications was incompatible with the right to privacy.

The Lisbon Treaty was intended to represent a milestone in the status and protection of fundamental rights within EU law. These reforms included commitments by the Council of the EU and the European Parliament to promote EU fundamental rights as a priority for future measures adopted at the EU level to counter terrorism and serious crime (area of freedom, security, and justice, AFSJ). Indeed, the European Commission stated that these reforms would promote a 'fundamental rights culture' and that the Charter would serve as a 'compass' for EU policies and their implementation by the Member States.[238] Within the area of EU data retention policymaking and the right to privacy, this book shows where there has been progress towards this more robust fundamental rights culture, and where the EU has fallen short. Chapters 5 to 9 specifically identify these gaps. This analysis also addresses how these gaps arose within the context of the mainstreaming of the right to private life in the e-Privacy Directive, Data Retention Directive, API Directive, and PNR Directive and provides policy recommendations in each chapter regarding how these challenges may be addressed in future.

From the tapping of landline telephones to the bulk retention of vast volumes of personal data using ML and other emerging AI technologies for analysis and profiling, Article 8 ECHR has been a benchmark for evolving data privacy standards for State surveillance of communications, including communications data. Despite the absence of any explicit reference to data protection within the ECHR itself, the ECtHR has long recognized in its case law that the protection of personal data forms part of the right to respect for private life and is of 'fundamental importance'. Hence, it is now well established that even the mere retention of information relating to private life, including communications data and biometric data, for law enforcement or national security purposes constitutes an interference with the protected interest of a private life.[239] This is a significant standard, among others, that has proven hugely influential for the landmark data retention and surveillance case law of the CJEU.

The Strasbourg Court itself often cites relevant instruments and standards from other legal systems, domestic and international, in its surveillance and data retention judgments in a rather boilerplate manner. Of course, there are times when the ECtHR will not explicitly cite, or discuss, any relevant EU or international framework. This does not mean that these texts have not been considered or have had no influence on the judgment. Nevertheless, it is often worth paying attention to the sources that the ECtHR does in fact choose to openly engage with in its assessment of data retention measures and their compatibility with Article 8 ECHR with respect to how the jurisprudence of the ECtHR may develop in future. Within this context, the ECtHR has given an increasingly special status in this area of case law

[238] European Commission, 'Strategy for the effective implementation of the Charter of Fundamental Rights by the European Union', COM(2010) 573 final, 2–4.
[239] See further Chapters 2 and 3.

to the relevance of data protection principles in its development and application of Article 8 ECHR. More recently, the ECtHR has referenced (often at length) relevant judgments by the CJEU and the plethora of reports published in the wake of the Snowden revelations by various international bodies on the regulation of surveillance for national security purposes. An emboldened CJEU has delivered a series of landmark cases over the past decade concerning data retention and State surveillance that cannot be ignored by the ECtHR.[240] In addition, relevant reports by the Venice Commission have also played a particularly influential role in the bulk interception case law of the ECtHR. Acknowledging the approach and standards of other legal systems (including even close engagement with corresponding CJEU case law) will not necessarily, however, be the writing on the wall for the conclusions of that particular ECtHR judgment.[241]

European human rights law remains at the forefront of privacy and data protection standards worldwide.[242] This status is further entrenched by the inextricable links between the ECHR and EU legal orders within the EU Charter and the ever-expanding global reach of EU data protection law and the related EU Digital Strategy.[243] Indeed, in an era of AI policymaking, the future development of these standards via the ECHR and EU legal systems have arguably never been so important. With so much communications data now collected concerning individuals' lives in the modern digital society, leading scholars describe the current era as the 'Golden Age of Surveillance'.[244] Article 8 ECHR will therefore continue to play a key role in the regulation and mainstreaming of the right to privacy in measures permitting surveillance and data retention by public authorities within the EU and beyond.

[240] See Chapters 5 and 9.

[241] On the evolving dialogue, and convergences and divergences, within this area of case law between the ECHR and EU legal systems, see Chapters 2 to 5.

[242] Graham Greenleaf and Bertil Cottier, 'International and Regional Commitments in African Data Privacy Laws' (2022) 44 Computer Law & Security Review; Christopher Kuner, 'Protecting EU Data Outside EU Borders Under the GDPR' (2023) 60 Common Market Law Review 77, 79; Bradford (n 51) 105–45; Orla Lynskey, 'Complete and Effective Data Protection' (2023) 76 Current Legal Problems 297, 298; Clifford (n 41) 27–28. See generally Anu Bradford, *The Brussels Effect* (OUP 2020).

[243] See further Chapters 4 and 5 and the European Commission, 'Shaping Europe's Digital Future', <https://digital-strategy.ec.europa.eu/en/policies/europes-digital-decade>. The ECHR and the COE 108 are also referenced in the preamble of the Draft COE Framework Convention on AI. The COE AI Convention is expected to be adopted in late 2024, making it the first international legally binding AI treaty. See further the Draft Framework Convention on artificial intelligence, human rights, democracy and the rule of law, CM(2024)52-prov1, 20 March 2024, <https://search.coe.int/cm#{%22CoEIdentifier%22:[%220900001680aee411%22],%22sort%22:[%22CoEValidationDate%20Descending%22]}>.

[244] See Swire (n 217); Walden (n 217).

2

The Approach of the Strasbourg Court

Article 8 ECHR and Interception of Communications

A. Introduction

The ECtHR has developed within its Article 8 ECHR case law an influential set of principles and minimum safeguards governing the secret surveillance of communications by public authorities. These requirements have played a pivotal role in shaping data privacy standards in legal systems within Europe and beyond. It is also well established in the jurisprudence that these standards apply when such measures are used for safeguarding national security. Thus, while the Strasbourg Court has recognized that national authorities enjoy a wide margin of appreciation in any matters concerning national security, the Court must still be satisfied that these surveillance powers when used in this context are subject to 'adequate and effective guarantees against abuse'.[1] Showing that important data privacy standards were not always the reserve of the CJEU and the EU Charter, this chapter identifies and examines these influential Article 8 ECHR standards developed within the ECHR legal order. The chapter also explains why they were long regarded by leading scholars and practitioners as 'an important driving force' in the scrutiny of domestic laws governing the secret monitoring of communications by public

[1] *Big Brother Watch and Others v United Kingdom* [2021] ECHR 439 [338]-[339] (GC); *Centrum för Rättvisa v Sweden* [2021] ECHR 440 [252]-[253] (GC). See generally on these leading bulk surveillance rulings: Marko Milanovic, 'The Grand Normalization of Mass Surveillance: ECtHR Grand Chamber Judgments in *Big Brother Watch* and *Centrum för Rättvisa*' *EJIL*, 26 May 2021: <https://ejiltalk.org/the-grand-normalization-of-mass-surveillance-ecthr-grand-chamber-judgments-in-big-brother-watch-and-centrum-for-rattvisa/>; Nora Ni Loideain, 'Not So Grand: The Big Brother Watch ECtHR Grand Chamber Judgment' *ILPC Blog*, 28 May 2021): <https://infolawcentre.blogs.sas.ac.uk/2021/05/28/not-so-grand-the-big-brother-watch-ecthr-grand-chamber-judgment/>; Mark Klamberg, 'Big Brother's Little, More Dangerous Brother' *VerfBlog*, 1 June 2021: <https://verfassungsblog.de/raettvisa/>; Graham Smith, 'Big Brother Watch/Rattvisa—a multi-factorial puzzle' *Cyberlegal*, 8 June 2021: <https://cyberleagle.com/2021/06/big-brother-watchrattvisa.html>; Juraj Safert, 'The Big Brother Watch and *Centrum för Rättvisa* judgments of the Grand Chamber of the European Court of Human Rights—the Altamont of Privacy?' *European Law Blog*, 8 June 2021, <https://europeanlawblog.eu/2021/06/08/big-brother-watch-and-centrum-for-rattvisa-judgments-of-the-grand-chamber-of-the-european-court-of-humanrights-altamont-of-privacy/>; Lorna Woods, '*Big Brother Watch v UK*' *EU Law Analysis*, 17 June 2021:<https://eulawanalysis.blogspot.com/2021/06/big-brother-watch-v-uk-ecthr-grand.html>; Bart van der Sloot, '*Big Brother Watch and others v. United Kingdom* & *Centrum för Rättvisa v. Sweden*' (2021) 7 European Data Protection Law Review 319; Monika Zalnieriute, '*Big Brother Watch and Others v the United Kingdom*' (2022) 116 American Journal of International Law 585. All URLs for this chapter were last accessed on 22 April 2024.

EU Data Privacy Law and Serious Crime. Nora Ni Loideain, Oxford University Press. © Nora Ni Loideain 2025.
DOI: 10.1093/oso/9780198837169.003.0002

authorities.[2] The rich case law dealing with Article 8 ECHR and the secret surveillance of communications examined in this chapter are also inherently linked to, and continue to shape, the approach of the ECtHR to the retention of personal data and its subsequent access and use by public authorities. Consequently, this analysis examines key legal standards relevant in the next chapter which focuses on how the ECtHR has applied these standards to the retention and use of communications data for countering crime and safeguarding national security.

This chapter further provides a critical examination of how the ECtHR's approach to these once lauded Article 8 ECHR principles and safeguards has changed in recent case law.[3] A clear departure from these standards is particularly evident in the landmark Grand Chamber judgments in 2021 dealing with bulk retention and surveillance measures (also referred to as 'signals intelligence' or SIGINT). *Big Brother Watch and Others v United Kingdom* and *Centrum för Rättvisa v Sweden* were not the first cases where the ECtHR had grappled with the compatibility of bulk surveillance with Article 8 ECHR. However, *Big Brother Watch* was the first to examine legal challenges to the previous legal regime permitting bulk interception in the UK following the groundbreaking revelations by former NSA contractor Edward Snowden in 2013.[4] *Centrum för Rättvisa* was in contrast a pre-Snowden era application that reached the ECtHR in 2008. The resulting Chamber judgment which was delivered in 2018 would later join *Big Brother Watch* in being reviewed by the Grand Chamber. This case concerned the current legal regime of bulk interception of communications in Sweden, particularly the Signals Intelligence Act enacted in 2008 (and since amended).

It is essential to note that these notable judgments in 2021 followed a long line of Article 8 ECHR cases since the 1970s that have gradually shaped domestic laws governing communications interception by public authorities across Europe, with legal challenges to the ECtHR previously resulting in notable legal reforms at the national level.[5] Enabling such limits on the use of State surveillance powers is a

[2] David Feldman, 'Secrecy, Dignity or Autonomy? Views of Privacy as a Civil Liberty' [1994] Public Law 41, 43; Christopher Kuner and others, 'An Unstoppable Force and an Immoveable Object? EU Data Protection Law and National Security' (2018) 8 International Data Privacy Law 1, 3; Christopher Vajda, 'Data Protection: Made in Europe and Exported Globally' (UKAEL Annual Lecture, 19 January 2023): <https://monckton.com/wp-content/uploads/2023/03/UKAEL-Lecture-Data-Protection-Made-in-Europe-and-Exported-Globally-final.pdf>.

[3] This chapter examines the approach of the ECtHR to measures permitting communications interception and their compatibility with Art 8 ECHR, not other relevant rights such as Art 10 ECHR.

[4] The UK enacted new legislation and a new oversight regime under the Investigatory Powers Act 2016 that was not the focus of the *Big Brother Watch* judgments. On the significance of the Snowden revelations concerning cross-border intelligence activities, see further Chapter 1.

[5] Many European countries have introduced reforms and adopted new surveillance and data privacy laws in response to ECtHR case law. See eg Lorena Winter, 'Telephone Tapping in the Spanish Criminal Procedure' (2007) 13 Jura 7; John Spencer, 'Telephone-Tap Evidence and Administrative Detention in the United Kingdom' in Marianne Wade and Almir Maljevic (eds), *A War on Terror?* (Springer 2010); TJ McIntyre and Ian O'Donnell, 'Criminals, Data Protection, and the Right to a Second Chance' (2017) 58 The Irish Jurist 27; Félix Tréguer, 'Intelligence Reform and the Snowden Paradox: The Case of France' (2017) 5 Media and Communication 17; Annual Report of the Investigatory Powers Commissioner 2022 (HM Stationery Office 2023) 16 (otherwise referred to as IPCO).

significant achievement for a supranational human rights court, especially in areas of such closely guarded sovereignty for the Contracting States of the ECHR such as national security. Scholars and practitioners have rightly recognized this impact by highlighting the major role played by previous Article 8 ECHR judgments in gradually entrenching and ratcheting up data privacy standards across Europe and within EU law.[6] A new chapter was then reached in the post-Snowden era when the ECtHR was invariably tasked with determining whether the unprecedented capabilities available to governments to monitor communications in the twenty-first century were compatible with Article 8 ECHR. Initially, the ECtHR openly acknowledged in its 2016 judgment of *Szabó and Vissy v Hungary* that the minimum safeguards required of States under its traditional Article 8(2) requirements may no longer be fit for purpose. This showed a court sensitive to the need for these standards 'to be enhanced' in response to the new and powerful technologies now being used for communications monitoring.[7] However, as discussed later, the Grand Chamber would later deliver a very different response to the calls for updating the Article 8 ECHR standards in 2021, which instead established that the ECtHR should determine the compatibility of bulk interception regimes with Article 8 ECHR by conducting a more holistic and deferential 'global assessment' of their operation.

It should, of course, be acknowledged that the fact that the surveillance techniques available to the State are always developing in their sophistication and reach into private life is far from novel. Since the dramatic rise of databases and automated data processing used by the public and private sectors from the 1960s onwards, concerns have consistently been raised about the preservation of privacy in the face of new pressures from communications technologies that may track, monitor, and profile individuals.[8] Consequently, in order for the Article 8 ECHR standards to remain relevant and capable of responding to such increasingly sophisticated surveillance capabilities, it is welcome that the ECtHR has acknowledged in its earlier case law the impact of key technological and social developments on the scope of intrusion to private life.[9] The ECtHR's approach in its

[6] Feldman (n 2); Paul de Hert, 'Balancing Security and Liberty Within the European Human Rights Framework [2005] Utrecht Law Review 68, 73; Ben Emmerson, Andrew Ashworth, and Alison Macdonald, *Human Rights and Criminal Justice* (3rd edn, Sweet & Maxwell, 2012) 315; Lee A Bygrave, *Data Privacy Law: An International Perspective* (OUP 2014) 86; Mary Arden, *Human Rights and European Law* (OUP 2015) 144; Marko Milanovich, 'Human Rights Treaties and Foreign Surveillance' (2015) 56 Harvard International Law Journal 81, 101; Nora Ni Loideain, 'Lawfulness and Police Use of Facial Recognition in the United Kingdom: Article 8 ECHR and *Bridges v South Wales Police*' in Rita Matulionyte and Monika Zalnieriute (eds), *Facial Recognition in the Modern State* (CUP 2024).

[7] *Szabó and Vissy v Hungary* (2016) 63 EHRR 3 [70]. See Eleni Kosta, 'Surveilling Masses and Unveiling Human Rights—Uneasy Choices for the Strasbourg Court', Tilburg Law School, Legal Studies Research Paper, 7 (15 December 2017) who noted that *Szabó and Vissy* provided the ECtHR with the opportunity to provide 'bold statements' in future surveillance cases (eg *Big Brother Watch*).

[8] See Chapter 1.

[9] See eg *Szabó and Vissy* (n 7); *Ekimdzhiev and Others v Bulgaria* [2022] ECHR 1 [394]. See generally Thérèse Murphy and Gearóid O'Cuinn, 'Works in Progress: New Technologies and the European Court of Human Rights' (2010) 10 Human Rights Law Review 601; Ni Loideain (n 6). As the ECtHR

earlier case law to dealing with these emerging technologies and their privacy implications resulted in two significant substantive developments.

First, there was the Court's recognition of data protection as a sub-right of Article 8 ECHR and its acknowledgement of the importance of related principles and safeguards of the Council of Europe's 1981 Convention on the Automatic Processing of Data (COE 108).[10] Secondly, the ECtHR has in previous landmark cases applied a heightened level of scrutiny to the impact on the interference with the rights enshrined in Article 8 ECHR posed by new surveillance capabilities and practices. This has resulted in the ECtHR reversing and reconsidering earlier jurisprudence in the light of recent technological developments that have dramatically expanded the scope (and thus the intrusiveness to private life) of modern communications surveillance. For instance, in its 2008 judgment of *Liberty v United Kingdom*, the ECtHR departed from its previous ruling in *Christie v United Kingdom* in holding that the same rule of law criteria developed for assessing regimes permitting the interception of individual (targeted) communications should also apply to general and indiscriminate (bulk) surveillance regimes.[11]

Thus, over a decade before its judgments in *Big Brother Watch*, the ECtHR had previously held that Article 8 ECHR requires intelligence agencies to provide with sufficient clarity in domestic law the scope and level of discretion available to public authorities to monitor communications outside the jurisdiction of the UK. This established that indiscriminate and general surveillance measures should be subject to the same foreseeability safeguards under the legality condition of Article 8(2), originally developed with respect to the targeted monitoring of individuals. This evolution in the case law was important for two key reasons. First, it demonstrated that both the scope of Article 8(1) and the safeguards of Article 8(2) were keeping pace at this time with modern technological and regulatory developments in the highly dynamic area of digital communications and secret surveillance. Secondly, *Liberty v United Kingdom* showed a court sensitive to the fact that the use of novel twenty-first-century surveillance powers should not evade the 'classic concerns', and robust scrutiny, previously applied

states in its 2022 judgment in *Ekimdzhiev* [394]: 'In view of the technological and social developments in the past two decades in the sphere of electronic communications, communications data can nowadays reveal a great deal of personal information. If obtained by the authorities in bulk, such data can be used to paint an intimate picture of a person through the mapping of social networks, location tracking, Internet browsing tracking, mapping of communication patterns, and insight into who that person has interacted with.'

[10] COE 108 has since been the subject of reform. On the modernized 'COE 108+', see Chapter 1.

[11] *Liberty v United Kingdom* (2008) 63 EHRR 3 [63]. The Court highlights this shift to a stricter approach to national security and its foreseeability in *Liberty* in contrast with its approach in *Christie v United Kingdom* [1994] ECHR 59. See Benjamin Goold, '*Liberty and others v United Kingdom*' (2009) 1 Public Law 5. The ECtHR previously considered the compatibility of signals intelligence regimes with Art 8 ECHR in its admissibility decision of *Weber and Saravia v Germany* [2006] ECHR 1173 and draws significantly from its analysis in *Weber* in *Liberty v United Kingdom*.

in the well-established and lauded Article 8 ECHR case law on communications interception.[12]

However, scholars have since raised concerns about the decline of these Article 8 ECHR standards and their progressive evolution by the ECtHR.[13] These criticisms stem from an initially gradual to a now very distinct shift (following its Grand Chamber judgments in 2021) within the ECtHR's level of scrutiny and approach in its examination of Article 8 ECHR in cases of secret surveillance, particularly its jurisprudence concerning novel and far-reaching surveillance regimes allowing for the indiscriminate monitoring and tracking of individuals using bulk collections of personal data. Indeed, warning signs were emerging before the controversial Grand Chamber judgments in *Big Brother Watch* and *Centrum för Rättvisa* that the ECtHR's approach to examining the compatibility of secret surveillance regimes with Article 8 ECHR was becoming less systematic and less strict—a change that has resulted in an increasing number of obfuscated and less rigorous assessments in judgments dealing with Article 8 ECHR and secret surveillance measures. Indeed, judges of the ECtHR itself have expressed concern over the Court's recent lax scrutiny of powerful surveillance and bulk data retention powers now available to public authorities and their compatibility with the right to private life as enshrined in Article 8 ECHR.[14]

There has relatedly been sharp criticism of the ECtHR for continuing to base its assessments of modern bulk interception regimes on what Smith aptly describes as 'old fashioned' safeguards developed between the 1970s and 1990s, particularly as the latter case law was developed long before the 'technological sea change' brought about by the twenty-first century.[15] This transformation in the reach of State surveillance has been enabled by access to AI-based systems in smart cities, mobile phones, facial recognition, modern predictive analytics, and highly sophisticated pattern-analysis and profiling capabilities. All this is made possible from the bulk

[12] Murphy and O'Cuinn (n 9) 636; Ni Loideain (n 6).

[13] See De Hert (n 6) 80; Marie-Helen Murphy, 'A Shift in the Approach of the European Court of Human Rights in Surveillance Cases' [2014] European Human Rights Law 507; Kirsty Hughes, 'Mass Surveillance and the European Court of Human Rights' [2018] European Human Rights Law 589; Woods (n 1); Paul De Hert and Gianclaudio Malgieri, 'One European Legal Framework for Surveillance' in Valsamis Mitsilegas and Niovi Vavoula (eds), *Surveillance and Privacy in the Digital Age* (Hart 2021) 255296; Ni Loideain (n 6); Valsamis Mitsilegas and others, 'Data Retention and the Future of Large-Scale Surveillance' (2023) 29 European Law Journal 176, 205. On legality within the ECHR system generally, see Geranne Lautenbach, *The Concept of the Rule of Law and the European Court of Human Rights* (OUP 2013).

[14] Ni Loideain (n 1); Smith (n 1); *Big Brother Watch v United Kingdom* [2018] ECHR 722, Partly Concurring, Partly Dissenting Opinion of Judge Koskelo and Judge Turković [29]; *Big Brother Watch* (n 1), Partly Concurring and Partly Dissenting Opinion of Judge Pinto De Albequeque [58]; on the Chamber judgment generally, see Bart van der Sloot and Eleni Kosta, '*Big Brother and Others v UK*' (2019) 5 European Data Protection Law Review 252 and Theodore Christakis, 'A Fragmentation of EU/ECHR Law on Mass Surveillance', *European Law Blog*, 20 September 2018: <https://europeanlawblog.eu/2018/09/20/a-fragmentation-of-eu-echr-law-on-mass-surveillance-initial thoughts-on-the-big-brother-watch-judgment/>.

[15] ibid.

collection of communications data created from our online lives and constant use of online devices. The above concerns are examined throughout this chapter with a view to addressing how Article 8 ECHR could return to its previously lauded role as an important driving force in the scrutiny of laws permitting the secret surveillance of communications in Europe.

B. Article 8(1): Interferences with Private Life

Article 8 guarantees the 'right to respect for private life' and forms part of the ECHR that protects numerous fundamental rights and freedoms.[16] The ECtHR has interpreted the scope of the protected interest of a 'private life' broadly under Article 8(1) with the aim of keeping up to date with emerging technologies and surveillance practices. Like certain other rights under the ECHR, the text of Article 8(2) clearly shows that the right to respect for private life is not absolute. Thus, the ECtHR is required to balance this qualified right alongside other competing rights and legitimate interests, including the prevention of crime and the protection of national security and public safety.[17] Article 8 ECHR imposes two different types of obligations (negative and positive). The approach of the ECtHR to the surveillance measure at issue will turn on which type of obligation arises.[18] The former imposes an obligation on a Contracting State to avoid interfering with any of the rights protected by Article 8(1) unless the conditions for justifying the interference under Article 8(2) are satisfied. The latter requires that the State take positive steps to protect the rights guaranteed under Article 8(1), particularly against interference by others. Both types of obligations have been found to apply to the secret surveillance of communications by the State. Ultimately, it is well established in the Article 8 ECHR case law that any surveillance by public authorities concerns 'the primary purpose' of the State under Article 8 ECHR not to interfere with the private life of the applicant unless justified with respect to the requirements of Article 8(2).[19]

[16] Council of Europe, Convention for the Protection of Human Rights and Fundamental Freedoms ETS No 005, 04.XI.1950 (ECHR): <https://www.coe.int/en/web/conventions/full-list/-/conventions/treaty/005>.

[17] Literature on Art 8 ECHR and secret surveillance is extensive. See David Feldman, *Civil Liberties and Human Rights* (2nd edn, OUP 2002) 523–42; Bernadette Rainey, Pamela McCormick, and Clare Ovey, *Jacobs, White and Ovey: The European Convention on Human Rights* (7th edn, OUP 2017) ch 16; David Harris and others, *Harris, O'Boyle, and Warbrick: Law of the European Convention on Human Rights* (4th edn, OUP 2018) ch 11; EU Agency for Fundamental Rights (FRA), *Surveillance by Intelligence Services, Vol II* (FRA 2017); FRA, *Surveillance by Intelligence Services* (updated report 2023); Ni Loideain (n 6). On the machinery of protection under the ECHR, see Chapter 1.

[18] See generally Jean-François Akandji-Kombe, *Positive Obligations under the European Convention on Human Rights* (COE 2007); Alisdair Mowbray, *The Development of Positive Obligations under the European Convention on Human Rights by the European Court of Human Rights* (Hart 2004); Malu Beijer, *The Limits of Fundamental Rights Protection by the EU* (Intersentia 2017).

[19] See eg Keir Starmer, *European Human Rights Law* (Legal Action Group 1999) 129; *MD and Others v Spain* [2022] ECHR 527 [52].

1. The two-stage test

Most legal challenges brought against secret surveillance measures under Article 8 ECHR concern negative obligations and are subject to a two-stage test.[20] First, the ECtHR will consider whether the complaint falls within the scope of Article 8(1). The ECtHR determines at this first stage whether the alleged interference by the Contracting State has engaged Article 8(1). If so, the ECtHR will then examine whether the interference meets the conditions of Article 8(2). The three conditions of this second stage concern: (1) whether the interference is 'in accordance with the law' (legality); (2) whether it pursues one of the several legitimate aims identified under Article 8(2); and (3) whether the measure is 'necessary in a democratic society' (proportionality). Positive obligations may also arise in cases concerning Article 8 ECHR and the notion of private life. The ECtHR has established that the principles relevant to a case being analysed in terms of a positive duty on the State to take reasonable and appropriate measures to secure the applicant's rights under Article 8(1), or in terms of a negative obligation to be justified in accordance with Article 8(2), are broadly similar.[21] The basis relied upon for the enforcement of these positive obligations has been the duty of the State to 'respect' the rights provided for under Article 8(1), with a view to ensuring that these rights are effectively safeguarded by the State.[22] In 2008, for instance, the ECtHR unanimously held in *KU v Finland* that the Contracting State had violated positive obligations guaranteed by the right to respect for private life of Article 8 ECHR due to its failure to prosecute an offence of malicious representation.[23]

The facts involved the applicant's photo being posted on an Internet dating website without his knowledge. He was twelve years old at the time and the advertisement included details of his age, physical profile, and a link to his own website.[24] Under the domestic law then in force, communication service providers could not be ordered to provide information identifying the offender. In line with common practice, there was no dispute between the parties that the matter before the ECtHR fell within the scope of private life. In particular, the ECtHR highlighted the 'potential threat' posed by the intrusion to the applicant's physical and mental welfare that fall under the areas of physical and moral integrity of an individual protected under Article 8(1).[25] Recognizing the difficulties involved in 'policing modern societies', the ECtHR noted that positive obligations should not be interpreted in a way that would place a disproportionate burden on the legislator.[26] Nevertheless,

20 Feldman (n 17) 665–67.
21 *Hatton v United Kingdom* (2003) 37 EHRR 611 (GC).
22 *Airey v Ireland* (1979–80) 2 EHRR 305 [32], [33]; *X and Y v The Netherlands* (1985) 8 EHRR 235 [23].
23 *K.U. v Finland* [2008] ECHR 1563.
24 ibid [7].
25 ibid [41].
26 ibid [48].

the ECtHR pointed out that Finland would have been aware at the material time that the 'anonymous character' of the Internet could be used for criminal purposes, including the widespread problem of child sexual abuse.[27] The public authorities had the opportunity, therefore, to create a system to protect child victims 'from being exposed as targets for paedophiliac approaches via the Internet'.[28] Not doing so culminated in the inability of the State to identify the offender and undertake an effective investigation. The ECtHR thus held that this constituted a violation of Article 8 ECHR as the positive obligation owed to the applicant to provide practical and effective protection of his right to private life through relevant legislation was not met.

Furthermore, in contrast to a literal interpretation of its wording, Article 8 ECHR is not limited to interferences with private life by government measures and has instead been interpreted as having horizontal application.[29] This means, in practice, that the application of human rights obligations also extends indirectly to the private sector.[30] That being said, any obligations placed on Contracting States in respect of private acts are only imposed indirectly through the medium of positive obligations.[31] Nevertheless, the importance of this implication cannot be overstated given the growing role of the private sector in providing public services through data-driven products and systems, particularly in the areas of criminal justice and national security.[32] Hence, while the principal aim of Article 8 ECHR is to protect the individual against arbitrary interferences by public authorities, it does not merely compel the State to abstain from such interference 'as there may be positive obligations inherent in effective respect for private life'.[33] As discussed in Chapter 3, this determination includes assessing what safeguards govern the retention, use, sharing, and deletion of information within a regime of secret communications surveillance, to ensure the effective protection of the right to respect for private life.

2. The temporal scope of examination: falling between two stools

A key element underpinning the operation of this two-stage test in practice is the temporal scope of the surveillance regimes under examination. Given the

[27] ibid [48].
[28] ibid [48].
[29] Harris and others (n 17) 26–27.
[30] Unlike the ECtHR, the US Supreme Court has not recognized a principle of positive obligation on the State to create protections against private parties. See Perry Keller, 'A Reconstruction of Privacy Through Law' (2019) 9 International Data Privacy Law 132.
[31] Harris and others (n 17) 27.
[32] See further Chapter 1.
[33] *Craxi v Italy (No 2)* (2004) 38 EHRR 995 [73].

numerous years that may often pass between when a secret surveillance measure took place, an application being lodged with the ECtHR, and the delivery of its judgment, the contested law may have been amended several times over this period. This is a particularly important factor in recent major judgments as bulk data retention and surveillance regimes across Europe have been subject to challenge and reform following the legal and political fallout of the Snowden revelations.[34] Some parties may identify the exact period in question for the scope of the examination based on the material time of when the surveillance took place.[35] That being so, the ECtHR may decide not to examine the legality of the regime at the material time when the surveillance occurred if new and more comprehensive legislation is enacted 'offering a broader scope of guarantees within *a relatively short time* after the events complained of'.[36] This questionable approach was applied in the 2009 judgment of *Kvasnica v Slovakia* and concerned a gap of over two years between the impugned law in force at the time of the mobile phone interception and the enactment of key reforms.[37] If no exact period for review is specified when examining the law and practice *in abstracto*,[38] the ECtHR may also adopt the approach of assessing the surveillance framework as it stands at the time of examination.[39] In such circumstances, potentially involving many legal changes, the ECtHR has pointed out that it cannot be required to examine the 'compatibility with the Convention before and after every single legislative amendment'.[40] The ECtHR does not elaborate on the reasoning for taking into account legal and policy developments that have occurred often many years after the material time of the surveillance.

In pursuing this pragmatic approach, it could be argued that the ECtHR is providing scrutiny of the most recent legal developments in communications surveillance within the relevant Contracting State. Thus, by doing so, the ECtHR is contributing to the development of the most up-to-date standards for all members of the Council of Europe in a rapidly evolving area of law and technology. On the other hand, this approach also serves to potentially undermine what is the cardinal issue before the ECtHR, which is determining whether an impugned surveillance law amounts to a justified interference under Article 8 ECHR. Indeed, this unsatisfactory situation has resulted in oversight gaps created between amended regimes (updated following the initiation of legal challenges) and the legality of the relevant frameworks in operation when it has been shown that violations of Article 8 ECHR have clearly taken place. Thus, the ECtHR's judgment in such

[34] See further Chapter 1.

[35] *Liberty* (n 11) [42], [69].

[36] *Kvasnica v Slovakia* [2009] ECHR 872 [84] (emphasis added). The mobile phone of the applicant (a lawyer) was tapped in order to investigate whether his clients had committed serious fraud.

[37] ibid [12], [42] (October 2000–May 2003).

[38] Applicants may still claim to be victims of an Art 8 ECHR violation due to the mere existence of the surveillance practice, without having to show that any concrete measures were taken against them.

[39] *Centrum för Rättvisa v Sweden* [2018] ECHR 520; *Big Brother Watch* (n 14).

[40] *Centrum för Rättvisa* ibid [98].

circumstances may fall between two stools by examining very different legal regimes for different periods of time. This poses the risk that regimes that were not Article 8 ECHR compliant at the material time (which in some cases have been decades) may inevitably escape any oversight or scrutiny by the ECtHR, effectively resulting in few—if any—consequences for unlawful and disproportionate State surveillance.

Such an approach arguably sends a deeply problematic message to public authorities granted very broad powers to use secret surveillance programmes that collect vast amounts of data, powers which by their very nature involve enormous risks of abuse. These gaps in oversight suggest that there may be no meaningful assessment of whether Article 8 ECHR safeguards remain adequate and effective in such cases. This approach consequently runs the risk of perpetuating a culture where public authorities believe they may act with impunity.

Consider, for instance, the first application in *Big Brother Watch*,[41] submitted to the ECtHR in 2013 shortly after the Snowden revelations took place.[42] By the time the ECtHR had delivered this judgment five years later in 2018, the UK had made major changes to the relevant legal regime in force in 2013. In submissions to the European Parliament in November 2013, oversight safeguards provided under the main statute in force at the time were sharply criticized, with one leading academic expert deeming them 'lax' and 'poor'.[43] Thus, in the intervening period between 2013 and the ECtHR Court hearings in 2017, several new legal policy documents were issued concerning surveillance powers that had never been revealed to key oversight bodies (including relevant Parliamentary Committees) or the public.[44] However, the fact remains that these surveillance programmes were only later made known to the public (or 'avowed') as a result of the Snowden revelations in 2013. This means that intelligence agencies effectively had a 'long-secret' power for obtaining 'regular feeds' of bulk communications data from communication service providers (CSPs)for twenty-nine years.[45] Nevertheless, both the Chamber and the Grand Chamber took into account findings from later reports, updated Codes of Practice, and domestic legal challenges concerning the avowed surveillance programmes from between 2013 and 2017.[46] The relevant Codes of Practice

[41] The *Big Brother Watch* application to the ECtHR was joined with two others in 2014 and 2015: *Big Brother Watch and Others v United Kingdom* (App No 58170/13); *Bureau of Investigative Journalism and Alice Ross v United Kingdom* (App No 62322/14); *10 Human Rights Organisations v United Kingdom* (App No 24960/15).

[42] 'Timeline of Events' *Big Brother Watch*, <https://privacynotprism.org.uk/assets/files/privacynotprism/Timeline%20of%20Events.pdf>.

[43] Iain Cameron, 'Speaking Notes: European Parliament Hearing on Mass Surveillance' (7 November 2013) 4. The relevant legislation at this time was the Regulation of Investigatory Powers Act 2000 (RIPA).

[44] Nora Ni Loideain, 'A Bridge Too Far? The Investigatory Powers Act and Human Rights' in Lilian Edwards (ed), *Law, Policy and the Internet* (2nd edn, Hart, 2018) 165–92.

[45] Graham Smith, *Internet Law and Regulation* (5th edn, Sweet & Maxwell 2019) 935.

[46] *Big Brother Watch* (n 14) [325]–[347]; *Big Brother Watch* (n 1) [366]. One later legal development revealed that GCHQ had retained intercepted emails of Amnesty International for longer than

had only materialized as a result of litigation initiated following the Snowden revelations. As Hughes and others rightly point out, the ECtHR did not then have to consider whether the impugned regime '*had* been operating on the basis of a clear, accessible and foreseeable legal framework, but rather whether in November 2017 it met the requirements of legality'.[47]

Consequently, with a view to enhancing legal certainty and the standard-setting role of the ECtHR in future related case law, it is argued here that the Strasbourg Court should apply the traditional temporal approach when applicants do not specify what legal framework (or material time) is to be examined. The Court's scope of examination would then be clearly limited to the specific material time when the impugned surveillance was in operation. More importantly, this means doing so at the point when the application was first lodged with the ECtHR—not when the Court's examination of the contested surveillance framework takes place (often several years later). Such an approach does not prevent the ECtHR from highlighting later reforms adopted by that Contracting State which subsequently address the previous issues of non-compliance with Article 8 ECHR. Indeed, this was the approach explicitly adopted in *Liberty v United Kingdom*.[48] Like *Big Brother Watch*, *Liberty* also concerned a legal challenge made *in abstracto* by civil society groups (NGOs) claiming victimhood status by virtue of the existence of the surveillance regime. The impugned law was the Interception of Communications Act 1985, which was later replaced by the Regulation of Investigatory Powers Act 2000 (RIPA) which was itself later the subject of legal challenge in *Big Brother Watch*.[49] The ECtHR focused its assessment in *Liberty* on the 'virtually unfettered' discretion then available to a Secretary of State to monitor communications external to the British Islands under the regime of the Act of 1985.[50] This absence of any limits in domestic law to avoid abuses of power was held to be a breach of the legality condition and therefore a violation of Article 8 ECHR.

Nevertheless, the ECtHR still took the opportunity in *Liberty* to highlight advances in the legal reforms adopted after the material time under examination. These included the UK making details from the regime governing this secret surveillance regime publicly accessible in a Code of Practice after RIPA had been adopted. A development which, the ECtHR rightly observed, 'suggests that it is possible for a State to make public certain details about the operation of a scheme

lawfully permitted, thus violating Art 8 ECHR: *Liberty and Others v GCHQ, SIS, Security Service* [2015] UKIPTrib 13_77-H_2.

47 Hughes (n 13) 593; Woods (n 1). The Grand Chamber judgment in 2021 also determined its review of the legislative regime as it stood on 7 November 2017: see *Big Brother Watch* (n 1) [270].

48 *Liberty* (n 11). See similarly *Benedik v Slovenia* [2018] ECHR 363 [131]. Contrast this with the deferential approach of the ECtHR in *Ekimdzhiev and Others v Bulgaria* [2022] ECHR 1 [293].

49 Much of RIPA has been amended by the Investigatory Powers Act 2016. See Smith (n 45) 875–975.

50 *Liberty* (n 11) [64].

of external surveillance without compromising national security'.[51] The ECtHR thus took the opportunity to highlight these welcome reforms without conflating its assessment of the different legislative regimes and time periods in its legal assessment. This approach enabled the ECtHR to avoid any oversight gaps in its examination of the contested provisions and their computability with Article 8 ECHR. The ECtHR was then still able to fulfil its lauded standard-setting role of acknowledging any legal developments that could be of guidance to other Council of Europe members when assessing the Article 8 ECHR compliance of their secret surveillance regime and legal frameworks.

3. The right to respect for private life

The ECtHR has long considered the notion of 'private life' as a term not susceptible to exhaustive definition. As a result, this concept has been interpreted broadly in cases involving Article 8 ECHR and secret surveillance of communications in general. Its scope of protection applies to the interests within the 'inner circle' of an individual's private life, including the right to identity and personal development and establishing relationships with others and the wider world.[52] The application of this protection also goes beyond this inner circle, extending to the 'zone of interaction' of an individual with others and their movements, even in a public context.[53] An interference with private life takes place therefore even if retained information on a 'person's whereabouts and moments' is collected from a public place.[54] This means that the ECtHR has established that information retained for the purpose of enabling State surveillance of an individual through their travel by plane, train, or car also constitutes an interference with the protected interest of private life of Article 8(1).[55]

Indeed, even if no physical intrusion into a private place occurs, surveillance can interfere with physical and psychological integrity and the right to respect for private life.[56] Put more simply, surveillance may take place if 'a police officer is just

[51] ibid [68]. The FRA followed suit in 2017 and recommended that States should explain their surveillance laws in clear and understandable codes of practice on intelligence services' websites: FRA (n 17) 45.

[52] *Niemietz v Germany* (1992) 16 EHRR 97 [29]; *P.G. and J.H. v United Kingdom* [2001] ECHR 546 [56]; *Peck v United Kingdom* (2003) 36 EHRR 719 [57]; *Von Hannover (No 2) v Germany* (2012) 55 EHRR 15 [95] (GC); *Breyer v Germany* [2020] ECHR 95 [73]; *Glukhin v Russia* [2023] EHRR 540 [64].

[53] As held in *Peck* ibid, a public authority sharing with the media CCTV footage identifying a distressed individual in a public space with a knife just before his attempted suicide, which was then broadcast to a wide TV audience, was found to constitute a serious interference with the right to respect for private life.

[54] *Shimovolos v Russia* (2014) 58 EHRR 26 [64]–[66]; *Glukhin* (n 52). See further Chapter 3.

[55] *Shimovolos* (n 54) [65].

[56] Nicola Moreham, 'The Right to Respect for Private Life in the European Convention on Human Rights: A Re-Examination' (2008) 3 European Human Rights Law Review 44, 53.

using his eyes when standing on the street or whether the same officer is targeting someone with binoculars'.[57] For an analogy in a more digital context, an interference with private life also occurs when a public authority is given access to the social media accounts or location data of an individual's mobile phone (in real time or historical) via their communications service provider to track that individual's movements, relationships, or daily routine. This applies whether they are at home, at work, or in an online (or offline) public space.[58]

This broad interpretation of private life by the ECtHR turns on the core of privacy, particularly in its context as a civil liberty, being underpinned by 'the very essence' of the ECHR, namely 'respect for human dignity and human freedom'.[59] In earlier cases, the ECtHR had generally examined whether the interception of communications in a particular application before it had fallen within the distinct protected interests under Article 8(1) of 'private life' and 'correspondence'.[60] Subsequently, however, the approach of the ECtHR has effectively shifted over time to primarily assessing whether a relevant secret surveillance measure has engaged and, if so, thereby amounts to an interference with the protected interest of private life. This notably contrasts with the more granular approach of the ECtHR in cases dealing with Article 8 ECHR and the retention and access to communications data by public authorities where both protected interests of private life and correspondence are generally subject to greater scrutiny. This is likely a response to the groundbreaking judgments on data retention by the CJEU. This stark contrast is particularly evident in the 2022 judgment of *Ekimdzhiev v Bulgaria* in which the ECtHR sidesteps any Article 8(1) assessment of the relevant interference posed by the contested secret surveillance measures. However, for its assessment of the contested provisions of the domestic law concerning the retention and access of communications data, there is a detailed assessment of how both the protected interests of private life and correspondence are engaged.[61]

[57] Akil Reed Amar, *The Constitution and Criminal Procedure* (Yale UP 1997) 8–9.

[58] In *Roman Zakharov v Russia* (2016) 63 EHRR 17 (GC), Russia laws permitting remote direct access to the databases of communication services providers to both security agencies and police were found to contain several 'defects' due to a lack of adequate and effective safeguards to ensure against abuse. Hence, the regimes were held to be in violation of Art 8 ECHR. See generally Lorna Woods, '*Zakharov v. Russia*' (2016) 55 International Legal Materials 207.

[59] *Pretty v United Kingdom* (2002) 35 EHRR 1 [65] (this case concerned the right to self-determination and assisted suicide). See Janneke Gerards, *General Principles of the European Convention on Human Rights* (CUP 2019) 61–62. On the approach to the concept of essence by the ECtHR generally, see Sébastien Van Drooghenbroeck and Cecilia Rizcallah, 'The ECHR and the Essence of Fundamental Rights' (2019) 20 German Law Journal 904.

[60] See eg *Klass v Germany* [1978] ECHR 4 [41]; *Huvig v France* (1990) 12 EHRR 547 [25]; *Valenzuela Contreras v Spain* (1999) 28 EHRR 483 [47].

[61] *Ekimdzhiev and Others* (n 9) [262], [372]–[376]. See further Chapter 3.

(a) Dignity and private life

Dignity is essential to an individual's development and flourishing which depends on the exercise of autonomy.[62] Secrecy, or exerting control over that information, serves the function of enabling the individual's development but—crucially—does not exhaust an individual's entitlement to dignity. Consequently, the scope of protection under Article 8 ECHR goes beyond relying on the value of freedom or the 'right to be let alone'.[63] The value of privacy is also plural for both the individual and society given the range of activities it protects that are important to the flourishing of both.[64] The ECtHR has increasingly given little weight, however, to the value of dignity and its role in assessing interferences with private life in recent surveillance case law. This can be seen in the narrow emphasis (if any) placed on the importance of private life interests as only relevant to the protection of the individual when balanced in a clear dichotomy against society's interest to protect national security interests.[65] Indeed, such an approach runs counter to the broad scope of the right to respect for private life that the ECtHR has previously recognized under Article 8(1).

From the perspective of legal certainty, it is necessary for the ECtHR to clearly highlight the broad scope of protection afforded to a wide range of activities under the right to private life under Article 8(1) in order to convey the value of those rights. Indeed, it is essential for this analysis to take place in order to establish what is lost when the right to private life (and indeed other human rights) is sacrificed 'for some other end'.[66] The key interests at stake include intimacy, friendship, dignity, individuality, human relationships, autonomy, freedom, self-development, creativity, freedom of thought, democracy, reputation, and psychological well-being.[67] Moreover, the dissemination of information from this zone by the individual (including its collection by others) is subject to the wider right of society to protect individuals within this zone and the interests of society as a whole outside it.[68] Thus, as Lynskey and other leading scholars point out, laws that rely solely on a 'notice and consent' model for the protection of individuals' zones of privacy are sorely outdated in an era of online data proliferation where individuals have little control over systematic data collection that tracks their online and

[62] Feldman (n 2) 55; Giovanni Buttarelli, 'Choose Humanity: Putting Dignity Back into Digital (2018) 4 European Data Protection Law Review VII.

[63] See Louis Brandeis and Samuel Warren, 'The Right to Privacy' (1890) 4 Harvard Law Review 193.

[64] Feldman (n 2) 55.

[65] *Zakharov* (n 58) [232]; *Centrum för Rättvisa* (n 39) [112]; *Big Brother Watch* (n 1) [314]; *Ekimdzhiev and Others* (n 9).

[66] Hughes (n 13) 598.

[67] Daniel J Solove, *Understanding Privacy* (HUP 2008) 98. On the chilling effect to freedom of thought and expression also posed by the threat of surveillance, see Jonathon W Penney, 'Chilling Effects: Online Surveillance and Wikipedia Use' (2016) 31 Berkeley Technology Law Journal 117; Daragh Murray and Pete Fussey, 'Bulk Surveillance in the Digital Age' (2019) 52 Israel Law Review 31, 43–47.

[68] Feldman (n 2) 55.

offline behaviours.[69] Similar concerns apply to relying on the concept of a reasonable expectation of privacy in relation to assessing the privacy harms posed by the increasing practice of public authorities collecting vast amounts of data that enables the bulk tracking or identification of individuals (online and offline).

An extensive and 'purposive' interpretation of Article 8(1) has invariably allowed the ECtHR great freedom to increase the scope of activities that interfere with private life in contrast to stricter limits placed on privacy doctrines in other jurisdictions (such as the US).[70] The ECtHR established as far back as 1978 that telephone conversations fall within the notions of private life and 'correspondence' and are protected under Article 8(1).[71] In order to keep up to date with rapid developments in communications technology and surveillance capabilities, the ECtHR has (in certain judgments) deftly used its broad interpretation of Article 8(1) to expand this scope of protection. Hence, the notion of private life has since been interpreted to cover access to communications data (online and offline),[72] communications within the home/business,[73] Internet usage (emails, online browsing),[74] mobile phones,[75] location data,[76] and mass surveillance programmes (including signals intelligence methods).[77] An interception of communications still constitutes 'a serious inference' with the right to respect for private life even if no use is subsequently made of the collected and stored material.[78]

This finding is significant as it shows that the ECtHR has recognized the different types, and varying levels, of interference to private life posed by each distinct stage of the surveillance life cycle from collection, retention, access, extent of use, sharing, efforts to anonymize data, and deletion.[79] That being said, it is important

[69] On consent and these power asymmetries generally, see Eleni Kosta, *Consent in European Data Protection Law* (Brill 2013); Gabriela Zanfir, 'Forgetting about Consent. Why the Focus Should be on "Suitable Safeguards" in Data Protection Law' in Serge Gutwirth and others (eds), *Reloading Data Protection* (Springer 2014) 239–44; Orla Lynskey, *The Foundations of EU Data Protection Law* (OUP 2015) 185–96; Chris Jay Hoofnagle, *Federal Trade Commission* (CUP 2016) 331–33. Regarding the right to data protection and power asymmetries, see Plixara Vogiatzoglou and Peggy Valcke, 'Two Decades of Article 8 CFR' in Eleni Kosta, Ronald Leenes, and Irene Kamara (eds), *Research Handbook on EU Data Protection Law* (Elgar 2022) 11–49; Damian Clifford, *Data Protection and Emotion* (OUP 2024).

[70] Milanovich (n 6) 131. Nicolas Bratza, 'Living Instrument or Dead Letter—the Future of the European Convention on Human Rights' (2014) 2 European Human Rights Law Review 116, 122. On the approach of the US Supreme Court to communications data surveillance and privacy and the narrowing of the 'third party doctrine', see *Carpenter v United States*, 138 S Ct 2066 (2018); Matthew Tokson, 'The Aftermath of *Carpenter*' (2022) 135 Harvard Law Review 1790.

[71] *Klass* (n 60) [41]; *Malone v United Kingdom* (1985) 7 EHRR 14 [64]; *Lambert v France* (2000) 30 EHRR 346 [21].

[72] *Malone* ibid; *Copland v United Kingdom* (2007) 45 EHRR 858.

[73] *Niemietz* (n 52) [29]; *Halford v United Kingdom* (1997) 24 EHRR 523 [44]; *Amann v Switzerland* [2000] ECHR 87 [44] (GC).

[74] *Copland* (n 72) [41]; *Szabó and Vissy* (n 7) [53].

[75] *Liberty* (n 11) [56]; *Szabó and Vissy* (n 7) [53].

[76] *Uzun v Germany* (2011) 53 EHRR 24 [52].

[77] *Liberty* (n 11); *Big Brother Watch* (n 1).

[78] *Kopp v Switzerland* (1999) 27 EHRR 91 [53], [72].

[79] The ECtHR has also employed this more careful strict-scrutiny approach in cases concerning the processing of data with respect to photographs and CCTV: *Peck* (n 52).

to note that the ECtHR does not always apply this more carefully considered and granular assessment of Article 8(1) when dealing with cases that involve multiple data privacy issues (such as length of data retention, distinguishing between the retention of content and communications data, access to intercepted data[80]). The ECtHR will often not identify what protected interests under Article 8(1) are specifically affected and/or the different levels of intrusiveness posed by each specific stage of data processing. This ambiguity consequently raises serious questions around the protection provided by Article 8 ECHR to new surveillance technologies such as 'emotion detection' that immediately profiles individuals but may not necessarily also store that captured information.[81] It would provide greater legal certainty if the ECtHR focused primarily on the exact private life interference, advertising tailored to an individual based on their emotional state, and the relevant affected interests (such as freedom of thought and psychological well-being) rather than on the specific technique used.

(b) A 'reasonable expectation of privacy'

The concept of a reasonable expectation of privacy has been applied inconsistently in Article 8 ECHR case law dealing with surveillance and data retention measures.[82] On the one hand, Hughes argues that the reasonable expectation of privacy test could prove useful in providing a more constructive and detailed examination of Article 8(1) within the context of secret surveillance if applied correctly.[83] In the specific context of State surveillance, this more holistic analysis would at least go beyond the current approach of the ECtHR where it 'simply declares' that certain types of communications monitoring have engaged Article 8(1).[84] Hughes concedes that there is always a risk that the ECtHR could interpret this test conservatively but argues that the holistic approach of also identifying the social norms relevant to the privacy intrusion at issue is significant for two major reasons. First, the ECtHR would not be putting itself in the position of having to exaggerate the extent of the privacy interference in order to establish that Article 8(1) had been engaged.[85] Secondly, the narrow private interests approach of the ECtHR leaves private life 'overly vulnerable' to competing interests, particularly the prevention of crime and national security if the only justification for protecting private life is limited to the individual.[86]

[80] See, for instance, *Zakharov* (n 58) [173]. See further Chapter 3.
[81] See Sam Stockwell and others, *The Future of Biometric Technology for Policing and Law Enforcement* (Alan Turing Institute 2024).
[82] *Halford* (n 73); *Von Hannover v Germany* (2005) 40 EHRR 1. See further Chapter 3.
[83] Kirsty Hughes, 'A Behavioural Understanding of Privacy and its Implications for Privacy Law' (2012) 75 Modern Law Review 806.
[84] ibid 825.
[85] This criticism also rings true for the approach of the CJEU in its data retention case law. See further Chapter 5.
[86] Hughes (n 83) 827.

However, other commentators have rightly questioned the use of the reasonable expectation of privacy criterion in secret surveillance cases. The principal concern being that relying on this concept to determine whether Article 8(1) is engaged runs the risk of undermining the human rights protection of those being monitored if the normative element of the test is indeed applied conservatively.[87] This is particularly so if that test is being applied by those who are also involved in the outcome of the deployment of the surveillance measure in question, such as public authorities or oversight bodies who have dual roles of authorization and review and therefore are not fully independent from the executive. Indeed, it is suggested that this risk of 'under-protection' is likely to be even higher in cases concerning secret surveillance and national security given the wide margin of appreciation granted to Contracting States which often coincides with a very narrow consideration of the privacy interests protected under Article 8(1).[88] Thus, given this risk, it is welcome that in certain cases concerning State surveillance, the ECtHR has 'whittled down'[89] the significance of a reasonable expectation of privacy to the status of a 'not necessarily conclusive' factor.[90]

This approach is evident in the 2018 judgment of *Benedik v Slovenia* where the law enforcement authorities tried (unsuccessfully) to rely on this problematic criterion to make the argument that the applicant's rights under Article 8 ECHR had not been engaged due to his activity falling outside the scope of private life.[91] The facts involved an international investigation into online child pornography where the Slovenian police acquired the name and address of the subscriber associated with a relevant dynamic IP address (the applicant's father) from an Internet Service Provider (ISP) but without a court order. Ultimately, in a notably robust judgment, the ECtHR rejected the argument that the applicant had waived any reasonable expectation of privacy by not concealing his use of a dynamic IP address from other users online.[92] In arriving at this determination, the ECtHR highlighted the importance of online anonymity for promoting the free flow of ideas and information online.[93] The ECtHR also pointed out that the applicant's online activity had in fact engaged 'a high degree of anonymity' as the dynamic IP address could only be traced to a specific computer (thereby identifying the applicant) following a request by the police to the ISP.[94]

Indeed, it is well established Article 8 ECHR case law that the collection and storing of data by public authorities on individuals for the aims of countering

[87] De Hert (n 6) 76; Lorna Woods, 'Automated Number Plate Recognition: Data Retention and the Protection of Privacy in Public Places' (2017) 2 Journal of Information Rights, Policy and Practice 1, 8.
[88] See eg *Centrum för Rättvisa* (n 1); *Big Brother Watch* (n 1).
[89] De Hert (n 6) 76.
[90] See eg *Peck* (n 52) [58]–[59]; *Glukhin* (n 52) [66].
[91] *Benedik* (n 48) [92].
[92] ibid [115], [119].
[93] ibid [105].
[94] ibid [117].

crime and safeguarding national security constitute an interference with those persons' private lives, even if that data exclusively concerns a person's public activities. However, it is noteworthy that the ECtHR has in more recent case law identified the compilation of data about an individual 'in a manner or degree beyond that normally foreseeable' as a factor when examining whether there has been an interference with Article 8(1) in the use of communications data where law enforcement is involved.[95] The latter development indicates a less strict approach in the scrutiny of the ECtHR to the retention and access of communications data by public authorities compared to the interception of the content of a person's communications.

(c) Cursory assessments of Article 8(1)

The examination of how a certain type of communications surveillance falls within the scope of Article 8(1), and thereby interferes with a person's private life, has been increasingly dealt with in an often brief and slavish manner that follows earlier judgments.[96] In the Grand Chamber judgment of *Zakharov v Russia,* the determination that mobile telephone communications fell within the scope of Article 8(1) took up no more than three sentences, with *Liberty v United Kingdom* cited as supporting authority.[97] This may be an understandable approach if the type of monitoring programmes and scope of privacy intrusion involved is the same as that dealt with in earlier case law, such as the interception of an individual's phone calls. However, while similar in their wide scope to intrude on private life, the surveillance regimes in *Zakharov* and those assessed a decade earlier in *Liberty* operated in strikingly different ways. The bulk monitoring regimes at issue in *Liberty* permitted the surveillance of all external commercial communications from the UK to Europe using State facilities, specifics of which were neither confirmed nor denied.[98] *Zakharov*, in contrast, was the first case where the ECtHR assessed the compatibility with Article 8 ECHR of a surveillance programme inter alia where CSPs in the private sector were required to design their systems in order to allow law enforcement authorities direct access to both the real-time content of their customers' mobile phone communications and location data.[99] This wide-ranging regime also required the private sector to retain other communications data, and subscriber data including payment details and passport numbers, on a database for future State access for up to three years.[100]

[95] *Uzun* (n 76); *Benedik* (n 48); *Breyer* (n 52). See further Chapter 3.
[96] *Zakharov* (n 58) [173]; *Big Brother Watch* (n 14) [93]; *Ekimdzhiev and Others* (n 9) [262].
[97] *Zakharov* (n 58) [173]. For another such example, see *Ekimdzhiev and others* (n 9) [291], where the ECtHR does not provide any Art 8(1) stage assessment in its secret surveillance assessment but instead provides a general reference to judgments dealing with different types of surveillance (bulk interception) that were not being examined in *Ekimdzhiev and others* (n 9).
[98] *Liberty* (n 11) [47].
[99] *Zakharov* (n 58) [118].
[100] ibid [132]–[133].

Another procedural factor reinforcing this cursory approach by the ECtHR to the Article 8(1) stage is that parties tend not to dispute that an interference with the right to private life has taken place. Instead, the more detailed examinations concerning Article 8(1) increasingly focus on the admissibility of the applicant's victim status and their submission of an application to the ECtHR. This shift in focus is also demonstrated in the often-combined examination of identifying the existence of an interference with Article 8(1) with the applicant's claim to victim status.[101] Assessing the significance of the privacy interest interfered with by the relevant surveillance measure is often then left (if addressed at all) to the wide-ranging examination of whether the interference is justified by reference to the conditions of Article 8(2). This cursory approach to Article 8(1) is proving to be highly problematic from the perspective of human rights protection and meaningful judicial scrutiny. This is evident in more recent judgments concerning secret surveillance where the lack of engagement and scrutiny of Article 8(1) has contributed to an unnecessary overloading of the more important next stage of scrutiny during which the ECtHR will ultimately determine whether a contested measure can be justified subject to the conditions of Article 8(2) and thus be deemed compatible with the ECHR.

This overloading of the Article 8(2) stage, perhaps invariably, often results in patchy scrutiny of the cardinal question before the ECtHR regarding whether the legality and proportionality requirements have been met by the contested surveillance framework.

4. Article 8(1): surveillance in an age of AI and technological 'sea change'

ECtHR judges and scholars have rightly criticized the distinct lack of engagement by the ECtHR in recent case law regarding how digitalized our lives have become and how this 'sea change' has made the power of bulk surveillance to look into our private lives so much greater.[102] Such an oversight gap is deeply problematic as clearly identifying the zones of private life protected by Article 8(1) against these interferences is critical in order to assess the importance of the activities, and thereby the extent (and justification) of the intrusion.[103] That being said, it has long been the practice of the ECtHR not to explore in depth the value of private life in cases concerning Article 8 ECHR and surveillance for national security purposes, particularly with respect to mass surveillance programmes. This more

[101] See eg ibid; *Centrum för Rättvisa* (n 39) [85]–[95]; *Ekimdzhiev* (n 9) [261]–[277]. On the admissibility of applications being the primary issue before the ECtHR within the context of bulk communications interception, see *Wieder and Guarnieri v United Kingdom* [2023] ECHR 668.

[102] See the previous analysis. For a brief but notable exception, see *Szabó and Vissy* (n 7) [53].

[103] Solove (n 67) 99.

rigorous analysis has instead been undertaken in certain legal challenges to surveillance measures (or long-term data retention) used for the purposes of countering serious crime or crime prevention in general. In a limited number of cases, the ECtHR has engaged in-depth with the scope of private life where a new type of surveillance or data processing is being examined.[104] Thus, given the novel and far-reaching scope of enhanced bulk surveillance regimes in the twenty-first century, it is a clear cause for concern that the ECtHR has departed from addressing the significance of these implications as part of its Article 8(1) analysis in its recent case law.

The cardinal issue in most cases is not the extent of the interference with the right to private life, irrespective of whether law enforcement purposes or national security are involved. Instead, the focus of the ECtHR's scrutiny is whether the impugned surveillance can be justified with reference to the conditions of Article 8(2).[105] EU law, in contrast, unlike the text of the ECHR, explicitly provides for the importance of an infringed interest to be examined using the criterion of what identifies the 'essence' of the right and its protected interests in Article 52 of the EU Charter of Fundamental Rights. One the one hand, it should also be noted that in practice the approach of the CJEU in applying this standard has been inconsistent in its judgments concerning data retention and surveillance generally. On the other hand, when the essence of the right to private life within a surveillance context has been examined by the CJEU, there have been significant implications for the protection of data privacy in certain landmark findings.[106] At the time of writing, however, the 'essence' test has not been applied to Article 8 ECHR within the context of State surveillance. Relevant Article 8 ECHR case law in this area has been a curious outlier in this respect as the ECtHR has examined interferences with the essence of other ECHR rights in related challenges dealing with secret surveillance, including the right to a fair trial.[107] This raises the question of why the ECtHR has to date avoided applying the same strict-scrutiny approach when assessing private life interferences under Article 8(1) in this area of its case law.

Dean Spielmann, a former President of the ECtHR, has stressed that Article 8 ECHR is shown no less respect in its assessment by the ECtHR than other rights.[108] Concerns nevertheless abound that the ECtHR (unlike the CJEU) has not yet properly examined new threats to private life posed by the use of modern

[104] *S and Marper v United Kingdom* (2009) 48 EHRR 50 [66] (GC) (indefinite DNA retention of individuals never convicted of a crime); *Uzun* (n 76) [43]–[44] (GPS tracking of a suspected terrorist's vehicle); *Glukhin* (n 52) [64]–[67] (alleged use of historical and real-time facial recognition).

[105] See eg *Klass* (n 60) [42]; *Mustafa Sezgin Tanrikulu v Turkey* [2017] ECHR 669 [49].

[106] See further Chapter 5.

[107] See Laura Hoyano, 'What Is Balanced on the Scales of Justice? In Search of the Essence of the Right to a Fair Trial' [2014] Criminal Law Review 4. Note the sole fleeting reference to the 'essence' of Art 8 ECHR when balancing the rights to privacy and freedom of expression in *Delfi AS v Estonia* (2016) 62 EHRR 6 [110] (GC).

[108] Dean Spielmann, 'Allowing the Right Margin: The European Court of Human Rights and the National Margin of Appreciation' (2012) 14 Cambridge Yearbook of European Legal Studies 381, 397.

bulk surveillance technologies in the increasingly data-driven era of the twenty-first century, particularly as the lack of scrutiny in recent cases departs from its lauded approach in previous Article 8 ECHR case law and the need to give special consideration to the impact of new technologies on an individual's private life.[109] This is a striking omission by the ECtHR given the vast amount of information that can now be revealed from monitoring our 'digitalized' lifestyles and societies using such novel surveillance measures.[110] Thus, recent judgments concerning bulk surveillance suggest that private life intrusions may not carry the same normative weight for the ECtHR as other rights threatened by communications surveillance.[111] This shift has significant implications for the already wide margin of appreciation applied in such cases at the crucial assessment stage of Article 8(2) when the ECtHR determines what level of scrutiny should apply to the review of surveillance measures used for national security purposes.

Ultimately, the level of protection being provided in the balancing of the individual's right to private life in recent related cases has been deeply unclear when weighed against other public interests carefully identified by the ECtHR. The latter have included the ECtHR highlighting 'the vital importance' and 'the intrinsic value for security operations' of bulk surveillance powers and their increased importance 'given the current threat level from both global terrorism and serious crime'.[112] Much legal uncertainty therefore persists around the adequate and effective protection of Article 8 ECHR in the rapidly evolving area of communications surveillance if the specific activities at stake protected by privacy are not even identified at the Article 8(1) stage. There are also clear opportunities here for the ECtHR to meaningfully address the relationship between the private life harms and data protection harms posed by bulk communications surveillance.

Security (and therefore privacy) risks posed by devices and systems essential to our digitalized lives due to the bulk collection and various transfers of huge amounts of communications data between the private and public sectors should thus be clearly identified as constituting a further interference within the scope of Article 8(1). The more data is collected and shared, the greater its value. Accordingly, the greater the incentive for bad actors to hack and gain access to these huge datasets held by both public and private sectors. Relatedly, there is the increasing need for strong encryption of data generally across society given its crucial role in protecting the exercise of all human rights online and offline.[113]

[109] Murphy and O'Cuinn (n 9). Indeed, the ECtHR had ample opportunity to do so in its Grand Chamber judgments in 2021 which specifically dealt with novel forms of bulk communications interception.

[110] See *Big Brother Watch* (n 14) Partly Concurring, Partly Dissenting Opinion of Judge Koskelo and Judge Turković [14]–[29]; *Big Brother Watch* (n 1), Partly Concurring, Partly and Dissenting Opinion of Judge Pinto De Albequeque [58].

[111] Hughes (n 13) 598.

[112] *Big Brother Watch* (n 1) [424]; *Centrum för Rättvisa* (n 1) [365]; *Big Brother Watch* (n 14) [386].

[113] The applicants submitted this very argument in *Breyer* (n 52) [67] but it was not addressed by the ECtHR. On the importance of strong encryption for the exercise of the rights to private life and

Consider, for instance, the major cyberattacks on Ukraine and its CSPs in 2023 where critical IT infrastructure was damaged and over twenty million people were put in danger of not receiving alerts of potential Russia air assaults.[114]

The ECtHR could identify potential future harms in its assessment of Article 8 ECHR posed by such unauthorized disruption and/or access to an individual's communications of these bulk surveillance systems as relevant to the activities protected by private life. Indeed, the Court has previously taken such a precautionary approach regarding the potential use of retained biometric data by public authorities.[115] The potential range of psychological and physical harms from long-term access from such security breaches are far from abstract as the latter could result in assault, harassment, blackmail, fraud, and theft.[116] Hacking and gaining access to an individual's mobile communications data for just a few months may reveal clear patterns of daily behaviour and location data. Such bad actors would be equipped with the knowledge to track homeowners to identify 'where they are, where they've been and where they are going'.[117] Irrespective of what sector collects them and for what purpose, huge datasets of location data alone may be a lucrative asset for hackers and others to enable fraud, identity theft, and many other serious crimes.

5. The mere existence of surveillance: an interference with private life

It is well established under Article 8 ECHR case law that the mere fact that a secret regime of monitoring exists constitutes an interference with the right to respect for private life as even the threat of surveillance creates 'a very real menace' for individuals. This privacy-focused and impressively prophetic determination was established by the ECtHR decades ago in 1978 which indicated the then clear sensitivity of the Strasbourg Court to the increasing threats posed by technological

data protection, see European Data Protection Board and European Data Protection Supervisor, Joint Opinion 4/2022 on the Proposal for a Regulation of the European Parliament and of the Council laying down rules to prevent and combat child sexual abuse (EDPB & EDPS, 28 July 2022) [96]–[102].

114 Max Hunder, Jonathan Landay, and Stefaniia Bern, 'Ukraine's top mobile operator hit by biggest cyberattack of war' *Reuters* (13 December 2023). Elsewhere, see relatedly Georgi Gotev, 'Two charged with "terrorism" over Bulgaria's biggest data breach' *Euractiv with Reuters* (25 July 2019).

115 *S and Marper* (n 104) [71].

116 Household IoT devices such as locks, thermostats, lighting systems, and cameras have been used to harass and control in situations of domestic violence. See further Chapter 1. On the rise of data breaches across various sectors, see generally Daniel J Solove and Woodrow Hartzog, *Breached!* (OUP 2022).

117 De Hert (n 6) 70. The compatibility with Art 8 ECHR of hacking by a State as an investigatory power (otherwise referred to as 'equipment interference') came before the ECtHR in 2020 but was not dealt with due to the application being deemed inadmissible: *Privacy International and Others v United Kingdom* (App No 46259/16) 7 July 2020 (admissibility decision).

advances in policing and national security in its early landmark case law.[118] Despite no evidence that the applicants had been the subject of surveillance, the ECtHR still found in its well-known case of *Klass v Germany* that the contested domestic legislation instituted a system of surveillance under which the mail and communications of all individuals could be monitored. Indeed, as the Court aptly highlights, this monitoring could occur in complete secrecy, 'without [individuals] ever knowing' unless some indiscretion or subsequent notification in judicial proceedings arose.[119] The ECtHR held therefore that the disputed legislation directly affected all users, or potential users, of the postal and telecommunication services.[120] The same approach was applied again in *Malone v United Kingdom* where it was held that the existence in England and Wales of laws and practices which permitted and established a system for effecting secret surveillance of communications amounted in itself to an interference.[121] Similarly, the mere existence of a SIGINT law in Sweden that 'institutes a system of secret surveillance' of *any* mobile phone of an Internet user whose data can be intercepted from a fibre-optic cable crossing the Swedish border also constitutes an interference with Article 8(1).[122] It is noteworthy that any reference to the clear 'menace' posed by bulk surveillance powers to the right to private life is absent from the more recent Grand Chamber judgments of *Big Brother Watch* and *Centrum för Rättvisa.*

The ECtHR thus established with impressive foresight in its early jurisprudence that the scope of Article 8 ECHR should recognize the rights of all those whose communications were monitored and who were not the primary focus of the surveillance. To not give such third parties standing to complain, the ECtHR explained, could result in very large groups of individuals being deprived of the protection of the law which would render the protective machinery of the ECHR 'largely devoid of substance' in practice.[123] This willingness in the earlier case law to consider future threats to privacy posed by emerging technologies earned the ECtHR plaudits for its 'role as an actor in the field of new technologies and human rights'.[124] As a result, an individual may under certain conditions claim to be the victim of a violation based on the mere existence of secret measures, or of

[118] *Klass* (n 60) Concurring Opinion of Judge Pinheiro Farinha); *Szabó and Vissy* (n 7) [53]; *Centrum för Rättvisa* (n 39) [92].

[119] *Klass* (n 60) [37].

[120] ibid. Ultimately, while the ECtHR determined that the right to respect for private life in Art 8(1) had been interfered with in *Klass*, it was held that this interference was justified as the law in question satisfied the conditions of Art 8(2). Despite being established case law, note that Contracting States continue to challenge applicants' claims of victimhood status being a violation of Art 8 ECHR caused by the mere existence of surveillance laws. See eg [384].

[121] *Malone* (n 71) [63].

[122] *Centrum för Rättvisa* (n 39) [94]–[95].

[123] *Lambert* (n 71) [38]. On the importance of adequate legal safeguards to protect against innocent individuals being 'randomly affected' by secret surveillance measures, see *Haščák v. Slovakia* [2022] ECHR 503.

[124] Murphy and O'Cuinn (n 9) 638.

legislation permitting secret measures, without having to allege that such measures were in fact applied to them.[125] An applicant will have to establish a reason as to why such provisions may apply to them and then whether as a result there has been an interference with their rights because of the threat posed to their effective enjoyment of them.[126]

As argued by the applicants in *Klass*,[127] and acknowledged since by the ECtHR, such a threat necessarily strikes at freedom of communication between users of the telecommunications services. This amounts in itself to an interference with the exercise of the applicants' rights under Article 8 ECHR, irrespective of any measures actually taken against them.[128] The relevant conditions are determined in each case according to the rights alleged to have been infringed, the secret character of the measures objected to, and the connection between the applicant and those measures.[129] If an applicant contends, however, in their complaint that they have actually been subject to secret measures of surveillance, they will have to meet a higher threshold and show a 'reasonable likelihood' that this has occurred.[130] Recognizing this victim status under Article 8 ECHR is of increasing importance in the twenty-first century given the growing use of bulk collection and surveillance powers, including SIGINT; the latter involving data being obtained from what is often a vast number of people not individually suspected of any particular crime. Using selectors or 'catchwords'[131] as search criteria with novel and powerful methods of data analysis (such as machine learning) to sift through vast amounts of content and communications data collected in these massive datasets may often prove to be a very useful and powerful tool for combating serious crimes and terrorism. Public authorities undertake these searches using either or both format-related selectors (such as telephone numbers or emails) and content-related selectors ('holy war'). More specific inferences may then be identified through having access to and being able to trawl through such large pools of data.

These inferences may then be used to fill in gaps when piecing together a specific narrative or profile of an individual or event when investigating a serious crime or identifying a terrorist network. The speeding up of this fact-finding process may also be critical to the prevention of these serious offences. Notably, there is empirical evidence that the need for data retention in such urgent cases within the UK national security context is most valuable within three months in 72 per cent of cases.

[125] *Klass* (n 60) [41]; *Kennedy v United Kingdom* [2010] ECHR 682 [124]; *Zakharov* (n 58) [170]–[172].
[126] Harris and others (n 17).
[127] *Klass* (n 60) [37].
[128] *Malone* (n 71) [64]; *Kennedy* (n 125) [120]; *Zakharov* (n 58) [171].
[129] *Klass* (n 60) [34].
[130] *Halford* (n 73).
[131] First dealt with by the ECtHR in *Weber and Saravia* (n 11). Although only an admissibility decision, the standards discussed by the ECtHR are often referred to as the '*Weber* criteria'. The first judgment where these standards were applied and resulted in a violation of Art 8 ECHR was in *Liberty* (n 11).

This value diminishes dramatically to data retention beyond twelve months (3 per cent).[132] As highlighted by the applicants in *Big Brother Watch*, these advances thereby increase the power and invasiveness of bulk data collection. Moreover, the ability to collect so much communications data and combine so many inferences about an individual's life with such sophisticated data mining for search criteria makes having access to content largely and/or increasingly irrelevant.[133]

While recognizing the legitimate aims of such powers, serious interferences with private life and due process implications invariably arise from their use.[134] Affected individuals, the vast majority of whom are innocent and of little interest to the police or intelligence agencies, are highly unlikely to have any awareness that they are under surveillance or of its consequences. This privacy interference may occur where individuals are being monitored by targeted powers or bulk surveillance (or both together). Proving that you have been swept up in one (or more) of these various wide nets of surveillance is also very difficult or impossible. One such request that public authorities may submit to communication service providers (such as a 'geofence' or 'reverse location search warrant') may collect information on all smartphones used at a particular location and time, as opposed to a specific individual's smartphone.[135] As noted earlier, in addressing this imbalance of power, the ECtHR established that an applicant may be a victim of an Article 8 ECHR violation in certain circumstances based on the mere existence of these measures. In *Zakharov v Russia*, the Grand Chamber made a point of clarifying the conditions (established in 1978) to be satisfied when such a claim is made.[136] In doing so, the Grand Chamber endorsed the approach taken by the ECtHR in its earlier 2010 judgment of *Kennedy v United Kingdom*.[137] This clarification by the Grand Chamber is welcome as case law dealing with the question of victim status under the examination stage of Article 8(1) has been less than consistent. Indeed, the issue has also been examined as part of the proportionality analysis of Article 8(2).[138]

[132] *Dwyer v Commissioner of An Garda Síochána* [2018] IEHC 685 (High Court of Ireland) [2.24]: citing evidence from David Anderson, former UK Independent Reviewer of Terrorism Legislation.

[133] *Big Brother Watch* (n 14) [296], [301]: submissions of Access Now and European Digital Rights (EDRi). See further Chapter 1.

[134] Kim A Taipale, 'Why Can't We All Get Along? How Technology, Security and Privacy Can Co-Exist in the Digital Age' in Jack M Balkin and others (eds), *Cybercrime: Digital Cops in a Networked Environment* (NYU Press 2006) 172–74.

[135] Jennifer Valentino De-Vries, 'Google's Sensorvault is a Boon for Law Enforcement. This is How It Works' *New York Times* (13 April 2019); Johana Bhuiyan, 'The New Warrant: how US police mine Google for your location and search history' *The Guardian* (16 September 2021).

[136] *Zakharov* (n 58) [171]. The ECtHR has since followed this approach. See eg *Centrum för Rättvisa* (n 39); *Centrum för Rättvisa* (n 1) [163]. Indeed, *Zakharov* has been described as 'revolutionary' for holding that the far-reaching secret surveillance system in Russia amounted to a violation of Art 8 ECHR despite the applicant's claim being made *in abstracto*. See Bart van der Sloot, 'The Quality of Law' (2020) 11 JIPITEC 160, 166.

[137] *Zakharov* (n 58) [171].

[138] See eg *Lambert* (n 71) [35].

As held in *Zakharov*, and followed subsequently by the Grand Chamber in 2021, the scope of the law permitting secret surveillance is the first condition to be considered in the light of whether the applicant can possibly be affected by it. An applicant could fall within the reach of the surveillance due to them being part of a group of individuals targeted by the impugned legislation (specified categories). Legal challenges have previously been brought against the combination of specific categories (prevention of serious crime and combating terrorism) which were broadly framed so as to effectively include every person who had received or sent any form communication outside the territory of a particular State.[139] In other words, allegedly targeted surveillance could in practice have been used for general and indiscriminate surveillance. Alternatively, the applicant could possibly be affected because the contested law could directly affect all users of communications due to it establishing a monitoring regime where anyone's communication can be intercepted (mass surveillance). Secondly, the ECtHR will assess the availability of remedies at the national level, with the degree of scrutiny being adjusted depending on the effectiveness of such remedies. Without effective remedies, the ECtHR observes that there would justifiably be widespread suspicion and concern among the general public that these secret surveillance powers are being abused.[140] Furthermore, in this situation, the applicant does not need to show any risk that these secret surveillance measures may have been applied to them.

However, if the national law in question is found to have provided effective remedies, the applicant is then required to show that they are 'potentially at risk' of being subjected to such measures.[141] The ECtHR has long established that one such remedy is to make provision to notify applicants affected by the surveillance as soon as this would no longer jeopardize the purpose for the surveillance. Such qualifications include combating serious crime and safeguarding national security.[142] The ECtHR has stressed that this *ex post* general duty to notify is 'inextricably linked' to effective remedies and the existence of effective safeguards against abuse.[143] It is worth noting, however, that *ex post* notification, although strongly encouraged by the ECtHR, is ultimately a non-essential safeguard as the ECtHR approach has always provided that the review and supervision of surveillance may come into play at different stages. These include when the surveillance is first ordered (namely its authorization), while it is being carried out, or after it has been terminated.[144] In contrast to the prescriptive approach adopted by the CJEU under EU law, this reflects the long-established and more flexible ECtHR standards with respect to the safeguards it requires of governments to ensure that

[139] *Liberty* (n 11).
[140] *Kennedy* (n 125) [124]; *Zakharov* (n 58) [172].
[141] *Big Brother Watch* (n 1) [467]; *Centrum för Rättvisa* (n 1) [274].
[142] *Klass* (n 60) [58]; *Big Brother Watch* (n 14) [310].
[143] *Zakharov* (n 58) [286]; *Big Brother Watch* (n 1) [337].
[144] *Zakharov* (n 58) [233].

secret surveillance systems are subject to adequate controls. It is noteworthy, however, that this level of scrutiny has been made more deferential since the Grand Chamber judgments in *Big Brother Watch* and *Centrum för Rättvisa* in which the ECtHR established that the Strasbourg Court will in future determine whether a bulk interception regime is Convention-compliant 'by conducting a *global* assessment of the operation of the regime'.[145]

If found to form part of the impugned surveillance law, a key factor for the ECtHR when measuring the effectiveness of this remedy will be the independence of the mechanism which determines whether these notifications may be permitted. A body appointed by Parliament, independent in its functions, and led by an individual qualified for judicial office, has long been considered sufficiently independent to ensure an effective notification mechanism.[146] In contrast, giving responsibility for issuing these notifications to the direct supervisor (a prosecutor or court) of those carrying out surveillance fails to meet the requirement of being sufficiently independent to ensure against an abuse of authority.[147] The inadequacy of this specific safeguard, alongside the lack of several other safeguards to ensure against arbitrariness and abuse, resulted in the Grand Chamber unanimously determining Russian law on the interception of mobile phone communications to be in violation of Article 8 ECHR in *Zakharov*.[148]

In practice, it is worth noting that many laws with such statutory requirements governing communications surveillance across Europe rarely produce such notifications. This is especially the case with respect to any measures concerning national security. Indeed, some countries have never issued any such notifications to affected individuals despite the existence of such a statutory duty.[149] This invariably raises questions regarding their role as an adequate and meaningful safeguard for enhancing transparency and accountability. In this situation, the ECtHR will consider whether other remedies are available to the applicant that would initiate an examination of the lawfulness of the secret surveillance system. The ECtHR has held that the lack of certain strongly encouraged *ex post* measures—such as notification or recourse to complain to a court specifically about the surveillance measure *in abstracto*[150]—will not violate Article 8 ECHR if the overall remedies combined are considered effective. Weight will then be given here to the oversight safeguard of *ex ante* authorization by a judicial/quasi-judicial body. Despite rarely leading to actual notifications, advocates of this oversight safeguard maintain that its existence may still assist in curbing abuse.

145 *Big Brother Watch* (n 1) [337]; *Centrum för Rättvisa* (n 1) [274] (emphasis added).
146 *Klass* (n 60) [57]; *Weber and Saravia* (n 11) [137]; *Big Brother Watch* (n 1) [316].
147 *Zakharov* (n 58) [292].
148 ibid [305].
149 See eg *Centrum för Rättvisa* (n 39) [59].
150 ibid [178].

This argument is made on two main grounds. First, the State will still have to justify its reasons for not informing the public to the relevant oversight body. Secondly, publishing such statistics may 'serve to assuage public concerns regarding the scale of surveillance'.[151] Critics, however, have rightly cast doubt on the inference that these statistics indicate the actual inhibition of unlawful surveillance. Instead, concern has been expressed that the low rate, or indeed complete absence, of notifications may in fact serve to undermine the public's trust in such a remedy given that they may then believe it to be 'void of any practical meaning'.[152] These concerns regarding the heavily qualified right of notification unquestionably serve to highlight the importance of an individual's right to seek redress and access to information concerning any systems of secret surveillance. Hence, it is welcome that the victim status for legal standing *in abstracto* continues to be recognized by the ECtHR. The rise in use of bulk surveillance measures by both national security agencies and law enforcement authorities demonstrates the ever-increasing significance of this standard when determining an interference with Article 8(1). Otherwise, as the ECtHR has long warned, where a State institutes secret systems of monitoring, the impact of which remains unknown to those affected, exercise of that power would effectively be 'unchallengeable'.[153]

C. Article 8(2): Justifying an Interference

1. The traditional approach to Article 8(2): overcoming a series of hurdles

Whether an interference with private life can be considered justified under the requirements of Article 8(2) remains the cardinal issue before the ECtHR when assessing whether a secret surveillance measure is compatible with Article 8 ECHR. The ECtHR has traditionally been rigorous in its application of the 'in accordance with the law' condition (or legality criteria) in cases involving the secret surveillance of communications.[154] This strict-scrutiny approach led leading scholars like McHarg to observe that Article 8(2) was clearly designed 'to give some priority to rights by raising hurdles which states must overcome in claiming public interest defences'.[155] Contracting States seeking to justify communications surveillance

[151] Council of Europe Venice Commission, Update of the 2007 Report on the democratic oversight of the security services and report on the democratic oversight of signals intelligence agencies, CDL-AD (2015) 006, 20–21 March 2015, [137].
[152] *Centrum för Rättvisa* (n 39) [162].
[153] *Klass* (n 60) [36]; *Lambert* (n 71) [38]; *Zakharov* (n 58) [171]; *Centrum för Rättvisa* (n 1) [166].
[154] Yutaka Arai-Takahashi, *The Margin of Appreciation Doctrine and the Principle of Proportionality in the Jurisprudence of the ECHR* (Intersentia 2002) 74.
[155] Aileen McHarg, 'Reconciling Human Rights and the Public Interest: Conceptual Problems and Doctrinal Uncertainty in the Jurisprudence of the European Court of Human Rights' (1999) 62 Modern Law Review 671, 685.

measures for countering serious crime, or threats to national security, were often held to have fallen foul of this first hurdle. Thus, the contested measure was held to have violated Article 8 ECHR without any consideration of the proportionality condition and criteria therein. The ECtHR consequently developed the approach whereby failing the first hurdle of Article 8(2) (the legality criteria) would obviate any need to examine whether the impugned surveillance measure had overcome the (third) proportionality hurdle.[156]

Mahoney and others have persuasively argued that this more formalistic style emerged from an earlier and more cautious period in the Court's history; a time when the ECtHR sought to avoid being perceived in its jurisprudence as overreaching its role as the Council of Europe's 'international watchdog' of human rights.[157] This careful approach would also have been an astute response to charges of judicial activism facing the ECtHR in the 1970s.[158] By the 1980s, the ECtHR seemed to have 'earned the confidence and respect' of the governments concerned and so the ECHR system became more accepted thereafter.[159] After carefully then assuring Contracting States of its capacity for 'judicial self-restraint',[160] the ECtHR incrementally (and deftly) seized opportunities to take a more emboldened approach in certain cases concerning data retention and surveillance measures and their compatibility with Article 8 ECHR.[161] The ECtHR delivered one such landmark judgment (sitting as the Grand Chamber) in the 2008 case of *S and Marper v United Kingdom* in which the Court held that the indiscriminate and indefinite retention of the biometric data (DNA profiles, cellular samples, and fingerprints) from persons suspected, but not convicted, of a criminal offence amounted to a disproportionate interference with the applicants' right to respect for private life.

This robust examination of the regime's compatibility with the proportionality hurdle turned on the basis that the questions in *Marper* were 'closely related to the broader issue of whether the interference was necessary in a democratic society'.[162] In doing so, the Grand Chamber drew at length from the applicants' detailed critique of the regime's blanket scope of retention of DNA profiles for law enforcement aims. The proportionality standards established in the lodestar judgment have proved highly influential in the subsequent case law of the ECtHR concerning the collection and retention of data relating to private life for countering

[156] *Malone* (n 71) [81]; *Valenzuela Contreras* (n 60) [62]; *Khan v United Kingdom* (2001) 31 EHRR 1016 [28]; *Association for European Integration and Human Rights and Ekimdzhiev v Bulgaria* [2007] ECHR 533 [23]; *Iordachi and Others v Moldova* [2009] ECHR 256 [53].

[157] See Paul Mahoney, 'Judicial Activism and Judicial Self-Restraint in the European Court of Human Rights: Two Sides of the Same Coin' (1990) 11 Human Rights Law Journal 57, 77; Helen Keller and Alec Stone Sweet (eds), *A Europe of Rights* (OUP 2008) 695.

[158] Ed Bates, *The Evolution of the European Convention on Human Rights* (OUP 2010) 385.

[159] ibid. On the history of the ECtHR, see further Chapter 1.

[160] Mahoney (n 157).

[161] *S and Marper* (n 104); *Liberty* (n 11); *Zakharov* (n 58); *Szabo and Vissy* (n 7); *Catt v United Kingdom* [2019] ECHR 76.

[162] *S and Marper* (n 104) [99]; *Catt* (n 161) [106].

crime and safeguarding national security. These standards have also significantly shaped the notable data retention case law of the CJEU and consequently the reform of EU data protection law and data transfers between the EU and non-EU countries.[163]

(a) The first hurdle: in accordance with the law

(i) *Accessibility and foreseeability* The traditional approach of the ECtHR when determining if an interference meets the legality condition under Article 8(2), requires that the contested measure satisfy two principles. The measure must have 'some basis in domestic law' and, secondly, must also comply with the rule of law. This second principle focuses on the 'quality' of the domestic law which involves meeting the tests of 'accessibility' and 'foreseeability'. As operation and use of surveillance measures by police and intelligence agencies by their very nature are not open to full scrutiny by those affected or the wider public, the ECtHR has rightly emphasized that it would be 'contrary to the rule of law for the legal discretion granted to the executive or to a judge to be expressed in terms of an unfettered power'.[164] Thus, as part of the Article 8(2) foreseeability test, the ECtHR developed 'minimum' safeguards that the basis in domestic law of a Contracting State should address in order to avoid misuse or abuses of power in the use of secret surveillance. These comprise: the nature of the offences where the measure may be applied; a definition of the categories of people who may be subjected to this measure; a limit on the duration of the measure; the procedures to be followed for the examination, use, and storage of the obtained data; precautions to be taken if data is shared with other parties; and the circumstances in which obtained data should be erased or destroyed.[165]

The ECtHR first developed these safeguards in the 1990s, many years before mobile smartphones and Internet access became ubiquitous. It was a very different time, when the prevailing mode of State surveillance was the monitoring of the then prevailing mode of communication—the now quaint fixed and analogue landline telephone. Although first applied in cases dealing with targeted interceptions in criminal investigations and specific individuals, the application of these minimum safeguards was later extended by the Strasbourg Court to its scrutiny of secret surveillance measures used for safeguarding national security.[166] However, the Grand Chamber departed from this case law in 2021. A new approach instead was established for examining the compatibility of bulk interception measures which waters down the six foreseeability safeguards of Article 8(2). An examination of whether

[163] See further Chapters 3, 5, and 8.

[164] *Weber and Saravia* (n 11) [94].

[165] *Huvig* (n 60) [34]; *Kruslin v France* (1990) 12 EHRR 547 [35]; *Valenzuela Contreras* (n 60) [46].

[166] *Weber and Saravia* (n 11) [95]–[101]; *Liberty* (n 11) [62]–[63]; *Zakharov* (n 58) [231]. Some refer to the six foreseeability safeguards as the '*Weber* criteria' following their application by the ECtHR to general and indiscriminate surveillance in the 2006 admissibility decision of *Weber and Saravia*.

a bulk interception regime is 'Convention compliant' is now based on a 'global assessment' of its operation, including the existence or absence of any evidence of actual abuse.[167] This broader and more general assessment of Article 8(2), as noted later, considers just four of the long-established six foreseeability safeguards and focuses primarily on whether the domestic legal framework 'is subject to "end-to-end" safeguards'.[168]

The ECtHR established in its early jurisprudence that the principle of having some basis in domestic law comprised legislation and judgments.[169] This more prescriptive approach has since changed. What the ECtHR now considers to constitute a basis in domestic law in this area of case law has been expanded quite significantly. To the extent, as Woods aptly points out, that it may now include non-legally binding documents that effectively share 'a connection with the domestic law'.[170] This more flexible approach to the rule of law standards of Article 8(2) is clearly demonstrated in the Grand Chamber judgment of *Big Brother Watch*. Here the Court holds that the Article 8 ECHR requirement of foreseeability requires that periods of retention for communications data acquired from bulk interception measures 'should be included in appropriate legislative and/*or other general measures*'.[171]

In another related example, the Court noted in the 2022 judgment of *Ekimdzhiev and Others v Bulgaria* that a Chief Prosecutor's instruction governing the deliberate or accidental use of special means of surveillance with respect to lawyers in Bulgaria was only published in the Supreme Bar Council's journal. Although not published by the public authorities, the ECtHR highlighted in *Ekimdzhiev* that the procedures governing the special surveillance of lawyers was still 'sufficiently accessible for the persons that it concerns—practising lawyers'.[172] The Court then went so far as to cast doubt on whether the instruction 'being a purely internal act' can be seen as 'law' for the purposes of Article 8(2) but the ECtHR did not identify this as a critical shortcoming in the Bulgarian legal regime.[173] However, there is a clear gap here in the reasoning of the ECtHR regarding affected persons. The reasons being that monitoring by law enforcement of these communications will not be limited to interfering with the private lives of just those practising lawyers; it will also result in the surveillance of those with whom they communicate. These

[167] *Big Brother Watch* (n 1) [360]; *Centrum för Rättvisa* (n 1) [274].

[168] *Big Brother Watch* (n 1) [348]–[360]; *Centrum för Rättvisa* (n 1) [274].

[169] *Huvig* (n 60) [28].

[170] See eg *Catt* (n 161). For related criticism of how this expansion may undermine traditional rule of law safeguards, see Lorna Woods, 'Automated Facial Recognition in the UK' (2020) 3 European Data Protection Law Review 455, 460; Ni Loideain (n 6).

[171] *Big Brother Watch* (n 1) [423] (emphasis added).

[172] *Ekimdzhiev* (n 9) [297]. Note that this judgment examined the compatibility with Art 8 ECHR of the legal frameworks in Bulgaria concerning targeted regimes of secret surveillance (not bulk interception) and the generalized and indiscriminate retention of communications data. The Court held that there had been violations of Art 8 ECHR with respect to both measures. See further Chapter 3.

[173] *Ekimdzhiev* (n 9) [333], [356].

third parties may range from their clients, potential witnesses relevant to an on-going investigation, to family, friends, and colleagues. Other members of the public therefore may be affected by these special surveillance measures and should thus be able to access the relevant basis in domestic law governing such State powers in a source easier to locate than a specific issue of a legal practitioner's journal.

The second principle of the 'quality' of the law governing the exercise of this secret power requires that the measure should comply with the rule of law and that the domestic law must provide protection against arbitrary interference with the rights of Article 8 ECHR.[174] These safeguards are crucial in the enabling of any meaningful accountability of public authorities as State surveillance by its very nature cannot be open to full public scrutiny, this being an area, as the ECtHR has rightly and consistently held, 'where abuse is potentially so easy in individual cases and could have such harmful consequences for democratic society as a whole'.[175] As a result, the domestic law should be sufficiently accessible and clear in its terms to give individuals 'an adequate indication' to foresee the circumstances and the conditions in which public authorities are empowered to resort to using the surveillance.[176] These clear and detailed rules on surveillance measures of the legality hurdle of Article 8(2) should also be accessible to the public and include the above foreseeability safeguards. The ECtHR has indicated that best practice is for such rules governing secret surveillance to satisfy the following criteria: be made 'publicly available'; constitute an official government publication; have been laid before and approved by Parliament; and available online on a relevant government website.[177]

Of course, what is exalted by the ECtHR as best practice is not an essential or minimum requirement under the legality condition of Article 8(2). Consequently, in *Zakharov*, publication by the Russian government of the addenda of an order, which set out the technical requirements for interception equipment to be installed by communications service providers, in an official magazine of the Ministry of Communications, and which was available on subscription and via a private website, was also held to meet the accessibility test. Nevertheless, in reaching this assessment, the Grand Chamber made clear that it rejected Russia's argument that no official publication was required due to these documents being 'technical in nature'.[178] Instead, the ECtHR held that these technical details were capable of

[174] *Zakharov* (n 58) [228]; *Big Brother Watch* (n 1) [333]; *Centrum för Rättvisa* (n 1) [247].

[175] *Zakharov* (n 58) [230]; *Big Brother Watch* (n 1) [336]; *Centrum för Rättvisa* (n 1) [250].

[176] *Malone* (n 71) [67]; *Big Brother Watch* (n 14) [306]; *Hambardzumyan v Armenia* [2019] ECHR 878 [60].

[177] See *Kennedy* (n 125) [157] (referring to the Interception of Communications Code of Practice 2002 then available on the UK Home Office website); *Centrum för Rättvisa* (n 1) [281]; *R.E. v United Kingdom* [2015] ECHR 947 [121] (referring to the Covert Surveillance Code of Practice being available online and the accessibility test). See *Ekimdzhiev* (n 9) [356] where the ECtHR criticized the lack of rules, not made publicly accessible, governing the storage and destruction of materials obtained via surveillance.

[178] *Zakharov* (n 58) [181].

affecting the right to private life as they required law enforcement authorities to have direct access to all data concerning the mobile telephone communications of all users and explicitly banned any record-keeping of these interceptions.[179] The addenda consequently had to be made accessible to the public. That said, it is noteworthy that the ECtHR has stressed in more deferential judgments dealing with serious crime and safeguarding national security a rather contrasting general approach to this effect. Specifically, that the safeguards to be met by a contested novel surveillance measure to satisfy the 'quality of law' criteria will depend on the nature and extent of the interference with the private life of the applicant.[180]

It is crucial to note at this juncture that the foreseeability test has understandable limits within the special context of secret surveillance measures adopted for protecting public safety. As the ECtHR rightly points out, ensuring foreseeability does not mean that an individual should be able to precisely anticipate when law enforcement authorities are likely to intercept their communications so that they can adapt their conduct accordingly, particularly within the sphere of national security.[181] Complete transparency would, of course, enable criminals and terrorists to avoid any surveillance measures and undermine the capacity of the State to prevent or investigate threats to public safety. This means that the foreseeability test should be viewed instead as a mechanism of accountability limiting the risk of abuse of surveillance powers by mandating the relevant law to have adequate safeguards, particularly by showing to the public 'the scope of any discretion conferred on the competent authority with sufficient clarity'.[182] This requirement is particularly relevant to the protection of private life within communications surveillance by the State in two ways. First, it acknowledges the inherent risk of arbitrariness involved in this area. Secondly, foreseeability demands a level of transparency in the otherwise secret exercise of this power by public authorities.[183] Another important effect of this foreseeability requirement is that the guarantees, which set out the scope of how the power will be exercised and monitored, must be set out and explained in detail within the relevant domestic legal framework.

In its case law where the ECtHR has applied its traditional approach to examining the distinct legality and proportionality conditions of Article 8(2), the domestic laws of several Contracting States have been found not to have overcome the 'in accordance with the law' hurdle of Article 8(2) due to the ECtHR determining

[179] ibid [241], [242].

[180] See eg *P.G. and J.H.* (n 52) [46]; *Big Brother Watch* (n 1) [340]–[347].

[181] *Leander v Sweden* (1987) 9 EHRR 433 [51]; *Zakharov* (n 58) [229]; *Centrum för Rättvisa* (n 1) [247].

[182] *Leander* (n 181) [51].

[183] For a comparative analysis of surveillance and the rule of law in Ireland, the UK, and US, see Maria Helen Murphy, *Surveillance and the Law: Language, Power, and Privacy* (Routledge 2019). As Iain Cameron, leading scholar and member of the Venice Commission, rightly highlights (n 43): '[u]nless external limits are imposed, and continually reimposed, then the natural tendency on all security and intelligence agencies is to over-collect information'.

that there was no legal framework governing the secret surveillance of communications, or a lack of an effective system to oversee the use of these powers, at the material time. One such example is *Halford v United Kingdom*, where there was no domestic law in place regulating surveillance by the State of internal communications systems operated by public authorities.[184] Interception of the applicant's telephone conversations in her place of work (police headquarters in this instance) had no basis therefore in domestic law and could not be in accordance with the law within the meaning of Article 8(2). States have also fallen at the first legality hurdle of Article 8(2) where laws governing the targeted (with prior suspicion) and bulk surveillance of communications (untargeted/without prior suspicion) did not indicate with sufficient clarity at the material time the extent of the discretion of the relevant public authorities, or the way in which this discretion should have been exercised.[185]

As held in *Liberty v United Kingdom*, the ECtHR noted that it is possible for Contracting States to provide 'certain details about the operation of a scheme of external surveillance' to the public in codes of practice, regarding what safeguards need to be observed by intelligence agencies 'without compromising national security'.[186]

(ii) *Oversight defects: a lack of independence and records* The Grand Chamber in *Zakharov* made clear that it was crucial for the interception bodies of a Contracting State to keep 'detailed records' of any surveillance measures. This procedural safeguard is essential in order for supervisory bodies to have effective access to clear information on the surveillance activities undertaken.[187] Without such logs, the Grand Chamber stressed that it would be 'impossible' for any supervising authority to fulfil its role of monitoring compliance with the relevant safeguards.[188] Hence, although other notable oversight 'defects' were identified,[189] the lack of any records of interceptions rendered the entire Russian oversight regime ineffective against abuse as it was 'incapable of detecting unlawful interceptions'.[190] Indeed, the explicit prohibition under Russian law not to retain these records was

[184] *Halford* (n 73).
[185] *Malone* (n 71); *Valenzuela Contreras* (n 60); *Liberty* (n 11).
[186] *Liberty* (n 11) [68].
[187] *Kennedy* (n 97) [165].
[188] *Zakharov* (n 58) [272]. The logging of activities concerning the use and overall lifecycles of secret surveillance and data retention systems by public authorities is instrumental for ensuring internal and external systems of oversight and for demonstrating the compatibility of such systems with Art 8 ECHR. Since the entry into force of the EU Law Enforcement Directive (EU) 2016/680, it is also a key accountability requirement for law enforcement data processing under EU data protection law. See Christopher Docksey and Kenneth Propp, 'Government Access to Personal Data and Transnational Interoperability' (2023) 10 Oslo Law Review 1, 13–14; Michael Veale, 'Article 25: Logging' in Eleni Kosta and others (eds), *The EU Law Enforcement Directive (LED): A Commentary* (OUP 2024) 399–410.
[189] *Zakharov* (n 58) [274]–[276]: these included the lack of any publicly available details on the exact role accorded to the Russian President in the oversight process.
[190] ibid [272].

held to be further exacerbated by the fact that the law allowed the police and intelligence agencies to directly intercept communications.[191] The lack of an independent institution that can effectively scrutinize any errors that could occur at the first stage of the surveillance measure is an element that has also fallen short of the legality hurdle.

To prevent this potential abuse of power, the ECtHR has long established that it is best for judges to carry out this supervisory role as this offers the best guarantees of independence, impartiality, and a proper procedure.[192] Consequently, in *Association for European Integration and Human Rights and Ekimdzhiev v Bulgaria*, the Minister of Internal Affairs was found to be an insufficiently independent supervisory control under the legality hurdle requirements of Article 8(2) for authorizing surveillance with the aims of countering serious crime and threats to national security. The ECtHR took particular issue with the minister being a political appointee and a member of the executive and his conflicting dual role of also being involved in the commissioning of surveillance generally.[193] Similarly, in *Szabó and Vissy v Hungary*, the ECtHR found that legislation permitting a Minister for Justice to issue authorization of surveillance by the security services was not an oversight mechanism that provided the necessary guarantees against abuse.[194] It is also settled Article 8 ECHR case law of the Strasbourg Court that supervisory bodies should be 'independent of the authorities carrying out the surveillance' and have sufficient competence and resources to exercise 'effective and continuous control'.[195]

That being said, while the ECtHR may exalt judicial control to be the optimal oversight process, it is settled Article 8 ECHR case law that this is not an essential requirement and thereby holds the status of best practice. As first held in its 1978 judgment of *Klass v Germany*, other safeguards provided for under legislation may be accepted as a replacement for judicial control.[196] In *Klass*, the alternative oversight control that satisfied the Article 8(2) legality hurdle consisted of initial control by an official qualified for judicial office and control provided by the 'G 10' Parliamentary Board and Commission appointed under the impugned statute.[197] Supervision that is provided by non-judicial bodies may thus be compatible with Article 8(2). This determination will turn on the extent to which the supervisory

[191] ibid [272].

[192] *Klass* (n 60) [55]; *Big Brother Watch* (n 1) [336]; *Ekimdzhiev and Others* (n 9) [301]. On the constitutional importance of such bodies being independent, see Paul F Scott, 'Hybrid Institutions in the National Security Constitution' (2019) 39 Legal Stud*ies* 432, 453–54.

[193] *Association for European Integration and Human Rights and Ekimdzhiev* (n 156) [87]–[93].

[194] *Szabó and Vissy* (n 7) [77].

[195] *Zakharov* (n 58) [275]; *Ekimdzhiev and Others* (n 9) [338]–[347]. See eg *Ekimdzhiev and Others* (n 9) [337], where the Court stated that the effectiveness of the oversight being provided by judges determining the authorization of warrants for secret surveillance was 'open to doubt' due to their 'high workload'.

[196] *Klass* (n 60) [56]; *Zakharov* (n 58) [275], [318]–[320].

[197] *Klass* (n 60) [56].

body is independent of the authorities carrying out the surveillance and whether the oversight regime is vested with sufficient powers and competence to exercise effective and continuous supervisory control.[198] The ECtHR has also taken into account the following factors: the legal status of the oversight body and the manner of its appointment; whether the members are parliamentary representatives of the government and opposition; and if those members are qualified for (or have held) judicial office or have any legal training.[199]

Despite the post-Snowden reforms, the language and scope of bulk surveillance measures as outlined in legislation, policy documents, and codes of practice continue to be highly complex and thus 'largely abstract to the public'.[200] Judges and senior legal experts with experience in this area of law are more likely to be familiar with the legal language used to describe the scope of such legal powers and their accompanying safeguards and limits. Additionally, given the increasing complexity of surveillance laws and governance, judges and senior legal experts may be in the best position (when supported by independent experts from other relevant disciplines) to properly scrutinize both the legal and technical terminology of surveillance laws and practices.[201] Put simply, those authorizing and reviewing its use should understand the actual reach, operation, and impact of such surveillance powers in practice, not just on paper.[202] Moreover, as Cameron rightly points out, 'independent authorisation is not enough: you need a follow-up stage to check that the agency is actually complying with the terms of the authorisation'.[203] It is therefore suggested that both the *ex ante* and *ex post* oversight stages of any secret surveillance framework should be independent of the executive with members who have expertise in various relevant disciplines. The latter should include (but by no means be limited to) law, computer science, forensic science, and sociology.

(b) The second hurdle: in pursuit of a legitimate aim

Satisfying the condition of whether a surveillance measure of communications interception was adopted in pursuit of a legitimate aim is rarely a difficulty for Contracting States. This is mainly due to two reasons. Applicants in these cases frequently concede the existence of a legitimate aim and, secondly, the broad terms

198 *Zakharov* (n 58) [275].

199 ibid [278]. Consequently, in *Ekimdzhiev and Others* (n 9) [338]–[347], the ECtHR was highly critical inter alia of the fact that several members appointed to one of the oversight bodies supervising the use of secret surveillance powers in Bulgaria had come from the security services, were not therefore sufficiently independent, and lacked any legal training (National Bureau).

200 Kristina Irion, 'Accountability Unchained: Bulk Data Retention, Preemptive Surveillance, and Transatlantic Data Protection' in Marc Rotenberg, Jeramie Scott, and Julia Horrowitz (eds), *Privacy in the Modern Age* (The New Press 2015) 83.

201 The key oversight body for bulk surveillance powers in the UK (IPCO) includes a 'Technical Advisory Board': Investigatory Powers Act 2016, s 245.

202 On judicial oversight as an effective legal safeguard, see generally Martin Scheinin, Helle Krunke, and Marina Aksenova (eds), *Judges as Guardians of Constitutionalism and Human Rights* (Elgar 2016).

203 Cameron (n 43) 4.

in which legitimate purposes are framed in the text of Article 8(2). As a result, even if the pursuit of a legitimate aim is contested by an applicant, the ECtHR is more likely to identify one of the aims under Article 8(2) and examine this as part of a general assessment of whether the surveillance measure was 'necessary in a democratic society'.[204] Relatedly, the ECtHR allows States a wide margin of appreciation in assessing what falls within the scope of the legitimate aim of their national security interests.[205] This approach is evident, for instance, in *Kennedy v United Kingdom* where the ECtHR states that by '*the nature of things*, threats to national security may vary in character and may be unanticipated or difficult to define in advance ... Similar considerations apply to the use of the term in the context of secret surveillance.'[206]

(c) The third hurdle: necessary in a democratic society

Under the traditional approach, the third hurdle of Article 8(2) requires that an interference must be 'necessary in a democratic society', as well as being lawful and in pursuit of a legitimate aim, to justifiably restrict a right enshrined in Article 8(1). The ECtHR established in its earlier case law that Contracting States could overcome this hurdle by showing that the contested surveillance measure is responding to 'a pressing social need' and the interference with the protected rights is no greater than is necessary to address that pressing social need.[207] This requirement is otherwise referred to as the test of proportionality and consists of four principles. The latter are addressed in detail later but essentially provide as follows: (1) 'necessary' does not equate to 'dispensable' or 'desirable'; (2) a certain 'margin of appreciation' will apply; (3) an interference must correspond to 'a pressing social need' and be 'proportionate' to the legitimate aim being pursued; and (4) any exceptions to rights guaranteed under the ECHR are to be 'narrowly interpreted'.[208]

First, the ECtHR has held that the adjective 'necessary' is not synonymous with 'indispensable' or as flexible as 'reasonable' or 'desirable'.[209] In practice, this means that powers allowing for any system of secret surveillance of communications in which the 'risk of abuse is inherent', whether for countering serious crime or the protection of national security, must have 'adequate' and 'effective guarantees' against arbitrariness and abuse.[210] The ECtHR makes a case-by-case

[204] See eg *Kennedy* (n 125) [147]–[155]; *Glukhin* (n 52) [61]–[84].
[205] Jack Beatson and others, *Human Rights: Judicial Protection in the United Kingdom* (Sweet & Maxwell 2008) 162; Janneke Gerards, *General Principles on the European Convention on Human Rights* (CUP 2023) 265. Article 8(2) provides for the following legitimate aims: 'the interests of national security, public security or the economic well-being of the country, for the prevention of disorder or crime, for the protection of health or morals, or for the protection or the rights and freedom of others'.
[206] *Kennedy* (n 125) [159] (emphasis added).
[207] *Silver v United Kingdom* (1983) 5 EHRR 347 [97]; *Leander* (n 181) [58].
[208] *Silver* (n 207) [97].
[209] *Handyside v United Kingdom* (1976) 1 EHRR 737 [48].
[210] *Weber and Saravia* (n 11) [106]; *Big Brother Watch* (n 1) [338]–[339]; *Centrum för Rättvisa* (n 1) [252]–[253]; *Ekimdzhiev* (n 9) [292]. The ECtHR has also applied the threshold of 'sufficient guarantees' in some of its more robust judgments. See eg *Marper* (n 104) [99]; *Glukhin* (n 52) [77].

assessment of the guarantees that a Contracting State has put in place in the framework governing the relevant surveillance measure. This review is context-dependent, meaning that it is well established case law that the Strasbourg Court may consider 'all circumstances of the case' including the nature, scope, and duration of the possible measures; the grounds required for ordering them; the authorities competent to authorize, carry out, and supervise them; and the kind of remedy provided by the domestic law.[211] These assessments may include further consideration of the six foreseeability safeguards from the legality requirements of Article 8(2). Scrutiny by the ECtHR of these foreseeability safeguards should be much more rigorous under the proportionality assessment as their operation in practice must be closely scrutinized in order to establish the actual effectiveness of those guarantees. More recently, the Grand Chamber has stressed the importance of 'end-to-end safeguards' and independent authorization when examining the Article 8 ECHR compatibility of bulk surveillance measures undertaken for safeguarding national security.[212] In the latter, as examined later, the Grand Chamber has expanded the scope of this already holistic examination from considering all of the circumstances of the case to that of an even broader 'global assessment'.[213]

Secondly, and perhaps most importantly, a 'margin of appreciation' will apply in assessing the existence and extent of such necessity.[214] The margin of appreciation is a tool developed from the Court's interpretation of the ECHR and its use has provoked controversy amongst some leading scholars, especially as a result of an increase in judgments where the ECtHR does not make clear the relationship between the scope of the margin of appreciation applied and the intensity of the Court's review.[215] At its core, the contested doctrine raises the question regarding the extent to which the ECtHR should defer to a State's interpretation of the situations it faces in permitting a limitation on the rights guaranteed by the ECHR.[216] The ECtHR has stressed that the scope of this margin is not unlimited. Or, as Legg aptly notes, the doctrine is not the 'result of servility' to States as it is subject

[211] *Klass* (n 60) [50].

[212] *Big Brother Watch* (n 1) [350]–[351]; *Centrum för Rättvisa* (n 1) [264]–[265].

[213] *Big Brother Watch* (n 1) [360]; *Centrum för Rättvisa* (n 1).

[214] *Silver* (n 207) [97]. See generally Howard Yourow, *The Margin of Appreciation Doctrine in the Dynamics of European Human Rights Jurisprudence* (Kluwer 1996); Andrew Legg, *The Margin of Appreciation in International Human Rights Law* (OUP 2012); Steven Greer, *Human Rights in the Council of European and the European Union* (CUP 2018); Gerards (n 205) 241–85. On the benefits of clarity and consistency to be gained by the parameters determining the scope of the margin of appreciation being clearly expressed by the ECtHR, see Janneke Gerards, 'Margin of Appreciation and Incrementalism in the Case Law of the European Court of Human Rights' (2018) 18 *Human Rights Law Review* 495.

[215] See eg Woods (n 1); De Hert (n 6); Gerards (n 214) who notes that despite increasing references to the margin of appreciation in the case law, 'such references are rather empty ... and the doctrine is seldom translated into clear standards of review'.

[216] Rainey, McCormick, and Ovey (n 17) 325.

ultimately to the final call of the ECtHR in deciding whether these restrictions are compatible with the ECHR.[217]

The ECtHR has therefore consistently stated that this assessment of 'European supervision' embraces both the legislation and the decisions applying it, including those given by the independent domestic courts.[218] Where there is no consensus within the Contracting States of the Council of Europe, either as to the relative importance of the interest at stake or as to the best means of protecting it, the margin of appreciation granted will be wider.[219] Thus, in cases concerning secret surveillance by public authorities, the ECtHR has tended to grant a wider margin to States in matters of national security in light of the sensitive and confidential nature of the information involved and the seriousness of the threat at the material time.[220] Factors identified by the ECtHR in recent cases that may widen this scope include threats from the 'scourge of global terrorism' and 'international networks of hostile actors' with access to increasingly sophisticated technology 'enabling them to communicate undetected'.[221] The margin will tend to be narrower (or restricted) in cases where the ECtHR identifies that 'a particularly important facet of an individual's existence or identity is at stake', including the ability of a public authority to infer an individual's ethnic origin from the retention of health data.[222]

Thus, the examination of the proportionality hurdle of Article 8(2) within the context of State surveillance will turn on the intensity of the review employed by the ECtHR which will ultimately depend on the scope of the margin of appreciation granted, whether or not the doctrine is explicitly referenced by the ECtHR. As Murphy observes, it is possible that restraint shown by the ECtHR in its criticism of State surveillance measures ensures that 'any compliance costs on Member States are extremely low and that is how it maintains its legitimacy in this sensitive area'.[223] Reception to the doctrine in general, however, remains understandably fraught by those who view it as undermining the protective minimum standard-setting role of the ECtHR. Such criticism has come from within the ECtHR itself by judges who have gone so far as to call for the Strasbourg Court to 'banish' the concept from its reasoning.[224] Thus, the doctrine reflects an ever-present challenge for the ECtHR in the form of a legal (and political) tightrope. This involves

[217] Legg (n 214) 23. On the doctrine being neither 'a gift nor a concession' to national courts, see Dean Spielmann, 'Whither the Margin of Appreciation?' (2014) 67 Current Legal Problems 49.

[218] *Kennedy* (n 125) [154]; *Zakharov* (n 58) [232]; *Gaughran v United Kingdom* [2020] ECHR 144 [85]; *Big Brother Watch* (n 1) [339].

[219] *S and Marper* (n 104) [102].

[220] *Klass* (n 60); *Segerstedt-Wiberg v Sweden* (2007) 44 EHRR 14; *Centrum för Rättvisa* (n 1) [237]; *Big Brother Watch* (n 1) [323].

[221] *Big Brother Watch* (n 14) [314]; *Centrum för Rättvisa* (n 1) [237].

[222] *L.B. v Hungary* [2023] ECHR 239 [118] (GC). See further the sensitivity of the Grand Chamber to the indefinite retention of DNA materials and profiles of unconvicted individuals that could be used by law enforcement to infer an individual's ethnic identity in *S and Marper* (n 104) [70]–[77], [118].

[223] Murphy (n 13) 517.

[224] See eg *Z v Finland* (1998) 25 EHRR 371 (Partly Dissenting Opinion of Judge De Meyer).

reconciling its crucial guiding role as a supranational human rights court setting minimal standards throughout Europe alongside its inherent dependence on national courts, public authorities, and regulators, to give these standards life beyond a specific judgment.

Thirdly, the phrase 'necessary in a democratic society' has been interpreted by the ECtHR in its general case law dealing with Article 8 ECHR as 'a pressing social need' which must be proportionate to the legitimate aim pursued if the interference is compatible with the ECHR. The ECtHR, however, rarely employs this particularly demanding necessity standard when examining the compatibility of secret surveillance measures with Article 8 ECHR. Instead, the Strasbourg Court has established that powers permitting the secret surveillance of individuals' communications for reasons of national security and countering serious crime may be permitted under Article 8 ECHR to the extent that they are 'strictly necessary' for safeguarding democratic institutions.[225] In judgments, however, dealing with more modern and increasingly powerful secret surveillance measures undertaken for protecting national security (such as machine learning pattern analysis and bulk interception), the proportionality assessment has not involved the 'strictly necessary' test. The ECtHR has instead applied the more general test of 'what is *necessary* in a democratic society'.[226] De Hert has criticized this explicitly less demanding standard, arguing that it indicates a reluctance by the ECtHR to require States to demonstrate the necessity of a surveillance measure with the result that this allows for contested surveillance regimes to be subject to a 'mild check of proportionality'.[227]

It should be noted that the ECtHR will still highlight in its (more robust) judgments dealing with secret surveillance the failure of States to strike a 'fair balance' between public and private interests or to show compliance with the 'strictly necessary' or 'pressing social need' tests. This is evident in cases where the ECtHR has been highly critical of surveillance and data retention measures involving a lack of clear limits and safeguards in the domestic law and/or the collection of biometric data (such as live facial recognition).[228] Express engagement by the ECtHR with these higher thresholds can prove to be an useful indicator for when a surveillance measure (bulk or targeted) will be subject to an assessment of greater depth with respect to its proportionality.[229] This heightened level of scrutiny has also included

[225] *Klass* (n 60) [42]; *Rotaru v Romania* [2000] ECHR 192 [47] (GC); *Kennedy* (n 125) [153]–[155]; *Mustafa Sezgin Tanrikulu* (n 105) [49].

[226] *Weber and Saravia* (n 11) [106]; *Zakharov* (n 58) [232]; *Big Brother Watch* (n 14) [308]; *Big Brother Watch* (n 1) [332]; *Centrum för Rättvisa* (n 39) 104]; *Centrum för Rättvisa* (n 1) [248]; (emphasis added). The UK regulator of intelligence agencies has stated that 'AI and machine learning will play an increasingly significant role in the work of the organisations we oversee': Investigatory Powers Commissioner's Office, Annual Report 2022 (IPCO 2023) 8.

[227] De Hert (n 6) 80. The 'necessity' test of the ECtHR also contrasts starkly with the stricter proportionality assessment of the CJEU in its landmark data retention case law. See Chapter 5.

[228] *S and Marper* (n 104); *M.K. v France* [2013] ECHR 341; *Szabó and Vissy* (n 7); *Mustafa Sezgin Tanrikulu* (n 105); *Glukhin* (n 52). See further Chapter 3.

[229] See eg *Szabó and Vissy* (n 7) [54], [73]; *Mustafa Sezgin Tanrikulu* (n 105) [49].

detailed examinations of whether use of a surveillance measure was allowed on the basis that the public authorities provided details to the relevant authorizing body showing that the investigation could not be conducted using less intrusive means. Details, as the ECtHR indicates in *Potoczká and Adamčo v Slovakia*, should amount to more than 'an offhand finding' in a warrant that obtaining the necessary evidence by other means was ineffective or impossible.[230]

2. The new approach to Article 8(2): combining hurdles and moving goalposts

The key principles and safeguards established under the traditional approach by the ECtHR in its examinations of Article 8 ECHR, secret surveillance and the interception of communications have long been lauded by leading scholars and practitioners. However, in more recent case law it is no longer standard practice for the ECtHR to determine that a State's failure to overcome the legality hurdle negates any requirement to also examine whether the proportionality condition of Article 8(2) has been satisfied.[231] This development aligns with a shift in approach by the ECtHR of combining its examination of the legality and proportionality hurdles when assessing the compatibility of secret surveillance measures with Article 8 ECHR. Scholars have raised serious concerns regarding the rise of this combined approach and highlighting that such examinations of data retention and surveillance regimes and their compatibility with Article 8 ECHR have become less systematic and structured, thereby resulting in less precise and robust assessments of the protection of private life.[232]

(a) A combined analysis of the legality and proportionality tests

The emergence of this combined approach to examining Article 8(2) is evident in the 2008 landmark judgment delivered by the Grand Chamber in *S and Marper*. Here the ECtHR assessed the domestic law in England and Wales permitting the indefinite retention of fingerprints and DNA for the prevention of crime on grounds of proportionality instead of legality. The ECtHR took this different approach to Article 8(2) based on the reasoning that the questions before it were 'closely related to the broader issue of whether the interference was necessary in a democratic society'.[233] Later, in *Kvasnica v Slovakia*, this time in a case dealing with communications

[230] See eg *Dragojević v Croatia* [2015] ECHR 28 [95]; *Mustafa Sezgin Tanrikulu* (n 105) [59]; *Potoczká and Adamčo v Slovakia* [2023] ECHR 14 [71]–[74]. Although the assessments in the latter cases resulted in violations of the legality condition of Art 8(2), the ECtHR also took into account proportionality considerations and the need for adequate and effective guarantees.

[231] See eg *Iordachi and Others v Moldova* [2009] ECHR 256; *Association for European Integration and Human Rights and Ekimdzhiev* (n 156); *Valenzuela* (n 60); *Malone* (n 71).

[232] De Hert (n 6); Murphy (n 13); Hughes (n 13); Ni Loideain (n 6).

[233] *S and Marper* (n 104) [99]; *Catt* (n 161) [106].

surveillance, the ECtHR again departed from its traditional approach of first examining the legality condition before proceeding to deal with questions of proportionality.[234] It did so following the same reasoning of the Grand Chamber in *Marper*, namely that the applicant's arguments concerning the measure's legality were 'closely related' to whether the proportionality condition had been satisfied.[235]

However, unlike its approach in *Marper*, the ECtHR decided in *Kvasnica* to *combine* its analysis of the legality and proportionality conditions. This combined assessment is now an established practice for the ECtHR in cases concerning secret surveillance measures for the aims of protecting national security and the prevention of crime.[236] The rationale first put forward by the ECtHR for this change in approach to the examination of Article 8(2) in *Kvasnica* turned specifically on the applicant's arguments concerning the requirements of the legality and the proportionality hurdles being 'closely related'. This indicates that the combined approach may be employed by the ECtHR in cases concerning secret surveillance measures and Article 8 ECHR depending on the facts and arguments at issue. In other words, the combined analysis of these hurdles will depend on the circumstances of the surveillance regime being challenged.

On the one hand, the logic behind this jurisprudential development is persuasive given the well-established overlap between the specific principles of the legality and proportionality conditions of Article 8(2).[237] There is a clear link, for instance, between the foreseeability safeguards under the legality hurdle and the broader assessment of the existence of adequate and effective guarantees against arbitrariness and abuse that (traditionally) takes place under the proportionality condition. It is suggested that there is therefore a strong argument to adopt an approach that proceeds directly to a strict-scrutiny assessment of the foreseeability test under the proportionality hurdle if either or both of the following circumstances arise. First, it has been accepted by both parties that the impugned surveillance regime in question is governed by a legislative framework that clearly satisfies the requirements of the accessibility test under the legality hurdle. Secondly, the proportionality of the measure has also been specifically challenged by the applicant, including whether the specific procedural safeguards provided for under statute are adequate and effective in practice.

Hence, applicants in the separate cases of *Kvasnica* and *Kennedy* had no dispute with there being a domestic basis in law for the impugned surveillance regimes or their accessibility to the public.[238] Their challenges instead focused on

[234] *Kvasnica* (n 36) [84].
[235] ibid.
[236] See eg *Kennedy* (n 125) [155]; *Dragojević* (n 230) [89]; *Zakharov* (n 58) [236]; *Szabó and Vissy* (n 7) [58]; *Centrum för Rättvisa* (n 39) [107].
[237] Iain Cameron, *National Security and the European Convention on Human Rights* (Kluwer 2000) 36.
[238] *Kvasnica* (n 36) [69]; *Kennedy* (n 125) [131].

whether the procedures in place to supervise the ordering and implementation of the relevant safeguards governing interception of communications were sufficient in practice. Thus, in *Kvasnica*, although interception required judicial authorization and the judge was required to examine on a continuous basis whether the grounds for it persisted, no evidence was provided showing that the judge had any means of checking how the interception was being carried out in practice. On this basis, in addition to several 'other shortcomings',[239] the ECtHR held that the lack of any evidence showing adequate compliance with the relevant law amounted to a disproportionate and thereby unjustified interference with Article 8 ECHR.[240]

However, the combined approach to Article 8(2) took another turn in 2015. Without explanation, the ECtHR (sitting as the Grand Chamber) in *Zakharov v Russia* departed from its approach established in *Kvasnica* by expanding the parameters for employing the combined approach when examining Article 8(2). Although relevant passages in *Kvasnica* and *Kennedy* are cited as supporting authority for jointly considering the legality and proportionality hurdles, these references are misleading. Instead of the combined approach being justified based on the circumstances of a specific case, the Grand Chamber departs from this requirement in *Zakharov* and establishes that the 'lawfulness' of any legislation permitting surveillance before the ECtHR is 'closely related' to the necessity of the interference.[241] The Grand Chamber has followed the broader approach established in *Zakharov* in both *Big Brother Watch* and *Centrum för Rättvisa*, expressly stating: 'where the legislation permitting secret surveillance is contested before the Court, the lawfulness of the interference is closely related to the question whether the "necessity" test has been complied with and it is therefore appropriate for the Court to address jointly the "in accordance with the law" and "necessity" requirements'.[242]

This major shift in approach means that the ECtHR no longer needs to explain why a combined analysis of the legality and proportionality conditions of Article 8(2) is appropriate in a particular case when examining the compatibility of a secret surveillance measure with the right to private life. There are circumstances in certain cases, as noted earlier, where this approach may be sensible. However, in practice, there are an increasing number of Article 8 ECHR cases dealing with secret surveillance and data retention where this joint approach has resulted in less robust assessments of key legality and proportionality standards and safeguards enshrined in Article 8(2), a development that raises clear concerns for the adequate protection of the right to private life at a time when the use of privacy-intrusive

[239] Including a lack of measures to safeguard communications subject to lawyer–client confidentiality.
[240] *Kvasnica* (n 36) [86]–[89].
[241] *Zakharov* (n 58) [236].
[242] *Big Brother Watch* (n 1) [334]; *Centrum för Rättvisa* (n 1) [248].

AI-based systems for communications surveillance, such as facial recognition and emotion recognition, are on the increase.

(b) Weakening the protection of the right to private life

Expanding the application of the combined approach to Article 8(2) could be welcomed on the basis that it gives the ECtHR greater discretion to engage more with assessments of proportionality. Indeed, the Strasbourg Court was criticized for not embracing this approach more in its earlier Article 8 ECHR case law. It could thus be argued that this enhanced engagement could serve as a useful starting point for ensuring the continued relevance of Article 8 ECHR safeguards at a time when communications surveillance has advanced with 'remarkable progress ... and reached a level of sophistication which is hardly conceivable for the average citizen'.[243] On the other hand, the application of this joint analysis to date in cases dealing with Article 8 ECHR and secret surveillance measures has shown its potential of blurring the functions and aims of both the legality and proportionality principles and safeguards of Article 8(2), a conflation that may serve to reduce the intensity of the Court's review and weaken the substantive protection of the right to private life under Article 8 ECHR.[244] Moreover, as Murphy rightly warns, this combined approach 'employed incautiously' also runs the risk of the necessity test being 'lost in the mire'.[245]

Another way in which the protection of Article 8 ECHR may be undermined is through hindering the development of the minimum safeguards of the foreseeability test and other established rule of law safeguards. This risk is particularly acute given the ECtHR's previous recognition in *Szabo and Vissy* that the current Article 8 ECHR safeguards 'need to be enhanced' in light of the capacity of State surveillance to now acquire detailed profiles of the 'most intimate aspects of individuals' private lives', resulting in particularly invasive interferences with private life.[246] In response to this robust commitment made in *Szabo and Vissy*, the Grand Chamber in 2021 chose not to re-examine the foreseeability minimum safeguards in light of the enhanced capacity of modern secret surveillance powers to see ever further into the private lives of individuals. The Grand Chamber, as discussed later,

243 *Szabó and Vissy* (n 7) [68].

244 Murphy (n 13) 513; Hughes (n 13). There is also a risk that use of the joint analysis approach can be a source of confusion, resulting in patchy and incomplete Art 8(2) assessments generally. See eg *Hambardzumyan* (n 176) where the 'quality' of the impugned domestic law was not assessed (as per the legality condition) but rather its effectiveness in practice (as per the proportionality condition) but the ECtHR then mistakenly stated that no proportionality analysis had taken place.

245 Murphy (n 13) 513. See eg the overall assessment of the secret surveillance regime in *Ekimdzhiev and Others* (n 9) [291]–[293], [356]–[358]. It is deeply unclear in this judgment what the Court considers to be the 'general principles' governing the question of when secret surveillance can be justified under Art 8(2), as opposed to what the Court considers to be the 'minimum safeguards against arbitrariness and abuse' in its highly case-specific joint assessment of the legality and proportionality requirements in Art 8(2).

246 *Szabó and Vissy* (n 7) [70].

instead reduced the significance of the foreseeability safeguards to 'principles' in its 'global assessment' of whether bulk interception measures are 'Convention compliant' in practice.[247]

However, by not clearly identifying the Article 8(2) conditions under examination, and the specific requirements and minimum safeguards to be met thereunder by Contracting States, invariably allows for these hurdles—previously lauded for giving priority to rights—to become moving goalposts for various public interest defences. Put simply, combining any hurdles makes overcoming them a less onerous task. This shift in approach invariably raises questions regarding the adequacy and effectiveness of the examination of any data retention and surveillance regime by the ECtHR. It also potentially hampers the capacity of Article 8 ECHR to ensure the existence of clear and detailed rules to safeguard against abuse and for its standards to remain relevant to present-day conditions and increasingly powerful surveillance capabilities now available to public authorities.

D. Bulk Interception and 'End-to-End' Safeguards

On 25 May 2021, the ECtHR (sitting as the Grand Chamber) delivered two landmark judgments in *Big Brother Watch* and *Centrum för Rättvisa*, rulings which will shape the future ECHR legal order and the approach of the ECtHR to future applications dealing with Article 8 ECHR and bulk communications interception. These significant judgments were highly anticipated for three main reasons. The first concerned the divergence in the outcomes of the previous Chamber judgments. Both examined the bulk interception regimes of the UK and Sweden and their compatibility with Article 8 ECHR. However, whereas the ECtHR held unanimously in *Centrum för Rättvisa* that there had been no violation of Article 8 ECHR, the ECtHR held that there had been a violation of Article 8 ECHR in *Big Brother Watch*. Secondly, the Grand Chamber's judgments were delivered in the wake of an ongoing series of notable judgments by the CJEU dealing with bulk data retention and access for the purposes of countering serious crime and national security matters. The jurisprudence of the CJEU sets out standards that are stricter and more prescriptive than those to be found in the well-established jurisprudence of the ECtHR dealing with Article 8 ECHR and secret surveillance.[248] Thirdly, the applicants in *Big Brother Watch* and *Centrum för Rättvisa* both urged the ECtHR to consider adopting at least some, if not all, of the stricter standards the CJEU continues to apply and develop in its case law; standards that have built

[247] *Big Brother Watch* (n 1) [347]. It is concerning that this general reframing (or downgrading) of all the legality and proportionality standards and safeguards of Art 8(2) as 'general principles' has since been extended by the ECtHR beyond the context of bulk interception and to the review of secret surveillance and communications data retention measures: see *Ekimdzhiev and others* (n 9) [291].

[248] See further Chapter 5.

on the previously lauded jurisprudence of the ECtHR dealing with Article 8 ECHR and secret surveillance.[249] This section examines the main determinations of the Grand Chamber in both judgments concerning Article 8 ECHR with a focus on novel developments in the case law. It then discusses their broader implications, including the ECtHR's departure from being an important driving force in setting minimum standards in the scrutiny of laws governing secret surveillance of communications across Europe.

1. Main findings by the Grand Chamber

(a) *Big Brother Watch v United Kingdom*

The Grand Chamber held unanimously in *Big Brother Watch and Others* that the former legal framework regulating bulk interception regimes of communications and communications data in the UK constituted a violation of Article 8 ECHR.[250] Consistent again with the Chamber judgment, the Grand Chamber also held (by a majority) that there had been no violation of Article 8 ECHR with respect to the intelligence-sharing regime. The ECtHR took a holistic approach through a newly established 'global assessment' and held that 'when viewed as a whole' the bulk interception regimes for both the content of communications and 'related communications data' did not contain sufficient 'end-to-end' safeguards to provide adequate and effective guarantees against arbitrariness and the risk of abuse.[251] Despite some 'robust' oversight safeguards, particularly the role of the Investigatory Powers Tribunal in the *ex post* oversight and access to remedies under the impugned legal framework,[252] the ECtHR identified three 'fundamental deficiencies'. These shortcomings were the absence of independent authorization, the failure to include the categories of selectors in the application for a warrant, and the failure to make selectors linked to an individual subject to prior internal authorization.[253] Overall, the Grand Chamber in *Big Brother Watch* does not identify any Article 8 ECHR issues with bulk interception that diverge in any significant way from the main holdings in the Chamber judgment under the former section 8(4) regime of RIPA.[254] Both express their 'greatest concern' over the role of

[249] See further Chapter 8.

[250] The impugned regime for bulk interception warrants under s 8(4) of RIPA has since been replaced by the Investigatory Powers Act 2016. See further Ni Loideain (n 44); Smith (n 45). On the judgment generally, see Woods (n 1).

[251] *Big Brother Watch* (n 1) [425]. On the significance of the judgment for measures which permit the bulk retention of communications data, see Chapter 3.

[252] *Big Brother Watch* (n 1) [413]–[415].

[253] ibid [425]. Note that the reference to the more robust language of 'fundamental deficiencies' in its legal assessment departs from the Court's more traditional hierarchy of identified 'shortcomings' in this area of Art 8 ECHR case law. See eg *Kennedy* (n 125); *Zakharov* (n 58); *Ekimdzhiev* (n 9).

[254] The Chamber judgment identifies two areas of concern in the s 8(4) regime. The first concerns the lack of oversight of the selection of bearers for interception, selectors used for filtering intercepted communications, and the process by which analysts selected intercepted communications for examination.

independent supervision, and safeguards for the 'selectors' and search criteria,[255] used to filter bulk intercepted communications for material that will be examined by a human analyst.[256]

However, there are some important departures from the Chamber judgment. The most significant being, as noted later, the introduction of a global assessment to examine bulk interception regimes and their compatibility with Article 8 ECHR. The Grand Chamber also considered how an interference with Article 8 ECHR takes place over what it identifies as the four stages of data processing within a bulk interception system: namely, the initial retention; application of selectors; examination of selected content/communications data by analysts; and subsequent data retention and use/data sharing of the 'final product'.[257] The ECtHR concluded that the 'degree of interference with privacy rights will increase as the process moves through the different stages' and that the need for safeguards will be at its highest at the examination stage involving an analyst.[258] On the one hand, this more granular Article 8(1) analysis is welcome, as the question of how a particular bulk interception regime constitutes an interference with the rights of Article 8 ECHR has often received little engagement by the ECtHR as noted earlier. However, this assessment on the extent to which bulk interception programmes interfere with Article 8 ECHR departs dramatically from long-established ECtHR case law, which provides that the mere existence of a bulk interference measure constitutes an interference with Article 8 ECHR. Subsequently accessing data (for whatever purpose, such as its use and sharing with other public authorities) acquired from a bulk interception system thereby constitutes 'a further separate interference' with the rights enshrined in Article 8 ECHR.[259] As the ECtHR has previously and rightly highlighted, this processing stage stands on its own regarding its distinct intrusion into private life, on the ground that it 'enlarges the group of persons with knowledge of the personal data intercepted and can lead to investigations being instituted against the persons concerned'.[260]

Secondly, the absence of any real safeguards applicable to the searching and selection for examination of communications data. On the latter, see Chapter 3.

[255] The Grand Chamber notes the use of (simple) selectors, such as emails and telephone numbers, used by automated systems to filter through bulk collections of data. However, intelligence agencies may also use more detailed 'complex selectors' in powerful algorithmic systems that combine multiple factors to find 'items of interest' for public authorities: David Anderson, *A Question of Trust: Report of the Investigatory Powers Review* (HM Stationery Office 2015) 109.

[256] *Big Brother Watch* (n 14) [347]; *Big Brother Watch* (n 1) [377]–[383]. Note that the Grand Chamber judgments (and related Chamber judgments) draw heavily from the main recommendations of the 2015 Report by the Venice Commission, *Democratic Oversight of Signals Intelligence Agencies*, which considered that the main interference with privacy occurs when stored personal data are accessed and/or processed by the agencies. See eg *Big Brother Watch* (n 1) [424].

[257] *Big Brother Watch* (n 1) [325].

[258] ibid [330]–[331].

[259] See eg *Weber and Saravia* (n 11) [79]; Ni Loideain (n 1).

[260] *Weber and Saravia* (n 11) [79]. Indeed, the ECtHR judges have also criticized the Grand Chamber's view that the initial bulk retention stage involving the communications of millions of

There is no explanation regarding why the Grand Chamber chose to depart from this well-established Article 8 ECHR standard which provides that the operation of a bulk surveillance system involves not one but a series of interferences with individuals' rights under Article 8 ECHR. That said, this whittling down by the Grand Chamber of the intrusiveness to the rights under Article 8(1) posed by the bulk interception regimes in *Big Brother Watch* is unsurprising for two noteworthy reasons. First, the analysis is consistent with the criticism, as noted previously, of the distinct lack of engagement by the ECtHR in taking into account how digitalized individuals' lives have become and how this sea change has made the power of bulk interception to look into a person's private life so much greater. Given the novel and far-reaching scope of modern, highly sophisticated, and AI-based surveillance powers, it is a cause for concern that the Grand Chamber omits any examination of this factor in its Article 8(1) assessment of the degree of interference posed by the operation of bulk interception regimes to the right to private life. Secondly, this deferential examination of Article 8(1) is evidence of the more general level of scrutiny, and wider margin of appreciation, granted by the Court in cases where it applies the increasingly criticized joint analysis approach to its examination of the legality and proportionality tests in Article 8(2).

This brings us to what was arguably the most significant question before the Grand Chamber which was the applicants' contention that bulk interception was 'in principle neither necessary nor proportionate within the meaning of Article 8 ECHR' and consequently did not fall within a State's margin of appreciation.[261] In particular, the applicants stressed that the availability of automated processing, its rapid advancement, and its use in the operation of bulk interception regimes, 'raised particularly severe privacy concerns and did not, as the Government contended, minimise any intrusion'.[262] Agreeing with the applicants' argument would have rendered such regimes an unjustified interference and a violation of Article 8 ECHR. Such a groundbreaking determination by the ECtHR would also have brought the Strasbourg jurisprudence into greater convergence with the stricter proportionality standards in the related case law of the CJEU.[263] No such convergence took place. Affirming the earlier judgment by the Chamber, the Grand Chamber rejected the applicants' argument and endorsed the principle of bulk interception, stating that the decision to operate a bulk interception regime in order to 'identify threats to national security or against essential national interests' is one which continues to fall within the margin of appreciation granted to Contracting States.[264]

individuals does not amount to 'a particularly significant interference'. See eg *Big Brother Watch* (n 1) Joint Partly Concurring Opinion of Judges Lemmens, Vehabović, and Bošnjak, 162.

261 *Big Brother Watch* (n 1) [277].
262 ibid [278].
263 See further Chapter 5.
264 *Big Brother Watch* (n 1) [340].

The applicants' other main argument concerned the need for the ECtHR to update its safeguards and existing approach when assessing the foreseeability test and bulk interception measures, including that of the UK. Their key grounds being that changes in both society and technology since the 2006 decision of *Weber and Saravia* required the Court to update its existing approach to ensure that Convention rights 'remained practical and effective' with the current approach being problematic as it dates back decades to a time when smartphones had 'limited functionality' and before people 'lived major parts of their lives online'. Modern smartphones therefore generate enormous amounts of communications data which are of significant value to public authorities for bulk surveillance. Consequently, the applicants stressed that the data gathered now are highly revealing even without the related content. It may also be structured in such a way that computers may process these huge datasets and 'search for patterns in them faster and more effectively than similar searches over content'.[265] These arguments echo findings in other official reports concerning the UK intelligence agencies, that 'the primary value to GCHQ [Government Communications Headquarters] of bulk interception [is] not in reading the actual content of communications, but in the information associated with those communications'.[266] Consequently, the applicants argued that the Grand Chamber should adopt the following Article 8(2) standards. First, domestic law permitting secret surveillance should require prior independent judicial authorization of warrants, the choice of selectors, and the selection of intercepted material for examination. Secondly, where selectors or search terms refer to a specified individual, there should be 'objective evidence of reasonable suspicion' in relation to that person. Thirdly, there should also be subsequent notification of any clearly defined surveillance target where it would not cause 'substantial harm' to the public interest.[267]

The Grand Chamber, following the Chamber judgment, ultimately rejected the applicants' two main arguments that bulk interception was in principle incompatible with Article 8 ECHR and that the Strasbourg Court's approach and related Article 8(2) safeguards needed to be enhanced by adopting the above necessary requirements. Indeed, the Grand Chamber made clear that the decision to operate a bulk interception regime with the aims of identifying 'threats to national security or against essential national interests' falls within the wide margin of appreciation granted to Contracting States by the Strasbourg Court. The Grand Chamber highlighted that this approach was consistent with certain previous cases (*Weber* and *Liberty*) and noted the 'proliferation of threats' that States currently face from

[265] ibid [280].

[266] The former Independent Reviewer of Terrorism Legislation had confirmed by 2016 that the UK intelligence agencies were using these highly sophisticated techniques (including pattern analysis) for examining bulk datasets of communications data and content: David Anderson, *Report of the Bulk Powers Review* (HM Stationery Office 2016) 53, 83–84.

[267] *Big Brother Watch* (n 1) [281].

networks of international actors and the existence of sophisticated technology which enables those actors to avoid detection.[268] However, despite the weight given by the applicants in their arguments to the more recent ECtHR judgment of *Szábo and Vissy*, the Grand Chamber does not mention this judgment in its assessment. This is a striking omission particularly as the ECtHR in *Szábo and Vissy* explicitly endorsed the approach of the CJEU that secret surveillance measures are only compatible with the ECHR if they are 'strictly necessary'.[269]

On the need to update its safeguards and existing approach when assessing the foreseeability test and bulk interception measures, the Grand Chamber adopted a very different approach to the applicants' proposals. In doing so, the Court held that the compatibility of bulk interception regimes with Article 8 ECHR now requires the ECtHR to apply an approach to the legality and proportionality tests under Article 8(2) that is even more general in scope than the previous 'as a whole' holistic test. This new approach involves a 'global assessment' of a bulk interception regime's operation that focuses primarily on whether the domestic law contains sufficient guarantees against abuse and end-to-end safeguards.

(b) *Centrum för Rättvisa v Sweden*

It is important to note that the bulk interception regime in *Centrum för Rättvisa* reviewed by the Grand Chamber and held (by a majority) to have been in violation of Article 8 ECHR was the law in operation at the time of the judgment. This contrasts with *Big Brother Watch* where the Grand Chamber's examination dealt with the legal framework in the UK under RIPA that since been replaced by the Investigatory Powers Act 2016. Another important element to bear in mind when comparing both judgments is the fact that this Grand Chamber judgment resulted in an outcome that clearly departs from the Chamber judgment, the latter of which had held (unanimously) that the Swedish bulk interception law was compatible with Article 8 ECHR and that there were no 'significant shortcomings' in the structure and operation of the regime.[270] The aims for which the contested powers under this still operational framework are permitted are twofold. The first aim encompasses a broadly framed list of eight 'foreign intelligence' purposes, while the second goes beyond foreign intelligence and deals with 'development activities'. Bulk interception by the Swedish public authorities for the latter is undertaken 'to monitor changes in the international signals environment'. This includes technical

[268] ibid [340].

[269] See particularly *Szábo and Vissy* (n 7) [73]: 'A measure of secret surveillance can be found as being in compliance with the Convention only if it is strictly necessary, as a general consideration, for the safeguarding the democratic institutions and, moreover, if it is strictly necessary, as a particular consideration, for the obtaining of vital intelligence in an individual operation. In the Court's view, any measure of secret surveillance which does not correspond to these criteria will be prone to abuse by the authorities with formidable technologies at their disposal.'

[270] *Centrum för Rättvisa* (n 39) [180]. On the basis that the law in Sweden is still in place, this section engages in greater detail with the main issues and determinations from this Grand Chamber judgment.

advances and to develop the technology needed for SIGINT. While the ECtHR has noted that these activities 'usually' do not focus on communications between individuals, information on individuals' identities may still be intercepted and the relevant public authority undertaking this monitoring (the FRA) may share experiences gained on technological issues with other authorities.[271]

In line with *Big Brother Watch*, the Grand Chamber rejected the applicant's argument that the principle of bulk interception itself is incompatible with Article 8 ECHR.[272] However, the ECtHR did determine that there were issues with the Swedish legal framework for general and indiscrimination communications interception. The Grand Chamber did not go so far as it did in *Big Brother Watch* to describe these as 'fundamental deficiencies' but nevertheless identified 'three shortcomings' deemed to amount to a violation of Article 8 ECHR.[273] These comprised: (1) the absence of a clear rule on destroying intercepted material which does not contain personal data; (2) the absence of a requirement in the domestic law that public authorities should give consideration to the privacy interests of individuals when making a decision to transmit intelligence material to foreign partners; and (3) the absence of an effective *ex post facto* review.[274] While this finding of an Article 8 ECHR violation by the Grand Chamber majority judgment marks a departure from the Chamber judgment, the three shortcomings criticized by the ECtHR sidestep most of the unresolved issues raised in the applicant's detailed arguments as described later; many of which, as judges of the ECtHR itself have criticized, mirror concerns raised in *Big Brother Watch* that bulk interception regimes should be subject to 'clear minimum safeguards' under Article 8 ECHR which are capable of protecting individuals against abuse of such surveillance powers.[275]

[271] The Swedish National Defence Radio Establishment (referred to as the 'FRA') is the public authority tasked with the bulk collection of communications following directives from the government, and other public authorities, including the armed forces and security police. The FRA may also conduct the same bulk interception for development activities. See *Centrum för Rättvisa* (n 39) [14]; *Centrum för Rättvisa* (n 1) [22].

[272] *Centrum för Rättvisa* (n 1) [254].

[273] *Centrum för Rättvisa* (n 39) [7]. The ECtHR defined signals intelligence as 'intercepting, processing, analysing and reporting intelligence from electronic signals. These signals may be processed to text, images and sound. The intelligence collected through these procedures may concern both the content of a communication and its associated communications data (the data describing, for instance, how, when and between which addresses the electronic communication is conducted). The intelligence may be intercepted over the airways—usually from radio links and satellites—and from cables. Whether a signal is transmitted over the airways or through cables is controlled by the communications service providers. A great majority of the traffic relevant for signals intelligence is cable-based ... the regulation of Swedish signals intelligence does not distinguish between the content of communications and their communications data or between airborne and cable-based traffic.'

[274] *Centrum för Rättvisa* (n 1) [369]. On the judgment generally, see Klamberg (n 1).

[275] *Big Brother Watch* (n 1). Joint Partly Concurring Opinion of Judges Lemmens, Vehabović, and Bošnjak, 159–62: '[W]hile the present judgment as a whole is elegantly structured and largely clear in its message, it has also missed an excellent opportunity to fully uphold the importance of private life and correspondence when faced with interference in the form of mass surveillance ... Consequently, the Grand Chamber should have ... introduced clear minimum safeguards capable of protecting individuals against arbitrary or excessive interference; and consequently (c) assessed the impugned bulk interception scheme in a stricter manner.'

These concerns have also been reiterated by several scholars who have taken the view that both judgments represent 'a grand normalization of mass surveillance'.[276]

The applicant's legal challenge in *Centrum för Rättvisa* when first lodged before the ECtHR in 2008 initially focused on the compatibility of the Swedish legal framework with the six foreseeability safeguards as applied in the earlier cases of *Weber* and *Kennedy*.[277] However, when before the Grand Chamber, no doubt influenced by the far stricter standards from the data retention case law of the CJEU delivered in the intervening years, the applicant further contested that bulk interception regimes are inherently incompatible with the ECHR.[278] Similar to the approach of the applicants in *Big Brother Watch*, it was argued in *Centrum för Rättvisa* that if the ECtHR considered bulk interception justified under the ECHR, that existing Article 8 ECHR standards would need to be adapted. The applicant argued that this would require the addition of the following 'robust minimum safeguards' given the 'elevated privacy risks' posed by more modern forms of untargeted surveillance.[279]

First, the main elements of the regime 'should be set out in sufficient detail in statute law'.[280] Secondly, regarding prior authorization, while the applicant accepted that the body entrusted with this task in Sweden is a judicial one, the NGO invited the ECtHR to move one step further in its case law and hold that prior authorization must always be judicial.[281] Thirdly, the authorizing body should be capable of verifying the 'existence of a reasonable suspicion' in relation to any person singled out or targeted and that use of personalized selectors to single out and collect data on an individual, albeit in the bulk interception context, should be subject to the same threshold as applied to targeted interception. Otherwise, it was argued that public authorities could use such selectors 'as a work-around method for targeting individuals'.[282] Fourthly, the applicant noted that in the alternative (where there are no predefined targets), the authorizing body should be capable of verifying that personal data used in selectors are only permitted to the extent that they are relevant 'to a narrowly specified foreign intelligence objective'. This safeguard being necessary, the applicant stressed, on the basis that 'use of selectors relating to specific individuals exposes them to distinct privacy risks'.[283]

Fifthly, the authorizing body should be provided with 'an indication' of how the data will be analysed and used. The applicant then suggests some examples of what could be provided to this body, including some of the data-driven tools

[276] See eg Milanovich (n 1); Klamberg (n 1); Woods (n 1); Zalnieriute (n 1).
[277] See the questions lodged before the ECtHR, 14 July 2008: <https://hudoc.echr.coe.int/eng?i=001-147946>.
[278] *Centrum för Rättvisa* (n 1) [182]. On the landmark case law of the CJEU, see Chapter 5.
[279] *Centrum för Rättvisa* (n 1) [183].
[280] ibid [184].
[281] ibid [185].
[282] ibid [186].
[283] ibid [187].

in the current bulk surveillance landscape, such as whether 'pattern-based or subject-based analysis' will be applied and whether profiles of individuals will be compiled.[284] Sixthly, the applicant accepted that the Swedish oversight bodies met the requirement of being sufficiently independent of the executive. The NGO argued, however, that such oversight bodies should be enhanced and given the following set of powers: they should be capable of issuing legally binding decisions, including the power to stop and remedy breaches and seek the liability of those responsible for said breaches; their supervision should extent to both content and communications data, the storage, transfer to foreign actors, and automated analysis of any such information; they should have access to classified documents; and they should function in a way that is 'open to public scrutiny'.[285] Finally, the applicant argued that effective remedies for individuals should be threefold. First, *ex post* notification of being part of a surveillance measure. Secondly, the possibility to request information about the surveillance. Thirdly, in addition to or in place of the latter, the existence of a body that can examine complaints without the individual being required to provide evidence.[286]

More specifically, the applicant found the following five elements of the Swedish legal framework to be particularly problematic in terms of its compliance with Article 8 ECHR. The applicant took issue with the 'wide discretion' granted to the Swedish public authorities regarding their use of, and in some cases direct access to, bulk intercepted data collected for 'development activities' that goes beyond the scope of foreign intelligence activities.[287] Secondly, despite warrants (otherwise referred to as 'permits') under the Swedish legislation having a 'clear expiry date', the applicant highlighted that there was no legal requirement that a warrant be cancelled if collection of the data was no longer necessary.[288] The applicant stressed that, given the sheer volume of information that could be obtained through bulk interception in that time, the lack of provision for the cancellation of permits when no longer needed 'opened the door to excessive and inappropriate surveillance for several months until the warrant eventually expired'.[289] Thirdly, the applicant criticized the scope of judicial review of the authorizing body (the Foreign Intelligence Court) as being 'too narrow to be effective'. The following grounds for this argument were of particular concern to the applicant: a lack of verification of 'a reasonable suspicion' regarding a person singled out for monitoring and 'the exceptional importance' criterion for justifying selectors relating directly to a person did not apply to the stage of collected data being further searched (only when selectors are used in the automated collection of data). In addition, the authorizing body was

[284] ibid [188].
[285] ibid [189]–[192].
[286] ibid [191].
[287] ibid [193].
[288] ibid [194].
[289] ibid [334].

not required to review the intended use of the data (such as the profiling of individuals or groups).[290]

Fourthly, the applicant identified what are described as 'two major flaws' in the Swedish legal framework concerning the storage, access, examination, use, and destruction of intercepted data. The first concerned the lack of a legal obligation for the FRA (the relevant public authority tasked with undertaking bulk interception for other public authorities and for development activities) to 'keep detailed records of the interception, use, and communication of data'. This was an issue for which the Swedish Data Protection Authority had consistently criticized the FRA. Secondly, the applicant criticized the lack of rules specific to bulk interception as opposed to general rules on data processing and the fact that as of March 2018 the Security Police may be granted direct access to the FRA's databases.[291] Fifthly, the applicant argued that 'legal persons' did not enjoy adequate protection since the FRA Data Processing Act only applied to intercept material containing personal data. This gap could thereby result in a situation where material not containing personal data 'may be kept forever' and used for purposes incompatible with the original purpose of collection.[292] In addition, the applicant was critical of several elements within the supervisory system, relevant remedies, and 'glaring' deficiencies in the law concerning transfers to foreign third parties. These included the fact that *ex post* notification and information requests under the Signals Intelligence Act was limited to natural persons, thereby excluding organizations, and may also be disapplied based on 'reasons of secrecy', rendering the remedy in practice 'theoretical and illusory'.[293]

The Grand Chamber takes a very different view to the applicant on the wide discretion granted to Swedish public authorities regarding their use of bulk interception for development activities. Regarding the bulk interception of signals for foreign intelligence (any content or communications data from the communication of text, images, sounds), most of which is collected from fibre optic cables, the Court noted the Swedish government's admission that separating 'domestic' from 'foreign' communications 'is not always possible'.[294] The Court then proceeds to highlight that signals interception measures in Sweden are also permitted under the domestic legislation for the purposes of 'development activities', which goes beyond the scope of the (eight) foreign intelligence purposes.[295] Earlier in

[290] ibid [195].
[291] ibid [196].
[292] ibid [197].
[293] See further ibid [198]–[200].
[294] ibid [290].
[295] The Signal Intelligence Act, Art 1(2) sets out these eight foreign intelligences purposes: (1) external military threats to the country; (2) conditions for Swedish participation in international peacekeeping or humanitarian missions or threats to the safety of Swedish interests in the performance of such operations; (3) strategic circumstances concerning international terrorism or other serious cross-border crime that may threaten essential national interests; (4) development and proliferation of weapons of mass destruction, military equipment, and other similar specified products; (5) serious external threats to society's infrastructure; (6) foreign conflicts with consequences for international

its judgment, it is stated that although interceptions undertaken for development activities 'usually do not focus on communications between individuals ... information on individuals' identities may be intercepted'.[296] Both of these factors are significant as they show that interception measures for these additional purposes that go beyond the scope of foreign intelligence may also include personal data concerning the citizens and residents of Sweden and those beyond Sweden's borders. The Court further acknowledges in its analysis that public authorities may access information collected *via* this additional interception route of development activities but stresses that it is 'undisputed' that such access is only possible subject to the following safeguards.[297]

However, the Court points out that any such information may only be used by the relevant public authorities if 'in conformity' with one of the eight foreign intelligence purposes and applicable 'tasking directives'. Undertaking any development activities is also subject to the Foreign Intelligence Court issuing a permit, supervision by the Inspectorate, including for compliance with the law and tasking directives approved by the Foreign Intelligence Court.[298] Although the principle of 'necessity' is notably not explicitly mentioned, the ECtHR relatedly holds that the government's reasons for monitoring 'very large segments of international signals traffic' beyond the eight permitted foreign intelligence purposes, such as the need to identify trends in new types of signals, 'appear convincing'. The ECtHR observes that public authorities 'must be able to react' to the evolution in technology and communication practices.[299] In addition, the Strasbourg Court expresses the view that the 'degree of interference with individuals' Article 8 rights engendered by such activities *appears to be* of a very low intensity' on the basis that the data thereby obtained 'is not in a form destined to generate intelligence'.[300] Based on the above, the ECtHR does not take issue with the use of development activities to monitor 'very large segments of international signals traffic' beyond the eight permitted foreign intelligence purposes. It holds that the legal framework governing these measures contains 'safeguards *capable* of preventing attempts to circumvent the legal restrictions' related to the grounds for which signals intelligence may be used and that the legal provisions set out with sufficient clarity the circumstances in which communications interceptions may take place.[301]

Regarding the lack of a 'clear expiry date' or legal requirement that a warrant for a bulk interception measure be cancelled if collection of the data was no longer

security; (7) foreign intelligence operations against Swedish interests; and (8) the actions or intentions of a foreign power that are of substantial importance for Swedish foreign, security, or defence policy.

296 *Centrum för Rättvisa* (n 1) [24].
297 ibid [291]–[293].
298 ibid [293].
299 ibid [292].
300 ibid [292] (emphasis added).
301 ibid [293]–[294] (emphasis added).

necessary, the Grand Chamber recognized that this was indeed a shortcoming. However, the ECtHR did not consider it sufficiently serious to amount to being one of the three 'shortcomings' that resulted in the ECtHR assessing the Swedish legal framework to be in violation of Article 8 ECHR.[302] The reasons of the Grand Chamber for this are twofold. First, the Court states that Swedish law provides relevant mechanisms that 'can lead to the cancellation of a bulk interception mission when ... it is no longer needed', including the possibility of a 'requesting authority' revoking an existing warrant.[303] Secondly, the Court takes the view that based 'by the nature of things' in the specific context of bulk interception for foreign intelligence aims, 'the implementation of a legal requirement to cancel a permit when no longer needed must in all likelihood be heavily dependent on internal operative assessments involving secrecy'. Consequently, the Court concludes that the existence of such supervision 'must generally be seen as providing similar legislative safeguards against abuse related to the duration of interception operations'.[304] In order words, the ECtHR effectively determined that such oversight thereby renders moot the necessity of a clear legal limit in a permit for the surveillance measure to be cancelled when no longer needed.

Given that there is no reference to any supporting 'material' or case law from the Swedish government showing that such measures are taken in practice, it is quite remarkable that the ECtHR treats the possibility of a public authority itself cancelling a bulk interception measure as an example of an alternative safeguard to an explicit limit in an authorizing permit.[305] This approach is unpersuasive on two grounds. First, it is contrary to the nature of how intelligence agencies operate and, secondly, it diverges from the Court's emphasis elsewhere in its judgment on the importance of independent oversight being a fundamental safeguard in bulk interception regimes.[306] The latter is evident elsewhere in the significant weight given by the ECtHR to the independence of the Foreign Intelligence Court, its *ex ante* authorization role, the requirement that necessity and proportionality are considered in the review of selected search terms for bulk interception measures, and the presence of 'a privacy protection representative'. These factors led the ECtHR to conclude that the pre-authorization regime and 'supervision exercised by an independent body in Sweden serve *in*

[302] ibid [336] [369].
[303] ibid [336]. Or a 'tasking directive' under Swedish law.
[304] ibid [336].
[305] The ECtHR highlights when it had 'material' concerning certain information provided to it by the Swedish government but also that the ECtHR was generally required to undertake its overall assessment of the operation of the Swedish regime based on 'limited information' and a lack of concrete examples: see ibid [237], [303], [320].
[306] See ibid [264]. As Iain Cameron, leading scholar and member of the Venice Commission, observes (n 43): '[u]nless external limits are imposed, and continually reimposed, then the natural tendency on all security and intelligence agencies is to over-collect information'.

principle to … limit the risk of disproportionate consequences affecting Article 8 rights'.[307]

On the remaining issues raised by the applicant, the Grand Chamber found some common ground on the following three shortcomings which were assessed as being 'not sufficiently compensated' by existing safeguards in the Swedish framework. Consequently, the Swedish bulk interception regime was held to have 'overstepped the margin of appreciation' left to the public authorities in Sweden.[308] The first concerned the absence of a clear rule on destroying material that does not contain personal data. However, the Court proceeds to note that in fact this shortcoming's 'potential for causing adverse consequences on Article 8 rights is limited' on the ground that Swedish law provides clear rules on the destruction of intercepted material in several circumstances.[309] It is curious, then, that what was viewed as a 'procedural shortcoming in the regulatory framework' earlier in the judgment goes on to be included in the key trifecta of shortcomings that pushed the Grand Chamber to depart from the Chamber judgment and find the Swedish regime to be in violation of Article 8 ECHR.[310] In contrast, the Grand Chamber attaches far greater weight to the second of these shortcomings and its potential to lead 'to very significant adverse consequences for affected individuals or organisations'.[311]

This 'substantive' and 'significant' shortcoming concerns the absence of a requirement in the Signals Intelligence Act, 'or other relevant legislation', that public authorities should give consideration to the 'privacy interests' of individuals when making a decision to transmit intelligence material to foreign partners.[312] The Court warns that this missing requirement may allow 'information seriously compromising privacy rights or the right to respect for correspondence to be transmitted abroad mechanically, even if its intelligence value is very low'. Consequently, the Court stresses that such transmission 'may therefore generate clearly disproportionate risks for Article 8 Convention rights' and that there is no legally binding obligation on the FRA to analyse and determine whether the foreign recipient of intelligence 'offers an acceptable minimum level of safeguards'.[313] The Grand Chamber proceeds to hold that the Swedish government 'had failed to convince the Court' that the supervisory body of the Foreign Intelligence Inspectorate monitored in practice the possible risks or disproportionate consequences of intelligence sharing on Article 8 ECHR rights. Departing from the deferential approach

[307] ibid [368]. Note that the Privacy Protection Representative does not attend any urgent proceedings before the Foreign Intelligence Court and that there is no right of appeal regarding its decisions which are final and confidential: ibid [297].
[308] ibid [373].
[309] ibid [370].
[310] ibid [370].
[311] ibid [371].
[312] ibid [326], [330], and [369].
[313] ibid [371].

of the Chamber, the Grand Chamber did not accept that this set of shortcomings in the regulatory framework were sufficiently counterbalanced by the supervisory elements of the Swedish regime.[314]

Thirdly, the Grand Chamber held the absence of an effective *ex post facto* review 'must be seen as a shortcoming' in the Swedish legal framework on bulk interception and be taken into account in the Court's assessment of its compatibility with Article 8 ECHR.[315] The Court was particularly critical of the Foreign Intelligence Inspectorate's dual role in supervising the FRA's activities (including authorization of the use of selectors and analysis of intercepted materials) and its *ex post facto* review of requests from individuals. Functions which, the Court noted, may lead to situations where the Inspectorate will have to assess its own activities on supervising bulk interception by the FRA.[316] In addition, the Court took issue with the lack of any possibility for members of the public to obtain reasoned decisions in some form in response to inquiries or complaints regarding the bulk interception of communications.[317] The Court also agreed with the applicant that the remedy in the UK before the Investigatory Powers Tribunal shows that it is possible 'to reconcile legitimate security concerns and the need to ensure a reliable *ex post facto* control of bulk interception activities'.[318] Finally, the Grand Chamber held that the lack of an effective review at the final stage of interception could 'not be reconciled with the Court's view' that the degree of interference with individuals' Article 8 ECHR rights increases as the process advances and falls short of the requirement of 'end-to-end' safeguards.[319]

2. Developing the case law on bulk interception: the new approach to Article 8 ECHR

(a) Reformulating the foreseeability requirements and reducing minimum safeguards to 'principles'

The applicants in *Big Brother Watch* and *Centrum för Rättvisa* both urged the ECtHR to adopt enhanced and 'robust minimum safeguards' in order to ensure that Article 8 ECHR standards on bulk interception regimes 'remained practical and effective'.[320] However, the Grand Chamber roundly rejected the argument that

[314] ibid [329] and [371].
[315] ibid [364].
[316] Similar risks of marking its own homework favourably arise from the dual roles of the UK's supervisory body established under the Investigatory Powers Act 2016. The Investigatory Powers Commissioner's Office (IPCO) is also tasked with jointly authorizing bulk interception warrants with the Secretary of State and undertaking their *ex post* review. See Ni Loideain (n 44) 187.
[317] *Centrum för Rättvisa* (n 1) [359]–[364].
[318] ibid [363].
[319] ibid [372].
[320] *Big Brother Watch* (n 1) [280]; *Centrum för Rättvisa* (n 1) [183].

changes in society and technology had resulted in a need for the Strasbourg Court to adopt any such minimum safeguards. The Court instead highlights that previous judgments dealing with bulk interception and Article 8 ECHR did not address the fact that 'it was dealing with surveillance of a different nature and scale from that considered in previous cases'.[321] In addition, the Grand Chamber attempts to distinguish the bulk interception regimes at issue in *Big Brother Watch* from those reviewed in the Court's earlier judgments in *Weber and Saravia* and *Liberty*.

The Court stressed that those judgments were over ten years old and thus the scope of surveillance activities then covered by those bulk interception regimes would have been 'much narrower' given the 'significantly larger volume of electronic communications' generated today.[322] The Grand Chamber then distinguishes between the level of interference in an individual's right to private life posed by targeted interception and bulk interception. The key argument being that the safeguards cannot be the same for both types of surveillance on the basis that bulk interception regimes are different and (as noted earlier) only pose increasing gradual degrees of intrusion into the Article 8 rights. This leads the Grand Chamber to take the view that the need for safeguards is 'at its highest' at the end of the bulk interception process 'where information about a particular person will be analysed or the content of the communications is being examined by an analyst'.[323]

The Grand Chamber as a result does not assess whether the six foreseeability safeguards previous applied by the ECtHR when examining the compatibility of bulk interception regimes with Article 8 ECHR are fit for purpose. Instead, the Court refers to what were previously 'minimum safeguards' as 'principles' that 'will have to be adapted to reflect the specific features of a bulk interception regime' and the increasing degrees of intrusion into the Article 8 ECHR rights of individuals through the different bulk interception stages.[324] This results in the Court determining that the first two of the six foreseeability safeguards has found 'in the context of targeted interception' should be defined clearly in domestic law in order to avoid abuses of power that 'are not readily applicable to a bulk interception regime'.[325] These concern the nature of offences which may give rise to an interception order and the categories of people liable to have their communications intercepted. Relatedly, the Court briefly notes that the requirement of 'reasonable suspicion', which can be found in the Court's case law on targeted interception in the context of criminal investigations is 'less germane in the bulk interception context'. This is based on the grounds that the purpose of bulk regimes is 'in principle preventive, rather than for the investigation of a specific target and/or an identifiable criminal offence'.[326]

[321] *Big Brother Watch* (n 1) [343].
[322] ibid [341].
[323] ibid [325]–[331]; *Centrum för Rättvisa* (n 1) [239]–[245].
[324] *Big Brother Watch* (n 1) [347]; *Centrum för Rättvisa* (n 1) [261].
[325] *Big Brother Watch* (n 1) [348]; *Centrum för Rättvisa* (n 1) [262].
[326] *Big Brother Watch* (n 1) [348]; *Centrum för Rättvisa* (n 1) [262].

The Grand Chamber then stresses that it 'considers it imperative' that 'domestic law should contain detailed rules on when the authorities *may* resort to such measures ... and the circumstances in which an individual's communications might be intercepted'.[327] It proceeds to note that the remaining 'four minimum safeguards' defined by the Court in its previous judgments are 'equally relevant to bulk interception'.[328] These four safeguards are then effectively incorporated into what the Court describes as a 'wider' eight-part set of criteria for assessing whether a bulk interception framework of a Contracting State has fallen within the 'margin of appreciation' and contains adequate and effective safeguards to meet the requirements of 'foreseeability' and 'necessity in a democratic society'.[329] This new approach draws from the controversial combined analysis of the legality and proportionality tests of Article 8(2), which the Grand Chamber refers to 'as the established approach in this area'.[330]

This new criteria will be applied by the Court to assess whether the domestic legal framework clearly defined: (1) the grounds on which bulk interception may be authorized; (2) the circumstances in which an individual's communications may be intercepted; (3) the procedure to be followed for granting authorization; (4) the procedures to be followed for selecting, examining, and using intercept material; (5) the precautions to be taken when communicating the material to other parties; (6) the limits on the duration of interception, the storage of intercept material, and the circumstances in which such material must be erased and destroyed; (7) the procedures and modalities for supervision by an independent authority of compliance with the above safeguards and its powers to address non-compliance; and (8) the procedures for independent *ex post facto* review of such compliance and the powers vested in the competent body in addressing instances of non-compliance.

The reasoning of the Grand Chamber and its reformulation (and effective watering down) of the foreseeability safeguards to 'principles' is problematic on two grounds. First, the requirement that domestic law should identify the circumstances when public authorities '*may* resort' to using bulk interception regimes falls under the scope of the first two foreseeability safeguards that the Court has held are no longer applicable to the examination of these regimes. Secondly, the Grand Chamber does not expressly address in its reasoning that all six foreseeability safeguards have previously been applied by the Court in more recent cases dealing with bulk interception, including the Grand Chamber judgment

327 *Big Brother Watch* (n 1) [348]; *Centrum för Rättvisa* (n 1) [262].

328 *Big Brother Watch* (n 1) [348]; *Centrum för Rättvisa* (n 1) [262]. These require that: domestic law should set out a limit on the duration of interception; the procedure to be followed for examining, using, and storing the data obtained; the precautions to be taken when communicating the data to other parties; and the circumstances in which intercepted data may or must be erased or destroyed.

329 *Big Brother Watch* (n 1) [361]; *Centrum för Rättvisa* (n 1) [275].

330 *Big Brother Watch* (n 1) [361]. For a critique of the joint analysis approach, see the earlier discussion.

of *Zakharov v Russia*. This is a significant omission in the reasoning of the judgment which also does not explain the major reversal of well-established Article 8 ECHR rule of law safeguards taking place in its reformulation of the foreseeability requirements. The Grand Chamber also omits to deal with its departure from the unanimous judgment of *Szabó and Vissy* in 2016 where the Court held that Article 8 ECHR safeguards needed 'to be enhanced' due to the capacity of State surveillance to now acquire detailed profiles of the 'most intimate aspects of individuals' private lives'.[331]

Indeed, other members of the Grand Chamber have highlighted these omissions and strongly criticized the new approach of the Court to examining bulk regimes on three main grounds. First, Judges Lemmes, Vehabović, and Bošnjak rightly observe that 'it is difficult to see why one should not expect the domestic legislation to clearly define' the possible national security threats and the circumstances in which those threats may trigger bulk interception.[332] Secondly, it is recognized that the requirement for defining categories of people liable to have their communications intercepted 'make little sense' in the first stage of bulk interception, when all communications running through certain bearers are intercepted indiscriminately. However, the judges rightly proceed to point out that the 'breadth of the interference should not be an excuse for abandoning a particular safeguard'. They note that the later stages of bulk interception become 'largely comparable to that of targeted interception', particularly when strong selectors are applied for the purpose of singling out and analysing the communications of an identified individual. Thus, they point out that expecting the legal framework to define the categories of people who can be targeted by the application of strong selectors 'would not be an excessive, but rather a fully appropriate, requirement'.[333] Thirdly, Judge Pinto de Albuquerque (in a separate opinion) highlights previous case law where the six foreseeability safeguards have been applied to bulk interception and notes that this jurisprudence was not given 'proper weight' by the Court.[334]

(b) End-to-end safeguards and a 'global assessment': no minimum safeguards

In another departure from previous case law, the Grand Chamber establishes that in future the operation of a bulk interception regime will be subject to 'a global assessment' that will focus 'primarily on whether the domestic legal framework contains sufficient guarantees against abuse' and has 'end-to-end safeguards'.[335] The exact details of what the 'global' nature of such an assessment will entail are not

331 *Szabó and Vissy* (n 7) [70].
332 *Big Brother Watch* (n 1), Joint Partly Concurring Opinion of Judges Lemmens, Vehabović, and Bošnjak, 164–65.
333 ibid 165.
334 ibid, Partly Concurring and Partly Dissenting Opinion of Judge Pinto de Albuquerque, 173.
335 ibid [360]; *Centrum för Rättvisa* (n 1) [274].

addressed. This is another striking lack of clarity in the reasoning of the Grand Chamber, particularly given the importance of how this new form of assessment will shape the future case law of the Strasbourg Court on Article 8 ECHR and secret surveillance. Instead, the Grand Chamber proceeds to highlight that 'in doing so' regard will be given to the more traditional proportionality requirement of examining the 'actual operation of the system … and the existence or absence of any evidence of actual abuse'.[336] More detail is, however, provided regarding how the bulk interception regimes of Contracting States may satisfy the requirement of 'end-to-end' safeguards. Specifically, the Grand Chamber states that in order 'to minimise the risk of the bulk interception power being abused', the process must be subject to end-to-end safeguards. The Court then proceeds to identify the three 'fundamental safeguards' which in the Court's view 'will be the cornerstone of any Article 8 compliant bulk interception regime'.[337] The first requires that an assessment should be made at each stage of the process of the necessity and proportionality of the measures being taken. Secondly, that bulk interception should be subject to prior independent authorization ('at the outset') when the object and scope of the surveillance operation are being defined. Lastly, the operation should also be subject to supervision and independent *ex post facto* review.

While there are those who have welcomed these 'end-to-end' safeguards, particularly the importance they place on *ex ante* independent authorization,[338] others have raised serious concerns regarding their actual legal status when the judgments of *Big Brother Watch* and *Centrum för Rättvisa* are viewed as a whole.[339]As Judge Pinto de Albuquerque states, although the Grand Chamber refers to these as 'fundamental safeguards', the Court has 'diluted these safeguards' through the establishment of the 'global assessment of the operation of the regime' which allows 'for a trade-off among the safeguards'.[340] This compensatory approach via the global assessment test thereby allows the Court to avoid having to assess whether any future contested bulk interception regime meets all of the so-called 'fundamental' end-to-end safeguards. Consequently, as Milanovic and Woods point out, these 'highly flexible' eight safeguards are part of a global assessment of the programme which means that a State 'failing one of the criteria can nonetheless compensate for that failing by being very good on some of the other criteria'.[341] Put another

[336] *Big Brother Watch* (n 1) [360].
[337] ibid [360]; *Centrum för Rättvisa* (n 1) [274].
[338] See eg European Data Protection Board, Opinion 5/2023 on the European Commission Draft Implementing Decision on the adequate protection of personal data under the EU–US Data Privacy Framework [142].
[339] See Milanovic (n 1); Ni Loideain (n 1); Smith (n 1); Woods (n 1). For an alternative view of the Grand Chamber judgments and the safeguards therein, see Vajda (n 1).
[340] See *Big Brother Watch* (n 1), Partly Concurring, Partly and Dissenting Opinion of Judge Pinto De Albequeque. As the judgment itself states, [370]: 'Consequently, in the Court's view, a regime which permits bulk interception to be ordered on relatively wide grounds may still comply with Article 8 of the Convention, provided that, when viewed as a whole, sufficient guarantees against abuse are built into the system to compensate for this weakness.'
[341] Milanovic (n 1); Woods (n 1).

way, these 'principles' are what the Grand Chamber would view as best practice in its overall holistic assessment of bulk interception regimes and their compatibility with Article 8 ECHR.

Thus, despite the robust language used in describing their significance as 'fundamental' and 'cornerstone', the safeguards underpinning this new global assessment are markedly deferential and lack a strict-scrutiny approach.

(c) Expanding the scope of permitted legitimate aims for bulk interception: protecting 'other essential national interests'

It has traditionally been an important role of the ECtHR to develop and apply minimum safeguards that will serve to limit the inherent risk of the misuse or abuse of secret surveillance measures by public authorities. It is in this vein that another clear example of divergence has arisen between the ECtHR and the CJEU concerning the area of secret surveillance and the right to private life, specifically the aims for which bulk retention and bulk interception measures may be permitted to protect national security and prevent crime. It is now well-established CJEU case law that Article 15(1) of the e-Privacy Directive 2002/58, read in the light of the EU Charter, precludes measures which provide as a preventive measure for the 'general and indiscriminate' retention of traffic and location data. The CJEU carved out a narrow exception for safeguarding national security from this requirement in its 2020 judgment of *La Quadrature du Net*. Nevertheless, such bulk retention must still be subject to 'foreseeable' time limits and is also limited to situations where 'a serious threat' to national security is 'shown to be genuine and present or foreseeable'. The CJEU also established in the groundbreaking judgment of *La Quadrature du Net*, and has reiterated since, that the retention and transfer of individual's communications data for national security should be the exception and not the rule.[342] In contrast, the Strasbourg Court later established a much more deferential approach in the Grand Chamber judgments of *Big Brother Watch* and *Centrum för Rättvisa*.

Regarding the test of whether an interference is 'necessary in a democratic society' in pursuit of a legitimate aim, the ECtHR has long recognized in its Article 8 ECHR case law that national authorities enjoy a wide margin of appreciation in choosing how best to achieve the legitimate aim of 'protecting national security'.[343] However, in the Grand Chamber judgments of 2021, the Strasbourg Court expanded the scope of this already wide margin for permitted uses of bulk interception to include not only the protection of national security but also 'other essential national interests'.[344] In doing so, the Grand Chamber has expanded what was an exhaustive, but still considerably broadly framed, list of legitimate aims under

342 See Chapter 5.
343 See eg *Leander* (n 181) [59].
344 See *Big Brother Watch* (n 1) [339]; *Centrum för Rättvisa* (n 1) [253]–[254].

Article 8(2) in this area of State surveillance measures.[345] This significant development in the case law of Article 8 ECHR is also noteworthy for its brevity and lack of reasoning. Indeed, this expansion of the wide margin of appreciation does not fall within the relevant part of the Court's analysis concerning the need to develop its case law but instead is swiftly mentioned in passing as part of its discussion of the general principles relating to secret surveillance measures. The only apparent source for this addition to the Article 8 ECHR case law is its transplantation from the provisions of the Swedish bulk interception domestic law (Signal Intelligence Act).[346]

In both *Big Brother Watch* and *Centrum för Rättvisa*, the Court makes another brief reference elsewhere in these judgments where it possibly appears to limit the scope of this new legitimate aim to 'other essential national interests *against serious external threats*'.[347] There is still, however, no explanation or reasoning underpinning this expansion of the legitimate aims of Article 8(2) with respect to when Contracting States are justified to use bulk interception in circumstances that are compatible with Article 8 ECHR. The lack of any reasoning or justification by the Grand Chamber for this expansion of the legitimate aims of Article 8(2) which has the effect of further enabling the use of bulk interception powers by Contracting States is striking. Furthermore, the ECtHR has effectively left the placing of any limits on the scope of the legitimate aims and expanded discretion conferred on relevant public authorities to the national courts, regulators, and national legislators.

(d) An assessment based on 'limited information': end-to-end safeguards 'in practice'?

The Grand Chamber highlights at various points in *Big Brother Watch* and *Centrum för Rättvisa* that it has been required to assess the end-to-end safeguards put in place to provide adequate and effective guarantees against arbitrariness and the risk of abuse based on 'limited information' of how these operate in practice.[348] Indeed, in *Big Brother Watch*, judges of the ECtHR in a concurring opinion criticized the lack of any information provided to the Grand Chamber regarding how the immediate discarding of intercepted communications is performed in practice, particularly the lack of transparency surrounding what criteria the intelligence

[345] Article 8(2) provides: 'There shall be no interference by a public authority with the exercise of this right except such as is in accordance with the law and is necessary in a democratic society in the interests of *national security, public safety or the economic well-being of the country, for the prevention of disorder or crime, for the protection of health or morals, or for the protection of the rights and freedoms of others*' (emphasis added).

[346] *Centrum för Rättvisa* (n 1) [22]: Signals Intelligence Act, s 1(2)(3) provides that electronic signals may be collected as part of foreign intelligence for the purpose of '... serious cross-border crime that may threaten essential national interests'.

[347] *Big Brother Watch* (n 1) [347] (emphasis added); *Centrum för Rättvisa* (n 1) [261].

[348] *Centrum för Rättvisa* (n 1) [237]; *Big Brother Watch* (n 1) [323].

services apply to 'separate rubbish from possibly useful material'. In the view of the judges of this concurring opinion, the lack of any detailed engagement in the judgment with this lack of information amounted to a 'important shortcoming' and the lack of transparency itself raised serious questions of compatibility with the requirement of foreseeability.[349]

Another example of this limited information is the lack of an effective *ex post facto* review in Swedish law on bulk interception where the Grand Chamber emphasized that this shortcoming was particularly relevant to the fact that the Court had 'insufficient information' about the practice of the Foreign Intelligence Court. This was specifically regarding its judicial pre-authorization of strong selectors, categories of selectors, and how the legal requirements on the destruction of intercepted material are applied under the Swedish legal framework in practice.[350] In addition, the Grand Chamber highlighted that it did not have 'sufficient information' on how the necessity to keep material containing personal data is assessed in practice—whether unprocessed intercepted material is always stored for the maximum period of one year, or if the necessity of continued storage is regularly reviewed. The Court further stated that this gap in evidence made it 'difficult to arrive at comprehensive conclusions' covering all aspects of the storage and deletion of intercepted material.[351]

Given the further lack of access of the Grand Chamber to any of the judgments of the Foreign Intelligence Court, as Klamberg rightly observes, there was a particularly stark lack of information for the ECtHR to examine when determining whether the Swedish bulk interception regime operated with end-to-end safeguards in practice.[352] This raises an important question regarding the general adequacy and effectiveness of the judicial review and capacity for meaningful scrutiny by the ECtHR of these national security regimes, in particular their operation in practice and the application of the end-to-end safeguards. For instance, how many times has the FRA self-authorized permits allowing it to undertake bulk interception of communications on the basis that prior authorization from the Foreign Intelligence Court 'might cause delay or other *inconveniences* of essential importance for one of the specified purposes of the signals intelligence'?[353] Such broadly framed justifications invariably raise questions of what in practice have these 'other inconveniences' been? Has the Foreign Intelligence Court ever revoked or amended a self-authorized permit as provided for under the Signals Intelligence Act?[354] What issues have the Privacy Protection Representatives

349 *Big Brother Watch* (n 1), Joint Partly Concurring Opinion of Judges Lemmens, Vehabović, and Bošnjak, 162–63.

350 *Centrum för Rättvisa* (n 1) [364].

351 ibid [343].

352 Klamberg (n 1).

353 *Centrum för Rättvisa* (n 1) [33] (emphasis added).

354 ibid [33].

raised (if any) before the Foreign Intelligence Court only to have those challenges rejected on the basis that there is no appeal of the Foreign Intelligence Court's decisions which are final?[355]

Consequently, there is a notable convergence between the CJEU and ECtHR that neither court is taking an evidence-based approach in its proportionality assessments of bulk retention and bulk interception measures by public authorities. This not entirely the fault, of course, of the courts. Both courts have indeed highlighted in recent pleadings and judgments a lack of information being provided by Contracting States in relation to the operation in practice of contested surveillance and data retention systems. However, two very different approaches are emerging from the courts, neither of which is welcome from the perspective of enabling the protection of the right to private life in practice and both of which permit public safety measures that are only adopted when shown to meet the legality and proportionality tests of the ECHR and EU legal orders. On the one hand, the Strasbourg Court in its creation of a holistic 'global assessment', that lacks any minimum safeguards, has provided an even wider margin of appreciation to Contracting States when examining whether their bulk interception regimes are compatible with Article 8 ECHR. Whereas on the other hand, the CJEU has consistently rejected any arguments put before it regarding the limits of expedited retention and its temporal and geographic targeting test for data retention. The CJEU considers, for instance, the former so-called 'quick freeze' of traffic and location data for the purpose of countering serious crime to be a viable alternative to the general retention of traffic and location data. However, its effectiveness (as several Member States and national courts have stressed to the CJEU) depends on the data being retained in the first place.[356]

More broadly, the lack of evidence in these cases showing the impact of surveillance conducted for national security measures in practice has major implications for the protection and mainstreaming of the right to private life and other affected human rights.[357] To raise one particularly burning question, how can supranational courts tasked with assessing the proportionality and compliance of bulk powers with the rule of law and human rights effectively fulfil this requirement without (at least some) access to such information? Relying solely on the information provided by national oversight bodies (such as annual reports) is insufficient as this provides only a snapshot of the entire legal framework and its compatibility with Article 8 ECHR in practice.[358]

[355] ibid [34].

[356] See further Chapter 5.

[357] See related concerns raised by Klamberg (n 1).

[358] The European Commission has also faced data collection challenges regarding its evaluations of related EU laws implemented by Member States concerning the retention of communications data, passenger name record (PNR) data, and the detection of Child Sexual Abuse Material, for countering terrorism and serious crime. See further Chapters 1, 8, and 9. Safert (n 1) also stresses the importance for the ECtHR to ask Contracting States for any empirical evidence which demonstrates the necessity and proportionality of bulk interception regimes. On the importance for policymakers to ensure greater

3. The ECtHR steps back: no longer setting minimum requirements for the scrutiny and oversight of bulk interception

In a joint concurring opinion, three judges of the ECtHR recognized that the Grand Chamber in *Big Brother Watch* had missed an opportunity to 'fully uphold the importance of private life' within the context of interferences posed by mass surveillance.[359] They highlight that while the ECtHR 'extensively describes' the nature of modern threats facing Contracting States and recognizes how valuable bulk interception can be in identifying and preventing those threats in its preliminary assessment, there is 'no similar emphasis on the importance of privacy or any other private interest'.[360] They stress that the development of new technologies enabling mass surveillance and more effective use of the information collected 'has increased threats to privacy as well as the risk of abuse of personal data'. This, and other considerations, should have led the Grand Chamber to attach 'significantly more weight' to the interests of private life and correspondence when weighing them in the balance against the legitimate interests of the respondent State in operating its bulk interception scheme. The opinion then proceeds to make three main criticisms of the ECtHR. First, the Strasbourg Court should have accurately identified and 'attached proper weight' to interferences with private life and correspondence. Secondly, clear minimum safeguards capable of protecting individuals against arbitrary or excessive interference should also have been introduced. Thirdly, the impugned bulk interception framework should have been assessed 'in a stricter manner'.[361]

Both Grand Chamber judgments in *Big Brother Watch* and *Centrum för Rättvisa* also have broader implications for the scrutiny of bulk interception regimes across Europe and the ECHR legal order. The first is the clear departure for the ECtHR as an important driving force and its previously lauded role for setting minimum standards in the review of laws governing State surveillance of communications across Europe. To date, it is only the CJEU that is consistently providing any novel safeguards to deal with the emerging threats to private life and data protection posed by surveillance measures that are underpinned by rapidly evolving technologies and systems. These include major developments such as machine learning models, automated decision-making, predictive analytics, and the increasing role of the private sector in data acquisition for public authorities

empirical assessment of privacy laws in general, see Kenneth A Bamberger and Deirdre K Mulligan, *Privacy on the Ground* (MIT Press 2015); Orla Lynskey, 'Complete and Effective Data Protection' (2023) 76 Current Legal Problems 297.

359 *Big Brother Watch* (n 1), Joint Partly Concurring Opinion of Judges Lemmens, Vehabović, and Bošnjak, 159.
360 ibid 159.
361 ibid 161–68.

and State surveillance.[362] Secondly, the general eight-part criteria and more lenient approach of the ECtHR's joint analysis assessment for bulk interception regimes (via the global assessment) provides that there is now a clear and significant divergence between the rights-based rules and safeguards of the ECHR and EU legal systems.

Thirdly, the Grand Chamber called a clear halt to any apparent shift by the ECtHR towards an outright finding that general and indiscriminate surveillance regimes may be incompatible with Article 8 ECHR, with the result that 'a clear line' has been drawn by both Grand Chambers in Strasbourg and Luxembourg between the approaches of the ECtHR and CJEU.[363]

E. Conclusions

For Article 8 ECHR standards to remain relevant and capable of responding to increasingly sophisticated surveillance capabilities, the ECtHR acknowledges in earlier case law the impact of key technological and social developments on the scope of intrusion to private life. The ECtHR's previous landmark cases applied a heightened level of scrutiny to the impact on the interference with the rights enshrined in Article 8 ECHR posed by new surveillance capabilities and practices. This included establishing that indiscriminate and general surveillance measures should be subject to the same foreseeability safeguards under the legality condition of Article 8(2), originally developed with respect to the targeted monitoring of individuals. This evolution in the Article 8 ECHR case law of the Strasbourg Court was important for two key reasons. First, it demonstrated that both the scope of Article 8(1) and the safeguards of Article 8(2) were keeping pace at this time with modern technological and regulatory developments in the highly dynamic area of digital communications and secret surveillance. Secondly, these developments showed a court sensitive to the fact that the use of novel twenty-first-century surveillance powers should not evade the robust scrutiny previously applied in the well-established and acclaimed Article 8 ECHR case law on communications interception. This chapter has identified and examined the gradual development of these standards and the landmark judgments from which they stemmed, showing why they were long regarded as an important driving force in the scrutiny of domestic laws governing the secret monitoring of communications by public authorities. For decades, these requirements played a pivotal role in shaping data privacy standards in legal systems within Europe, the EU legal order, and beyond.[364]

[362] See further Chapters 1, 5, and 9.

[363] Christopher Docksey and Kenneth Propp, 'Government Access to Personal Data and Transnational Interoperability' (2023) 10 Oslo Law Review 1, 8.

[364] See Chapters 5–9.

Times, however, have changed. The Strasbourg Court no longer holds the mantle of being the ultimate guardian of data privacy in Europe when it comes to the scrutiny and review of communications surveillance by public authorities. This change is particularly evident in the controversial and highly deferential Grand Chamber judgments of *Big Brother Watch* and *Centrum för Rättvisa.* Here the ECtHR abandoned its role of setting minimum standards in the review of laws governing State surveillance of communications across Europe. Moreover, the Court rejected calls to enhance its Article 8 ECHR standards in response to the unprecedented capabilities now available to governments to monitor communications, comprehensively predict and profile, and intrude upon the private lives of individuals and communities in the twenty-first century. That said, serious concerns had already been mounting before these widely criticized rulings in 2021 that the ECtHR's approach to examining the compatibility of secret surveillance regimes with Article 8 ECHR was becoming less systematic and less strict. The result of this decline being that the CJEU is now considered to be the ultimate guardian of data privacy in Europe following its vanguard data retention judgments.[365]

There may come a time in the future when the ECtHR could return to its previously lauded role as an important driving force in the scrutiny of laws permitting secret surveillance in Europe. Of the various proposals put forward here to enable this shift,[366] the following four will be paramount. First, in an era of AI, mass biometric tracking and online data proliferation, where individuals and their online and offline communications are ubiquitously tracked, it is essential that the Court should apply its 'emerging technologies' rule of law requirement as a minimum mandatory safeguard. Under the previously lauded standards of Article 8 ECHR, this has traditionally required that police use of emerging technologies 'must be based on a law that is particularly precise' as the technology available for use is continually becoming more sophisticated. This would involve the ECtHR explicitly considering the impact of key technological and social developments on the scope of intrusion to private life posed by modern forms of communications surveillance at both the Article 8(1) and Article 8(2) stages of legal assessment. It is not enough for the ECtHR to make a general reference to the importance of this requirement when setting out the 'general principles' relevant to a particular case. This risks reducing what should be a minimum mandatory safeguard to the status of a general principle which may (or may not) be applied by the Court in its actual

[365] Several factors within the ECHR legal order, as noted earlier, contributed to this shift. On the contributing factors within the EU legal order, including the elevation to EU law of the EU Charter of Fundamental Rights and the impact of the Snowden revelations, see Chapters 4 and 5.

[366] See eg the previous recommendation that the ECtHR's scope of examination when assessing a secret surveillance regime and its Art 8 ECHR compatibility should be clearly limited to the specific material time when the impugned surveillance regime was in operation. Such an approach does not prevent the ECtHR from highlighting later reforms adopted by that Contracting State which subsequently address previous issues of non-compliance with Art 8 ECHR.

legal assessment.[367] Furthermore, this safeguard should be applied when assessing the compatibility with Article 8 ECHR of secret surveillance measures (targeted or bulk) used for countering crime and safeguarding national security. This approach aligns with the view of the ECHR as 'a living instrument' capable of fundamental change and to be interpreted in the light of present-day conditions.[368]

Secondly, and relatedly thirdly, the ECtHR should re-establish treating the six foreseeability requirements as 'minimum safeguards' in this area of case law and abandon the combined approach to assessing the legality and proportionality conditions under Article 8(2). Of course, this would by extension mean abandoning the highly flexible and deferential global assessment test introduced by the Grand Chamber in the controversial judgments of *Big Brother Watch* and *Centrum för Rättvisa*. This increasingly criticized joint approach has to date diluted and weakened the protections provided by each of these distinct tests of legality and proportionality. It hampers the capacity of Article 8 ECHR in two main ways. The first is to ensure its standards remain relevant to present-day conditions and the increasingly powerful surveillance capabilities available to public authorities and, secondly, to ensure the development of clear and detailed rules to safeguard against the abuse of such intrusive measures. Fourthly, the Court should consider the extent to which the current safeguards under Article 8 ECHR are fit for purpose and what additional minimum safeguards should be introduced for future assessments of secret surveillance measures and their compatibility with Article 8 ECHR. This should include that empirical evidence forms part of the pleadings put before the ECtHR in order that it may assess the adequacy of safeguards in practice and the pressing social need of the contested surveillance measure. If this evidence is not provided in any form from the Contracting State, the ECtHR should make clear that it could not provide an informed assessment regarding the proportionality of a contested surveillance measure (if this is the condition of Article 8(2) being contested by the applicants in the relevant case).

It is time for the Strasbourg Court to build on the lauded standards it developed in the last century in its case law dealing with Article 8 ECHR and the secret surveillance of communications by public authorities. This jurisprudence must address the impact of the technological changes in the twenty-first century and the resulting extended reach of State surveillance into the private lives and communications of individuals. A seismic change in the relationship between individuals and governments enabled by access to AI-based systems in smart cities,

[367] See eg *Big Brother Watch* (n 1) [333] where the Grand Chamber notes the importance of domestic laws providing 'clear and detailed rules' for surveillance measures where the available technology is continually becoming more sophisticated (and is thus a greater threat to individuals' private lives). However, this principle, denoting greater privacy interferences posed by increasingly powerful surveillance measures, is then not applied by the Grand Chamber as part of the actual legal analysis in its Art 8(2) compatibility assessment.

[368] Nicolas Bratza, 'Living Instrument or Dead Letter—the Future of the European Convention on Human Rights' (2014) 2 European Human Rights Law Review 116. See further Chapter 3.

mobile phones, facial recognition, modern predictive analytics, highly sophisticated pattern-analysis, and profiling capabilities. Otherwise, the Court's approach in its review and scrutiny of laws permitting such surveillance will fall so far behind these changes that the standard of protection provided under Article 8 ECHR risks becoming more illusory than real.

3

The Approach of the Strasbourg Court

Article 8 ECHR and Communications Data

A. Introduction

It is hard to overstate the seismic shift that has taken place in electronic communications and data-driven monitoring in the modern digital age. From the last century's era of analogue and fixed communication devices to the era of AI, this is a brave new world encompassing a slew of mobile Internet-enabled devices. Today, personal data about an individual's movements and communications are ubiquitously collected from mobile phones, cars, glasses, watches, toys, homes, offices, and CCTV. As early as 1984,[1] the ECtHR examined cases dealing with analogue landline phones and the then relatively unknown power of public authorities to acquire communications data (or metadata).[2] *Malone* was one of two judgments delivered before the arrival of the modern 'smartphone' where the Court examined the use of communications data for countering crime.[3] Communications data in these early cases concerned the contextual information revealed by calls made using landline telephones and the information collected for telephone billing. Police would acquire this from the relevant communications service provider (CSP) which had used a technique known as 'metering',[4] collecting what would be considered today as very limited and basic communications data generated by a device with a fixed landline location. This information revealed only the numbers

[1] *Malone v United Kingdom* (1985) 7 EHRR 14. It was not until thirty years later in *Digital Rights Ireland* that the CJEU would deliver its first judgment in an ongoing series of landmark cases on data retention measures for countering crime, terrorism, and protecting national security. See further Chapters 5 and 9. All URLs for this chapter were last accessed 22 April 2024.

[2] The term 'communications data' used throughout this book is broadly interpreted and refers to all categories of non-content information processed due to a communication transmission. This scope includes traffic data, location data, subscriber data, and 'data relating to the civil identity of users'. On the evolving definition(s) of communications data in EU law and beyond, see Chapters 1 and 5.

[3] *Malone* (n 1) (handling of stolen antiques); *Valenzuela Contreras v Spain* (1999) 28 EHRR 483 (harassment).

[4] *Malone* (n 1) [56]. Decades after *Malone*, the significance of communications data for law enforcement across the EU was clearly demonstrated in the adoption of the Data Retention Directive 2006/24/EC. This required Member States to mandate the storage of various types of communications data by the private sector for up to two years on the basis that it could be required for countering serious crime. The CJEU held this controversial Directive to be invalid under EU law and struck down the legislation in 2014. See further Chapters 5–8.

EU Data Privacy Law and Serious Crime. Nora Ni Loideain, Oxford University Press. © Nora Ni Loideain 2025.
DOI: 10.1093/oso/9780198837169.003.0003

dialled, who owned the phoneline, when, how often, and the length of the calls made. Telephone 'tapping' and 'metering' being the most common methods of police surveillance of communications between the 1960s and 1990s.

Of course, this is no longer the case as the Internet has transformed modern communications. We now live in a data-driven mobile world of instant messaging, across various connected devices and environments, with smart CCTV systems and AI chatbots that can constantly monitor and record a person's movements and communications. In today's era of AI-powered systems and mass biometric surveillance, public authorities may access and monitor increasingly detailed and sensitive information about a person's private life and communications like never before; especially when data is collected from online sources, in vast volumes, and subject to sophisticated forms of machine learning, automated processing, and profiling (such as pattern recognition and predictive analytics). One such capability is the collection of abundant amounts of communications data as part of 'signals intelligence', through intercepting the online communications of millions of people carried over international submarine fibre optic cables. This is to the extent that the communications data alone reveals so much about a person's private life that it is often unnecessary for public authorities to require access the content of their communication. At the same time, technologies available to criminals and terrorists to evade surveillance have also increased and become more sophisticated. One such example are encryption technologies. These are essential to protecting the privacy and security of online communications but may also be accessed by bad actors.[5]

From the perspective of the protection of the right to private life, it is therefore welcome that the ECtHR has developed a rich body of jurisprudence dealing with the compatibility of such intrusive monitoring powers with Article 8 ECHR. Some of these landmark judgments on the retention and access by public authorities to personal data for countering crime and safeguarding national security were delivered decades ago. Nevertheless, standards established in those cases continue to play a key role in more recent legal challenges concerning sophisticated modern surveillance techniques in the ECtHR, the CJEU, and in national courts across Europe.[6] The ECtHR has delivered various judgments examining the vast range

[5] See *Big Brother Watch v United Kingdom* [2021] ECHR 439 [14]–[60], [342] (GC); Marko Milanovich, 'Human Rights Treaties and Foreign Surveillance' (2015) 56 Harvard International Law Journal 81, 121–22. In 2023, a majority of surveyed Europeans (82 per cent) stated that they expected digital technologies to be central for connecting with people, friends, and family online by 2030: European Commission, *The Digital Decade Report: Special Barometer 532* (EU 2023), <https://europa.eu/eurobarometer/surveys/detail/2959>. On the Snowden revelations and the value of collecting and accessing communications data in bulk for law enforcement and national security purposes, see Chapter 1. On signals intelligence (SIGINT), see Chapter 2.

[6] eg the landmark data retention judgment of *S and Marper v United Kingdom* (2009) 48 EHRR 50 (GC) is still cited by the ECtHR and the CJEU.

of data-driven surveillance powers now available to public authorities. These cases range from assessing the compatibility with Article 8 ECHR of measures that can track a protestor via live facial recognition, using GPS to monitor a car, and real-time tracking of mobile phones in a drug-trafficking investigation,[7] to indiscriminately gathering the communications data of millions of individuals across Europe and beyond.[8] As a result, recent jurisprudence from the Strasbourg Court has dealt with the retention and acquisition of increasingly varied amounts and types of communications data. Given the rapidly increasing capacity to monitor a person's online and offline life, it is welcome to see the Court making its view clear in the 2022 case of *Ekimdzhiev and Others* that when collected in bulk 'communications data can nowadays reveal a great deal of personal information'.[9] Moreover, as the ECtHR has noted elsewhere, much may now be revealed about a person's private life by having access to just a single item of their communications data. Internet browser settings (type, security settings, language), a billing address, a phone number, for example, may act as a 'key' to identify any person, such as a journalist or whistle-blower, and consequently enable 'the attribution of possibly sensitive information to an identifiable person'.[10]

Three key factors have steered the evolution of this rich Strasbourg jurisprudence on communications data. First, with the emergence of the Internet, and the rise of data collection systems that can ubiquitously track a person's every online communication and activity, data protection law has played an increasingly significant role in national surveillance laws across Europe and within the EU and ECHR legal orders. Secondly, the ECtHR has increasingly referenced within its judgments relevant data protection instruments and policies of the Council of Europe (COE) and the EU, and the data retention case law of the CJEU, often citing at length from these notable judgments of the Luxembourg Court.[11] Thirdly, the interception of telephone calls (and the 'pager') was the prevailing method of communication

[7] *Glukhin v Russia* [2023] ECHR 540; *Uzun v Germany* (2011) 53 EHRR 24; *Ben Faiza v France* [2018] ECHR 153.

[8] *Big Brother Watch* (n 5); *Centrum för Rättvisa v Sweden* [2021] ECHR 440. See further Chapter 2.

[9] *Ekimdzhiev and Others v Bulgaria* [2022] ECHR 1 [394]. The Court further highlights in its reasoning the important impact of the 'technological and social developments in the past two decades'.

[10] See *Breyer v Germany* [2020] ECHR 95, Dissenting opinion of Judge Carlo Ranzoni (facts involved the general and indiscriminate retention of subscriber information for countering crime and protecting national security). On identifying a person through web browser 'fingerprinting' and companies using IP addresses to identify whistle-blowers and journalists, see Nadezhda Purtova, 'From Knowing by Name to Targeting' (2022) 12 International Data Privacy Law 163, 171; Emily Baker-White, 'TikTok Spied on Forbes Journalists' *Forbes* (24 April 2023), <https://forbes.com/sites/emilybaker-white/2022/12/22/tiktok-tracks-forbes-journalists-bytedance/>.

[11] Of course, as demonstrated in the Grand Chamber judgments of *Big Brother Watch* (n 5) and *Centrum för Rättvisa* (n 8), lengthy references to relevant CJEU judgments do not always equate to an endorsement of the legal standards established therein. On the complex dialogue between the Luxembourg and Strasbourg Courts on the right to private life, data retention, and secret surveillance, see Chapter 4.

worldwide for most of the twentieth century. It was thus the prevailing State surveillance measure and the focus of the earlier communications data case law of the ECtHR.[12]

This chapter critically examines the evolving approach of the ECtHR to Article 8 ECHR and the retention and interception of communications data (*via* targeted and bulk measures) for the legitimate aims of preventing crime and protecting national security. In doing so, the analysis considers the principles and approach of the ECtHR in its broader related jurisprudence dealing with data protection, and the retention and access of other types of personal data by these public authorities. The Court has examined various measures in its extensive jurisprudence used for these legitimate aims and their compatibility with Article 8 ECHR. These include biometric data (DNA profiles, fingerprints, facial recognition),[13] data relating to criminal records and proceedings,[14] intelligence files on political activities,[15] and passenger travel records.[16] This proceeds to a critical analysis of how the role of data protection standards, developed with respect to the secret surveillance of communications content, have informed and shaped the approach of the ECtHR to the retention and use of communications data; standards that have long been underpinned by the view that accessing communications content is always more intrusive than its communications data (irrespective of type or scale).[17]

While such reasoning made sense in the pre-Internet era, to now argue that access to content data remains exclusively at the top of the hierarchy of intrusiveness to a person's private life is increasingly unpersuasive and technologically anachronistic. In addition, advocating for the continued existence of this problematic principle has significant implications for the protection of privacy life, including the argument that a lower level of safeguards should be applied for when public authorities access and use traffic and location data. Such as there being no requirement that accessing communications data (irrespective of type or amount) should be subject to prior authorization by a judge or independent body. Or that less strict limits on the data's deletion should apply when its storage and use has

[12] Pagers were a popular radio message transmitter in the 1990s. See *Taylor-Sabori v United Kingdom* (2003) 36 EHRR 17 where the UK failed to satisfy the legality hurdle of Art 8(2) for not enacting legislation at the material time regulating the interception of pager messages.

[13] *Van der Velden v The Netherlands* [2006] ECHR 1174 (admissibility decision); *Marper* (n 6); *Gardel v France* (App No 16428/05) 17 December 2009; *M.K. v France* [2013] ECHR 341; *Aycaguer v France* [2017] ECHR 587; *Gaughran v United Kingdom* [2020] ECHR 144; *Glukhin* (n 7).

[14] See *N.F. and Others v Russia* [2023] ECHR 669; *M.M. v United Kingdom* [2012] ECHR 1906; *Dimitrov-Kazakov v Bulgaria* (App No 11379/03) judgment of 10 February 2011 (violation of Art 8 ECHR held due to inclusion of applicant's name in police record of 'offenders' despite only being questioned in relation to a rape investigation).

[15] *Segerstedt-Wiberg v Sweden* (2007) 44 EHRR 2; *Catt v United Kingdom* [2019] ECHR 76.

[16] *Shimovolos v Russia* (2014) 58 EHRR 26.

[17] The CJEU has taken the same approach in its data retention case law, particularly with respect to its approach of what constitutes a violation of the 'essence' of the right to private life. See further Chapters 5 and 9.

gone beyond what is justified or necessary for an investigation or intelligence operation.[18] Thus it is welcome to see the ECtHR pushing back against such arguments (in certain cases) by adopting a more nuanced and granular approach to the enhanced capacity of the State to monitor an individual's communications and private life in the data-driven world of the twenty-first century.[19] The most significant bright spot to date in this regard being the Court's determination in *Ekimdzhiev and Others* that the acquisition of communications data in bulk on a general and indiscriminate basis 'can be *just as intrusive* as the bulk acquisition of the content of communications'.[20]

Despite these positive developments, this chapter shows how the overall approach of the ECtHR has subjected far-reaching retention obligations on the private sector, and the bulk interception of communications data, to questionable levels of scrutiny when examining their compatibility with the legality and proportionality requirements of Article 8 ECHR. Analysis of recent case law shows that the Strasbourg Court is still heavily influenced by the principle that public authorities' access to content data is always more privacy-intrusive than accessing communications data, irrespective of any evidence-based factors, including the type or quantities of communications data in question, its reuse for different purposes, or its subsequent processing and aggregation with other vast datasets. In other words, this is a highly problematic fallacy when the reality today is that access to large volumes of communications data will often render access to content data obsolete. Access to the content of a person's telephone calls from one day will reveal less about a person's private life as opposed to accessing the location data and traffic data from their mobile phone use over a year. Instead, the scrutiny of Article 8 ECHR, and the safeguards enshrined therein, need to adapt and evolve to respond to this fundamental change in communications monitoring and the level of privacy-intrusiveness that comes with accessing communications data in the modern digital age.[21]

[18] Some Member States across the EU have continued to apply this lower standard to the long-term retention of traffic and location data (often a retention period of twelve months) despite this being clearly contrary to the safeguards established by the CJEU in its data retention case law. Others have since enacted reforms in their national laws which adopt some of these safeguards. See eg the Communications (Retention of Data) (Amendment) Act 2023 which came into force in Ireland on 26 June 2023: <https://irishstatutebook.ie/eli/2023/si/287/made/en/print>.

[19] Civil society have also commended this acknowledgement of technological developments in recent cases such as *Ekimdzhiev and Others* (n 9). See Statewatch, 'ECHR: Strasbourg Court provides a strong standard on data retention and secret surveillance' 28 January 2022, <https://statewatch.org/news/2022/january/echr-strasbourg-court-provides-a-strong-standard-on-data-retention-and-secret-surveillance/>.

[20] *Ekimdzhiev and Others* (n 9) [394] (emphasis added).

[21] On these concerns but also bright spots where there has been some pushback in certain ECtHR judgments on the need to review and update current Article 8 ECHR standards, see further Chapter 2. On the starkly contrasting approach and rapidly evolving data privacy standards of the CJEU, see Chapters 5 and 9.

B. Collection, Storage, and Use of Personal Data

The ECtHR has gradually recognized in its case law that there are distinct stages of data processing that are all significant within the lifecycle of any secret surveillance regime.[22] Relatedly, the Court has acknowledged that the interference with private life that stems from why public authorities seek to access certain personal data is linked to its initial retention when the context concerns crime and national security.[23] This is an important normative development as different processing stages, their length (tracking a person's communications and movements over a day, month, year), and scope (bulk or targeted) each pose distinct and varying degrees of intrusion to one or more private life interests protected by Article 8 ECHR. Cases with this more comprehensive and strict-scrutiny approach tend to involve a careful examination by the ECtHR of particular factors, including the nature of the personal data, such as the type of information, scale of collection, and potential future applications.[24] As the Grand Chamber held in its landmark ruling of *S and Marper*, personal data stored over lengthy periods is subject to greater risk and technologies 'which cannot be anticipated with precision today'.[25]

1. Data retention: one of the 'crucial stages' of (bulk) surveillance

The ECtHR has held that there are 'various crucial stages at which data protection issues' under Article 8 ECHR may arise, including the retention, access, (future) use, and management of that data.[26] Although data retention is not 'mass surveillance' in and of itself, monitoring and associated techniques, such as profiling or predicting future conduct, would not be possible without the collected data (or access to the collected data). The act of data retention is therefore an instrumental part of most surveillance programmes whether it is initially collected by a public authority or the private sector. Thus, the ECtHR has held that there must be at '*each stage* ... appropriate and adequate safeguards which reflect the principles elaborated in applicable data protection instruments and prevent arbitrary and

[22] *M.M.* (n 14); *Catt* (n 15). For a notable departure from this approach within the context of bulk interception, see *Big Brother Watch* (n 5) and *Centrum för Rättvisa* (n 8). See further Chapter 2.

[23] See eg *Benedik v Slovenia* [2018] ECHR 363 [109]: '[W]hat would appear to be peripheral information sought by the police, namely the name and address of a subscriber, must in situations such as the present one be treated as inextricably connected to the relevant pre-existing content revealing data ... To hold otherwise would be to deny the necessary protection to information which might reveal a good deal about the online activity of an individual, including sensitive details of his or her interests, beliefs and intimate lifestyle.'

[24] See regarding the police collection of biometric data: *Marper* (n 6) [71]; *Gaughran* (n 13) [81]; *Glukhin* (n 7) [86]–[87] (the Court also considers implications of facial recognition for freedom of expression).

[25] *Marper* (n 6).

[26] *M.M.* (n 14) [195]; *Catt* (n 15) [95].

disproportionate interference with Article 8 rights'.[27] This requirement reflects settled jurisprudence that the protection of personal data is of 'fundamental importance' to an individual's right to respect for private as guaranteed under Article 8 ECHR.[28] Moreover, the need for this protection is 'all the greater' where data has been subject to automated processing, profiling, or other analytics for the purposes of law enforcement or national security.[29]

It is also well-established case law that the *mere* storage of data 'relating to the private life of an individual', for the prevention of crime, serious crime, or the safeguarding of national security, constitutes an interference with the right to respect for private life.[30] Furthermore, the ECtHR Grand Chamber has stated that it is irrelevant if this information collected by interception or other secret measures has not been subsequently accessed, used, or disclosed.[31] This means that even if the purposes for data retention involve national security, the subsequent use of this stored information has no impact on this finding under Article 8(1).[32] Thus, once intelligence services intercept a signal concerning the public's communications and start collecting data, they have interfered with the right to respect for private life. Despite this legal standard being well established under both ECHR and EU law, some governments have continued to argue that retention alone does not interfere with private life in any meaningful away.[33] Instead, they have posited that an interference has taken place only when public authorities have accessed and analyse the collected data.[34]

The ECtHR has nevertheless held (in its more robust data retention judgments) that it is 'essential' that the retention and sharing of any 'record data' by law enforcement have clear and detailed procedural rules governing the scope, data management, and use of these measures.[35] While it has not adopted a rule of binding precedent, the ECtHR has repeatedly stated the guiding principle that, 'it is in the interests of legal certainty, foreseeability and equality before the law that it should not depart without good reason from precedent laid down in previous cases'.[36] The Grand Chamber further held in the seminal case of *Marper* that these rule of law

27 *M.M.* (n 14) (emphasis added).

28 *Z v Finland* (1997) EHRR [95]; *LL v France* (App No 7508/02) 10 October 2006 [44]; *Marper* (n 6) [103]; *Aycaguer* (n 13) [38].

29 *Marper* (n 6) [103]; *M.K.* (n 13) [35]; *Aycaguer* (n 13) [38]; *Glukhin* (n 7) [75].

30 *Leander v Sweden* (1987) 9 EHRR 433 [48]; *Rotaru v Romania* [2000] ECHR 192 [43]; *Catt* (n 15) [93]; *Ekimdzhiev and Others* (n 9) [372].

31 *Amann v Switzerland* [2000] ECHR 87 [69] (GC).

32 ibid [69].

33 EU Agency for Fundamental Rights (FRA), *Surveillance by Intelligence Services*, Vol II (FRA 2017) 34.

34 See eg CJEU, Opinion 1/15 on the Draft Agreement between Canada and the EU on the transfer and processing of Passenger Name Record Data, Opinion of Advocate General Mengozzi, judgment of 8 September 2016 (ECLI:EU:C:2016:656) [171]–[172].

35 *Marper* (n 6) [99]; *M.M.* (n 14) [195].

36 Nicolas Bratza, 'Living Instrument or Dead Letter—the Future of the European Convention on Human Rights' (2014) 2 European Human Rights Law Review 116, 123.

safeguards should include the six minimum foreseeability requirements developed in its notable cases on the interception of communications.[37]

2. Article 8 ECHR and data protection

(a) Of 'fundamental importance' to private life

It is now settled case law that the ECtHR recognizes that the protection of personal data plays 'a primordial role' and is of 'fundamental importance' in the exercise of an individual's right to private life.[38] However, this was not the Strasbourg Court's initial approach. Although 'informational aspects to privacy' were not considered to fall within the ambit of Article 8 ECHR in its early jurisprudence, the ECtHR gradually adopted a broad interpretation of the scope of the right to respect for private life in relation to personal data.[39] This major development is evidence of the ECtHR taking the view of the ECHR as 'a living instrument' capable of fundamental change and to be interpreted in the light of present-day conditions.[40] The ECtHR has thus since held that the aim of data protection standards under EU law,[41] and those under the Council of Europe Data Protection Convention,[42] correspond with the broad interpretation of the right to respect for private life.[43] The establishment of such a link is significant as it requires that all ECHR Contracting States provide every individual with their 'right to privacy, *with regard* to automatic processing of personal data relating to [them] ... such personal data being defined as any information relating to an identified or identifiable individual'.[44] At the same time, it is crucial to note that the ECtHR has interpreted this standard subject to a key caveat that the relevant information must concern the applicant's private life in order to fall under the scope of protection guaranteed under Article 8 ECHR.[45]

This means that the ECtHR will consider the specific circumstances of the data that has been processed by a public authority when assessing whether this

[37] *Marper* (n 6) [99].

[38] See *Glukhin* (n 7) [75]; *L.B. v Hungary* [2023] ECHR 239 [103] (GC). *L.B.* is the first case where the ECtHR examined to what extent the imposition of a statutory obligation, to publish taxpayers' personal data (including their home address), is compatible with Art 8 ECHR.

[39] David Feldman, 'Information and Privacy' in Jack Beatson and Yvonne Cripps (eds), *Freedom of Expression and Freedom of Information* (OUP 2000) 306–08.

[40] Bratza (n 36). See further Chapter 2.

[41] The 1995 Directive was replaced by the EU GDPR: Regulation (EU) 2016/679 of the European Parliament and of the Council of 27 April 2016 on the protection of natural persons with regard to the processing of personal data and on the free movement of such data, repealing Directive 95/46/EC [2016] OJ L119/1 (GDPR).

[42] Convention of 28 January 1981 for the Protection of Individuals with regard to Automatic Processing of Personal Data, ETS No 108 (Convention 108). On the modernization of Convention 108, see further Chapter 1.

[43] *Rotaru* (n 30) [43]; *Benedik* (n 23) [102]; *Breyer* (n 10) [74].

[44] *Amann* (n 31) [65] (emphasis added).

[45] See *Marper* (n 6) [67].

requirement has been satisfied before determining whether the protected interest of private life under Article 8(1) ECHR has been engaged. As discussed later, the examination involves a case-by-case analysis, including the type of information at issue and how it has been treated and used by the public authorities in question.[46] Moreover, there are three other important factors to always bear in mind in Article 8 ECHR cases dealing with data retention, the prevention of crime, and/or national security. First, the ECtHR has in many cases treated the protection of personal data as a sub-right, or 'part of the rights', that fall under the scope of protection of Article 8 ECHR.[47] Secondly, the weight given by the ECtHR to the safeguards applicable to each step in the data processing cycle (retention, access, use, deletion) varies greatly depending on how intrusive the Court views the public authorities' access and use of the relevant personal data. Thirdly, and relatedly, whether the ECtHR applies the generally less strict 'joint analysis approach' to the Article 8(2) examination stage and to what extent a 'margin of appreciation' has been granted to the Contracting State.[48]

(b) Data protection: a sub-right of Article 8 ECHR

Although there is considerable overlap in the scope of each, the related rights of private life and data protection differ in various ways and are not treated as identical within the ECHR and EU legal systems.[49] One way in which the right to the protection of personal data is treated differently under the scope of rights protected under Article 8(1) ECHR when compared with the right to data protection under EU law is the lack of a general right to access personal data.[50] This is a significant distinction as the right to access constitutes one of the core rights of data protection law.[51] Instead, the ECtHR has recognized that a right to access information from public authorities (and others) is highly context-dependent under Article 8 ECHR and relies on several factors. This means that the right to access to personal data may be limited in certain circumstances, provided that compliance with Article 8

[46] It has been argued that this case-by-case approach may lead to the application of Art 8 ECHR having a narrower scope than EU data protection law. See Orla Lynskey, *The Foundations of EU Data Protection Law* (OUP 2015) 125.

[47] See EU FRA and Council of Europe, *Handbook on European Data Protection Law* (FRA 2018) 23. However, it is notable to see the ECtHR increasingly taking into account data protection considerations in its assessments of data processing by public authorities with regard to the transposition of EU data protection law and its link to the contested domestic law. See further Chapter 4.

[48] On the examination of the Art 8(2) requirements in cases of secret surveillance, see further Chapter 2.

[49] Juliane Kokott and Christoph Sobotta, 'The Distinction Between Privacy and Data Protection in the Jurisprudence of the CJEU and the ECtHR' (2013) 3 International Data Privacy Law 222; Lynskey (n 46) 125–29.

[50] *Gaskin v United Kingdom* (1990) 12 EHRR 36 [37]; *Godelli v Italy* [2012] ECHR 347.

[51] See Jef Ausloos and Pierre Dewitte, 'Shattering One-Way Mirrors—Data Subject Access Rights in Practice' (2018) 8 International Data Privacy Law 4; Orla Lynskey, 'Complete and Effective Data Protection' (2023) 76 Current Legal Problems 297, 324.

ECHR has been secured by other means, with the 'choice' of these means falling within the Contracting State's margin of appreciation.[52]

For instance, in the case of *Leander*, the Court held that a lack of access to information stored on a secret police file regarding why an applicant did not satisfy the national security clearance requirements for a post involving access to a restricted military zone in a naval museum amounted to a justified interference with his rights under Article 8 ECHR.[53] The ECtHR found the Swedish law to be otherwise accessible (with details of an ordinance published in an official journal and publicly available) and foreseeable. The latter meaning that the ordinance provided 'explicit and detailed' provisions on the use and sharing of the data and relevant safeguards.[54] Moreover, the ECtHR held that a clear 'pressing social need' existed with respect to protecting national security in these circumstances, namely assessing the suitability of candidates for employment for posts of importance to national security.[55] Following this reasoning, the ECtHR held in a later challenge to the same Swedish law that refusal of 'full access' to a secret police register is necessary where the State 'may legitimately fear' that such access may jeopardize the efficacy of a secret surveillance system designed to protect national security.[56] Both outcomes are unsurprising given the wide margin of appreciation granted by the ECtHR to Contracting States in cases dealing with Article 8 ECHR and national security.[57]

(c) Data protection and data retention systems: holistic assessments and muddy standards

When dealing with Article 8 ECHR and the retention and access to private life information for law enforcement or national security purposes, the highly contextual and case-by-case approach to the role of data protection standards has produced some unclear judgments. This leads to some confusion regarding what specific data protection principles and safeguards should be met by data retention systems adopted for law enforcement and national security purposes in order to be compatible with Article 8 ECHR. While the traditional approach of the ECtHR when examining a law's compatibility with the Article 8(2) in this area of law will involve consideration of the six 'minimum safeguards' of foreseeability, there are no such minimum safeguards for data protection law. The ECtHR will instead take certain established data protection principles into account in various judgments.

[52] See *Godelli* (n 50) where the ECtHR held that the failure of Italian authorities to attempt any balancing of the right of a person to access information about their origins, against the interests of their mother in remaining anonymous, overstepped the margin of appreciation granted and amounted to a violation of Art 8 ECHR.

[53] *Leander* (n 30).

[54] ibid [53]–[57].

[55] ibid [59].

[56] *Segerstedt-Wiberg* (n 15) [102].

[57] See further Chapter 2.

Sometimes this is done clearly with explicit references to data protection law and the relevant principles but at other times this may be done without any mention of data protection law. In other cases, the ECtHR has often not identified (or scrutinized): each of the specific types of personal data retained; the specific rights engaged under Article 8(1) and the level of intrusiveness; and how each of the different relevant stages of data processing (retention, access, use, deletion) are compatible with the Article 8(2) requirements.[58] Consequently, as Bygrave and others have highlighted, judgments dealing with Article 8 ECHR and data protection may often come across as 'confusing'.[59]

Mirroring its criticized combined assessment of the legality and necessity requirements of Article 8(2) taken in judgments dealing with secret surveillance measures, these assessments by the ECtHR will often proceed swiftly to the question of whether the contested measure is compatible with Article 8(2).[60] It has been argued that allowing for such ambiguity raises critical questions around the specific type and scope of protection provided by Article 8 ECHR to new surveillance technologies.[61] One such novel type of processing is 'emotion detection', which may immediately profile an individual but may not necessarily also store that captured information.[62] Clarity of the relevant standards applicable to emerging technologies and their consistent application in the analytical approach of the ECtHR going forward are critical to such a dynamic area of regulation and technology. The muddiness surrounding the adequate level of safeguards otherwise risks undermining effective compliance by relevant public authorities. Indeed, an ad hoc approach that is completely holistic in its approach, without any minimum standards or safeguards, also risks under-protecting privacy and impeding the necessary development of Article 8 ECHR rule of law requirements that are fit for purpose in the twenty-first century.

There are two ways in which legal certainty could be significantly improved in these judgments. First, the ECtHR could focus on providing more systematic and clearly structured assessments of the different stages of Article 8(1) and Article 8(2).[63] Examining the Article 8(1) stage would entail examining the specific threat

[58] *Roman Zakharov v Russia* (2016) 63 EHRR 17 [173] (GC); *Benedik* (n 23) [103], [120]; *Catt* (n 15) [93]; *Ekimdzhiev and Others* (n 9).

[59] See eg Lee Bygrave, 'Data Protection Pursuant to the Right to Privacy in Human Rights Treaties' (1998) 6 International Journal of Law and Information Technology 247, 283; Raphaël Gellert and Serge Gutwirth, 'The Legal Construction of Privacy and Data Protection' (2013) 29 Computer Law and Security Review 522. For an example of where the data protection principle of storage limitation was implicitly considered concerning public disclosure of individuals' former employment with the KGB, see *Sõro v Estonia* [2015] ECHR 761 [56]–[64].

[60] See further Chapter 2.

[61] ibid.

[62] On data protection and the monitoring of emotions, see generally Damian Clifford, *Data Protection Law and Emotion* (OUP 2024).

[63] This would require the ECtHR abandoning its controversial 'joint assessment' approach to the legality and necessity requirements in this area of its Art 8 ECHR case law. See further Chapter 2.

to private life (such as tracking protestors' movements and interactions using facial recognition) and identifying the affected interests at stake (privacy and dignity, freedom of expression, freedom of assembly) and thereby the extent of the level of intrusiveness with private life ('a serious interference'). Secondly, the ECtHR could engage in more depth, and more explicitly, with its settled jurisprudence in its actual assessment of the instant case (instead of the 'general principles'). A more granular approach could also be taken regarding the related but separate data protection issues that arise from particular programmes of secret data processing by public authorities.[64] This would serve to reduce confusion arising from when the ECtHR departs from settled criteria it has cited from earlier judgments that it will rely on, but then departs from without any clear explanation with respect to the facts of the relevant judgment under review.[65]

Catt v United Kingdom is one such data retention judgment criticized for 'lacking in firmness as well as consistency'.[66] The facts involved the incorrect retention of records on a domestic extremism database. Ultimately, the ECtHR held that the applicant 'had done no more than exercise his democratic right of peaceful protest' and that the data retention system used constituted a disproportionate interference with Article 8 ECHR.[67] The ECtHR was also particularly critical of the failure by public authorities to delete the applicant's personal data from the database. In a robust *obiter dictum*, the Court stated: 'it would be entirely contrary to the need to protect private life under Article 8 if the Government could create a database in such a manner that the data in it could not be easily reviewed or edited, and then use this development as a justification to refuse to remove information from that database.'[68] This determination clearly indicates that in order to be compatible with Article 8 ECHR, any such data retention systems for policing or national security purposes should be designed with the capacity to review and edit any collected data therein.[69] However, the ECtHR did not consider the lack of any publicly accessible statutory framework that provided a clear 'legal basis for the collection of applicant's personal data', and thereby for the creation of the database, to be incompatible with the legality requirements of Article 8(2).[70] This runs

[64] Leading cases with this more comprehensive assessment include *Marper* (n 6); *M.M.* (n 14); *M.K.* (n 13).

[65] See later for the critical analysis of the proportionality assessment in *Breyer* (n 10) and the Art 8(2) assessment of the bulk retention of communications data in *Ekimdzhiev and Others* (n 9).

[66] See *Catt* (n 15) and the Concurring Opinion of Judge Koskelo, joined by Judge Felici. See further Nora Ni Loideain, 'Lawfulness and Police Use of Facial Recognition in the UK: Article 8 ECHR and *Bridges v South Wales Police*' in Rita Matulionyte and Monika Zalnieriute (eds), *Facial Recognition in the Modern State* (CUP 2024) 161–65.

[67] *Catt* (n 15) [33], [124]–[128].

[68] ibid [127].

[69] On the lack of transparency in accessing data collected by such systems, see Chapter 1.

[70] *Catt* (n 15) [106]. Although the ECtHR does not formally make assessments based on precedent, its judgments are in practice based on the previous standards and criteria developed in its earlier related jurisprudence and landmark judgments. See generally Janneke Gerards, *General Principles of the European Convention on Human Rights* (2nd edn, CUP 2023).

contrary to settled case law which has established that domestic law must 'lay down the manner in which such evidence may be obtained', which is 'accessible to the person concerned and foreseeable as to its effect'.[71]

Catt departs significantly, therefore, from previous Article 8 ECHR case law where the 'absence of a clear legislative framework for the collection and storage of data' was previously held to constitute a critical shortcoming for ensuring sufficient safeguards that protect private life.[72] Moreover, *Catt* represents a growing trend where the ECtHR has sidestepped dealing with clear deviations by Contracting States from 'minimum' foreseeability safeguards that measures were previously required to meet to satisfy the legality condition of Article 8(2).[73] In *Catt*, this was the lack of a clear legal basis for the creation of a domestic extremism database, a gap that would not have existed if the minimum foreseeability requirements in the earlier (and generally stricter) case law of the ECtHR had been met by the contested measure. Not identifying a specific purpose clearly in law for such data collection enables public authorities to use such powers with unfettered discretion. As the ECtHR has held elsewhere, this means that the law did not indicate with sufficient clarity at the material time the extent of the authorities' discretion, or how it should be exercised, and fell short of 'the minimum degree of legal protection to which citizens are entitled under the rule of law in a democratic society'.[74]

(d) Publicly available information may fall within the protection of Article 8 ECHR

Private-life issues may also arise from the collection of information from open sources, or in the public domain, for the prevention of serious crime or national security purposes if any systematic or permanent record comes into existence based on this material. Bulk collection of such information from public or open-source datasets is now common practice by national and EU intelligence agencies and is otherwise known as 'OSINT'. Opportunities for public authorities and EU agencies—such as GCHQ and Europol—to collect such publicly accessible information have dramatically expanded in the modern digital era, especially since the arrival of social media and the increasingly integral role of digital platforms in accessing services from the public and private sectors. It is also a source of information that public authorities increasingly use to train models of machine learning and AI to produce 'actionable intelligence'.[75] Such public information in

[71] *Rotaru* (n 30) [52]–[53]; *Marper* (n 6) [99]; *M.M.* (n 14) [195]–[206].

[72] *M.M.* (n 14) [206].

[73] See the analysis later, and Chapter 2, on the shift away from scrutinizing 'minimum' rule of law safeguards in secret surveillance measures and the rise of the joint analysis approach to the legality and proportionality requirements of Art 8(2).

[74] *Malone* (n 1) [79]; *Valenzuela Contreras* (n 3) [61].

[75] See German Federal Commissioner for Data Protection and Freedom of Information, Activity Report 2022 (Berlin 2023) 87: <www.bfdi.bund.de/EN/Service/Publikationen/Taetigkeitsberichte/taetigkeitsberichte_node.html>; David Anderson, Independent Review of the Investigatory Powers Act

cases to date before the ECtHR have included the retention of records concerning education and engagement in political activities.[76] Drawing from data protection standards, the ECtHR has also held that the retention of personal data that reveals political opinions, DNA, and criminal records to constitute 'sensitive data' which fall within the protection of private life.[77] The length of retention, and the existence of independent oversight assessing the need for continued retention, are often key factors when assessing if these regimes are Article 8 ECHR-compliant, especially if the information concerns a person's distant past.[78] Thus, as the ECtHR has stressed with respect to convictions and caution records, once this information 'recedes into the past, it becomes a part of the person's private life which must be respected'.[79]

This determination implicitly acknowledges the importance of a right to erasure and the principle of data minimization, a procedural right and key requirement under European data protection law that are inherently linked. As noted earlier, despite the absence of any explicit reference to data protection within the ECHR, the ECtHR has established in its jurisprudence that the aims of Article 8 ECHR correspond with that of Convention 108. The ECtHR has, for instance, been critical when examining the proportionality of data retention regimes in related cases if no adequate deletion procedures (or retention limits) have been put in place by the public authorities.[80] Indeed, as the ECtHR has held, the ability for an individual to delete such records is inter alia an important safeguard and remedy that contributes to ensuring 'that the data storage period is proportionate to the nature of the offences and the aims of the restrictions'.[81] The lack of any distinction in criminal record systems between the retained files of those never convicted of a crime, as opposed to those who have, has also been held as a disproportionate interference with private life. In line with the rule of law and the presumption of innocence, this is based on the risk of stigmatization to individuals who have never convicted not being fairly treated as innocent.[82]

The collection of public information that does not directly identify an individual but is included in a government file concerning them, has also been held to relate to their private life and thus an interference with the right to private life under Article 8(1). In other words, public information may fall within the scope of

2016 (June 2023) Annex 7, <https://gov.uk/government/publications/independent-review-of-the-investigatory-powers-act-2016-2>.

[76] See generally *Rotaru* (n 30); *Segerstedt-Wiberg* (n 15); *Catt* (n 15).

[77] *M.M.* (n 14) [188]; *Glukhin* (n 7) [67], [75]–[77].

[78] *Rotaru* (n 30) [43]; *Cemalettin Canlı v Turkey* [2008] ECHR 1458 [33]; *M.M.* (n 14) [187].

[79] *M.M.* (n 14) [188].

[80] See eg *Marper* (n 6) [107], [119]; *M.M.* (n 14) [206]–[207]; *Aycaguer* (n 13) [45]; *Catt* (n 15) [127]. On the right to erasure generally, see Jef Ausloos, *The Right to Erasure in EU Data Protection Law* (OUP 2020).

[81] *Aycaguer* (n 13) [44].

[82] *Marper* (n 6) [122]; *M.K.* (n 13) [36], [42]–[47].

private life 'where it is systematically collected and stored in files held by the authorities'.[83] The ECtHR adopted this broad interpretation of the scope of Article 8(1) in *Segerstedt-Wiberg* where the security file of an applicant contained police records (reports, newspaper cutting, photographs) concerning letter bombs that had been sent to her, another individual, and the Swedish national radio station.[84] While some documents contained in her file identified the applicant, others did not. As the Swedish government highlighted when arguing that these did not fall within the scope of private life, the applicant's file included documents that 'did not concern her own activities but the activities of other persons, namely those responsible for the letter bombs that had been sent to her and others'.[85] Dismissing this argument, the ECtHR focused on the purposive element at issue that engaged the protection of private life and gave weight to the context regarding why the public authorities sought the retention of what would otherwise appear to be peripheral information. This involved the collection of information to be stored on a secret police register concerning the applicant for the prevention of serious crime and national security interests, namely protecting her life. The ECtHR thus held that the scope of Article 8(1) 'embraces even those parts of the information that were public since the information had been systematically collected and stored in files held by the authorities'.[86]

This important precedent has broader implications for future Article 8 ECHR cases dealing with the data collection which underpin predictive policing, mass biometric surveillance, and the development of AI-based systems. These powerful measures rely on access and analysis of various and vast datasets and may identify real-time and historical patterns and profiles or make predictions about individuals, groups, and communities. They draw from personal data collected, or inferred from, previously unstructured datasets, intelligence gathered from social media (SOCMINT), and open-source data (OSINT), from a wide range of sources (census information, medical research statistics, news archives, etc).[87]

[83] *Cemalettin Canlı* (n 78) [33].

[84] *Segerstedt-Wiberg* (n 15) [11]. One of the applicants in this case was a well-known public figure and former chairperson of the UN Association of Sweden.

[85] *Segerstedt-Wiberg* (n 15) [71].

[86] ibid [72]–[73].

[87] These examples are just the tip of the iceberg of what is publicly available. Eg the US government's Open Data system currently provides access to over 290,000 datasets: <https://data.gov/>. There is also the matter of commercially available data (CAI). This includes the long-established practice of US data brokers selling vast datasets to public authorities in the US and Europe (eg the Netherlands and the UK), concerning US and non-US citizens, their private lives, social media presence, and relationships. See David Anderson, *A Question of Trust: Report of the Investigatory Powers Review* (HM Stationery Office 2015) 200–01; Justin Sherman, *Data Brokers and Sensitive Data on US Individuals* (Duke UP 2021); Kevin Collier, 'US government buys data on Americans with little oversight, report finds' *NBC News* (13 June 2023); Jan-Jaap Oerlemans and Sander Langenhuijzen, 'Balancing National Security and Privacy: Examining the Use of Commercially Available Information in OSINT Practices' (2024) 37 International Journal of Intelligence and CounterIntelligence, <https://doi.org/10.1080/08850607.2024.2387850>. On the risks of using Big Data approaches and machine learning for intelligence-gathering and law enforcement purposes (eg the aggregation and combining of SIGINT and OSINT datasets), see Chapters 1 and 9.

(e) Contracting States should ensure retained data is accurate and secure

In determining whether personal data retained by public authorities involves any of the private life aspects mentioned earlier, the ECtHR will have due regard to the following factors: the specific context in which the information has been recorded and retained; the nature of the records; the way in which these records are used and processed; and the results that may be obtained.[88] This assessment is underpinned by the requirement that 'respect for private life' means not only that the State refrain from interfering with private life but also entails certain positive obligations on the State to ensure effective enjoyment of this right.[89] Contracting States also have a positive obligation to ensure accurate and secure storage of personal data about an individual collected for law enforcement purposes or protecting national security.[90] Disclosing this retained information about an individual may therefore also interfere with the informational aspects of private life and may amount to a violation of Article 8 ECHR, particularly if the information shared is inaccurate or published in breach of domestic law.[91] Of course, a margin of appreciation will apply to public authorities in striking a fair balance between the relevant public and private interests. The scope of this margin will depend on the nature and seriousness of the interests at stake and the gravity of the interference.[92]

Khelili is a good example of when the margin of appreciation has been narrowed due to public authorities clearly having failed to fulfil this positive obligation. The facts concerned inaccurate entry of the applicant's profession as 'prostitute' (instead of dressmaker) on a police record. Moreover, despite requests to correct the record, this false information was retained for several years in other police files. The Court ultimately held that this to amount to an unjustified and disproportionate interference with Article 8 ECHR.[93] While the ECtHR acknowledged that retaining an individual's personal data on the ground that they may commit another offence could be relevant to the assessment of proportionality, the allegation of unlawful prostitution here was not supported by sufficiently concrete facts.[94] Thus, the public interest of crime prevention in *Khelili* was not shown to be a pressing social need when balanced against the implications that this inaccurate

[88] *Friedl v Austria* (1995) 21 EHRR 83; *Peck v United Kingdom* (2003) 36 EHRR 719 [57]–[63]; *L.B.* (n 38) [103].

[89] *K.U. v Finland* (2009) 48 EHRR 1169 [42].

[90] This positive obligation on States to ensure against the unauthorized access of information concerning an individual's private life has also been applied to medical data: *I v Finland* [2008] ECHR 623. On negative and positive obligations under Art 8 ECHR generally, see Chapter 2.

[91] *Craxi v Italy (No 2)* (2004) 38 EHRR 47 [74]; *X and others v Russia* (App No 78042/16) 14 January 2020; *L.B.* (n 38) [123]. See also *Cemalettin Canlı* (n 78) where the police mis-identified the applicant as a member of an illegal organization in their records, inaccurate information that was later published by the media.

[92] See eg *Segerstedt-Wiberg* (n 15); *M.K.* (n 13).

[93] *Khelili v Switzerland* (App No 16188/07) 18 October 2011.

[94] The Court was particularly critical of the low threshold of evidence relied on by police, namely that the recording of such inaccurate information was based on an unsubstantiated allegation and not a recorded previous conviction.

record posed to the applicant's reputation and her right to the presumption of innocence. Moreover, the Court highlighted that the extent of the risks to the private interests of the applicant is greater in modern society because records from this police database were subject to automated processing, thereby facilitating greater distribution and access to this data for other public authorities. The legal assessment also considered in detail how each stage of the data processing cycle, from the entering of inaccurate data to its long-term retention, can affect an individual's private life interests. The ECtHR consequently held that the applicant had a significant interest in having the word 'prostitute' deleted from the police records. This clear and strict-scrutiny analysis in *Khelili* is a notable 'bright spot' in this area of case law dealing with Article 8 ECHR, highlighting the significant implications to a person's private life posed by the long-term inaccurate retention of data by public authorities.[95]

3. Indefinite and blanket retention of DNA: beyond an 'acceptable margin of appreciation'

(a) *S and Marper*: landmark judgment and lesser-known outlier

The ECtHR's most influential case to date concerning data retention and the prevention of crime is the 2008 Grand Chamber judgment of *Marper*.[96] In this unanimous and now famous judgment, the ECtHR held that the indefinite and blanket retention of fingerprints and DNA data from suspects, irrespective of whether they were later charged or convicted, violated Article 8 ECHR as it 'overstepped' any acceptable margin of appreciation.[97] As highlighted by Nicolas Bratza, former President of the ECtHR, the Court was particularly struck by the fact that England and Wales was the only European jurisdiction to expressly allow this systematic and indefinite retention regime.[98] Moreover, in stark contrast to the approach of the highest national court, the ECtHR held that the interference with private life was far from minimal.[99] For the UK, the judgment resulted in key reforms to

[95] Marie-Helen Murphy, 'A Shift in the Approach of the European Court of Human Rights in Surveillance Cases' [2014] European Human Rights Law 507, 514. On related 'bright spots' in this area of Art 8 ECHR case law and proportionality, see the analysis later concerning *Gaughran* (n 13) and developments in facial recognition.

[96] Literature on this landmark case is extensive. See eg Kate Beattie, '*S and Marper v UK*: Privacy, DNA, and Crime' (2009) 2 European Human Rights Law Review 229; Ian Brown, 'Communications Data in an Evolving Internet' (2011) 19 International Journal of Law and Technology 95; Hillary Biehler, 'The Right to Privacy and the Retention of DNA Profiles—Getting the Balance Right' (2014) 5 European Human Rights Law Review 479, 483.

[97] *Marper* (n 6) [125].

[98] eg Scotland had a much more limited and proportionate retention regime for the DNA storage of unconvicted individuals: *Marper* (n 6) [109]–[110].

[99] Nicolas Bratza, 'The Relationship Between the UK Court and Strasbourg' (2011) 5 European Human Rights Law Review 505, 509.

the scope and oversight of a framework previously described as 'an overgrown system of DNA retention'.[100] As Woods highlights, *Marper* also departed from previous Article 8 ECHR cases on data retention for a lesser-known development.[101] Specifically, the ECtHR appears to have adopted the view that concern for the storage of data by public authorities should be limited to only 'personal information' that involves any of the 'private life aspects' specifically set out in *Marper*.[102] This 'outlier' view of an otherwise lauded judgment is a notable and somewhat confusing departure from the ECtHR's other leading cases concerning data retention by the State. Instead, the previous long line of case law provided that the 'mere storage of information' amounted to an interference with an individual's 'private life where it is systematically collected and stored in files held by the authorities'.[103]

Although this opposing line of case law is explicitly affirmed and cited in *Marper*, the ECtHR nonetheless appears to add a further test which requires that the storage of such data by the State must be linked to a particular private life interest.[104] This additional test in *Marper* limits the scope of private life which runs contrary to the well-established requirement under Article 8 ECHR case law (and indeed that of the CJEU) which requires that the term 'private life' should not be interpreted restrictively.[105] While it has not adopted a rule of binding precedent, the ECtHR has repeatedly stated that although not bound by its previous judgments, 'it is in the interests of legal certainty, foreseeability and equality' before the law that it should not depart without good reason from precedent laid down in previous cases.[106] Thus, it is always in the interests of legal certainty for reasons to be given for departing from (or updating) previous standards if the ECtHR seeks to establish new requirements concerning Article 8 ECHR in its data retention case law.[107] Greater clarity and engagement by the ECtHR on the critical question of what constitutes an interference with Article 8 rights would be welcome, particularly given the increasing capacity of AI-based policing systems to infer highly sensitive personal data from the analysis of vast volumes of non-personal datasets and OSINT.[108]

[100] Beattie (n 96) 229. These reforms were enacted under the Protection of Freedoms Act 2012 and included the establishment of an independent commissioner to review the retention and use of biometric material for policing (in England and Wales) and national security across the UK. This regulatory role has since been combined with a second oversight role and is now the 'Biometrics and Surveillance Camera Commissioner'. See further <https://gov.uk/government/publications/biometrics-and-surveillance-camera-commissioner-report-2022-to-2023>.

[101] Lorna Woods, 'Automated Number Plate Recognition: Data Retention and the Protection of Privacy in Public Places' (2017) 2 Journal of Information Rights, Policy and Practice 1, 9.

[102] *Marper* (n 6) [67].

[103] *Segerstedt-Wiberg* (n 15) [72]; *Cemalettin Canlı* (n 78) [33]; *M.M.* (n 14) [187]; *Catt* (n 15) [93].

[104] *Marper* (n 6) [67].

[105] Kokott and Sobotta (n 49) 223.

[106] Bratza (n 36) 123.

[107] As the Court clarified eg in *Liberty v United Kingdom* (2008) 63 EHRR 3 [63]. See Chapter 2.

[108] Janneke Gerards and Raphaële Xenidis, *Algorithmic Discrimination in Europe* (European Commission 2020) 80–82.

(b) DNA profiles: 'nothing more than a sequence of numbers . . .'

In attempting to justify the indefinite retention of DNA profiles from individuals never convicted of an offence, it was argued before the ECtHR in *Marper* that this data reveals very little information. The Contracting State went so far as to argue that DNA profiles are in fact 'nothing more than a sequence of numbers or a barcode containing information of a purely objective and irrefutable character and that the identification of a subject only occurs in case of a match with another profile in the database'.[109] The Court (sitting as the Grand Chamber) was clearly unpersuaded by this reasoning. Instead, the Court stressed that the processing of DNA profiles 'through automated means allows the authorities to go well beyond neutral identification', consequently producing an analysis that police can then use to identify 'substantial' and 'highly sensitive' amounts of personal data, including the ethnic origins of the donor.[110] Moreover, the Grand Chamber gave particular weight to the threat to private life posed by the possible use of the retained DNA for profiling, and joined ranks with the higher threshold of protection under data protection law accorded to 'sensitive' personal data[111] and the 'precautionary principle'.[112] In doing so, the Court held that the possibility of this DNA being used for profiling, and to create inferences that may identify an individual's ethnicity, made their 'retention all the more sensitive and susceptible of affecting the right to private life'.[113] At the critical Article 8(2) assessment stage of *Marper*, the ECtHR undertook a comprehensive examination of whether the indefinite and blanket retention of DNA materials from unconvicted individuals had overcome the proportionality hurdle of Article 8 ECHR; ultimately holding that the indefinite and blanket retention of fingerprints and DNA data from individuals never subject to a conviction failed 'to strike a fair balance between the competing public and private interests', and thus constituted a violation of Article 8 ECHR.[114]

(c) The legacy of *Marper* and clear applications to communications data

The four key factors assessed by the ECtHR in *Marper* in its determination of whether the retention of DNA data and other biometric data in England and Wales constituted an interference with the broad scope of private life were drawn from its settled case law.[115] First, that due regard will be given to the specific context within

109 *Marper* (n 6) [74].
110 ibid [75]–[76].
111 Article 9(1) of the GDPR (EU) 2016/679 now refers to these as 'special categories', the broad scope of which includes personal data which reveal: racial or ethnic origin; political opinions, religious or philosophical beliefs, or trade union membership, the processing of genetic data, biometric data for the purpose of uniquely identifying a natural person, health data, and data concerning a person's sex life or sexual orientation.
112 On the precautionary principle and EU data protection law, see Raphaël Gellert, 'Data Protection: A Risk Regulation?' (2015) 5 International Data Privacy Law 3, 17–19.
113 *Marper* (n 6) [76].
114 ibid [125]–[129]. On the judgment generally, see Beattie (n 96).
115 *Friedl* (n 88); *Peck* (n 88) [57]–[63]; *Amann* (n 31) [46].

which the relevant data has been recorded and retained. Secondly, the ECtHR will consider the nature of the data in question. Thirdly, consideration will be given to the way in which the records are used and processed. Finally, the Court will take into account the results that 'may' be obtained from this data.[116] The third and fourth factors are particularly pertinent to the potential threats to private life posed by the retention and subsequent use of communications data in the modern digital age of the twenty-first century as the latter is, essentially, the building block (or DNA) for producing detailed profiles, inferences, and predictions about the attributes and behaviours of individuals and groups from their online and offline lives in a data-driven society—especially when combined with other sources of data and subject to increasingly sophisticated analysis using AI-based systems and machine learning.

The continuing influence of *Marper* is also evident in later cases where the ECtHR has held regimes permitting the indiscriminate and indefinite retention of biometric data (including photographs) for the prevention of crime to be incompatible with Article 8 ECHR.[117] For instance, in *Gaughran v United Kingdom*, the Court held unanimously in 2020 that the indefinite retention of DNA profiles, fingerprints, and custody images concerning any *convicted* person on the police national database amounted to a disproportionate interference with Article 8(2). Drawing often and at length from *Marper*,[118] the Court found that the indiscriminate nature of the retention regime of the applicant's DNA profile, fingerprints, and photograph, without reference to the seriousness of the offence, 'the need for indefinite retention and in the absence of any real possibility of review', failed to strike a fair balance between the competing public and private interests.[119] In addition, the ECtHR stressed in *Gaughran* with respect to the margin of appreciation granted to Contracting States that there were 'compelling reasons' for the Strasbourg Court to provide its own assessment of the factual details concerning the proportionality of the retention powers in the case despite the extensive amount of judicial scrutiny at the domestic level. Although the proportionality of the measure was scrutinized by the domestic courts (including the Supreme Court), the ECtHR noted that the courts had made their assessment concerning the retention of the applicant's photograph on the basis that it was held on a local database and could not be searched against other photographs. The Strasbourg Court then assessed this conclusion by the domestic courts to no longer be relevant

[116] *Marper* (n 6) [67].

[117] *M.K.* (n 13); *Gaughran* (n 13); *Trajkovski and Chipovski v North Macedonia* [2020] ECHR 143.

[118] See *Gaughran* (n 13) [63]–[65], [73]–[83], [88].

[119] ibid [9], [96]. The applicant pleaded guilty to the offence of driving with excess alcohol in 2008. He was fined £50 and suspended from driving for twelve months. No custody time was served. His conviction was 'spent' after five years. Following a request that his biometric data no longer be retained, the Police Service of Northern Ireland (PSNI) destroyed his DNA samples in 2015 but continue to retain, and intend to retain indefinitely, the applicant's records of his DNA profile, fingerprints, and photograph. At the time of writing in 2024, the PSNI retention powers remain unchanged.

due to it being 'superseded by technological developments' in facial recognition in the UK.[120]

Furthermore, the ECtHR seized the opportunity in *Marper* to explicitly highlight the requirements of data quality, and time limits, for data retention programmes created for policing purposes.[121] By directly incorporating key data protection principles into its proportionality assessment, the ECtHR clarified the Article 8 ECHR principles applicable to data retention regimes in general, stating that domestic law 'should notably ensure that such data are relevant and not excessive in relation to the purposes for which they are stored; and preserved in a form which permits identification of the data subjects for no longer than is required for the purpose for which those data are stored'.[122] The ECtHR also recognized, drawing from the influential UN Convention on the Rights of the Child, that the retention of data concerning unconvicted individuals may be especially harmful for juveniles given their 'special situation and the importance of their development and integration in society'.[123] Thus, the Grand Chamber established the principle that public authorities should pay 'particular attention' to 'the protection of juveniles from any detriment that may result from the retention by the authorities of their private data'.[124] Otherwise, indefinite and blanket data retention policies similar to those struck down in *Marper* may result in the 'over-representation' in police databases of young persons and ethnic minorities who have not been convicted of any crime.[125]

The close-scrutiny examination of the above private life interests in *Marper* clearly demonstrates the capacity of the ECtHR to robustly examine the proportionality implications of data retention regimes established without clear evidence of need or a 'just in case' basis.[126] Thus, before addressing how the ECtHR has dealt with Article 8 ECHR and the retention and use of communications data, it is crucial to consider these standards within the legacy of the leading judgment of the ECtHR on data retention for law enforcement purposes. Moreover, as Brown and

[120] *Gaughran* (n 13) [69]–[70], [85]–[86]. On the regulation of law enforcement use of facial recognition and AI-based biometric systems in the UK, see generally Sam Stockwell and others, *The Future of Biometric Technology for Policing and Law Enforcement* (Alan Turing Institute 2024).

[121] Cécile De Terwangne, 'Principles Relating to Processing of Personal Data' in Christopher Kuner and others (eds), *The EU General Data Protection Regulation (GDPR): A Commentary* (OUP 2020) 309–20.

[122] *Marper* (n 6) [103].

[123] ibid [124]. On this UN Convention, see further Simone van der Hof and Eva Lievens, 'The Importance of Privacy by Design and Data Protection Impact Assessments in Strengthening Protection of Children's Personal Data Under the GDPR' (2018) 23 Communications Law 33.

[124] *Marper* (n 6) [124].

[125] ibid [124]. Use by police databases of machine learning analytics, which essentially make decisions concerning individuals drawing from profiles of groups that these analytics associate with that individual, often based on biased datasets, raises clear risks for groups already subject to unfair discrimination or 'over-policing': EU FRA, *Bias in Algorithms: AI and Discrimination* (FRA 2022); EU FRA, *Addressing Racism in Policing* (FRA 2024) 48–50. See further Chapter 1.

[126] See more recently *Gaughran* (n 13) [121].

others point out, key privacy concerns and Article 8 ECHR standards in *Marper* regarding the long-term retention and future use of DNA profiles have 'clear applications to the detailed information revealed about an individual's private life by communications data'.[127] This link is particularly evident in the following three ways. First, the retention and use of both sets of information concern an individual's private life and enable public authorities to profile those individuals, their related communities, and their connections to others in an individual's immediate and wider networks. As noted previously, communications data is essentially the building block (or DNA) for producing detailed records, inferences, and predictions about the attributes and behaviours of individuals and groups, particularly when combined in bulk with other datasets that can then be sifted through for various types of profiling, patterns, and connections using search terms and other algorithmic analytics. Thus, irrespective of whether the retained data has been accessed or subsequently used, the mere storage of information that could provide the power of profiling (or, in some cases, ubiquitous monitoring) to the State has been held to amount to an interference with Article 8 ECHR.

Secondly, the above determination in *Marper* shows recognition of the fact that, although important, the retention of data concerning an individual's private life is only one of various stages of data processing that make up any programme of secret monitoring and data collection by the State. This resulted in the Grand Chamber applying the standard that any subsequent use(s) of this retained data amounts to an additional interference with the right to private life. Thus, the ECtHR has held in data retention cases that each stage of the surveillance cycle (retention, access, use) should be underpinned by adequate safeguards which reflect core data protection principles and prevent arbitrary and disproportionate interferences with the right to private life. Thirdly, this more granular approach to the different data processing stages of the surveillance cycle highlights the fundamental role and relevance of data protection principles in cases concerning Article 8 ECHR, emerging technologies, and data retention in a criminal justice context. As the ECtHR has consistently held, the need for data protection safeguards is 'all the greater' where retained data has been subject to automated processing.[128]

Drawing from well-established principles in European data protection law, the ECtHR established key requirements in *Marper* to be met by EU and domestic laws on data retention in order for such measures to be deemed compatible with Article 8 ECHR. These included the need to ensure the retention of relevant (not excessive) amounts of data in relation to specified legitimate aim, suitable data security measures for enabling identification of an individual for no longer than

[127] See Brown (n 96) 102; Sheldon Krimsky and Tania Simoncelli, *Genetic Justice* (Columbia University Press 2012) 322; Nora Ni Loideain, 'Surveillance of Communications Data and Article 8 ECHR' in Serge Gutwirth, Ronald Leenes, and Paul de Hert (eds), *Reloading Data Protection* (Springer 2014) 183–209; Anderson (n 87) 147.

[128] *Marper* (n 6) [99] [103] *M.K.* (n 13) [35]; *Aycaguer* (n 13) [38].

necessary, and adequate guarantees to protect against the misuse or abuse of the retained data. *Marper* has also played a significant role in shaping the landmark standards of the CJEU concerning bulk data retention and public authorities' acquisition and use communications data.[129] In stark contrast, as discussed later, the ECtHR Grand Chamber took a very different approach in its equivalent rulings in 2021, establishing instead a new approach and set of principles that depart from the above key factors in *Marper* in the most important post-Snowden Article 8 ECHR judgments to date dealing with the retention and bulk interception of communications data.

C. Retention and Interception of Communications Data

This section critically examines the key developments and approach of the ECtHR in its case law dealing with Article 8 ECHR and the retention and interception of different types of communications data for the prevention of crime and safeguarding national security. Since the Snowden revelations in 2013 and the increasing practice of bulk data collection directly and indirectly from the private sector, cases challenging the Article 8 ECHR compatibility of laws that permit the acquisition of communications data by public authorities are on the rise. The following analysis considers the approach of the ECtHR to the interferences with Article 8 ECHR posed by the subsequent access and use of different types of communications data for law enforcement and national security purposes. This highly dynamic area of surveillance, technology, and human rights law in the post-Snowden era became a decisive issue in various landmark cases before the CJEU and subsequently the ECtHR.[130] Given their importance for the future development and protection of the right to private life within the ECHR and EU legal orders, this section concludes with an analysis of the relevant findings from the Grand Chamber judgments in *Centrum för Rättvisa* and *Big Brother Watch*.

1. Article 8(1): interferences with the rights to respect for private life and correspondence

(a) Traffic data and location data: access in real time and historical

Early Article 8 ECHR case law dealt with police acquiring traffic data in a time long before AI chatbots, social media, and smartphones, namely the use of landline telephones by specific individuals as part of a related criminal investigation.[131]

[129] See further Chapters 5 and 8.

[130] On the case law of the CJEU and the impact on EU law of the Snowden revelations, see Chapters 1 and 5.

[131] *Malone* (n 1); *Valenzuela Contreras* (n 3); *P.G. and J.H. v United Kingdom* [2001] ECHR 546.

On the basis that traffic data contains information, 'in particular the numbers dialled, which is an integral element in the communications made by telephone', the ECtHR held in 1984 that the release of communications data to the police without a customer's consent amounted to an interference with 'a right guaranteed by Article 8'.[132] By not identifying which specific right under Article 8 ECHR had been interfered with, as noted previously, the ECtHR was initially unclear in its first case dealing with law enforcement access to communications data about the exact privacy harm and the extent of its intrusiveness posed by this investigatory power. The Strasbourg Court has since moved away from this hesitant approach, recognizing in later judgments that access and use of traffic data and location data for the prevention of crime, and safeguarding national security, constitutes an interference with the right to respect for private life.

It is now settled case law that such an interference has occurred when public authorities have acquired traffic data or location data for these aims from various modes of communications. These include landline phones in a home or business, interception of online communications from satellites or submarine cables, Internet use (such as social media activities), mobile phone usage, and monitoring a GPS transmitter secretly installed on a car).[133] The ECtHR has generally provided greater clarity in its assessment of the intrusiveness of communications data in more recent cases. *Ekimdzhiev and Others* is the most significant bright spot to date in this respect, particularly as the Court held without qualification in this 2022 judgment that the acquisition of communications data through bulk interception can 'be just as intrusive as the bulk acquisition of the content of communications'.[134] Furthermore, the Court held that the storage of any communications data—from any type of electronic communications—also amounts to an interference with the right to respect for correspondence, and any access to said data constitutes a further interference.[135] This clarification on what rights protected under Article 8(1) are affected by such measures is welcome as it shows a court that is sensitive to the need of keeping pace with rapid developments in technology and surveillance practices and the specific privacy interests that are consequently at risk from harm.

These include the collection (real time and historical) of vast amounts of personal data and highly sensitive private life information, which can now be captured and analysed from accessing the traffic and location data constantly generated from communications made via multiple Internet-enabled and ubiquitously pinging devices used daily (mobile phones, cars, watches).[136] But is real-time access to this

[132] *Malone* (n 1) [84] (emphasis added).
[133] See *Valenzuela* (n 3) [47]; *P.G. and J.H.* (n 131) [42]; *Uzun* (n 7) [52]; *Benedik* (n 23) [120]; *Ben Faiza* (n 7) [68]; *Breyer* (n 10) [76]; *Big Brother Watch* (n 5) [375].
[134] *Ekimdzhiev and Others* (n 9) [394].
[135] ibid [373]–[376].
[136] See further Chapter 1.

traffic and location data more intrusive than the more established police practice of historical access? It appears that the ECtHR has adopted this view in its case law as evident in *Ben Faiza*. Here the applicant was suspected of being involved in a major drug trafficking operation and was consequently the subject of various forms of surveillance by French investigators, one of which was monitoring his real-time location via GPS and the traffic and location data generated from his mobile phone use.[137] As part of its key findings in *Ben Faiza*, the ECtHR held that live access to an individual's geographical position (real-time data) constitutes a more significant intrusion to the right to respect for private life than access to mobile phone tracking revealing a person's prior movements (historical data).[138] Two key questions arise from this approach of the ECtHR which has since been followed by the CJEU.[139]

First, as Hughes and others have rightly questioned, at what point does real-time data concerning a person's private life and movements become historical data?[140] Further clarity on this distinction is required to ensure that real-time access is only permitted if a higher threshold of safeguards is met under the relevant law if such measures are to comply with the legality requirements of Article 8(2). Secondly, the view that real-time access to an individual's current movements is inherently more intrusive and more revealing than having knowledge of their prior movements (particularly over a lengthy period of time)—whatever the circumstances—is suspect. The analysis in *Ben Faiza* is particularly unpersuasive given the lack of any clear reasoning for this sweeping finding.[141] The significance of an individual's movements (or lack thereof) in a particular moment/real time depends entirely on context. Moreover, being able to access the historical location data from a person's mobile phone, thereby having a detailed record of *all* of their movements from yesterday, last week, last month, etc, reveals far more about an individual's private life. From a security perspective, the various surveillance measures employed in *Ben Faiza*, and other relevant cases, also indicate that law enforcement require access to both types of communications data to track the ongoing movements of individuals suspected of being involved in a serious crime or future terrorist attack. In *Uzun*, various historical and real-time measures were both used for monitoring

[137] *Ben Faiza* (n 7). On the judgment generally, see Katrien Keyaerts, '*Ben Faiza v France*' (2019) 5 European Data Protection Law Review 120.

[138] *Ben Faiza* (n 7) [74]. Although the Chamber judgment in *Big Brother Watch* does not share its own view on the matter, the Court notes the assessment in *Ben Faiza* that public authorities' access of a person's location in real time is more privacy-intrusive than identifying the past geographical position of a person.

[139] See further Chapter 4.

[140] Kirsty Hughes, 'Mass Surveillance and the European Court of Human Rights' [2018] European Human Rights Law Review 589, 595; Ni Loideain (n 66). On this argument within the context of the EU AI Act and live facial recognition, see EDPS & EDPB, Joint Opinion 5/2021 on the proposal for a Regulation of the European Parliament and of the Council laying down harmonised rules on artificial intelligence (AI Act) 11.

[141] Keyaerts (n 137) 126.

suspects subsequently convicted for the attempted murder of members of the German Parliament.[142]

(b) The value of subscriber data: linking IP addresses and mobile phone numbers

A CSP assigns (or leases) a 'dynamic IP address' to an Internet-enabled device, such as a mobile phone, every time it connects to the Internet. This differs from static IP addresses, in that dynamic IP addresses are not permanent and can change if the Internet connection is reset. Similar to a person's mobile phone number, much can be revealed from tracking dynamic IP addresses once they can be linked to the subscriber/device user as the Internet usage during the particular period before it is reset could be several hours or days. This information may reveal when and where the Internet was accessed, for how long, how often, and what websites or networks that individual used during that particular time of Internet use.[143] Within a criminal justice context, however, the ECtHR has been reluctant to apply established Article 8 ECHR standards from cases concerning larger collections of traffic data (retained over certain time periods) to recent cases where one specific type of traffic data can be used to identify and link an individual with a particular set of communications.[144] Instead, the ECtHR has often relied on its data protection judgments as the most relevant line of precedent for examining when 'subscriber data' is used to link IP addresses and mobile phone numbers for the purpose of identifying a specific individual and connecting them with their online and offline activities.[145]

In essence, 'subscriber information' (or subscription data) concerns personal data held or obtained by a CSP about persons to whom the CSP provides or has provided a communications service. This may also include people who subscribe to a communications service without using that service and a significant number of people who use a communications service without necessarily subscribing to it (such as free Wi-Fi hotspots),[146] for instance criminals may easily obtain and use mobile phones anonymously by using mobile phone cards obtained from third parties.[147] Distinguishing strictly between the categories of 'traffic data' and subscription data is also a grey area in terms of definitional clarity for laws governing communications data as the bulk retention of subscription data also invariably includes traffic data, such as telephone numbers and IP addresses.[148] These are needed as part of the information provided by the parties to enable transmission

[142] *Uzun* (n 7) [14]–[17]. These included communications interception, GPS tracking of shared vehicle, police visual surveillance, and camera surveillance outside their homes.
[143] See further *Benedik* (n 23).
[144] ibid [120]; *Breyer* (n 10) [81].
[145] *Benedik* (n 23) [120]; *Breyer* (n 10) [81].
[146] *Big Brother Watch* (n 5) [117].
[147] *Breyer* (n 10) [15].
[148] See further Chapter 1.

of a communication (call/message via mobile phone) and therefore fall within the scope of traffic data.[149] One item of traffic data is, of course, much more limited than the increasing reams of traffic data produced by a person's communications over a matter of hours, days, months, etc. Nevertheless, it still means that the bulk retention of subscription data concerning pre-paid SIM cards for mobile phones still includes a phone number linked to an individual or legal entity and thus involves the retention of traffic data.[150] It is also impossible to separate traffic data from subscriber data, as traffic data alone does not make any sense if the person behind those data is not identified—the latter information is thus 'an extremely important element of communication privacy'.[151]

Finally, although subscriber data is generally considered the most limited and least intrusive type of communications data, the amount of information transferred by CSPs to public authorities may in fact involve a great range of personal data depending on how its scope has been defined under the relevant law.[152] Under the contested surveillance legislation in *Zakharov*, for instance, this included the retention and access to the subscriber's name, address, payment details, passport number (ie form of ID used for purchase), their company name if relevant, and the names of all employees using that service.[153] At the time of writing, the wide-ranging scope of personal data that the specific concept of 'subscriber data' may encompass in a particular data retention programme has not yet been addressed by the ECtHR or the CJEU when assessing the level of intrusiveness to private life.[154] The ECtHR first dealt with Article 8 ECHR and the linking of dynamic IP addresses with subscriber data for the prevention of crime in the 2008 judgment of *K.U.*[155] However, the Court did not examine whether placing a mandatory obligation on CSPs to divulge the identity of the holder of a dynamic IP address to police was compatible with Article 8 ECHR. When reviewing various secret surveillance laws in *Zakharov*, the Grand Chamber did not specifically examine the compatibility with Article 8 ECHR of legal provisions requiring all CSPs to retain the subscriber data of all their mobile phone customers for up to three years.[156]

149 On the approach of the CJEU to the retention and access to various types of communications data by public authorities, see Chapter 4.

150 Note that the CJEU has held that dynamic IP addresses registered by a CSP when a customer accesses a website constitute personal data: Case C-582/14 *Breyer*, judgment of 19 October 2016 (ECLI:EU:C:2016:779).

151 A salient argument made by the Slovenian Information Commissioner in *Benedik* (n 23) [26].

152 Time will tell if the approach in the more recent judgment of *Ekimdzhiev and Others* (n 9) [373] is applied in future cases, where the ECtHR indicated that all types of communications data retained and accessed by public authorities constitute interferences with the rights to private life and correspondence.

153 *Zakharov* (n 58) [133]. See also *Breyer* (n 10) [27] for the different types of subscription data subject to mandatory bulk retention by CSPs in Germany including: name, home address, data of birth, phone number.

154 On related case law of the CJEU concerning the similarly ambiguous category of 'data relating to the civil identity of users', see Chapter 4.

155 *K.U. v Finland* [2008] ECHR 1563.

156 *Zakharov* (n 58).

At the time of writing, the ECtHR had dealt with the Article 8 ECHR compatibility of legal regimes permitting the retention and/or access to subscriber data used to link individuals with their communications for countering serious crime in two cases in 2018 and 2020.[157] However, largely due to the wide margin of appreciation granted in cases involving Article 8 ECHR, data retention, and national security, the reasoning and outcomes of both judgments diverge considerably. The first judgment of *Benedik* concerned the disclosure of information concerning a dynamic IP address to law enforcement to identify a particular user of the relevant Internet service.[158] The applicant was the son of the subscriber whose Internet usage made him a person of interest to law enforcement. The Slovenian police had already acquired the dynamic IP address from the Swiss police as part of a cross-border investigation concerning a peer-to-peer file-sharing network that permitted the sharing of illegal content where each of the connected computers acted as a client and a server. The Slovenian government argued that acquiring subscriber data from the CSP did not interfere with Article 8 ECHR on the basis that the applicant had waived any expectation of privacy through his Internet usage and compared the subscriber data request to consulting a public phone directory.[159]

Following a lengthy analysis that took into account similar cases in Canada, Germany, and the CJEU, and in line with its broad interpretation of what falls within the scope of private life, the ECtHR unequivocally rejected these arguments.[160] In a robust and normative assessment, the ECtHR held (by a majority) that it 'cannot ignore [that] ... [t]he sole purpose of obtaining the subscriber information was to identify a particular person behind the independently collected content revealing data he had been sharing'.[161] The ECtHR further clarified that the zone of interaction a person has with others falls within the scope of private life and that information on such activities engages Article 8(1) 'the moment it is linked to or attributed to an identified or identifiable individual'.[162] This means that subscriber data constitutes personal data and when sought by the police in these circumstances 'must ... be treated as *inextricably connected* to the relevant pre-existing content revealing data'.[163] The ECtHR held that to not adopt this purposive approach 'would be to deny the necessary protection to information which might reveal a good deal about the online activity of an individual, including sensitive details of his or her interests, beliefs and intimate lifestyle'.[164]

[157] *Benedik* (n 23); *Breyer* (n 10).
[158] *Benedik* (n 23).
[159] ibid [98]–[108].
[160] See generally Nataša Pirc Musar, '*Benedik v Slovenia*: Dynamic IP and Communication Privacy' (2018) 4 European Data Protection Law Review 554.
[161] *Benedik* (n 23) [98]–[108].
[162] ibid [98]–[108].
[163] ibid [109].
[164] ibid [109].

The Article 8(1) analysis in *Benedik* is a model of clarity. Moreover, it shows the standards of Article 8 ECHR keeping pace with how advances in communications technology have changed the types and scale of information now required by law enforcement to identify those linked to serious criminal activity. By specifically identifying the protected interest and interference with the right to respect for the applicant's private life under Article 8(1), the ECtHR also avoided the risk of overstating the inevitable interference to private life and data protection posed by any legitimate criminal investigation. That said, despite emphasizing the inextricable link between the interference with the right to private life and access to the content of an applicant's online communications made by the identifying subscriber data, the ECtHR refrains from determining that this also amounts to an interference with the right to correspondence under Article 8(1). This curious omission indicates a distinct cautiousness in an otherwise comprehensive legal assessment of Article 8(1). Furthermore, it suggested a reluctance by the ECtHR (at that time)[165] to treat the monitoring of an individual's Internet use as being capable of revealing the same, or more, about an individual's private life than intercepting their mobile phone conversations or online communications.

The second case of *Breyer* concerned an ultimately unsuccessful challenge to the law in Germany which required CSPs to retain all customers' 'subscriber information' for various broadly framed aims that conflate the prevention of crime, serious crime, and protecting national security. These aims ranged from performing intelligence duties, 'warding off dangers', and prosecuting criminal offences, to regulatory offences.[166] The applicants' arguments in this 2020 judgment focused on the bulk retention of customers' personal data from the purchase of pre-paid ('pay-as-you-go') mobile-telephone SIM cards, the storage of which is otherwise not necessary for billing purposes.[167] In contrast with *Benedik*, the examination in *Breyer* of the Article 8(1) stage is far narrower in scope. Moreover, the ECtHR took pains to emphasize throughout its judgment in *Breyer* that the interference with Article 8 ECHR '*only* concerns the storage of subscriber data' and that the contested legislative provision 'does not extend to traffic data, location data or data which reveals the content of communications'.[168] The Contracting State in its arguments also deftly avoided dealing with the status of mobile phone numbers as traffic data by narrowly defining traffic data as 'data *originating* in the course of a communication process' and departing from its broader definition under the relevant EU law (as cited in *Breyer*).[169] The ECtHR does not challenge this interpretation. There is

[165] See the contrasting approach in the 2022 case of *Ekimdzhiev and Others* (n 9) where the ECtHR has held that all types of communications data retained and accessed by public authorities constitute interferences with the rights to private life and correspondence.
[166] *Breyer* (n 10) [87], [98].
[167] ibid [7].
[168] ibid [61] (emphasis added).
[169] ibid [61] (emphasis added). Note that Art 2(b) of the e-Privacy Directive 2002/58/EC defines traffic data broadly as 'any data *processed* for the purpose of the conveyance of a communication on an electronic communications network or for the billing thereof' (emphasis added). See further Chapter 1.

furthermore no reference to the related Article 8 ECHR analysis in *Benedik* which dealt with the identification of an Internet user through obtaining the subscriber data associated with a dynamic IP address.[170]

Perhaps most importantly, the ECtHR in *Breyer* does not examine the scale of this general and indiscriminate retention obligation as part of its Article 8(1) assessment. Instead, the ECtHR noted that none of the parties disputed the finding that an interference had occurred with the right to respect for private life on the basis that a mandatory obligation was placed on CSPs to store their users' personal data.[171] It then reiterated the settled Article 8 ECHR standard that the 'mere storing of data relating to the private life of the individual' constitutes an interference within the meaning of Article 8 ECHR.[172]

(c) Retention obligations and bulk interception: from silence to some decisiveness

The first time the ECtHR had the opportunity to examine Article 8 ECHR and legal obligations on CSPs to store the personal data of all their mobile phone customers for the prevention of crime and national security purposes was the Grand Chamber judgment of *Roman Zakharov*. This landmark case in 2015 dealt with various secret surveillance laws in Russia, including requirements for CSPs to install equipment enabling the bulk interception and acquisition of communications data concerning all their customers.[173] One of these laws required all CSPs operating in Russia to retain and update all communications data about their mobile phone customers 'and the services provided to them' and to store said data for three years.[174] CSPs were also mandated to ensure that a wide range of law enforcement authorities and intelligence agencies had the ability to access this database remotely at all times (within 30 seconds of a request).[175] The impugned legal framework provided public authorities in Russia with two types of real-time monitoring: 'total interception' and 'statistical monitoring'.[176] The former allowed

[170] Although the ECtHR takes a case-by-case approach in its assessment and is not formally led by precedent, its reasoning is in practice based on previous related judgments (see further Chapter 2). Omission of the relevant analysis in *Benedik* is highlighted by Judge Ranzoni in his Dissenting Opinion in *Breyer* (n 10) 44.

[171] *Breyer* (n 10) [81].

[172] ibid [81].

[173] See further Chapter 2.

[174] *Zakharov* (n 58) [132]–[133]. See the details here on Order No 538.

[175] ibid [117]–[119].

[176] ibid [117]–[119]. Specifically, the installed equipment by CSPs was required to ensure '(a) interception of all the incoming and outgoing calls of the interception subject; (b) *access to information about his or her whereabouts*; (c) maintenance of interception capability where an ongoing connection is transferred between the networks of different mobile network operators; (d) maintenance of interception capability in cases involving supplementary services, such as call forwarding, call transfer or conference calls, with the possibility of registering the number or numbers to which the call is routed; (e) *collection of communications data concerning all types of connections, including fax, short messaging (SMS) or other*; (f) access to information about the services provided to the interception subject' (emphasis added).

real-time interception of the contents of all communications and the interception of communications data, while statistical monitoring applied to 'real-time monitoring of communications data only'. In other words, this Russian law allowed public authorities to access and monitor any mobile phone user's real-time communications data (and content) and to do so without prior independent authorization.

In a notably robust judgment, the Grand Chamber unanimously held that the overall regime underpinning these secret surveillance programmes in Russia violated Article 8 ECHR for not satisfying either the legality or proportionality requirements under Article 8(2).[177] The Court was especially critical of the fact that the framework enabled the secret services and police to directly intercept the communications of every citizen without requiring them to show an interception authorization to CSPs or anyone else. This made such monitoring 'particularly prone to abuse' and the need for adequate safeguards to prevent this abuse 'particularly great'.[178] However, the ECtHR provided an overall assessment of the far-reaching secret interception measures of mobile phone communications which was silent on any determination regarding the retention measures and the real-time interception of location data and other types of communications data.[179] It would not be until the Chamber judgment of *Big Brother Watch* in 2018 when the ECtHR would examine a legal obligation on CSPs to retain various types of communication data and provide public authorities with subsequent access to this traffic data, location data, and subscription data.[180]

That said, this element of the ECtHR's assessment in this highly anticipated post-Snowden ruling was limited in two respects. First, the regime of retention notices issued by the Secretary of State under the contested law for CSPs to retain communications data was only challenged within the context of public authorities' acquisition of the data, subject to such access being authorized by a prior review by a court or independent body and for its use to be limited for countering serious crime (not the prevention of crime). Neither the indiscriminate and general scope of the retention nor the scale of data being acquired by public authorities were examined by the ECtHR. Secondly, the Court was silent on what is traditionally addressed under the Article 8(1) stage of its legal assessment: the identification of what rights enshrined in Article 8 ECHR were interfered with by the impugned data retention regime and the related access.[181] The Grand Chamber judgment in 2021 was also silent on these issues on the grounds that the parties did not contest

[177] *Zakharov* (n 58) [304]–[305]. On the legality and proportionality requirements in secret surveillance cases, see further Chapter 2.

[178] ibid [270].

[179] ibid [269]. These measures are briefly mentioned in the overall examination of the facts and circumstances of the case.

[180] Note that the 2020 judgment in *Breyer* (n 10) was limited to CSPs being required to retain only the subscriber information of all their mobile phone users (excluding traffic and location data).

[181] *Big Brother Watch v United Kingdom* [2018] ECHR 722 [460]–[468]. See further Chapter 2.

the determination by the Chamber judgment that the UK law at the material time (as interpreted by the domestic authorities in light of recent judgments of the CJEU) had violated Article 8 ECHR.

The Strasbourg Court has nevertheless become less hesitant overall to recognize the intrusiveness of public authorities' acquisition and use of communications data in recent judgments. Observing that communications interception 'represents one of the gravest intrusions' into an individual's private life,[182] both the Chamber and Grand Chamber in *Big Brother Watch* held that they were 'not persuaded' that the acquisition of communications data through bulk interception 'is necessarily less intrusive than the acquisition of content'.[183] The ECtHR went further again in its 2022 judgment of *Ekimdzhiev and Others*. There the Court held that the acquisition of communications data through bulk interception can be '*just as intrusive* as the bulk acquisition of the content of communications'.[184] Secondly, the Court established in *Ekimdzhiev and Others* that the storage of any communications data, from any type of electronic communications, amounts to an interference with the right to respect for private life and the right to respect for correspondence. Moreover, any access to the data constitutes further interferences with those rights.[185] Finally, in contrast to its brief Article 8(1) analysis in *Breyer*, the ECtHR further clarified in *Ekimdzhiev and Others* that the legally mandated retention of communications data of all communication service users was an interference with their right to respect for correspondence. Moreover, although carried out by private persons, the interference was still 'attributable to the Bulgarian State'.[186]

2. Article 8(2) and accessing content and communications data: same safeguards but two-tier scrutiny

Two key developments in its Article 8 ECHR case law have contributed to the departure of the ECtHR from its previously lauded role for setting minimum standards in the review of laws permitting public authorities' use of secret surveillance and data retention across Europe. The first deals with the influential safeguards for governing the secret surveillance of communications under its Article 8 ECHR case law. Here concerns have been raised with respect to a shift away from these standards through a joint assessment by the ECtHR that combines and conflates

[182] ibid [350].
[183] ibid [350]; *Big Brother Watch* (n 5) [363]. The Chamber judgment did not explicitly limit this comparison to the acquisition of related communications data to the context of 'bulk interception'.
[184] *Ekimdzhiev and Others* (n 9) [394] (emphasis added).
[185] ibid [373]–[376].
[186] ibid [374]–[375]. Note the ECtHR cited as supporting authority the relevant case law of the CJEU in *Digital Rights Ireland*. On the latter, see further Chapters 5 and 8.

the legality and proportionality conditions at the Article 8(2) assessment stage.[187] In particular, scholars have warned that this à la carte approach to the traditionally distinct requirements and different tests concerning the rule of law, and the necessity of an interference with Article 8 ECHR, often results in diluting the scope and intensity of the Court's review of these previously acclaimed standards.[188] This controversial approach to the cardinal question of whether a Contracting State can show that a measure is a justified interference with Article 8 ECHR has been increasingly applied in cases dealing with the retention, acquisition, and use by public authorities of communications data.[189]

Secondly, it has become a settled principle in the case law dealing with secret surveillance that the scope of safeguards required to satisfy the conditions of Article 8(2) will depend on the nature and extent of the interference with the right to private life. This means that the ECtHR may not apply the same strict-scrutiny approach regarding which requirements must be met by interferences it considers to be less intrusive and thus affect an individual's rights under Article 8(1) less seriously. For example, the Court may entirely omit examining certain interferences at the Article 8(2) stage that were identified at the Article 8(1) stage.[190] The influence of this principle is also clear in the case law of the ECtHR concerning its assessment of data retention and bulk interception regimes involving communications data.[191] Despite the Court's recent statements to the contrary that public authorities' access to communications data should be subject to the same safeguards as their access to content, the reality has been a two-tiered approach where the ECtHR is still subjecting the latter to stricter scrutiny than the former.

(a) The hierarchy of intrusiveness and communications data in early case law

Long before the joint analysis approach to Article 8(2) emerged in the case law of the ECtHR, underpinning a less rigorous approach to public authorities' access and use of communications data has been the view that the degree of intrusion to a

[187] On the settled case law of the ECtHR dealing with secret surveillance and the distinct principles and safeguards that underpin the three conditions of Art 8(2) of legality, legitimate aim, and proportionality, see Chapter 2.

[188] Ni Loideain (n 66). See further Chapter 2.

[189] On the retention of other types of personal data for law enforcement purposes in *Catt* (n 15) where members of the Strasbourg Court itself have criticized the joint approach assessment of Art 8(2) for not examining relevant issues concerning the rule of law and ambiguous police powers, see Ni Loideain (n 66).

[190] See eg *Ekimdzhiev and Others* (n 9) where the ECtHR does not examine any legality or proportionality issues with respect to the scope of retention permitted by the impugned communications data regime under Bulgarian law.

[191] Referred to by this author as the 'hierarchy of intrusiveness': Ni Loideain (n 66). The ECtHR has also held surveillance of a legal consultation in a police station to constitute 'an extremely high degree of intrusion into a person's right to respect for his or her private life and correspondence'. To the extent that the Court 'will expect the same safeguards to be in place to protect individuals from arbitrary interference with their Article 8 rights as it has required in cases concerning the interception of communications'. See *R.E. v United Kingdom* [2015] ECHR 947 [131].

person's private life is simply not comparable to that caused by the interception of content.[192] The *P.G. and J.H.* case provides a good example of when the Court has been influenced by this principle.[193] Here the applicants were convicted of a serious crime (conspiracy to commit armed robbery) following an investigation that relied on various forms of secret surveillance, including police access to over two months of landline phone usage acquired from the itemized billing of one of the applicant's phone lines. No warrant was required for the disclosure of this traffic data from the CSP, instead the safeguards to be met by the police (as required by the CSP) involved a data protection form countersigned by a police superintendent and details explaining the reason for the request. In this case, the police stated that the information was necessary to assist in the identification of members of a team of suspected armed robbery.[194] The acquired traffic data proved useful in two ways: (1) by identifying one of the suspects and (2) as corroborating evidence in court confirming a record of the times and dates for when the police used a covert listening device in the home of one of the applicants.[195]

The issue before the ECtHR focused on whether the relevant legal framework setting out the circumstances and conditions by which the police were empowered to resort to such a measure was compatible with the legality condition of Article 8 ECHR. None of the parties disputed that the disclosure to the police of the billing information met the first principle of having a 'basis in domestic law'. The crux of the challenge lay instead with the second principle under the legality condition of Article 8(2), namely the 'quality of the law'.[196] The applicants argued that the latter had not been satisfied due to the relevant legislation (the Telecommunications Act 1984 and the Data Protection Act 1984) lacking any foreseeable safeguards concerning the use, storage, and destruction of the acquired traffic data. For instance, the applicants highlighted that neither statute stipulated any of the restraints on abuse which were to be found in the relevant legislation concerning covert recordings (as provided in the Police Act 1997). The legal framework in the UK at that time did not therefore provide an adequate indication to the public as to the circumstances in which and conditions under which the public authorities were empowered to resort to such a measure.[197] Based on the strongly held view that

[192] This hierarchy of intrusiveness principle has also been applied in the data retention case law of the CJEU. See further Chapters 5 and 9.

[193] *P.G. and J.H.* (n 131).

[194] The police made a request to BT (British Telecommunications PLC) for itemized billing in relation to the telephone number of one of the applicants for the period between 1 January 1995 and 14 March 1995.

[195] *P.G. and J.H.* (n 131) [13].

[196] The traditional approach of the ECtHR when determining if an interference meets the legality condition under Art 8(2) requires that the contested measure satisfy two principles. The measure must have 'some basis in domestic law' and must also comply with the rule of law. This second principle focuses on the 'quality' of the domestic law which involves meeting the tests of 'accessibility' and 'foreseeability'. See further Chapter 2.

[197] *P.G. and J.H.* (n 131) [39].

the nature and extent of the intrusion to the applicants' private lives was strictly limited, however, the ECtHR dismissed this argument in its entirety.

In doing so, the ECtHR provided a highly cursory assessment of the legality requirements under Article 8(2) and whittled down its consideration of the 'quality of law' criterion to what was required by way of a singular 'safeguard'.[198] This allowed the Court to forego examining or even mentioning the six 'minimum' foreseeability safeguards applied in previous cases involving the acquisition of landline phone traffic data (otherwise known as metering).[199] The Court explained that the information obtained concerned the telephone numbers called from the flat of one of the applicants fell between 'two specific dates'.[200] By not mentioning the specific period of time when considering the question of intrusiveness, this allowed the Court to sidestep examining the two-month duration and thereby scope of the acquired traffic data records in the legality assessment. The Court also stressed that the itemized billing 'did not include any information about the contents of those calls, or who made or received them' thus making the use of the information 'strictly limited'.[201] The applicants further contested the lack of any legally binding safeguards governing the storage and destruction of the traffic data. Again, there is no scrutiny of this clear lack of foreseeability in the domestic law and the Court simply states that it was 'not persuaded that the lack of such detailed formal regulation raises any risk of arbitrariness or misuse'.[202]

The ECtHR furthermore took no issue with the fact that these safeguards were only to be found in the 'internal policy guidelines' of the relevant police force or that the scope of the guidance permitted the traffic data to be retained effectively on an indefinite basis ('for six years or longer') at the discretion of a detective inspector, thereby also lacking any *ex ante* or *ex post* independent oversight.[203] This incomplete Article 8(2) assessment in *P.G. and J.H.* clearly jars with the settled rule of law standards developed by the Court in its established jurisprudence dealing with Article 8 ECHR and communications monitoring. As the ECtHR itself has recognized, given the operation and use of secret surveillance measures by public authorities by their very nature are not open to full scrutiny by those affected or the

[198] ibid [46].

[199] See, in contrast, the detailed legality assessment in *Valenzuela Contreras* (n 3). The settled Art 8 ECHR case law at that time set out the six 'minimum' safeguards to be provided in the statute or case law of Contracting States as follows: (1) a definition of the categories of people liable to have their telephones monitored; (2) the nature of the offences which may give rise to such an order; (3) a limit on the duration of telephone tapping; (4) the procedure for drawing up the summary reports containing intercepted conversations; (5) the precautions to be taken in order to communicate the recordings intact and in their entirety for possible inspection by the judge and by the defence; and (6) the circumstances in which recordings may or must be destroyed. See further Chapter 2.

[200] *P.G. and J.H.* (n 131) [46].

[201] ibid [46]. The Court omits in its assessment of Art 8(2) that the traffic data obtained was in fact used to identify one of the suspects in the investigation.

[202] ibid [47].

[203] ibid [46].

wider public, it would be 'contrary to the rule of law for the discretion granted to the executive or to a judge to be expressed in terms of an unfettered power'.[204]

(b) Lax scrutiny under the joint analysis approach to Article 8(2) in recent case law

It is now settled case law that public authorities' acquisition of communications data amounts to an interference with the right to private life as enshrined in Article 8(1) and must therefore be shown to be justified with respect to the requirements of Article 8(2). This applies irrespective of how public authorities acquired the communications data[205] or what legitimate aim was being pursued, such as the prevention of crime, protecting the rights and freedoms of others, or safeguarding national security. Consistent with the early jurisprudence of the ECtHR dealing with Article 8 ECHR and secret surveillance,[206] there have been some cases where measures allowing public authorities to access communications data have been found to be in violation of Article 8 ECHR based solely on their incompatibility with the legality condition. The settled two requirements of the latter stipulate that there is some basis in domestic law for accessing communications data and that this framework is compatible with the rule of law and meets the 'quality of law' tests of 'accessibility' and 'foreseeability'.[207] In *Copland*, for instance, the Court held that there was a violation of Article 8 ECHR where no domestic law existed at the relevant time regulating the circumstances in which a public body could monitor the communications data from an employee's Internet usage, email, and telephone.[208] In *Benedik*, where the Slovenian police sought access to subscriber data in order to link an individual with an IP address involved in an online file-sharing network, the law was found not to have satisfied the test of foreseeability. Specifically, the Court criticized the lack of any legal rules setting out the conditions for the retention of the data or safeguards against abuse by the police in accessing this data. The ECtHR further highlighted the lack of evidence of any independent supervision of the use of these police powers at the relevant time.[209]

More recently, however, the ECtHR has increasingly undertaken a joint analysis of the Article 8(2) conditions of legality and proportionality in cases dealing with

[204] *Malone* (n 1) [68]; *Zakharov* (n 58) [230]. See further Chapter 2.

[205] eg these methods include public authorities obtaining communications data from a communications service provider (digital data that exists due to a mandatory legal obligation imposed on CSPs to retain said data for possible future use by the public authorities) or public authorities acquiring this data directly through methods of bulk interception via satellites or submarine cables controlled by CSPs.

[206] See further Chapter 2.

[207] ibid.

[208] *Copland* v *United Kingdom* [2007] ECHR 253 [45]–[49].

[209] *Benedik* (n 23) [130]–[134]. See *Valenzuela Contreras* (n 3) [50]–[61] where the Spanish law which dealt with the secret surveillance and monitoring of traffic data by Spanish police from landline phones ('metering') in a harassment case was held not to be 'foreseeable' as it did not indicate with sufficient clarity at the material time the extent of the authorities' discretion in the domain concerned or the way in which it should be exercised.

the acquisition of communications data for preventing crime and safeguarding national security. While some of these judgments have resulted in the identification of a number of decisive 'shortcomings' in these contested measures,[210] the Court's scrutiny when examining Article 8(2) in this way is often less robust, invariably resulting in greater leeway granted to States regarding to what extent any contested collection or use of communications data is assessed in terms of its legality and proportionality. The difference in the judicial restraint of the ECtHR is particularly stark when compared to the level of detail and stricter scrutiny applied in its review of bulk regimes that involve the interception of content data. This less robust approach to the previously lauded safeguards of Article 8(2) is evident, as discussed later, in the famous and complex rulings of the Grand Chamber in *Centrum för Rättvisa* and *Big Brother Watch*. Another important example of where the controversial joint analysis approach was applied to the bulk retention of communications data (specifically subscription data) for preventing crime and safeguarding national security is *Breyer*, as noted earlier, which was delivered just a year before the latter.

(c) *Breyer*: an important harbinger for the deferential judgments of the Grand Chamber

(i) *Accessibility and foreseeability: a brief and split assessment* The ECtHR found no issue in *Breyer* at the Article 8(2) stage of its assessment regarding the existence of some basis in domestic law. This is a sound finding as the retention, access, and use of the data were all explicitly provided for under a legally binding statutory regime.[211] Instead, the need for a closer examination of the more detailed six foreseeability safeguards in *Breyer* was particularly acute on the basis that, in addition to police and intelligence agencies, a broad array of public authorities were permitted access to the bulk data retention system, which thereby increased the risks of arbitrariness and misuse of such access.[212] However, the Court applied a less rigorous review with respect to the 'quality of the law' requirement. Consistent with *P.G. and J.H.*, the overall legality assessment in *Breyer* is brief and simply states that the data retention regime was 'sufficiently clear and foreseeable' with respect to the amount of data stored, the duration, and the 'technical side of the storage'.[213] By applying the joint analysis approach to the Article 8(2) stage, this

[210] See *Big Brother Watch* (n 181); *Big Brother Watch* (n 5); *Ekimdzhiev and Others* (n 9).

[211] *Breyer* (n 10) [84]. The ECtHR only examined the law concerning the Telecommunications Act in force on 1 January 2008, as subsequent amendments to the relevant legislation were the subject of proceedings pending before the Federal Constitutional Court. On why the temporal scope of the court's review is an important factor, see further Chapter 2.

[212] *Breyer* (n 10) [29], [87], and [98]. Eg non-criminal offences for which access was permitted included administrative offences under the Telecommunications Act and the Unfair Competition Act. See also *Ekimdzhiev and Others* (n 9) on the use of the joint analysis approach to Art 8(2) and the broad scope of public authorities permitted access to communications data.

[213] *Breyer* (n 10) [84].

allowed the Court to refrain from specifically determining whether the contested general and indiscriminate scope of retention affecting millions of German citizens satisfied the foreseeability test. Furthermore, as is now the trend with the joint analysis approach in this area of Article 8 ECHR case law, no detailed reasoning is provided in *Breyer* for the whittling down of these settled rule of law safeguards. The ECtHR instead stated that the foreseeability issues would be considered in combination with the necessity issues on the basis that there were 'in the present case closely related to the broader issues of whether the interference was necessary in a democratic society and proportionate'.[214]

(ii) *Whittling down the 'pressing social need' test and the scale of interference* On the proportionality of the legal obligation requiring CSPs to store the subscription data of all their customers in Germany, the applicants had three main arguments. First, they questioned the effectiveness of the system as the identification of individuals at the relevant time could be easily circumvented by submitting false names or using stolen, second-hand, or foreign SIM cards. Secondly, it was posited that less intrusive measures for realizing the pursued legitimate aims were available, as other investigatory measures could have identified suspected mobile telephone users. Thirdly, the applicants were particularly critical of the indiscriminate scope of the retention, arguing that the interference was very serious and constituted 'mass pre-emptive storage of personal data' of everyone who used telecommunications. A vast majority of people who did not present any danger to public safety were affected, with no exceptions for confidential communications, such as between lawyers and their clients. The applicants also stressed that the bulk data storage increased the risk of misuse, data leaks, and identity fraud.[215] The Contracting State conceded that the regime constituted an interference with the right to private life but stressed that the storage was limited and 'effective safeguards against abuse' when retrieving said data had been put in place under relevant legislation.[216] Specifically, the regime complied with the data protection requirements established in *Marper* as the stored data was limited to what was 'absolutely necessary' for identification and the retention period was 'clearly defined' and limited to a maximum term not exceeding the term necessitated by the purpose being pursued. Moreover, a 'relatively broad' margin of appreciation applied as the German government had to balance various competing ECHR rights and

[214] ibid [85]. On the 'watering down' of the Art 8(2) legality test by the ECtHR in *Breyer*, see generally Paul De Hert and Georgios Bouchagiar, 'Adding and Removing Elements of the Proportionality and Necessity Test to Achieve Desired Outcomes. *Breyer* and the Necessity to End Anonymity of Cell Phone Users' (2021) 7 European Data Protection Law Review 304. On the origins and development of the joint analysis approach to legality and proportionality in the case law dealing with Art 8 ECHR and secret surveillance, see Chapter 2.

[215] *Breyer* (n 10) [66]–[67].

[216] Citing the Telecommunications Act, ss 112 and 113. Section 111 of the Act provided the legal basis for the imposed mandatory retention on CSPs.

obligations and there was no European consensus on the obligation to store subscriber data when acquiring pre-paid mobile phone SIM cards.[217]

The wide margin of appreciation accorded by the ECtHR in its joint analysis of Article 8(2) in *Breyer* is demonstrated in its highly deferential approach and general scrutiny of the proportionality issues. This is evident is the diluted application of the long-established 'pressing social need' requirement. The Court begins its analysis by stating that an interference will be considered necessary in a democratic society for a legitimate aim 'if it answers a "pressing social need" and if it is proportionate to the legitimate aim pursued'.[218] The mere reference to this (usually demanding) high threshold test for proportionality is surprising as most cases examining the Article 8 ECHR compatibility of a measure used for national security will apply the less strict standard of what is 'necessary' in a democratic society.[219] Indeed, explicit engagement with the higher thresholds of 'a pressing social need' or 'strictly necessary' is more often than not a reliable indicator for a robust proportionality assessment by the ECtHR (and indeed by the CJEU). This is not what occurs in *Breyer*. The Court instead reiterates what legitimate aims are being pursued by the bulk retention system as identified earlier in its Article 8(2) assessment and simply states that 'the fight against crime, and in particular against organised crime and terrorism ... constitute "pressing social needs"'.[220]

There is therefore no actual application in *Breyer* of the traditional 'pressing social need' test. Application of the latter would instead have involved the ECtHR carefully examining whether the relevant interference (in this instance, the bulk retention of subscription data) had corresponded to a social need sufficiently pressing to outweigh the right to private life.[221]

(iii) *General and indiscriminate retention of subscription data: compatible with Article 8 ECHR* Regarding the seriousness of the interference with private life, the ECtHR takes pains to explain in *Breyer* why it views the general and indiscriminate retention regime of the subscription data concerning millions of Germans, to be 'a limited data set ... of a rather limited nature'.[222] The Strasbourg Court rightly highlights that the nature of the stored data does not include any 'highly personal information', such as health data or location data from mobile telephone subscribers.[223] The Court also emphasizes that the bulk retention of subscription

[217] *Breyer* (n 10) [68]–[71].
[218] ibid [88].
[219] See further Chapter 2.
[220] *Breyer* (n 10) [88]. Note that Judge Ranzoni in his Dissenting Opinion in *Breyer* observed that the interference posed by the retention regime with the applicants' Art 8 ECHR rights did not correspond to the 'pressing social need' test and was consequently not proportionate, particularly due to the domestic legislation not being confined to measures against terrorism or other serious crimes or to issues of national security.
[221] *Sunday Times v United Kingdom* (1979) 2 EHRR 245 [67]. See further Chapter 2.
[222] *Breyer* (n 10) [95]–[103].
[223] ibid [92]. The ECtHR also states that the storage of the personal data at issue does not 'allow the creation of personality profiles'. However, this regime permits various public authorities in Germany to

data differs significantly in scope from the larger, and unquestionably more far-reaching, datasets of communications data examined by the CJEU in *Digital Rights Ireland* and *Tele2*[224]—judgments that deal with the combined retention of traffic data, location data, and subscriber data as was required by the since struck down Data Retention Directive 2006/24/EC. After making this distinction, the ECtHR determines that the 'data at issue' in *Breyer* instead bears greater resemblance to the CJEU judgment in *Ministerio Fiscal* which does not deal with access to traffic data and location data over a given period and 'does not therefore allow precise conclusions to be drawn concerning the private lives of the persons whose data is concerned'.[225] Consequently, the ECtHR concludes, drawing from the CJEU's holdings in *Ministerio Fiscal*, that the interference in *Breyer* is also 'of a rather limited nature'.[226]

At first blush, there is some logic to the above reasoning. Closer scrutiny of the facts in these relevant judgments, however, shows that equating the intrusiveness of the 'data at issue' in both cases with the overall 'interference' in *Breyer* is misleading and unpersuasive. As Judge Ranzoni rightly highlights in his dissenting opinion, the majority judgment by the ECtHR neglects to point out the 'major differences' between the level of intrusiveness at issue in *Ministerio Fiscal* with the seriousness of the interference in *Breyer*.[227] First, *Breyer* does not 'directly concern' access to the 'data at issue' which is the focus of *Ministerio Fiscal*. The scope of the interference under review in *Breyer* is in fact far broader. Indeed, it concerns the establishment of a legal regime which places mandatory obligations on all CSPs within Germany to retain and make available the subscriber data of all their customers to numerous public authorities.[228] Secondly, the facts in *Ministerio Fiscal* deal with allowing certain public authorities access to a very specific set of subscriber data (SIM cards from one telephone) used over a limited period (12 days).[229] *Breyer*, in contrast, does not relate to access to a particular set of data for a specific criminal investigation but rather the bulk retention of personal data relating to millions of people stored for a much longer period.[230] Thirdly, the scope of access to this personal data in *Breyer* is not limited to the police for the purpose of a criminal investigation. The German legal regime instead allows far broader access across a range

access this data and use it for a broad range of legitimate aims which could involve its aggregation with other datasets. In other words, the vast storage of subscription data collected in *Breyer* may be used to enable the building of profiles of various individuals or groups. See the earlier discussion of the use of such datasets by intelligence agencies for training AI-based and machine learning models and systems.

224 *Breyer* (n 10) [93].
225 ibid [94].
226 ibid [95].
227 ibid Dissenting Opinion of Judge Ranzoni [13].
228 ibid [14].
229 ibid [14].
230 ibid [14].

of purposes, including regulatory offences, and other general purposes pursued by customs investigation services and emergency services.[231]

Moreover, the majority judgment in *Breyer* makes no reference to the key findings of *Benedik* discussed earlier which links police access to subscriber data with its future use. In *Benedik*, the ECtHR held that the sole purpose of obtaining the subscriber information in this 2018 judgment was to identify a particular person behind independently collected content (an IP address) and when sought by police in these circumstances must 'be treated as *inextricably connected* to the relevant pre-existing content revealing data'.[232] The ECtHR then rightly holds in *Benedik* that not adopting this purposive approach would 'deny the necessary protection to information which might reveal a good deal about the online activity of an individual, including sensitive details of his or her interests, beliefs and intimate lifestyle'.[233] Consequently, the lack of any reference in *Breyer* to this relevant jurisprudence in *Benedik* is curious particularly as the majority judgment draws at length from the 2018 CJEU case of *Ministerio Fiscal* which, as in *Benedik*, also focuses on targeted access to subscription data.[234] The omission and lack of engagement with the Court's own case law is even more questionable given the later observation in *Breyer* that the ECtHR 'cannot consider the proportionality of the interference without closely assessing the future possible access to and *use* of the data stored'.[235] Future judgments before the ECtHR (or indeed the CJEU) dealing with the bulk retention or acquisition of subscription data would ideally engage with the findings and analysis in *Benedik*.

In addition to this perplexing analysis of the seriousness of the interference at issue in *Breyer*, the examination of the data security issues posed by the scale and duration of the retention regime is inconsistent. The ECtHR states that the applicants have not alleged that the data storage at issue was subject 'to any technical insecurities'.[236] It also finds that the data retention period of one year following the end of a customer's contract with a CSP does 'not appear inappropriate' given that investigations into criminal offences may take some time and extend beyond the end of the contractual relationship.[237] However, the Court's overall scrutiny of these factors is again questionable. First, the applicants do in fact argue in their submissions to the Court that the data storage constitutes a threat to data security due to the increased risk of misuse and data leaks and thereby the risk of identity fraud.[238] Nevertheless, the ECtHR does not examine the privacy interest at

[231] ibid [14].
[232] *Benedik* (n 23) [109].
[233] ibid [109].
[234] The striking lack of any engagement by the ECtHR in *Breyer* with the key holdings of *Benedik* is also highlighted by Judge Ranzoni in his Dissenting Opinion.
[235] *Breyer* (n 10) [97] (emphasis added).
[236] ibid [96].
[237] ibid [96].
[238] ibid [67].

stake there as part of its balancing test. Secondly, as with the retention period, the ECtHR heavily emphasizes the fact that the indiscrimination scope of the retention programme only applies to subscription data. It is, however, silent again on the bulk nature of the system and the specific risks raised by the vast scale of such retention that interferes by its very operation with the right to private life of millions of people across Germany.

Official records state that the number of datasets retrieved by public authorities from the automated system increased from 26 million in 2008 to over 34 million in 2015.[239] The German government also noted that the automated retrieval process was of 'primary importance', with manual retrievals directly from CSPs amounting to no more than 5 per cent of the number of automated retrievals at the material time.[240] Following a request from one of the several public authorities enabled to do so, the Federal Network Agency via the automated system retrieves subscriber data and telephone numbers from customer databases using search terms in order to match individual communications with the subscriber's details.[241] As noted previously, the ECtHR is right to highlight that the bulk retention system under review in *Breyer* is less intrusive than the combined bulk retention of not only subscription data but also traffic data and location data, as examined by the CJEU in *Tele2*. However, in contrast to *Tele2*, the proportionality analysis in *Breyer* is incomplete as it fails to deal with the harms posed by the general and indiscriminate retention of the personal data of millions of innocent individuals and their rights protected under Article 8 ECHR. This is therefore another clear private interest not addressed by the ECtHR in its examination of whether the respondent State 'struck a fair balance' between the competing public and private interests.[242]

(iv) ***No assessment of 'adequate and effective guarantees against abuse'*** The ECtHR has long recognized in its Article 8 ECHR cases dealing with secret surveillance and data retention that the 'possibility of improper action by a dishonest, negligent or over-zealous official can never be completely ruled out whatever the system'.[243] This has led the ECtHR (in its more robust judgments) to assess not just the Article 8 ECHR compatibility of the 'adequate safeguards' provided in the domestic law but to also scrutinise the actual operation of the system in practice.[244] However, the ECtHR does not adopt this strict scrutiny approach in *Breyer*. The ECtHR instead reduces the threshold of its proportionality assessment to the 'legal basis for information requests and the safeguards available' and draws at length from the holdings of the national court. This less strict-scrutiny approach is based on the Court's view that the seriousness of the interference to the right to private

239 ibid [23], [67].
240 ibid [13].
241 ibid [29].
242 ibid [91].
243 *Klass v Germany* [1978] ECHR 4 [59]; *Zakharov* (n 58) [270]; *Big Brother Watch* (n 181) [319].
244 See eg *Zakharov* (n 58) [285], [303]; *Ekimdzhiev and Others* (n 9) [357].

life posed by the public authorities' access to the bulk retention regime in *Breyer* is limited.[245]

Deferring to the 'double door concept' of the national court,[246] the ECtHR observes that the retained data is 'further protected against excessive or abusive information requests' because public authorities must rely on 'independent enabling legislation' in order to collect any data retrieved for them by another public authority (Federal Network Agency) or the CSP.[247] This approach certainly contributes to the well-established rule of law safeguards under Article 8(2) requiring that procedures to access personal data from bulk retention systems be accessible and clear.[248] The Strasbourg Court does not explain, however, how exactly this so-called double door has to date safeguarded against abusive requests in practice. Instead, somewhat confusingly, the Court immediately shifts its analysis to the settled Article 8(2) requirement for retention limits, stating that the necessity requirement is safeguarded 'by a general obligation' for the authorities retrieving the information to erase any data they do not need without undue delay.[249]

The ECtHR proceeds to highlight the Federal Constitutional Court's determination that the necessity threshold for public authorities retrieving datasets for prosecuting criminal or regulatory offences should involve 'at least an initial suspicion'.[250] Furthermore, the ECtHR shares the view that the obligation to submit a written request to service providers in order to retrieve customer data from the rarely used manual request system was 'likely to encourage' public authorities to obtain information only when sufficiently needed.[251] In sum, following the national court's review, the ECtHR accepts that there are 'sufficient limitations' to the power to request information and that the necessity requirement is not only inherent in the relevant legal provisions in *Breyer* but also in German and European data protection law.[252] This deferential and terse assessment, however, does not address how the operation of these safeguards in practice contribute to compliance with the necessity requirement or how they enable the detection of excessive

[245] *Breyer* (n 10) [103].
[246] ibid [14]. As the Federal Constitutional Court explains (emphasis added): 'Provisions which give authority for government authorities to deal with personal data as a rule create a number of encroachments which build on each other. In this respect, a distinction must in particular be made between the collection, storage and use of data ... the legislature must open not only the door for the transmission of data, but also the door for their retrieval. It is only both legal bases together, *which must operate together like a double door*, which give authority to exchange personal data. This does not exclude—subject to the system of competencies and the requirements of clear drafting—the possibility of both legal bases being contained in one provision.'
[247] *Breyer* (n 10) [12], [100].
[248] See further Chapter 2.
[249] *Breyer* (n 10) [100].
[250] ibid [100].
[251] ibid [101].
[252] ibid [100].

information requests.[253] Put simply, the proportionality analysis is notably vague on any assessment of the actual adequacy of the stated safeguards.

No prior independent authorization is required when a public authority in Germany seeks to retrieve subscription data from these bulk customer databases using the automated system or from the rarely used option of a direct request to a service provider. This is not problematic factor for the ECtHR. Although regarded as best practice within the context of secret surveillance, and retention regimes, it is well established under Article 8 ECHR case law that the prior supervision of secret surveillance measures (bulk or targeted) when the interference is first ordered is not a mandatory safeguard.[254] The ECtHR has instead established in a long line of case law that a system may be compatible with Article 8 ECHR provided that some independent oversight comes into play at one of three different stages: when the interference is first ordered (*ex ante*); while it is being carried out; or after it has been terminated (*ex post*).[255] As the ECtHR explains in *Breyer*, these well-established Article 8 ECHR standards traditionally require that it is essential that the supervisory procedures 'should themselves provide adequate and equivalent guarantees safeguarding the individual's rights'.[256] The ECtHR, however, then departs from these established oversight standards based on the reasoning that the previous cases on which this jurisprudence draws concerned more serious and intrusive interferences with the right to respect for private life than that at issue in *Breyer*.[257] Consequently, the Court observes that while the level of review and supervision provided in *Breyer* should be considered important, it does not amount to a 'decisive element in the proportionality assessment [given] the collection and storage of such a limited data set'.[258]

The ECtHR proceeds to explain what other types of oversight safeguards apply to this bulk retention system. This includes the existence of some ad hoc internal supervision, namely that the Federal Network Agency may review the admissibility of a data access request from another public authority if it has 'a special reason' to do so.[259] Regarding external independent oversight, the ECtHR notes that certain types of information concerning each retrieval are recorded for the purposes of general data protection supervision conducted by the Federal and provincial (*Länder*) data protection authorities (DPAs).[260] The latter being responsible for

[253] As Judge Ranzoni rightly queries in his Dissenting Opinion in *Breyer*: 'what do the safeguards actually consist of? In my view, to put it simple, they consist of general provisions for data retrieval which, according to the majority, are "protected" by a general necessity requirement, which is "safeguarded" by a further general obligation. I fail to see any real protection against possible misuse and abuse'.
[254] See further Chapter 2.
[255] *Breyer* (n 10) [102].
[256] ibid [102].
[257] ibid [103].
[258] ibid [103].
[259] ibid [104].
[260] ibid [105]. These records show: time of retrieval; data used in the process; data retrieved; information identifying the person retrieving the data; requesting authority; reference number; and information identifying the person requesting the data. Note, however, that these records do not include the

monitoring data protection compliance by all public authorities and can also be appealed to by anyone who believes their rights have been interfered with via the collection, processing, or use of their personal data.[261] The ECtHR considers the general supervision provided by these DPAs to constitute review by an independent authority as anyone can lodge an appeal. Consequently, the Court takes the view that the lack of any *ex post* notification to affected mobile phone users of access to their personal data by public authorities 'does not raise an issue under the Convention'.[262] Highlighting the margin of appreciation which Germany does not overstep in *Breyer* in choosing the means for achieving the legitimate aims of 'protecting national security and fighting crime', the bulk retention regime is held to be proportionate and therefore 'necessary in a democratic society'.[263]

There are striking gaps in the Strasbourg Court's assessment, however, regarding the weight attached to the protection provided by the double door concept and the adequacy of the disparate oversight regime to safeguard against any excessive requests or data retrievals in practice. The records held by public authorities for the review of DPAs, for instance, do not contain the reason(s) why a particular retrieval by a public authority was in fact necessary. Without logging this essential information, in addition to the ad hoc supervision of the Federal Network Agency and the general oversight of already inundated provincial DPAs, it is unclear how these bodies had the capacity to adequately detect, or indeed protect against, 'excessive or abusive information requests' by the relevant public authorities.[264]

3. *Centrum för Rättvisa* and *Big Brother Watch*: communications data and key outcomes

This section examines four key outcomes from these landmark judgments dealing with Article 8 ECHR and the acquisition of communications data within the contexts of law enforcement and national security and their significant implications for the ECHR and EU legal orders.

(a) From clear divergence to convergence: violations of Article 8 ECHR

On 25 May 2021, the ECtHR (sitting as the Grand Chamber) delivered its judgments in *Centrum för Rättvisa* and *Big Brother Watch*—rulings which will shape the approach of its future case law dealing with Article 8 ECHR and the bulk

specific reason (or necessary justification) for the public authority's acquisition of the relevant personal data of the affected individual(s).

[261] ibid [105].
[262] ibid [107].
[263] ibid [109]–[110].
[264] ibid [100].

interception, and acquisition, of communications data. The latter of which had considered some of the secret surveillance programmes used by the NSA, and other intelligence agencies, brought to light by whistle-blower Edward Snowden (such as PRISM and Upstream), revelations that have since led to major policy reforms in the US and Europe.[265] These notable judgments were also highly anticipated for three other important reasons. The first concerned the distinct divergence in the overall outcomes of the initial Chamber judgments delivered in 2018. Amongst other contested measures, both cases examined regimes of the UK and Sweden permitting the bulk interception of content and communications data and their compatibility with Article 8 ECHR. Both judgments held unequivocally that a 'wide' margin of appreciation applied to the types of bulk interception regimes these Contracting States had decided were necessary for identifying present-day threats 'posed by global terrorism and serious cross-border crime as well as the increased sophistication of communications technology'.[266] However, while the ECtHR held unanimously in *Centrum för Rättvisa* that there had been no violations of Article 8 ECHR, the Court determined shortly after that there had been violations of Article 8 ECHR in *Big Brother Watch*.

Secondly, the Grand Chamber's judgments were delivered amid an ongoing series of groundbreaking rulings by the CJEU concerning EU law. The latter line of case law also dealing with related measures of bulk data retention and mass surveillance powers adopted for the aims of countering serious crime and protecting national security.[267] Although built on the well-established jurisprudence of the ECtHR dealing with Article 8 ECHR, data retention, and secret surveillance,[268] this rapidly-evolving jurisprudence of the CJEU has established data privacy standards applicable to EU Member States and third countries that are far stricter. Thirdly, and relatedly, the applicants in *Big Brother Watch* and *Centrum för Rättvisa* had urged the ECtHR to consider adopting at least some, if not all, of the standards set out by the CJEU in its case law concerning the retention of communications data.[269] The Grand Chamber ultimately held in 2021 that there had been violations of Article 8 ECHR in both cases.[270] Yet, the Strasbourg Court in doing so essentially dismissed the applicants' arguments that current Article 8 ECHR standards need to be updated in line with the stricter case law of the CJEU, with the result

[265] On the Snowden revelations and their legacy, see Chapter 1.

[266] *Centrum för Rättvisa v Sweden* [2018] ECHR 520 [179]; *Big Brother Watch* (n 181) [314], [387].

[267] eg in 2020, the CJEU had struck down (for the second time) the European Commission's adequacy decision covering data transfers between the EU and US for its incompatibility with EU law in the landmark judgment of *Schrems II*. One key issue being the lack of actionable rights of redress under US law for EU data subjects whose personal data may have been the subject of US surveillance programmes. See further Chapter 5.

[268] See Chapters 2, 3, and 8.

[269] On the role of NGOs across Europe in initiating these landmark judgments before both courts, see Edoardo Celeste and Giulia Formici, 'Constitutionalizing Mass Surveillance in the EU' (2024) 25 German Law Journal 427, 431–32.

[270] On the judgments generally and further analysis, see Chapter 2.

that stark divergences now exist between the approach and data privacy safeguards applied by the Grand Chambers of both courts in their respective jurisprudence concerning general and indiscriminate surveillance and data retention measures.

Notwithstanding the implications of this problematic divide for the protection of European human rights law and legal certainty, the Grand Chamber rulings did converge with respect to violations of Article 8 ECHR being held in both *Centrum för Rättvisa* and *Big Brother Watch*. There was also a clear alignment on the following important and decisive Article 8 ECHR standard that both reflects the vanguard case law of the CJEU and recognizes the evolving role of communications data in State surveillance within the modern digital age.

(b) Bulk interception of communications data: not 'necessarily less intrusive' than content

Both judgments of the Grand Chamber in 2021 made clear that the Court was 'not persuaded that the acquisition of … communications data through bulk interception is necessarily less intrusive than the acquisition of content'.[271] Moreover, the Strasbourg Court thus considered that the interception, retention, and searching of communications data 'should be analysed by reference to the same safeguards as those applicable to content'.[272] It is hard to overstate the importance of this recognition by the Strasbourg Court of the much greater role communications data now plays in the leading surveillance measures of the modern digital age, especially when compared to the lack of engagement and highly deferential approach to this development in the earlier Chamber judgment in *Centrum för Rättvisa*. Here the issue of the intrusiveness to private life posed by public authorities' access and use of modern communications data when acquired in bulk was barely scrutinized. Indeed, the omission of this analysis in this judgment remains puzzling, particularly given the applicant's arguments that the scope of bulk communications data collected by the relevant Swedish public authority (FRA) is often greater than content due to the use of 'broader search terms' which may then result in more individuals being affected. In addition, Swedish law allows information obtained from this bulk interception measure to be used for purposes beyond foreign intelligence.[273]

Nevertheless, in a whittled-down assessment at the Article 8(1) stage, the Court in *Centrum för Rättvisa* did not distinguish between the bulk interception and different uses by the Swedish public authorities of content and communications data. The Court instead combined its analysis of the privacy intrusiveness of these measures with the question of the applicant's victim status. This was proceeded by a brief and vague determination that the 'mere existence' of the Swedish signals intelligence law constituted 'an interference with the exercise of the applicant's rights

[271] *Big Brother Watch* (n 5) [363]; *Centrum för Rättvisa* (n 8) [277].
[272] *Big Brother Watch* (n 5) [363]; *Centrum för Rättvisa* (n 8) [277].
[273] *Centrum för Rättvisa v Sweden* [2018] ECHR 520 [116]–[122].

under Article 8'.[274] In its analysis at the Article 8(2) stage, the Court noted that the bulk collection of communications data was 'essential' to developing Sweden's signals intelligence capacity and technology. However, other than a fleeting reference to the potential privacy harms that 'may' arise from 'the operation of a signal intelligence scheme', the Court did not deal with the specific privacy interferences that result from the bulk interception of communications data.[275] The ECtHR then took a very different approach to the issue of public authorities' access and use of communications data acquired from bulk interception in the Chamber judgment of *Big Brother Watch* delivered just months later; one that represented a clear departure from *Centrum för Rättvisa* regarding the Article 8(2) stage of the foreseeability and necessity requirements.

In *Big Brother Watch*, the Court even considered how the bulk acquisition of communications data in the modern digital age may reveal more about a person's private life than that of content data, as addressed in the detailed analysis provided by the ECtHR of one of the contested regimes—a measure which permitted the bulk interception of content and communications data which fell within the broadly defined category of 'external communications' (a communication sent or received outside the British Islands) if deemed necessary by the Secretary of State for national security interests or countering serious crime. Following the Snowden revelations, the 'counter-intuitive' scope of what constituted 'external communications' and what could in fact be captured by a section 8(4) warrant became public knowledge,[276] the breath of which involved a huge volume of online communications including emails between individuals in the UK, emails to/from overseas servers (such as California), or any Internet search hosted by an overseas server.[277] These warrants under section 8(4) of the Regulation of Investigatory Powers Act 2000 (RIPA) also did not impose any explicit limit on the number of external communications that could be intercepted. Section 8(4) warrants additionally did not have to name or describe a person as the interception subject or a single set of premises as the target of the interception. This very wide scope reflects the fact that such general and indiscriminate warrants represented general powers of 'intelligence gathering' as opposed to an investigative tool only used once a particular person for interception is identified.[278]

[274] ibid [95].

[275] ibid [122]–[179]: 'The Court is mindful of the potentially harmful effects that the operation of a signals intelligence scheme may have on the protection of privacy. Nevertheless, the Court acknowledges the importance for national security operations of a system such as the one examined in the present case.'

[276] Anderson (n 87) [6.52].

[277] ibid.

[278] As highlighted by the regime's then oversight body: Interception of Communications Commissioner, *Annual Report for 2015* (HC255, September 2016) [6.24]. This body was replaced by the Investigatory Powers Commissioner's Office (IPCO) under the Investigatory Powers Act 2016. IPCO inspects the following nine intercepting agencies annually: Security Service (MI5); Secret Intelligence Service (SIS/MI6); GCHQ; HM Revenue and Customs; Metropolitan Police Service; Ministry of Defence; National Crime Agency; Police Scotland; and Police Service of Northern Ireland.

However, the relevant safeguards set out in this section of RIPA for these significant intelligence-gathering capabilities only applied to the content of what was intercepted. Any communications data acquired under such a warrant could therefore 'be searched and selected for examination without restriction'.[279] The Contracting State submitted to the ECtHR that access to communications data was necessary to give effect to the relevant safeguards and to determine whether a person is outside the British Islands. It was further argued that as communications data 'is less intrusive than data relating to content', its interception, storage, and use should not be subject to the same six minimum requirements under the foreseeability test of Article 8 ECHR (as apply to content). The Contracting State then concluded on these grounds that the Court should apply a less strict test for the bulk acquisition of communications data and 'simply ask whether the law was sufficiently clear to give the individual adequate protection against arbitrary interference'.[280] The Strasbourg Court acknowledged that communications data is a valuable resource for the UK intelligence services as such data enabled public authorities to determine a person's location and could be 'analysed quickly to find patterns that reflect particular online behaviours associated with activities such as a terrorist attack ... making it invaluable in fast-moving operations'.[281]

The Court nevertheless held that it was 'a matter of some concern' that public authorities could search and examine this communications data apparently without restriction.[282] Dismissing the argument that 'only ever traffic data' was obtained, the Court rightly underlined that the scale of communications data collected by the contested regime represented 'a significant quantity of data'.[283] The Court then made clear that it was 'not persuaded that the acquisition of related communications data is necessarily less intrusive than the acquisition of content'.[284] Furthermore, the Court gave the example of where the content of an electronic communication is encrypted and, even if decrypted, might not reveal anything of note about the sender or recipient, whereas communications data could reveal the

[279] *Big Brother Watch* (n 181) [348]. See ss 8, 16, and 20 of RIPA. Certain parts of RIPA have since been replaced by the Investigatory Powers Act 2016. Although the Grand Chamber takes the enactment of the Act of 2016 into account, its ruling only applied to the operation of the RIPA regime at the material time before these reforms. See further Chapter 2.

[280] *Big Brother Watch* (n 181) [349]. On the foreseeability requirement of Art 8 ECHR and the 'minimum' safeguards for secret surveillance measures, see Chapter 2.

[281] *Big Brother Watch* (n 181) [353]. It is important to note that general and indiscriminate retention of communications data and bulk interception warrants are not the exclusive domain of the intelligence agencies but are frequently used by other UK public authorities. In 2022, eg, UK law enforcement agencies (LEAs) continued to have larger numbers of authorizations due to their use of communications data powers; 332,442 interceptions warrants and authorizations were issued with 310,592 issued to LEAs. See IPCO, *Annual Report 2022* (IPCO 2024) 100–01.

[282] *Big Brother Watch* (n 181) [355].

[283] Indeed, the Court set out the scale of this scope as defined in the Code of Practice which covered what would traditionally be described as not just 'traffic data' but also location data, dynamic IP addresses, and basic web browsing. See ibid [355].

[284] ibid [356].

identities and location of the relevant parties and equipment by which the communication was made.[285] Closely mirroring the data retention case law of the CJEU, the ECtHR proceeded to highlight that when collected in bulk the degree of intrusion is then magnified, explaining that the emerging 'patterns could be capable of painting an intimate picture of a person through the mapping of social networks, location tracking, Internet browsing tracking, mapping of communication patterns, and insight into who a person interacted with'.[286] The Court therefore held that the public authorities had not struck a fair balance between the competing public and private interests by exempting the bulk acquisition of communications data entirely from the safeguards applicable to the searching and examining of content.[287]

When the matter came before the Grand Chamber, the UK challenged this assessment alongside three other intervening governments in *Big Brother Watch*. All contested the argument that accessing communications data could reveal as much about a person's private life as that of content.[288] The Grand Chamber nevertheless embraced the more robust standard of the Chamber judgment. Moreover, this recognition of the increased level of intrusiveness to private life posed by public authorities' access and use of bulk communications data is set out in both *Big Brother Watch* and *Centrum för Rättvisa*.[289] Commentators welcomed the emphasis placed by the Grand Chamber on the role now played by communications data in monitoring the lives and communications of individuals in the twenty-first century. As Woods rightly observes, recognition by the ECtHR of changes in State surveillance facilitated by technological change 'is an important prerequisite for ensuring effective protection of individuals' rights'.[290] The ECtHR has since built on this standard regarding the intrusiveness of bulk communications data in its 2022 judgment of *Ekimdzhiev and Others*. Here the Court omitted the Grand Chamber's more cautious framing of this Article 8 ECHR standard being 'necessarily' the case. Establishing instead in *Ekimdzhiev and Others* that

[285] ibid [356].
[286] ibid [356].
[287] ibid [357].
[288] See these arguments made by the governments of the UK, France, the Netherlands, and Norway, in *Big Brother Watch* (n 5) [295], [302]–[310]. Note the related argument also raised by the government of Norway that the Strasbourg Court should 'refrain from importing concepts and criteria from the CJEU'.
[289] As the Grand Chamber states in *Big Brother Watch* (n 5) [341]–[342]; *Centrum för Rättvisa* (n 8) [255]–[256]: 'Lives are increasingly lived online, generating both a significantly larger volume of electronic communications, and communications of a significantly different nature and quality, to those likely to have been generated a decade ago ... This is equally so with related communications data ... since every piece of content is surrounded by multiple pieces of communications data.'
[290] See Lorna Woods, 'Big Brother Watch v UK' *EU Law Analysis* (17 June 2021), <https://eulawanalysis.blogspot.com/2021/06/big-brother-watch-v-uk-ecthr-grand.html>. On the other hand, commentators also criticized the lack of clarity surrounding the highly flexible 'global assessment' criteria established by the Grand Chamber for determining the Art 8 ECHR compatibility of any bulk interception regimes (including communications data) and its clear departure from the 'minimum safeguards' of the CJEU. See further Chapter 2.

the acquisition of communications data when captured in bulk on a general and indiscriminate basis can be '*just as intrusive* as the bulk acquisition of the content of communications'.[291]

(c) Of 'a different character'? Content still treated as more intrusive than communications data

Unfortunately, the wings of the above jurisprudential breakthrough to strengthen the protection afforded by Article 8 ECHR to when public authorities access communications data collected from bulk interception programmes were promptly clipped in *Big Brother Watch*, the fall of which concerned the 'cardinal issue' for any Article 8 ECHR assessment by the ECtHR. This is whether a contested surveillance measure meets the conditions of Article 8(2) and can thus be deemed to constitute a justified interference with the right to private life. On the one hand, the Grand Chamber held that the 'interception, retention and searching of communications data should be analysed by reference to *the same safeguards* as those applicable to content'.[292] This groundbreaking standard for the ECHR legal order was then limited when the Court determined that as long as the same safeguards apply, the legal provisions governing the treatment of communications data 'may not necessarily have to be identical in every respect' as those applied to content.[293] The Court briefly stated that this less strict approach to communications data is based on two factors. One being 'the different character' of communications data and the other being 'the different ways' intelligence services use this information.[294] In other words, the Court held that the legal limits in the domestic laws of Contracting States to the ECHR allowing public authorities' access and use of content from bulk interception need not be as strict when it comes to their (often much greater) use of communications data.

The Grand Chamber began its assessment of the public authorities' access and use of communications data in the UK under the relevant surveillance programme (s 8(4) of RIPA) by first referencing its earlier analysis of the accessed content. In doing so, the Court stressed that both were treated identically in 'most respects' and the deficiencies concerning content applied equally to communications data.[295] Three 'fundamental deficiencies' were the absence of independent authorization, failure to include the categories of 'selectors' in the warrant application to the Secretary of State,[296] and failure to make selectors linked to an individual

291 *Ekimdzhiev and Others* (n 9) [394] (emphasis added).
292 *Big Brother Watch* (n 5) [363]; *Centrum för Rättvisa* (n 8) [277] (emphasis added).
293 *Big Brother Watch* (n 5) [364]; *Centrum för Rättvisa* (n 8) [278].
294 *Big Brother Watch* (n 5) [364]; *Centrum för Rättvisa* (n 8) [278].
295 *Big Brother Watch* (n 5) [416].
296 Selectors are akin to search criteria. When combined with novel and powerful methods of automated data analysis (eg machine learning algorithms) they allow public authorities to sift through vast amounts of content and communications data collected in these huge bulk datasets. These may involve different types of selectors, including format-related selectors (eg telephone numbers or emails) and/or

subject to prior internal authorization.[297] The Court then acknowledged that there were 'two principal ways' by which acquired content and communications data were in fact treated differently. The first concerned intelligence analysts not being required to have the necessity and proportionality of using a selector to search through bulk communications data approved by the Secretary of State for a person known to be in the British Islands. Secondly, any results from examined content which did not match a strong selector or complex query were destroyed immediately. Any communications data, on the other hand, not matching this test met a different fate. This information was not deleted immediately but was instead stored for up to 'several months'.[298]

Rather than examine the Article 8(2) implications of this less strict approach to communications data, the Grand Chamber takes pains to dwell on the argument before it that some alternative non-legislative safeguards applied to this intelligence gathering.[299] These were provided under the Interception of Communications Code of Practice which set out statutory guidance to public authorities wishing to examine communications data. The Code stated that public authorities in the UK were required to complete a written record explaining why the communications data was necessary and proportionate. These records later formed part of an overall *ex post* audit by the then independent oversight body.[300] The Contracting State further argued that it would not have been feasible to have required analysts to certify the necessity of searching communications data with the Secretary of State in advance of doing so (as done for content). The key reason for this? Analysts used this intelligence-gathering programme to search these vast volumes of data captured from transmitted communications around the world via fibre-optic cables and satellites primarily for their communications data. Indeed, at a rate 'significantly higher' than the queries made against content, 'possibly many thousands in any given week'.[301] Applying the same authorization requirement for communications data would therefore have delayed these searches as they had 'a temporal quality' and 'would seriously risk undermining their use in intelligence terms'.[302] The Court does not question the highly pragmatic reasoning regarding why this

content-related selectors ('holy war'). More specific inferences, patterns, and profiles about individuals or groups may then be identified. See further Chapter 2.

[297] *Big Brother Watch* (n 5) [416], [425]. The more robust language of 'fundamental deficiencies' here departs from the Court's more traditional hierarchy of 'shortcomings' (procedural or substantive) in this area of Art 8 ECHR case law. Eg the Grand Chamber identified only shortcomings with respect to the incompatibility with Art 8 ECHR of the regime in *Centrum för Rättvisa* (n 8) [373]. See further Chapter 2.

[298] *Big Brother Watch* (n 5) [419].

[299] The Court noted that s 16(2) of RIPA was the 'principal statutory safeguard' for limiting the process of selecting intercepted material for examination by analysts.

[300] *Big Brother Watch* (n 5) [420].

[301] ibid [420].

[302] ibid [420].

safeguard was not applied. Thus, despite its frequent use by the intelligence agencies, the Court taking a holistic approach held that the lack of external authorization for the search terms applied to bulk communications data should not 'carry decisive weight in the overall assessment'.[303]

The Grand Chamber also took no issue with the public authorities not applying the other key safeguard to the analysed communications data, namely that any results which did not match a strong selector or complex query were not destroyed immediately; it notwithstanding that this was a principal safeguard for any examined content by analysts under the section 8(4) intelligence-gathering programme which did not meet this threshold. The crux of the Contracting State's argument was that more analysis of communications data was necessary to discover 'unknown unknowns' and 'that discovery could involve ... [forming] a "jigsaw" revealing a threat, and would include the possible examination of items that initially appeared to be of no intelligence interest'.[304] Put another way, the Court accepted the argument that results from any examined communications data from this intelligence gathering should be stored based on its future potential value. The Court was critical of one element specific to the use of communications data under section 8(4) of RIPA. This concerned the transparency surrounding the retention period of any examined communications data, the scope of which had only been disclosed before the Court and had not been previously set out in any legislation or publicly accessible policy. The Court stated that in order to meet the 'foreseeability' requirement of Article 8 ECHR, these retention periods 'should be included in appropriate legislative and/or other general measures'.[305] Nevertheless, the Court held that the storage provisions 'were sufficiently robust' based on the arguments being 'objectively and reasonably justified' and the storage reportedly not going beyond 'several months' in practice.[306]

There are three striking omissions in the Grand Chamber's notably deferential analysis. First, rather than scrutinizing the reasons why the same safeguards for content were not applied to communications data, the Court was at pains to insist that alternative safeguards were applied. In line with its highly holistic 'global assessment' approach,[307] the Court gave the example of the Interception of Communications Code of Practice. The Code provided that intelligence analysts were required to complete a written record explaining why examining the communications data was necessary and proportionate and such records later formed part of an *ex post* audit by the then independent oversight body. However, the Court

[303] ibid [421].
[304] ibid [422].
[305] ibid [423]. On the conflation, and reduced levels of scrutiny, of the rule of law tests of accessibility and foreseeability in recent case law dealing with Art 8 ECHR and State surveillance resulting from the 'joint analysis' approach to Art 8(2), see further Chapter 2.
[306] *Big Brother Watch* (n 5) [423].
[307] On the controversial 'global assessment' test concerning the foreseeability and necessity requirements under Art 8(2) and its important implications for this area of Art 8 case law, see Chapter 2.

does not mention in its Article 8(2) analysis that the relevant Code was only published in 2016. It is also not explained that as a result these alternative safeguards arrived many years after RIPA became law in 2000 and long after public authorities had access to these bulk warrant powers. This means that the safeguards did not exist for over than a decade. Moreover, they were only publicly accessible after legal challenges to the surveillance powers had been brought to the ECtHR following the Snowden revelations.[308] Secondly, the Court is silent on how exactly the 'different character' of communications data influenced its assessment, despite this being one of the two factors justifying the Court's view why there may be fewer legal safeguards applicable to public authorities' use of communications data collected from regimes which allow for the general and indiscriminate interception of online communications.[309]

Thirdly, the Grand Chamber does not address how the security-driven approach to discover 'unknown unknowns' with respect to retaining all examined communications data under this intelligence-gathering regime was justified and 'necessary in a democratic society'. This is a notable omission when the lack of results from content warranted the contrasting strict approach of immediate destruction if no matches linked to a strong selector or complex query were found. The application of a clear policy approach during this period can be discerned here, namely that the relevant public authorities in the UK simply viewed and treated the access and use of communications data as being less privacy-intrusive. Thus, they applied less strict safeguards to the use of communications data than were applied to content. Indeed, as noted earlier, the UK, and other governments, all made this exact argument in their submissions to the Grand Chamber in *Big Brother Watch*. There was therefore an opportunity for the Court to make two determinations in its Article 8(2) analysis as part of its role for minimum standard-setting as a guardian of European human rights law. One being that these two principal safeguards were absent due to this now anachronistic standard that access to communications data is inherently less privacy-intrusive than accessing content. Secondly, such an approach is not compatible with Article 8 ECHR based on the earlier reasoning of the Court regarding how access to communications data may now reveal just as much about a person's private life as access to content and the findings that public authorities' use of communications data is extensive and is relied on more than content.

These findings and analysis in *Big Brother Watch* have important implications. Both judgments clearly establish that public authorities in the UK view their access

[308] *Big Brother Watch* (n 5) [95]. In contrast to the silence of the Grand Chamber majority judgment on this point, Judge Pinto de Albuquerque makes clear in his Partly Concurring and Partly Dissenting Opinion that UK domestic law on various mass surveillance powers was not in any way publicly accessible before the UK made disclosures to the Strasbourg Court in 2014 (see fn 152).

[309] The so-called 'different character' of communications data is also referenced but not explained in *Centrum för Rättvisa* (n 8).

and analysis of communications data as highly valuable to their operations to safeguard the public and relied on its use frequently. Indeed, since the Snowden revelations, the intelligence agencies have consistently asserted that access to communications data is 'integral' to their daily operations.[310] However, the safeguards for accessing this information when captured in huge volumes came long after. The finding that the bulk interception of communications data under this intelligence-gathering programme was exempt from key safeguards under section 16 of RIPA resulted in a situation whereby intelligence analysts could search and select from a vast quantity of individuals' communications without restriction. Moreover, domestic legislation during the relevant time (2000–16) did not require intelligence agencies to justify the necessity of their use of communications data, as they did for content, under this intelligence-gathering programme. In addition, the use, storage, and deletion of this retrieved communications data was subject to fewer safeguards. These represent significant gaps in the legality and proportionality standards of Article 8 ECHR.

Finally, one finding cuts across all the above. The Grand Chamber held that the legal limits in the domestic laws of Contracting States allowing public authorities' access and use of communications data from bulk interception need not be as strict as the rules for content.[311] The Court arrived at this determination despite findings in both *Big Brother Watch* and *Centrum för Rättvisa* that public authorities' use of communications data from bulk interception was far greater and the number of people affected was thus likely to be larger.[312] Furthermore, the Court's highly holistic assessment in *Big Brother Watch* concluded that the missing safeguards and oversight for acquired communications data under the above intelligence-gathering regime was not decisive—an approach that is clearly inconsistent with the principle that public authorities' access to content and modern communications data, when collected on a general and indiscriminate basis, should be treated in a manner that reflects its capacity to intrude upon a person's privacy. In contrast, this shows a Court still heavily influenced by the view that public authorities' access to content is always more privacy-intrusive than accessing communications

[310] As stated, eg, by the MI5 Director General: 'comms data is very often one of the early means we can use to determine whether and where to focus our investigation'. See Intelligence and Security Committee, *Privacy and Security: A modern and transparent legal framework* (UK Parliament Report 2015) 47–48.

[311] It is notable that the Court held the same lower standard with respect to communications data acquired from bulk signals intelligence programmes under Swedish law in *Centrum för Rättvisa* (n 8) [278]: 'In view of the different character of related communications data and the different ways in which they are used … the legal provisions governing their treatment may not necessarily have to be identical in every respect to those governing the treatment of content.'

[312] In *Centrum för Rättvisa*, the Grand Chamber jointly examined the bulk interception of communications content and communications data. The Parliamentary Committee overseeing the use of signals intelligence in Sweden that search terms used for the interception of communications data were 'less specific' than those used for content, noting that public authorities could thus be storing the communications data of 'a larger number of individuals'.

data irrespective of type (traffic data, location data, subscriber data) or scale (targeted or bulk).

(d) Bulk interception of communications data and bulk retention of subscription data: proportionate and compatible with Article 8 ECHR

The Strasbourg Court has to date carefully avoided ruling directly on the data retention standards that have led to a constitutional crisis between the CJEU and EU Member States. Specifically, whether imposing mandatory obligations on CSPs to retain traffic and location data on a general and indiscriminate basis for countering serious crime, or national security interests, is disproportionate and thus incompatible with the right to private life.[313] The Grand Chamber judgments in 2021 did not weigh in on the matter. There were, however, understandable reasons for not doing so. In *Centrum för Rättvisa*, these mandatory obligations involving the private sector in Sweden did not fall within the scope of the contested signals intelligence legal framework before the Strasbourg Court.[314] In *Big Brother Watch*, the issue of public authorities accessing this retained data from the bulk retention regime in the UK had already been examined in the Chamber judgment and held to be in violation of Article 8 ECHR due to its incompatibility with EU law. None of the parties therefore raised the matter before the Grand Chamber.[315] Although not directly relevant, it is worth noting that the Grand Chamber in *Big Brother Watch* took no issue with the bulk interception of communications data by public authorities being permitted for a wide range of legitimate aims. These included protecting national security, preventing disorder and crime, and protecting the rights and freedoms of others.[316] This entrenchment of the traditionally wide margin of appreciation granted by the ECtHR to States in any matters concerning national security and surveillance was a 'huge disappointment' to the NGOs who had urged the Court to update its Article 8 ECHR case law and follow the stricter standards of the CJEU.[317]

The ECtHR has had other opportunities to consider the compatibility with Article 8 ECHR of States imposing mandatory obligations on CSPs to retain their

[313] On the case law of the CJEU dealing with data retention, State surveillance, and the complex standards and limited exceptions therein, see Chapters 5 and 9.

[314] This Swedish data retention law was the subject of a preliminary reference before the CJEU in *Tele2 Sverige and Watson*. See further Chapter 5.

[315] On the role of EU law in the ECtHR case law dealing with Art 8 ECHR and data retention, see Chapter 4.

[316] *Big Brother Watch* (n 5) [365]. Article 8(2) provides: 'There shall be no interference by a public authority with the exercise of this right [to private life] except ... in the interests of national security, public safety or the economic well-being of the country, for the prevention of disorder or crime, for the protection of health or morals, or for the protection of the rights and freedoms of others.'

[317] See eg Article 19, 'UK: European Court decision in *Big Brother Watch* case does not go far enough to protect free expression and privacy' *Article 19* (25 May 2021). The applicants in *Big Brother Watch* contended that bulk interception was in principle neither necessary nor proportionate within the meaning of Art 8 ECHR. See further Chapter 2.

customers' communications data on a general and indiscriminate basis. In the 2015 judgment of *Zakharov*, as noted previously, the Court (sitting as the Grand Chamber) provided an overall assessment of the far-reaching secret surveillance regime of mobile phone interception in Russia. The Court did not, however, avail itself of the chance to examine the retention measures concerning communications data, or the real-time interception of location data, regarding their compatibility with Article 8 ECHR. This omission is somewhat surprising as *Zakharov* was delivered after the CJEU's first groundbreaking data-retention ruling, which was referenced (at length) in *Zakharov*.[318] In 2020, *Breyer* was silent in its assessment on the proportionality of imposing mandatory obligations for the bulk retention of traffic and location data. However, as discussed earlier, the Court did deliver a highly deferential ruling where it held that the German law imposing a mandatory obligation on CSPs to retain their customers' subscription data on a general and indiscriminate basis for countering crime, and other aims, was compatible with Article 8 ECHR.

To date, the most significant judgment where the Strasbourg Court came close to dealing with this thorny issue was in its 2022 judgment of *Ekimdzhiev and Others*. Here the Court held that the legal regimes in Bulgaria permitting secret surveillance and imposing a mandatory obligation on CSPs to retain traffic and location data for national security purposes, countering serious crime, and other aims were both in violation of Article 8 ECHR.[319] The laws governing the retention of communications data by CSPs, and its access by the authorities, were found to have 'significantly improved' following the Bulgarian Constitutional Court's examination of same in 2015 after the CJEU's judgment in *Digital Rights Ireland*. However, the ECtHR held that the law when applied in practice fell short of the 'minimum safeguards against arbitrariness and abuse'.[320] Thus, the Court held that there had been a breach of Article 8 ECHR on the basis that the domestic laws did not fully meet the quality of law requirement. The law was therefore 'incapable' of keeping the interference entailed by the system of retention and accessing of communications data in Bulgaria to what is necessary in a democratic society.[321]

Following the Grand Chamber rulings in *Zakharov*, *Big Brother Watch*, and *Centrum för Rättvisa*, the Court applied a joint assessment of the legality and proportionality requirements under Article 8(2) in its holistic examination of the communications data retention regime, the focus of which was not the retention of the communications data (and its scope) but rather the accessibility and effectiveness of certain safeguards underpinning public authorities' access.

[318] On the significance of *Digital Rights Ireland*, see Chapters 5 and 8.
[319] *Ekimdzhiev and Others* (n 9) [435].
[320] ibid [419], [435].
[321] ibid [420]–[421]. On the conflation of the legality and proportionality requirements of Art 8(2) in the secret surveillance case law of the ECtHR, and criticism thereof, see further Chapter 2.

Consequently, in a striking omission, the Court sidestepped examining the compatibility of the general and indiscriminate scope of the data's retention with the foreseeability and necessity requirements of Article 8 ECHR, despite the Bulgarian government raising this very question in its arguments to the ECtHR and the applicants' complaint that 'the retained data enabled the profiling of all persons in the country'.[322] Indeed, the Contracting State very pointedly defended the scope of its retention law within the context of the proportionality requirements under Article 8(2). In so doing, it highlighted the deep divisions on the matter between the CJEU and EU Member States by stressing to the ECtHR that 'there was no European consensus about the need to retain communications data or its modalities'.[323]

There are several reasons why the Strasbourg Court may not want to address this constitutional crisis. One understandable ground, as Gerards rightly notes, is that only twenty-seven of the forty-six States to the ECHR are bound by EU law. The matter is thus far from 'common ground' for all its members.[324] Sidestepping the data retention issue, on the other hand, through increasingly holistic assessments and not identifying what minimum safeguards should be met by States to be compatible with Article 8 ECHR also has grave implications. One is the risk that in allowing diverging case law, such conflicting obligations arise for States that the protection of the right to private life is undermined due to legal uncertainty and non-implementation of essential safeguards and oversight by public authorities.[325] Another is the Court's (increasing) departure from its formerly lauded standard-setting role as a guardian of the right to privacy across Europe in its case law dealing with secret surveillance and data retention.[326] Time will tell if the Article 8 ECHR case law of the Strasbourg Court will take a clear stance on what Vadja describes as the 'position of high principle' established by the CJEU in its stricter case law,[327] that there can be no general and indiscriminate retention of data for countering crime and safeguarding national security.[328]

[322] *Ekimdzhiev and Others* (n 9) [364].

[323] ibid [390].

[324] Janneke Gerards, *General Principles of the European Convention on Human Rights* (CUP 2019) 102. See further Chapter 4.

[325] ibid.

[326] On the influence of this case law in the EU, eg the evaluation of the Data Retention Directive by the European Commission, the CJEU ruling in *Digital Rights Ireland*, and beyond Europe, see Chapters 1 and 8.

[327] Christopher Vajda, 'Data Protection: Made in Europe and Exported Globally' (UKAEL Annual Lecture, 19 January 2023), <https://monckton.com/wp-content/uploads/2023/03/UKAEL-Lecture-Data-Protection-Made-in-Europe-and-Exported-Globally-final.pdf> (former judge of the CJEU between 2012 and 2020). On the case law of the CJEU and its exceptions to this principle, see Chapter 5.

[328] At the time of writing, a judgment concerning this very question was forthcoming in 2024. See the Chamber Hearing of *Pietrzak and Bychawska-Siniarska v Poland* (App Nos 72038/17 and 25237/18) 27 September 2022.

D. Conclusions

Public authorities tasked with protecting national security, and public safety more broadly, view measures permitting the bulk retention and analysis of communications data as invaluable to their daily operations. They are also in a technological arms race against criminals and terrorists. As the European Data Protection Supervisor (EDPS) has recognized in recent investigations, 'the context of criminal investigations and criminal intelligence operations is not limited anymore to targeted data collection but also increasingly includes the collection of large datasets'.[329] In line with the expanding role of the private sector within national security and policing,[330] the number of cases before the Strasbourg Court involving State-imposed obligations mandating the general and indiscriminate retention of communications data by CSPs is on the rise.[331] Consequently, we now have the following security and legal landscape. The combined uses of vast datasets of communications data and others (census data, travel records, city crime data) with AI-based automated decision-making for profiling and pattern analysis techniques are now the backbone of an increasingly data-driven approach to policing and national security at the EU and national levels. However, any new surveillance system used by public authorities in Europe, including the shift in focus towards capturing and inferring data in order to identify, monitor, and profile individuals and groups from vast collections of communications data, must be shown to be lawful, proportionate, and compatible with the right to private life.

It is welcome, therefore, from a human rights-based perspective that the previous analysis shows the ECtHR is keeping (better) pace with the widespread use of these highly sophisticated surveillance tools that are open to the risks of abuse, misuse, and overreach into individuals' private lives. The Court has shown itself in key judgments to be less hesitant in recognizing the intrusiveness of public authorities' acquisition and use of communications data. For instance, after stressing that communications interception represents one of the gravest intrusions into an individual's private life, the Chamber and Grand Chamber in *Big Brother Watch* proceeded to highlight that they were not persuaded that the acquisition of communications data through bulk interception is necessarily less intrusive than that of content. Indeed, the Court went further in its 2022 judgment of *Ekimdzhiev and Others*. Here the Court held that the acquisition of communications data through bulk interception can be 'just as intrusive' as the bulk acquisition of content.[332]

[329] Letter from EDPS Director to Europol Executive Director, 'EDPS Decision on the own initiative inquiry on Europol's Big Data Challenge', Brussels, 18 September 2020, 4. On related actions concerning the EDPS and Europol, see Case T-578/22 *EDPS v European Parliament and Council of the EU* (ECLI:EU:T:2023:522) order of the general court of 6 September 2023, and the pending appeal to the CJEU (Case C-698/23 P).

[330] See further Chapter 1.

[331] See earlier, eg, *Zakharov* (n 58), *Breyer* (n 10), *Ekimdzhiev and Others* (n 9).

[332] *Ekimdzhiev and Others* (n 9) [394].

The Court also indicated in *Ekimdzhiev and Others* that the storage of any communications data, from any type of communications, amounts to an interference with not just the right to respect for private life but also the right to respect for correspondence.

On the other hand, this chapter shows how recent developments in the overall approach of the Strasbourg Court raise several concerns. First, the Court has subjected far-reaching retention obligations on the private sector, and the bulk interception of communications data, to questionable levels of scrutiny when examining the cardinal issue of any contested measure's compatibility with the Article 8(2) requirements of Article 8 ECHR. The Court, despite asserting otherwise, is still heavily influenced by the argument that public authorities' access to content data is always more privacy-intrusive than accessing communications data, irrespective of any evidence-based factors, including the type or quantities of communications data in question, its reuse for different purposes, or its subsequent processing and aggregation with other vast datasets. This is a highly problematic stance when the reality today is that access to large volumes of communications data will often render access to content data obsolete. Access to the content of a person's telephone calls from one day, for instance, will in almost all circumstances reveal far less about a person's private life as opposed to accessing both the location data and traffic data from their mobile phone use over a week, month, or year. The latter will most certainly reveal precise details about a person's private life, thereby making it possible to discern highly sensitive information, including their most frequent communications and movements, closest relationships, and even their health, religious beliefs, and politics.

In addition, the Court continues to focus disproportionately on the private life implications posed by the subsequent access by public authorities to these vast databases of communications data for the broad aims of protecting national security and preventing crime, with far less scrutiny being applied to the issues of legality and proportionality that specifically arise from other stages in this surveillance life cycle. These far less scrutinized areas include the acquisition and retention of vast volumes of personal data from the private sector, their processing by various public authorities and private sector bodies, and their sharing between governments via cross-border transfers.[333] Going forward, the assessment of Article 8 ECHR, and the safeguards enshrined therein, must adapt and evolve to respond to this fundamental change in communications monitoring and the level of privacy-intrusiveness that comes with retaining and accessing communications data in the modern digital age. Another future challenge to be addressed by the Court is its decision to steer clear from engaging directly with the data retention

[333] As noted previously, this gap persists despite being raised in the arguments of applicants before the Court (see eg *Breyer, Big Brother Watch, Ekimdzhiev and Others*) and in Dissenting Opinions that depart from the majority judgments of the Grand Chamber (*Big Brother Watch*).

constitutional crisis between the CJEU and EU Member States. This has grave implications, notably the risk of diverging case law leading to conflicting obligations for States and the undermining of the protection of citizens' right to private life due to legal uncertainty and the failure to implement essential safeguards and oversight by public authorities. Additionally, this omission is undermining the Strasbourg Court's formerly applauded standard-setting role as a guardian of the right to private life across Europe in its case law dealing with secret surveillance and data retention.[334]

Such shortcomings invariably put the protection afforded by the right to private life in this area of Article 8 ECHR case law at risk of becoming more illusory than real. In the glaring light of the rapidly evolving standards being established by the CJEU, rulings that still embrace the fallacy of content always revealing more than communications data about a person's private life cast doubt on whether the ECtHR is applying the same levels of scrutiny to the same societal developments that are shaping how government surveillance now operates. The final pressing issue for the Court to address is consequently whether current standards applicable to the retention and acquisition of communications data for public safety within the ECHR legal order reflect the social and technological realities of the twenty-first century.

[334] See eg criticism of this decline by Mitsilegas and others: '[I]t is hoped that the seemingly more lenient approach of the ECtHR will not lead to further downgrading of the standards of protection as elaborated by the CJEU': Valsamis Mitsilegas and others, 'Data Retention and the Future of Large-Scale Surveillance' (2023) 29 European Law Journal 176, 211. See further Chapter 2.

4

The Evolving Dialogue between Luxembourg and Strasbourg

A. Introduction

The enactment and review of data retention law and policymaking within Europe has always taken place in the shadow of two linked but also diverging bodies of jurisprudence: the right to private life, as interpreted and applied by ECtHR and the CJEU.[1] These systems are set to become more intertwined once the ECHR becomes formally binding on the EU following its accession to this international human rights treaty.[2] After the Lisbon Treaty entered into force in 2009,[3] the EU-ECHR accession should have resulted in EU acts being subject to the direct scrutiny of the ECtHR and to the EU being formally subject to the same system of international human rights oversight as its Member States. However, much to the 'disappointment' of the Strasbourg Court,[4] the CJEU held (as it had previously) that the draft agreement providing for EU accession to the ECHR was incompatible with EU law. This second ruling in 2014 'threw a very significant spanner in the works' regarding the integration of the EU into the ECHR system.[5] Indeed, at the time of writing, process towards this significant reform is still beyond reach as negotiations between the EU and Council of Europe remain ongoing.[6]

[1] The CJEU before 2009 was known as the European Court of Justice (ECJ). The ECJ was renamed the 'Court of Justice of the EU' under the Lisbon Treaty. Under Art 19(1) of the Treaty on European Union (TEU), the CJEU is the collective term for the three separate courts of the EU—the upper tier of the Court of Justice and lower tier of the General Court (formerly the Court of First Instance) and the Civil Service Tribunal. For consistency, this book refers to the Luxembourg Court throughout as the 'CJEU' and the 'EC' as the 'EU'. All URLs for this chapter were last accessed on 22 April 2024.

[2] Consolidated version of the Treaty on the Functioning of the European Union (TFEU/Lisbon Treaty) [2010] OJ C83/47, Art 6(2) (Art 6 TEU). The TFEU, also known as the 'Reform Treaty', was the response of the EU institutions to the unsuccessful passing of the proposed Constitutional Treaty. The TFEU came into force from 1 December 2009.

[3] Article 6(2) TEU: 'The European Union shall accede to the European Convention for the Protection of Human Rights and Fundamental Freedoms.'

[4] President Dean Spielmann, *2014 Annual Report of European Court of Human Rights* (ECtHR Registry 2015) 6.

[5] Gráinne de Búrca, 'The Evolution of EU Human Rights Law' in Paul Craig and Gráinne de Búrca, *The Evolution of EU Law* (3rd edn, OUP 2021) 496; Opinion 2/94, *Accession to the ECHR*, 28 March 1996 (ECLI:EU:C:1996:140). Accession negotiations began in 2010. After Opinion 2/13, *Accession to the ECHR*, 18 December 2014 (ECLI:EU:C:2014:2454), negotiations were postponed and resumed in June 2020. EU Member States are all Contracting Parties to the ECHR.

[6] In 2024, the Belgian Presidency of the Council of the EU (January–June 2024) stated in its programme of policy priorities for the EU that it would 'closely follow up' on the EU-ECHR accession, <https://belgian-presidency.consilium.europa.eu/media/3kajw1io/programme_en.pdf>.

EU Data Privacy Law and Serious Crime. Nora Ni Loideain, Oxford University Press. © Nora Ni Loideain 2025.
DOI: 10.1093/oso/9780198837169.003.0004

Notwithstanding this long and winding road to accession, it is noteworthy that it forms just one part of an overall robust commitment made by the EU under the Lisbon Treaty to prioritize fundamental rights. Moreover, it is hard to overstate how much the EU legal order has departed from the almost non-existent legal status accorded to human rights at the beginning of what was the EU in the 1950s. This chapter explains the complex and dynamic dialogue between the ECHR and EU systems before and after the seismic reforms for EU human rights law took place following the entry into force of the Lisbon Treaty. The analysis addresses the controversial blocking of the EU-ECHR accession by the CJEU and the significant implications for the role of Article 8 ECHR within EU law posed by the elevation in legal status of the EU Charter. The discussion also explores how the post-Lisbon dialogue between both Courts has evolved within the context of their case law dealing with the right to private life, data retention, and surveillance.

Two groundbreaking developments have arisen from this complicated interplay between the Courts and their distinctly diverging lines of jurisprudence on State surveillance and data retention. These changes have also fundamentally reshaped the status of both supranational Courts as guardians of the right to private life in the modern digital age. The first is the departure of the Strasbourg Court from its previously lauded role as an important driving force in the scrutiny of laws permitting the secret surveillance of communications in Europe. This has enabled the second major development, namely the rise of the CJEU as the vanguard legal institution for both data retention policymaking and supranational judicial scrutiny in Europe.[7] Despite the clear divergences and tensions underpinning the long road to the EU-ECHR accession, there are several areas where the data retention and surveillance jurisprudence of the Luxembourg and Strasbourg Courts continue to converge. Indeed, the same challenges that lie at the heart of the complex EU-ECHR accession process, such as the autonomy of the EU legal order, have also played a key role in the dialogue between the CJEU and the ECtHR in their respective case law on data retention.

This is to be expected given the constitutional links between the right to private life enshrined in Articles 7 and 52(3) of the Charter and the benchmark standards set by the rich jurisprudence of the ECtHR concerning its corresponding right in Article 8 ECHR (much of which long predates the Charter).[8] Consequently, notwithstanding the divergences in the levels of scrutiny applied in their approaches

[7] On this rapidly evolving area of CJEU case law, see Chapters 5 and 9.

[8] Charter of Fundamental Rights of the European Union [2016] OJ C202/389, Art 52(3) CFR mirrors Art 53 ECHR which states that Contracting States to the ECHR may provide additional protection to the minimum human rights standards set by the ECtHR. Article 52(3): 'In so far as this Charter contains rights which correspond to rights guaranteed by the Convention for the Protection of Human Rights and Fundamental Freedoms, the meaning and scope of those rights shall be the same as those laid down by the said Convention. This provision shall not prevent Union law providing more extensive protection.'

and standards, both Courts continue to influence the case law of the other within the ongoing saga of data retention policymaking across Europe.

B. The Pre-Lisbon Dialogue

1. EU fundamental rights law: from silence to a cacophony

In the beginning, the Strasbourg Court alone had jurisdiction governing the supranational protection of human rights in Europe. This changed when the CJEU held in 1969 in order to preserve the supremacy of Community law that EU law (or EC law as it then was) was subject to fundamental rights.[9] That said, for decades afterwards, the CJEU would continue to turn to the ECHR, and the more experienced human rights court of the ECtHR, for 'guidelines' and 'inspiration' in the development of its own catalogue of fundamental rights under the 'general principles' of Community law.[10] Despite more recent assertions to the contrary, it is questionable whether the dialogue between the Strasbourg and Luxembourg systems regarding the protection of human rights standards was ever truly one of 'peaceful convergence' prior to Opinion 2/13.[11] Instead, it is argued here that once the CJEU took on the mantle of being an adjudicator of human rights in the 1970s, a Pandora's box of issues was opened involving questions of coherence, hierarchy, and autonomy to be managed by both Courts in their protection of human rights and dialogue with one another. And there has been no going back.

The ECHR began as a legal nonentity for the 'Communities' (the EU as it then was) when first created due to the focus on economic cooperation and because the first six Member States were not all part of the ECHR.[12] Consequently, in 1957, despite being out of step with most constitutions in Europe at the time, the EEC and Euratom Treaties were cautiously drafted and contained no reference to human rights.[13] As Williams and others highlight, the reception to fundamental rights generally, and the ECHR, within the early legal landscape of the EU was thus

[9] Case 29/69 *Stauder v City of Ulm* [1969] ECR 419 [7]; Case 11/70, *Internationale Handelsgesellschaft* [1970] ECR 1125 [4].

[10] Case C-260/89 *ERT* [1991] ECR I-2925 [41]. On the interplay between the general principles and the scope of EU law, see Michael Dougan, 'Judicial Review of Member State Action Under the General Principles and the Charter' (2015) 52 Common Market Law Review 1201.

[11] For the contrasting view that Opinion 2/13 interrupted an otherwise 'peaceful convergence' between ECtHR and CJEU case law, see Xavier Groussot and Gunnar Thor Pétursson, 'Je t'aime … moi non plus: Ten years of application of the EU Charter of Fundamental Rights' (2022) 59 Common Market Law Review 239, 252.

[12] See generally Luis J Gordillo, *Interlocking Constitutions* (Hart 2012).

[13] On the detailed provisions for a human rights system contained in the draft 'European Political Community Treaty' that was abandoned by the founding Member States of what was then the EU in 1953 (European Coal and Steel Community), see Gráinne de Búrca, 'The Evolution of EU Human Rights Law' in Paul Craig and Gráinne de Búrca, *The Evolution of EU Law* (3rd edn, OUP 2021) 484–86.

'subliminal' at best.[14] The establishment of the EEC that followed was 'legitimated by goals that were to a large extent neutral with regard to constitutional issues'.[15] A reference in the preamble of the EEC Treaty of 1957 'to lay the foundations of *an ever closer union* among the peoples of Europe' suggests an inevitable departure from this neutral approach.[16] Nevertheless, it should be acknowledged that this lukewarm approach to human rights within the early EU project was not unique among other transnational organizations of the time. Even the ECHR had a lowly status in Strasbourg until the late 1960s.[17] This was partly due to the dearth of case law before the Strasbourg Court and that it took until the end of that decade for Strasbourg to find the first official violation of the ECHR.[18]

From 1969, however, notable changes were afoot with the CJEU's recognition that 'fundamental human rights' were part of, and protected under, the general principles of EU law.[19] This was the first major step in recognizing a role for human rights within the EU.[20] In the landmark judgment of *Internationale Handelsgesellschaft*, the CJEU confirmed its expansion of the 'general principles of community law' and the creation of its own doctrine of 'fundamental rights'.[21] This innovative and deft approach provided the CJEU with the discretion to develop its own approach to the protection of fundamental rights as part of EU law, whilst also effectively giving regard to the equivalent provisions of national constitutions as part of the EU legal framework. Indeed, although the Opinions of Advocate Generals have at times been a driving force for change in EU law,[22] some of the

[14] Andrew Williams, 'Respecting Fundamental Rights in the New Union' in Catherine Barnard (ed), *The Fundamentals of EU Law Revisited* (OUP 2007) 71; Martin Kuijer, 'The Challenging Relationship Between the European Convention on Human Rights and the EU Legal Order' [2020] The International Journal of Human Rights 998, 999.

[15] Armin von Bogdandy, 'Doctrine of Principles' (Jean Monnet Working Paper 9/03, Max Planck Institute for Comparative Public Law and International Law, Heidelberg, 24–27 February 2003) 9.

[16] Emphasis added. On this argument, see Philip Alston and Joseph HH Weiler, 'An "Ever Closer Union" in Need of a Human Rights Policy' (1998) 9 European Journal of International Law 658; Gráinne de Búrca, 'The Road Not Taken: The EU as a Global Human Rights Actor' (2011) 105 American Journal of International Law 649.

[17] Ed Bates, *The Evolution of the European Convention on Human Rights* (OUP 2010) 179–215. See generally Henri Rolin, 'Has the European Court of Human Rights a Future?' (1965) 11 Howard Law Journal 442.

[18] Bates (n 17).

[19] Case 29/69 *Stauder v City of Ulm* [1969] ECR 419 [7]; Case 11/70 *Internationale Handelsgesellschaft v Einfuhr und Vorratsetelle fur Getriede und Futtermittel* [1970] ECR 1125; Case 4/73 *Nold v Commission* [1974] ECR I-491. The early development of fundamental rights under the general principles of EU law (then EC law) is the subject of much commentary. See eg Francis G Jacobs, 'The Protection of Human Rights in the Member States of the Community' in James O'Reilly (ed), *Human Rights and Constitutional Law* (Round Hall 1992); Jason Coppel and Aidan O'Neill, 'The European Court of Justice: Taking Rights Seriously?' (1992) 29 Common Market Law Review 669; Joseph HH Weiler and Nicholas JS Lockhart, '"Taking Rights Seriously" Seriously' (1995) 32 Common Market Law Review 51 and 579 (Parts I and II).

[20] Jacobs (n 19) 244.

[21] *Internationale Handelsgesellschaft* (n 19).

[22] See Takis Tridimas, 'The Role of the Advocate General in the Development of Community Law' (1997) 34 Common Market Law Review 1349; Cyril Ritter, 'A New Look at the Role and Impact of Advocates-General—Collectively and Individually' (2006) 12 Columbia Journal of European Law 751;

most recent and boldest rulings concerning the rights to privacy and data protection are attributable to the Luxembourg Court alone.[23]

Two main factors brought about the incorporation of fundamental rights into the general principles of EU law to act as a check on EU legislation and policy-making. The first concerned the CJEU coming to the defence of the principle of supremacy. This principle was firmly established within the EU legal order by the early 1970s and provides that EU law takes precedence over the domestic laws of Member States.[24] The principle's development was in response to challenges by the German and Italian Constitutional Courts. The conflict between the CJEU and these national courts concerned the resistance of the CJEU to accept that EU law should be bound by fundamental rights, whilst still requiring that Member States be subject to EU law.[25] The German Federal Constitutional Court (Bundesverfassungsgericht) recognized in 1967 the supremacy of EU law over national law.[26] However, in 1974, the Bundesverfassungsgericht held that this was not the case in the area of fundamental rights.[27] The German Court determined that it was its responsibility to safeguard fundamental rights as no bill of rights existed within EU law.

This meant that EU law would have to be examined at national level to ensure that it was compatible with the protection afforded to German citizens under their national constitution. After a similar reversal of approach by the Italian Constitutional Court, the German Constitutional Court recognized that the CJEU had developed a greater commitment to fundamental rights protection since its earlier finding to the contrary.[28] The Bundesverfassungsgericht thus held that it would maintain effective protection of rights for people in Germany but would do so in a cooperative rather than confrontational relationship with the CJEU.[29] Essentially, this now famous '*Solange*' doctrine has established that domestic courts will refrain from reviewing the compatibility of EU law with rights under their

Carlos Arrebola, Ana Júlia Maurício, and Héctor Jiménez Portilla, 'An Econometric Analysis of the Influence of the Advocate General on the Court of Justice of the EU' (2016) 5 Cambridge International Law Journal 82.

[23] This applies especially to the post-Lisbon Treaty era landmark case law of the CJEU on EU data protection law. See further Chapter 5.

[24] Case 26/62 *Van Gend en Loos* [1963] ECR 1; Case 6/64 *Costa v ENEL* [1964] ECR 585; Bruno de Witte, 'Direct Effect, Supremacy and the Nature of the Legal Order' in Paul Craig and Gráinne de Búrca (eds), *The Evolution of EU Law* (OUP 1999) 197. See generally Michael Dougan, 'The Primacy of Union Law over Incompatible National Measures' (2022) 59 Common Market Law Review 1301; Matteo Bonelli, 'Growing Pains: Direct Effect, Primary, and Fundamental Rights after *Lin*' (2024) 61 Common Market Law Review 1045.

[25] Stephen Weatherill and Paul Beaumont, *EU Law* (3rd edn, Penguin 1999) 443–49.

[26] Jochen A Frowein, '*Bundesverfassungsgericht*. Second Senate. Decision of July 5, 1967' (1968) 5 Common Market Law Review 481.

[27] Jochen A Frowein, 'Solange II (BVerfGE 73, 339)' (1988) 25 Common Market Law Review 201.

[28] Giorgio Gaja, '*Spa Granital v Administrazione delle Finanze dello Stato*' (1984) 21 Common Market Law Review 756; Frowein (n 27) 205.

[29] David Feldman, *Civil Liberties and Human Rights* (2nd edn, OUP 2002) 76.

respective national constitutions. Note that such restraint rests on these courts being of the view that the CJEU is adequately protecting fundamental rights.[30]

The second factor that led to the recognition of fundamental rights by the CJEU was the inevitable consequence from the EU's rapid expansion into areas beyond the purely economic. As early as 1976, the European Commission asserted that the development of an EU fundamental rights doctrine was inherently linked with the aim of greater market integration and the need to protect individuals by virtue of the increasing detailed rules affecting their lives beyond the economic sphere.[31] The Commission promised that EU policy would meet the optimum, and not the lowest common denominator, of the standards of fundamental rights in the Member States.[32] Weatherill and others viewed the decision of the Court to effectively read an unwritten bill of rights into EU law as a striking contribution to the EU legal order and for the relationship of the EU with its citizens.[33] Of course, this was just the beginning. The later arrival of the EU Charter of Fundamental Rights would transform this engagement with human rights by the EU, and notably the CJEU, from 'silence to a cacophony'.[34]

2. The Strasbourg perspective

(a) The *Bosphorus* presumption: indirect review of implemented EU law

The Strasbourg legal order was initially reluctant to review any matter related to the EU.[35] As demonstrated in the 1978 judgment of *Confederation Francaise Democratique du Travail (CFDT)*, the European Commission on Human Rights

[30] Solange II, BVerfGE 73, 339 2 BvR 197/83 (1986) and BVerfGE 2 BvL 1/97 of 7 June 2000. On related dialogue between the CJEU and the national courts in Germany and France where the primacy of EU law has been questioned, see generally Lucia Serena Rossi, 'A "new course" of the Bundesverfassungsgericht in the context of constitutional complaints' *EU Law Analysis* (16 April 2020), <https://eulawanalysis.blogspot.com/2020/04/a-new-course-of-bundesverfassungsgerich.html>; Eleanor Spaventa, 'Fundamental Rights in the EU' in Catherine Barnard and Steve Peers (eds), *European Union Law* (3rd edn, OUP 2020); Mattias Wendel, 'The Two-Faced Guardian—Or How One Half of the German Federal Constitutional Court Became a European Fundamental Rights Court' (2020) 57 Common Market Law Review 1383; Araceli Turmo, 'National Security as an Exception to EU Data Protection Standards' (2022) 59 Common Market Law Review 203.

[31] European Commission, 'The protection of fundamental rights as Community law is created and developed', COM (76)37 final, 4 February 1976, Bulletin of the EC: Supplement 5/76, [28]. See eg at that time on issues of employment equality, Case 43/75 *Defrenne v SABENA (Defrenne II)* [1976] ECR 455. Here the CJEU held that a private party comply with the requirement in Art 119 of the EEC Treaty for equal pay of equal work by men and women.

[32] European Commission (n 31).

[33] See eg Stephen Weatherill, *Law and Integration in the EU* (Clarendon Press 1995) 42; Andrew Williams, 'Respecting Fundamental Rights in the New Union: A Review' in Catherine Barnard (ed), *The Fundamentals of EU Law Revisited* (OUP 2007) 107.

[34] Williams (n 33) 107.

[35] Jan Klabbers, *Treaty Conflict and the EU* (CUP 2009) 167; Paul Gragl, *The Accession of the European Union to the European Convention on Human Rights* (Hart 2013) 65.

held that to the extent that the application was directed against the EU,[36] the consideration of the applicant's complaint fell outside the Commission's jurisdiction *ratione personae* on the basis that the EU was not a Contracting Party to the ECHR. However, *CFDT* raised the difficult question of whether EU Member States, also Contracting Parties to the ECHR, could be held responsible for legal measures implemented in order to give effect to EU law.[37] In *M & Co*, it was found that such a transfer of power to a supranational organization was compatible with the ECHR, provided that within that organization fundamental rights would receive 'equivalent protection'.[38] *M & Co* thus introduced a new concept, derived from the '*Solange*' principle, to the dialogue between Strasbourg and Luxembourg.[39]

Subsequently, 'a stony silence' was adopted regarding the degree to which a Member State's margin of discretion must be taken into account when transposing EU Directives into national law.[40] Nevertheless, a few years later, Strasbourg indicated its increasing willingness to review EU measures implemented by its Member States with considerable scrutiny,[41] even where the national law of the Member State adopted an EU Directive almost word for word.[42] As observed by a former President of the Strasbourg Court, this departure from the deferential approach in *CFDT* was widely regarded as a 'warning shot' across the jurisdictional bow of the EU.[43] A warning from Strasbourg which notably coincided with the roundly criticized opinion delivered by the CJEU which stated that the EU could not accede to the ECHR without an amendment to the founding EU Treaties.[44] Gragl has argued that these actions towards Luxembourg were influenced by an interest in restraining the EU's increasing powers and to prevent ECHR violations by the EU. The latter, of course, the Strasbourg Court, was then unable to review given its lack of jurisdiction *ratione personae*.[45]

[36] *Confederation Francaise Democratique du Travail (CFDT) v The European Communities Case* (App No 15073/77) 10 July 1978, [3]. The ECHR originally created two part-time bodies in the 1950s to ensure the observance of States that had ratified the ECHR (the Commission and the Court). In 1998, following an amendment to the ECHR under Protocol 11, both entities were replaced with a new permanent court. See further Bates (n 17) 213–21.

[37] Gragl (n 35) 66.

[38] *M & Co v Federal Republic of Germany* (App No 13258/87) 9 February 1990.

[39] Laurent Scheeck, 'The Relationship Between the European Courts and the Integration of Human Rights' (2005) 65 Heidelberg Journal of International Law 837, 858.

[40] Gragl (n 35) 66.

[41] See *Procola v Luxembourg* (1995) 22 EHRR 193; *Cantoni v France* [1996] ECHR 52 (GC).

[42] *Cantoni* (n 41) [30].

[43] Dean Spielmann, 'Human Rights Case Law in the Strasbourg and Luxembourg Courts' in Philip Alston (ed), *The EU and Human Rights* (OUP 1999) 773.

[44] Opinion 2/94, *Accession to the ECHR* [1996] ECR I-1759. There is considerable literature on Opinion 2/94, and even more regarding its fraught sibling (Opinion 2/13). See eg Joseph HH Weiler, 'Human Rights, Constitutionalism and Integration' (2001) 3 International Law Forum du droit internationale 227, 235; Bruno de Witte, 'The Use of the ECHR and Convention Case Law by the European Court of Justice' in Patricia Popelier, Catherine Van de Heyning, and Piet Van Nuffel (eds), *Human Rights Protection in the European Legal Order* (Intersentia 2011) 17.

[45] Gragl (n 35) 68.

Tensions arose again in *Matthews v United Kingdom* where it was alleged by the applicant that there had been a violation of her right to free elections and who subsequently brought an action against the UK.[46] The ECtHR (sitting as the Grand Chamber) held that the impugned law (Direct Elections Act) was brought about as a result of an international treaty (the Maastricht Treaty), freely entered into by the respondent State. Consequently, the UK was held to be responsible *ratione materiae* under Article 1 ECHR and Article 3 of Protocol No 1 ECHR for the consequences of said Treaty.[47] The ECtHR held there had been a violation of the applicant's right to vote under Article 3 of Protocol No 1. *Matthews* therefore established that in areas where a Member State retained some discretion when transposing EU law, the State would be held responsible for ECHR violations even if the violations were the result of EU law. *Matthews* was also significant for highlighting the unanswered question of what consequences would arise for EU measures implemented by Member States where said States had no discretionary power in this undertaking.[48] The landmark case of *Bosphorus* v *Ireland* would address this issue.[49]

The facts of *Bosphorus* involved a UN Security Council measure adopted in response to human rights violations that had occurred in the former Yugoslavia.[50] The EU implemented the UN Resolution as Council Regulation 990/93.[51] Public authorities in Ireland transposed the EU Regulation and consequently impounded two passenger aircraft which Bosphorus Airways (a Turkish airline company) had leased from a Yugoslavian airline company. Bosphorus brought a challenge to the impoundment before the Irish Supreme Court. The domestic court then sought a preliminary reference from the CJEU. Consequently, the CJEU held that the infringement of the company's fundamental rights was appropriate and proportionate in the light of the main objective of dissuading the Federal Republic of Yugoslavia from further violating the integrity and security of the Republic of Bosnia-Herzegovina.[52] Bosphorus then brought an application against Ireland before the ECtHR claiming that the impoundment amounted to a violation of the right to property under Article 1 of Protocol No 1 ECHR. According to Article 1 ECHR, the impounded act was held to have fallen within the jurisdiction of the respondent State.[53] However, the ECtHR (sitting as the Grand Chamber) held that the alleged ECHR infringement had its origins in the impoundment which was based on the EU Regulation. The latter was a binding and directly applicable legal

[46] *Matthews v United Kingdom* (1999) 28 EHRR 361.
[47] ibid [33].
[48] Klabbers (n 35) 170.
[49] *Bosphorus v Ireland* (2006) 42 EHRR 1 (GC).
[50] UNSC S/RES/820 (1993), 17 April 1993 (Resolution 280).
[51] Council Regulation (EEC) No 990/93, 26 April 1993.
[52] Case C-84/95 *Bosphorus v Minister for Transport, Energy and Communications* [1996] ECR I-3953, [25]–[26].
[53] ibid [135].

act which crucially afforded no discretion to the domestic public authorities, thus leaving Ireland to choose between violating its obligations flowing from the ECHR or EU law.

The ECtHR was faced with reconciling two principles. A contracting party was not prevented from transferring powers to an international organization and, secondly, a Contracting Party cannot be allowed to avoid its responsibilities under the ECHR because of this transfer.[54] In resolving this conflict, the ECtHR relied on the principles it had established in *M & Co* and held that the 'equivalent protection' presumption applied.[55] The Court held that the equivalent protection formula could be rebutted if it is considered that the ECHR rights within the legal order of the relevant international organization were 'manifestly deficient'.[56] This formula would only apply to cases where the relevant State has no discretion in implementing the legal act in question. Ultimately, it was held that the equivalent protection presumption had not been rebutted. The Court came to this conclusion based on two grounds: substantive protection of human rights was provided under the general principles of EU law and the EU Charter of Fundamental Rights (despite not being part of EU law at the time) which recognizes the ECHR as establishing minimum human rights standards. In addition, all are effectively observed under the 'control mechanism' of the CJEU's preliminary reference procedure.[57] Application of the *Bosphorus* presumption is thus subject to two conditions: the absence of any margin of manoeuvre on the part of a Member State's public authorities and, secondly, deployment of the full potential of the supervisory mechanisms provided for by EU law. When both conditions are fulfilled, compatibility with the ECHR is presumed. The presumption is rebutted if it is shown (in the relevant case) that the protection of ECHR rights was 'manifestly deficient'.[58]

On the one hand, the approach of the ECtHR in *Bosphorus*, the leading authority on the jurisdiction of the Strasbourg legal order concerning EU obligations, was deft. Whilst managing not to allow the protection of human rights standards under the ECHR to become hypothetical, the ECtHR straddled the difficult line between maintaining its position as the final arbiter on the adjudication of human

[54] Tobias Lock, 'The ECJ and the ECtHR' (2009) 8 The Law and Practice of International Courts and Tribunals 375, 378.

[55] *Bosphorus* (n 52) [155]. Equivalent meaning 'comparable' and not 'identical' as the latter standard could run counter to the interest of pursuing international cooperation.

[56] ibid [156].

[57] ibid [159].

[58] Koen Lenaerts, Piet Van Nuffel, and Tim Corthaut, *EU Constitutional Law* (OUP 2021) 672–74. See further *Avotiņš v Latvia* (2017) 64 EHRR 2 (GC). On the legacy of *Bosphorus*, see Catherine Van de Heyning, '*PO Kokkelvisserij*' (2009) 46 Common Market Law Review 2117; Paul Gragl, 'An Olive Branch from Strasbourg? Interpreting the European Court of Human Rights' Resurrection of *Bosphorus* and Reaction to Opinion 2/13 in the *Avotiņš* Case' (2017) 13 European Constitutional Law Review 551; Tobias Lock, 'EU Accession to the ECHR' in Steve Peers and others (eds), *The EU Charter of Fundamental Rights: A Commentary* (Hart 2021) 1878–90.

rights in Europe and respecting the status quo of its dialogue with the CJEU.[59] Nevertheless, as Gragl and others rightly highlight, *Bosphorus* is not without flaws. The high threshold of a manifestly deficient test bestows a privileged status upon ECHR Contracting Parties who are EU Member States (when acting within the scope of EU law).[60] This invariably raises questions of fairness and consistency regarding the approach of the ECtHR with respect to legal challenges concerning non-EU Contracting Parties. Secondly, *Bosphorus* provides that the Court could hold EU Member States responsible for measures of EU policy.[61] Douglas-Scott describes this as the 'price for Strasbourg achieving a level of control over the EU, while respecting its autonomy as a separate legal order'.[62]

Thirdly, by establishing a clear hierarchy between the two legal systems, *Bosphorus* threatens the principle of legal certainty as the ECtHR reserved the right to determine on a case-by-case basis if the system's protection level is comparable to that of the EU.[63] Consequently, as Gordillo warns, in order to avoid claims before the ECtHR, Member States might be tempted to refrain from applying EU law in certain cases.[64] Fourthly, as the EU is not (yet) a party to the ECHR, it cannot intervene directly if any EU matters come before the review of the Strasbourg Court or appoint a judge to the ECtHR.[65]

(b) Drawing from the CJEU? A rare but increasing practice in the pre-Lisbon era

Despite an established practice of referring to international human rights treaties and the jurisprudence of other international courts in its interpretation of the ECHR, the ECtHR tended not to closely engage with CJEU case law in the pre-Lisbon era.[66] This is unsurprising for two main reasons. One is the general scarcity of CJEU jurisprudence concerning human rights and data protection at this time, especially before the EU Charter became legally binding in 2009. Secondly, there was the frequently applied 'light-touch' level of scrutiny by the CJEU which was effectively underpinned by a shared view between the legal orders that Strasbourg was Europe's leading supranational human rights court.[67] Explicit references

[59] See Luzius Wildhaber, 'The European Convention on Human Rights and International Law' (2007) 56 International and Comparative Law Quarterly 217, 230; Catherine Van de Heyning and Rick Lawson, 'The EU as a Party to the ECHR' in Popelier, Van de Heyning, and Van Nuffel (n 44) 53.

[60] Gragl (n 35) 73; Sionaigh Douglas-Scott, 'A Tale of Two Courts' (2006) 43 Common Market Law Review 629; Leonard FM Besselink, 'Should the European Union ratify the European Convention on Human Rights?' in Andreas Føllesdal, Birgit Peters, and Geir Ulfstein (eds), *Constituting Europe* (CUP 2013) 306; Gordillo (n 12) 183–84.

[61] Besselink (n 60) 306.

[62] Douglas-Scott (n 60) 639.

[63] Gordillo (n 12) 184.

[64] ibid 183.

[65] ibid.

[66] Van de Heyning and Lawson (n 59) 39.

[67] On the 'light-touch' standard of judicial review applied by the CJEU concerning its rights review of the EU institutions and EU law in the pre-Lisbon era, see Bruno de Witte, 'The Past and Future Role of the European Court of Justice in the Protection of Human Rights' in Alston (n 43) 866–69;

to the jurisprudence of the CJEU by the ECtHR were gradually on the rise from 2007.[68] Of the few references between the entry into force of the EU Data Retention Directive in 2006, and that of the Lisbon Treaty in 2009, most were approving.[69] Additionally, the ECtHR continued its fairly deferential approach to the EU generally by shoring up EU legal principles of supremacy and uniformity. The Court, for instance, rejected applications asserting an ECHR right to a preliminary reference to the CJEU and criticized Member States for failing to follow EU law.[70] A notable exception to this otherwise respectful approach, most notably the autonomy of the CJEU, arose with respect to the EU Charter. While its legal status within the EU was still uncertain, and for some a source of controversy, the ECtHR was the first of the two Courts to refer to the Charter.[71] In other words, the Strasbourg Court did not wait for the CJEU to share its public view on the Charter.

Harpaz and others note that pre-Lisbon era relations between Strasbourg and Luxembourg were based on a self-conscious dialogue that served both the self-interest and shared values of both systems in this area of human rights.[72] Within this context, while the ECtHR did indeed acknowledge EU law as an autonomous international legal order, it still considered itself as the 'ultimate guardian' of human rights in Europe.[73] This argument carries weight following the *Bosphorus* doctrine where the ECtHR held that consequences could arise for EU measures implemented by EU Member States (which had no discretionary power in their undertaking) if in the circumstances the relevant human rights standards were 'manifestly deficient'.[74] At the same time, the ECtHR was more willing to give the CJEU a special status in its express references to relevant international materials in the pre-Lisbon era. This is demonstrated, for instance, by the CJEU being openly referred to by the ECtHR more often than other legal jurisdictions, such as the US Supreme Court.[75] Other elements also reinforce this view of the Courts' relationship at this time. The EU and the ECHR essentially share the same community of Member States. While the EU itself is not yet party to the ECHR, all its Member States have acceded to the ECHR. Secondly, the EU and the ECHR are

Douglas-Scott (n 60) 641; Darren Harvey, 'From Low- to High Intensity Review in the Protection of EU Fundamental Rights' (2024) 31 Maastricht Journal of European and Comparative Law 171, 173–76.

[68] Van de Heyning and Lawson (n 59) 46.

[69] See eg Case C-13/94 *P v S* [1996] ECR I-2143 in *Goodwin v United Kingdom* (2002) 35 EHRR 447 (GC) and *Scoppola v Italy (No 2)* (2010) 51 EHRR 12 (GC).

[70] See eg *Hornsby v Greece* (1997) 24 EHRR 250.

[71] *Goodwin* (n 69); *Bosphorus* (n 52); *Scoppola* (n 69).

[72] Guy Harpaz, 'The European Court of Justice and Its Relations with the European Court of Human Rights' (2009) 46 Common Market Law Review 105, 106; AG Toth, 'The EU and Human Rights' (1997) 34 Common Market Law Review 491; Iris Canor, '*Primus inter pares*. Who is the Ultimate Guardian of Fundamental Rights in Europe' (2000) 25 European Law Review 3.

[73] Toth (n 72) 503 and Canor (n 72) 21.

[74] *Bosphorus* (n 52) and *PO Kokkelvisserif v The Netherlands* (App No 13645/05) 20 January 2009 (admissibility decision).

[75] Douglas-Scott (n 60) 641; Gragl (n 35) 54.

both engaged in a 'common project of European integration' where the aims of the promotion and protection of human rights are important for both systems, albeit from within different constitutional frameworks.[76] Thirdly, by giving this special status to the EU, the ECtHR may have been working to enable a more constructive dialogue between both systems in order assist with the substantive and procedural complexities that would inevitably arise from the (still pending) EU-ECHR accession process.

3. The Luxembourg perspective

(a) The ECHR in the pre-Lisbon era: 'a special source of inspiration' for the EU

Express references to the ECHR by the EU institutions, and in EU Treaty law, occurred at a gradual pace.[77] These began as general mentions to the instrument of the ECHR, moving to more specific references to Article 8 ECHR, reliance, and even deference to ECtHR jurisprudence. The approach of the CJEU to the ECHR was first given expression in EU law in the preamble to the Single European Act in 1986.[78] However, the position of the ECHR within Treaty law was only made clearly concrete with an amendment under the Amsterdam Treaty in 1997, promulgating the general principles underlying the EU.[79] Nevertheless, until 2000, the CJEU consistently relied on the ECHR as the primary source for its gradual development of a minimum human rights standard in its review of EU law and policy. The CJEU's engagement with other international human rights instruments was, and has remained, limited in comparison.[80] The European Commission adopted this approach in its treatment of international human rights treaties as far back as the 1970s, stressing that the development of the Court's fundamental rights doctrine was 'particularly relevant' to the ECHR.[81] This view was based on the existing recognition in all Member States of the binding nature of the ECHR, which in turn, the Commission emphasized, despite not being part of the ECHR itself, means that EU institutions were also bound to comply with the ECHR.[82]

[76] ibid.

[77] Bernadette Rainey, Elizabeth Wicks, and Clare Ovey, *Jacobs, White and Ovey: The European Convention on Human Rights* (6th edn, OUP 2014) 325; EU Agency for Fundamental Rights (FRA), *Fundamental Rights Report 2020* (FRA 2020) 7. See generally Tobias Lock, *The European Court of Justice and International Courts* (OUP 2015); Clara Rauchegger and Sarah Lambrecht, 'European Union: The EU's Attitude to the ECHR' in Patricia Popelier, Sarah Lambrecht, and Koen Lemmens (eds), *Criticism of the European Court of Human Rights* (Intersentia 2017) 41–72.

[78] Single European Act, 17 February 1986 [1987] OJ L169/01.

[79] Treaty of Amsterdam, 2 October 1997 [1997] OJ C340/01; Spielmann (n 43) 759.

[80] See Williams (n 14); Giuseppe F Mancini, 'The Making of a Constitution for Europe' (1989) 26 Common Market Law Review 595; Sara Iglesias Sánchez, 'The Court and the Charter' (2012) 49 Common Market Law Review 1565.

[81] European Commission (n 31) [28].

[82] ibid.

Given the exalted political status attributed to the ECHR by the EU institutions, it is unsurprising that the CJEU maintained this approach and increasingly gave priority to the ECHR over other sources of international human rights.[83] By 1989, the CJEU had firmly established that fundamental rights were an integral part of the general principles of EU law.[84] Hence, the CJEU had undertaken to ensure that these general principles would be observed in accordance with constitutional traditions common to the Member States and that the ECHR was of particular significance in that regard. The CJEU was thus regularly highlighting the special significance of the ECHR and the rulings of the Strasbourg Court as a key source of inspiration for the general principles of EU law before the EU Charter became legally binding in 2009.[85]

Indeed, despite the EU not being part of the ECHR, the CJEU had already committed itself to upholding principles drawn from the ECHR in reviewing EU law during the drafting of the 2004 EU–US Passenger Name Record (PNR) Adequacy Decision and the Data Retention Directive 2006/24/EC.[86] The Court had also addressed the extent to which the actions of Member States are subject to review for compatibility with the ECHR when implementing or enforcing EU measures, not just as a standard assessing the legality of the acts of EU institutions.[87] By stopping short of holding that the ECHR was formally binding on the EU, while at the same time stressing its special role, the Court allowed itself both to assert the autonomy and supremacy of EU law and to avoid being accused of incorporating international agreements into EU law without the consent of Member States.[88] This deft approach provided the CJEU with the capacity early on in its fundamental rights case law to go beyond the ECHR in recognizing rights as part of EU law which may not have warranted the same protection under the ECHR.[89]

(b) Drawing from Strasbourg jurisprudence

Before the Charter became a part of EU law in 2009, it was standard practice by the CJEU to openly engage with and draw from the ECHR, and the case law of the ECtHR, for guidance in its adjudication of fundamental rights. The Court

[83] Allan Rosas, 'Fundamental Rights in the Luxembourg and Strasbourg Courts' in Carl Baudenbacher, Per Tresselt, and Thorgeir Örlygsson (eds), *The EFTA Court* (Hart 2005) 168–69. On the CJEU expressly referring to the special status of the ECHR in its development of EU fundamental rights, see eg Joined Cases 46/87 and 222/88 *Hoechst v Commission* [1989] ECR 2859; Case C-260/89 *ERT* [1991] ECR I-2925; Case C-274/99 *P Connolly v Commission* [2001] ECR I-1611.

[84] *Hoechst* (n 83) 53.

[85] Rosas (n 83) 169.

[86] See further Chapters 5 and 9.

[87] Case C-5/88 *Wachauf* [1989] ECR 2609; Case C-101/01, *Bodil Lindqvist*, judgment of 6 November 2003 (ECLI:EU:C:2003:596).

[88] Paul Craig and Gráinne de Búrca, *EU Law* (5th edn, OUP 2011) 369.

[89] See eg Case C-155/79 *AM and S Europe Ltd v Commission* [1982] ECR 1575, where the Court does not engage with the standards under the relevant ECtHR case law and relies instead on its interpretation of recital 11 from the contested Regulation in the light of 'common criteria' from the Member States' national laws on the confidentiality of communications between lawyers and clients.

expressly referred to the ECHR for the first time in 1974,[90] holding soon after that the ECHR constituted guidelines to be followed within the EU legal order.[91] That said, it took more than twenty years until the CJEU began to openly refer to case law from the Strasbourg Court.[92] Given the relative inexperience of the CJEU in adjudicating fundamental rights issues in depth at this time, it makes sense that the Court continued this interface with the rich human rights jurisprudence developed by the ECHR system in Strasbourg since the 1950s in order to develop its own fundamental rights framework within EU law. Accordingly, the CJEU referred to the jurisprudence of the ECtHR in its leading pre-Lisbon fundamental rights case law.[93] *Kadi* was one such landmark judgment dealing with the relationship between EU law and the international legal order.[94]

The facts of *Kadi* primarily involved a challenge by an individual to EU legislation that had implemented several UN Security Council Resolutions,[95] which identified him as being involved with terrorism, thereby requiring the freezing of his assets. The Court (sitting as the Grand Chamber) held that the implementing measures had violated fundamental rights protected under EU law. In its assessment of the right to property and the right to effective judicial protection, the Luxembourg Court relied on the ECHR and case law of the ECtHR.[96] However, the Court distanced EU law from the international legal order, particularly the UN, in its adjudication of the fundamental rights at issue in *Kadi*. The Court made clear that 'a constitutional guarantee stemming from the EC Treaty as an autonomous legal system ... cannot be prejudiced by an international agreement'.[97] In the pre-Lisbon era, the Court had rarely departed from the case law of the ECtHR and had never openly contradicted it. The approach in *Kadi* towards the possibility that the UN legal system could encroach upon the Luxembourg Court's interpretation, and application, of EU law raised fears that the ECHR, and the case law of the ECtHR could be treated in a similar manner.

Consequently, as de Búrca and others have noted, *Kadi* represented a significant (and consistent) departure from the status of the EU as an organization whose actions were underpinned by a commitment to the international legal order.[98]

[90] Case C-4/73 *Nold v Commission* [1974] ECR 491.

[91] Case C-36/75 *Rutili* [1975] ECR 1219.

[92] Case C-13/94 *P v S* [1996] ECR I-2143.

[93] De Witte (n 44) 24.

[94] Joined Cases C-402/05 P and C-415/05 P *Kadi* [2008] ECR I-6351 (GC). Literature on this judgment is extensive. See eg Guy Harpaz, 'Judicial Review by the European Court of Justice of UN "Smart Sanctions" Against Terror in the *Kadi* Dispute' (2009) 14 European Foreign Affairs Review 65; Gráinne de Búrca, 'The European Court of Justice and the International Legal Order after *Kadi*' (2010) 51 Harvard International Law Journal 1.

[95] Council Regulation (EC) No 881/2002 of 27 May 2002 was adopted to give effect to the Council Common Position 2002/402/CFSP [2003] OJ L53/62, in order to implement several UN Security Council Resolutions (1267 of 1999, 1333 of 2000, and 1390 of 2002).

[96] *Kadi* (n 94) [344], [360]–[368].

[97] ibid [316].

[98] de Búrca (n 94) 2; Gragl (n 35) 263. Aside from the ECHR, scholars have consistently criticized the CJEU for selectively and rarely engaging with, or even citing, other sources of international human

4. Article 8 ECHR in the pre-Lisbon era

(a) CJEU: 'special status' of Article 8 ECHR begins decline

It was well established by the time of the drafting of the Data Retention Directive in 2005 that the CJEU had recognized the right to respect for private life, guaranteed under Article 8 ECHR, as a fundamental right under the general principles of EU law.[99] Article 8 ECHR was also one of the most often quoted provisions of the ECHR by the CJEU. When politically declared into existence in 2000, Article 7 of the EU Charter (CFR) gave full recognition to these rights by effectively reproducing the wording of Article 8(1) ECHR: 'Everyone has the right to respect for his or her private and family life, home and communications'. There is no reference to Article 8(2) ECHR in Article 7 CFR as similar conditions for relevant measures falling within the scope of EU law must be met under Article 52(1) CFR.

However, the Court had already previously held in *Hoechst* that the conditions to be satisfied under Article 8(2) ECHR, in order for an interference by a public authority with a right guaranteed under Article 8 ECHR to be justified, 'must be recognized as a general principle' of EU law.[100] The applicant in *Hoechst* was a company that challenged various decisions by the European Commission which resulted in the ordering of an investigation into the company's affairs on the basis that it was suspected of undertaking anti-competitive practices. The investigatory powers of the Commission in this area were very wide and allowed the Commission to investigate and make searches and to impose significant financial sanctions. However, the CJEU did not confirm that the safeguards of Article 8(2) ECHR were part of the general principles of EU law until *Hoechst*. The applicant's rights challenge in *Hoechst* was ultimately unsuccessful as the Court did not extend the scope of protection afforded to the home under Article 8(1) ECHR to business premises.

Essentially, the approach of the Luxembourg Court went beyond just turning to the Strasbourg Court and its Article 8 ECHR case law for guidance. The Court deferred to this line of jurisprudence of the ECtHR as it was not prepared to go beyond the scope established by the ECtHR in this area, and expressly referred to the fact that there was no guidance on the matter from the Strasbourg Court at this time.[101] Again, the Luxembourg Court took the same deferential approach in the

rights law beyond the EU Charter in its post-Lisbon case law. See eg Olivier De Schutter, *The Future of Europe: International Human Rights in European Integration* (UN Human Rights Regional Office for Europe 2020), <https://europe.ohchr.org/sites/default/files/2023-07/FutureOfEurope.pdf>.

[99] Case C-136/79 *National Panasonic v Commission* [1980] ECR 2033; Case C-145/83 *Stanley Adams v Commission* [1985] ECR 3539; Case C-249/86 *Commission v Germany* [1989] ECR 1263; *Hoechst* (n 83); Case C-76/93 *P Scaramuzza v Commission* [1994] ECR I-5713; Case C-139/01 *Österreichischer Rundfunk and Others* [2003] ECR I-4989.

[100] *Hoechst* (n 83) [19].

[101] ibid [18]. Others have expressed the view (including Allan Rosas, former judge of the CJEU) that the Luxembourg Court has only ever treated the ECHR, and other international sources of law, as

case of *Roquettes Frères* after the ECtHR had extended the scope of this protection to business premises in its Article 8 ECHR case law.[102] *Roquettes Frères* was another judgment of the Court concerning the powers of the European Commission when investigating companies for anti-competitive practices. The Court highlighted its earlier finding in *Hoechst* that the tests of legality, necessity, and proportionality to be met by a public authority, in order to justify an interference with the right to respect for private life guaranteed under Article 8 ECHR which constituted a general principle of EU law. The Court further stressed in *Roquettes Frères* that the jurisprudence of the ECtHR since *Hoechst* had to be taken into account for the purposes of determining the scope of that principle in relation to the protection of business premises. Thus, the CJEU established in *Roquettes Frères* that protection of the home, as provided under Article 8 ECHR, also extended to business activities and premises, as part of the general principles of EU law.

This clear role played by Article 8 ECHR in the development of the right to privacy under EU law shows that the CJEU took no issue with looking towards the ECtHR for guidance in its pre-Lisbon case law, including being a significant influence on the way in which the CJEU interpreted EU data protection law.[103] In *Rundfunk*, for instance, the Court held that provisions under the Data Protection Directive 95/46/EC that governed the processing of personal data liable to infringe fundamental freedoms 'reflect rights of privacy protected under the ECHR and must be interpreted in that light'.[104] *Rundfunk* involved a challenge by a State-administered broadcasting company regarding a domestic statutory obligation on public authorities, subject to the control of the Court of Audit (Rechnungshof), to publicly report the salaries and pensions of their employees to the Rechnungshof. The aim of the provision was intended to guarantee the efficient and appropriate use of public funds by the administration. Several public companies contested the provision of this personal data to the Rechnungshof relying primarily on the Data Protection Directive 95/46/EC and the right to respect for private life guaranteed under Article 8 ECHR. The Austrian Constitutional Court (Verfassungsgerichtshof) submitted a preliminary ruling to the CJEU to ascertain whether the contested statutory obligation was compatible with EU law. The Verfassungsgerichtshof stated that it did not consider that the 'mere public interest' of such information met the test of proportionality required under Article 8(2)

'guidelines or sources of inspiration': see Allan Rosas, 'The Court of Justice of the European Union: A Human Rights Institution?' (2022) 14 Journal of Human Rights Practice 204, 206.

102 Case C-94/00 *Roquettes Frères* [2002] ECR I-9011; *Niemietz v Germany* (1992) 16 EHRR 97; *Peck v United Kingdom* (2003) 36 EHRR 41.

103 Herke Kranenbourg, 'Access to Documents and Data Protection in the European Union' (2008) 45 Common Market Law Review 1079, 1085.

104 *Rundfunk* (n 99) [68]; *P Connolly* (n 83) [37]; Craig and de Búrca (n 88) 382. The fundamental right to data protection was later confirmed as a general principle of EU law in Case C-275/06 *Promusicae* [2008] ECR I-271.

ECHR. Accordingly, the legal provision was argued to be in breach of Article 8 ECHR.[105] The European Commission, the Rechnungshof, and several Member States contested this claim, arguing that the aim of the measure did not amount to being disproportionate within the meaning of Article 8(2) ECHR.[106]

Like the ECtHR, the CJEU has adopted a broad interpretation for the scope of the protected interest of 'private life' under Article 8(1) ECHR.[107] This is evident in *Rundfunk*, where the CJEU held in one of its early privacy cases that the collection of an individual's income, with a view to communicating that information to third parties, falls within the scope of Article 8 ECHR.[108] Furthermore, the CJEU determined, drawing from the jurisprudence of the ECtHR, that the communication of this information to third parties constitutes a further interference with Article 8(1) ECHR.[109] The CJEU applied a level of detailed scrutiny comparable to that of the ECtHR in its review of the case. However, its threshold regarding what constituted a legitimate aim was considerably lower than the standard suggested by the Verfassungsgerichtshof, which was in line with Article 8 ECHR standards. The national court was unequivocally of the view that 'mere public interest' did not meet the identified legitimate aim under Article 8(2) ECHR of furthering the 'economic well-being of the country'. In contrast, the CJEU found that monitoring the 'proper use of public funds ... serves the public interest' and thereby constituted a legitimate aim under Article 8(2).[110] The CJEU ultimately held that the issue of proportionality was a matter for the Austrian Constitutional Court to examine.[111]

Rundfunk gives weight to strong criticism by de Witte and others of the CJEU in its pre-Lisbon case law that while it rarely refused to include an alleged right into its 'capacious bag of general principles', the Court was cautious of finding an actual violation of those rights and embracing a right-based approach to data protection.[112] The CJEU had still nevertheless made it clear for EU policymakers that any law drafted at this time (such as the Data Retention Directive 2006/24/EC) was required to be compatible with Article 8 ECHR, which formed part of the fundamental rights within the general principles of EU law.[113] Moreover, a far more

[105] *Rundfunk* (n 99) [21].
[106] ibid [50].
[107] See further Chapters 2 and 5.
[108] *Rundfunk* (n 99) [73].
[109] ibid [74]; *Amann v Switzerland* [2000] ECHR 87.
[110] *Rundfunk* (n 99) [81]–[85].
[111] ibid [89]–[90].
[112] De Witte (n 67) 869; Feldman (n 29) 77. On this hesitant approach in its early data protection case law, see Orla Lynskey, *The Foundations of EU Data Protection Law* (OUP 2015) 50–58; Damian Clifford, *Data Protection Law and Emotion* (OUP 2024) 24–25. On the deferential approach to the national courts, or as Dalla Corte notes the 'initial timidness', of the CJEU in its early data protection case law in its proportionality assessments, see Lorenzo Dalla Corte, 'On Proportionality in the Data Protection Jurisprudence of the CJEU' (2022) 12 International Data Privacy Law 259, 270; Felix Bieker, *The Right to Data Protection* (Springer 2022) 51–69.
[113] On the pre-legislative rights scrutiny of EU data retention policy in the pre-Lisbon era dealing with the retention of communications data and passenger information (API and PNR), see Chapters 6 and 9.

emboldened right-based approach by the Court to privacy and data protection would emerge after the EU Charter became legally binding, particularly its scrutiny of EU data retention law.[114]

On the cusp of this seismic shift by the CJEU, its pre-Lisbon case law dealing with the protection of data privacy suggests a decline in regard for the special significance of Article 8 ECHR and the related case law of the ECtHR. This constitutes an exception from the line of literature that the CJEU was increasingly relying on the ECHR and the jurisprudence of the ECtHR in its assessment of fundamental rights up until the Lisbon Treaty entered into force in 2009.[115] A number of reasons may explain the decline in explicit citations of Article 8 ECHR, and the related case law of the ECtHR in this area of its jurisprudence. The first concerns the long-established procedural and jurisprudential approach followed by the CJEU, one that involves a single collegiate judgment with 'a formulaic ... and fairly minimalist style of judicial reasoning in most cases'.[116] While exceptions to this methodology were beginning to take place in fundamental rights cases just prior to 2009, these more comprehensive assessments were usually limited to certain high-profile Grand Chamber cases.[117]

Kadi, for instance, was one of the most important judgments concerning fundamental rights which indicated the (declining) influence of the international legal order on the Luxembourg system. The whittled-down approach to Article 8 ECHR in its late pre-Lisbon privacy cases following *Rundfunk* (such as *Bavarian Lager, Promusicae, Satamedia, Ireland v Parliament and Council*) may therefore simply have been due to this default minimalist style of judicial reasoning employed by the CJEU. However, these 'significant rulings concerning privacy' were all high profile given the Court's analysis of the right to private life and data protection and their reconciling with the competing rights and interests of access to information, freedom of expression, copyright infringement, and law enforcement.[118] Despite the fact that three of these judgments were delivered by the Grand Chamber, it

[114] See Chapter 5.

[115] See eg Douglas-Scott (n 60) 650; Harpaz (n 72) 109.

[116] Gráinne de Búrca, 'After the EU Charter of Fundamental Rights' (2013) 20 Maastricht Journal 168, 176.

[117] ibid. See generally Vlad F Perju, 'Reason and Authority in the European Court of Justice' (2009) 49 Virginia Journal of International Law 307.

[118] Peter Oliver, 'The Protection of Privacy in the Economic Sphere Before the European Court of Justice' (2009) 46 Common Market Law Review 1443, 1444. See Case T-194/04 *Bavarian Lager v Commission* [2007] ECR II-4523 (concerning whether the European Commission had to give access to the full minutes of a meeting it had organized); Case C-275/06 *Promusicae*, judgment of 29 January 2008 (ECLI:EU:C:2008:54) (GC) (concerning the retention and disclosure of certain traffic data for copyright protection); Case C-73/07 *Satakunnan Markkinapörssi and Satamedia*, judgment of 16 December 2008 (ECLI:EU:C:2008:727) (GC) (concerning annual publication in newspaper of earnings and taxes of individuals with high incomes); Case C-301/06 *Ireland v Parliament and Council*, judgment of 10 February 2009 (ECLI:EU:C:2009:68) (GC). On the reconciling of data protection with these other rights, see Lynskey (n 112) 135–60. On the importance of Case C-301/06 for the Data Retention Directive, see Chapter 6.

was the judgment delivered by the lower Court (Court of First Instance, CFI) in *Bavarian Lager* that provided a rich and discursive examination of the relevant fundamental rights issues.[119] Given these factors, the argument for the vacuum of express references to Article 8 ECHR being merely coincidental is unpersuasive.

The second possible explanation for the apparent shift at this time in the approach from openly acknowledging the significance of Article 8 ECHR when assessing matters concerning private life and data processing by public authorities concerns the need of the CJEU to maintain the legitimacy and autonomy of the EU legal order. After all, while the ECHR was then of special significance as 'an authoritative guideline' to the Court in the development of its own fundamental rights regime, the fact remains that the ECHR was (and is still) not a binding legal instrument for the EU.[120] Accordingly, until the entry into force of the Lisbon Treaty in 2009, and the elevation to EU law of the Charter, the CJEU may have straddled a difficult line between striving to draw guidance from the extensive case law of the more experienced court of human rights in Europe in the development of its own legitimate fundamental rights framework, while simultaneously maintaining that its regard for this legal authority external to the EU was discerning and not a blind adoption of the same human rights standards. Of course, as Harpaz rightly argues, the opposite approach of 'automatic reliance' would be ill-advised with the risk that it could result in the duplication of procedural errors, to the adoption of standards which would contradict and undermine the protection of EU fundamental rights law.[121]

On the one hand, while there was a dearth of substantive engagement with Article 8 ECHR regarding the protection of private life and personal data, only one judgment (*Satamedia*) lacked any reference to the ECHR. This clearly clashes with the idea of the CJEU seeking to operate in complete isolation from the Strasbourg legal order. On the other hand, despite references to the ECHR and ECtHR case law being generally standard practice at this time in the overall rights jurisprudence of the CJEU,[122] only the CFI in *Bavarian Lager* engaged at length with Article 8 ECHR and the ECtHR case law in its interpretation and application of Article 8 ECHR.[123] In contrast, the Grand Chamber judgments in *Promusicae* and *Satamedia* indicated a shift away from the CJEU directly relying on ECtHR case law to merely referring to the ECHR 'at a certain distance' and only once 'filtered through' the EU legal order.[124] The approach of the CJEU towards Article 8 ECHR

[119] This 2007 judgment was successfully appealed by the Commission in Case C-28/08 *Bavarian Lager* (ECLI:EU:C:2010:378) (GC).

[120] Allan Rosas, 'The EU and Fundamental Rights/Human Rights' in Catarina Krause and Martin Scheinin (eds), *International Protection of Human Rights* (Åbo Akademi University 2009) 457.

[121] Harpaz (n 72) 123.

[122] De Witte (n 44) 24.

[123] *Bavarian Lager* (n 118) [113]–[118].

[124] Editorial, 'Relations Between International Courts and Community Courts: Mutual Deference or Subordination?' (2005) 42 Common Market Law Review 581, 585. On a brief reference to Art 8 ECHR, see *Promusicae* (n 118) [64]. On Art 10 ECHR being referenced but not Art 8 ECHR despite the focus

in its late pre-Lisbon case law concerning the protection of private life and data protection thus indicated a growing move towards less systematic use of Article 8 ECHR and ECtHR case law, a change which perhaps was unsurprising given the pending elevation of the Charter to EU law accompanied by the lack of any special treatment by the ECtHR towards the CJEU at this time in its related case law dealing with Article 8 ECHR and data protection.

(b) Strasbourg approach to data retention: no special status for EU law

In its pre-Lisbon case law dealing with Article 8 ECHR, secret surveillance, and data retention, the ECtHR adopted a dialogue towards the EU by which the EU had no special status and was explicitly acknowledged in the briefest terms. In other words, the EU legal order was effectively accorded the same status by the ECtHR of any relevant national, or international, legal source. This approach is clearly demonstrated in the following two cases. First, the ECtHR (sitting as the Grand Chamber) in its landmark judgment of *Marper* briefly cites the Data Protection Directive 95/46/EC and the 2008 Council Framework Decision on the protection of personal data processed in the framework of police and judicial co-operation in criminal matters.[125] This reference sits next to several other briefly cited 'relevant' international materials. Sources from other jurisdictions include materials from the Council of Europe (primarily Convention 108), the national law and practice of Contracting States, case law from the Supreme Court of Canada, and the UN Convention on the Rights of the Child 1989.[126]

K.U. v Finland was another judgment during this period where the ECtHR expressly referred to the EU data protection legal framework as a relevant source of 'international law'.[127] *K.U.* dealt with Article 8 ECHR and the processing of personal data and included a brief reference to the Data Retention Directive 2006/24/EC. The focus of the applicant's complaint involved a violation of the positive obligations guaranteed by the right to respect for private life regarding the failure to prosecute an offence of malicious representation, not secret surveillance. Nevertheless, *K.U.* is still an important judgment to note given that the ECtHR adopted the same general approach to the weight it accorded to EU data protection law in *Marper*. Aside from brief references to Directive 95/46/EC in *Marper* and the Data Retention Directive in *K.U.* to merely reaffirm existing ECtHR case law, there was no meaningful engagement with EU law in the assessment of these measures and their compatibility with Article 8 ECHR. The apparent shift in the above

of the complaints by the affected individuals being the breach of their right to privacy, see *Satamedia* (n 118) [8], [31].

[125] *S and Marper v United Kingdom* (2009) 48 EHRR 1169 [50]–[53]. On *Marper* and its importance for the data retention standards of the ECHR and EU legal orders, see Chapters 3 and 8.

[126] ibid [41]–[55].

[127] *K.U. v Finland* (2009) 48 EHRR 52.

approach by the CJEU between 2006 and 2009 with respect to Article 8 ECHR in this specific area of case law thus seems most likely down to the interaction between Strasbourg and Luxembourg being based on a self-conscious dialogue that serves both the self-interest and shared values of both systems.

It is clear the ECtHR did not consider itself to be operating in isolation from the EU legal order in this specific area of case law during this period. However, given the scarcity of references to EU law and CJEU case law, it seems that while the ECtHR acknowledged the existence of the EU as an autonomous legal system, it did not consider itself by any means beholden to EU law standards when it came to assessing the compatibility of secret surveillance and data retention with Article 8 ECHR. In the light of its long-established case law dealing with Article 8 ECHR and secret surveillance,[128] and the nascent rights-approach of the CJEU at this time, it is unsurprising that the ECtHR would have perceived itself as the more experienced court in human rights and ultimate guardian of the right to privacy.

5. The EU Charter and a constitutional crisis

It was decided at the Cologne European Council in 1999 that fundamental rights 'scattered across primary and secondary sources' of EU law should be consolidated for greater clarity and thereby made more evident.[129] This resulted in the political endorsement of the 'EU Charter of Fundamental Rights' through proclamation by the Council of the EU, the European Commission, and Parliament at the Nice Summit in 2000.[130] The need for such an instrument within the EU legal order was questioned by some leading scholars at the time and criticized for being little more than a codification of existing rights.[131] Consequently, during the drafting of the controversial Data Retention Directive and the various Passenger Name Record Agreements between the EU and various third countries which all raised privacy and data protection concerns,[132] the legal status of the Charter was deeply uncertain. Despite being cited by the CFI and Advocates General in their Opinions to the CJEU the Charter was not legally binding.[133] Indeed, the very relevance of the

128 On this rich Art 8 ECHR case law dating back to the 1970s, see Chapters 2 and 3.

129 Catherine Barnard, *The Substantive Law of the EU* (3rd edn, OUP 2010) 421.

130 Charter of Fundamental Rights of the European Union [2000] OJ C364/01.

131 See eg Gráinne de Búrca, 'The Drafting of the European Union Charter of Fundamental Rights' (2001) 26 European Law Review 126; Francis G Jacobs, 'Human Rights in the EU' (2001) 26 European Law Review 331; Joseph HH Weiler, 'Does the European Union Truly Need a Charter of Rights?' (2000) 6 European Law Journal 95. For a contrasting view, see Armin von Bogdandy, 'The European Union as a Human Rights Organization?' (2000) 37 Common Market Law Review 1307; Koen Lenaerts and Eddy de Smijter, 'A "Bill of Rights" for the European Union' (2001) 38 Common Market Law Review 273.

132 See further Chapters 6 and 9.

133 Opinion of AG Jacobs in Case C-50/00 *Union de Pequenos Agricultores v Council of the European Union* [2002] ECR I-6677; Opinion of AG Geelhoed in Case C-224/98 *D'Hoop v Office National d'Emploi* [2002] ECR I-6191; Case T-177/01 *Jégo Quéré et Cie SA v European Commission* [2002] ECR II-2365.

Charter in cases concerning the interpretation and application of fundamental rights before the CJEU was the subject of challenge.[134]

Controversial data-driven measures to combat serious crime adopted at the EU level were therefore entering into force at a time of constitutional crisis for EU policymakers and Member States. As Harpaz aptly observes, the EU integration project was in 'the midst of a soul-searching exercise'.[135] Major efforts were made under the proposed Constitution Treaty to establish a new EU fundamental rights policy, which included placing the Charter of Fundamental Rights on the same footing as EU Treaty law and providing for the accession of the EU to the ECHR.[136] However, the draft Treaty was rejected in 2005.[137] Following the abandonment of the proposed Constitution by the EU institutions, there was a sense of urgency among policymakers that the accession should go ahead as soon as possible.[138] Before these two major reforms could be ensured under the Lisbon Treaty,[139] the EU was criticized for its lack of a comprehensive human rights policy and its ambiguous interface with the ECHR legal system.[140] One way in which the CJEU could have indicated its approach to the ECHR, and the case law of the ECtHR during this difficult period, was through the framework of the Charter of Fundamental Rights, the Luxembourg system's own autonomous catalogue of rights.

However, due to its uncertain legal status, the Luxembourg Court was slow to engage with the Charter in its adjudication of matters concerning EU fundamental rights before the instrument became legally binding in 2009.[141] In contrast, the Advocates General displayed no such hesitation and referred to the Charter increasingly more frequently and comprehensively between 2006 and 2009.[142] A shift began to happen from 2006 when the Court (sitting as the Grand Chamber) made its first

[134] See eg the written observation of the UK questioning the relevance of the legally non-binding Charter in *Rundfund* (n 99) [56]. On the UK's consistent resistance of the Charter until its repeal under UK law post-Brexit, see Catherine Barnard, 'So Long, Farewell, *Auf Wiedersehen, Adieu*: Brexit and the Charter of Fundamental Rights' (2019) 82 Modern Law Review 350.

[135] Harpaz (n 72) 131.

[136] Treaty Establishing a Constitution for Europe, 16 December 2004 [2004] OJ C310, Art I-9.

[137] The rejections by referendums in France (29 May 2005) and the Netherlands (1 June 2005) led to the abandonment of the draft Constitution Treaty: 'Dutch say "devastating no" to EU Constitution', *The Guardian* (2 June 2005).

[138] See Jean-Claude Juncker, 'Council of Europe–European Union: "A sole ambition for the European Continent"' (11 April 2006), <https://pace.coe.int/en/files/11264/html>.

[139] Ireland initially rejected the Treaty but subsequently voted for its approval in another referendum: Henry McDonald, 'Ireland votes yes to Lisbon Treaty', *The Guardian* (3 October 2009). Pending the success of the second referendum, the Lisbon Treaty did not enter into force until 1 December 2009.

[140] Harpaz (n 72) 114; de Búrca (n 5) 480.

[141] See eg Case C-117/01 *KB* [2004] ECR I-541, where despite relying upon the ECtHR judgment of *Goodwin* which cited the Charter, the Court made no explicit reference in *KB* to the Charter. See generally Iris Canor, 'Case C-117/01, *KB*' (2004) 41 Common Market Law Review 1113.

[142] See Opinion of AG Kokott in Case C-540/03 *Parliament v Council* [2006] ECR I-5769; Opinion of AG Poiares Maduro in Case C-305/05 *Ordre des barreaux* [2007] ECR I-5305; Opinion of AG Ruiz-Jarabo Colomer in C-553/07 *Rijkeboer* [2009] ECR I-3889.

direct reference to the Charter.[143] For the purpose of reaffirming, or confirming, fundamental rights previously established under EU law, the Court found referring to mentions of the Charter in secondary legislation, and references by parties to the Charter, as acceptable.[144] On the other hand, a more dynamic approach could have run the risk of raising accusations of judicial activism.[145] The Court nevertheless gradually became bolder and began openly citing the Charter independently of explicit references to the Charter made by the legislature in secondary EU legislation.[146]

For a non-binding legal instrument, the approach by the CJEU towards the Charter before the Lisbon Treaty came into force raises an interesting issue for the dialogue between the Strasbourg and Luxembourg Courts given the pending accession of the EU to the ECHR. It is striking that the Court should have accorded any recognition to the Charter given its unclear legal status, particularly when the Court could have referred and drawn from its legally binding fundamental rights jurisprudence developed under the general principles of EU law. On the other hand, the ECtHR had already taken the lead by being the first of the two Courts to refer to the Charter and may have done so as a preparatory step towards the accession of the EU to the ECHR. The CJEU may therefore have followed suit for the purpose of strengthening the ongoing dialogue between both systems and felt that it had the legitimacy to do so given the previous approach to the Charter by the ECtHR, the more experienced human rights court.

Alternatively, either Court citing the Charter before it was made legally binding under EU law could be interpreted as evidence of an early warning sign of conflict with respect to the autonomy and hierarchy between the two systems. Before 2000, there was only one codified catalogue of human rights that underpinned the protection of human rights across the EU—the ECHR. Since the declaration of the Charter, the EU has been essentially governed by two 'Bills of Rights'.[147] Until the Lisbon Treaty entered into force, the ECHR, as interpreted within the general principles of EU law, effectively outranked the Charter as the leading source of fundamental rights within EU law given the non-binding legal status of the Charter. Nevertheless, as the previous findings clearly highlight, the Charter was beginning to influence EU law before it formally became part of EU primary law.[148]

[143] *Parliament v Council* (n 142) [38]: 'While the Charter is not a legally binding instrument, the Community legislature did, however, acknowledge its importance by stating, in the second recital in the preamble to the Directive [2003/86/EC], that the Directive observes the principles recognised not only by Art 8 of the ECHR but also in the Charter.' The Court of First Instance (now known as the 'General Court') first referred to the Charter in Case T-54/99 *Max.mobil* [2002] ECR II-313.

[144] *Parliament v Council* (n 142) [31]; *Promusicae* (n 118) [64] refers to Art 8 ECHR and Arts 7 and 8 CFR; *Ordre des barreaux* (n 142) [12].

[145] Iglesias Sánchez (n 80) 1571.

[146] ibid 1572; Case C-432/05 *Unibet v Justitiekanslern* [2007] ECR I-2271 [37] (GC); Case C-438/05 *International Transport Workers' Federation v Viking Line ABP* [2007] ECR I-10779 [44] (GC); *Kadi* (n 94) [335].

[147] De Witte (n 44) 24.

[148] Thomas Streinz, 'The Europeanization of Data Protection Law' in Craig and de Búrca (n 5) 911.

The increasing number of judicial references to the legally ambiguous Charter thus suggests an (uneasy) acknowledgement by each legal order of the pending switch in priority that would take place between the ECHR and the Charter in the post-Lisbon era.

C. The Post-Lisbon Dialogue and Article 8 ECHR

The entry into force of the Lisbon Treaty introduced three major reforms for the legal status of the Charter, and the role of Article 8 ECHR, in the drafting, implementation, and review of EU data retention law. First, the obligation of the EU to accede to the ECHR became legally binding under Article 6(2) TEU.[149] Secondly, and most importantly for the purposes of this chapter, the Charter was elevated to the status of EU primary law. Thirdly, the protection of personal data became an autonomous fundamental right under primary EU law, as guaranteed by both Article 8 CFR and Article 16 TFEU.[150] As a result, the Lisbon Treaty established a much more comprehensive human rights policy for the EU. A key consequence of these substantial reforms, especially the rise of the Charter, was the expansion of the role of the CJEU as a human rights adjudicator. This was further achieved through two other major developments under the Lisbon Treaty; one being the increase in the scope of EU powers and competences and the other extending the jurisdiction of the CJEU, thus allowing for the making of preliminary references by national courts to the Court in the area of freedom, security, and justice (AFSJ).[151] The last reform has proved particularly significant given the need for ensuring the scrutiny and monitoring of the right to private life, and other related human rights such as non-discrimination, in what continues to be a rapidly expanding field in EU law.[152]

[149] Article 6(3) TEU also reaffirms that the ECHR is inherently part of the general principles of EU law: 'Fundamental rights, as guaranteed by the European Convention for the Protection of Human Rights and Fundamental Freedoms and as they result from the constitutional traditions common to the Member States, shall constitute general principles of the Union's law.'

[150] On the development of data protection by the CJEU as an autonomous right as enshrined in Art 8 CFR and the lack of clarity regarding its scope and rationale to date, see Chapter 5.

[151] de Búrca (n 116) 170. On how the current EU constitutional framework for the protection of human rights hinders the overall capability of the EU, and its other institutions, to monitor and scrutinize the implementation of EU law by its Member States in practice, see de Búrca (n 5) 494–95. For analysis of how these gaps have arisen specifically within the area of EU data retention law and the mainstreaming of the right to private life in related secondary legislation, see Chapters 5 and 9.

[152] Note eg the link established by the Lisbon Treaty between the AFSJ and border security within the context of establishing a 'common EU asylum system'. As Costello argues, this complex policy development has been riddled with rights issues due to the deep tensions between ensuring freedom of movement within the EU for most asylum seekers and the security concerns stemming from a minority of illegal immigrants: Cathryn Costello, *The Human Rights of Migrants and Refugees in European Law* (OUP 2015) 17–24. See generally Evangelia (Lilian) Tsourdi and Cathryn Costello, 'The Evolution of EU Law on Refugee and Asylum' in Craig and de Búrca (n 5) 793–823; Steve Peers, *EU Justice and Home Affairs Law—Vol I: EU Immigration and Asylum Law* (5th edn, OUP 2023).

The interconnected importance of these major constitutional developments became resoundingly clear in 2014. This was a historic year for the post-Lisbon dialogue between the Luxembourg and Strasbourg Courts with respect to two notable cases concerning the EU-ECHR accession and the compatibility of data retention with EU law. In the first of these groundbreaking and influential judgments in *Digital Rights Ireland*, the Court (sitting as the Grand Chamber) held that the Data Retention Directive 2006/24/EC was invalid under EU law and was struck down in its entirety for its incompatibility with Articles 7, 8, and 52(1) CFR.[153] The second concerned the famous and controversial Opinion 2/13 delivered in December 2014 wherein the CJEU (sitting as the Full Court) identified numerous reasons regarding why accession of the EU to the ECHR, as provided for under the Draft Accession Agreement, was incompatible with EU law.[154] This section addresses what obstacles Opinion 2/13 placed in the path towards the EU-ECHR accession and the progress made since this controversial and roundly criticized ruling.

The analysis then turns to the Charter's elevation to becoming the 'reference text' and 'starting point' for the CJEU in its assessment of EU fundamental rights and the implications of this major shift for the status of Article 8 ECHR in the privacy and data protection case law of the CJEU.[155] The scene is then set to examine the divergences and convergences in the complex dialogue between the Luxembourg and Strasbourg Courts in their case law dealing with data retention and the right to private life.

1. The long and winding road to accession

(a) The Draft Accession Agreement

In response to Opinion 2/94,[156] Article 6(2) TEU requires that the EU shall accede to the ECHR.[157] Dating back to the origins of the European Community itself,[158]

[153] Joined Cases C-293/12 and C-594/12 *Digital Rights Ireland and Seitlinger*, judgment of 8 April 2014 (ECLI:EU:C:2014:238). See further Chapters 5 and 8.

[154] Opinion 2/13 (n 5). On the meetings of the EU-ECHR accession process, see the COE, EU Accession to the ECHR ('46+1' Group), <https://coe.int/en/web/human-rights-intergovernmental-cooperation/accession-of-the-european-union-to-the-european-convention-on-human-rights#{%2230166137%22:[14]}>.

[155] Joint Communication from Presidents Costa and Skouris, 24 January 2011, <https://echr.coe.int/documents/d/echr/ue_communication_costa_skouris_eng>.

[156] Opinion 2/94 (n 5). The Court held that EU law at the time required an amendment to the EU Treaties for the competence to accede to the ECHR. On the ruling generally, see Giorgio Gaja, 'Opinion 2/94' (1996) 33 Common Market Law Review 975.

[157] Article 6(2) TEU [2016] OJ C202/19: 'The Union shall accede to the European Convention for the Protection of Human Rights and Fundamental Freedoms. Such accession shall not affect the Union's competences as defined in the Treaties.'

[158] Rosas (n 101) 207. Debates on accession to the ECHR go back over seventy years. They formed part of the drafting of the human rights provisions in the draft European Political Community Treaty which was abandoned in 1953: see de Búrca (n 5) 484 and Jean-Paul Jacqué, 'The Accession of the EU to

this 'long and winding' road from divisive debates to negotiations on the accession of the EU to the ECHR had finally reached the stage of a draft agreement in 2011.[159] These negotiations also followed the entering into force of Protocol No 14 ECHR in 2010 which amended Article 59 ECHR in order that the EU could accede to the ECHR.[160] Contentious issues for the negotiators included the creation of a mechanism that avoided the ECtHR becoming 'the judge of the division of power and competences within the EU ... as a consequence of an applicant's choice', the appointment of a judge to the ECtHR, and the future of the *Bosphorus* doctrine.[161] The general principles guiding the work on the Draft Accession Agreement (DAA) were thus threefold: (1) preserving the principle of equal rights of all individuals under the ECHR; (2) the rights of applicants in the procedure; and (3) the equality of all High Contracting Parties.[162] The accession for the ECtHR would be like no other given that the EU will be the first supranational organization to accede to the ECHR.[163]

Fears concerning the loss of the EU's autonomy following accession to the ECHR underpinned the year-long DAA negotiations process. Consistent with its approach to the EU's ratification of the UN Convention on Disability Rights,[164] the CJEU in particular stressed the need to ensure the autonomy of EU law when reconciling the requirements of the EU and ECHR systems.[165] As Gragl and others have argued, this strongly-held view shows that the CJEU has—and will—protect the legal autonomy of the EU 'at any cost'.[166] It is a stance that has subsequently

the ECHR' (2011) 48 Common Market Law Review 995. EU-ECHR accession was also a policy priority for the European Commission in the 1970s: Bulletin of the European Communities, Memorandum on the accession of the European Communities to the ECHR, Supplement 2/79, COM (79) 210 final, 2 May 1979, <https://aei.pitt.edu/6356/>.

159 Council of Europe, Draft agreement on the accession of the EU to the Convention, CDDH-UE (2011) 04, 25 February 2011, 3 (Draft Accession Agreement). On the final report containing the draft accession instruments finalized in April 2013, see <https://echr.coe.int/documents/d/echr/UE_Report_CDDH_ENG>.

160 Council of Europe, Explanatory report to the draft agreement on the accession of the EU to the Convention, Strasbourg, CDDH-UE (2011) 05, 25 February 2011, 4 (Draft Accession Agreement Report).

161 Gordillo (n 12) 187.

162 Draft Accession Agreement Report (n 160) 3.

163 In contrast, following its ratification of the UN Convention on Disability Rights, the EU-ECHR accession will not be the first time that the EU has become a party to a comprehensive international human rights instrument. See Gráinne de Búrca, 'The EU in the Negotiation of the UN Disability Convention' (2010) 35 European Law Review 174.

164 de Búrca, ibid 194.

165 See Gaja (n 156) 989; Tobias Lock, 'Walking on a Tightrope: The Draft ECHR Accession Agreement and the Autonomy of the EU Legal Order' (2011) 48 Common Market Law Review 1025. It has also been argued that arguments made in Opinion 2/94 show that, in addition to the CJEU, not all Member States at the time were 'warm' towards to the idea of accession, a factor which may have influenced the Court.

166 Gragl (n 35) 261. The origins of the autonomy principle, as noted earlier, run deep within the EU integration project and date back to the jurisprudence of the Luxembourg Court from the early 1960s: see Opinion 2/13 (n 5) [157]. It is also important to note that preserving the autonomy of the EU has not been the exclusive domain of the CJEU. Eg 'several Member States' during the drafting of the EU

played a clear role in the EU-ECHR accession debates and in shaping the human rights dialogue between the Luxembourg and Strasbourg Courts more broadly.[167] One especially fraught issue in negotiations was the involvement of the ECtHR in the interpretation and application of EU law and thus having to rule on the division of competences between the EU and Member States.[168] Consequently, the CJEU's demands during the first set of EU-ECHR accession negotiations that an 'internal review' be undertaken before the ECtHR should scrutinize an EU measure showed its concern that the preservation of autonomy of the EU should be at the core of the accession process.[169]

Nevertheless, a draft agreement was reached in 2011. The Steering Committee for Human Rights (CCDH) noted in its report to the Committee of Ministers of the Council of Europe that most delegations from EU and non-EU countries considered the DAA to be 'an acceptable and balanced compromise'.[170] There was also a general consensus amongst scholars that the DAA had managed to preserve the autonomy of EU law by making only necessary adaptations to the ECHR system in three significant ways.[171] First, the DAA did not create new competences for the EU. Secondly, the complex 'co-respondent' mechanism had 'largely ensured' that cases would be correctly directed either against the EU or its Member States.[172] Thirdly, the autonomy of the EU's legal order, and the position of the CJEU as the ultimate guardian of EU law (as provided for in the EU Treaties), were preserved.[173] What happened three years later came as a great surprise to many. The CJEU in its long-awaited ruling held the DAA to be incompatible with EU law to the extent that some questioned whether EU accession to the ECHR is 'a mission impossible'.[174]

Charter objected to there being any reference in Arts 53 and 52(3) of the Charter to the case law of the ECHR: see de Búrca (n 5) 497.

[167] ibid; Lock (n 165) 1047.

[168] Gragl (n 35) 76–79.

[169] Discussion document of the Court of Justice of the European Union on certain aspects of the accession of the European Union to the European Convention for the Protection of Human Rights and Fundamental Freedoms, Luxembourg, 5 May 2010, [7]; Lock (n 165) 1047.

[170] CDDH Report (2011) 009, 14 October 2011, [9]: <https://eerstekamer.nl/eu/documenteu/cddh_2011_009_report_to_the/f=/vitoilq0djvs.pdf>. The CCDH conducts the intergovernmental work of the Council of Europe on human rights.

[171] See eg Xavier Groussot, Tobias Lock, and Laurent Pech, 'EU Accession to the ECHR' (Robert Schuman Foundation Policy Paper Series, 7 November 2011), <https://server.www.robertschuman.eu/storage/en/doc/questions-d-europe/qe-218-en.pdf>; Tobias Lock, 'End of an Epic? The Draft Agreement on the EU's Accession to the ECHR' (2012) 31 Yearbook of European Law 162; Paul Craig, 'EU Accession to the ECHR: Competence, Procedure and Substance' (2013) 36 Fordham International Law Journal 1114.

[172] Groussot, Lock, and Pech (n 171) 16. For a detailed and persuasive critique of the voluntary nature of the proposed co-respondent procedure, and the challenges posed by its application in practice, see Lock (n 171).

[173] ibid.

[174] Editorial, 'The EU's accession to the ECHR—a "No" from the ECJ!' (2015) 52 Common Market Law Review 1, 14; Sionaidh Douglas-Scott, 'Opinion 2/13 on EU accession to the ECHR: a Christmas bombshell from the European Court of Justice', UK Constitutional Law Association (24 December 2014),

(b) Opinion 2/13: CJEU calls accession to a halt

On 18 December 2014, the CJEU (sitting as a Full Court) delivered what the then President of the Strasbourg Court described as an 'unfavourable opinion' and 'a great disappointment' for the project of accession.[175] The ruling in Opinion 2/13 held that the DAA was incompatible with the EU Treaties, thereby bringing a halt to the accession of the EU to the ECHR. Opinion 2/13 prompted a widespread response of shock and criticism by EU and human rights law scholars, particularly given the far-reaching consensus between the representatives of Member States and EU institutions involved in the draft agreement proceedings, many of whom had already accepted its compatibility with EU law at the hearings of the Opinion in May 2014.[176] The ruling also represented a significant departure from the analysis of Advocate General Kokott who concluded overall that the DAA was not fundamentally flawed and thus compatible with EU law.[177]

Throughout Opinion 2/13, however, the CJEU stressed the lack of compliance with the two key qualifications underpinning the legal obligation for the EU's accession to the ECHR as required under Article 6(2) TEU and Protocol No 8 ECHR. These provisions require that the accession agreement shall not affect the EU's competences as defined in the Treaties and, secondly, that the framework for EU accession to the ECHR will make provision for preserving the specific

<https://ukconstitutionallaw.org/2014/12/24/sionaidh-douglas-scott-opinion-213-on-eu-accession-to-the-echr-a-christmas-bombshell-from-the-european-court-of-justice/>; de Búrca (n 5) 496.

[175] European Court of Human Rights, *Annual Report 2014* (COE 2015) 6.

[176] Commentary and literature on this topic are extensive. See eg Steve Peers, 'The CJEU and the EU's accession to the ECHR: a clear and present danger to human rights protection' (18 December 2014), <https://eulawanalysis.blogspot.co.uk/2014/04/the-data-retention-judgment-cjeu.html>; Douglas-Scott (n 174); Martin Schenin, 'CJEU Opinion 2/13: Three Mitigating Circumstances' (26 December 2014), <https://verfassungsblog.de/cjeu-opinion-213-three-mitigating-circumstances-2/>; Piet Eeckhout, 'Opinion 2/13 on EU Accession to the ECHR and Judicial Dialogue: Autonomy or Autarky?' (2015) 38 Fordham International Law Journal 955; Eva Nanopoulos, 'Killing Two Birds with One Stone? The Court of Justice's Opinion on the EU's Accession to the ECHR' (2015) 74 Cambridge Law Journal 185; Benedict H Pirker and Stefan Reitemeyer, 'Between Discursive and Exclusive Autonomy—Opinion 2/13, the Protection of Fundamental Rights and the Autonomy of EU Law' (2015) 17 Cambridge Yearbook of European Legal Studies 168; Tobias Lock, 'The Future of EU Accession to the ECHR after Opinion 2/13: Is It Still Possible and Is It Still Desirable?' (2015) 11 EU Constitutional Law Review 239; Bruno de Witte and Sejla Imamovic, 'Opinion 2/13 on Accession to the ECHR: Defending the EU Legal Order Against a Foreign Human Rights Court' (2015) 40 European Law Review 683; de Búrca (n 5) 495–500; Jörg Polakiewicz, 'Accession to the European Convention on Human Rights—An Insider's View Addressing One by One the CJEU's Objections in Opinion 2/13' (2016) 36 Human Rights Law Journal 10; Jörg Polakiewicz, 'EU Accession to the ECHR: How to square the circle?' (Conference Paper, Council of Europe, 9 March 2020), <https://coe.int/en/web/dlapil/-/eu-accession-to-the-echr-how-to-square-the-circle-#_ftn19>; Tobias Lock, 'EU Accession to the ECHR' in Steve Peers and others (eds), *The EU Charter of Fundamental Rights: A Commentary* (Hart 2021) 1871–90. On the minority views that defended Opinion 2/13, see Catherine Barnard, 'Opinion 2/13 on Accession of the EU to the ECHR: looking for the silver lining' (18 December 2014), <https://eulawanalysis.blogspot.co.za/2015/02/opinion-213-on-eu-accession-to-echr.html>;Daniel Halberstam, '"It's the Autonomy, Stupid!"' (2015) 16 German Law Journal 105.

[177] AG Kokott, Opinion 2/13, view of 13 June 2014 (ECLI:EU:C:2014:2475) [278].

characteristics of the EU and EU law. Overall, the CJEU identified seven aspects of the draft agreement that rendered it incompatible with Article 6(2) TEU and Protocol No 8 ECHR—including elements that will prove challenging to secure in future renegotiations of the DAA. The first four aspects dealt with the compliance of Member States with EU law and the relationship between the Member States; the fifth and sixth focused on the protection of the EU legislature and the integrity of the CJEU; and the final point involved the oversight of EU law and policy in Common Foreign and Security Policy (CFSP).[178]

First, the CJEU held that the coordination of the relationship between Article 53 ECHR[179] and Article 53 CFR[180] requires clarification. Following its widely-criticized judgment of *Melloni*,[181] the Court made clear that the application of national standards with respect to the protection of fundamental rights under the ECHR and the constitutions of Member States must not compromise the level of protection provided under the Charter or the 'primacy, unity and effectiveness of EU law'.[182] Accordingly, the CJEU observed that the DAA must be reviewed in light of the risk posed to the autonomy of EU law by this ambiguity. The likelihood of such a clash between the national courts and the CJEU, however, and thus the need for such a review of this aspect of the draft agreement, has been questioned. More specifically, the CJEU has been sharply criticized for the lack of trust accorded to Member States' courts not to overstep the limits of their powers and jurisdiction and the lack of confidence of the CJEU in the EU legal order itself.[183] Despite Article 53 ECHR, national courts of EU Member States would still be bound to comply with the primacy of EU law in cases raising issues concerning the interpretation and application of EU law and, by extension, EU fundamental rights when acting within the scope of EU law.

178 Editorial (n 174) 8.

179 Article 53 ECHR provides: 'Nothing in this Convention shall be construed as limiting or derogating from any of the human rights and fundamental freedoms which may be ensured under the laws of any High Contracting Party or under any other agreement to which it is a party.'

180 Article 53 CFR provides: 'Nothing in this Charter shall be interpreted as restricting or adversely affecting human rights and fundamental freedoms as recognised, in their respective fields of application, by Union law and inter- national law and by international agreements to which the Union, the Community or all the Member States are party, including the European Convention for the Protection of Human Rights and Fundamental Freedoms, and by the Member States' constitutions.'

181 See Case C-399/11 *Melloni*, judgment of 26 February 2013 (GC). Here the CJEU held that Member States could not apply higher fundamental rights standards than the EU Charter in cases where the EU has harmonized the relevant law. On *Melloni* being the subject of considerable criticism for allowing the supremacy of EU law to effectively trump strengthening human rights standards, see Leonard Besselink, 'The Parameters of Constitutional Conflict after "*Melloni*"' (2014) 39 European Law Review 531; Daniel Sarmiento, 'Who's Afraid of the Charter?' (2013) 50 Common Market Law Review 1267; Eleanor Spaventa, 'Should We "Harmonize" Fundamental Rights in the EU? Some Reflections about Minimum Standards and Fundamental Rights Protection in the EU Composite Constitutional System' (2018) 55 Common Market Law Review 997.

182 Opinion 2/13 (n 5) [189].

183 See Pirker and Reitemeyer (n 176).

Secondly, the CJEU determined that the draft agreement fails to secure recognition of the 'principle of mutual trust' between Member States, save in exceptional circumstances, to consider all Member States as compliant with EU law. This principle is of particular relevance to EU fundamental rights and the EU AFSJ that covers measures such as criminal matters which, following the Lisbon Treaty, are now subject to the review of the CJEU and thus no longer the exclusive preserve of Member States.[184] In its failure to recognize this principle, the CJEU found that the DAA had treated the EU as any other Contracting Party to the ECHR, thereby posing a threat to the autonomy of EU law and ignoring 'the intrinsic nature of the EU'.[185] By maintaining an exclusive focus on the autonomy and primacy of EU law without any attempt to align EU law fundamental rights standards with that of the ECHR, critics have warned that such a rigid approach blindly sustains an already strained principle of mutual trust 'at all costs'.[186]

Thirdly, the CJEU criticized the lack of clarity concerning the potential interference posed by Protocol No 16 ECHR to the preliminary ruling procedure pursuant to Article 267 TFEU, otherwise described by the CJEU as the 'keystone' of the EU judicial system.[187] A significant reform for the ECHR legal order when it entered into force in 2018,[188] Protocol No 16 allows the ECtHR to provide an 'advisory opinion' in response to a request from certain of the highest courts and tribunals of a Contracting State before an application to the Strasbourg Court is submitted. At the time of writing, the ECtHR had delivered numerous such opinions but none concerned questions of EU law.[189] When Opinion 2/13 was delivered in 2014, this major reform of the ECHR legal order had not yet taken place. It was not therefore a consequence of the accession and subsequently took place regardless of the EU's accession to the ECHR. This raises the question, as Eeckhout and others have highlighted, of why the CJEU even considered the matter to fall within its jurisdiction when reviewing the framework of the DAA.[190] Nevertheless, the CJEU took issue in two ways with respect to how Protocol No 16 could interfere with the operation of Article 267 TFEU.

The CJEU highlighted that following accession national courts could proceed directly to the ECtHR for an advisory opinion on a matter concerning EU fundamental rights instead of referring the case to the CJEU.[191] As accession would turn ECHR rights into EU law, this would then amount to referring a question of EU law to the ECtHR given that it would implicate the EU's own ECHR obligations

[184] Opinion 2/13 (n 5) [191]–[194].
[185] ibid [191]–[194].
[186] See Peers (n 176); Pirker and Reitemeyer (n 176).
[187] Opinion 2/13 (n 5) [176].
[188] See Síofra O'Leary, 'Advisory Opinions and Judicial Dialogue Strasbourg style' (2022) 59 Common Market Law Review 87.
[189] ibid. On the importance of Protocol No 16 ECHR and its operation to date, see Chapter 1.
[190] Eeckhout (n 176) 971.
[191] Opinion 2/13 (n 5) [196].

and therefore, it is argued, creates 'a real risk of undermining the EU's preliminary reference procedure'.[192] However, the CJEU omitted any reference to the fact that such an advisory opinion would not be binding on the national court as provided under Article 5 of Protocol No 16. Hence, through what has been described as the 'exclusively autonomous' approach of the CJEU, Opinion 2/13 highlights again the lack of trust in Member States' highest courts in the latter's potential use of the procedure under Protocol No 16 ECHR.[193]

Furthermore, as highlighted by the Advocate General, the solution to this problem lies with Article 267(3) TFEU which requires national courts to refer questions of EU law to the CJEU within the framework of the preliminary reference procedure.[194] This provision of the Treaties takes precedence over national law and thus also over any international agreement that may have been ratified by individual Member States of the EU, including Protocol No 16 ECHR.[195] Alternatively, in order to further ensure against any mistaken requests from Member State courts to the ECtHR that fall within the competence of the CJEU, a binding unilateral declaration could provide a clear legal basis for the ECtHR to refuse jurisdiction should this circumstance arise.[196] The second issue posed by the advisory opinion under Protocol No 16 ECHR for the CJEU was that it could trigger the prior involvement of the CJEU and thereby create the risk of the Article 267 TFEU procedure being 'circumvented'.[197] However, as Lock observes, the CJEU did not address the fact that in the matter of an advisory opinion there is no respondent as prior involvement by the EU would arise within the co-respondent mechanism.[198]

Fourthly, the CJEU expressed concern regarding the compatibility of Article 5 of the DAA with Article 344 TFEU on the basis that Article 5 enables the EU or Member States to submit an application to the ECtHR under Article 33 ECHR[199] concerning an alleged violation by a Member State or the EU relating to EU law.[200] In line with settled case law, Article 344 TFEU requires that Member States undertake not to submit a dispute concerning the interpretation or application of the EU Treaties to any method of settlement other than those provided for therein. As a result, the CJEU concluded, in line with its 'exclusively autonomous' approach in Opinion 2/13,[201] that the DAA be amended to include a provision that expressly excludes the ECtHR's jurisdiction under Article 33 ECHR within the scope of EU

192 Halberstam (n 176).
193 Eeckhout (n 176) 972.
194 AG Kokott (n 177) [141].
195 ibid [141].
196 Halberstam (n 176).
197 Opinion 2/13 (n 5) [198].
198 Lock (2015) (n 176).
199 Article 33 ECHR provides: 'Any High Contracting Party may refer to the Court any alleged breach of the provisions of the Convention and the Protocols thereto by another High Contracting Party.'
200 Opinion 2/13 (n 5) [207].
201 Pirker and Reitemeyer (n 176).

law being compatible with Article 344 TFEU.[202] While sharing the concern of the CJEU regarding the threat posed by Article 5 of the DAA to the monopoly of the CJEU over interstate disputes, the Advocate General adopted a much more narrow 'notion of conflict' and arrived at an arguably more 'convincing ... and discursive solution'.[203]

Instead, AG Kokott considered the possibility of bringing infringement proceedings against Member States that submit their disputes concerning EU law before international courts other than the CJEU,[204] with the added possibility that interim measures may be prescribed within those proceedings[205] being 'sufficient to safeguard the practical effectiveness of Article 344 TFEU'.[206] In other words, as critics have highlighted, the CJEU's issue regarding Article 344 TFEU relates more to obligations of Member States and their courts that flow from the EU Treaties, which are then enforced with EU legal instruments as opposed to warranting an amendment in the framework governing the EU's accession to the ECHR.[207] The CJEU's approach in this instance regarding its exclusive jurisdiction has thus been further questioned for not being conducive to a 'genuine judicial dialogue' with Member States' national courts, again indicating a lack of trust in these institutions and in the EU legal order itself.[208]

The fifth and sixth points concerned the protection of the EU legislature and the integrity of the CJEU, specifically in relation to the provisions in the DAA on the co-respondent mechanism and the prior involvement procedure. Regarding the former, the CJEU took issue with the ECtHR's influence over the 'division of powers' between the EU and Member States, particularly where either would request leave to intervene as a co-respondent,[209] and the ECtHR's attribution of acts, and responsibility of acts, to either the EU or Member State which was also considered problematic.[210] Regarding one of the most controversial measures for European human rights law advocates,[211] the Court maintained that the prior involvement procedure must fall to a 'competent EU institution' and not the ECtHR to examine whether the CJEU has already given a ruling on the same question of law at issue in the proceedings before the ECtHR.[212] Arrangements should be made, according to the CJEU, that would 'fully and systematically inform' this

202 Opinion 2/13 (n 5) [213].
203 Eeckhout (n 176) 974; Pirker and Reitemeyer (n 176).
204 See Arts 258 to 260 TFEU.
205 See Art 279 TFEU.
206 AG Kokott (n 177) [118].
207 Editorial (n 176) 11.
208 Eeckhout (n 176) 972; Lock (2015) (n 176).
209 As opposed to being invited by the ECtHR, as provided under Art 3(3) of the DAA.
210 Opinion 2/13 (n 5) [220]–[230].
211 See eg the contrasting views of Aida Torres Pérez, 'Too Many Voices? The Prior Involvement of the Court of Justice of the EU' in Vasiliki Kosta, Nikos Skoutaris, and Vassilis P Tzevelekos (eds) *The EU Accession to the ECHR* (Hart 2014) and Roberto Baratta, 'Accession of the EU to the ECHR: The Rationale for the ECJ's Prior Involvement Mechanism' (2013) 50 Common Market Law Review 1305.
212 Opinion 2/13 (n 5) [238].

competent EU institution in its assessment of whether the CJEU has previously given a ruling on the relevant question at issue and, if it has not, to arrange for the prior involvement procedure to be initiated.[213]

The CJEU also stipulated that the scope of its prior involvement be extended to cases involving the interpretation of secondary EU law (in addition to cases concerning the validity of secondary law and the interpretation of a provision of primary law).[214] Following its examination of these points, the CJEU determined that the provisions of the draft agreement concerning the co-respondent mechanism and prior involvement procedure did not ensure that the specific characteristics of the EU and EU law were preserved.[215] Commentators have endorsed the reasoning of the Advocate General in relation to there being insufficient information concerning the notification of possible proceedings before the ECtHR, including participation as a co-respondent.[216] An amendment to the DAA therefore is necessary in order to ensure that the ECtHR is responsible for such notification as the procedural rights of potential co-respondents must not depend on their finding out indirectly from other parties (EU/Member State) in proceedings pending before the ECtHR.[217] However, in what has been described as its 'wholly inadequate' assessment of the co-respondent mechanism concerning the allocation of powers and responsibility, the CJEU has been criticized for confusing the attribution of international responsibility with the EU's internal division of powers.[218]

The former is based on the attribution of a breach and focuses on acts or omissions not on questions of competence. Consequently, while the DAA may be amended to address the encroachment on the EU's requirements of autonomy by removing the power of the ECtHR to apportion joint or sole responsibility, this will need to be carefully reviewed in order to reflect the very purpose of the accession agreement—external control of the EU legal order by the ECtHR.[219] In relation to the prior involvement procedure, some commentators have considered the calls of the CJEU for amending the draft agreement to ensure greater clarity and legal certainty in this procedure's scope and application as well founded.[220] In stark contrast, others have questioned the need for such clarifications; specifically, why the CJEU would not already be aware of proceedings pending before the ECtHR having already decided to become a co-respondent and how proceedings would ever come before the ECtHR where only the interpretation of EU law, but not the compatibility of EU law, with the ECHR was required.[221]

[213] ibid [241].
[214] ibid [243].
[215] ibid [235].
[216] AG Kokott (n 177) [222]–[228]; Lock (2015) (n 176).
[217] ibid.
[218] Eeckhout (n 176) 984.
[219] ibid; Lock (2015) (n 176).
[220] Editorial (n 174) 12; Halberstam (n 176).
[221] Lock (2015) (n 176); Eeckhout (n 176) 986.

The final and seventh point dealt with the judicial review of CFSP matters. As highlighted by the CJEU in Opinion 2/13, the Lisbon Treaty provides that the scope of the jurisdiction of the CJEU in the area of CFSP is very restricted.[222] These limits provide that the Luxembourg Court may only review the legality of decisions providing for 'restrictive measures' against natural or legal persons and allows the CJEU to police the boundaries between CFSP and TFEU competences.[223] However, CFSP measures are covered by the ECHR and the EU would be held responsible either on the basis of Article 1(3) of the DAA or as a co-respondent in accordance with Article 1(4) in proceedings concerning such matters before the ECtHR. Following its earlier case law, the CJEU stressed that jurisdiction to undertake a judicial review of acts, actions, or omissions by the EU cannot be conferred exclusively on an international court which is outside the institutional and judicial framework of the EU.[224]

The CJEU acknowledged that this was a consequence of the EU Treaties and not the DAA. Nevertheless, the Court maintained that this provision of the draft agreement governing the judicial review of the conduct of the EU in CFSP matters failed to have regard to the specific characteristics of EU law.[225] The major implication that the EU cannot accede to the ECHR as long as the CJEU is restricted in its jurisdiction to review CFSP matters has been roundly criticized.[226] Moreover, scholars expressed particular concern for the resulting cost to the protection of EU citizens' human rights. The major implication of the CJEU's reasoning in Opinion 2/13 being that it is 'preferable that no court should have jurisdiction over CFSP matters' rather than the ECtHR.[227]

(c) EU-ECHR accession negotiations resume: still a mission impossible?

Following the controversial and roundly criticized CJEU ruling in Opinion 2/13, prospects for the 'never-ending story' of EU accession to the ECHR receded substantially for many years.[228] A renewed impetus on making this legally mandated reform by the Lisbon Treaty a reality emerged with accession negotiations resuming in 2020.[229] Major progress was made in 2023 with negotiators reaching

[222] Opinion 2/13 (n 5) [249].
[223] Editorial (n 174) 11.
[224] Opinion 2/13 (n 5) [256].
[225] ibid [253]–[257].
[226] Douglas-Scott (n 174); Editorial (n 174) 13; Eeckhout (n 176) 987–88; Peers (n 176).
[227] See Pirker and Reitemeyer (n 176) 18; Schenin (n 176); Mark Dawson, 'What Does it Mean to Say that the Court of Justice is not a Human Rights Institution? A Critical Appraisal' (2022) 14 Journal of Human Rights Practice 215, 220.
[228] Polakiewicz (2020) (n 176); de Búrca (n 5) 481.
[229] In October 2019, EU Member States made clear their political will in a decision of the EU Council to reaffirm the authorization for the European Commission to negotiate and to issue amended negotiating directives on the EU-ECHR accession process: see Rosas (n 101) 207.

a provisional agreement on the revised draft accession texts.[230] However, at the time of writing, issues remained to be resolved by the EU internally regarding the jurisdictions of the Courts and the CFSP before the opinion of the CJEU[231] and the relevant ratifications from the European Parliament and Member States could be sought.[232] While there are those who remain 'cautiously optimistic' about the prospects of accession,[233] Lock and others warn that if this fully incorporated the CJEU's autonomy-driven vision in Opinion 2/13, the system of external accountability provided by the ECHR would be weakened and potentially lower the standard of human rights protection.[234] These challenges aside, one outcome is certain—it will again be for the CJEU to assess the compatibility with EU law of this third draft agreement and whether there will be a new chapter for the protection of human rights in the EU.

2. The EU Charter and Article 8 ECHR

(a) Charter swiftly becomes leading source on rights in EU legal order

The binding legal nature of the Charter elevated the status of what was effectively the EU's Bill of Rights to become the principal source for the CJEU in its assessment of EU fundamental rights within the EU legal order. Following this major change, the Court increasingly draws from and enforces the relevant provisions of the Charter. This has resulted in the CJEU relying less on the ECHR as a source of law in its fundamental rights jurisprudence.[235] Indeed, in its early post-Lisbon case law, the CJEU based its reasoning on the Charter rather than

230 On the texts of the revised draft agreement, see: <https://coe.int/en/web/human-rights-intergovernmental-cooperation/accession-of-the-european-union-to-the-european-convention-on-human-rights>.

231 The CJEU strongly criticized the possibility that the ECtHR ('a non-EU body') would have the 'exclusive' jurisdiction to assess the compatibility with the ECHR of certain activities falling within the scope of CFSP areas that would remain outside the jurisdiction of the CJEU: see Opinion 2/13 (n 5) [254]–[258].

232 On the accession procedural requirements, see Art 218 TFEU. See generally Šejla Imamović, Elin Börjedal, and Elenora Di Franco, 'The Future of EU Fundamental Rights' (2024) 31 Maastricht Journal of European and Comparative Law 137.

233 See eg Rosas (n 101) (former judge of the CJEU) and Polakiewicz (2020) (n 176) (Legal Counsel at the Council of Europe).

234 See Tobias Lock, 'EU Accession to the ECHR' in Steve Peers and others (eds), *The EU Charter of Fundamental Rights: A Commentary* (Hart 2021) 1890; Robert Harmsen, 'The (Geo-)Politics of EU Accession' in Vasiliki Kosta, Nikos Skoutaris, and Vassilis P Tzevelekos (eds), *The EU Accession to the ECHR* (Hart 2014) 217. Lock also highlights three reasons why EU accession to the ECHR should take place. Accession would provide for greater accountability of the EU, and its institutions, via external review by the ECtHR and allow individuals to bring cases directly against the EU, as opposed to using Member States as proxies. Secondly, the EU would have the opportunity to better defend its own position and its legal order. Thirdly, accession would address the remaining gaps in responsibility established by the ECtHR in its case law, notably the *Bosphorus* doctrine: see Lock (n 234) 1878.

235 See Sionaidh Douglas-Scott, 'The European Union and Human Rights after the Treaty of Lisbon' (2011) 11 Human Rights Law Review 645; De Búrca (n 13) 499; Rosas (n 101) 208.

the ECHR, even where the ECHR was relevant to the relevant case or right.[236] This avid prioritization of the Charter was demonstrated again in the reliance by the CJEU on this formal source of EU fundamental rights without any reference to the issue of temporal applicability.[237] Despite not being legally binding before the entry into force of the Lisbon Treaty, unlike the general principles of EU law, the validity of EU law in force before 2009 was considered by the CJEU in light of provisions under the Charter in several cases.[238] This retroactive application of the Charter ran counter to the principles of legality and legal certainty and was thus clearly problematic from a rule of law perspective.[239] Moreover, the prioritization of the Charter over the ECHR and the general principles of EU law aligns with an increasingly emboldened CJEU in its autonomy-driven post-Lisbon case law.[240]

(b) CJEU no longer defers to Article 8 ECHR case law: coherence versus autonomy

Where data retention and surveillance measures are concerned, there are three key differences when it comes to assessing what constitutes a justified interference with the right to respect for private life under the systems of the EU Charter and the ECHR. First, and perhaps most importantly, the Charter—unlike the ECHR—explicitly provides for a distinct right to the protection of personal data in Article 8(1).[241] The novel introduction of an autonomous right to the protection of personal data to the European human rights *acquis* in Article 8 CFR is a particularly striking reminder that the Charter is far from 'a mere copy' of the ECHR.[242] Its creation also invariably raised the risk of incoherence between the standards and safeguards of the ECHR and the EU legal orders within the respective bodies of jurisprudence of the ECtHR and the CJEU concerning data protection.[243] Although the protection of data privacy guaranteed by Article 7 CFR clearly overlaps with the fundamental right to the protection of personal data, as enshrined in Article 8 CFR, there is no corresponding right in the ECHR. Similarities in the scope of each are, of course, evident but the related rights of private life and data protection

236 See eg Case C-403/09 PPU *Deticek* [2009] ECR I-12193; Case C-407/08 P *Knauf Gips* [2010] ECR I-6375; Joined Cases C-92/09 and C-93/09 *Volker und Markus Schecke* [2010] ECR I-11063 (GC).

237 Iglesias Sánchez (n 80) 1573.

238 *Deticek* (n 236) (Council Regulation (EC) No 2201/2003); *Volker* (n 236) (Council Regulations (EC) No 1290/2005 and No 259/2008).

239 Iglesias Sánchez (n 80) 1575.

240 See, as noted earlier, the role played by the autonomy of the EU legal order in Opinion 2/13 delivered by the CJEU (sitting as the Full Court) five years after the Charter became legally binding.

241 Article 8(1) CFR provides: 'Everyone has the right to the protection of personal data concerning him or her.'

242 Rosas (n 101) 212.

243 This divergence between the standards of the EU and ECHR legal orders, as noted later, became abundantly clear in the novel data protection safeguards established by the CJEU in its interpretation of Art 8 CFR in *Digital Rights Ireland* and its data protection case law thereafter. See Chapter 5.

differ in many ways and are not treated as identical within the ECHR and EU legal orders.[244]

Secondly, like Article 8 ECHR, the rights to private life and data protection guaranteed under Articles 7 and 8 CFR are not absolute. In contrast to Article 8(2) ECHR, however, the conditions that must be met if limitations are placed on the rights guaranteed by Articles 7 and 8 CFR are set out in an entirely separate provision under Article 52(1) CFR. The latter contains overlapping, but also additional, requirements that must be satisfied if the exercise of these rights are restricted by a measure the CJEU determines falls within the scope of EU law. For instance, unlike the text of the ECHR, Article 52 CFR explicitly provides for a privacy interference to be examined based on the 'essence' of the right and its protected interests.[245] Thirdly, Article 52(3) gives statutory expression to the pre-existing status under the EU general principles of law which recognize equivalent rights under the ECHR as providing minimum human rights standards within EU law. The Charter thus enshrines, as Craig and de Búrca highlight, the long-established idea that the scope of protection and safeguards of Article 8 ECHR represent 'a floor' but crucially 'not a ceiling' for the interpretation and application of Article 7 CFR.[246]

In a 2011 Joint Communication by the Presidents of the ECtHR and the CJEU, a 'parallel interpretation' of the ECHR and the EU Charter was endorsed by both systems in order to ensure the greatest coherence between these legal instruments where the meaning and scope of corresponding rights are involved.[247] Effectively, this novel extra-judicial statement highlighted the need for both Courts to engage in a constructive dialogue in order inter alia to address the complexities and differences between the ECHR and the Charter, one such novel provision being Article 8 CFR. Despite expressing a commitment to follow the jurisprudence of the ECtHR when interpreting Charter rights that correspond with rights under the ECHR, explicit consideration by the CJEU of this case law, including Article 8 ECHR, has sharply declined.[248] Rosas argues that 'less frequent' references to the ECHR and Strasbourg jurisprudence was to be expected once the status of the EU Charter was elevated to binding primary law and thus part of the EU constitutional order.[249] However, as noted previously, an emboldened CJEU was already distancing itself from Article 8 ECHR, and from the Strasbourg Court, in its privacy and data protection case law before the Charter was legally binding.

[244] On the interplay of Arts 7 and 8 CFR, see Chapter 5. On the approach of the ECtHR to the treatment of data protection as a sub-right of Art 8 ECHR, see Chapter 3.

[245] On Art 52 CFR and the significance of the essence requirement for Art 8 ECHR and Arts 7 and 8 CFR in the data retention case law of the CJEU and ECtHR, see Chapter 5.

[246] Craig and de Búrca (n 88) 367.

[247] Joint Communication (n 155).

[248] See Iglesias Sánchez (n 80) 1604; de Búrca (n 14) 498; Bieker (n 112) 69–78.

[249] Rosas (n 101) 208.

In line with the explanations of the Charter,[250] the CJEU has consistently acknowledged Article 52(3) CFR as requiring that it takes into account the corresponding rights guaranteed by Article 8 ECHR when interpreting those guaranteed by Article 7 CFR 'as the minimum threshold of protection'.[251] The Court has also, however, highlighted in its landmark data retention case law that this benchmark 'floor' threshold, and other constitutional links between the Luxembourg and Strasbourg systems, is subject to a potentially far-reaching caveat. This concerns the aim of Article 52(3) CFR as 'intended to ensure the necessary consistency between the rights contained in the Charter and the corresponding rights guaranteed in the ECHR, *without adversely affecting* the autonomy of EU law and that of the Court of Justice'.[252] In line with its post-Lisbon rights jurisprudence more broadly,[253] the CJEU has made clear that despite the close institutional links between the EU and the ECHR in the EU legal order, its interpretation and application of the right to private life have changed drastically. Within the tight constraints of this autonomy-driven interpretation of the Charter, the approach of deference by default to the Article 8 ECHR case law of the ECtHR has been rendered a relic of the CJEU's pre-Lisbon jurisprudence.

(c) Early post-Lisbon rulings on Article 8 ECHR and the Charter raise concerns

Bavarian Lager and *Volker* were two major judgments concerning the protection of private life and personal data delivered by the CJEU (sitting as the Grand Chamber) in its the early post-Lisbon era. Both were also the subject of strong criticism with respect to the CJEU's interpretation and application of Article 8 ECHR and Articles 7 and 8 CFR.[254] In *Bavarian Lager*, the European Commission

[250] Explanations relating to the Charter of Fundamental Rights [2007] OJ C303/17, 33. Article 52(3) CFR: 'is intended to ensure the necessary consistency between the Charter and the ECHR by establishing the rule that, in so far as the rights in the present Charter also correspond to rights guaranteed by the ECHR, the meaning and scope of those rights, including authorised limitations, are the same as those laid down by the ECHR. This means in particular that the legislator, in laying down limitations to those rights, must comply with the same standards as are fixed by the detailed limitation arrangements laid down in the ECHR ... without thereby adversely affecting the autonomy of Union law and of that of the Court of Justice.'

[251] See eg Case C-694/20 *Orde van Vlaamse Balies and Others*, judgment of 8 December 2022 (ECLI:EU:C:2022:963) [26] (GC) (concerning the validity of Flemish legislation on administrative cooperation in the field of taxation and legal professional privilege).

[252] See Joined Cases C-203/15 and C-698/15 *Tele2 Sverige and Watson*, judgment of 21 December 2016 (ECLI:EU:C:2016:970) [129]; Joined Cases C-511/18, C-512/18, and C-520/18 *La Quadrature du Net and Others*, judgment of 6 October 2020 (ECLI:EU:C:2020:791) [124] (emphasis added) (concerning an assessment of the right to liberty and security as enshrined in Art 6 CFR and Art 5 ECHR); *Orde van Vlaamse Balies* (n 251) [26] (specific assessment of Art 7 CFR and Art 8 ECHR).

[253] On the CJEU's autonomous interpretation of the fundamental rights of the Charter, which are influenced, but not fully determined, by the ECHR in its recent case law, see Charlotte Langenfeld, 'The "Autonomization" of EU Fundamental Rights Protection' (2024) 31 Maastricht Journal of European and Comparative Law 188.

[254] See eg Sionaidh Douglas-Scott, 'The European Union and Human Rights after the Treaty of Lisbon' (2011) 11 Human Rights Law Review 645; Juliane Kokott and Christoph Sobotta, 'The Distinction Between Privacy and Data Protection in the Jurisprudence of the CJEU and the ECtHR'

appealed the judgment of the General Court to the Grand Chamber on the main ground that the General Court had erred in its interpretation of the EU legislation that governed exemptions to the right of access to documents involving the conduct of EU institutions. Specifically, it was argued that the General Court had misinterpreted Regulation No 1049/2001 as the Court did so only 'in light of Article 8 ECHR and the case law based thereon', excluding any consideration of EU data protection legislation.[255] The CJEU stressed in its judgment that the General Court's assessment of the protection of the '*right* to privacy with respect to the processing of personal data' should not have been split between an analysis of Article 8 ECHR and the relevant EU legislation concerning the protection of personal data.[256]

In upholding the appeal, the Grand Chamber stated that the Commission had not infringed EU law by disclosing redacted minutes of a meeting that concerned the business of the applicant on the ground that consent authorizing the disclosure of the identities of all participants had not been obtained. The General Court had previously held that disclosing the identities of the five individuals in question did not amount to an interference with their right to respect for private life. This was based on the reasoning that the relevant personal data did not fall within the scope of 'private life' and therefore the disclosure was not 'capable of undermining the private life of the person concerned'.[257] However, unlike the General Court, the CJEU did not address the need to reconcile the relevant conflicting interests of the right of access to documents and the right to respect for private life. Instead, the Grand Chamber simply stated that the applicant 'had not shown any express and legitimate justification or any convincing argument in order to demonstrate the necessity for those personal data to be transferred'.[258] This reasoning, or lack thereof, is confusing given that the appeal directly concerned, as observed by the CJEU earlier on in its judgment, the '*right* to privacy with respect to the processing of personal data'. Consequently, there was a major gap in the fundamental rights analysis in *Bavarian Lager* concerning the absolute application of the protection of private life and personal data and its lack of justification for the non-disclosure of the relevant personal data. Ultimately, as Lynskey rightly observes, this glaring lacuna raised the question of what interest was being protected by the Court in *Bavarian Lager* 'if not privacy'?[259]

(2013) 3 International Data Privacy Law 222; Maria Tzanou, 'Data Protection as a Fundamental Right Next to Privacy?' (2013) 3 International Data Privacy Law 88; Lynskey (n 112) 131–75; Bieker (n 112) 71–72. On the combined readings of Arts 7, 8, and 52(1) CFR by the CJEU in its more recent data protection case law, see further Chapter 5.

[255] Case C-28/08 *Commission v Bavarian Lager* [2010] ECR I-6055, [58].
[256] ibid [60] (emphasis added).
[257] ibid [119].
[258] ibid [78].
[259] Orla Lynskey, 'Deconstructing Data Protection: The "Added-Value" of a right to Data Protection in the EU Legal Order' (2014) 63 International and Comparative Law Quarterly 569, 579.

Like *Bavarian Lager*, the main issue before the CJEU in *Volker* was the protection of personal data processed by the EU institutions but also dealt with the issue of data retention. The specific facts concerned the validity of EU legislation that required the publication on a publicly accessible Internet website of personal data identifying the applicants as recipients of funding from the EU common agriculture policy and other related information. The applicants sought to prevent any publication of this personal data. In its questions to the CJEU, the national court requested in this preliminary reference to that the Court should review the validity of the (already highly controversial) Data Retention Directive 2006/24/EC to enable its assessment of whether the contested retention of personal data in *Volker* was lawful. However, the CJEU held that there was no need to consider the validity of the retention required by Directive 2006/24/EC on the grounds of its lack of relevance to the proceedings.[260]

In a departure from the lack of engagement with Article 8 ECHR in *Bavarian Lager*, the fundamental rights analysis in *Volker* involved much closer engagement with Article 8 ECHR and the case law of the ECtHR. This was framed, however, within the context of the validity of the impugned EU legislation in the light of Articles 7 and 8 CFR, provisions of which were not legally binding before the entry into force of the Lisbon Treaty and thus did not apply to the disputes which had occurred before 2009. Although the CJEU acknowledged that when the national court had specifically requested whether the publication of the relevant personal data constituted an unjustified interference with the right to the protection of personal data, it referred 'essentially to Article 8 of the Convention', the CJEU did not address the issue of the temporal applicability of the Charter.[261] Instead, the CJEU disregarded the principles of legality and legal certainty, and the approach of the national court, and instead held that the validity of the relevant pre-Lisbon legislation should be assessed in light of the provisions of the Charter.[262] This retroactive application of the Charter by the CJEU clearly demonstrates the legally unsound prioritization of Articles 7 and 8 CFR over the source of fundamental rights that the CJEU should have relied on when assessing the protection of personal data in *Volker*, the authoritative guidance of which was Article 8 ECHR as guaranteed by the general principles of EU law.

Instead, the entrenchment and elevation of the Charter as the leading source of EU fundamental rights clearly takes priority in *Volker* over considerations of legal certainty and coherence. Further evidence of this approach can be seen in the CJEU taking particular care in *Volker* to replace any explicit references to Article 8 ECHR, and the relevant case law of the ECtHR, by self-referencing its own case

[260] On the difficult and fraught dialogue between the national courts and the CJEU on the validity of the Data Retention Directive with EU law, see Chapter 7.

[261] *Volker* (n 236) [44].

[262] ibid [46].

law. In its identification of Article 8 CFR as a qualified right, the Grand Chamber cites its previous judgment in *Schmidberger*.[263] However, the exact passage from *Schmidberger* relies on jurisprudence explicitly drawn from the ECtHR and its Article 8 ECHR case law which define the conditions that apply to qualified rights guaranteed by the ECHR. Here the CJEU indirectly relies on the rich jurisprudence of the ECtHR in its development of Article 8 CFR. Following, and curiously not before, its prior indirect reference to the Strasbourg system, the CJEU highlights the requirement of Article 52(3) CFR which provides that the meaning and scope of fundamental rights under the Charter, which correspond to rights guaranteed by the ECHR, are to be the same.

Subsequently, the fundamental rights analysis concerning the right to respect for private life and the protection of personal data in *Volker* becomes riddled with inconsistency and inaccuracy. In particular, the Grand Chamber determined that the right to respect for private life regarding the processing of personal data 'recognised by Articles 7 and 8 of the Charter, concerns *any information* relating to an identified or identifiable individual'.[264] This passage is significant for three reasons. First, the focus of the fundamental rights analysis of the CJEU shifted from the scope of Article 8 CFR to the protection of personal data as a subset of the right to respect for private life, as guaranteed by both Article 7 and Article 8 CFR. The CJEU thus appears to have reverted back to its confusing approach in *Bavarian Lager* of conflating its analysis of the rights guaranteed by Article 7 and Article 8 CFR.

Secondly, the CJEU relies again on the case law of the Strasbourg system in its interpretation of the scope of the *right* to respect for private life regarding the processing of personal data as guaranteed under the Charter. However, on this occasion, the CJEU has done so by engaging with the Strasbourg system directly and discursively by discussing and expressly citing the jurisprudence from the ECtHR judgments of *Amann* and *Rotaru*.[265] Thirdly, the CJEU interpreted the ECtHR case law as meaning that the protected interest of private life under Article 8(1) ECHR includes the protection of all personal data ('any information relating to an identified or identifiable individual'). This interpretation may have seemed correct based on a cursory glance of the established case law of the ECtHR concerning the right to respect for private life and the processing of personal data. However, as Kokott and Sobotta highlight, 'a closer inspection' of the relevant case law at that time shows that the protection of personal data under Article 8 ECHR requires an additional element of privacy in order for personal information to be included in the scope of private life.[266] Consequently, based on this erroneous interpretation of

[263] Case C-112/00 *Schmidberger* [2003] ECR I-5659 [80].
[264] *Volker* (n 236) [52].
[265] *Amann v Switzerland* [2000] ECHR 87 [65]; *Rotaru v Romania* [2000] ECHR 192 [43].
[266] Kokott and Sobotta (n 254) 224.

Article 8 ECHR, the CJEU held in *Volker* that the online publication of the names and amounts received by the applicants constituted 'an interference with their private life' within the meaning of Article 7 CFR.[267]

In determining the cardinal issue of whether the interference with Article 7 CFR was justified in line with the criteria of Article 52(1) CFR, the CJEU ultimately held that an unjustified interference had taken place. The Court arrived at this determination based on the lack of any evidence showing that the EU legislature had taken into account 'methods of publishing information on the beneficiaries concerned consistent with the objective of such publication while at the same time causing less interference with those beneficiaries right to respect their private life in general and to the protection of their personal data in particular'.[268] The publication of personal data could therefore have been limited to the frequency, or nature, of the amounts received. Accordingly, the EU legislature exceeded the limits which compliance with the principle of proportionality imposes by requiring the publication of names of all natural persons who were recipients of EU funding in this instance.[269]

Volker was a milestone judgment for the EU Charter. It will always be well known for being the first ruling where the validity of an EU act assessed in light of the Charter resulted in the striking down of that contested part of EU law.[270] On the other hand, underlying this jurisprudential landmark for EU fundamental rights is an inaccurate interpretation of the right to respect for private life as guaranteed by Article 8(1) ECHR and an inconsistent examination and retroactive application of the Charter. Moreover, far from being a leading case for the protection of private life within the EU legal order, the judgment also suggests that the CJEU had a high threshold for allowing long-term data retention.[271] Concerns expressed at this time regarding a permissive approach by the CJEU in its post-Lisbon case law dealing with data retention measures turned out to be short-lived. Instead, the CJEU has subsequently positioned itself at the vanguard of EU data retention policymaking and supranational judicial human rights scrutiny in Europe.[272]

[267] *Volker* (n 236) [58].

[268] ibid [81].

[269] ibid [88].

[270] Iglesias Sánchez (n 80) 1581. In addition, *Volker* has been described as 'a remarkable judgment' with respect to transparency laws in the management of the EU agricultural funding: Theodore Konstadinides, 'Destroying Democracy on the Ground of Defending It?' (2011) 36 European Law Review 722, 735.

[271] See Konstadinides (n 270) 735. These concerns also stemmed from what Docksey describes as the 'jurisdictional approach' adopted by the CJEU in its pre-Lisbon case law concerning State surveillance and data retention. This approach involves the Court dealing solely with the legal basis of an impugned measure regardless of its broader consequences and giving little explicit consideration to any rights issues raised for its scrutiny: Christopher Docksey, 'The European Court of Justice and the Decade of Surveillance' in Hielke Hijmans and Herke Kranenborg (eds), *Data Protection Anno 2014: How to Restore Trust?* (Intersentia 2014) 97. See further Chapter 6.

[272] On the details and legal impact of the Snowden revelations, see Chapters 1 and 5.

D. Article 8 ECHR in the Post-Snowden Era

Emboldened by the enactment of the Charter at the height of the Snowden revelations, *Digital Rights Ireland* was the first time an entire instrument of EU legislation was struck down by the CJEU for its incompatibility with the Charter.[273] This notable judgment followed considerable pressure from national courts and growing challenges to the *Solange* doctrine raising questions regarding the capacity of the CJEU to ensure adequate protection of human rights within the EU legal order.[274] Streinz has further argued that competition between the CJEU and the ECtHR in the 'highly topical area' of data protection may have 'propelled Luxembourg to embrace a fundamental rights-protective stance' that it did not advance comparatively in other areas of EU law.[275] Thus, in its first of many groundbreaking judgments on bulk data retention measures, the Court firmly established in *Digital Rights Ireland* that the Directive constituted a 'wide-ranging and particularly serious interference' with the rights to privacy and data protection.[276] The Court held that this amounted to an unjustified interference on the key ground that the Directive had failed to satisfy the proportionality requirements under Article 52(1) CFR and had thereby permitted a regime of general and indiscriminate retention. The access to said data by public authorities also lacked clear and precise rules to ensure the extent that the interference with the rights guaranteed by Articles 7 and 8 CFR was limited to what was 'strictly necessary'.[277]

By declaring in *Digital Rights Ireland* that the controversial Data Retention Directive was invalid under law, and not limiting the temporal effect of its judgment, the declaration of invalidity took effect from the date on which the former Directive entered into force. This robust rights-based assessment by the CJEU thus resulted in the Directive being erased from existence without 'an immediate successor'.[278] Through the establishment of strict rules concerning bulk data retention, and the subsequent legislative lacuna in EU law, *Digital Rights Ireland* marked the beginning of a shift by the Court towards using 'the fundamental right guarantees of the Charter as a means to extend the reach and impact of EU legislation' in the areas of law enforcement and national security.[279]

[273] See eg Orla Lynskey, 'The Data Retention Directive is Incompatible with the Rights to Privacy and Data Protection and is Invalid in Its Entirety' (2014) 51 Common Market Law Review 1789; Martin Nettesheim, 'The CJEU's Decision on the Data Retention Directive' in Burhard Hess and Cristina M Mariottini (eds), *Protecting Privacy in Private International and Procedural Law and by Data Protection* (Nomos 2015) 57–71. See further Chapter 8.

[274] See Chapter 7.

[275] Other such areas have notably included EU immigration law and policy: see Streinz (n 148) 911; Peers (n 152).

[276] Joined Cases C-293/12 and C-594/12 *Digital Rights Ireland and Seitlinger*, judgment of 8 April 2014 (ECLI:EU:C:2014:238) [65]. On the judgment generally and related case law, see Chapters 5 and 8.

[277] ibid [62]–[65].

[278] Lynskey (n 273) 1789.

[279] See Nettesheim (n 273) 66.

The CJEU has since established a reputation for its robust and expansive interpretation and application of EU fundamental rights, and data protection law, largely due to the highly prescriptive standards it has continued to develop in this area of case law.[280]

1. CJEU becomes the vanguard court for data retention scrutiny: built on Article 8 ECHR standards

Since *Digital Rights Ireland*, the dialogue between the CJEU and the ECtHR regarding the role and influence of Article 8 ECHR in this groundbreaking area of jurisprudence continues to be rich and complex. There can be no doubt regarding the instrumental role played by the principles and standards of the Article 8 ECHR case law of the ECtHR in the development of the landmark standards of Articles 7 and 8 CFR first established in *Digital Rights Ireland*.[281] In line with the requirement in Article 52(3) CFR that any fundamental rights standards must be interpreted as providing 'a minimum threshold of protection' with respect to corresponding rights under the ECHR,[282] the Court has based many of its EU rules concerning data retention on long-established Article 8 ECHR standards. These include the strict proportionality approach applied by the ECtHR in its leading data retention judgment in *Marper* to blanket and indiscriminate retention, and the need for 'greater' safeguards where personal data is subject to automatic processing and when the latter is used for 'police purposes'.[283] The CJEU in *Digital Rights Ireland* also engages in detail with the importance of these Article 8 ECHR standards and explicitly draws from the related case law of the ECtHR dealing with retention measures and access to data for countering serious crime and national security matters in its reasoning.[284] These standards have gone on to shape the cardinal question for the CJEU in its later notable cases on data retention and law enforcement access, all of which have primarily focused on the proportionality of the contested frameworks and

[280] On the major legal impacts of these evolving judicial standards in related subsequent rulings that have shaped provisions in the GDPR, the LED, and other regimes permitting international data transfers, and the surveillance of passenger name records within the EU, see Chapters 5 and 9.

[281] See Marie-Pierre Granger and Kristina Irion, 'The Court of Justice and the Data Retention Directive in Digital Rights Ireland' (2014) 39 European Law Review 835, 847. See further Chapter 8.

[282] Note the Advocate General's Opinion which explicitly drew from and cited the relevant Art 8 ECHR case law of the ECtHR (though strikingly not *Marper*). See Opinion of AG Cruz Villalón, Case C-293/12 *Digital Rights Ireland* (ECLI:EU:C:2013:845) [68]–[73].

[283] On the legacy of *Marper* and the relevant CJEU case law, see Chapters 3 and 5.

[284] *Digital Rights Ireland* (n 276) [35], [47]–[55]. Strasbourg case law cited included: *Weber and Saravia*; *Rotaru*; *S and Marper*; *M.K.*; and *Liberty and Others*. On the standards and safeguards developed by this Art 8 ECHR case law and their importance, see Chapters 2 and 3.

whether they meet the 'strictly necessary' criteria as enshrined in Articles 7, 8, 11, and 52(1) CFR.[285]

Of course, the stricter approach and additional safeguards applied in the CJEU case law show that these EU data retention rules have gone far beyond the 'floor' of the standards previously developed by the ECtHR in its rich Article 8 ECHR case law. These clear divergences from the Strasbourg jurisprudence were directly brought to the attention of the CJEU by the Court of Appeal for England and Wales in *Tele2*. Here the Luxembourg Court was asked to confirm whether its interpretation of the scope of Articles 7 and 8 CFR in *Digital Rights Ireland* had been expanded 'beyond' that of Article 8 ECHR as established in the jurisprudence of the ECtHR.[286] In responding to this question, the CJEU goes beyond simply pointing to the scope afforded to it by Article 52(3) CFR which clearly states that EU law is not precluded 'from providing protection that is more extensive then the ECHR'.[287] Instead, two years after the shock of Opinion 2/13 for the Council of Europe and the EU, the Court takes the opportunity to highlight the role of the autonomy of EU law and the current legal status of Article 8 ECHR therein within the particular context of its data retention jurisprudence.

The CJEU begins by explaining that although Article 6(3) TEU confirms that fundamental rights recognized by the ECHR constitute general principles of EU law, 'the ECHR does not constitute, *as long as the European Union has not acceded to it*, a legal instrument which has been formally incorporated into EU law'.[288] Thus, the Court reasons that the interpretation of the e-Privacy Directive 2002/58, the EU legislation under review in *Tele2*, must accordingly be undertaken '*solely* in the light of the fundamental rights guaranteed by the Charter'.[289] It is only then that the Court refers to Article 52(3) CFR which clearly states that EU law is not precluded from providing protection that is more extensive than the ECHR. In addition, the Court highlights another key difference between the ECHR and the Charter, noting that Article 8 CFR concerns a fundamental right which is distinct from that enshrined in Article 7 CFR and 'which has no equivalent in the ECHR'.[290] It is noteworthy that the CJEU in *Tele2* engaged with this question from the national court at such length particularly as the Court ultimately deems it to be 'inadmissible'.[291] Consequently, this detailed response and its reasoning clearly show

[285] See eg the proportionality assessments and the 'strictly necessary' safeguards in Opinion 1/15, *Schrems II*; *La Quadrature du Net*; *SpaceNet*; and *Ligue des droits humains*. On these CJEU judgments and their importance for EU data protection law more broadly, see Chapters 5 and 9.

[286] Joined Cases C-203/15 and C-698/15 *Tele2 Sverige and Watson*, judgment of 21 December 2016 (ECLI:EU:C:2016:970) [126].

[287] ibid [129].

[288] ibid [127] (emphasis added). Notably, the CJEU does not mention Opinion 2/13 in its reasoning though there is a clearly an implicit reference being made here to the controversial ruling.

[289] ibid [128] (emphasis added).

[290] ibid [129].

[291] ibid [133].

some sensitivity on the part of the CJEU to its jurisprudence being challenged for its divergence from Strasbourg case law.

The CJEU has continued to engage with the Article 8 ECHR and the related case law of the ECtHR in its subsequent data retention judgments.[292] However, explicit references to Strasbourg jurisprudence now tend to occur on a more ad hoc basis. Here we see the CJEU giving the case law of Article 8 ECHR the status of persuasive authority in its reasoning and thus placing the Charter centre stage as its main source of EU law in its fundamental rights analysis. This shift has taken place in tandem with the Court self-referencing the same standards previously incorporated into Articles 7 and 8 CFR by citing its own case law, particularly when expanding the application of these strict standards beyond the original scope of the Data Retention Directive. As Kuner and others highlight, the Court continues to cite and build on its groundbreaking precedents in *Digital Rights Ireland* and *Tele2*, extending these standards to other areas, including international data transfers, passenger name records, and national security.[293]

An overarching development in the dialogue between Strasbourg and Luxembourg is therefore clearly evident: the Charter has become 'both a point of departure and an end station' for the CJEU when examining any issues concerning the right to private life in this high-profile and rapidly evolving area of its data protection case law.[294] While Article 8 ECHR, as part of the general principles of EU law, still holds greater weight within the EU legal order than other sources of international human rights law, the CJEU no longer accords the same 'special' status to the ECtHR case law on data retention and surveillance that applied before the enactment of the EU Charter.

2. The Strasbourg response: an elevated status for the vanguard case law of the CJEU and a departure from its minimum safeguards setting role

An emboldened CJEU has delivered a series of cases since *Digital Rights Ireland* concerning data retention and State surveillance that the ECtHR cannot ignore when it reviews the compatibility of such measures with Article 8 ECHR. Indeed,

[292] Opinion 1/15 (citing *Marper*); *Tele2* (citing *Zakharov*; *Szabo and Vissy*); Joined Cases C-511/18, C-512/18, and C-520/18 *La Quadrature du Net and Others*, judgment of 6 October 2020 (ECLI:EU:C:2022:702) (citing inter alia *Amann*; *Ben Faiza*; *Breyer*); *SpaceNet* (citing *Big Brother Watch*; *Centrum för Rättvisa*). On these judgments, see further Chapters 3 and 5.

[293] See Christopher Kuner, 'International Agreements, Data Protection, and EU Fundamental Rights on the International stage: Opinion 1/15, *EU Canada PNR*' (2019) 55 Common Market Law Review 857; Dominique Moore, 'Article 23: Restrictions' in Christopher Kuner and others (eds), *The EU General Data Protection Regulation: A Commentary* (OUP 2020) 543–54; Elif Mendos Kuşkonmaz, 'The Grand Gala of PNR Litigations' (2023) 19 European Constitutional Law Review 294, 317. See further Chapters 5 and 9.

[294] Rosas (n 101) 208.

civil society and others have specifically urged the ECtHR to update its Article 8 ECHR standards and incorporate the stricter principles and safeguards that the CJEU has established in this dynamic body of jurisprudence.[295] The view of the Court has also been sought on the altogether contrasting topic of whether these high data retention standards set by the CJEU conflict with the scope of the margin of appreciation as granted to Contracting States in the Article 8 ECHR case law of the ECtHR. In this vein, one Contracting State very pointedly defended the scope of its retention law in its submissions to the ECtHR within the context of the proportionality requirements under Article 8(2). In so doing, it highlighted the ongoing constitutional crisis on the matter between the CJEU and EU Member States by stressing to the ECtHR that 'there was no European consensus about the need to retain communications data or its modalities'.[296]

Two main developments have consequently taken place within the related case law of the ECtHR and its dialogue with the Luxembourg Court that have fundamentally reshaped the status of both supranational Courts as guardians of the right to private life in the modern digital age. The first is the elevated status now held by the case law of the CJEU in the judgments of the ECtHR dealing with Article 8 ECHR and measures permitting the retention of communications data and other State surveillance measures. Following *Digital Rights Ireland*,[297] it is increasingly the exception that such case law would not include any mention of EU data protection law or the case law of the CJEU concerning data retention or surveillance measures for law enforcement or national security purposes. In addition to the EU law and policy and CJEU jurisprudence cited (often at length), the ECtHR has increasingly been engaging with the standards of the CJEU in its reasoning and review of related case law on data retention, law enforcement access, and State surveillance.[298] The ECtHR has therefore adopted in this specific line of post-Lisbon jurisprudence dealing with Article 8 ECHR a dialogue by which the EU legal order

[295] This was one of the key arguments made to the ECtHR in the Grand Chamber judgment of *Big Brother Watch*: see Chapter 2.

[296] *Ekimdzhiev and Others v Bulgaria* [2022] ECHR 1 [390]: 'Even after the CJEU's judgments in *Digital Rights Ireland and Others* and *Tele2* ... many member States of the European Union had not fully repealed their laws providing for the generalised retention of communications data, since that was a valuable instrument for combatting serious crime. A more restrictive approach could prevent the proper operation of that instrument. The CJEU had not altogether dismissed the importance of retaining communications data, and the matter remained within the States' margin of appreciation.' See further Chapter 3.

[297] See eg the post-Lisbon judgment delivered before the Snowden revelations in *Uzun v Germany* [2010] ECHR 2263 which makes no reference to EU data protection law (facts concerned use of GPS to monitor vehicles, in addition to other historical and real-time measures, for monitoring suspects subsequently convicted for the attempted murder of members of the German Parliament).

[298] See eg *Szabó and Vissy v Hungary* (2016) 63 EHRR 3 [68], [70], [73]; *Roman Zakharov v Russia* (2016) 63 EHRR 17 [145]–[147] (GC); *Benedik v Slovenia* [2018] ECHR 363 [53]–[62]; *Breyer v Germany* [2020] ECHR 95 [47]–[56], [93]–[94]; *Big Brother Watch and Others v United Kingdom* [2021] ECHR 439 [202]–[241] (GC); *Ekimdzhiev and Others v Bulgaria* [2022] ECHR 1 [230]–[245], [390], [419]; *Glukhin v Russia* [2023] ECHR 540 [38]–[39]. On the increased level of engagement with this CJEU case law and related EU data retention law, see further Chapters 2 and 3.

has a special status compared to other sources of international law or national legal systems.

The second major development underpinning the Strasbourg response concerns the departure of the ECtHR from its previously lauded role as an important driving force in the scrutiny of laws permitting the secret surveillance of communications in Europe. The ECtHR, in stark contrast to the stricter standards of the CJEU, has taken a far more holistic and deferential turn in its most important judgments delivered in the wake of the Snowden revelations dealing with data retention and mass surveillance. These less strict principles and standards are particularly evident in the Grand Chamber judgments of *Big Brother Watch* and *Centrum för Rättvisa*.[299] In addition, the ECtHR has to date carefully avoided ruling directly on the same jurisprudential requirements that have led to a constitutional crisis between the CJEU and Member States within the EU legal order. Specifically, whether mandatory obligations on the private sector to retain traffic and location data for countering serious crime (or national security interests) are disproportionate and thereby incompatible with Article 8 ECHR due to this retention being general and indiscriminate in its scope.[300] Time will tell if the ECtHR will take a clear stance on what Vadja describes as the 'position of high principle' established by the CJEU in its stricter case law,[301] that there can be no general and indiscriminate retention of data for countering crime and safeguarding national security.[302]

3. Clear convergences and deep divergences

Since the establishment of strict EU rules set by the CJEU governing data retention and surveillance measures that fall within the scope EU law, some clear convergences have emerged in the approaches and standards of the Luxembourg and Strasbourg case law. First, both Courts apply an evolving 'hierarchy' of public interest objectives in their respective judgments when assessing the compatibility of these measures with the right to private life. These permitted legitimate aims range from countering crime, countering serious crime, safeguarding public security, safeguarding national security, 'other essential national interests', and

[299] On the weakening of these Art 8 ECHR standards as a result inter alia of the rise of the controversial joint analysis of the legality and proportionality requirements in Art 8(2) ECHR, and the 'global assessment' test established by the Grand Chamber in these judgments for assessing the compatibility of bulk interception regimes with Art 8 ECHR, see Chapters 2 and 3.

[300] See Chapter 3.

[301] Christopher Vajda, 'Data Protection: Made in Europe and Exported Globally' (UKAEL Annual Lecture, 19 January 2023), <https://monckton.com/wp-content/uploads/2023/03/UKAEL-Lecture-Data-Protection-Made-in-Europe-and-Exported-Globally-final.pdf> (former judge of the CJEU between 2012 and 2020). On the case law of the CJEU and its exceptions to this principle, see Chapter 5.

[302] At the time of writing, a judgment concerning this very question was forthcoming in 2024. See the Chamber Hearing of *Pietrzak and Bychawska-Siniarska v Poland* (App Nos 72038/17 and 25237/18) 27 September 2022.

serious threats to national security.[303] Secondly, a 'hierarchy of intrusiveness' to the right to private life is also applied by both Courts. Here the ECtHR and the CJEU have clearly established in their respective jurisprudence that access to the content of communications constitutes the most intrusive type of communications surveillance with respect to the rights enshrined in Articles 7 and 8 CFR (and Art 8 ECHR). This is where the data retention case law of the CJEU and the ECtHR converge with a shared assumption that access and analysis of communications data will always reveal less (irrespective of the type, scale, or circumstances) about an individual's private life than content.[304]

This approach is particularly evident in the Court's leading data retention judgments where different requirements are applied to different types of communications data. Thus, at the other end of the spectrum, both Courts have ranked the retention of 'data relating to the civil identity of users' or 'subscriber data' as last within this intrusiveness hierarchy. Consequently, the bulk retention (and subsequent access and use) of this specific type of communications data may be authorized for a wide range of public interest purposes and is subject to fewer limits and safeguards when compared to the stricter rules that apply when public authorities seek to intercept the content of an email.[305] Both the ECtHR and CJEU have also shown greater sensitivity to the intrusiveness of real-time tracking of location data.[306] For instance, in *La Quadrature du Net*, the CJEU explicitly relies on and draws from the same assessment made by the ECtHR in a previous case (*Ben Faiza v France*) which also determined that real-time access of location data is unequivocally more intrusive than historical data.[307]

Thirdly, both Courts have shown some convergence in their cardinal assessment of whether an indiscriminate and general data retention measure can ever constitute a justified interference with the right to private life that is compatible with the requirements of the ECHR and Article 52(1) CFR. In *La Quadrature du Net*[308] and *Ligue des droits humains*, for instance, the CJEU has clearly established that such bulk regimes can 'in principle' be compatible with EU fundamental rights law.[309] Relatedly, as Mitsilegas and others have highlighted, there is also 'some alignment' to be found in the jurisprudence of each Court when it comes to certain oversight

[303] See Chapters 2 and 5.

[304] See further Chapters 3 and 5.

[305] As clearly established in *Breyer v Germany* (ECtHR) and subsequently in *La Quadrature du Net* (CJEU): see Chapters 3 and 5.

[306] See Chapters 3 and 5.

[307] On *Ben Faiza v France*, see further Chapter 3.

[308] On the view that *La Quadrature du Net* represents 'an ambivalent response to political pressure', see Monika Zalnieriute, 'A Struggle for Competence: National Security, Surveillance and the Scope of EU Law at the CJEU' (2022) 85 Modern Law Review 198.

[309] See further Chapters 5 and 9 on the exceptions made by the CJEU with respect to certain types of communications data and specific contexts (eg 'a serious threat to national security') and the less strict approach of the CJEU to the bulk retention of passenger name record (PNR) data in *Ligue des droits humains*.

safeguards for bulk retention and data collection regimes adopted for national security purposes.[310] This is evident in the considerable weight given by both Courts to the importance of public authorities' access to vast volumes of data being subject to *ex ante* 'independent' authorization by a judge or an independent administrative body that is also provided with the sufficient resources and capacity necessary to fulfil its oversight tasks.[311]

Fourthly, following the ECtHR, the CJEU has also applied the 'joint analysis' approach when assessing the legality and proportionality requirements enshrined in Article 52(1) CFR. The specific question of what the 'provided for by law' requirement entails under Article 52(1) has as a result been overlooked by the CJEU in certain data retention cases. Instead, the primary focus for the Courts that results from this joint analysis approach is frequently whether a particular data retention regime had complied with the principle of proportionality. This is clearly demonstrated in *Digital Rights Ireland*, *Tele2*, and *GD* where the Court sidesteps any detailed examination of the legality test and conflates any rule of law considerations within its proportionality analysis. The ECtHR has increasingly adopted a joint analysis approach in its post-Snowden case law dealing with secret surveillance and bulk data retention. However, this approach departs from previously acclaimed Strasbourg case law and has been criticized for weakening the substantive protection provided by the right to respect for private life in surveillance and data retention cases.[312]

Some convergences have therefore clearly emerged in the approaches and standards of the Luxembourg and Strasbourg Courts in this highly topical area of case law,[313] but these remain outweighed by numerous significant differences. Indeed, as judges, regulators, and scholars have observed,[314] deep divergences persist between the levels of rights scrutiny and proportionality standards applied by both Courts to data retention and mass surveillance measures. The overarching principle established in the landmark case law of the CJEU is arguably the most important of these differences. This provides that the imposition of bulk retention measures on the private sector concerning traffic and location data for countering

[310] See Valsamis Mitsilegas and others, 'Data Retention and the Future of Large-Scale Surveillance' (2023) 29 European Law Journal 176, 209–11.

[311] ibid. See further Chapters 2 and 5.

[312] See Chapters 2 and 3. Given the concerns surrounding this controversial approach, it is welcome that the CJEU is beginning to stress the importance of the 'quality' of law requirements of Art 52(1) in some of its case law (eg Opinion 1/15 and *Schrems II*): see further Chapters 5 and 9.

[313] Many of these convergences, as noted earlier, are unsurprising given the constitutional links between the right to private life enshrined in Arts 7 and 52(3) CFR and the benchmark standards set by the rich jurisprudence of the ECtHR concerning its corresponding right in Art 8 ECHR, much of which long predates the Charter.

[314] See eg Vajda (n 301); European Data Protection Board, Opinion 5/2023 on the European Commission Draft Implementing Decision on the adequate protection of personal data under the EU–US Data Privacy Framework (adopted 28 February 2023) 31–37; Mitsilegas and others (n 310); Christopher Docksey and Kenneth Propp, 'Government Access to Personal Data and Transnational Interoperability' (2023) 10 Oslo Law Review 1, 8.

serious crime, serious threats to public security, or safeguarding national security is 'the exception and not the rule'.[315] In stark contrast to this robust rights-based approach, the ECtHR in its recent case law dealing with bulk interception and data retention has moved towards a more deferential and holistic approach to the right to private life than previously applied by the Strasbourg Court.

The judgments of the Strasbourg Court (sitting as the Grand Chamber) in *Big Brother Watch* and *Centrum för Rättvisa* make particularly evident that 'a clear line' has been drawn between the jurisprudence of the ECtHR and CJEU.[316] This divergence has broader implications for the scrutiny of bulk interception regimes across Europe and the ECHR legal order. The first is the clear departure for the ECtHR as an important driving force and its previously impressive role for setting minimum standards in the review of laws governing State surveillance of communications across Europe. To date, it is only the CJEU that is consistently providing any novel safeguards to deal with the emerging threats to private life and data protection posed by data retention and surveillance measures that are underpinned by rapidly evolving technologies and systems. These include major developments such as machine learning models, automated decision-making, predictive analytics, and the increasing role of the private sector in data acquisition for public authorities and State surveillance.[317] Secondly, the holistic eight-part criteria and more lenient approach of the ECtHR's joint analysis assessment for bulk interception regimes (via the novel 'global assessment' test) provides that there is now a clear and significant divergence between the rules and safeguards of the ECHR and EU legal systems.

The ECtHR has as a result subjected far-reaching retention obligations on the private sector, including the bulk retention and bulk interception of communications data, to far lower levels of scrutiny than the CJEU when examining the legality and proportionality requirements of Article 8 ECHR. For instance,[318] the Grand Chamber in 2021 held that the legal limits in the domestic laws of Contracting States allowing public authorities' access and use of traffic and location data from bulk interception need not be as strictly applied as the rules for content.[319]

[315] As held by the Grand Chamber in *La Quadrature du Net* (n 292) [142]; Case C-140/20 *G.D. v Commissioner of An Garda Síochána*, judgment of 5 April 2022 (ECLI:EU:C:2022:258) [65]; Joined Cases C-793/19 and C-794/19 *SpaceNet and Deutsche Telekom*, judgment of 20 September 2022 (ECLI:EU:C:2022:702) [74]: 'In view of the sensitive nature of the information that traffic and location data may provide, the confidentiality of those data is essential for the right to privacy … and, secondly, the seriousness of the interference entailed by such retention, it is necessary, within a democratic society, that retention be the exception and not the rule, as provided for in the system established by Directive 2002/58, and that those data should not be retained systematically and continuously.'

[316] Docksey and Propp (n 314) 8.

[317] See Chapters 5 and 9.

[318] Chapter 3 also provides other examples: see *Breyer v Germany* [2020] ECHR 95 where the ECtHR held the bulk retention of the subscription data concerning millions of mobile phone customers to be 'of a rather limited nature'; see *Ekimdzhiev and Others v Bulgaria* [2022] ECHR 1 where the ECtHR does not examine the proportionality of the relevant regime which permitted the bulk retention of traffic and location data for the purposes of countering serious crime.

[319] See Chapter 3.

The Court arrived at these determinations despite finding in both *Big Brother Watch* and *Centrum för Rättvisa* that public authorities' use of this communications data from bulk interception was far greater than their use of content, and the number of people affected was thus likely to be larger.[320] This approach is clearly inconsistent with the principle in CJEU case law that public authorities' access to content or communications data, when collected on a general and indiscriminate basis that may enable the possibility of profiling, should be treated in a manner that reflects their capacity to intrude upon a person's privacy.[321]

Finally, these Grand Chamber judgments both called a clear halt to the adoption of any 'minimum safeguards', or any shift by the ECtHR towards an outright finding that general and indiscriminate retention (or surveillance) regimes may be incompatible in principle with Article 8 ECHR.[322]

E. Conclusions

The entry into force of the Lisbon Treaty in 2009 introduced three major reforms of importance for the legal status of the Charter and for the role of Article 8 ECHR in the drafting, implementation, and review of EU data retention law and policy-making. First, Article 6(2) TEU provided a legal basis for the accession of the EU to the ECHR and places an obligation of the EU to fulfil this requirement. Secondly, and most importantly for the purposes of this chapter, the entry into force of the Lisbon Treaty elevated the Charter to the status of EU primary law, leading it to become the reference text for the CJEU in its assessment of EU fundamental rights. Thirdly, and relatedly, data protection became an autonomous and binding fundamental right under primary EU law, as guaranteed by both Article 8 CFR and Article 16 TFEU.

The first of these Lisbon reforms is intended to make EU law subject to the external review of the ECHR system, thereby making the ECtHR the final arbiter and ultimate guardian of European human rights law. Although negotiations have since resumed, over a decade has passed since the CJEU halted the accession process held in Opinion 2/13 when it assessed the Draft Accession Agreement as incompatible with EU law. This has left many to question whether accession is still legally feasible or even desirable. Concerns arising from the current geo-political context have also prompted some to argue that the negotiations are of great importance

320 ibid.

321 See Chapter 5.

322 See Chapters 2 and 3. Note the four (main) minimum safeguards enshrined in Arts 7, 8, 11, and 52(1) CFR as established in the case law of the CJEU: (1) there can be no general and indiscriminate retention of *traffic and location data* from electronic communications—measures must be 'targeted'; (2) access is subject to prior review by a court or independent administrative body; (3) such targeted measures are restricted to fighting serious crime (not crime); (4) retained data must be stored within the EU. Strict exceptions apply for certain public security and national security purposes: see Chapter 5.

in bringing both legal systems closer together to respond to Europe's 'rule of law crisis'.[323] On the other hand, scholars rightly point out that the goal is ultimately not EU-ECHR accession itself. Rather, as Harmsen has noted, it is an instrument to be adopted if it 'enhances the overall protection of human rights' across Europe and to only be pursued once the right balance is struck between this fundamental aim and the autonomy of the EU legal order.[324] Lock similarly argues that even if the status quo is imperfect, those in favour of stronger human rights protection need to ask whether the many conditions set by the CJEU in Opinion 2/13 are a price worth paying. Thus, it must be carefully considered whether meeting these requirements may do equal damage and 'weaken the credibility of the ECHR regime' if this results in large carve-outs of responsibility for the EU in sensitive areas such as cooperation in criminal matters.[325]

As a result of the second and third of these Lisbon reforms, the CJEU no longer defers or accords the same special status to the Article 8 ECHR case law of the ECtHR in its review of matters dealing with data retention and State surveillance. This shift in the status for Article 8 ECHR in the post-Lisbon jurisprudence of the CJEU makes sense in the light of key legal and political developments that inherently link both legal orders. These notably include the rise of the Charter, the autonomy-driven approach of the CJEU, the delayed EU-ECHR access process, and the departure of the ECtHR from its previously lauded role as an important driving force in the scrutiny of laws permitting secret surveillance in Europe.[326] Despite some convergences between the approach and standards of the Courts in this area, these developments have led to the CJEU becoming the vanguard legal institution for both data retention policymaking and supranational judicial scrutiny in Europe. The next chapter examines this landmark case law of the CJEU and the challenges posed by this dual role for the mainstreaming of the right to privacy in EU data retention law.

[323] See eg Robert Spano, *Annual Report 2021 of the European Court of Human Rights* (Council of Europe 2022) 18 (Former President of the Strasbourg Court 2020–21).

[324] Harmsen (n 234) 217.

[325] Lock (n 234) 1890.

[326] Another important factor has been the lack or limited *ex post* review and rights scrutiny thereof by the European Commission in its evaluations of EU data retention laws and related AFSJ measures: see Chapters 8 and 9.

5

The Approach of the Court of Justice

Article 8 ECHR and Data Retention

> Article 15(1) of Directive 2002/58, read in the light of Articles 7, 8 and 11 and Article 52(1) of the Charter, does not prevent a Member State from adopting legislation permitting, as a preventive measure, the targeted retention of traffic and location data for the purposes of combating serious crime, preventing serious threats to public security and equally of *safeguarding national security*, provided that such retention is limited, with respect to the categories of data to be retained, the means of communication affected, the persons concerned and the retention period adopted, to what is strictly necessary.
>
> *La Quadrature du Net and Others* (2020)[1]

A. Introduction

The right to private life and the EU Charter of Fundamental Rights (CFR) both play a significant role within the EU legal order (and beyond) within the contexts of data retention and surveillance measures adopted for countering serious crime and safeguarding national security. These evolving rules are based on a series of landmark judgments by the CJEU which primarily stem from the interpretation of the scope of Article 15(1) of the e-Privacy Directive 2002/58, when read in the light of the EU Charter. The CJEU's data retention jurisprudence has been lauded by scholars and civil society.[2] Indeed, as discussed later, there

[1] Joined Cases C-511/18, C-512/18, and C-520/18 *La Quadrature du Net and Others*, judgment of 6 October 2020 (ECLI:EU:C:2022:702) [147] (emphasis added). As reiterated subsequently by the Grand Chamber, see eg: Joined Cases C-793/19 and C-794/19 *SpaceNet and Deutsche Telekom*, judgment of 20 September 2022 (ECLI:EU:C:2022:702) [72]. All URLs for this chapter were last accessed on 22 April 2024 unless otherwise stated.

[2] See Marie-Pierre Granger and Kristina Irion, 'The Court of Justice and the Data Retention Directive in *Digital Rights Ireland*—Telling Off the EU Legislator and Teaching a Lesson in Privacy and Data Protection' (2014) 39 European Law Review 835; Federico Fabbrini, 'Human Rights in the Digital Age: The ECJ Ruling in the Data Retention Case and Its Lessons for Privacy and Surveillance in the US' (2015) 28 Harvard Human Rights Journal 65; Edoardo Celeste, 'The Court of Justice and the Ban on Bulk Data Retention' (2019) 15 European Constitutional Law Review 134; Chloé Berthélémy, 'Data Retention? Advocate General says "Asked and Answered!"' *EDRi* (1 December 2021), <https://edri.org/our-work/data-retention-advocate-general-says-asked-and-answered/>.

EU Data Privacy Law and Serious Crime. Nora Ni Loideain, Oxford University Press. © Nora Ni Loideain 2025.
DOI: 10.1093/oso/9780198837169.003.0005

is much to welcome from a fundamental rights perspective. This includes the high level of scrutiny applied by the CJEU in successive judgments examining the specific intrusions to private life posed by the retention of communications data and the strict safeguards developed by the Court concerning large-scale profiling and automated decision-making.[3] Previously, laws allowing retention and access to communications data (data revealing the context of a communication) for law enforcement purposes had long been treated by governments as a far lesser intrusion of a person's private life with limited regulatory safeguards.[4] However, scholars and national courts have also raised ongoing concerns regarding the highly prescriptive nature of this jurisprudence, its inconsistency with previous case law, and how some of these standards may serve to hinder, rather than enhance, the protection of EU fundamental rights in practice.[5] Indeed, we see clear evidence of this in the stark criticism of the CJEU's alternative solutions of targeted retention and geographical profiling for fighting serious crime which the French Council of State and the Irish Supreme Court have deemed as 'unworkable'.[6]

This chapter identifies and critically examines in detail the development of this rapidly evolving area of EU rules established by the landmark and rights-affirming data retention jurisprudence of the CJEU and the key role of Article 8 ECHR therein. The analysis begins by identifying and explaining the relationship between Article 8 ECHR and the fundamental rights to private life and the protection of personal data as enshrined in Articles 7 and 8 CFR. This is followed by a detailed examination which sets out and navigates this highly complex patchwork of EU rules stemming from the CJEU's jurisprudence dealing with the retention of communications data by communication service providers (CSPs) within the private sector on behalf of public authorities. The influence and importance

[3] For related developments and the CJEU's case law concerning passenger name records, see Chapter 9. On the concept of 'automated individual decision-making' under Art 22 GDPR within the context of 'scoring' future behaviour and a person's creditworthiness, see Case C-634/21 *SCHUFA*, judgment of 7 December 2023 (ECLI:EU:C:2023:957).

[4] See further Chapter 1.

[5] See eg Orla Lynskey, 'The Data Retention Directive is Incompatible with the Rights to Privacy and Data Protection and is Invalid in Its Entirety' (2014) 51 Common Market Law Review 1789; Iain Cameron, 'Metadata Retention and National Security: *Privacy International* and *La Quadrature du Net*' (2021) 58 Common Market Law Review 1433; Juraj Sajfert, 'Bulk data interception/retention judgments of the CJEU—A victory and a defeat for privacy' *European Law Blog* (26 October 2020); Xavier Tracol, 'The Grand Chamber is Trying Hard to Square the Circle of Data Retention' (2021) 41 Computer Law & Security Review; Maria Tzanou and Spyridoula Karyda, '*Privacy International* and *Quadrature du Net*: One Step Forward Two Steps Back in the Data Retention Saga?' (2022) 28 European Public Law 123.

[6] *Graham Dwyer v Commissioner of An Garda Síochána* [2020] IESC 4 [5.5]; Conseil d'État Press Release, 'Connecting Data: the Council of State conciliates the implementation of European Union law and the effectiveness of the fight against terrorism and crime', 21 April 2021. On the critical responses of the Irish and French courts, see Araceli Turmo, 'National Security as an Exception to EU Data Protection Standards' (2022) 59 Common Market Law Review 203; Anastasia Iliopoulou-Penot, 'The Construction of a European Digital Citizenship in the Case Law of the CJEU' (2022) 59 Common Market Law Review 969, 991–94.

of Article 8 ECHR, as interpreted by the ECtHR in its data retention case law, on these groundbreaking EU rules is also addressed.[7]

In conclusion, some critical reflections are provided on three key developments that threaten the mainstreaming of the right to private life across all stages of EU policymaking concerning data retention and the protection of EU fundamental rights law in practice more broadly. These concern the converging and diverging approaches and standards of the CJEU and the ECtHR, the fraught dialogue between the CJEU and national courts, and the CJEU as the vanguard EU institution for both data retention policymaking and supranational judicial scrutiny in Europe.

B. The EU Charter and Article 8 ECHR

1. The Charter and Article 8 ECHR: corresponding rights but different standards

Despite the EU not yet acceding to the ECHR as required under the Lisbon Treaty, these supranational legal systems have been inextricably intertwined for decades.[8] We see further recognition of these close links in the EU's cornerstone legislation on data protection, the General Data Protection Regulation (GDPR) and the Law Enforcement Directive (LED), which explicitly recognize that any restrictions to data protection principles and rights must comply with the Charter and the ECHR.[9] Where data retention and surveillance measures are concerned, however, there are two key differences when it comes to assessing what constitutes a justified interference with the right to respect for private life under the systems of the ECHR and the Charter.

First, like Article 8 ECHR, the rights to private life and data protection guaranteed under the EU Charter are not absolute. They are qualified rights and must be assessed 'in relation to their function in society'.[10] In contrast to Article 8(2) ECHR, however, the conditions that must be met if limitations are placed on the rights guaranteed by Articles 7 and 8 CFR are set out in an entirely separate

[7] On ECtHR case law dealing with Art 8 ECHR and data retention, see Chapter 3.

[8] See further Chapter 4.

[9] Regulation (EU) 2016/679 of the European Parliament and Council of 27 April 2016 on the protection of natural persons with regard to the processing of personal data and on the free movement of such data, and repealing Directive 95/46/EC [2016] OJ L119/1 (GDPR), recital 73; Directive (EU) 2016/680 of the European Parliament and Council of 27 April 2016 on the protection of natural persons with regard to the processing of personal data by competent authorities for the purposes of the prevention, investigation, detection or prosecution of criminal offences or the execution of criminal penalties [2016] OJ L119/89 (LED), recital 46.

[10] Case C-311/18 *Data Protection Commissioner v Facebook Ltd*, judgment of 16 July 2020 (ECLI:EU:C:2020:559) (*Schrems II*) [172]; Case C-140/20 *G.D. v Commissioner of An Garda Síochána*, judgment of 5 April 2022 (ECLI:EU:C:2022:258) [48].

provision under Article 52(1) CFR. The latter contains overlapping, but also additional, requirements that must be satisfied if the exercise of these rights are restricted by a measure the CJEU determines falls within the scope of EU law. These limitations must: be provided for by law; respect the essence of those rights; and, in compliance with the principle of proportionality, be necessary and genuinely meet objectives of general interest recognized by the EU, or the need to protect the rights and freedoms of others.[11]

Unlike the text of the ECHR, Article 52 CFR explicitly provides for the importance of an infringed interest to be examined using the criterion of what identifies the 'essence' of the right and its protected interests. If the essence of a right under the Charter is found to be compromised, it has been observed that such a limitation on that right goes 'so far that it empties the right of its core elements and thus prevents the exercise of the right'.[12] This is a significant determination since limitations of the essence of the right render that measure 'automatically disproportionate' thereby halting any examination of the other rule of law and proportionality requirements under Article 52(1).[13] Although the ECtHR has examined the notion of essence as part of its proportionality assessment in certain cases concerning other ECHR rights, such as Article 6 ECHR, this has not been the approach in Article 8 ECHR cases dealing with State surveillance and data retention.[14]

Secondly, Article 52(3) CFR gives statutory expression to the pre-existing status under the EU general principles of law which recognize equivalent rights under the ECHR as providing minimum human rights standards within EU law. As Craig and de Búrca highlight, it is therefore enshrined in the Charter that the scope of protection and standards of Article 8 ECHR represent 'a floor' but crucially 'not a ceiling' for the interpretation and application of Article 7 CFR.[15] This means that the CJEU can establish further requirements that must be satisfied in order for a limitation to the rights enshrined in Article 7 CFR to be assessed as compatible with the Charter, in addition to the Article 8 ECHR standards set by the ECtHR.[16]

[11] *La Quadrature du Net* (n 1) [121].

[12] European Data Protection Supervisor (EDPS), 'EDPS Guidelines on assessing the proportionality of measures that limit the fundamental rights to privacy and the protection of personal data', 19 December 2019, 8.

[13] Koen Lenaerts, 'Limits on Limitations: The Essence of Fundamental Rights in the EU' (2019) 20 German Law Journal 779, 781. See further Tuomas Ojanen, 'Making the Essence of Fundamental Rights Real' (2016) 12 European Constitutional Law Review 318, 325; Maja Brkan, 'The Essence of the Fundamental Rights to Privacy and Data Protection' (2019) 20 German Law Journal 864, 867–69; Lorenzo Dalla Corte, 'On Proportionality in the Data Protection Jurisprudence of the CJEU' (2022) 12 International Data Privacy Law 259, 273–75.

[14] Laura Hoyano, 'What Is Balanced on the Scales of Justice? In Search of the Essence of the Right to a Fair Trial' [2014] Criminal Law Review 4. See further Chapters 2 and 3.

[15] Paul Craig and Gráinne de Búrca, *EU Law* (5th edn, OUP 2011) 367.

[16] Charter of Fundamental Rights of the European Union [2016] OJ C202/389, Art 52(3) CFR mirrors Art 53 ECHR which states that Contracting States to the ECHR may also provide additional protection to the minimum human rights standards set by the ECtHR. See further Alec Stone Sweet, 'The European Convention on Human Rights and National Constitutional Reordering' (2012) 33 Cardoza Law Review 1859; Bruno de Witte, 'Article 53' in Steve Peers and others (eds), *The EU Charter of Fundamental Rights* (2nd edn, Bloomsbury 2022).

Following the Charter's elevation to EU primary law and the Snowden revelations, the CJEU has fully embraced this principle in an ongoing series of landmark data retention cases, each one adding to the list of prescriptive 'minimum safeguards' that EU and national law must satisfy if such measures are to be considered compatible with Articles 7, 8, 11, and 52(1) CFR.[17]

2. Articles 7 and 8 CFR: distinct fundamental rights

The protected interests under Article 7 CFR, namely the right to respect for 'private and family life, home, and communications', provide the same rights as guaranteed by Article 8 ECHR. In line with the well-established case law of the ECtHR dealing with State surveillance,[18] the CJEU has also adopted a broad interpretation of the right to private life under Article 7 CFR that is not exhaustive. Thus, the scope of Article 7 CFR has been interpreted to apply to the retention, access, and use of personal data for law enforcement purposes. This includes: communications data (traffic and location data);[19] biometric data for passports;[20] personal and sensitive information revealed from passenger name record data (including information relating to health, financial status, religion);[21] and non-EU public authorities having indiscriminate powers to access the communications of individuals within the EU.[22] This consistent line of case law shows the protection of data privacy guaranteed by Article 7 CFR clearly overlaps with the fundamental right to the protection of personal data enshrined in Article 8 CFR.

However, although similarities in the scope of each are evident, the related rights of private life and data protection differ in various ways and are not treated as identical within the ECHR and EU legal systems.[23] In addition to explicitly providing for a guaranteed right to the protection of personal data in Article 8(1), Article 8 CFR contains two further sections of additional guarantees that reflect more granular standards that have emerged from Article 8 ECHR case law, and other data protection instruments, since the 1950s. The EU Charter explanations state that these requirements are based on a variety of sources, including Article 16 TFEU and Article 8 ECHR.[24] Article 8(2) CFR also explicitly guarantees

[17] Joined Cases C-293/12 and C-594/12 *Digital Rights Ireland and Seitlinger*, judgment of 8 April 2014 (ECLI:EU:C:2014:238) [54]; Joined Cases C-203/15 and C-698/15 *Tele2 Sverige and Watson*, judgment of 21 December 2016 (ECLI:EU:C:2016:970) [109], *La Quadrature du Net* (n 1) [132].

[18] See further Chapter 3.

[19] *Digital Rights Ireland* (n 17); *Tele2* (n 17).

[20] Case C-291/12 *Schwarz v Stadt Bochum*, judgment of 17 October 2013 (EU:C:2013:670).

[21] Opinion 1/15 *EU–Canada PNR Agreement*, opinion of 26 July 2017 (ECLI:EU:C:2017:592).

[22] Case C-362/14, *Schrems v Data Protection Commissioner*, judgment of 6 October 2015 (ECLI:EU:C:2015:650).

[23] On the approach of the ECtHR, see Chapter 3.

[24] Council of the EU, Charter of Fundamental Rights of the European Union: Explanations relating to the complete text of the Charter, December 2000; Explanations relating to the Charter of Fundamental Rights [2007] OJ C303/17, 20.

protection under EU primary law to two of the procedural rights provided to data subjects under EU data protection legislation—the right of access to data which has been collected concerning them and the right of rectification. Finally, Article 8(3) provides that the 'rules' of Article 8(1) and Article 8(2) must be subject to control of an independent authority.[25] The CJEU has consistently recognized these independent bodies as 'an essential component' for ensuring the effective protection of individuals with respect to the processing of personal data.[26] This standard also requires Member States to ensure that these oversight authorities operate and function free of any external influence.[27]

The CJEU has also adopted an expansive interpretation of the fundamental right to data protection by determining that any measure which 'provides for the processing of personal data' amounts to an interference with Article 8(1).[28] Personal data has been interpreted very broadly by the Court in this context to mean 'any data that identifies' an individual or makes them 'identifiable'.[29] This means any collection, use, or sharing of personal data for law enforcement purposes within the scope of EU law falls under the protection of, and constitutes an interference with, the right to protection of personal data enshrined in Article 8(1) CFR. The following measures have thus been held to constitute interferences with Article 8 CFR: storing of fingerprints to prevent passport fraud; transfer of personal data between EU and third countries for ensuring public security; automated assessment of passenger name records; and retention or transfer of communications data, such as IP addresses, traffic data, and location data, by private parties for countering crime, safeguarding public security, and national security.[30]

These Article 8 CFR jurisprudential developments are welcome as they recognize the need for protecting data at every stage of the surveillance cycle given the increased risks to privacy and the rule of law that come with the transformed scope and scale of data that may now be accessed and shared in this era of connected digitalization.[31] In no particular order, the Internet is clearly playing an ever larger role—especially since the lockdowns of the pandemic—in how we all work, play, read, watch, and think. This process of integrating online technology, and algorithmic decision-making into many if not all aspects of life is profoundly transforming social and economic life, as well as practices of governments worldwide.[32]

[25] These bodies are also described as 'quasi-judicial' due to their oversight functions.

[26] Case C-518/07 *Commission v Germany*, judgment of 9 March 2010 (ECLI:EU:C:2010:125) [23]–[25]; *Schrems* (n 23) [41]; Case C-746/18, *Prokuratuur*, judgment of 2 March 2021 (ECLI:EU:C:2021:152) [53].

[27] ibid.

[28] *Digital Rights Ireland* (n 17) [36]; Opinion 1/15 (n 21) [126].

[29] *La Quadrature du Net* (n 1) [171].

[30] *Schwarz* (n 20) [30]; Opinion 1/15 (n 21) [125]; *Schrems II* (n 10) [170]–[171]; *La Quadrature du Net* (n 1) [115], [139], [153]–[159]; *G.D.* (n 10) [44], [73]; Case C-817/19 *Ligue des droits humains*, judgment of 21 June 2022 (ECLI:EU:C:2022:491) [111].

[31] See further Chapter 2.

[32] Gráinne de Búrca, *Reframing Human Rights in a Turbulent Era* (OUP 2021) 194. See generally Ad hoc Committee on Artificial Intelligence, *Towards Regulation of AI Systems* (Council of Europe 2020);

Inevitably, this includes the wide-ranging use and sharing of data and analytical tools between law enforcement and the private sector.[33]

Europol has, for instance, used software from US data analytics company Palantir for the 'operational analysis of all counter-terrorism related data' for identifying new lines of investigation in support of competent authorities in EU Member States and beyond.[34] Indeed, major reforms to the Europol Regulation 2016/794 were finalized in 2022 that significantly increase the agency's legal powers to directly request data from private parties.[35] These changes were the subject of understandable criticism as the significant reforms were made before any evaluation of the effectiveness (or shortcomings) of Regulation 2016/794 was conducted.[36] The reforms also follow an admonishment by the EDPS of Europol's processing of large datasets which the EU's data protection oversight body determined was disproportionate and posed high risks to the fundamental rights of individuals not linked to any criminal activity.[37]

Given the rapid pace of these data-driven developments in EU law enforcement, there are pressing questions to be addressed by the CJEU on what intrusions to the right to personal data of individuals are safeguarded against by the autonomous right in Article 8 CFR that are not covered by Article 7 CFR. As Kranenborg observes, examining whether there has been a justified interference with the special formulation of Article 8 CFR gives rise to a 'peculiar' situation.[38] Article 8(2) already requires that any processing of personal data, if not based on consent, must be based on law. This means that Article 52(1) CFR allows for the rules of Article 8(2) and Article 8(3) CFR to be restricted but only if this is provided for by law and complies with the other conditions of Article 52(1) CFR.[39]

Annual Report of the United Nations High Commissioner for Human Rights, The right to privacy in the digital age, A/HRC/48/31, 2021.

[33] Orla Lynskey, 'Criminal Justice Profiling and EU Data Protection Law' (2019) 15 International Journal of Law in Context 162; Eleni Kosta and Magda Brewczyńska, 'Government Access to User Data' in Rosa-Maria Ballardini, Olli Pitkänen, and Petri Kuoppamäki (eds), *Regulating Industrial Internet through IPR, Data Protection and Competition Law* (Kluwer Law International 2019). See generally, Valsamis Mitsilegas and Niovi Vavoula (eds), *Surveillance and Privacy in the Digital Age* (Hart 2021).

[34] Answer on behalf of European Commission, Parliamentary Questions (Reference: E-000173/2020) 9 June 2020, <https://europarl.europa.eu/doceo/document/E-9-2020-000173-ASW_EN.html>.

[35] Council of the EU, 'Europol: Council adopts legislation entrusting new tasks to the agency' Press Release, 24 May 2022. See particularly amendments made to Regulation (EU) 2016/794, Art 26.

[36] Niovi Vavoula and Valsamis Mitsilegas, 'Strengthening Europol's Mandate', European Parliament Commissioned Study, PE 694.200, May 2021, 70.

[37] EDPS, 'EDPS Decision on the own initiative inquiry on Europol's big data challenge', 18 September 2020; EDPS, 'EDPS orders Europol to erase data concerning individuals with no established link to criminal activity', 10 January 2022 (concluding 2019 inquiry).

[38] Herke Kranenborg, 'Article 8—Protection of Personal Data' in Steve Peers and others (eds), *The EU Charter of Fundamental Rights: A Commentary* (Hart 2014) 259. See generally Maria Tzanou, 'Data Protection as a Fundamental Right Next to Privacy? "Reconstructing" a Not So New Right' (2013) 3 International Data Privacy Law 88.

[39] Kranenborg (n 38). On the development of data protection as an autonomous right as enshrined in Art 8 CFR, see Gloria González Fuster and Raphael Gellert, 'The Fundamental Right of Data Protection in the EU' (2012) 26 International Review of Law, Computers & Technology 73; Felix

National courts have understandably sought clarification from the CJEU regarding how the guarantees of Article 8 CFR are to be assessed in the light of Article 7 CFR and Article 52(1) when determining what constitutes an interference with the right to data protection and the safeguards therein.[40] The CJEU has to date adopted a combined reading of all provisions. In doing so, the Court treats Articles 8(2) and 8(3) as requirements that need to be satisfied, in addition to those under Article 52(1), in order for a contested limitation on the exercise of the right to data protection to be assessed as justified.[41] As Brkan and others point out, however, this approach does not address how the guarantees of Article 8 CFR interact with *specific* requirements of Article 52(1) such as whether non-compliance with any of these distinct guarantees could compromise the 'essence' of Article 8 CFR.[42]

Little light to date has been cast on the relationship between the generally elusive essence requirement of Article 52(1) and the guarantee set out in Article 8(3) which provides that the rules of Article 8(1) and Article 8(2) must be subject to control of an independent authority.[43] The CJEU has clearly established, as noted earlier, that Article 8(3) constitutes 'an essential component' of the right to data protection. Nevertheless, despite several cases before the CJEU dealing with data retention regimes that lacked independent oversight, it remains unclear why non-compliance with this so-called essential component has not been held to compromise the essence of the right to data protection as enshrined in Article 8 CFR.[44] Some clarity from the CJEU on the relationship between Article 8(3) and Article 52(1) would be welcome, especially in light of the importance of this safeguard for monitoring the fundamental rights compliance of increasingly data-driven law enforcement tools and systems.[45] Given the restrictions on alternative safeguards (right of access), the rise of public–private partnerships, and profiling systems reliant on the analysis of communications and biometrics, robust independent oversight with adequate resources is indeed essential to ensuring effective supervision of these powers.

Bieker, *The Right to Data Protection* (Springer 2022) 69–132; Orla Lynskey, 'Complete and Effective Data Protection' (2023) 76 Current Legal Problems 297.

[40] See eg *Digital Rights Ireland* (n 17) [21]; *Tele2* (n 17) [59].

[41] *Tele2* (n 17) [124]; Opinion 1/15 (n 21) [137]–[138], [142]–[145].

[42] Brkan (n 13) 880–81; Plixara Vogiatzoglou and Peggy Valcke, 'Two Decades of Article 8 CFR' in Eleni Kosta, Ronald Leenes, and Irene Kamara (eds), *Research Handbook on EU Data Protection Law* (Elgar 2022) 49; Dalla Corte (n 13).

[43] ibid.

[44] See *Schrems* (n 23); Opinion 1/15 (n 21); *Prokuratuur* (n 26).

[45] See further European Commission, 'Proposal for a Regulation of the European Parliament and of the Council Laying Down Harmonised Rules on Artificial Intelligence (Artificial Intelligence Act) and Amending Certain Union Legislative Acts', COM(2021) 206 final. Of course, independent oversight is by no means the only safeguard needed to ensure the adequate monitoring of regulatory compliance in a data-driven society. See generally Julie E Cohen, *Between Truth and Power* (OUP 2019).

C. Retention and Use of Communications Data

1. Affirming EU fundamental rights and data retention

(a) An emboldened Court and the Data Retention Directive

Commitments made by the EU under the Lisbon Treaty to a more robust culture of fundamental rights have moved in tandem with the adoption of laws providing for the retention, analysis, and sharing of personal data that allow public authorities to monitor the communications and movements of individuals within and beyond the EU.[46] In response to these developments and its strict-scrutiny review of data retention regimes, the CJEU has gained a reputation for its increasingly purposive and expansive interpretation and application of EU fundamental rights.[47] This is particularly evident in the strict proportionality standards applied by the Court to ensure that the rights enshrined in Articles 7 and 8 CFR are 'fully respected' since its striking down of the controversial Data Retention Directive in *Digital Rights Ireland*.[48]

Under the weight of considerable political pressure for increased counter-terrorism powers worldwide following terrorist attacks on Madrid and London in 2004 and 2005, the Data Retention Directive was rapidly drafted, passed, and entered into force by the EU legislator in 2006.[49] Directive 2006/24 required that traffic data, location data, and related data necessary to identify the subscriber, derived from the communications of every natural person and legal entity within the EU, be retained and made available for the purposes of 'the investigation, detection and prosecution of serious crime' as defined by each Member State in its national law. This blanket scope thus imposed a mandatory duty on Member States to require CSPs to store all their customers' communications data for up to two years and facilitate access if required by relevant competent public authorities.[50]

Following pressure from several national courts, including challenges to the *Solange* doctrine concerning the capacity of the CJEU to ensure adequate protection of EU fundamental rights, the Court held that the Directive constituted a 'wide-ranging and particularly serious interference' with the rights to privacy and data protection.[51] The Court held that this regime permitted general and

[46] LED (n 9); Directive (EU) 2016/681 of the European Parliament and Council of 27 April 2016 on the use of passenger name record data (PNR) data for the prevention, detection, investigation and prosecution of terrorist offences and serious crime [2016] OJ L119/132 (PNR Directive). See further Chapter 9.

[47] See eg Lee Bygrave, 'Information Concepts in Law' (2015) 35 Oxford Journal of Legal Studies 91, 110; Nora Ni Loideain and others, 'An Unstoppable Force and an Immoveable Object? EU Data Protection Law and National Security' (2018) 8 International Data Privacy Law 1; Christopher Docksey and Hielke Hijmans, 'The Court of Justice as a Key Player in Privacy and Data Protection' (2019) 5 European Data Protection Law Review 300.

[48] *La Quadrature du Net* (n 1) [106]. On the importance of *Digital Rights Ireland*, see Chapter 9.

[49] On the legislative life cycle of the Data Retention Directive, see Chapters 7–9.

[50] *Digital Rights Ireland* (n 17) [16].

[51] ibid [37].

indiscriminate retention and access and lacked clear and precise rules to ensure the extent of the interference with Articles 7 and 8 CFR was 'actually limited to what is strictly necessary'.[52] Accordingly, this amounted to an unjustified interference with the proportionality requirements of Article 52(1) and marked the first time an entire instrument of EU secondary legislation was struck down by the Court for its incompatibility with the Charter.[53]

Emboldened by the legally binding status of the Charter and the Snowden revelations, *Digital Rights Ireland* and its subsequent legacy of groundbreaking data retention standards are a far cry from early data protection cases which 'were hardly likely to set the pulses of EU lawyers racing'.[54] These evolving, far-reaching, and often novel legal requirements have consequently had significant implications for the reform and operation of data retention regimes across the EU.[55] While welcomed by civil society,[56] these standards have also resulted in considerable legal uncertainty for law enforcement, policymakers, and industry when it comes to the actual implementation, oversight, and evaluation of these evolving data retention rules at the EU and national levels.[57] One such crucial question requiring clarification after the first landmark ruling in *Digital Rights Ireland* was whether the CJEU had in fact established that the very measure of indiscriminate data retention itself was incompatible with the Charter, thereby rendering any enabling national legislation derogating from the 2002 e-Privacy Directive invalid under EU law. Furthermore, if these standards under Articles 7, 8, and 52(1) CFR extended to national legislation by falling within the scope of the e-Privacy Directive, were Member States required to implement all safeguards set out in *Digital Rights Ireland* in order to comply with EU law?

The CJEU responded, as discussed later, affirmatively to these questions in a series of judgments that continue to dramatically expand the scope and substance of these data retention standards.[58] In doing so, the Grand Chamber has consistently held that the 'general and indiscriminate retention of traffic and location data' for the purpose of combating serious crime exceeds the limits of what is strictly necessary and cannot be considered justified within a democratic society.

[52] ibid [62]–[65].

[53] See further Chapter 9.

[54] Christopher Kuner, 'International Agreements, Data Protection, and EU Fundamental Rights on the International Stage: Opinion 1/15, *EU Canada PNR*' (2019) 55 Common Market Law Review 857, 857.

[55] Iain Cameron, 'European Union Law Restraints on Intelligence Activities' (2020) 33 International Journal of Intelligence and Counter Intelligence 452, 456.

[56] See Granger and Irion (n 2).

[57] The Commission has consulted with Member States several times on devising possible solutions which comply with the Court's judgments, address law enforcement needs, and fully respect fundamental rights: European Commission, 'EU Strategy to Tackle Organised Crime', COM(2021) 170 final, 24.

[58] *Tele2* (n 17); Case C-207/16 *Ministerio Fiscal*, judgment of 2 October 2018 (ECLI:EU:C:2018:788); *La Quadrature du Net* (n 1); Case C-623/17 *Privacy International*, judgment of 6 October 2020 (ECLI:EU: C:2020:790); *Prokuratuur* (n 26); *G.D.* (n 10).

Furthermore, this jurisprudence has established that the bulk retention of traffic and location data is only valid under EU law in very limited situations, namely the safeguarding of national security due to the nature and particular seriousness of those specific threats.[59] The Court stresses, however, that the latter constitutes 'the exception and not the rule' and that data should not be retained systematically and continuously.[60] Thus, despite EU Treaty law explicitly placing national security matters of Member States outside the material scope of EU law, the CJEU has nevertheless entered 'the stage as an important regulator of intelligence activities'.[61]

The following sections examine the rapidly evolving data retention case law of the CJEU that has indeed set the pulses of EU lawyers racing. This analysis will also discuss how the Court has both deftly drawn, and dramatically diverged, from the ECtHR's considerable body of corresponding Article 8 ECHR case law in the development of its more prescriptive and novel data retention standards. Some critical reflections are then provided on the implications posed by the divergence between the standards of the CJEU and the ECtHR. This analysis concludes by considering the broader implications posed by the CJEU being the vanguard EU institution for data retention policymaking and fundamental rights protection in Europe.

(b) National legislation on data retention falls within scope of EU law

The fundamental rights requirements and 'minimum safeguards' concerning data retention established in *Digital Rights Ireland* have raised several thorny questions for policymakers at the EU and national levels. Arguably, the most significant question (then) was whether the CJEU had in fact held in *Digital Rights Ireland* that the very measure of indiscriminate data retention itself was incompatible with the EU Charter, thereby rendering any enabling national legislation derogating from the e-Privacy Directive invalid under EU law. The Court had the opportunity to address this and other key questions on scope in *Tele2 and Watson*.[62]

(i) Tele2 *and* Watson*: in search of 'an 'unequivocal ruling'* This notable judgment concerned two joined cases, from the national courts of Sweden and the UK (C-203/15 and C-698/15) seeking further clarity on the extent and effect of the privacy and data protection standards established in *Digital Rights Ireland*. The Swedish case arose following a decision by a Swedish CSP (*Tele2 Sverige*) that it would no longer retain communications data in line with the CJEU judgment of *Digital Rights Ireland*. Moreover, *Tele2 Sverige* also stated that it would erase

[59] *La Quadrature du Net* (n 1) [136]; *Privacy International* (n 58) [74]–[75].

[60] *G.D.* (n 10) [65]; *La Quadrature du Net* (n 1) [142]; *Privacy International* (n 58) [59].

[61] Cameron (n 55) 461. Opinion 1/15 (n 21) [122]–[123]; *La Quadrature du Net* (n 1) [136]; *Privacy International* (n 58) [61].

[62] *Tele2* (n 17). On the judgment, see further Iain Cameron, 'Balancing Data Protection and Law Enforcement Needs: *Tele2 Sverige and Watson*' (2017) 54 Common Market Law Review 1467; Isabella Buono and Aaron Taylor, 'Mass Surveillance in the CJEU' (2017) 76 Cambridge Law Journal 250.

any such data retained for law enforcement purposes prior to the date of the Data Retention Directive being deemed invalid under EU law in *Digital Rights Ireland*.[63]

The Swedish Minister of Justice thus subsequently appointed a special reporter to examine the Swedish legislation in the light of *Digital Rights Ireland* following a complaint from the Swedish Police Authority. The 2014 report concluded that the Swedish legislation was compatible with both EU and ECHR law. More importantly, the report contested that *Digital Rights Ireland* could not be interpreted 'as meaning that the general and indiscriminate retention of data was to be condemned as a matter of principle' or be understood as meaning that the 'set of criteria all of which had to be satisfied if legislation was to be able to be regarded as proportionate'.[64] The Swedish Telecommunications Authority promptly issued an order to the CSP to again commence its data retention obligations under Swedish law but this was not to be as the case would later be referred to the CJEU. In the preliminary reference, the referring court sought 'an unequivocal ruling' from the CJEU on whether general and indiscriminate communications data retention is incompatible with Articles 7 and 8 and Article 52(1) CFR. Alternatively, should the compatibility of such a regime be assessed in light of provisions relating to access to the data, the protection and security of the data, and the duration of retention?[65]

No parties before the Court in *Tele2* argued that the general data retention obligations did not fall within the scope of Article 3 of the e-Privacy Directive 2002/58 which concerns the 'processing of personal data in connection with the provision of publicly available electronic communications services' by CSPs in the EU. Instead, the Czech, French, Polish, and UK governments submitted that the general data retention obligations fell within the scope of *exclusions* provided in Article 1(3) of the e-Privacy Directive concerning 'public security, defence, State security (including the economic well-being of the State when the activities relate to State security matters) and the activities of the State in areas of criminal law'.[66] The European Commission attempted to carve out a middle ground between the need to ensure the protection of fundamental rights within EU law and the effect of the scope of Article 15(1) of the e-Privacy Directive for national legislation enabling general and indiscriminate data retention.

In doing so, the Commission argued that only national rules relating to the *retention* of data, and not those relating to the *access* of the national authorities to that data, should fall within the scope of the e-Privacy Directive as the retention deals with processing by CSPs not State authorities. Although, the Commission proceeded, rules governing access should be given weight by the Court when assessing whether national legislation governing the retention of data by CSPs constitutes a

63 *Tele2* (n 17) [44].
64 ibid [46].
65 ibid [50].
66 AG Henrik Saugmandsgaard Øe, Opinion of 19 July 2016 in Joined Cases C-203/15 and C-698/1 *Tele2 Sverige and Watson* (ECLI:EU:C:2016:572) [87]–[88].

proportionate interference with the rights enshrined in Articles 7 and 8 CFR.[67] The Advocate General's Opinion to the CJEU endorsed this middle ground approach put forward by the Commission, and certain other Member States, that in light of Article 1(3), provisions governing access to retained data did not fall within the scope of the Charter's application.

Another key argument for the Advocate General which justified limiting the scope and effect of Article 15 of the e-Privacy Directive, and thus the level of strictness by which the requirements established in *Digital Rights Ireland* should be applied, turned on the provision itself not being 'classified as a derogation'.[68] Thus, if Article 15(1) is not considered by the Court to be a derogation then the absence of the requirement of strict interpretation would then mean that Member States would not be precluded from adopting general data retention obligations. The Advocate General arrived at this determination based on two grounds. First, the Advocate General draws attention to the explicit provision in the wording of Article 15(1) permitting Member States to adopt 'legislative measures providing for the retention of data for a limited period ... confirms that such obligations are not in themselves inconsistent with the regime established by Directive 2002/58'.[69]

There is certainly an elegant and coherent logic to this approach of literal interpretation. However, the rushed drafting and lack of pre-legislative scrutiny of Article 15(1) following considerable political pressure post-9/11 casts doubt over the claim that such a reference goes so far as to 'confirm' that the wording of Article 15(1) is consistent with other key provisions of the Directive, especially the principle of confidentiality.[70] The second ground put forward by the Advocate General, that he purports limits the scope and effect of Article 15(1), concerns the non-binding nature of recital 11 which states that the Directive does not address issues of fundamental rights protection related to activities outside the scope of EU law. It does not, therefore, 'alter the existing balance' between the individual's right to privacy and the possibility for Member States to take the measures referred to in Article 15(1).[71]

There is, however, no endorsement for this middle ground on the scope of the e-Privacy Directive. The CJEU instead departs entirely from the analysis of the Advocate General and adopts a purposive approach to this key question, underpinned by a very general interpretation which takes 'into consideration, *inter alia*, the general structure' of the e-Privacy Directive.[72] This analysis first draws attention to one of the aims of the Directive, namely to provide for harmonization of national legislation 'to ensure an equivalent level of protection of fundamental rights

[67] *Tele2* (n 17) [66].
[68] AG Opinion in *Tele2* (n 66) [109].
[69] ibid [106].
[70] See Chapter 7.
[71] AG Opinion in *Tele2* (n 66) [108].
[72] *Tele2* (n 17) [67].

and freedoms, and in particular the right to privacy and confidentiality, with respect to the processing of personal data in the electronic communications sector'.[73] Notably, the emphasis placed by the Court in *Tele2* on the aim of the e-Privacy Directive to provide such legislation ensures an equivalent level of fundamental rights protection, mirrors exactly its purposive and equally broad interpretation of the Data Retention Directive in *Digital Rights Ireland.* In the latter, the CJEU linked the main objective of Directive 2006/24, of harmonizing Member State laws on data retention, with non-binding recitals concerning Charter compliance.[74]

The Court's analysis in *Tele2* then proceeds to note that Article 3 of the e-Privacy Directive applies to the processing of personal data by CSPs and their provision of electronic communications services in public communications networks within the EU, which means that the Directive 'must be regarded as regulating the activities' of such CSPs.[75] Admittedly, the Court recognizes that the objectives referred to in Article 15(1)—including safeguarding national security, defence and public security, and the prevention, investigation, detection, and prosecution of criminal offences—'overlap substantially' with the activities that fall outside the scope of the e-Privacy Directive, as provided under Article 1(3).[76] However, based on its interpretation of 'the general structure' of the Directive, the Court simply states that Article 1(3) cannot take precedence over Article 15(1) of the e-Privacy Directive 'for otherwise that provision would be deprived of any purpose'.[77] The Court further holds that Article 15 when 'read together' with Article 3 of the e-Privacy Directive 'must be interpreted as meaning' that any national measures adopted and referred to in Article 15(1), including data retention by CSPs and allowing national authorities access to such data, fall within the scope of the e-Privacy Directive.[78]

The analysis of the Court then comes back full circle to what has become its normative cornerstone in later data retention judgments concerning the aim of the e-Privacy Directive to protect the right to privacy and confidentiality.[79] It is here that the Court emphasizes that the protection of the confidentiality of electronic communications and related traffic data guaranteed in Article 5(1) applies to the measures taken by all persons other than users 'whether private persons or bodies or State bodies'.[80] Consistent with its fundamental rights approach in *Digital Rights Ireland*, which linked the data retention permitted under the Data Retention Directive with its purpose of enabling access of its use to public authorities, the Court applies the same reasoning to the e-Privacy Directive in *Tele2*.[81]

[73] ibid [68].
[74] *Digital Rights Ireland* (n 17) [24].
[75] *Tele2* (n 17) [70].
[76] ibid [72].
[77] ibid [73].
[78] ibid [74]–[76].
[79] *Ministerio Fiscal* (n 58); *Privacy International* (n 58); *La Quadrature du Net* (n 1).
[80] *Tele2* (n 17) [77].
[81] ibid [79].

(ii) La Quadrature du Net: ***EU law and safeguarding national security*** Rather than clearly limit its examination of the application of the e-Privacy Directive to data retention for the purpose of combating serious crime, the Court left open the question of whether data retention for all the legitimate aims provided under Article 15(1) must comply with the requirements and safeguards established in *Tele2*. Indeed, as rightly highlighted by Advocate General Campos Sánchez-Bordona, *Tele2* contains several 'explicit references' to the fight against terrorism that 'can be extended to any other threat to national security'.[82] These references posed significant implications for the primacy of EU law, the competence of EU Member States, and the shared role between EU institutions and national courts to ensure the effectiveness of EU fundamental rights within a highly sensitive area of national sovereignty. In other words, national courts were effectively again left to seek another 'unequivocal ruling' from the CJEU. This time on whether the e-Privacy Directive (and if so, to what extent), read in light of Article 4(2) TEU, applies to the data retention by CSPs for the 'purpose of safeguarding national security' in the landmark judgments of *Privacy International* and *La Quadrature du Net*.[83]

Privacy International deals with one case (C-623/17) in a series of legal challenges brought by an international civil society organization (Privacy International) against the Secretary of State for Foreign and Commonwealth Affairs and other public authorities in the UK regarding their respective powers concerning State surveillance. The preliminary reference was submitted to the CJEU in October 2017 by the UK Investigatory Powers Tribunal (IPT) which reviews complaints concerning the surveillance programmes of the UK's law enforcement, security, and intelligence agencies.[84] At this time, the UK was still an EU Member State. The judgment of *La Quadrature du Net* concerns three joined cases, two from the Conseil d'État of France (C-511/18 and C-512/18) and one from the Constitutional Court of Belgium (C-520/18), regarding the extent and effect of the requirements and standards established in *Tele2*. Due to the number and detail of the questions submitted in these three joined cases, *La Quadrature du Net* is by far the most comprehensive and wide-ranging judgment on EU rules governing data retention by the Court. Its significant implications for the fundamental rights standards of the Charter concerning the retention of various types of communications data, and their subsequent access and analysis for law enforcement and national security purposes, are discussed below.

The Court holds in both judgments that national legislation requiring CSPs to process traffic data and location data for the safeguarding of national security to

[82] AG Campos Sánchez-Bordona, Opinion of 15 January 2020 in Joined Cases C-511/18 and C-512/18 *La Quadrature du Net* (ECLI:EU:C:2020:6) [60].
[83] On these judgments generally, see Cameron (n 5); Tzanou and Karyda (n 5).
[84] For all documents relating to this preliminary reference, see the IPT website <www.ipt-uk.com/judgments.asp?id=41> accessed 1 May 2021.

public authorities falls within the scope of the e-Privacy Directive 2002/58.[85] In reaching this determination, the Court's analysis closely follows its purposive interpretation of the e-Privacy Directive in *Tele2* and *Ministerio Fiscal*.[86] The Court thus again adopts an expansive interpretation of the e-Privacy Directive and its aim as provided under Article 1(1). The latter stating 'inter alia for the harmonisation of national provisions required to ensure an equivalent level of protection of fundamental rights' with respect to the processing of personal data in the communications sector. The Court goes on to recognize that Article 1(3) of the e-Privacy Directive provides that the Directive shall not apply to activities which fall outside the scope of EU law including 'activities *concerning* public security, defence, State security'.[87]

However, the Court then proceeds to highlight that Article 3 of the Directive provides that its scope also applies to the processing of personal data in connection with the provision of publicly available electronic communications services in the EU and 'thereby the directive must be regarded as regulating the activities of the providers of such services'.[88] Article 15(1) of the Directive provides that Member States may adopt, subject to the conditions therein, legislative measures to restrict the scope of the rights and obligations provided for in Articles 5 to 9 of the Directive.[89] This brings us to the key determination by the Court that Article 15(1) 'necessarily presupposes' that these national laws fall within the scope of the e-Privacy Directive. The reasoning being that it is expressly provided that such laws may only be adopted if the conditions laid down in the Directive are met and that these measures also regulate the activities of CSPs.[90] Contrary to a literal interpretation of Article 1(3), these considerations form the grounds for the Court to instead conclude that activities by CSPs undertaken for the purpose of safeguarding national security 'must be interpreted' as falling within the scope of the e-Privacy Directive. To do otherwise, as consistently emphasized by the Court, would be to deprive Article 15(1) of 'any practical effect'.[91]

Given the purposive reasoning of the Court in *Tele2*, this determination in *Privacy International* and *La Quadrature du Net* is far from surprising. But the Court had not dealt in *Tele2* with the issue of the material scope explicitly set out in Article 4(2) TEU that national security remains the sole responsibility of each Member State. Thus, as argued by the French and UK governments, and other

[85] *Privacy International* (n 58) [39], [49]; *La Quadrature du Net* (n 1) [104]. This processing includes the retention, transmission, and/or granting of access to such communications data.
[86] *La Quadrature du Net* (n 1) [91]. See further *Tele2* (n 17) [67]–[81]; *Ministerio Fiscal* (n 58) [31]–[35].
[87] Emphasis added.
[88] *La Quadrature du Net* (n 1) [93].
[89] ibid [95].
[90] ibid [96].
[91] ibid [97].

Member States,[92] it was contended in *La Quadrature du Net* that intelligence services' activities, insofar as they relate to the maintenance of public order and to the safeguarding of internal security and territorial integrity, are part of the essential functions of the Member States and, consequently, are within their exclusive competence as provided by Article 4(2) TEU.[93] Moreover, several Member States argued that such legislation does not fall within the scope of the e-Privacy Directive in light of previous case law, in particular the 2006 judgment of *Parliament v Council and Commission*.[94] Countering this argument, La Quadrature du Net, Privacy International, and other civil society organizations submitted that Article 4(2) TEU should not have any effect on the reasoning of the Court given its more recent case law, *Tele2* and *Ministerio Fiscal*. Arguing therefore that both the retention of data and access to retained data for the objective of safeguarding national security falls within the scope of the e-Privacy Directive, whether that access takes place in non-real time or in real time, as this objective is 'expressly mentioned' in Article 15(1) of the Directive.[95] In response to these opposing arguments, the Advocate General's Opinion deftly put forward a middle ground based on 'a holistic interpretation' covering the starkly contrasting judgments of *Parliament v Council and Commission* and *Tele2*.[96]

The Advocate General takes pains to point out that Article 4(2) TEU may still be respected in light of the standards established in *Tele2* based on an interpretation of the e-Privacy Directive that extends its scope to the activities undertaken by CSPs for the safeguarding of national security but excludes any activities 'undertaken by the public authorities themselves'.[97] In order to ensure, however, that 'EU privacy law' is not deprived of its effect, the Advocate General emphasizes that the concept of national security must be 'interpreted narrowly'.[98] This, he explains, may be achieved by setting out what specific activities fall within this scope of exclusion by way of legislation and is an approach that complies with both Article 15(1) of the e-Privacy Directive and Article 23 of the GDPR.[99] The reasoning of the Advocate General is laudable for its clarity. Moreover, it represents an admirable attempt to

[92] Further submissions on this point to the Court were submitted by the Czech government, Estonia, Ireland, Cyprus, Hungary, Poland, and Sweden.

[93] *La Quadrature du Net* (n 1) [89].

[94] ibid [90].

[95] ibid [87]. Further submissions on this point were submitted by Fédération des fournisseurs d'accès à Internet associatifs, Igwan.net, and the Center for Democracy and Technology.

[96] AG Campos Sánchez-Bordona, Opinion of 15 January 2020 in Case C-623/17 *Privacy International* (ECLI:EU:C:2020:5) [25].

[97] AG Opinion in *La Quadrature du Net* (n 82) [79]. The EDPS made a similar argument in its submission to the CJEU. See Pleading Notes of the European Data Protection Supervisor, Joint hearing in Case C-623/17 (*Privacy International*) with Joined Cases C-511/18 and C-512/18 (*La Quadrature du Net and Others*) and Case C-520/18 (*Ordre des barreaux francophones et germanophone and Others*), 9–10 September 2019, 2: <https://statewatch.org/media/documents/news/2019/sep/eu-cjeu-data-ret-edps.pdf> accessed 1 May 2021.

[98] AG Opinion in *La Quadrature du Net* (n 82) [80]–[89].

[99] ibid.

strike a balance between recognizing the competence of national Member States as provided by Article 4(2) TEU concerning national security whilst requiring that this scope be clearly limited so as not to undermine the EU fundamental rights standards of *Tele2* that apply to data retention regimes adopted for the objective of combating serious crime.

The Grand Chamber does not, however, follow the Advocate General's holistic approach. Indeed, the Court departs entirely from the Advocate General's interpretation of Article 4(2) TEU, read in the light of Directive 2002/58 and Article 23 of the GDPR. Consistent with its purposive reasoning in *Tele2* that Article 15(1) 'necessarily presupposes' that the national legislative measures referred to therein fall within its scope as it expressly authorizes Member States to adopt them only if the conditions laid down in the e-Privacy Directive are met, the Court determines that Article 4(2) TEU 'cannot invalidate that conclusion'.[100] As the Court itself puts it: 'the mere fact that a national measure has been taken for the purpose of protecting national security cannot render EU law inapplicable and exempt the Member States from their obligation to comply with that law'.[101] On the other hand, the Court recognizes that there is also a precedent for such an exemption in the 2006 judgment of *Parliament v Council and Commission*.[102]

Although the processing at issue in that case was undertaken by the private sector, the Court held that the *transfer* of personal data by airlines to the public authorities of a third country (the US in this instance) for 'safeguarding public security and for law-enforcement purposes' did not fall within the scope of the EU data protection rules then in force. The decisive reasoning for the Court, in what is a notably brief judgment, turned on the finding that the transfer of passenger name records (PNR) data fell 'within a framework established by the public authorities that relates to public security' which concerns personal data processing that Article 3(2) of the Data Protection Directive 95/46/EC excludes from the scope of the 1995 Directive.[103] In a notable contrast with its post-Lisbon cases, the Court in *Parliament v Council and Commission* did not deal with the fundamental rights issues posed by the PNR data transfer regime but narrowed its assessment instead to the issue of jurisdiction and the lack of a correct legal basis for the data processing.[104]

In light of its findings in *Tele2*, however, the Court determines that *Parliament v Council and Commission* 'cannot be transposed to the interpretation of Article 1(3)' which provides that the e-Privacy Directive shall not apply to activities which

[100] *La Quadrature du Net* (n 1) [99].
[101] ibid [99].
[102] ibid [100].
[103] Joined Cases C-317/04 and C-318/04 *Parliament v Council and Commission*, judgment of 30 May 2006 (ECLI:EU:C:2006:346) [57]–[59].
[104] Christopher Docksey, 'The European Court of Justice and the Decade of Surveillance' in Hielke Hijmans and Herke Kranenborg (eds), *Data Protection Anno 2014* (Intersentia 2014) 97–116. See further Chapter 9.

fall outside the scope of EU law including activities concerning public security, defence, and State security.[105] Furthermore, the Court points out that the EU Directive at issue in *Parliament v Council and Commission* has since been repealed and replaced by the GDPR.[106] The Court then proceeds to interpret Article 23(1) of the GDPR in line with its purposive approach of Article 15(1) of the e-Privacy Directive in *Tele2*, thereby concluding that national legislation requiring CSPs to retain traffic and location data for the purposes of protecting national security and combating crime falls within the scope of the e-Privacy Directive.[107]

La Quadrature du Net thus confirms that retention of traffic and location data constitutes a derogation from the qualified prohibition of Article 5 of Directive 2002/58 requiring Member States to adopt legislation that ensures against the storage or surveillance of communications and related traffic data 'by persons other than users'.[108] Consistent with its strict-scrutiny approach in *Tele2*, the Court takes pains to stress that restrictions permitted under Article 15(1) of Directive 2002/58 concerning traffic and location data represent exceptions that 'cannot ... become the rule'.[109] By contrast, the Court also clarifies that Article 15 of Directive 2002/58 does not apply where CSPs are not involved and Member States directly implement any data retention measures that derogate from Article 5 of Directive 2002/58. These measures are instead subject to national law, the LED (where applicable), and the requirements of the ECHR.[110] As Tzanou and Karyda point out, this distinction makes clear that the Court's jurisdiction now extends to assessing the compatibility with EU law of national security measures and public–private partnerships which involve private entities.[111]

(c) Interferences with the Charter: Articles 7, 8, and 11

Most of the landmark data retention case law of the CJEU focuses on regimes dealing with the long-term and general and indiscriminate retention of two particular types of communications data: traffic data and location data.[112] This stems from, as noted earlier, the provisions of the Data Retention Directive 2006/24/EC struck down in *Digital Rights Ireland*, which required CSPs to retain data on the communications (excluding content) made by all of their customers, for between a minimum of six months and maximum of two years, for the objective of countering serious crime. These specific data retention regimes have been held to constitute particularly serious interferences with the fundamental rights to respect for private life, communications, and the protection of personal data, as enshrined in

105 *La Quadrature du Net* (n 1) [101].
106 ibid [102].
107 ibid [104].
108 *Digital Rights Ireland* (n 17) [32]; *Tele2* (n 17) [85]; *La Quadrature du Net* (n 1) [115].
109 *Tele2* (n 17) [104]; *La Quadrature du Net* (n 1) [115].
110 *La Quadrature du Net* (n 1) [103].
111 Tzanou and Karyda (n 5) 129.
112 On the evolving scope of communications data and its use by law enforcement, see Chapter 1.

Articles 7 and 8 CFR.[113] In addition, the CJEU has established that such regimes are also liable to deter users of electronic communications systems from exercising their freedom of expression, as guaranteed in Article 11 CFR.[114]

The Court has also, however, examined various other data retention regimes and their compatibility with the Charter. In addition to the establishment of new EU standards set by the Court governing data retention that falls within the ever-expanding scope of EU law, a 'hierarchy of intrusiveness' to fundamental rights has also emerged in the application of these high standards to certain types of communications data. Here we see the data retention jurisprudence of the CJEU and the ECtHR clearly converge with a shared assumption that access and analysis of communications data will always reveal less—whatever the circumstances—about an individual's private life than content.[115] There are also, of course, some significant differences between the data retention standards of both Courts, most notably the slew of far stricter standards set out by the CJEU in a series of notable judgments concerning national security matters.

(i) *Indiscriminate and long-term retention of traffic and location data* Since *Digital Rights Ireland*, the Court has held that measures permitting the indiscriminate and long-term retention of traffic and location data constitute a 'far reaching' and 'particularly serious' interference with the fundamental rights enshrined in Articles 7 and 8 CFR.[116] Moreover, the interferences with these rights take place irrespective of whether the information in question relating to private life is sensitive or whether the persons concerned have been inconvenienced in any way on account of that interference.[117] This means that any further access or processing of that data (such as profiling or its sharing with other public authorities) constitutes 'a further interference' with those fundamental rights.[118] The lack of any requirement for applicants to show that a tangible harm from a bulk surveillance or retention measure has occurred, in order for there to be an *interference* with the right to respect for private life, has been long-established within the EU and ECHR legal orders.

This is evident in both the early data protection cases of the CJEU and the earlier case law of the ECtHR.[119] It is well established under Article 8 ECHR case law that the mere fact a secret regime of bulk monitoring exists constitutes an interference with the right to respect for private life as even the threat of surveillance creates 'a very real menace' for individuals.[120] This determination was made as early as

[113] *La Quadrature du Net* (n 1) [115], [118], [139].

[114] *Tele2* (n 17) [93]; *La Quadrature du Net* (n 1) [118]; *G.D.* (n 10) [46].

[115] See further Chapter 4.

[116] *Digital Rights Ireland* (n 17) [33]–[37]; *Tele2* (n 17) [100]; *Ministerio Fiscal* (n 58) [25]; *La Quadrature du Net* (n 1) [115]–[118]; *Prokuratuur* (n 26) [33].

[117] *Schrems II* (n 10) [171]; *Prokuratuur* (n 26) [40]; *Ligue des droits humains* (n 30) [96].

[118] *Digital Rights Ireland* (n 17) [35]; Opinion 1/15 (n 21) [125].

[119] See eg Case C-465/00 *Rundfunk and Others*, judgment of 20 May 2003 (ECLI:EU:C:2003:294) [75], citing *Amann v Switzerland* (2000) 30 EHRR 843.

[120] See further Chapter 2.

1978 and indicates the sensitivity of the ECtHR to the increasing threats posed by technological advances in policing and national security in its lauded traditional approach to Article 8 ECHR and surveillance.[121] Thus, despite no evidence that the applicants had been the subject of surveillance, the ECtHR still found in its seminal case of *Klass v Germany* that the contested domestic legislation instituted a system of surveillance under which the mail and communications of all individuals could be monitored. This is an important safeguard as otherwise a requirement to show evidence of harm would prevent most individuals being able to seek effective redress, particularly as *ex post* notification of being part of a bulk surveillance measure rarely occurs in the context of national security. The CJEU has also extended these EU fundamental rights standards regarding the intrusiveness of private companies retaining, in order to provide possible future access to these communications data to public authorities, to the transferring of other data between EU and third countries, including PNR data.[122]

Although the retention and access to traffic data and location does not directly reveal the content of a communication, the CJEU's assessment of the level of interference to private life and data protection has consistently placed considerable weight on two main elements with respect to its seriousness. As the Court notes in *G.D.*, these effectively aggravating factors concern the breath, and the capacity for profiling, that any large-scale collection of such communications data 'taken as a whole' may reveal highly sensitive information about a person's private life.[123] Furthermore, in light of the 'significant quantity' of data involved, the manner of its retention ('general and indiscriminate'), and the sensitive nature of the information that may be gleaned, the Court has held that the mere retention of such data by CSPs alone 'entails a risk of abuse and unlawful access'.[124] The purposive approach of the CJEU in its fundamental rights analysis is clearly demonstrated here through its consideration of what *may* be revealed about an individual's private life beyond the retaining and access of this communications data but following its combined analysis when 'taken as a whole'.

Despite no interference with Article 11 CFR being found in *Digital Rights Ireland*, the Court later held in *Tele2* and more recent cases that obligations imposed on CSPs by Member States via national legislation for the general and indiscriminate retention of traffic and location data, and making said data accessible to competent national authorities, also constitutes an interference with Article 11 CFR.[125] In this normative approach, the Court highlighted the risk of what scholars describe as the 'chilling effects' of surveillance and held that indiscriminate communications

[121] ibid. Note that this notable approach in the well-known case law of the ECtHR contrasts starkly with its more deferential judgments in *Big Brother Watch*.

[122] Opinion 1/15 (n 21) [124]–[126].

[123] *G.D.* (n 10) [45]; *La Quadrature du Net* (n 1) [117]–[118]; *Tele2* (n 17) [99].

[124] *La Quadrature du Net* (n 1) [119].

[125] *Digital Rights Ireland* (n 17) [31]; *Tele2* (n 17) [101]; *G.D.* (n 10) [46].

data retention not only interferes with the rights to private life and data protection but also with the right to freedom of expression.[126] This specific potential harm concerns individuals being deterred from exercising their rights enshrined in Articles 7, 8, and 11 CFR based on the feeling that they are being subject to secret measures of 'constant surveillance'.[127] This was a surprising determination by the Court in *Tele2* given that neither the Swedish nor UK national courts in their preliminary references, or the Advocate General, raised any questions for the review of the Court concerning Article 11 CFR.

On the other hand, this addition of Article 11 CFR to the EU data retention standards is another clear example of the CJEU's expansive interpretation and application of EU data protection law, and EU fundamental rights more broadly, in a decade of notable landmark cases concerning data retention and State surveillance. From a rights perspective, it is welcome that the Court is giving greater weight to the extent of the intrusions into the right of private life being caused by bulk surveillance programmes. It does so by referencing the risk of the chilling effect on how individuals may be more cautious in how they manage their relationships with wider society, in this instance through their communications with others. In contrast, the ECtHR has shown less sensitivity to the increasing threats posed by technological advances in policing and national security to privacy in its more recent case law, such as *Big Brother Watch*.[128]

(ii) *Automated 'screening' of traffic and location data* National legislation of EU Member States may also provide for other types of data processing to be requested of CSPs before public authorities access any retained traffic and location data. The CJEU reviewed the compatibility of such regimes with EU law in *La Quadrature du Net* with respect to the relevant law in France, the Code de la sécurité intérieure (Internal Security Code, CSI). The automated analysis at issue essentially requires CSPs to undertake 'a screening' of all retained traffic and location data concerning their customers based on parameters set by the competent national authorities.[129] Due to the need for the screened data to be verified, the Court held that this 'must be considered as involving' general and indiscriminate processing by CSPs on behalf of public authorities.[130] The Court notes that this falls within the scope of 'processing' as defined by Article 4(2) GDPR.

Crucially, the CJEU then determines that this processing stage is '*independent* of the subsequent collection of data relating to the persons identified following that automated analysis' authorized by different provisions of the French law.[131]

[126] *Tele2* (n 17). See generally Jon Penney, 'Chilling Effects: Online Surveillance and Wikipedia Use' (2016) 31 Berkeley Technology Law Journal 117.
[127] *Tele2* (n 17) [100]–[101]; *La Quadrature du Net* (n 1) [118].
[128] See Chapter 2.
[129] *La Quadrature du Net* (n 1) [172].
[130] ibid [172].
[131] ibid [172] (emphasis added).

The Court thus holds that this automated analysis of traffic and location data by CSPs derogates from the principle of confidentiality as provided by Article 5 of the e-Privacy Directive and constitutes an interference with the rights enshrined in Articles 7 and 8 CFR regardless of the subsequent use of the data.[132] Such legislation, the Court adds, is also likely to have a deterrent effect on the exercise of freedom of expression enshrined in Article 11 CFR. This interference was found to be 'particularly serious' based on two key factors. First, its scope is general and indiscriminate and therefore extends to the screening of innocent individuals' communications and, secondly, the data when analysed is likely to reveal the nature of the information consulted online.[133]

(iii) ***Real-time collection of traffic and location data*** The CJEU has reviewed the compatibility with EU law of real-time access to the traffic and location data of a person 'previously identified as potentially having links to a [terrorist] threat ... or more persons belonging to the circle' of the person of interest in *La Quadrature du Net*.[134] Consistent with previous case law, the Court has held that such monitoring 'taken as a whole' enables the profiling of all of these individuals thereby producing information 'that is no less sensitive ... than the actual content of communications'.[135] The Court has shown that it considers measures which allow competent public authorities access to real-time location data to be particularly intrusive.[136] Indeed, the Court states that this distinguishes access to an individual's prior movements, as revealed in historical traffic and location data, from real-time access as the Court views the latter as being more intrusive in that it allows for monitoring that is 'virtually total'.[137]

The CJEU in arriving at this determination explicitly relies on the same assessment made by the ECtHR in the case of *Ben Faiza v France*, which also held that real-time location data is unequivocally more intrusive than historical location data.[138] Two key questions arise, however, from this questionable assessment. First, as Hughes points out, this novel legal standard raises the pressing question of at what point real-time data become historical data.[139] Further clarity on this distinction is required for some semblance of legal certainty and consequently to

[132] ibid [173].
[133] ibid [174].
[134] ibid [183].
[135] ibid [184]. Note that the 'taken as whole' test is inconsistently applied by the Court when assessing the level of intrusiveness to the rights enshrined in Arts 7 and 8 CFR posed by subsequent processing of the collected data. It is not applied in *G.D.* (n 10) to data concerning a user's civil identity or to PNR data: see *Lingue des droits humains* (n 30) [120].
[136] *La Quadrature du Net* (n 1) [187].
[137] ibid [187].
[138] See further Chapter 4.
[139] Kirsty Hughes, 'Mass Surveillance and the European Court of Human Rights' [2018] European Human Rights Law Review 589, 595. Similar concerns have been raised regarding the provisions on law enforcement use of remote real-time biometric identification systems in the Draft EU AI Act: Nora Ni Loideain, 'A Trustworthy Framework that Respects Fundamental Rights? The Draft EU AI Act and Police Use of Biometrics' *Information Law & Policy Centre* (4 August 2021).

ensure that real-time access to location data is only permitted if a higher threshold of safeguards is met under the relevant law. Secondly, and more importantly, the reasoning that real-time access to an individual's current location is inherently more intrusive and more revealing than having knowledge of their prior movements—whatever the circumstances—is suspect.

The significance of an individual's movements, or lack thereof, today compared to their movements yesterday depends entirely on context and law enforcement has indeed confirmed the utility of historical data in the identification of terrorist networks.[140] Having access to the historical records of an individual's movements over the past six months will also reveal far more about their private life (a profile no less of their daily activities and relationships) than one immediate real-time snapshot. Indeed, it seems the Court does in fact agree that it is the *combined* access to both real-time and historical data that is particularly intrusive to private life given its reasoning that the privacy harm stems from an intrusion that is ongoing or permanent. As the Court itself puts it: 'the real-time collection of data that allows terminal equipment to be located appears particularly serious, since that data provides . . . a means of accurately and *permanently tracking* the movements of users of mobile telephones'.[141]

(iv) ***IP addresses and rights of the Internet user*** The CJEU does not distinguish between different types of IP addresses (static/dynamic) when examining regimes mandating their bulk retention on behalf of public authorities in *La Quadrature du Net*.[142] Instead, the Court states that IP addresses 'are part of traffic data' and mainly serve to identify, through CSPs, the natural person who owns the terminal equipment from which an Internet communication is made.[143] IP addresses are therefore considered by the Court to be 'less sensitive' than other traffic data because 'no information about third parties' who were in contact with the person who made the communication is disclosed.[144] It is curious why the Court in its assessment does not treat the reduced collection of traffic data as amounting to a less significant limitation on the rights enshrined in Articles 7 and 8 CFR as opposed to *less sensitive*. Indeed, the latter assessment seems to suggest that the Court ranks higher the right to respect to communications (between individuals) than an individual's right to respect for private life when they are online.

[140] On historical travel data, eg, see European Commission, 'Report on the review of Directive 2016/681 on the use of passenger name record (PNR) data for the prevention, detection, investigation and prosecution of terrorist offences and serious crime', SWD(2020) 128 final, 22.

[141] *La Quadrature du Net* (n 1) [187] (emphasis added).

[142] For further details on dynamic IP addresses and when they constitute 'personal data' under EU data protection law, see Case C-582/14 *Breyer*, judgment of 19 October 2016 (ECLI:EU:C:2016:779).

[143] *La Quadrature du Net* (n 1) [152].

[144] ibid [152].

The Internet is clearly playing an ever-larger role in how we all work, play, read, watch, and think.[145] Access then to data revealing an individual's Internet usage is arguably just as intrusive (if not more so) as data revealing their contacts. This curious reasoning aside, the Court does proceed to recognize that the retention and analysis of IP addresses may be used to 'track an Internet user's complete click-stream and, therefore, his or her entire online activity' thus enabling a detailed profile to be produced.[146] The Court thus determines that the combined intrusion of the retention and analysis of IP addresses thereby amounts to a serious interference with the 'fundamental rights of the Internet user' enshrined in Articles 7 and 8 CFR.[147] Given the lack of clarity regarding the exact privacy harms at issue and the pace of legal and technological developments, further clarity from the Court on what precise fundamental rights have been interfered with by the retention and analysis of these IP addresses would be welcome.

(v) ***'Data relating to the civil identity of users'*** The CJEU has clearly established in its jurisprudence that access to the 'actual content of communications' constitutes the most intrusive type of communications surveillance with respect to the fundamental rights enshrined in Articles 7 and 8 CFR.[148] Consequently, the Court has treated this as the key metric by which the intrusiveness of other regimes permitting the processing of personal data are measured, including the retention, access, and analysis of various types of communications data. At the other end of the spectrum, both the Court and the ECtHR have effectively placed the retention of 'data relating to the civil identity of users' as last within this intrusiveness hierarchy.[149] This analysis rests entirely on the reasoning that this sub-category of communications data does not, 'in itself', make it possible to ascertain any traffic or location data about a user's communications.[150] Consequently, the Court concludes that such data 'does not provide, apart from the contact details of those users, such as their addresses, any information on the communications sent and, consequently, on the users' private lives', thereby the interference entailed by its retention cannot be classified as serious.[151]

Three issues arise from this reasoning in *La Quadrature du Net*. First, the Court is entirely right to point out that the retention, and subsequent access, to data relating to the civil identity of users will not reveal 'in itself' the traffic data and location data generated by the communications made by the user. That said, as the

[145] See generally Tim Wu, *The Attention Merchants* (Vintage 2016); Yuval Noah Harari, *21 Lessons for the 21st Century* (Penguin 2018); James Williams, *Stand Out of Our Light: Freedom and Resistance in the Attention Economy* (CUP 2018); Suzie Alegre, *Freedom to Think* (Atlantic Books 2022).
[146] *La Quadrature du Net* (n 1) [153].
[147] ibid [153].
[148] *Digital Rights Ireland* (n 17) [39]; *Schrems* (n 23) [94]; *Tele2* (n 17) [99]; *La Quadrature du Net* (n 1) [117].
[149] On the approach of the ECtHR, see *Breyer v Germany* [2020] ECHR 95.
[150] *La Quadrature du Net* (n 1) [157].
[151] *Ministerio Fiscal* (n 58) [60]; *La Quadrature du Net* (n 1) [157]; *Prokuratuur* (n 26) [34].

Court itself has consistently highlighted, if any personal data is combined with other traffic or location data, and/or is then subject to automated analysis, this enables a detailed profile of an individual's private life to be produced. It is unclear why the Court does not give any weight to this normative factor, consistently applied to other types of communications data in its case law, when assessing the real-world application and consequent level of intrusiveness posed by the combination of the retention and analysis of data relating to the civil identity of users.

Secondly, it is questionable for the Court in *La Quadrature du Net* to effectively rely on *Ministerio Fiscal* as a relevant supporting authority when assessing the intrusiveness of regimes requiring CSPs to indefinitely retain data relating to the civil identity of all users of their electronic communications systems.[152] It is difficult to understand how the Court can equate a data retention regime affecting millions of users with a targeted request by police in Spain for accessing the numbers and subscription data of SIM cards used on one stolen mobile phone in *Ministerio Fiscal*.[153] Thus, given the stark difference in the purposes and scale of data collected and fundamental rights impact, this is an ill-fitting supporting authority as the overall circumstances at issue in both cases are so markedly different. Again, in adopting this assessment, the CJEU in *La Quadrature du Net* is following the approach of the ECtHR in its earlier judgment of *Breyer v Germany*.[154]

Thirdly, the scope of what constitutes 'data relating to the civil identity of users' in *La Quadrature du Net* has since been dramatically expanded in the Grand Chamber judgment of *G.D.* but without any engagement by the CJEU on what minimum safeguards now apply to its retention and access. The Court had stated rather fleetingly in *La Quadrature du Net* and in *Prokuratuur* that this sub-category of communications data concerns only 'the contact details of those users, such as their addresses'.[155] This may have been a deft attempt by the Court to make clear that this very limited sub-category of communications data should not be confused with 'evidence of a commercial transaction' held for lawful business practices regulated under Directive 2002/58 and the GDPR, otherwise known as subscriber data.[156] Hence, there is a lack of any explicit requirement regarding limits to its retention by public authorities.

However, the Court has since established in its judgment of *G.D.* that the 'general retention of data relating to civil identity' that may be used for the purposes of combating crime in general extends beyond a user's contact details. Specifically, the Court held that this sub-category of communications data concerns the 'check of official documents establishing the purchaser's identity and the registration, by the seller, of that information' when a user purchases 'a means of electronic

152 *La Quadrature du Net* (n 1) [157]–[158].
153 *Ministerio Fiscal* (n 58).
154 *Breyer* (n 149). See further Chapter 4.
155 *La Quadrature du Net* (n 1) [157]; *Prokuratuur* (n 26) [34].
156 See Directive 2002/58, Art 5(2) and recital 23.

communications (such as a pre-paid SIM card)'.[157] However, the purchase of a means of electronic communications covers a very broad range of possible transactions, from buying a pre-paid SIM card to a mobile phone contract. The official documents required for purchasing the latter may, for example, involve collection of a customer's credit history of several years or proof of ID which goes far beyond the mere retention of their contact details or address.

We thus now find ourselves in a situation of 'subscriber data by any other name' with this dramatically expanded definition established by the CJEU in *G.D.* of what constitutes data relating to civil identity. This is a significant development given the far less strict standards governing the retention of this sub-category of communication data in the CJEU's jurisprudence. As confirmed in related cases before the ECtHR, regimes mandating what subscriber data must be retained by CSPs for law enforcement purposes may involve a great range of personal data.[158] Similar data retention regimes for law enforcement purposes have required, for instance, the subscriber's name, address, payment details, ID used for purchase (such as passport numbers), their company name if relevant, and all employees using this service.[159] Consequently, in the interests of legality and proportionality, and for countering the risk of excessive data collection, clarity from the Court on what safeguards now apply to this rapidly expanding sub-category of communications data would be welcome.

(d) Limitations on rights must satisfy the requirements of Article 52(1)

The rights to private life, data protection, and freedom of expression enshrined in Articles 7, 8, and 11 CFR are qualified rights. This means that they are not absolute and may be subject to limitations provided that such restrictions satisfy the conditions set out in Article 52(1) CFR. As the CJEU highlights, restrictions to these rights permitted under Article 15(1) of the e-Privacy Directive 2002/58, allowing for the adoption of data retention measures on behalf of public authorities, are an example of these limitations and 'must be considered in relation to their function in society'.[160] This means that the Court when interpreting Article 15(1), in light of the Charter, must take into account the importance of the affected rights, other related rights, positive obligations to protect private life, and 'the objectives of protecting national security and combating serious crime in contributing to the protection of the rights and freedoms of others'.[161] In cases dealing with data retention or communications surveillance before the Court (or the ECtHR), all parties will generally concede that there has been an interference with the relevant rights, particularly the right to respect for private life.[162]

157 *G.D.* (n 10) [72].
158 *Zakharov v Russia* [2016] EHRR 17; *Breyer* (n 149).
159 *Zakharov* (n 158) [133].
160 *Schrems II* (n 10) [172]; *La Quadrature du Net* (n 1) [120]; *G.D.* (n 10) [48].
161 *La Quadrature du Net* (n 1) [122]; *G.D.* (n 10) [49]–[50].
162 See further Chapters 2 and 3.

The cardinal issue in practice for the Court is then to determine whether the contested data processing satisfies the requirements of Article 52(1) and thereby constitutes a measure (or a data retention regime in this instance) that is justified and therefore compatible with EU law. Article 52(3) CFR also requires, as noted earlier, that any fundamental rights standards must be interpreted as providing 'a minimum threshold of protection' with respect to corresponding rights under the ECHR, such as the right to respect for private life enshrined in Article 7 CFR and Article 8 ECHR.[163] Consequently, the Court has based most of its requirements concerning data retention on long-established Article 8 ECHR standards.[164] The influential role of the latter is not always apparent, however, as explicit references to relevant ECtHR case law become notably ad hoc once incorporated into the requirements of the Charter.[165]

(i) *Limitations are 'provided for by law'* The well-established Article 8 ECHR jurisprudence of the ECtHR provides that compliance with the condition of legality for EU Member States under Article 8(2) ECHR requires meeting two key principles. First, the data processing must have a domestic legal basis. Secondly, the 'quality of the law' requires that the measure must comply with the rule of law and provide protection against arbitrary interference with an individual's rights under Article 8 ECHR.[166]

These are important safeguards for constraint and accountability as bulk data collection for law enforcement and national security reasons by its very nature of secrecy cannot be open to full public scrutiny.[167] Satisfying the rule of law requirement traditionally consists of two key tests for states: accessibility and foreseeability. This means that the domestic law must be sufficiently accessible and clear in its terms to give individuals an adequate indication to foresee the circumstances in which public authorities are empowered to retain, access, or use the relevant data.[168] Moreover, in line with the principle of the rule of law, it is essential that data retention measures (bulk or targeted) must be based on law that is particularly precise with clear and detailed rules as the technology available for use is continually becoming more sophisticated.[169]

However, the specific question of what 'provided for by law' actually entails, under Article 52(1) CFR, was initially overlooked by the CJEU in its data retention cases. The primary focus for the Court in its examination of Article 52(1) in these landmark judgments has instead been whether a particular data retention regime

[163] *La Quadrature du Net* (n 1) [124].
[164] *Digital Rights Ireland* (n 17) [54]–[55]; Opinion 1/15 (n 21) [141]; *La Quadrature du Net* (n 1) [115]–[116].
[165] On the complex relationship and dialogue between the CJEU and the ECtHR, see Chapter 4.
[166] See further Chapter 3.
[167] ibid.
[168] ibid.
[169] See further Chapter 4.

has complied with the principle of proportionality. This is clearly demonstrated in *Digital Rights Ireland* and *Tele2* where the Court sidesteps any specific examination of the legality condition and conflates any rule of law considerations within its proportionality analysis.[170] It is likely that the CJEU adopted this combined approach because the ECtHR employed the same in its well-known data retention ruling in *S and Marper*.[171] *Marper* was consequently a huge influence on the CJEU's analysis in *Digital Rights Ireland* and provided the normative foundation for the strict proportionality standards later reaffirmed and expanded on in *Tele2*.[172]

The ECtHR has increasingly adopted a joint-assessment approach in its case law dealing with secret surveillance and bulk data retention. However, this joint-assessment approach departs from its established (and lauded) Article 8 ECHR jurisprudence and is criticized for weakening the substantive protection of the right to respect for private life.[173] Given the concerns surrounding this controversial approach, it is welcome that the CJEU is beginning to stress the importance of the 'quality' of law requirements of Article 52(1) *before* it proceeds to examine whether the measure satisfies the relevant proportionality requirements.[174] This shift towards a more systematic and clearly defined approach is evident in its leading case law concerning regimes permitting data transfers between the EU and third countries for use by public authorities. As the Court highlights, as any limitation on the exercise of fundamental rights must be provided for by law this 'implies that the legal basis which permits that interference must itself define the scope of the limitation on the exercise of the right concerned'.[175] In *La Quadrature du Net* and *Privacy International*, this requirement also forms part of the Article 52(1) assessment of regimes requiring CSPs to carry out general and indiscriminate transmission and/or analysis of traffic data and location data on behalf of intelligence agencies for safeguarding national security.[176]

It is noteworthy that this requirement in CJEU jurisprudence harks back to the more stringent legality standards in the acclaimed Article 8 ECHR case law, standards that the ECtHR itself has departed from in its increasingly à la carte approach to rule of law standards in its recent case law dealing with data retention and surveillance.[177]

170 *Digital Rights Ireland* (n 17) [52]–[54]; *Tele2* (n 17) [109]. See, however, the AG's Opinion which examines the 'quality of law' requirements of Art 52(1) CFR at length: AG Cruz Villalón, Opinion of 12 December 2013 in Joined Cases C-293/12 and C-594/12 *Digital Rights Ireland and Seitlinger* (ECLI:EU:C:2013:845) [108]–[131].

171 See further Chapter 4.

172 On *Digital Rights Ireland*, see Chapter 9.

173 See Chapters 3 and 4.

174 Although this is not always the case. See eg *G.D.* (n 10) [54], where the CJEU Grand Chamber combines its analysis of the legality and proportionality tests.

175 Opinion 1/15 (n 21) [139]; *Schrems II* (n 10) [175].

176 *La Quadrature du Net* (n 1) [175]; *Privacy International* (n 58) [65]; *Ligue des droits humains* (n 30) [114].

177 This is particularly evident in the controversial judgment of *Catt v United Kingdom* (2019) 69 EHHR 7. See further Chapter 3.

(ii) *Limitations must 'respect the essence of those rights'* The CJEU has examined the essence requirement of Article 52(1) in a limited number of judgments.[178] Comparatively detailed analysis, however, on the conditions by which the essence of the rights to private life and data protection may be affected can be found in its landmark cases dealing with bulk data retention and State surveillance.[179] *Schrems* has been the one judgment to date where the CJEU held that the essence of the right to respect for private life as enshrined in Article 7 CFR was compromised.[180] The 2015 case of *Schrems* concerned the EU–US data sharing adequacy decision, which was issued in 2000 ('Safe Harbour'), being deemed invalid due to non-compliance with EU data protection law when read in light of the Charter. In its reasoning, which draws at length from the strict proportionality standards set out in *Digital Rights Ireland*, the Grand Chamber was particularly critical of legislation that allows 'public authorities to have access on a generalised basis to the *content* of electronic communications'.[181] There has been no case to date where the essence of the right to the protection of personal data has been held to be adversely affected. However, the CJEU has explained that a data retention or transfer regime may avoid such a determination concerning Article 8 CFR if two requirements are satisfied. First, the relevant framework should include limits on the purposes for which the data may be processed.[182] Secondly, the same regime should also include rules that ensure '*inter alia*, the security, confidentiality and integrity of that data' and protect it against unlawful access and processing.[183]

Meanwhile, there has yet to be a case where the essence of the rights enshrined in Articles 7 and 8 CFR has been held to be compromised by regimes permitting the bulk retention of communications data by public authorities within the EU. This is problematic for two main reasons. First, it sits uneasily with the CJEU's own fundamental rights standards. In particular, the reasoning runs contrary to the Court's (consistently expressed) view that information produced from analysing traffic and location data is 'no less sensitive than the actual content of communications'.[184] Brkan and others have thus rightly criticized the 'muddled maze' of logic underpinning the analysis and inconsistent application of the essence requirement

[178] European Data Protection Supervisor (EDPS), 'EDPS Guidelines on assessing the proportionality of measures that limit the fundamental rights to privacy and the protection of personal data' (December 2019) 7.

[179] Laura Drechsler and Irene Kamara, 'Essential Equivalence as a Benchmark for International Data Transfers after *Schrems II*' in Eleni Kosta and Ronald Leenes (eds), *Research Handbook on EU Data Protection* (Elgar 2021). See *Digital Rights Ireland and Seitlinger* (n 17) [39]–[40]; *Tele2* (n 17) [101]; Opinion 1/15 (n 21) [150]–[151].

[180] See Loïc Azoulai and Marijn van der Sluis, 'Institutionalizing Personal Data Protection in Times of Global Institutional Distrust: *Schrems*' (2015) 53 Common Market Law Review 1343.

[181] *Schrems* (n 23) [94] (emphasis added).

[182] Opinion 1/15 (n 21) [150]. Otherwise known as 'purpose specification', one of the key principles of data protection law: see GDPR (n 9) Art 5(1)(b); LED (n 9) Art 4(1)(b).

[183] *Digital Rights Ireland* (n 17) [40]; Opinion 1/15 (n 21) [150].

[184] *Tele2* (n 17) [99]; *La Quadrature du Net* (n 1) [184]; *G.D.* (n 10) [45].

and Article 7 CFR.[185] Secondly, this disparity has led to the Court being accused of applying stricter fundamental rights standards in its scrutiny of bulk data retention and surveillance regimes in third countries than would be applied to the same within an EU Member State.[186]

There are those, however, who argue that the Court should no longer be accused of such 'double standards' following the Grand Chamber judgments delivered in *La Quadrature du Net* and *Privacy International*.[187] The latter holding, as noted previously, that any regimes permitting the bulk retention, access, and analysis of traffic and location data for safeguarding national security in EU Member States fall within the scope of Article 15(1) of the e-Privacy Directive 2002/58, as read in light of the Charter.[188] It is therefore contended that Member States will now be subject to the same high standard of protection under the Charter as have been applied to the surveillance programmes of third countries.[189] However, neither *La Quadrature du Net* nor *Privacy International* cast any light on the Court's adherence to the anachronistic fallacy that accessing communications data will always—irrespective of scale and data type—reveal less about an individual's private life than access to content. This means that the CJEU views public authorities accessing communications content as a more serious interference with private life than having the means to accurately and permanently track the movements of mobile phone users via real-time location data.[190]

The Court's assumption of content being inherently more revealing is additionally flawed in the national security context given the latter's powers to collect communications data in bulk and enabling the detailed profiling of an individual's life using various algorithmic tools, thus rendering access to content largely irrelevant.[191] *La Quadrature du Net* and *Privacy International* are also notably silent on whether the essence of the right to protection of personal data is adversely affected by any of the reviewed regimes permitting bulk retention and access to communications data.[192] The same gaps and ad hoc examination of the essence requirement arise in *Schrems II* where the Court invalidated an EU–US data sharing adequacy decision for its incompatibility with EU law for the second time in five years.[193]

185 See Brkan (n 14).

186 Peter Swire, '*Schrems II*—backs the European legal regime into a corner' *IAPP* (16 July 2020). See generally Orla Lynskey 'The Extraterritorial Impact of Data Protection Law through an EU Law Lens' in Federico Fabbrini, Edoardo Celeste, and John Quinn (eds), *Data Protection Beyond Borders* (Hart 2021).

187 Theodore Christakis and Fabien Terpan, 'EU–US Negotiations on Law Enforcement Access to Data' (2021) 11 International Data Privacy Law 81, 105.

188 *La Quadrature du Net* (n 1); *Privacy International* (n 58). These standards draw at length and build from the earlier Grand Chamber judgments in *Digital Rights Ireland* (n 17) and *Tele2* (n 17).

189 Christakis and Terpan (n 187).

190 *La Quadrature du Net* (n 1) [187].

191 See further Chapter 1.

192 The applicants do in fact raise the issue of a lack of adequate data security for the review of the CJEU in their submissions: *La Quadrature du Net* (n 1) [75].

193 *Schrems II* (n 10) [201]. A third EU–US adequacy agreement under the GDPR, the 'EU–US Data Privacy Framework' (DPF), was adopted to address the concerns raised in *Schrems II*. On the

However, despite *Schrems II* offering the ideal opportunity to do so, the Court sidesteps expanding upon the benchmark standard established in its sibling judgment of *Schrems* on when the essence of the right to private life is compromised without any clear explanation.[194] Indeed, the Court deftly avoids even mentioning this groundbreaking precedent that legislation (not just US law) which permits generalized access by public authorities to communications content adversely affects the essence of the right to private life.

The Court does so by limiting its Article 52(1) assessment to the question of proportionality on whether the US ensures an adequate level of protection for personal data essentially equivalent to that guaranteed in the EU by the GDPR, when read in light of the Charter.[195] The EU–US Privacy Shield was struck down with immediate effect on the main grounds that access and use of data by US intelligence authorities were not limited to what was strictly necessary and the relevant oversight and redress safeguards were not essentially equivalent to the 'minimum safeguards' required under the Charter.[196] That said, the rolling back on any examination of the essence of the rights to private life and data protection enshrined in Articles 7 and 8 CFR in these three landmark judgments that scrutinize data processing regimes for national security purposes (both within and outside the EU) is far from incidental.[197]

First, these omissions do give some weight to the argument that the CJEU should no longer be criticized for imposing a stricter level of scrutiny on data retention and surveillance regimes in third countries. Secondly, the primary focus on adequate safeguards in *Schrems II* suggests a glint of recognition by the CJEU that effective enforcement of EU data protection law, in practice, cannot be achieved by formalistic measures alone. As Kuner rightly points out, for these strict legal standards to be considered legitimate, they must also be enforceable in practice or suffer the fate of being mere illusions.[198] An EU–US data transfer regime based

judgement generally and the DPF, see Maria Helen Murphy, 'Assessing the Implications of *Schrems II* for EU–US Data Flows' (2022) 71 International and Comparative Law Quarterly 245; Janvier Parewyck, '*Schrems II* Judgment C-311/18' (2023) 1 Review of European Administrative Law; Bjørn Aslak Juliussen and others, 'The Third Country Problem Under the GDPR' (2023) 13 International Data Privacy Law; Christopher Kuner, 'Protecting EU Data Outside EU Borders Under the GDPR' (2023) 60 Common Market Law Review 77; Christopher Docksey and Kenneth Propp, 'Government Access to Personal Data and Transnational Interoperability' (2023) 10 Oslo Law Review 1.

194 The Court notes that the issue of proportionality was raised in the referral by the Irish High Court but so indeed was the question of whether the relevant data processing violated the 'rights of individuals' under Arts 7 and 8 CFR. See *La Quadrature du Net* (n 1) [68], question 4.

195 *Schrems II* (n 10) [178].

196 ibid [184]–[185], [202]. On the CJEU's (questionable) view that the derogations under Art 49 of the GDPR prevent any resulting legal vacuum, see EDPB, 'Recommendations 01/2020 on measures that supplement transfer tools to ensure compliance with the EU level of protection of personal data' (finalized version adopted in 2021).

197 This contrasts starkly with the detailed analysis of same by AG Saugmandsgaard Øe, Opinion of 19 December 2019 in Case C-311/18 *Schrems II* (ECLI: EU:C:2019:1145) [272]–[282].

198 Christopher Kuner, 'Reality and Illusion in EU Data Transfer Regulation Post *Schrems*' (2017) 18 German Law Journal 881, 913.

on enhanced safeguards and remedies is thus, as Murphy aptly notes, imminently more reachable than demanding 'total cessation of generalised surveillance of data originating from the EU'.[199]

Thirdly, the lengthy examination in *Schrems II* scrutinizing whether the essence of the right to an effective remedy was compromised (as opposed to the right to private life) clearly echoes the heavy emphasis on adequate safeguards found in the cases of the ECtHR dealing with Article 8 ECHR and national security. Practitioners and scholars will often highlight the notable divergences between both systems in this area of jurisprudence.[200] One such inescapable sharp divergence, of course, is the gulf between the strict-scrutiny approach applied to bulk data retention for national security purposes in *La Quadrature du Net* and the strikingly deferential judgments regarding the same by the ECtHR Grand Chamber in *Big Brother Watch* and *Centrum för Rättvisa*.[201] However, the CJEU's shift from boldly admonishing generalized surveillance regimes in *Schrems* to its focus on 'necessary limitation and safeguards' in *Schrems II* and other recent cases is a clear reminder of the deep links between the EU and ECHR legal orders and the ongoing influence of Article 8 ECHR standards in CJEU jurisprudence.

(iii) *Limitations must comply with the 'principle of proportionality'* In line with the traditional approach of the ECtHR in its Article 8 ECHR jurisprudence, any limitations to the right to private life must be proportionate, in addition to satisfying the legality test and pursuing a legitimate aim.[202] Indeed, the key issue for the CJEU when examining Article 52(1) in its data retention case law has been whether the contested regime has satisfied the proportionality test. As Article 52(1) provides, any limitations to fundamental rights are permitted only if they are 'necessary and genuinely meet objectives of general interest recognised by the Union or the need to protect the rights and freedoms of others'. Due to the seriousness of the interference with the rights enshrined in Articles 7 and 8 CFR, as noted earlier, it is well established in the Court's case law that particularly strict proportionality standards apply to such measures that involve the general and indiscriminate processing of traffic and location data.[203]

This means that the application of the fundamental rights standards established by the Court go beyond the retention (and subsequent transmission) of this data

[199] Murphy (n 193) 257. On the shift of the CJEU adopting a more pragmatic and 'proceduralist' approach to mass surveillance following *Schrems*, see generally Edoardo Celeste and Giulia Formici, 'Constitutionalizing Mass Surveillance in the EU' (2024) 25 German Law Journal 427.

[200] See eg AG Campos Sánchez-Bordona, Opinion of 18 November 2021 in Case C-817/19 *G.D.* (ECLI:EU:C:2021:942) [38]; Tzanou and Karyda (n 5) 141.

[201] Nora Ni Loideain, 'Not so grand: The *Big Brother Watch* ECtHR Grand Chamber judgment' *Information Law & Policy Centre* (28 May 2021).

[202] On the gradual shift away from the notable traditional approach of the ECtHR, see Chapters 2 and 3.

[203] *Digital Rights Ireland* (n 17); *Tele2* (n 17); *La Quadrature du Net* (n 1); *Prokuratuur* (n 26). Note that the term 'processing' covers the retention, access, transmission, analysis, and sharing of such communications data by, or on the behalf of, any public authorities.

by the private sector and extend to governing its access and use by public authorities.[204] While the Court has indeed recognized that safeguarding national security and fighting serious crime constitute objectives of general interest to the EU, and contribute to the protection of the rights and freedoms of others, they cannot in and of themselves justify the adoption of the latter.[205] Instead, the Court has robustly established that the protection of the right to privacy requires that the bulk retention of traffic and location data involve limitations on the protection of personal data that apply only insofar as is 'strictly necessary'.[206]

This brings us to the critical question of how an interference with the rights enshrined in Articles 7 and 8 CFR (and by extension Art 11) may be considered limited to what is strictly necessary and thus satisfy the requirement of proportionality. In undertaking this Article 52(1) assessment stage, the Court will examine whether the contested data retention measure meets the following criteria of minimum safeguards and principles. The first, and most significant, strict standard precludes (safeguarding national security being an exception) legislation which provides, as a preventive measure, for the general and indiscriminate retention of traffic and location data.[207] The Court has built and expanded on this restriction in its case law. In particular, it has established that measures allowing access to a set of traffic or location data liable to provide information regarding a user's electronic communications or the location of terminal equipment they use, which may be used to draw precise conclusions concerning their private life, are not permitted for the purpose of fighting crime.[208] This restriction applies regardless of the length of the period in respect of which access to the traffic or location data is sought or the quantity or nature of the data.[209]

Secondly, access by competent national authorities to a retained set of traffic or location data should, except in cases of validly established urgency, be subject to a prior review by a court or an independent administrative authority. This *ex ante* oversight standard also requires public authorities to submit a reasoned request to the latter institution before any such authorization is granted.[210] In a welcome acknowledgement by the Court of the time often involved in this process in practice, it has held that such reviews should take place within 'a short time' in urgent cases.[211] In line with settled case law of the ECtHR, the Court has also rightly stressed the importance for such bodies to be independent and for their decisions to be binding.[212] The CJEU points out that the very aim of this review is to verify

204 *Tele2* (n 17) [125]; *Privacy International* (n 58) [77].
205 *Tele2* (n 17) [103]; *La Quadrature du Net* (n 1) [122].
206 *Digital Rights Ireland* (n 17) [56]; *La Quadrature du Net* (n 1) [130].
207 *G.D.* (n 10) [55]–[58]; *Prokuratuur* (n 26) [30]; *La Quadrature du Net* (n 1) [168].
208 *Prokuratuur* (n 26) [45].
209 ibid [45].
210 Opinion 1/15 (n 21) [202]; *Tele2* (n 17) [120].
211 *Prokuratuur* (n 26) [51].
212 See further Chapter 3.

that the situation justifying use of such measures does in fact exist and that public authorities are staying within the terms of the authorization and following all necessary safeguards.[213]

Furthermore, as noted previously, the CJEU has consistently held that the establishment of an independent supervisory authority is 'an essential component' of the protection of individuals with regard to the processing of personal data.[214] Where an independent administrative body carries out this review, the Court has thus ruled that it must have the status to be able 'to act objectively and impartially when carrying out its duties' and be free from any external influence.[215] This entails that the authority entrusted with the prior review must be a third party in relation to the authority (such as law enforcement, an intelligence agency) which requests access to the data and must not be involved in the conduct of any relevant investigation.[216] Thus, following the recommendation of the Advocate General, the Grand Chamber determined in *Prokuratuur* that the Estonian public prosecutor's office could not satisfy these requirements.[217] This ruling was based on the grounds that the office directs investigating procedure and is tasked not of ruling on a case 'in complete independence' but acting as prosecutor in the proceedings of putting it before a court with jurisdiction.[218]

The CJEU applied the same independence and impartiality requirements in its review of an authorization regime in *G.D.*, which allowed a police officer (not below the rank of chief superintendent) to authorize the prior review of requests for access to data issued by the police investigation services and to request the CSPs to transmit the data that they retain to those services. Notwithstanding that said officer is assisted in that duty by a police unit (which benefits from a certain degree of autonomy in the exercise of its duties), the Court held that they still do not have the status of a third party in relation to those services enabling 'it to act objectively and impartially when carrying out its duties and must, for that purpose, be free from any external influence'.[219] Accordingly, irrespective of the *ex post* review safeguards of the competent police officer in the form of a complaint procedure, and a procedure before a judge responsible for examining the application of the law, the Court held the Irish legislation as incompatible with Article 15(1) of Directive 2002/58, read in the light of Articles 7, 8, 11 ,and 52(1) CFR.[220]

Thirdly, in line with lauded landmark Article 8 ECHR case law of the ECtHR, public authorities to whom access to communications data has been granted must

[213] *La Quadrature du Net* (n 1) [139], [179].
[214] *Schrems* (n 23) [41]; Opinion 1/15 (n 21) [229]; *Schrems II* (n 10) [186]–[188].
[215] *Prokuratuur* (n 26) [53].
[216] ibid [54].
[217] AG Pitruzzella, Opinion of 21 January 2020 in Case C-746/18 *Prokuratuur* (ECLI:EU:C:2020:18) [129].
[218] *Prokuratuur* (n 26) [55]–[57].
[219] *G.D.* (n 10) [108]–[111].
[220] ibid [114].

notify affected persons.[221] The Court stresses that this *ex post* notification is necessary for an individual to exercise their rights under Articles 7 and 8 CFR to request access to their personal data that has been the subject of those measures and to have the latter rectified or erased.[222] It is also necessary to enable the persons affected to exercise their right to a legal remedy, as provided for in Article 15(2) of Directive 2002/58, and the right to an effective remedy enshrined in Article 47 CFR.[223] However, this safeguard comes with a major caveat as the notification is only allowed if it is 'no longer liable to jeopardise the investigations being undertaken by those authorities'.[224]

Many laws governing communications surveillance across Europe with such statutory requirements rarely produce such notifications in practice, especially where national security interests arise.[225] This is unsurprising given the wide limitations of this remedy's application. What is surprising, however, as Cameron rightly points out, is the CJEU's decision to further expand the already far-reaching limits on this safeguard in *La Quadrature du Net*.[226] Thus, the limited effectiveness of this safeguard highlights the importance of other rights and safeguards that enable individuals to challenge secret surveillance regimes to which they are subject, notably the recognition of victim status for legal standing *in abstracto*.[227]

Fourthly, in a complete departure from ECtHR standards dealing with Article 8 ECHR and State surveillance, the CJEU has established as a minimum safeguard the implementation of 'data localization' rules.[228] This novel standard requires that EU and national laws must provide that communications data retained by service providers for the aim of fighting serious crime be kept within the EU to fully ensure its oversight by EU data protection authorities.[229] No doubt reignited by the Snowden revelations, privacy concerns posed by the extra-territorial reach of US public authorities (further enabled by the global dominance of US-based cloud providers) were considered to be one of the driving factors for the introduction of this fundamental rights safeguard.[230] As Drechsler and Kamara note, however,

[221] See further Chapter 2.
[222] *La Quadrature du Net* (n 1) [190].
[223] *Tele2* (n 17) [121]; Opinion 1/15 (n 21) [220]–[224].
[224] *Tele2* (n 17) [121]; Opinion 1/15 (n 21) [220].
[225] See research findings of the EU Fundamental Rights Agency (FRA), *Surveillance by Intelligence Agencies, Vol II Report Summary* (FRA 2018) 7–11.
[226] As highlighted by Cameron (n 5) 1463, the ruling that there is no obligation to notify if this jeopardizes the tasks for which the investigating body are responsible is 'a (much) wider, and longer-lasting, ground for refusing notification than jeopardizing the particular investigation'.
[227] See further Chapter 2.
[228] See generally Wai Kuan Hon, *Data Localization Laws and Policy* (Elgar 2017).
[229] *Digital Rights Ireland* (n 17) [68]; *Tele2* (n 17) [122]–[123].
[230] Christopher Kuner and others, 'Internet Balkanization Gathers Pace' (2015) 5 International Data Privacy Law 1; Mirelle Hildebrandt, *Law for Computer Scientists and Other Folk* (OUP 2020) 24; Ian Walden, 'Accessing Data in the Cloud' in Christopher Millard (ed), *Cloud Computing Law* (2nd edn, OUP 2021) 442–43; Damian Clifford, *Data Protection Law and Emotion* (OUP 2024) 26–28. Of course, it should be noted that law enforcement in jurisdictions other than the US make similar demands of CSPs.

data localization may not in fact safeguard against the bulk interception systems of third countries as mandatory storage of online communications within the EU will not prevent this data from being accessed during the data transfer process.[231]

Finally, the CJEU has made clear that the legality requirements of Article 52(1), as noted earlier, must be met to ensure that the principle of proportionality is also satisfied. This means that any data retention measure—and its safeguards—must be provided for in the same piece of legislation under domestic law.[232] This framework must also set out clear and precise rules governing its scope and application, including the imposition of minimum safeguards. One such safeguard, again in line with ECtHR standards, is the 'irreversible destruction' of the data at the end of the data retention period,[233] the key aim being that these rules and safeguards will thereby ensure that the persons whose personal data is affected have sufficient guarantees that the data will be effectively protected against the risk of abuse.[234] The Court has consistently emphasized that the need for such rule of law safeguards is all the greater where personal data is subjected to automated processing, particularly where there is a significant risk of unlawful access to that data.[235] Those considerations apply especially where the protection of highly sensitive personal data is at stake.[236]

(iv) ***Not an exact formula: communications data and the proportionality test*** It is essential to note that the Court's application of the above criteria in its data retention case law is far from an exact formula. Instead, like the approach of the ECtHR, the detail and level of scrutiny in the proportionality analysis undertaken by the CJEU is context-dependent and will vary depending on the circumstances of the relevant case.[237] Influential factors include: the category of communications data being processed (traffic data, location data, IP addresses, personal data identifying the user/subscriber); length and scale of retention; type of access (real time or historical); and purposes for access (prevention of crime, safeguarding national security).[238] This means that some, but not all, of these criteria may be applied where the Court examines whether the processing of a certain type of communications

[231] Drechsler and Kamara (n 179). Millard also argues that a key factor in protecting personal data from unauthorized access will be how strongly encrypted the data is and the security of the server, irrespective of whether the data is stored in the EEA: Christopher Millard, 'Data Protection in the Clouds' in Mark Graham and William H Dutton (eds), *Society & The Internet* (2nd edn, OUP 2019) 159. On whether encrypted data falls within the scope of personal data under the GDPR, see the following: Case T-557/20 *SRB v EDPS*, judgment of 26 April 2023 (ECLI:EU:T:2023:219). At the time of writing, an appeal of this judgment to the CJEU is forthcoming.

[232] In this respect, as noted earlier, the CJEU has interpreted the legality requirements far more strictly in its recent case law than the corresponding Art 8 ECHR case law of the ECtHR, the latter of which does not require that the relevant 'law' take the form of binding legislation. See Chapters 2 and 3.

[233] *Tele2* (n 17) [122]; Opinion 1/15 (n 21) [210]; *Catt* (n 177) [119].

[234] *Prokuratuur* (n 26) [48].

[235] *Digital Rights Ireland* (n 17) [55]; *Tele2* (n 17) [122]; Opinion 1/15 (n 21) [141].

[236] *G.D.* (n 10) [54]; *La Quadrature du Net* (n 1) [132].

[237] On the case law of the ECtHR, see Chapter 3.

[238] See eg the wide range of data retention regimes reviewed in *La Quadrature du Net* (n 1).

data on behalf of public authorities complies with the principle of proportionality under Article 52(1) CFR.

It is now settled case law, for instance, that Article 15(1) of the e-Privacy Directive 2002/58, read in light of Articles 7, 8, and 11, and Article 52(1) CFR, precludes measures which provide as a preventive measure for the 'general and indiscriminate' retention of traffic and location data.[239] While the Court has carved out a narrow exception for safeguarding national security, such retention must still be subject to 'foreseeable' time limits and also limited to situations where a serious threat to national security is 'shown to be genuine and present or foreseeable'.[240] Otherwise, this far-reaching and controversial minimum safeguard issued by the Court only allows for the 'targeted retention' of traffic and location data for the purposes of combating serious crime and preventing serious threats to public security.[241] Thus, the Court has made it clear that the objective of fighting crime is not capable of justifying public authorities having access to a set of traffic or location data given the seriousness of the intrusion to the rights to private life, data protection, and freedom of expression.[242] Given the rich profiling of an individual enabled by accessing this vast amount of communications data, to allow public authorities extensive use of this highly intrusive investigatory power for dealing with far less serious criminal offences, such as the illegal dumping of waste by homeowners, as opposed to murder, is indeed suspect.[243]

The implications for countering serious crime, and safeguarding national security, posed by this far-reaching safeguard, however, are far less clear given the overlap of both aims in dealing with the same threats to public safety, including terrorism.[244] Where targeted data retention is permitted, the Court has established that the scope of such retention measures must be limited to what is 'strictly necessary' with respect to the categories of retained data, the means of communication affected, persons concerned, and the retention period.[245] Any relevant legislation for such measures must be based on 'objective evidence' which makes it possible to target persons whose data is likely to reveal a link (at least indirectly) with

[239] *La Quadrature du Net* (n 1) [141], [168]; *Prokuratuur* (n 26) [30]. This also applies to measures requiring the bulk transmission of traffic and location data by CSPs to public authorities for the purpose of safeguarding national security: *Privacy International* (n 58) [82].

[240] *La Quadrature du Net* (n 1) [137]–[139]. This exception echoes that proposed by AG Campos Sánchez-Bordona, Opinion of 15 January 2020 in Case C-520/18 *Ordre des barreaux francophones et Germanophone* (ECLI:EU:C:2020:7) [105].

[241] *Tele2* (n 17) [108]; *La Quadrature du Net* (n 1) [147]. Confusingly, the Court makes the opposite determination later in *Prokuratuur* (n 26) ([33]) and states that 'general and indiscriminate' retention of traffic and location data is also justified for the purposes of combating serious crime and preventing serious threats to public security.

[242] *Prokuratuur* (n 26) [60].

[243] As Andrew Murray rightly argues here: 'AG Saugmandsgaard Øe on Mass Data Retention: No Clear Victory for Privacy Rights', *Verfassungsblog* (20 July 2016).

[244] Indeed, the CJEU has recognized that combating terrorism falls under both aims of fighting serious crime and safeguarding national security: *Tele2* (n 17) [103]; *La Quadrature du Net* (n 1) [135].

[245] *La Quadrature du Net* (n 1) [147].

serious criminal offences, that contributes 'in one way or another' to combating serious crime, or preventing a serious risk to public security, or a risk to national security.[246]

In an attempt to assist law enforcement overcome the difficulties posed by no longer having access to general and indiscriminate data retention powers, the Court has consistently proposed that data retention measures could be made more targeted if public authorities made use of geographical profiling and targeted specific communities.[247] Despite serious criticism rightly expressed by scholars and national courts of such a controversial, discriminatory, and thus questionably legal endorsement,[248] more detail was provided on how this geographical criterion could be applied in *La Quadrature du Net*. This advice suggests 'places with a high incidence of serious crime, places that are particularly vulnerable to the commission of serious criminal offences, such as places or infrastructure which regularly receive a very high volume of visitors, or strategic locations, such as airports, stations or tollbooth areas'.[249] The Court also highlights in *La Quadrature du Net* (responding perhaps to the above criticisms), and reiterates in *G.D.*, that the use of any such geographical criterion should be made on the 'basis of objective and non-discriminatory factors'.[250]

Notwithstanding the Court's concession of the difficulties posed by its proposed policy solution,[251] it is still difficult to understand how States can be expected to implement targeted retention regimes, which rely on profiling communities 'particularly vulnerable to serious crime', that is not discriminatory or will not result in the over-policing of already marginalized groups. Furthermore, Advocate General Campos Sánchez-Bordona highlights another key contradiction inherent in the preventive targeted retention of a specific community or place, namely that it is impossible to know in advance the perpetrators of criminal offences or where and when those offences will be committed.[252] This valid criticism also extends to expedited retention (quick freeze) regimes of traffic and location data put forward by the CJEU in *La Quadrature du Net*.[253] These regimes remain relevant and may be useful for law enforcement. However, the key challenge is that in most cases where a serious criminal offence is committed, such as rape or murder, public authorities will not be in the position of being able to identify a suspect *in advance* of the crime being committed and thus request (in advance of the crime) the suspect's mobile phone location data. Indeed, Cameron goes as far as to argue that *La Quadrature du Net*, the Court's most comprehensive data retention ruling on electronic

[246] *Tele2* (n 17) [111]; *La Quadrature du Net* (n 1) [148]; *G.D.* (n 10) [55].
[247] *Digital Rights Ireland* (n 17); *Tele2* (n 17); *La Quadrature du Net* (n 1).
[248] Buono and Taylor (n 62) 251; Lynskey (n 33) 174; Tzanou and Karyda (n 5) 144.
[249] *La Quadrature du Net* (n 1) [150].
[250] *La Quadrature du Net* (n 1) [150]; *G.D.* (n 10) [78]; see also *Tele2* (n 17) [111].
[251] *G.D.* (n 10) [79].
[252] AG Opinion in *La Quadrature du Net* (n 1) [89].
[253] *La Quadrature du Net* (n 1) [165].

communications to date, 'offers States no further guidance on how to redraft their laws on data retention in ways which preserve the value of data retention to law enforcement'.[254]

Finally, the CJEU tends to be more explicit in its application of a balancing test in cases where the retention and/or access to communications data by the public authorities is deemed proportionate and thus Charter-compliant. The key factors to be reconciled in these circumstances are the importance of the public interest objective pursued against the affected rights at issue and the seriousness of the interference entailed by the limitation.[255] This means that less strict standards will apply to data retention measures the Court does not classify as amounting to a serious interference with the rights enshrined in Articles 7 and 8 CFR.[256] Thus, the Court makes clear in *La Quadrature du Net* that it is not opposed to the bulk retention of communications data in certain circumstances and thereby general retention programmes in principle.

Instead, the Court (in line with the approach of the ECtHR) has shown itself to be particularly sensitive to the intrusiveness posed by the retention and analysis of *specific types* of communications data. Stricter proportionality standards apply, for instance, to the automated pre-screening and real-time collection of traffic or location data.[257] These include limiting the use of such measures to persons where there is a valid reason to suspect that they are involved in terrorist activities. Application of this investigatory power is also subject to a prior review, carried out either by a court or by an independent administrative body, to ensure the authorization takes place only within the limits of what is strictly necessary.[258]

In contrast, the Court also established in *La Quadrature du Net* that EU law does not prohibit measures that impose a mandatory requirement on CSPs to retain the personal data of millions of their customers for the broad purposes of preventing crime and the safeguarding public security. Due to the interference entailed by this measure not being considered as serious by the Court, far less strict standards apply to its retention, access, and use.[259] The Court has effectively ruled that this expanding sub-category of communications data may be retained by CSPs for various purposes for no less than indefinitely as no 'specific time limit' is required.[260] As discussed previously, this lax approach by the CJEU to what is essentially 'subscriber data' follows the same less strict standards applied by the ECtHR in its deferential review of the legal regime permitting bulk retention of the same in Germany.[261]

254 Cameron (n 5) 1463.
255 *La Quadrature du Net* (n 1) [130]–[131].
256 *Ministerio Fiscal* (n 58); *La Quadrature du Net* (n 1).
257 *La Quadrature du Net* (n 1) [192].
258 ibid [188]–[189]; *Prokuratuur* (n 26) [51]–[54]; *G.D.* (n 10) [106]–[110].
259 *La Quadrature du Net* (n 1) [157].
260 ibid [159]; *G.D.* (n 10) [71]–[72].
261 *Breyer* (n 149). See further Chapter 3.

This strikingly lenient review by the CJEU departs entirely from its previous proportionality jurisprudence on the minimum safeguards required under Article 52(1) CFR to ensure the effective protection of personal data. As the Court itself has consistently held regarding the use by public authorities of 'legitimately retained personal data', such laws 'must also lay down the substantive and procedural conditions governing that use'.[262] The need for such safeguards, as already noted, is all the greater where personal data is subject to automated processing.[263] Applying less strict standards to the less intrusive privacy interference posed by the retention and access to subscriber data is logical. At the same time, however, the lack of *any* clear and precise minimum safeguards to govern these regimes that allow for the mass and indefinite retention of the personal data of millions of users across the EU runs contrary to the rule of law and falls far short of the Court's own fundamental rights standards.[264]

2. A floor but not a ceiling: ECHR and EU standards

Article 52(3) CFR requires that equivalent rights under the ECHR provide minimum human rights standards within EU law. Accordingly, as noted previously, the scope of protection and standards guaranteed by Article 8 ECHR represent a floor but crucially *not a ceiling* for the interpretation and application of Article 7 CFR. The CJEU has embraced this principle in its landmark data retention jurisprudence through its strict proportionality assessments and establishing a high level of safeguards. In doing so, the CJEU has both built on existing Article 8 ECHR standards and further ratcheted up these requirements by applying a more prescriptive approach and making mandatory what the ECtHR now views as best practice.[265]

This approach is well demonstrated in *Digital Rights Ireland* and *Tele2* where the CJEU adopted and expanded the strict proportionality standards established by the ECtHR in its leading data retention judgment of *S and Marper*.[266] The CJEU had an obvious opportunity to distinguish, and thus distance, the strict standards applied in the latter from its ruling in *Digital Rights Ireland* as the facts and analysis in *Marper* concerned the retention of biometrics and DNA materials (not communications data). Nevertheless, the CJEU incorporated all the safeguards and principles as set out in *Marper* into its fundamental rights analysis in *Digital Rights Ireland* which were then reiterated in *Tele2*. The CJEU further expands these

262 See *Schrems* (n 23) [91]; Opinion 1/15 (n 21) [192]; *Schrems II* (n 10) [176].
263 ibid.
264 *Prokuratuur* (n 26) [34]; *La Quadrature du Net* (n 1) [168].
265 See further Chapters 2 and 3.
266 See further Chapter 3.

safeguards in both judgments to also apply to national authorities' access to the retained communications data, a processing stage the ECtHR explicitly refused to rule on in *Marper*.[267]

Another example of the CJEU's more expansive and prescriptive approach concerns the settled Article 8 ECHR standard that prior (*ex ante*) authorization by a court, or independent administrative body, allowing public authorities access to retained data is an important safeguard against abuse. The ECtHR has also established, however, that it is not an essential safeguard in its case law dealing with Article 8 ECHR and State surveillance.[268] A data retention measure may thus be assessed by the ECtHR as compliant with Article 8 ECHR provided that an *ex post* review by a court or independent body exists to compensate for lack of the former.[269] In contrast, the CJEU has taken a far more robust approach and has established that prior review by a judge, or independent administrative body, is one of the key minimum safeguards to be met in order to satisfy the principle of proportionality.[270] This divergence between the Courts' standards is clearly demonstrated in *Prokuratuur* and *G.D.*, where the CJEU Grand Chamber, responding to a specific question on the matter from the Supreme Courts of Estonia and Ireland, rejects the approach of the ECtHR. Instead, the CJEU states in both that a subsequent review alone would not enable the aim of a prior review which is to ensure that authorization of access to the relevant data does not exceed what is strictly necessary.[271]

At the same time, rather than go its own way, the CJEU has also unequivocally followed the unpersuasive approaches and reasoning of the ECtHR and indeed vice versa. Both Courts have shown, for instance, that they consider measures which allow competent public authorities access to real-time location data to be particularly intrusive but reach this conclusion without any detailed justification. The CJEU in arriving at this determination explicitly relies on the same vague reasoning used by the ECtHR in the case of *Ben Faiza v France* which also held that real-time location data is unequivocally more intrusive than historical location data.[272] However, as noted earlier, two key questions arise from this questionable assessment that are yet to be addressed by the CJEU or the ECtHR. First, at what point does real-time data become historical data? Further clarity on this distinction is required for some semblance of legal certainty and consequently to ensure that real-time access to location data is only permitted if a higher threshold of safeguards is met under the relevant law. Secondly, the argument that real-time access to an individual's location is inherently more intrusive, and thereby more

[267] *S and Marper v United Kingdom* (2009) 48 EHRR 50 [125].
[268] See further Chapter 2.
[269] *Big Brother Watch v United Kingdom* [2018] ECHR 722 [318]–[320].
[270] *Tele2* (n 17) [134]; *Privacy International* (n 58) [52].
[271] *Prokuratuur* (n 26) [58]; *G.D.* (n 10) [110].
[272] *La Quadrature du Net* (n 1).

revealing, than having knowledge of their prior movements (whatever the circumstances) is far from persuasive.

Finally, there is a clear convergence between the data retention case law of the CJEU and the ECtHR in the form of both being underpinned by the (now) outdated and misguided assumption that accessing communications data will always reveal less about an individual's private life than content.[273] This is particularly evident in the 'hierarchy of intrusiveness' to fundamental rights that has emerged from the CJEU's application of its high standards to particular types of communications data. The Court has clearly established in its jurisprudence, as already noted, that access to the content of communications constitutes the most intrusive type of communications surveillance with respect to the fundamental rights enshrined in Articles 7 and 8 CFR. At the other end of the spectrum, both Courts have ranked the retention of 'data relating to the civil identity of users' and 'subscriber data' as last within this intrusiveness hierarchy. This questionable assessment rests entirely on the reasoning that this sub-category of communications data does not 'in itself' make it possible to ascertain any traffic or location data about a user's communications.[274]

However, as discussed previously, three major issues arise from this reasoning set out by the CJEU in *La Quadrature du Net*. First, the Court is right to point out that the retention of, and subsequent access to, data relating to the civil identity of users will not in itself reveal the traffic data and location data generated by the communications made by the user. However, if this data is combined with any type of communications data (traffic and location data, IP addresses) and/or is then subject to automated analysis, this enables a detailed profile of an individual's private life to be produced. It is unclear why the Court does not give any weight to this normative factor which has been consistently applied when assessing the intrusiveness to fundamental rights posed by the analysis of other types of communications data in its jurisprudence. Secondly, the Court has yet to address what distinguishes the concept of 'data relating to the civil identity of users' from that of subscriber data when assessing the level of intrusiveness such retention and access to this information poses to the right to private life.

Thirdly, but not at all least, neither the CJEU nor the ECtHR have scrutinized in any detail what minimum safeguards, or level of adequate oversight, should apply to programmes that provide for the indefinite and bulk retention of data relating to the civil identity of users' and/or subscriber data.[275] As the ECtHR points out, where the State has 'put itself at the limit of the margin of appreciation in allocating to itself the most extensive power of indefinite retention, the existence and functioning of certain safeguards becomes decisive'.[276] Consequently, the lack

[273] See further Chapters 1–3.
[274] *La Quadrature du Net* (n 1) [157].
[275] *Breyer* (n 149); *La Quadrature du Net* (n 1). See further Chapter 3.
[276] *Gaughran v United Kingdom* [2020] ECHR 144 [88].

of analysis identifying what safeguards should be put in place to govern such regimes that enable the mass and indefinite retention of the personal data of millions of users across the EU is troubling and falls short of the settled case law of both Courts.

It can be concluded that since the elevation of the Charter to the status of EU law there has to date been more divergence than convergence between the EU and ECHR legal orders in this rich and complex dialogue between the Courts. One notable divergence being the far stricter standards that the CJEU has established in its landmark judgments concerning bulk retention measures and national security. This contrasts starkly with the lack of any shift by the ECtHR in its recent case law towards an outright finding that general and indiscriminate surveillance regimes may be incompatible with Article 8 ECHR.[277] However, within the former, and in relation to the use of communications data for law enforcement purposes, the corresponding standards of the ECHR legal order clearly continue to play a key role in shaping the case law of the CJEU within this important area of EU law.

3. EU fundamental rights and data retention: achievements and future challenges

(a) At the vanguard of data retention policymaking in Europe

For most of the EU's existence, the story of human rights in the EU has been led by the dialogue between the Luxembourg and Strasbourg Courts.[278] However, this has changed dramatically in more recent times. Following the rise of the EU Charter and the Snowden revelations, an emboldened CJEU has placed itself at the vanguard of data retention policymaking and human rights scrutiny in Europe. The landmark jurisprudence set out by the CJEU is rapidly evolving and extending into areas previously regarded as the sole remit of national courts, including national security and the admissibility of evidence. Indeed, the CJEU has now consistently held in three Grand Chamber rulings that national criminal courts, subject to certain circumstances, should disregard information and evidence obtained by means of the general and indiscriminate retention of traffic and location data in breach of EU law.[279] Thus, with each judgment, the Court continues to expand these far-reaching standards thereby entrenching its role as a de facto lawmaker.[280]

Civil society has welcomed these standards and put them forward as the yardstick by which the ECtHR should assess and update its corresponding Article

277 See further Chapters 2 and 3.

278 See further Chapter 4.

279 *La Quadrature du Net* (n 1) [225]–[228]; *Prokuratuur* (n 26) [41]–[44]; *G.D.* (n 10) [128].

280 For other areas of EU law where the CJEU's jurisprudence has taken on a regulatory dimension, see Oliver Gerstenberg, 'Constitutional Reasoning in Private Law: The Role of the CJEU in Adjudicating Unfair Terms in Consumer Contracts' (2015) 21 European Law Journal 599.

8 ECHR standards.[281] Indeed, by building on the previously lauded case law of the ECtHR,[282] the CJEU is now an important driving force in this area, setting minimum standards in the review of data retention and State surveillance laws across Europe and beyond. The CJEU is also holding the EU legislature far more to account for its responsibility to ensure human rights compliance in the implementation and evaluation of EU measures in these areas.[283] This is a welcome development towards ensuring the effective mainstreaming of fundamental rights across EU lawmaking. It also responds to calls by leading scholars for the Court to 'lay more responsibility for human rights compliance at the doorstep of the European legislator'.[284]

One key factor that the CJEU has given greater weight to in its legal assessment, far more consistently than the ECtHR, is how digitalized our lives have become in the twenty-first century and how this has enhanced the monitoring capacity of bulk retention and communications surveillance regimes.[285] The CJEU is right to closely examine and identify the specific harms posed to fundamental rights in the light of risks posed by present-day pervasive surveillance technologies and data analytics, such as real-time location tracking and automated profiling systems.[286] Otherwise, these legal safeguards run the risk of providing only illusory protection. This reflects the CJEU's transformative interpretation of the Charter preamble in Opinion 1/15 that it is necessary 'to strengthen the protection of fundamental rights in the light of changes in society, social progress and scientific and technological developments'.[287] The requirement that fundamental rights be fit for purpose in order to provide adequate protection from modern surveillance measures is welcome. Although not explicitly acknowledged by the CJEU, this transformative interpretation of the Charter clearly draws from the long-established 'living instrument' doctrine created by the ECtHR.[288]

The CJEU has further emphasized the risks posed by the growing role of the private sector in law enforcement and national security activities. This is evident

[281] See Chapter 3.

[282] ibid.

[283] See particularly *Digital Rights Ireland* (n 17) and *Schrems* (n 23).

[284] Bruno de Witte, 'The EU's Human Rights Agenda' in Vasiliki Kosta, Nikos Skoutaris, and Vassilis P Tzevelekos (eds), *The EU Accession to the ECHR* (Hart 2014) 353. See also Elise Muir, 'The Court of Justice: A Fundamental Rights Institution among Others' in Mark Dawson, Bruno de Witte, and Elise Muir (eds), *Judicial Activism at the European Court of Justice* (Elgar 2013).

[285] See also Chapter 1 on efforts by the European Parliament to address the use of Pegasus and increasing trade in other unregulated spyware technology. It has also been argued that this case law is a recognition of the rise of a 'European Digital Citizen': see generally Iliopoulou-Penot (n 6).

[286] *La Quadrature du Net* (n 1) [180]–[189]; *Ligue des droits humains* (n 30).

[287] Opinion 1/15 (n 21) [135]; *Ligue des droits humains* (n 30) [179]. The preamble does refer to the justification for the Charter's adoption. However, contrary to the CJEU's analysis, it does not state that the Charter should be interpreted in the light of societal changes: '[I]t is necessary to strengthen the protection of fundamental rights in the light of changes in society, social progress and scientific and technological developments *by making those rights more visible in a Charter*' (emphasis added).

[288] See further Chapters 2 and 3.

in the Court's determination that the bulk retention of communications data by the private sector itself, on behalf of public authorities, entails a risk of abuse and unlawful access. Examination of the seriousness of the interference with the rights enshrined in Articles 7 and 8 CFR posed by this includes the aggravating factors of the 'significant scale' of the retained data and 'the sensitive nature of the information that may be gleaned from that data'.[289] Thus, the Court has consistently held that laws permitting such data retention must provide rules that not only protect this information against unlawful access and disproportionate processing but also rules to ensure the data security, confidentiality, and integrity of that data.[290]

Finally, given the accountability challenges raised by the growing role of industry in law enforcement and national security,[291] the CJEU should be applauded for highlighting the risk that bulk retention regimes pose to the legal protections provided to whistle-blowers and the need for strengthening these safeguards.[292] The latter is unquestionably an oversight safeguard of increasing significance across both public and private sectors given the rising use of powerful and complex AI and algorithmic systems provided by industry to public authorities.[293]

(b) Challenges to legal certainty and the protection of EU fundamental rights

Much disarray has unsurprisingly arisen in the wake of the CJEU's highly complex and dynamic jurisprudence and in the absence of long overdue reforms to Article 15 of the e-Privacy Directive 2002/58, the regime's fraying legislative linchpin. While in the process of reviewing their laws and awaiting further reforms from both the CJEU and the EU legislature, most Member States have continued to permit the bulk retention of communications data for combating serious crime.[294] Work by the European Commission in consultation with Member States remains ongoing at the time of writing to set out possible solutions that are in line with the Court's judgments and fully respect fundamental rights.[295] At the same time,

[289] *G.D.* (n 10) [46]; *La Quadrature du Net* (n 1) [119].

[290] Opinion 1/15 (n 21) [150]; *Digital Rights Ireland* (n 17) [66]; *Tele2* (n 17) [122].

[291] See generally Simon Chesterman, 'We Can't Spy … if We Can't Buy!' The Privatization of Intelligence and the Limits of Outsourcing "Inherently Governmental Functions"' (2015) 19 European Journal of International Law 1055; Vavoula and Mitsilegas (n 36) 70–71; Cameron (n 5) 1459.

[292] *La Quadrature du Net* (n 1) [118]; *Privacy International* (n 58) [72].

[293] European Parliament, Special Committee on Artificial Intelligence in a Digital Age, 'AIDA Working Paper on AI and Bias' (November 2021) 2–3. See generally Amélie Lachapelle, 'Data Protection Enforcement in the Era of the Directive on Whistleblowers' in Eleni Kosta, Ronald Leenes, and Irene Kamara (eds), *Research Handbook on EU Data Protection Law* (Elgar 2022); Dimitrios Kagiaros, 'Reassessing the Framework for the Protection of Civil Servant Whistleblowers in the European Court of Human Rights' (2021) 39 Netherlands Quarterly of Human Rights 220.

[294] FRA, *Fundamental Rights Report 2020* (FRA 2020) 155.

[295] Communication from the Commission, 'On the EU Strategy to tackle Organised Crime 2021–2025', COM(2021) 170 final, 24. The European Data Protection Board (EDPB) advises that the e-Privacy Regulation must comply with the CJEU's 'latest case law': EDPB, Statement 03/2021 on the ePrivacy Regulation, 9 March 2021.

Member States have the intractable task of drafting national data retention laws that comply with the CJEU's evolving and expanding data retention standards in a clear and precise manner that also satisfies the rule of law and ensures legal certainty.[296] Consequently, the extent of compliance by most EU Member States to date with these landmark judgments of the CJEU has been limited. Any detailed evidence to assess their impact on the protection of EU fundamental rights, and the constraints placed on the use of data retention by law enforcement, have been confounded.[297]

The current ad hoc set of jurisprudential rules governing EU data retention law thus poses three significant challenges for the rule of law, legal certainty, and ultimately the protection of EU fundamental rights in practice. First, this fragmented framework consists of a highly complex patchwork of rules delivered by the CJEU on a case-by-case basis with minimum standards that are not always applied clearly or consistently. Secondly, the pace of change by which these jurisprudential standards are updated and expanded poses notable challenges for any public authority or industry body seeking certainty from the laws they are expected to comply with. This lack of clarity and confusion invariably threatens to create gaps in the protection of fundamental rights.[298] Thirdly, the CJEU's case law is increasingly encroaching upon the remit and role of the national courts as guardians of EU fundamental rights particularly in areas concerning national security and the admissibility of evidence.

4. National courts as guardians of EU fundamental rights

National courts have a constitutional duty in ensuring the legal certainty of EU law and maintaining public confidence in EU law at the domestic level. They must also take into account the CJEU's already heavy caseload becoming overloaded with references.[299] Accordingly, this has led the CJEU and commentators to acknowledge the key role of national courts, which establish the facts and ultimately apply the law in each case, as guardians of fundamental rights and the entire EU constitutional system.[300] This shared jurisdiction with the national courts also enables the

[296] At the time of writing, there are further preliminary references to the CJEU on data retention and law enforcement access from national courts. See eg from Germany (Joined Cases C-793/19 and C-794/19).

[297] FRA, *Fundamental Rights Report 2021* (FRA 2021) 191; European Commission, *Study on the retention of electronic communications non-content data for law enforcement purposes—Final report* (Publications Office of the EU 2020) 21.

[298] For a contrasting view that the legal certainty of a 'web of legislation … testable in court' is sufficient to govern emerging and complex policing technologies (including facial recognition), see Kit Malthouse, Minister of State for Crime and Policing, 'New Technologies and the application of the Law', Oral Evidence (House of Lords, 12 January 2022) Q110: <https://committees.parliament.uk/oralevidence/3287/html/>.

[299] See further Chapter 7.

[300] ibid.

judicial branch of Member States to hold their executives on the European Council to account for their part in developing EU policies that raise both domestic and EU legal concerns.[301] The CJEU and the national courts have therefore a joint role in providing 'legitimate and effective judicial intervention'[302] that ensures the effective protection of EU fundamental rights.

However, despite a raft of preliminary references, it is questionable whether a shared and constructive dialogue that advances fundamental rights is taking place between the national courts and the CJEU regarding the latter's expanding jurisdiction and prescriptive patchwork of data retention rules.[303] Indeed, the dialogue could be described as taking on a more combative and divisive tone. We see evidence of this in the critical reception given to the CJEU's solutions of expedited, targeted retention, and geographical profiling for fighting serious crime, which the French Council of State and the Irish Supreme Court have deemed as unworkable. The Irish Supreme Court in *G.D.* also raised concerns to the CJEU that expedited retention is only useful where it has already been possible to identify a suspect in the early stages of a serious crime investigation.[304]

In response, the CJEU observes in *G.D.* that the effectiveness of criminal proceedings generally 'depends not on a single means of investigation but on all the means of investigation available to the competent national authorities for those purposes'.[305] The Court also stresses that there are bulk regimes compatible with EU law that may still be used for countering serious crime. These include IP addresses and data relating to the civil identity of electronic communications users.[306] Again, as held in *La Quadrature du Net*, the Court points out that Directive 2002/58, read in light of Articles 7, 8, and 11 CFR, means law enforcement are not limited to requesting targeted and expedited retention of only *suspects* in serious crime investigations.[307] As commentators have pointed out, these other means of investigation do not address the issue of digital trails 'gone cold', mainly due to police being unable to access traffic and location data that no longer exist in an investigation where the identification of key suspects or witnesses takes several weeks or months.[308]

The complexity and pace of the CJEU's evolving data retention standards have put referring national courts in a constitutional crisis. On the one hand, national courts are faced with the decision of striking down data retention laws in their

[301] Theodore Konstadinides, 'Destroying Democracy on the Ground of Defending It?' (2011) 36 European Law Review 722, 736.
[302] Joanne Scott and Susan P Sturm, 'Courts as Catalysts' (2007) 13 Columbia Journal of European Law 565.
[303] Since *Tele2*, preliminary references have been submitted by the courts in Belgium, Estonia, France, Germany, Ireland, Spain, and the UK.
[304] *G.D.* (n 10) [26].
[305] ibid [69].
[306] ibid [70].
[307] ibid [75].
[308] Cameron (n 5) 1463.

entirety due to their incompatibility with the CJEU's jurisprudence.[309] On the other hand, national courts have been given the role of de facto lawmaker by being tasked with determining to what extent the application of these EU rules should apply within domestic law.[310] These national courts have, however, had little input in the actual impact and piecemeal development of these far-reaching and increasingly prescriptive data retention rules. The preliminary reference system traditionally involves the CJEU giving a ruling on 'the interpretation or the validity of a rule of EU law' as proposed or enacted by the EU legislature.[311]

In this context, the referrals to the CJEU are serving a very different purpose going far beyond judicial review and scrutiny of an existing legislative framework. Instead, the CJEU and (to a far lesser extent) the national courts via the preliminary reference system are effectively playing the role of de facto lawmakers in a highly complex and dynamic area of law and technology and producing questionable results which lack any basis in evidence or practice. The problematic patchwork of EU data retention law ultimately demonstrates the limits of judicial review through the inevitable challenges that arise for courts seeking to uphold the rule of law and the protection of human rights whilst also exercising the role of de facto lawmaker. This raises the question of the responsibility of the EU legislature (and indeed the Member States) in regulating data retention and mainstreaming fundamental rights across EU policymaking. It is this question to which we now turn.

5. The roles of the EU legislature and the CJEU

A stalemate of EU policymaking, and a major expansion of EU competence in the form of EU fundamental rights adjudication by the CJEU, has followed in the wake of *Digital Rights Ireland*. No new comprehensive data retention legislation has since been put forward by the EU legislator. Many Member States have also either resisted or been slow to adopt national laws that fully comply with all the legal standards established by the CJEU.[312] Legislatures at both the EU and

[309] The Belgian Constitutional Court has, for instance, struck down two national data retention laws following judgments by the CJEU in 2015 and 2021.

[310] *Tele2* (n 17) [124].

[311] *Schrems II* (n 10) [73].

[312] See Niklas Vainio and Samuli Miettinen, 'Telecommunications Data Retention after Digital Rights Ireland' (2015) 23 International Journal of Law and Information Technology 290; Jürgen Kühling and Sonja Heitzer, 'Returning Through the National Back Door? The Future of Data Retention after the ECJ Judgment on Directive 2006/24 in the UK and Elsewhere' (2015) 40 European Law Review 263; Privacy International, *Report on National Data Retention Laws since the CJEU's Tele-2/Watson Judgment* (2017); Cian Murphy, 'EU Counter Terrorism Law' (2019) 21 Cambridge Yearbook of European Legal Studies 217; Council of the EU, 'Data retention—situation in Member States', WK 3103/2019 INIT, 6 March 2019; Matthew White, 'Is the Incompatibility of UK Data Retention Law with EU Law Really a Victory?' (2021) 41 Legal Studies 130; Valsamis Mitsilegas and others, 'Data Retention and the Future of Large-Scale Surveillance' (2023) 29 European Law Journal 176.

national levels have also yet to deal with the growing legal vacuum and increasing legal uncertainty left by the striking down of the Data Retention Directive in *Digital Rights Ireland* and the overdue reform of the e-Privacy Directive 2002/58. It should also be noted that the European Commission had sidestepped its role in the mainstreaming of human rights in the governance of EU data retention law, long before *Digital Rights Ireland*, due to its incomplete evaluation of the Data Retention Directive in 2010.[313] We see the outsourcing of this legislative role to the CJEU again in subsequent preliminary references, including *G.D.* and *SpaceNet*. The referring courts insisting in these cases that the CJEU respond to their preliminary references rather than issue an order based on Article 99 of the CJEU's Rules of Procedure. This is despite the substance of their questions already having been addressed in *La Quadrature du Net* and *Prokuratuur*.[314] Hence, the de facto law-maker role of the CJEU in this area is not solely of its own making.

A view could be taken here that the EU legislature and Member States have effectively left it to the CJEU (and national courts) to deal with the fundamental rights issues raised by the bulk retention of communications data. The CJEU was left with no other choice in *Digital Rights Ireland* than to take on the role of de facto lawmaker whilst retaining its primary role as a guardian of EU fundamental rights in its scrutiny of data retention measures. Another view reflects the more challenging reality of the current situation which is that the CJEU has no need to step back from this regulatory role or to give national courts a role in the impact of its rulings.[315] This is demonstrated in the Court's determination in *G.D.* that the primacy of EU law precludes a national court (even under exceptional circumstances) from limiting the temporal effects of an EU law declared invalid but already transposed into national law.[316] Simultaneously, the CJEU continues to extend its data retention standards far beyond EU laws governing the mandatory retention of communications data for countering serious crime. These areas include international data transfers, national security, retention, access, automated processing of passenger

[313] The Commission stated that its evaluation of the Data Retention Directive would comprise two parts. The second dealing with issues of proportionality. However, this was never published. The Commission also made no recommendations for the reform of the EU PNR Directive despite the standards set by the CJEU on PNR data retention and access in Opinion 1/15 (n 21). See further Chapter 9.

[314] AG Opinion in *G.D.* (n 200) [7]; AG Campos Sánchez-Bordona, Opinion of 18 November 2021 in *SpaceNet* (n 1).

[315] This appears to be the Court's own view. Note the Court's following reasoning in its assessment of the legality requirements of Art 52(1) CFR in *Ligue des droits humains* (n 30) [114]: '[T]he Court may, where appropriate, specify, by means of interpretation, the actual scope of the limitation in the light of the very wording of the EU legislation in question as well as its general scheme and the objectives it pursues, as interpreted in view of the fundamental rights guaranteed by the Charter.'

[316] *G.D.* (n 10) [118]–[123]. Note, however, that the Grand Chamber has held in other cases that the CJEU could restrict the temporal limits of its judgment's effects if two essential criteria are fulfilled, 'namely that those concerned should have acted in good faith and there should be a risk of serious difficulties ... resulting from the interpretation adopted by the Court'. See Case C-439/19 *Latvijas Republikas Saeima (Penalty points)*, judgment of 22 June 2021 (ECLI:EU:C:2021:504) [132]–[136]; *Ligue des droits humains* (n 30) [294].

name records, and any personal data (such as financial data) retained as part of derogations that fall within the scope of Article 23 of the GDPR.[317]

By doing so, the Court invariably compromises its primary role of providing judicial scrutiny that will ensure the protection of the rule of law, legal certainty, and EU fundamental rights. The Court's ongoing shift towards a more regulatory role is also unsustainable and undermines the effective mainstreaming of fundamental rights across the entire legislative cycle of any EU data retention framework.[318] The latter is the responsibility of the EU legislature. It is also a complex governance process that should be underpinned by evidence-based policymaking, with comprehensive statistics from Member States, and robust independent oversight of all legislative stages from the drafting of a law, its implementation, and its review. As advised in the Opinions of Advocate General Campos Sánchez-Bordona, it is for the EU legislature and Member States to now act and 'to point the cursor in the right direction for striking a balance between the preservation of security and the fundamental rights protected by the Charter'.[319]

The CJEU bears some responsibility for the far-reaching regulatory role it has created for itself in its case law since its decision in *Digital Rights Ireland* to strike down the Data Retention Directive 2006/24 from legal existence *ab initio*. Indeed, the more the Court embraces this regulatory role, the more responsibility it must accept for the standards it establishes. Rather than continually expanding its capacity as de facto lawmaker, it is time for the Court to focus on its primary role as a guardian of EU fundamental rights. The Court's role and impact in providing legitimate judicial oversight to ensure the EU, and Member States, are held accountable for the protection of EU fundamental rights in practice, otherwise risks being merely illusory. At a time when the ECtHR has departed from its previously lauded standard-setting role,[320] the CJEU should accept that both great power and responsibility come with being Europe's vanguard supranational court for scrutinizing State surveillance and data retention laws.

D. Conclusions

This chapter examined the seismic shift in the approach of the CJEU and its rights-based scrutiny of data retention systems following the Snowden revelations and the elevation of the EU Charter to its legally binding status under EU law. The previous analysis also addresses the relationship between the EU and ECHR legal orders with respect to the approach of both concerning data retention standards.

[317] *Schrems* (n 23); *Schrems II* (n 10); Opinion 1/15 (n 21); *Ligue des droits humains* (n 30); *La Quadrature du Net* (n 1) [209]–[211].

[318] On the mainstreaming of rights in the legislative cycle of EU data retention law, see Chapters 6–9.

[319] AG Opinion in *G.D.* (n 200) [49].

[320] See further Chapters 2 and 3.

This landmark jurisprudence demonstrates that, while there is still some convergence, it is resoundingly clear that the CJEU no longer defers by default to the Article 8 ECHR case law of the ECtHR. The CJEU has also extended its data retention standards far beyond EU legislation governing the mandatory retention of communications data for countering serious crime. Finally, the analysis also shows that the CJEU is not opposed to all regimes that entail general and indiscriminate retention of personal data.

Instead, the Court (in line with the ECtHR) has shown itself to be particularly sensitive to the intrusiveness to private life posed by the retention and analysis of *certain types* of communications data. This is clearly demonstrated, for instance, in the Grand Chamber judgment of *Ligue des droits humains*. Briefly citing the aims pursued by the PNR Directive (EU) 2016/681 as its underpinning *ratio*, the Court reasons in a circular and unpersuasive way that the bulk retention of all air passenger name records for six months does not go beyond what is strictly necessary, insofar as it allows necessary searches to be carried out 'for the purposes of identifying persons who were not suspected of involvement in terrorist offences or serious crime'.[321] This, and the above findings, have significant implications for the Court's future judgments on the retention, access, and processing of other types of personal data within the contexts of law enforcement and national security.

The next chapter looks back to a very different era in EU policymaking, exploring how Article 8 ECHR played a key role in the origins and development of the Data Retention Directive before the CJEU placed the standards of the EU Charter at the vanguard of data retention policymaking in Europe.

[321] *Ligue des droits humains* (n 30) [255]. On the PNR Directive and this judgment, see Chapter 9.

6
The Data Retention Directive and Article 8 ECHR

A. Introduction

Terrorist attacks on Madrid and London in 2004 and 2005 provided the political impetus for the Data Retention Directive 2006/24/EC.[1] However, the Directive was also a response to the need for a more comprehensive right-based framework to be put in place[2] in order to replace the voluntary data retention regime established under a controversial amendment to the e-Privacy Directive 2002/58.[3] This chapter examines the first stage of the Data Retention Directive's legislative cycle and focuses on the influence of Article 8 ECHR on shaping this legislative process and the substantive provisions of the Directive. The analysis highlights the complex legal relationship with the e-Privacy Directive and the since invalidated Data Retention Directive. Also discussed are the ways in which national and international interests in the post-9/11 world impinged on the drafting (and critically the redrafting) of the Data Retention Directive. The analysis then proceeds to closely examine the contested legislative basis of Directive 2006/24/EC and the implications of this choice of legal framework finally agreed upon between the EU institutions and the role that Article 8 ECHR ultimately played in its drafting.

Much is revealed here regarding the approach of the EU institutions towards the standards of Article 8 ECHR, particularly the efforts made by the different EU institutions to 'mainstream' human rights across EU regulation and policymaking generally during the drafting stage of the controversial Data Retention Directive.[4]

[1] Cian Murphy, *EU Counter Terrorism Law* (Hart 2012) 168. All URLs for this chapter were last accessed on 22 April 2024 unless otherwise stated.

[2] European Parliament and Council Directive 2006/24/EC of 15 March 2006 on the retention of data generated or processed in connection with the provision of publicly available electronic communications services or of public communications networks and amending Directive 2002/58/EC [2006] OJ L105/54.

[3] European Parliament and Council Directive 2002/58/EC of 12 July 2002 concerning the processing of personal data and the protection of privacy in the electronic communications sector [2002] OJ L201/37, as amended by Directive 2009/136/EC (e-Privacy Directive 2002/58). Currently being revised as a draft EU Regulation since January 2017. See further Chapter 1.

[4] Council of Ministers and European Commission, *EU Annual Report on Human Rights 2006* (Office for Official Publications of the EC 2006). On the EU in its role as regulator, see generally Mark Dawson and Floris de Witte, *EU Law and Governance* (CUP 2022) 73–101.

EU Data Privacy Law and Serious Crime. Nora Ni Loideain, Oxford University Press. © Nora Ni Loideain 2025.
DOI: 10.1093/oso/9780198837169.003.0006

Mainstreaming is essentially an attempt by policymakers to ensure that the 'rights review' of law happens throughout the ongoing legislative cycle of a legal instrument and crucially is not then solely a matter for judicial review.[5] In other words, scrutiny of a law's compatibility with human rights standards, such as the rights to private life and data protection, should take place at each stage of the legislative cycle. This involves the drafting stage of the law, its implementation, and review. At the heart of this mainstreaming process is the aim that the protection of human rights should not be an area left solely to judicial exclusivity. This is especially important in the era of AI-based systems and other emerging technologies concerning the monitoring and secret surveillance of individuals and their communications, as retrofitting safeguards into such complex systems once implemented is very difficult or often impossible.

Particular attention is given in this chapter to the significance of the European Commission's drafting practice between 2001 and 2006 and the mainstreaming of the right to private life within the pre-legislative scrutiny of the e-Privacy Directive 2002/58 and the Data Retention Directive 2006/24/EC. This drafting practice primarily involved the Commission including a standard recital in draft legislation that would indicate compliance with the EU Charter of Fundamental Rights, notwithstanding that the Charter was not legally binding at this time.[6] Recitals are effectively the non-binding explanatory memorandum of an EU Regulation or Directive. The approaches of the EU institutions during the drafting stage of the Data Retention Directive's legislative cycle also reveal the different roles, key tensions, and aims of each EU institution with respect to reconciling the competing interests of the protection of the rights to private life and data protection and that of countering serious crime.

[5] These terms were coined by one of the leading political science scholars on legislative rights review: Janet L Hiebert, 'Interpreting a Bill of Rights: The Importance of Legislative Rights Review' (2005) 35 British Journal of Political Science 235, 236. For further detail, see Janet L Hiebert, *Charter Conflicts: What is Parliament's Role?* (McGill-Queen's UP 2002); David Feldman, 'The Impact of Human Rights on the UK Legislative Process' (2004) 25 Statute Law Review 91; Janet Hiebert and James Kelly, *Parliamentary Bills of Rights: The Experiences of New Zealand and the United Kingdom* (CUP 2015). See similar arguments made within the specific context of 'institutional pluralism' and constitutional interpretation regarding the CJEU in Gareth Davies, 'Legislative Control of the European Court of Justice' (2014) 51 Common Market Law Review 1579. For recent analysis on the importance of rights protection being shared between the executive, legislature, and courts, see generally Aileen Kavanagh, *The Collaborative Constitution* (CUP 2023).

[6] A drafting practice established under the following memorandum issued by the President of the Commission and the then European Commissioner for Justice and Home Affairs to all departments within the European Commission: Memorandum from the President and Mr Victorino, 'Application of the Charter of Fundamental Rights of the European Union', SEC (2001) 380/3, Brussels, 13 March 2001.

B. The Origins of Directive 2006/24/EC

1. Data retention: from the 'exception' to the 'rule'

In 2001, an independent advisory group primarily composed of data protection supervisory authorities from EU Member States[7]—the Article 29 Data Protection Working Party—unequivocally opposed a proposal from several Member States within the Council of the EU for reform of the then EU data protection framework.[8] Before proceeding to address these concerns, however, we must first briefly discuss the role, remit, and evolution of this important EU oversight body for data protection.

The Article 29 Working Party was until 2018 an independent body that acted in an advisory capacity. Its members consisted of representatives from the data protection supervisory authorities designated by EU Member States, a representative of the authority established for the EU institutions, and a representative from the European Commission. The tasks of the Working Party are outlined in Article 30 of the Data Protection Directive 95/46/EC (since replaced by the GDPR) and Article 15(3) of the e-Privacy Directive 2002/58. These included providing expert opinion from the EU Member State level to the Commission on questions of data protection and the promotion of the uniform application of the general data protection principles of Directive 95/46/EC in all Member States through cooperation between data protection supervisory authorities. Significantly, the Working Party also advised the Commission on any EU measures affecting the fundamental rights and freedoms of natural persons with regard to the processing of personal data. The Working Party also made highly influential policymaking recommendations to EU institutions on matters relating to the rights to privacy and data protection in the EU. With the entry into force of the GDPR in May 2018, the Working Party was replaced by the European Data Protection Board (EDPB). While the EDPB has effectively the same composition and carries on the key tasks of the Working Party, its new legal status and wider set of roles and responsibilities (particularly within the new pan-EU enforcement regime) make it a very different and more powerful oversight body.[9] Given the focus of this chapter, reference will only be made here to

[7] European Parliament and Council Directive 1995/46/EC of 24 October 1995 on the protection of individuals with regard to the processing of personal data and on the free movement of such data [1995] OJ L281/31 (Data Protection Directive 95/46/EC) established the then Article 29 Data Protection Working Party (Article 29 Working Party).

[8] Article 29 Working Party, 'Letter to Acting President of the Council of the EU', 7 June 2001, <https://statewatch.org/news/2001/jun/07Rodota.pdf>.

[9] Regulation (EU) 2016/679 of the European Parliament and of the Council of 27 April 2016 on the protection of natural persons with regard to the processing of personal data and on the free movement of such data, and repealing Directive 95/46/EC [2016] OJ L119/1 (GDPR), Arts 68–76. See further Christopher Docksey, 'Article 68 European Data Protection Board' in Christopher Kuner and others (eds), *The EU General Data Protection Regulation (GDPR): A Commentary* (OUP 2020) 1041–54; Giulia Gentile and Orla Lynskey, 'Deficient by Design? The Transnational Enforcement of the GDPR' (2022) 71 International Comparative Law Quarterly 799.

the EDPB's predecessor as it was the Article 29 Working Party that exercised a key role in the pre-legislative scrutiny of the Data Retention Directive 2006/24/EC and its compatibility with Article 8 ECHR standards.

The controversial 2001 proposal contested by the Article 29 Working Party was put forward by the telecommunications body within the Council of the EU. Proposed reforms included significantly increasing the scope of 'communications data' retained by the private sector for law enforcement purposes. The concept of communications data is broad and its capacity to reveal various aspects of an individual's private life continues to expand at a rapid pace in the twenty-first century given the growing use of household (AI virtual personal assistants) and mobile devices and environments that are Internet-enabled. Essentially, communications data is the *context* of a communication and consists of information generated or processed as a result of a communication's transmission. Traditionally, its scope is considered not to extend to the content of the communication in question. The communications data/content distinction in regulation has often been justified by public authorities worldwide on the basis that having access to the content of a communication poses a much greater level of intrusion to private life. This argument certainly carried weight decades before the tracking capabilities of Internet-enabled devices and environments became so embedded in the daily communications and movements of individuals and the practice of access to large-scale sets of communications data became a standard tool for law enforcement and intelligence purposes. Access to communications data in the twenty-first century now, however, is often more revealing, or just as revealing, as accessing the content to an individual's communications.[10]

Back in 2001, the obstacles posed by the different legal and technical data retention requirements in EU Member States for communication service providers (CSPs) was claimed to be one of the main factors that led to the adoption of the Data Retention Directive.[11]After Directive 2006/24/EC became law, a trend emerged among policymakers and commentators in the EU showing an increased use of the term 'communications data'.[12] In addition, the standard practice of service providers at this time was to keep data concerning their customers' communications usage for billing purposes for a period of six months.[13] The measure proposed by the Council of the EU on the other hand proposed increasing this period of retention of 'communications data' from faxes, emails, Internet, and mobile and landline telephony use for up to seven years.[14] The Article 29 Working Party

[10] On the evolving scope of communications data and its value for public authorities, see Chapter 1.

[11] Data Retention Directive 2006/24/EC, recital 5.

[12] See further Chapter 1.

[13] Paul Durrant, 'Data Retention Directive—Some ISP Observations' (Privacy and Data Retention Directive 2006/24/EC Conference, Irish Centre for European Law, Dublin, 19 July 2006).

[14] Karlin Lillington, 'Government support for data plans at odds with own policies', *The Irish Times* (3 August 2001).

was resolute in its criticism and maintained, in a letter to the Council, that the scope of the impugned proposal was unacceptable on the basis that 'systematic and preventive storage' of communications data would significantly undermine fundamental human rights to privacy and data protection.[15]

Between 2000 and 2002, the European Parliament and the Council were in the process of finalizing their positions on the Commission's proposal for a new Directive on privacy and protection of personal data in electronic communications. The EU legal framework governing the processing and protection of personal data in the telecommunications sector fell under the principal Data Protection Directive (95/46/EC) and the Telecommunications Data Protection Directive (97/66/EC).[16] The latter Directive was otherwise referred to as the Integrated Services Digital Network (ISDN) Directive reflecting the weight of the impact associated with the introduction of ISDN to the operation of the EU telecommunications industry. Essentially, ISDN provides a telecommunications network through which sound, images, and data can be transmitted as digitized signals. This network enabled what are now ubiquitously accessed Internet services, including video on demand (such as YouTube). One of the main purposes of Directive 97/66/EC was to ensure that the use of these services fell under the EU data protection framework so as not to undermine the confidence of users that their personal data would be at risk.[17] The Telecommunications Data Protection Directive did this by translating the principles set out in the Data Protection Directive 95/45/EC into specific rules for the telecommunications sector.

The aim of the European Commission in drafting new legislation in 2001 was again to ensure that the EU data protection framework adapted to subsequent economic and technological developments in the telecommunications sector. This would be achieved through drafting the legal provisions in a manner that was 'technology neutral'. It was then intended that such an approach would provide 'an equal level of protection of personal data and privacy for users of publicly available electronic communications services, regardless of the technologies used'.[18] These reforms were a specific response to the impact of digitization on the telecommunications sector and particularly advances in electronic communications services. Essentially, the objective of the Commission was merely to update the EU data protection framework in force at the time by replacing the Telecommunications Data Protection Directive with a new legal instrument that would 'particularize and complement' the principal Data Protection Directive 95/46/EC.[19] However, the controversial proposal from the Council deviated considerably from this policy.

[15] Article 29 Working Party (n 8).

[16] European Parliament and Council Directive 97/66/EC of 15 December 1997 concerning the processing of personal data and the protection of privacy in the telecommunications sector [1997] OJ L24/1.

[17] Directive 97/66/EC, recital 3.

[18] e-Privacy Directive 2002/58, recital 4.

[19] ibid Art 1(2).

In June 2001, the Article 29 Working Party maintained that exemptions to provisions under the draft of what would become the e-Privacy Directive guaranteeing the confidentiality of communications and the deletion of traffic data after completion of the communication had already been provided for under Article 15(1). Additionally, this existing draft of Article 15(1) also complied with the relevant human rights requirements. To extend the scope of this provision, the Article 29 Working Party warned, would be to 'change this balance in favour of increasing the possibilities of law enforcement authorities, beyond the scope of what the European Court on Human Rights has accepted in the course of its case law on Article 8 of the European Convention on Human Rights'.[20] The Council's proposed amendment to Article 15(1) of the draft e-Privacy Directive was subsequently reconstituted as a non-binding recital. This result is perhaps unsurprising given the lack of unanimous support that the controversial proposal had from within the Council itself (Greece, Italy, and the Netherlands all opposed the amendment).[21] Nevertheless, a sweeping amendment to the draft e-Privacy Directive would soon be made following the terrorist attacks on New York and Washington DC in September 2001.

2. 9/11 and the e-Privacy Directive 2002/58

The overview of the origins of Directive 2006/24/EC as noted above indicates that pressure was already building from within the EU institutions to significantly expand the retention and use of communications data for law enforcement purposes prior to the events of 9/11. As Goold rightly highlights, 'although the events of 9/11 were enormously significant in terms of shifting the balance in the security-rights debate, many of the threats to individual freedom and autonomy that now appear so clearly have in fact been present for a very long time'.[22] Shortly thereafter, the President of the US sent a letter to the European Commission containing a lengthy list of proposals for US—EU counter-terrorism cooperation.[23] Of the forty proposals therein, three concerned the reform of EU data protection law. These recommendations urged the EU to: (1) 'consider data protection issues in the context of law enforcement and counterterrorism imperatives'; (2) 'establish adequate capabilities for investigating terrorism cases that involve the use of the internet'; and (3) 'revise draft privacy directives that call for mandatory destruction to permit the

[20] Article 29 Working Party (n 8).
[21] Lillington (n 14).
[22] 'Privacy, Identity and Security' in Benjamin J Goold and Liora Lazarus (eds), *Security and Human Rights* (Hart 2007) 69.
[23] United States Mission to the President of the European Commission, Letter concerning Proposals for US–EU Counter Terrorism Cooperation, 16 October 2001 (US Mission), <www.statewatch.org/news/2001/nov/06Ausalet.htm>.

retention of critical data for a reasonable period'.[24] These calls for major policy reform did not go unheard. In early 2002, the Council would adopt the view that the ban on data retention for purposes other than billing should be deleted from the draft e-Privacy Directive.[25]

More than thirty leading NGOs expressed concern to the Council regarding the threat to the right to respect to private life posed by this unprecedented measure.[26] In particular, it was highlighted that such a policy would be 'inconsistent with well-established international norms for communications privacy, such as Article 8 of the European Convention on Human Rights'.[27] Despite these criticisms, the Council proposed the inclusion of a provision requiring the retention of data for law enforcement.[28] NGOs urged the European Parliament to reject the proposal on the basis that such a measure should only be employed in exceptional cases and in accordance with the ECHR and the case law of the ECtHR.[29] Nevertheless, the Parliament approved this far-reaching amendment to the draft e-Privacy Directive on 30 May 2002.[30] Article 15(1) of the e-Privacy Directive consequently provides that Member States can restrict the scope of traditional privacy safeguards and adopt legislative measures for the retention of communications data. Such a restriction may be adopted if it constitutes 'a necessary, appropriate and proportionate measure within a democratic society to safeguard national security (ie State security), defence, public security, and the prevention, investigation, detection and prosecution of criminal offences or of unauthorised use of the electronic communication system'.

Article 15(1) of Directive 2002/58 was therefore the most important harbinger of what would later be adopted as the Data Retention Directive 2006/24/EC, the latter originating from a commitment by the European Commission to address the raft of concerns raised by EU regulators and the NGO community regarding the legality and proportionality of Article 15(1) of Directive 2002/58. This response came in the form of a draft Directive. However, as discussed later, the Commission's proposal received an unwelcome reception from some quarters. Indeed, the resulting legislative proposal would provoke so much resistance from the Council and certain Member States that its legal basis would later be challenged before the CJEU when adopted as the Data Retention Directive 2006/24/EC. This chapter

[24] ibid (emphasis added).
[25] Commission Response (10 December 2002) to Written Question E-3081 by Erik Meijer, OJ C155 E: <http://eurlex.europa.eu/LexUriServ/LexUriServ.do?uri=CELEX:92002E3081:EN:HTML>.
[26] Global Liberty Internet Campaign, 'Letter to the EU Council of Ministers', 12 November 2001, <http://gilc.org/verhofstadt_letter.html>.
[27] ibid.
[28] European Parliament, 'On the Council common position for adopting a European Parliament and Council Directive', Session Document, Doc A5-130/2002, 23 May 2002, 3.
[29] Global Liberty Internet Campaign, 'Letter to the President of the European Parliament', 22 May 2005, <http://gilc.org/cox_en.html> accessed 19 January 2019.
[30] Karlin Lillington, 'Poor Irish showing at Brussels vote a severe blow for e-Privacy', *The Irish Times* (7 June 2002).

will discuss the first of two major challenges before the CJEU concerning the compatibility of this controversial legal framework with EU law.[31]

C. The Legislative Basis

1. First or third pillar?

The Data Retention Directive 2006/24/EC was intended to harmonize the national laws of Member States governing the retention of communications data by the private sector for the purpose of tackling serious crime across the EU. A significant policy change introduced under the Directive was the mandatory requirement that it placed upon Member States. This is a stark departure from the e-Privacy Directive 2002/58 which provided that Member States were free to voluntarily adopt data retention regimes.[32] As Article 1(1) of Directive 2006/24/EC mandated, Member States were required to ensure that CSPs retained communications data 'for the purpose of the investigation, detection and prosecution of serious crime, as defined by each Member State in its national law'. The original drafting of this mandatory EU data retention regime took the form of a 'Council Framework Decision' and was designed for the purpose of harmonizing national measures in Member States across the EU regulating the retention of traffic data for the much wider purpose of criminal investigations, including but not limited to terrorism.[33] Before the entry into force of the Lisbon Treaty in 2009, a Council framework decision was a measure that fell under the 'third pillar' of what was then referred to as the EU 'legal pillar' framework. A directive, on the other hand, fell under the 'first pillar'. Essentially, first pillar measures concerned matters relating to the economic harmonization of the EU, namely Article 95 EC (now Art 114 TFEU), whereas matters of criminal justice fell under the remit of the 'third pillar'.[34]

This was later confirmed by the CJEU (then referred to as the ECJ) in a challenge to the legal basis of the Data Retention Directive where Ireland asked the Luxembourg Court to annul the Directive on the ground that it was incorrectly

[31] For the second legal challenge which focused on the compatibility of Directive 2006/24/EC with the rights to private life and data protection under EU law, see Chapter 8.

[32] This practice must now be in line with the strict standards established in a series of landmark judgments by the CJEU concerning Art 15(1) of the e-Privacy Directive 2002/58 and the EU Charter, particularly Arts 7 and 8 CFR. See further Chapter 5.

[33] Council of the EU, 'Draft Framework Decision on the Retention of Data Processed and Stored in Connection with the Provision of Publicly Available Electronic Communication Services or Data on Public Communications Networks for the Purpose of Prevention, Investigation, Detection and Prosecution of Crime and Criminal Offences including Terrorism', Doc 8958/04, 28 April 2004.

[34] On the pre-Lisbon EU legislative pillar system, see Gráinne de Búrca, 'Giving Effect to European Community Directives' (1992) 55 Modern Law Review 215; Alexander Stubb, 'A Categorisation of Differentiated Integration' (1996) 34 Journal of Common Market Studies 283; Alan Dashwood 'The Constitution of the European Union after Nice' (2001) 26 European Law Review 215.

adopted under Article 95 EC. Specifically, the main question before the Court (sitting as the Grand Chamber) involved determining whether Directive 2006/24/EC was adopted on the ground that its main objective consisted of 'fighting crime and terrorism', rendering it the legal basis for the Directive, a 'third pillar' measure, as opposed to the objective of harmonizing the internal market for communication service providers, a 'first pillar' measure.[35] The Court rejected this challenge. Instead, the Court determined that the adoption of the legislation under the first pillar as a Directive was satisfactory for the harmonization of legislation between Member States following the disparity of previous laws on data retention introduced under Article 15 of the e-Privacy Directive 2002/58. Ultimately, the Court held that Directive 2006/24/EC regulated 'operations which are independent of ... the issue of access to data by the competent national law-enforcement authorities'.[36]

In other words, the Court determined that the legislative foundation of the Data Retention Directive was primarily concerned with the harmonization of Member States' provisions concerning the obligations of private telecommunications operators with respect to the retention of certain data generated or processed by them. It is noteworthy that this judgment has been roundly criticized, particularly for its application of the distinctions within the competences under the EU pillar system and its departure from previous jurisprudence concerning the third pillar.[37]

2. Data retention and EU governance *à la carte*

In 2004, France, Ireland, the UK, and Sweden put forward a legislative proposal solely concerned with the retention of data for law enforcement purposes in the form of a framework decision. This measure fell under the then EU institutional framework's third pillar of justice and home affairs (JHA).[38] The choice of legal basis in EU legislation under the three-pillar structure would have had significant implications for the domestic legislation of Member States. Under the third pillar measure of a framework decision on data retention, such legislation would have been binding only on Member States that would have agreed to comply with such a measure. In other words, Members States would have been free to opt out of such an action. However, in the case of a first pillar measure of a directive on

[35] Case C-301/06 *Ireland v Parliament and Council*, judgment of 10 February 2009 (ECLI:EU:C:2009:68) [35] (GC).

[36] ibid [83].

[37] See eg Theodore Konstadinides, 'Wavering Between Centres of Gravity: Comment on *Ireland v Parliament and Council*' (2010) 35 European Law Review 88; Ester Herlin-Karnell, 'Case C-301/06, *Ireland* v. *Parliament and Council*' (2009) 46 Common Market Law Review 1667; Christopher Docksey, 'The European Court of Justice and the Decade of Surveillance' in Hielke Hijmans and Herke Kranenborg (eds), *Data Protection Anno 2014* (Intersentia 2014) 97–116.

[38] Council of the EU (n 33).

data retention, the freedom and flexibility of Member States would be far more limited. Stubb aptly describes this former model of EU policymaking as an 'Europe *à la carte*' arrangement given its 'mode of differentiated integration'. Respective Member States were therefore able to select 'from a menu' which policy area they would like to participate in, whilst simultaneously committing only to a minimum number of common objectives.[39]

Another major implication arising from the adoption of a directive is that the European Parliament would have had greater involvement in the development and scrutiny of the legislation. Under the legal basis of a directive, Parliament would be allowed the right of co-decision,[40] thus providing the only democratically elected body in the EU with an enhanced role in the legal instrument's scope, objectives, and application. Consequently, the key feature of the co-decision procedure when introduced was that the Council was for the first time prevented from passing legislation against the will of the Parliament.[41] The third pillar measure on data retention, in striking contrast, as proposed by the Council, would have limited the role of Parliament to a right of consultation,[42] leaving the development of a pan-European measure on data retention without 'the more democratic co-operation procedure'.[43] Each of the three separate sets of legal advice sought by the Council,[44] the Commission, and Parliament recommended that a legislative measure on data retention should be dealt under a first pillar measure based on the rationale that a third pillar framework decision cannot impact upon the provisions of a first pillar Directive.[45] If enacted, the third pillar framework decision on data retention would have amended the e-Privacy Directive 2002/58. The Council was therefore advised that any challenge before the CJEU to a framework decision on data retention

[39] Stubb (n 34) 285.

[40] Article 251 (ex Art 189b) of EC Treaty, introduced by the Treaty of Maastricht in 1992, later modified by the Treaty of Amsterdam in 1997 and Treaty of Nice in 2002. The Lisbon Treaty would further consolidate the role of Parliament as co-legislator with the Council when its provisions came into effect in 2009. See further Laurent Pech, 'The Institutional Development of the EU Post-Lisbon' in Diamond Ashiagbor, Nicola Countouris, and Ioannis Lianos (eds), *The European Union after the Treaty of Lisbon* (CUP 2012) 7–46.

[41] Stephen Weatherill and Paul Beaumont, *EU Law* (3rd edn, Penguin 1999) 138. On the distinct role of the 'European Council' as a formal EU institution in steering EU policymaking as provided under Art 15(1) TEU, see Pech (n 40).

[42] Article 39(1) TEU (Nice version), Title VI.

[43] Catherine Barnard, *The Substantive Law of the EU* (OUP 2004) 501. See further Karen Bradley, 'Comitology and the Law' (1992) 29 Common Market Law Review 693; Paul Craig, 'Democracy and Rulemaking within the EC' (1997) 3 European Law Journal 105.

[44] Presidency of the EU to the Council, 'Draft Framework Decision on the retention of data processed and stored in connection with the provision of publicly available electronic communications services or data on public communications networks for the purpose of... investigation, detection and prosecution of crime and criminal offences including terrorism', Doc 8864/1/05, 24 May 2005, 5–6.

[45] Committee on Civil Liberties, Justice and Home Affairs, 'Report on the initiative by the French Republic, Ireland, the Kingdom of Sweden and the United Kingdom for a Draft Framework Decision on the retention of data processed and stored in connection with the provision of publicly available electronic communication services or data on public communications networks for the purpose of prevention, investigation, detection and prosecution of crime and criminal offences including terrorism', Doc RR\569187EN, 31 May 2005, 6–7 (Alvaro Report).

was likely to succeed.[46] In addition, the European Parliament expressed several reservations regarding the Council's proposal in a report published shortly before the Parliament's rejection of the draft framework decision.[47] The Parliament's main concerns being the choice of legal basis, doubts regarding the proposal's proportionality, and the incompatibility of the proposal with Article 8 ECHR.[48] Subsequently, Parliament rejected a second framework decision proposal on data retention shortly after in September,[49] expressing 'sizeable doubts' regarding the legality of a third pillar measure on data retention.[50]

In September 2005, the European Commission put forward a first pillar proposal for a Directive on data retention for approval by both the Council and Parliament.[51] Despite numerous rejections of their proposal by both the Commission and Parliament, the Council resisted this alternative legislative approach at first and only began to reconsider withdrawing their third pillar initiative in October.[52] Even then, the Council made clear to Parliament that its framework decision initiative would 'remain on the table'.[53] The Council's support for a directive on data retention was also conditional upon agreement being reached between the Commission, Parliament, and the Council on the provisions of a directive within a notably tight deadline of two months. The pervasive sense of urgency established by the Council regarding the adoption of a directive is echoed in a statement by the then President of the Council, Charles Clarke. Mr Clarke stressed at this juncture: 'I remain personally committed to reaching agreement on a first pillar instrument if it can be done by the end of the year'.[54] The tentative acceptance by the President of the Council of adopting a first pillar measure on data retention instead of the Council's third pillar proposal was most likely the result of political pressure from both within and outside the EU institutions. Three significant factors are likely to have contributed to this capitulation.

[46] Presidency of the EU to the Council, 'Data Retention', Doc 13036/05, 10 October 2005, 2.
[47] Alvaro Report (n 45) 6–9.
[48] ibid.
[49] The Parliament rejected an earlier proposed framework decision on data retention (draft of 28 February 2005) on the 7 June 2005: Council of the EU, 'Draft Framework Decision on the retention of data processed and stored in connection with the provision of publicly available electronic communications services or data on public communications networks for the purpose of investigation, detection and prosecution of crime and criminal offences including terrorism', Doc 12894/1/05, 10 October 2005, 2.
[50] BBC News, 'EU phone record proposal rejected', 27 September 2005.
[51] Commission of the EC, 'Proposal for a Directive of the European Parliament and of the Council on the retention of data processed in connection with the provision of public electronic communication services and amending Directive 2002/58/EC', COM(2005)438 final, 2005/0182 (COD), 21 September 2005 (Commission Draft Directive Proposal).
[52] Presidency of the EU to the Council (n 46).
[53] Charles Clarke, 'Letter to the Chairman of the LIBE Committee, European Parliament', United Kingdom Home Office, 17 October 2005, <www.statewatch.org/news/2005/oct/data-ret-clarke-to-cavada-17-10-05.pdf>.
[54] ibid.

First, legal advisors to the Council and the European Parliament had both cast the legality of the draft framework decision into doubt and warned that the CJEU would likely determine the same. The advice to both EU institutions was therefore that a high likelihood existed that the framework decision would be deemed to be incompatible with EU law if challenged before the Court. Secondly, largely based on this legal advice, the Parliament rejected two different drafts of the framework decision. It was also likely to reject a third draft given that the Commission had put forward an alternative legal framework in the form of a draft directive. Finally, considerable political pressure was building outside the EU institutions for a legislative response to the terrorist attacks in London that had recently taken place. According to interviews conducted with MEPs at the time, the two largest Parliament parties (the European People's Party and the Party of European Socialists) agreed to fast track the co-decision procedure for the passing of the draft Directive as they were wary of the negative publicity Parliament would receive for delaying legislation that could assist the investigation of similar atrocities in future.[55] Such political pressure would have been particularly acute in the UK following the terrorist attacks in July 2005 and no doubt exerted pressure on the national government to respond in its capacity as the holder of the European Presidency at this time.

3. Impact of European Parliament: a limited role

Even though the co-decision procedure provided the European Parliament with an enhanced role in the development of legislation, only a handful of the amendments proposed by Parliament influenced the final draft of the Data Retention Directive. This is evident in Parliament's initial report to the European Commission which contained many proposals restricting the scope, amount of data, access to data, and the period of retention as proposed by the Council.[56] In this initial report, there were calls for the retention of individuals' communications data from the use of phone, email, or other Internet telephony, to be available only for the 'investigation, detection and prosecution' of *serious* crimes and not the broader purpose of the '*prevention*, investigation, detection and prosecution' of crime.[57] Parliament was successful in narrowing the overall scope of the legislation by excluding the

[55] Rik de Ruiter and Christine Neuhold, 'Early Agreement in the Co-Decision Procedure' (2012) 18 European Law Journal 536, 548–49. On the tensions between the legal and political roles of the EU institutions generally, see Dawson and De Witte (n 4).

[56] Committee in Civil Liberties, Justice and Home Affairs, 'Draft Report on the proposal for a directive of the European Parliament and of the Council on the retention of data processed in connection with the provision of public electronic communication services and amending Directive 2002/58/EC (COM (2005) 0438-C6-0293/2005/0182(COD))', Doc PR\583793, 19 October 2005 (EU Parliament Draft Report on Data Retention).

[57] ibid 7 (emphasis added).

objective of 'prevention' from the draft Data Retention Directive based on the rationale that the additional concept was vague and made the retained data more vulnerable to the risk of abuse.[58]

Two subsequent attempts to amend the sweeping scope of the draft Directive were less successful. First, Parliament submitted that access to the retained data should be restricted to a more limited number of public authorities and that access should be limited to 'competent law enforcement authorities' which Parliament defined as 'judicial authorities responsible for the detection, investigation and prosecution of serious criminal offences'.[59] The Council appears to have ignored this restriction of the proposed measure's scope, proposing instead that access to data be made available to an undefined, and therefore inherently wider, group of 'competent national authorities'.[60] Secondly, the different periods of data retention put forward by each EU institution illustrate another significant disparity between the proposals of the Council and Parliament. While the latter proposed a retention period of three months, the former recommended what became the required retention period under Article 6 of Directive 2006/24/EC—between a minimum of six months and a maximum of two years.[61] Eventually, the European Parliament conceded and approved, by a majority vote of 378 to 197, this jointly amended version of the Commission's draft Directive proposal in December 2005.[62]

D. Mainstreaming Article 8 ECHR and the Directive

Much criticism and many human rights concerns preceded the establishment of a general communications data retention regime under Article 15(1) of the e-Privacy Directive 2002/58. Ensuring compliance with the requirements of Article 8 ECHR also played a decisive role in the dialogue between the Council, the European Commission, and the European Parliament during the development, drafting, and overall rights review of the Data Retention Directive. The following analysis of the drafting process of Directive 2006/24/EC examines the efforts of the EU institutions at this time to mainstream human rights across EU policymaking generally. The significance of the Commission's drafting practice during the pre-legislative scrutiny of Directive 2008/24/EC is closely examined, particularly the Commission's policymaking practice from 2001 of including a standard recital

[58] Committee in Civil Liberties, Justice and Home Affairs, 'Report on the proposal for a directive of the European Parliament and of the Council on the retention of data processed in connection with the provision of public electronic communication services and amending Directive 2002/58/EC (COM (2005)0438-C6-0293/2005/0182(COD))', Doc RR\589565, 25 November 2005, 9 (EU Parliament Report on Draft Directive).

[59] EU Parliament Draft Report on Data Retention (n 56) 13.

[60] Council of the EU, 'Data Retention', Doc 13789/05, 28 October 2005, 7.

[61] ibid 11.

[62] BBC News, 'EU approves data retention rules', 14 December 2005.

in a proposed Directive or Regulation highlighting its compliance with the EU Charter of Fundamental Rights. This is an important shift in EU law and human rights mainstreaming as the EU Charter was not legally binding at this time. Nevertheless, it was clearly an instrument on the rise within the EU legal order and European human rights law more broadly.[63]

1. The draft framework decisions: 'clandestine surveillance' incompatible with Article 8 ECHR

Following the amendment to Article 15 of the e-Privacy Directive 2002/58, the next stage in the development of the draft Data Retention Directive occurred in April 2004. It was at this time that France, Ireland, Sweden, and the UK (on behalf of the Council) put forward a legislative proposal solely concerned with the retention of data for law enforcement purposes in the form of a framework decision under the third pillar of justice and home affairs of the EU three-pillar institutional framework.[64] The scope of communications data set out in the draft framework decision was drawn from the definitions provided under Article 2 of the e-Privacy Directive. This provision covers many types of information, such as traffic data, location data, user data, and the subscriber data of the device/service being used (eg mobile phones and Internet services). Even from prevailing modes of communications at the turn of the twenty-first century which may now seem quaint, much could be revealed about the transmission of a communication from the collection and analysis of these types of data including: 'latitude, longitude and altitude of the sender's or recipient's terminal, direction of travel ... any naming, numbering or addressing information, volume of a communication, network on which the communication originates or terminates, and the beginning, end or duration of a connection.'[65]

The draft framework decision also adopted and extended the broad scope provided under the e-Privacy Directive 2002/58 regarding the range of law enforcement purposes for which the data could be retained and accessed to include 'criminal offences including terrorism'.[66] This reference to terrorism incorporated

[63] See further Chapters 4 and 5.

[64] Council of the EU, Doc 8958/04 (n 33).

[65] Jason M Young, 'Surfing While Muslim: Privacy, Freedom of Expression and the Unintended Consequences of Cybercrime Legislation' (2004) 7 Yale Journal of Law and Technology 346, 374. See further Chapter 1 on how much more valuable access to communications data has become in the era of AI-based systems, smart cities, and mass biometric surveillance.

[66] Compare Art 15(1) of the 2002 e-Privacy Directive 2002/58/EC with Art 1(1) of the draft framework decision (n 59): 'This Framework Decision aims to facilitate judicial co-operation in criminal matters by approximating Member States' legislation on the retention of data processed and stored by providers of a publicly available electronic communications service or a public communications network, *for the purpose of prevention, investigation, detection and prosecution of crime or criminal offences including terrorism*' (emphasis added).

the policy commitment made a month earlier by the Council in its Declaration of Combating Terrorism 'to examine measures for establishing rules on the retention of communications traffic data by service providers'.[67] Regarding the compatibility of the draft framework decision with Article 8 ECHR, recital 10 of the proposal acknowledged that such retention may constitute an interference with the private life of the individual.[68] However, the provision carefully highlighted that the scope of the retention in question did not 'violate the international rules applicable with regard to the right to respect to privacy and the handling of personal data' contained particularly under the legality, necessity, and proportionality tests of the ECHR.[69] While it is acknowledged in the recital that the proposed retention regime 'may' amount to an interference with the private life of the individual, the cautious tone of the provision then changes promptly. The language becomes considerably more forthright, asserting that no violation of the requirements under Article 8 ECHR occurs as a result of the establishment of such a measure. This contrasts with the initial hesitation in clearly confirming that law enforcement access to such personal data would amount to an interference with the right to respect for private life and correspondence.

However, there was no uncertainty at this time within the ECHR legal order and the relevant Article 8 ECHR jurisprudence of the ECtHR regarding whether such conduct constituted an interference with the right to respect to private life under Article 8(1) ECHR when the framework decision was being drafted. The ECtHR had in fact clearly established in its case law since 1984, and had reiterated subsequently, that the release of such communications data to the police, without the consent of the individual in question, amounted to an interference with the rights guaranteed under Article 8(1) ECHR.[70] In the most recent of these judgments at the relevant time in 2001, the Strasbourg Court had held unequivocally that the obtaining by the police of records relating to a person's telephone conversations (such as the phone numbers dialled, how often, when, and the duration of the call) interfered with their right to respect for private life guaranteed under Article 8(1).[71] There was, therefore, no doubt in the case law of the ECtHR during

[67] Declaration on Combating Terrorism adopted by the European Council on 25 March 2004. See also recital 4 of the preamble of draft framework decision of 28 April 2004 (n 33).

[68] Draft framework decision, Doc 8958/04 (n 33) recital 10.

[69] ibid.

[70] *Malone v United Kingdom* (1985) 7 EHRR 14; *Valenzuela Contreras v Spain* (1999) 28 EHRR 483; *P.G. and J.H. v United Kingdom* [2001] ECHR 546. See further Chapter 3.

[71] *Malone* (n 70) [83]; *P.G. and J.H.* (n 70) [42]. In the 1980s, this process was known as 'metering' and involved the use of a device (a meter check printer) which registered the numbers dialled on a particular telephone and the time and duration of each call. In *Malone*, while not provided for in legislation, a voluntary practice existed involving the Post Office (then the main telecommunications provider for the UK) providing such records to the police on request without the consent of the subscriber if the information was essential for investigating a serious crime and could not be obtained from other sources.

this period regarding whether the retention of communications data for the subsequent use of countering crime had amounted to an interference with Article 8 ECHR.[72]

The legality, necessity, and proportionality conditions to be met under Article 8(2) ECHR in order for an interference with the right to respect for private life to be tolerated in a democratic society are referred to indirectly in the Council's draft framework decision. However, no further specifications are provided regarding how the proposal will satisfy these requirements. There is an express commitment under Article 6 of the draft proposal of compliance with the general principles of the then Data Protection Directive 95/46/EC. In contrast, the draft contains no equivalent commitment to the principles and requirements of Article 8 ECHR. This absence is striking in light of the fact that EU law expressly provided at that time that the EU must respect the rights guaranteed under the ECHR.[73] Accordingly, EU legal measures, including framework decisions, were also required to be compatible with the ECHR.[74] The clear lack of explicit consideration to compliance with specific requirements of Article 8 ECHR gives weight to concerns expressed by leading commentators that the creation of adequate and sufficient safeguards to govern EU counter-terrorism measures under the third pillar was not a priority for the EU legislature.[75]

Under the Treaty of Amsterdam 1997, the European Parliament's opinion had to be sought but was not binding for police and judicial cooperation measures adopted under the third pillar.[76] As part of the limited role afforded to Parliament under this consultation procedure, a critical report by the Committee on Civil Liberties, Justice and Home Affairs for Parliament (otherwise known as the 'Alvaro Report' after its rapporteur) recommended that Parliament reject the draft framework decision.[77] The Report contained many reservations regarding the scope, aim, and application of the Council's proposal and focused on three key issues: the legal basis, the proportionality of the measure, and its compatibility with Article 8 ECHR. In particular, the Report stressed that there were 'sizeable doubts'

[72] Although there was some dispute regarding the seriousness of the intrusion with the right private life as enshrined in Art 8 ECHR when compared to the interception of communications content. See further Chapter 3.

[73] As Art 6(2) TEU (Nice version), provided: 'The Union shall respect fundamental rights, as guaranteed by the European Convention for the Protection of Human Rights and Fundamental Freedoms signed in Rome on 4 November 1950 and as they result from the constitutional traditions common to the Member States, as general principles of Community law.'

[74] Patrick Breyer, 'Telecommunications Data Retention and Human Rights' (2005) 11 European Law Journal 365, 366.

[75] See eg Hielke Hijmans and Alfonso Scirocco, 'Shortcomings in EU Data Protection in the Third and the Second Pillars?' (2009) 46 Common Market Law Review 1485, 1496; Murphy (n 1) 151.

[76] Since the Lisbon Treaty entered into force, unless otherwise provided, all third pillar measures are subject to the ordinary legislative procedure (formerly referred to as the 'co-decision procedure') giving Parliament and the Council the same weight in the decision-making process. See generally, Paul Craig and Gráinne de Búrca, *EU Law* (7th edn, OUP 2020).

[77] Alvaro Report (n 45). Also known as the LIBE Committee.

regarding the legal basis proposed and the measure's proportionality on the basis that the provisions were 'neither appropriate nor necessary and unreasonably harsh towards those concerned'.[78] The proposal's questionable proportionality with respect to infringing 'the personal data of individuals' is also highlighted.[79] No clarification, however, is provided in the 2005 Report regarding whether this analysis concerned the right to respect for private life and personal data guaranteed under Article 8 ECHR, or under the protection of human rights under the general principles of EU law (then referred to as EC law).

The crux of the proportionality concerns raised in the Alvaro Report was that there appeared to be a more 'suitable and more milder option' already available in the adoption of the model of data preservation provided under the 2001 Council of Europe's Convention on Cybercrime.[80] This alternative option essentially provides for specific requests for data storage in individual cases. On the other hand, the proposed draft framework decision, unlike the Cybercrime Convention, required indiscriminate and mandatory retention of all communications data. The Council contended that the model of data retention under the COE Cybercrime Convention would not be sufficient to meet the needs of the security, intelligence, and law enforcement authorities in the fight against modern criminals and terrorists. Storage for a specified purpose, the Council highlighted, would never aid in the investigation of a person who is not already suspected of involvement with a criminal or terrorist organization.[81] The authors of the Alvaro Report responded to this justification by expressing their concern that the more far-reaching model raised the question of the compatibility of the proposed data retention regime with the principle of the presumption of innocence.[82]

Again, the tension between Parliament and the Council on this point is demonstrated in the Report's recommendation that Member States should produce a study proving 'the unquestionable need' for such a sweeping data retention measure.[83] This evidence-based request aptly drew attention to an earlier questionnaire to Member States.[84] Strikingly, the results from this research found that a third of the participants responded negatively when asked if the absence of blanket data retention, as put forward in the proposed framework decision, had ever obstructed the work of their national law enforcement authorities. Notably, in addition to Greece, Italy, Luxembourg, and Sweden, Ireland (one of the four proponents of the draft framework decision) was among the Member States who responded negatively in the earlier questionnaire. In addition to a study demonstrating the necessity of the

[78] ibid 6–7.
[79] ibid 8.
[80] ibid.
[81] ibid.
[82] ibid.
[83] ibid 9.
[84] Council of the EU, 'Answers to questionnaire on traffic data retention', Doc 14107/02, 20 November 2002.

Council's proposed data retention regime, the Alvaro Report recommended that the data retention obligation and scope of data to be retained should be dealt with under a separate legal instrument, namely a Directive.[85] The Alvaro Report also observed that the negative implications for the internal market raised questions regarding the proportionality of the draft framework decision. This focused also on the financial burdens that telecommunications providers (especially small to medium-sized businesses) would be subject to, and the resulting lack of harmony from distortions in competition, as issues that could prevent the completion of a single European market.[86]

Finally, the Alvaro Report was unequivocal in its finding that the proposal was incompatible with Article 8 ECHR. In a reference to the Article 8 ECHR jurisprudence of the ECtHR, the Report observes that the Strasbourg Court 'has stressed that the contracting states do not have unlimited discretion to subject individual within their territory to clandestine surveillance'.[87] The passage clearly invokes *Klass v Germany*,[88] one of the Court's still influential judgments on Article 8 ECHR and State surveillance of communications. As the ECtHR held in 1978: '[p]owers of secret surveillance of citizens, characterising as they do the police state, are tolerable under the Convention only in so far as strictly necessary for safeguarding the democratic institutions'.[89]

The Alvaro Report's review of the draft framework decision and its compatibility with Article 8 ECHR concludes with the critical assessment that it was 'debatable, to say the least', whether the proposal met any of the conditions of Article 8(2), including the tests of legality or necessity. That said, the Alvaro Report adopted a similar approach to the language of the Council's draft framework decision as it also drew quite generally and loosely from the jurisprudence of the ECtHR in its analysis of Article 8 ECHR. From the perspective of mainstreaming human rights and the right to private life, it is noteworthy that neither EU institution made any explicit reference to the ECtHR line of case law of greatest relevance to the draft framework decisions that directly address the compatibility of obtaining communications data for the subsequent use of national law enforcement authorities with Article 8 ECHR.[90] Nevertheless, as noted earlier, Parliament rejected a second draft framework decision proposal on data retention put forward by the Council a few months later in September.[91] Both rejections clearly indicate that compatibility with the rights and conditions of Article 8 ECHR was a decisive factor in the European Parliament's review of the Council's proposals.

85 Alvaro Report (n 45) 9.
86 ibid.
87 ibid.
88 *Klass v Germany* (1978) 2 EHRR 214 [49].
89 ibid [42], [59].
90 *Malone* (n 70); *Valenzuela Contreras* (n 70); *P.G. and J.H.* (n 70).
91 BBC News (n 50).

2. Drafting the Data Retention Directive and the role of Article 8 ECHR

In September 2005, the European Commission put forward a proposal for a draft directive that would impose a mandatory obligation on Member States to require CSPs to retain communications data across the EU.[92] The proposal contained no mention of Article 8 ECHR. This was a striking omission especially considering the role Article 8 ECHR played in the rights review of both the European Parliament and the Council with respect to legal shortfalls in the previous draft framework decisions on data retention. Instead, the draft Directive referred to the ECHR within the very general context of the need to respect fundamental rights. This is evident in recital 16 of the draft Directive which required that Member States adopt legislative measures to ensure that data retained under the Directive should only be provided to competent national authorities in accordance with national legislation 'in full respect of the fundamental rights of the persons concerned'. The Commission's proposal stated that these measures should include the appropriate conditions, limits, and safeguards in order to ensure the conformity of the provision of the data retained with fundamental rights 'as guaranteed in particular in the European Convention for the Protection of Human Rights and Fundamental Freedoms'.[93] Approval from Parliament of the Commission's draft Directive then turned on the incorporation of several amendments embracing these safeguards. These concerned restricting the proposal's scope, the amount of data collected, narrowing the list of authorities with access to said data, and shortening the period of retention.[94]

The European Parliament then adopted a curious approach to the specific standards of Article 8 ECHR whereby it appears to have considered the general commitment provided by the Commission to the ECHR to be sufficient. This is suggested by the absence of any efforts by Parliament to amend this provision. Instead, Parliament focused its attention on strengthening the commitment guaranteed in the draft Data Retention Directive to the fundamental rights to respect for private life and the protection of personal data under Articles 7 and 8 CFR, provisions which at the time had no binding force in EU law. In its amendment to the relevant provision, the Parliament substituted the status of the express commitment to the Charter in the Commission's proposal from ensuring 'full respect' to ensuring 'full compliance'.[95] Notably, the same level of scrutiny was not applied regarding the draft Directive's commitment to the requirements of the ECHR as no amendment for ensuring 'full compliance' with the ECHR was sought by

[92] Commission Draft Directive Proposal (n 51).
[93] ibid.
[94] EU Parliament Draft Report on Data Retention (n 56). On the substantive provisions of Directive 2006/24/EC, see Chapter 8.
[95] EU Parliament Draft Report on Data Retention (n 56) 9.

Parliament. This approach represents a significant departure from the emphasis placed on the importance of the compatibility of Article 8 ECHR by Parliament in its earlier review of the draft framework decisions.

Hence, Parliament followed the Commission in making the EU Charter of Fundamental Rights a more prominent source than the legally binding general principles of EU law and the established jurisprudence of the ECtHR for the legal framework of privacy protection governing the operation of the draft Directive. The adoption of the Charter was proclaimed into existence by the EU institutions and given politically approval by Member States at the Nice Council Summit in December 2000.[96] However, its legal status was deliberately left undetermined in light of the expected passing of the Constitutional Treaty in 2005.[97] The subsequent non-ratification of this treaty meant that the Charter would not be upgraded to the same legal binding status as the EU Treaties until the entry into force of the Lisbon Treaty from 1 December 2009. Consequently, during the drafting of the Data Retention Directive, the legal status of the Charter as a source of EU human rights law at this time was ambiguous at best and at worst irrelevant. More importantly, any jurisprudence concerning the interpretation and development of this human rights instrument, compared to that of Article 8 ECHR and the ECtHR, would remain largely undeveloped until the Charter became legally binding in 2009.

In a similar approach to Article 8 ECHR, the Council's response to the Commission's draft Directive contained no mention of Article 8 ECHR or even the ECHR itself.[98] However, it did include a recital that invoked the legality, necessity, and proportionality conditions of Article 8(2) ECHR:

> In an area of freedom, security and justice, obligations upon Industry to retain data are justifiable only if necessary to preserve important interests within a democratic society. This necessity arises from the importance of analyzing specific historic data in the investigation, detection and prosecution of terrorist crimes and other serious offences. Where that data may provide the only approach for an effective resolution of such crimes, its availability for a determined period of time may be reliably ensured only with a statutory storage obligation.[99]

In its final report to the Commission and Council,[100] Parliament made a much more robust amendment to the same recital in the Commission's draft requiring

[96] See further Chapter 4.

[97] See eg Commission of the EC, 'The Fundamental Rights Agency Public consultation document', COM(2004) 693 final, 25 October 2004, 7: 'The Charter of Fundamental Rights ... brings together a package of rights, freedoms and principles which will, when the Constitutional Treaty enters into force, bind the EU institutions and the Member States when they apply EU law.'

[98] Council of the EU, Doc 13789/05 (n 60).

[99] ibid 13.

[100] EU Parliament Draft Report on Data Retention (n 56).

compliance with the case law of the Strasbourg Court (the highlighted text is included in the original document):

> (19) This Directive *could better* respect the fundamental rights and the principles recognised, in particular, by the Charter of Fundamental Rights of the European Union; in particular, this Directive together with Directive 2002/58/EC, *and* seek to ensure full respect of the fundamental rights to respect the private life and communications of citizens and the protection of personal data (Articles 7 and 8 of the Charter) *as well as the judgments of the European Court of Human Rights.*

The European Parliament again applied this more robust human rights approach by supporting this amendment with explicit references to ECHR case law.[101] The latter clearly established that the storage of personal data concerning an individual's private life, and the access to such data by public authorities, both constitute interferences with the right to respect for private life guaranteed under Article 8 ECHR.[102] Following an exceptionally swift fast tracking of the co-decision procedure,[103] Parliament approved the controversial draft Directive following a first reading agreement with the Council less than two months later in December 2005.[104]

3. General principles of EU law and the e-Privacy Directive 2002/58

In 2002, an international coalition of leading NGOs wrote to the President of the European Parliament urging him to vote against amending Article 15 of the draft e-Privacy Directive.[105] Ultimately, Parliament voted in favour of the adoption of this controversial amendment. In addition to the ECHR and the case law of the ECtHR, the EU Charter of Fundamental Rights was among the sources of EU human rights law referred to by the coalition in its failed plea to Parliament when highlighting the conditions where the retention of communications data may be tolerated in a democratic society.[106] Significantly, the document gives no explicit consideration to the case law of the ECJ or the right to respect for private life guaranteed under the general principles of EU law (then EC law). Article 15(1) of the e-Privacy Directive 2002/58 does, however, contain an express commitment to comply with the general principles of EU law:

[101] ibid 11–12.
[102] *Malone* (n 71); *Amann v Switzerland* [2000] ECHR 87.
[103] De Ruiter and Neuhold (n 55).
[104] BBC News (n 62).
[105] Global Liberty Internet Campaign (n 29).
[106] ibid.

> Member States may adopt legislative measures to restrict the scope of the rights and obligations provided for in Article 5, Article 6, Article 8(1), (2), (3) and (4), and Article 9 of this Directive when such restriction constitutes a necessary, appropriate and proportionate measure within a democratic society to safeguard national security (i.e. State security), defence, public security, and the prevention, investigation, detection and prosecution of criminal offences or of unauthorised use of the electronic communication system, as referred to in Article 13(1) of Directive 95/46/EC. To this end, Member States may, *inter alia*, adopt legislative measures providing for the retention of data for a limited period justified on the grounds laid down in this paragraph. All the measures referred to in this paragraph shall be in accordance with the general principles of Community law, including those referred to in Article 6(1) and (2) of the Treaty on European Union.

Recital 2 of the preamble of Directive 2002/58 also states that it seeks to ensure full respect for the right to respect for private life and the right to protection of personal data enshrined in Articles 7 and 8 CFR. However, the legal significance accorded to recitals and articles are fundamentally different. Articles are the main provisions of a directive or regulation and, most importantly, are legally binding upon Member States. In contrast, recitals form part of the preamble of a directive; they are neither binding nor sufficient as a ground to challenge derogations from actual binding provisions.[107] Nevertheless, recitals still play an important role in the implementation process through assisting Member States by explaining and clarifying the main provisions of the EU legislation in question. The CJEU,[108] including the Advocates General,[109] and the European Commission[110] have all given weight to the substance of recitals when interpreting the nature and aims of EU legislation.

Ultimately, for the EU legislature to require within the legally binding articles of the e-Privacy Directive 2002/58 that any legislative measures voluntarily adopted by Member States under Article 15 of said Directive should be 'in accordance' with the general principles of EU law attributes much more importance to the requirements of Article 8 ECHR as guaranteed in CJEU case law as opposed to the ECtHR. This requirement consequently places the general principles of EU law at the top of the hierarchy of human rights standards for ensuring the right to respect

[107] Case C-162/97 *Criminal proceedings against Gunnar Nilsson* [1998] ECR I-07477 [54]; Case 215/88 *Casa Fleischhandels* [1989] ECR 2789 [31]; Case C-136/04 *Deutsches Milch-Kontor* [2005] ECR I-10095 [32].

[108] Case C-101/01 *Lindqvist* [2003] ECR I-12971 [46], [64], [79], [95]; Case C-465/00 *Österreichischer Rundfunk* [2003] ECR I-4989 [70]; Case C-275/06 *Promusicae* [2008] ECR I-271 [64]. See further Chapter 5.

[109] Opinion of AG Tizzano in *Lindqvist* (n 108) [7], [39]; *Österreichischer Rundfunk* (n 108) [6], [51].

[110] See Opinion of AG Tizzano (n 109) [32], where the European Commission relied on the preamble of the Data Protection Directive 95/46/EC in its argument that the Directive was intended to regulate the free movement of personal data as a social activity not just economic activities.

for private life and the protection of personal data that could be subject to interference as a result of any measures permitted under the e-Privacy Directive 2002/58.

4. General principles and the Data Retention Directive

In the same vein as the e-Privacy Directive 2002/58, the Data Retention Directive expressed commitments of compliance with Article 8 ECHR and Articles 7 and 8 CFR within recitals 9 and 22. However, the standard of human rights protection and mainstreaming between both Directives differed significantly for two major reasons. First, Article 4 of Directive 2006/24/EC, a legally binding provision of EU law, explicitly required Member States to comply with the necessity and proportionality requirements of Article 8 ECHR:

> Member States shall adopt measures to ensure that data retained in accordance with this Directive are provided only to the competent national authorities in specific cases and in accordance with national law. The procedures to be followed and the conditions to be fulfilled in order to gain access to retained data in accordance with necessity and proportionality requirements shall be defined by each Member State in its national law, subject to the relevant provisions of European Union law or public international law, and *in particular the ECHR as interpreted by the European Court of Human Rights.*[111]

It is noteworthy that Article 4 of Directive 2006/24/EC was the result of a political compromise between the EU institutions during the drafting of the Data Retention Directive regarding what human rights standards would govern the subsequent access and use of the communications data by public authorities following its initial retention and processing by CSPs. Indeed, as Bignami rightly highlights, Article 4 is comparatively 'skeletal' in its scope compared to what was originally sought by the European Parliament and data protection authorities across the EU during the drafting of the Data Retention Directive.[112]

Secondly, the most important distinction between the e-Privacy Directive 2002/58 and the Data Retention Directive 2006/24/EC is the striking absence of any specific reference to the general principles of EU law. There is no requirement either within the recitals or the main articles of the Data Retention Directive that the retention of communications data under the Directive must comply with the fundamental rights recognized and guaranteed by the general principles of EU law. The sole reference to the 'relevant provisions of EU law' related only to the

[111] Emphasis added.

[112] Francesca Bignami, 'Privacy and Law Enforcement in the European Union: The Data Retention Directive 2006/24/EC' (2007) 8 Chicago Journal of International Law 233, 243.

human rights standards to be complied with by Member States regarding the procedures and conditions to be met with respect to the access of the data retained under Article 4 of Directive 2006/24/EC. However, the retention of communications data under the Data Retention Directive was subject only to the non-binding requirements of Article 8 ECHR, as interpreted under the ECtHR system, and the EU Charter of Fundamental Rights. It is crucial to note that these human rights instruments commanded much less legal certainty within the EU legal order at this time.

5. Drafting the Directive: Article 8 ECHR and the Charter

Decades before the drafting of the Data Retention Directive in 1977, the EU institutions announced in a Joint Declaration that the 'prime importance they attach to the protection of fundamental rights' derive in particular from 'the constitutions of the Member States and the [ECHR]' in the exercise of their powers.[113] Although the Declaration was useful for endorsing the fundamental rights jurisprudence of the CJEU (then the ECJ), it 'remained more a symbol than a tool' to strengthen the integration of fundamental rights in the EU law and policymaking process.[114] Consequently, in 2005, during the final drafting stages of the Data Retention Directive, while the EU institutions had the case law of the CJEU to draw from, there was an absence of a legally binding and clear reference point that consolidated the EU fundamental rights patchwork which then existed within the EU legal order.[115]

The CJEU was at this time in the practice of routinely citing the special significance of the ECHR and the rulings of the Strasbourg Court as a key source of inspiration for its interpretation of fundamental rights under the general principles of EU law. However, the ECHR standards were still not legally binding on EU institutions despite its unique status within the EU legal order at this time.[116] Additionally, any policy tools requiring, or supporting, the mainstreaming of EU fundamental rights within each EU institution had only reached a developmental stage of operation. For instance, the European Commission's practice of undertaking *ex ante* assessments of the economic, social, and environmental impacts (including compatibility with the Charter of Fundamental Rights) of EU policy proposals had only been launched a few years earlier in 2002.[117] This system of

[113] [1977] OJ C103/01.
[114] Olivier De Schutter, 'The Implementation of the Charter by the Institutions of the European Union' in Steve Peers and others (eds), *The EU Charter of Fundamental Rights: A Commentary* (Hart 2014) 1641.
[115] ibid.
[116] See further Chapter 4.
[117] Commission of the EC, 'Communication from the Commission on Impact Assessment', COM(2002)276 final, 5 May 2002.

'impact assessment' was introduced but it was done so on a gradual basis, with the stated intention that it was only expected to be 'fully operational' by 2005.[118] It was only having arrived at this point that the Commission then adopted a new set of internal guidelines overhauling the methodology it had previously used for its impact assessments.[119] Moreover, it was only in 2005 that the European Parliament and Council, the other two EU institutions comprising the EU trilogue process, then undertook responsibility for assessing the impact of their own policymaking and legislative scrutiny.[120]

In other words, the *ex ante* evaluation of the Data Retention Directive's compatibility with human rights took place during what was effectively the teething period of each EU institution's approach to mainstreaming fundamental rights and years before the Charter of Fundamental Rights became legally binding.[121] Much legal uncertainty surrounded the 'controversial' Charter between its political proclamation in 2000 until it was eventually given binding legal status by the Lisbon Treaty in 2009.[122] These difficulties notwithstanding, the drafting stage of the Data Retention Directive 2006/24/EC highlights the increasing efforts by the EU institutions to establish the Charter as an instrumental policy tool for the mainstreaming of fundamental rights in the intervening period. Notably, although the Commission's impact assessment and its draft Directive proposal both refer to the Charter, neither key policy document mentions the protection of fundamental rights as guaranteed under the general principles of EU law or Article 8 ECHR.[123]

Moreover, as examined in detail previously, in contrast to the e-Privacy Directive 2002/58, there was a striking absence of any specific reference to the protection of fundamental rights as guaranteed under the general principles of EU law within the finalized draft of the Data Retention Directive 2006/24/EC. That said, the recitals of both Directives refer to Articles 7 and 8 CFR.[124] This approach by the Commission reflects its drafting practice since 2001 with regard to recitals, in which a standard recital would be included in legislation to indicate compliance with the Charter.[125] Nevertheless, the inclusion of this reference in a recital does not necessarily impute that the Charter was to be binding in the long term.

[118] ibid.

[119] European Commission, 'Impact Assessment Guidelines', SEC(2005)791, 15 June 2005.

[120] European Commission, 'Proposal for an Interinstitutional Agreement on Better Regulation', COM(2015)216 final, 19 May 2005.

[121] Commission of the EC, 'Proposal for a Directive of the European Parliament and of the Council on the retention of data processed in connection with the provision of public electronic communications services and amending Directive 2002/58/EC: Extended Impact Assessment', SEC(2005)1131, 21 September 2005 (Commission Impact Assessment).

[122] Francis G Jacobs, 'Human Rights in the European Union: the Role of the Court of Justice' [2001] European Law Review 331, 331. See further Chapter 4.

[123] Commission Impact Assessment (n 121); Commission Draft Directive Proposal (n 51).

[124] Data Retention Directive 2006/24/EC, recital 22; e-Privacy Directive 2002/58/EC, recital 2.

[125] European Commission, 'Application of the Charter of Fundamental Rights of the European Union', SEC(2001)380/3, 13 March 2001.

Notably, those involved in the drafting of the Charter understood that they were involved in 'the drafting of a political declaration' with the aim of 'increasing the visibility' of the status then held by human rights within the EU legal order rather than the legally binding instrument that the Charter eventually became.[126]

As explained by the UK Government representative shortly after the Nice European Summit in December 2000 where the EU institutions solemnly proclaimed the Charter as a political non-binding declaration, there were two reasons for this decision. First, it was easier to show in a political declaration 'a clear statement of values which people can understand without the qualifications and exceptions necessary in a written law'.[127] Secondly, the Charter lacked 'the precision of language necessary' to allow it legal force.[128] When the proposed Data Retention Directive by the Commission was published in September 2005, the legal status (and future) of the Charter was deeply uncertain. This precarious position was due to the rejections of the Constitutional Treaty by French and Dutch voters only months earlier which if ratified would have made the Charter legally binding. Furthermore, two factors cast doubt on the fact that mention of the Charter in the finalized draft of the Data Retention Directive meant that it carried any weight in ensuring that the principles and safeguards of the rights to respect for private life and the protection of personal data were taken into account by the EU institutions during the drafting process.

First, as examined previously, the data retention framework decision (the legislative instrument initially proposed by the Council) had been the subject of considerable scrutiny for its fundamental rights compatibility by the European Parliament immediately prior to the Commission proposing a draft Directive.[129] Despite taking place between 2004 and 2005, when the Charter was expected to become legally binding following the ratification of the Constitutional Treaty, this extended legal dialogue between the Council and the Parliament contained no mention of the Charter. Instead, the Parliament's Report (published in May 2005) focused specifically on the questionable compliance of the framework decision with the legality, necessity, and proportionality conditions of Article 8 ECHR, particularly the proportionality of the framework decision's scope.[130]

Hence, there is no evidence that the Charter carried any weight in the only rigorous period of assessment and dialogue between the Council and the European Parliament regarding the fundamental rights compatibility of an EU-wide policy

[126] House of Commons European Scrutiny Committee, 'The Application of the EU Charter of Fundamental Rights in the UK: a state of confusion', 43rd Report of Session 2013–2014 (HC 979, 2014), 14; Gráinne de Búrca, 'The Drafting of the European Union Charter of Fundamental Rights' (2001) 26 European Law Review 126, 130.

[127] Lord Goldsmith, 'A Charter of Rights, Freedoms and Principles' (2001) 38 Common Market Law Review 1201, 1215.

[128] ibid.

[129] As addressed in the Alvaro Report (n 45).

[130] ibid 8–9.

on data retention for the purpose of countering serious crime. Secondly, despite the Charter's emergence as the principal reference point for fundamental rights under the Commission's draft Data Retention Directive, there was little opportunity for any rigorous rights scrutiny of the proposal due to the fast tracking of the co-decision procedure. Indeed, both the Council and the majority of Parliament reached a first-reading agreement on the draft Directive within the notably short period of three months.[131] This followed the urgency created by the London bombings in July 2005, combined with the UK's Presidency of the Council thereafter, and data retention legislation being one of its priorities during its Presidency. Despite its limited role in the actual drafting process, even reference by the EU legislature to the Charter in the finalized draft of the Data Retention Directive raises questions regarding the efforts of the EU institutions at this time to mainstream human rights across EU policymaking.

While the practice of referring to rights might suggest that the rights are becoming mainstreamed, the specific drafting circumstances surrounding what became Directive 2006/24/EC indicate that mainstreaming (or pre-legislative rights review) within the pre-Lisbon period of EU policymaking was far from robust. However, for this ambitious norm of decision-making to be effective in any democratic political process, there must exist 'a political willingness' that emphasizes the importance of confronting how proposed legislation implicates rights adversely and engaging in reasoned judgement about whether the initiative should be amended or is justified despite its potentially adverse effects for rights.[132] Perhaps unsurprisingly, serious doubts have been expressed regarding whether the mainstreaming of rights in this sense can ever be fully effective as it requires fundamentally reorienting 'political behaviour and legislative decision-making in a manner commensurate with the idealised notion of proactive rights protection'.[133] Consequently, it has been observed that such systematic engagement with fundamental rights can only work within a democratic political process in a specific context. This is when, as Feldman highlights, the protection of human rights 'is seen as a goal of all institutions, executive, legislative and judicial, working towards a common goal when exercising their different but complementary functions'.[134]

Hiebert, one of the leading scholars in this field of governance, has also identified more specific requirements that are essential for ensuring effective pre-legislative rights review.[135] These recommendations are relevant not only to

[131] De Ruiter and Neuhold (n 55) 549.

[132] Janet L Hiebert, 'Legislative Rights Review: Addressing the Gap between Ideals and Constraints' in Murray Hunt, Hayley J Hooper, and Paul Yowell (eds), *Parliaments and Human Rights: Redressing the Democratic Deficit* (Hart 2015) 40; Kent Roach, 'Varied Role of Courts and Legislatures' in ibid 420.

[133] Roach (n 132) 420.

[134] Feldman (n 5) 92.

[135] Hiebert (n 132) 49–55. These recommendations are based on a detailed examination of the work to date of the Joint Committee on Human Rights (the UK Parliament's legislative rights review body). The Committee has been criticized for its 'fairly dense and legalistic' reporting style which requires considerable time from overworked members of parliaments and their staff. Nevertheless, the

policymakers mainstreaming rights within EU law but also at the national level for Member States. First, the Parliament must exercise a significant role in its robust scrutiny of drafted legislation. This oversight should also have a particular focus on whether these proposed laws are compatible with particular rights under a specific human rights instrument.[136] With respect to the EU in the post-Lisbon era, this would be the EU Charter of Fundamental Rights. Such a requirement is particularly important for making sure that arguments and concerns are consistently framed within the same fundamental rights, principles, and safeguards. Hence, the practice of reviewing policy proposals in light of their Charter compatibility could consequently develop into a coherent and systematic part of the drafting and impact assessment process across (and within) each EU institution. Therefore, EU policymakers should avoid making references, or raise questions of compatibility, that tend to be 'framed in the more general and abstract language of civil liberties'[137] which do not draw specifically from the Charter.

Secondly, the Parliament must exert substantial pressure on the executive branch to provide detailed arguments and evidence-based reasons that explain and justify policy proposals that implicate rights or reports which assert that a policy proposal complies with fundamental rights.[138] This persistent pressure contributes to the establishment and entrenchment of a 'norm of justification' which in turn may result in the executive adopting adequate safeguards to ensure that the policy implementation process is rights-compatible.[139] Thirdly, an assessment of rights compatibility should begin at the earliest opportunity in the policymaking process (or the legislative cycle).[140] Scrutiny of an existing draft law may be too late to effect change as legislators across the relevant institutions may be reluctant to agree to 'amendments that could renew internal conflicts'[141] (or conflicts with non-governmental stakeholders) which could then add significant delays to the drafting stage. If such rights-based scrutiny could take place earlier, legislators may be more amenable to changes because 'agreeing to rights-inspired amendments would not carry the same political liabilities'.[142]

More effective mainstreaming of rights should make judicial challenges largely unnecessary although there will always be borderline cases. Accordingly, while the drafting of the Data Retention Directive raises questions concerning the

Committee has been described as the 'gold standard' which other jurisdictions interested in legislative rights review seek to emulate: Janet L Hiebert and Stephen Gardbaum, *The New Commonwealth Model of Constitutionalism* (CUP 2013) 224.

136 Hiebert (n 132) 49.
137 ibid 51.
138 ibid.
139 ibid.
140 ibid 52.
141 ibid.
142 ibid.

effectiveness of the mainstreaming of rights within the EU institutions in this pre-Lisbon period, the CJEU existed then (as it does now in the post-Lisbon period) as an important guardian of fundamental rights. The contribution of the judiciary to the legislative rights review process is to assess the quality of how the legislative decision was made and to ensure that the relevant rights have not been 'unduly compromised'.[143] Within the legal framework of a post-Lisbon EU, the legally binding Charter of Fundamental Rights provides the CJEU with 'legal standards against which to test the legality of the acts of the EU's institutions'.[144] While some contend that this guardianship should be the exclusive or prevailing remit of the courts,[145] to do so would be to adopt an approach of considerable deference to an institution that can also be 'a source of rights violations'.[146]

Normalizing the substitution of the collective judgement of elective representatives and thereby compromising the democratic ideal of transparent governance through discussion and debate is clearly problematic in a liberal democratic society.[147] Parliaments and legislators should also be encouraged, and indeed expected, to engage in legislative rights review given that the cycle of legislative rights review should not begin or end at the stage of judicial review. The norm of justification established during pre-legislative rights review should additionally contribute to the post-legislative rights review that follows when the courts have ruled that legislation is not rights-compliant. At this stage, pressure should then be put on legislators 'to develop and introduce remedial measures' in response to the court's judgment.[148] Moreover, legislators should also ensure that the requirements established by the judiciary to be met in order to ensure compliance with the principles and safeguards of the relevant rights are followed in any subsequent related policymaking.

E. Conclusions

This chapter has shown that the drafting of the Data Retention Directive reveals a period when the EU institutions were clearly grappling with their mainstreaming of fundamental rights in the EU policymaking process before the EU Charter of Fundamental Rights became legally binding. Moreover, the fast tracking of the drafting of Directive 2006/24/EC also shows a disregard of the need for EU legislation to comply with the specific principles and safeguards under the right to

[143] Janet L Hiebert, *Limiting Rights: The Dilemma of Judicial Review* (McGill-Queen's University Press 1996) 155.

[144] Kenneth Armstrong, *Governing Social Inclusion* (OUP 2010) 249.

[145] On this widely held review, see Ronald Dworkin, *Taking Rights Seriously* (HUP 1978) 149; Roach (n 132).

[146] Hiebert (n 143) 152; Hiebert (n 5) 236.

[147] Hiebert (n 5) 236; Jeremy Waldron, *The Dignity of Legislation* (CUP 1999) 239.

[148] Hiebert (n 132) 50.

respect for private life as guaranteed by the then EU legal order. Both factors cast serious doubt over the existence of a robust fundamental rights culture operating within the EU at this time. At the same time, it is also evident from this discussion that Article 8 ECHR and the related case law of the ECtHR clearly played a role in the drafting process of the Data Retention Directive, particularly in the early stages. Both the Council and European Parliament drew from the jurisprudence of the ECtHR during the draft framework decision stages and in the drafting of the Directive. Furthermore, Parliament stressed the need for the Directive to comply with the rights and conditions guaranteed under the ECHR as interpreted and applied by the ECtHR.

However, Article 8 ECHR, in addition to other sources of EU fundamental rights, was ultimately reduced to playing a rather limited role in the rushed final stages of the drafting process. Parliament relied heavily on the requirements of Article 8 ECHR when highlighting the questionable necessity and proportionality of the data retention scope that resulted in its rejection of the Council's draft framework decisions. Nevertheless, most of these concerns were not reflected in the wide scope of the data retention regime adopted following a fast-tracked first-reading agreement on the draft Directive that had been reached between the Council and the majority of Parliament within the notably short period of three months. This gives weight to the concern that little consideration was given to the compatibility of the Directive with EU fundamental rights during the final drafting stages.

Unquestionably, the strongest source for the protection of Article 8 ECHR in 2006 within the EU legal order was its status as one of the fundamental rights recognized and protected under the general principles of EU law.[149] By the time of the development and drafting of Directive 2006/24/EC, the CJEU had recognized human rights as being part of the general principles of Community law for several decades. In particular, the Luxembourg Court had come to regard the ECHR—once an inconsequential international human rights instrument to the EU legal framework—as a special source of inspiration warranting protection by the Court as part of the unwritten general principles of EU law. However, the data retention regime imposed under the Data Retention Directive, in striking contrast to the e-Privacy Directive 2002/58, contained no requirement for compliance with the general principles of EU law. Like the approach of the CJEU, despite recognizing the ECHR as a source of fundamental rights protection within EU law during the drafting process, the EU institutions as a whole did not prioritize ensuring compliance with the standards of Article 8 ECHR in the binding provisions of the Data Retention Directive. This lack of coherent scrutiny regarding Article 8 ECHR casts clear doubt on whether fundamental rights protection within the EU policy-making process at this time amounted to anything more than high rhetoric.

[149] On the status of Art 8 ECHR within the general principles of EU law and the EU Charter, see Chapters 4 and 5.

Consequently, much uncertainty surrounded the Data Retention Directive and its commitment to ensuring full compliance with the established human rights standards under Article 8 ECHR developed to protect the private life and correspondence of individuals across the EU. This examination of the first stage of the Data Retention Directive's legislative cycle also shows the EU institutions grappling with the mainstreaming of fundamental rights in the EU legislative and policymaking process in this pre-Lisbon period. In other words, the *ex ante* evaluation of the Directive's compatibility with fundamental rights took place during the teething period of each institution's approach to mainstreaming fundamental rights and before the EU Charter of Fundamental Rights became legally binding. Furthermore, the fast tracking of the drafting of the Directive also shows a disregard of the need for EU legislation to comply with the specific principles and safeguards under the right to respect for private life and the protection of personal data as guaranteed by the then EU legal order. Hence, both factors cast serious doubt over the existence of a robust fundamental rights culture operating within the EU at this time.

7
The Data Retention Directive and the National Courts

> It follows from settled case-law of the Court that it is solely for the national court before which the dispute has been brought, and which must assume responsibility for the subsequent judicial decision, to determine, in the light of the particular circumstances of the case, both the need for a preliminary ruling in order to enable it to deliver judgment and the relevance of the questions which it submits to the Court. Consequently, where the questions referred concern the interpretation or the validity of a rule of EU law, the Court is in principle bound to give a ruling. It follows that questions referred by national courts enjoy a presumption of relevance.
>
> *Data Protection Commissioner v Facebook Ltd* (2020)[1]

A. Introduction

Under the weight of considerable political pressure for increased surveillance powers that followed the events of 9/11 and the Madrid and London bombings in 2004 and 2005, the controversial Data Retention Directive was rapidly drafted, passed, and entered into force in May 2006.[2] During its implementation by Member States, the same major concerns raised regarding the Directive's compatibility with the right to respect for private life (as guaranteed by Article 8 ECHR), which were not fully addressed during the drafting stage, emerged again.[3] Subsequently, several constitutional courts across the EU rejected the national laws implementing the data retention regime mandated by Directive 2006/24/EC. Furthermore, most of these national courts relied on the human rights standards of Article 8 ECHR and the related case law of the ECtHR. These judgments show the challenges that may arise from the constitutional dialogue between the national courts and the

[1] Case C-311/18 *Data Protection Commissioner v Facebook Ltd* (*Schrems II*), judgment of 16 July 2020 (ECLI:EU:C:2020:559) [73]. All URLs for this chapter were last accessed on 22 April 2024.

[2] Directive 2006/24/EC of the European Parliament and of the Council of 15 March 2006 on the retention of data generated or processed in connection with the provision of publicly available electronic communications services or of public communications networks and amending Directive 2002/58/EC [2006] OJ L105/54 (Data Retention Directive).

[3] See further Chapter 6.

EU Data Privacy Law and Serious Crime. Nora Ni Loideain, Oxford University Press. © Nora Ni Loideain 2025.
DOI: 10.1093/oso/9780198837169.003.0007

EU system, particularly in relation to reconciling the supremacy of EU law, national sovereignty, and the protection of human rights.[4] This chapter addresses how the national courts have contributed to this dialogue within the judgments concerning the challenges at national level and focuses on the influence of Article 8 ECHR within this conversation on what has been described as a 'thorny' transposition process for the Directive.[5] First, the main provisions of the Data Retention Directive are explained, followed by an examination of the threats posed by this framework to the right to respect for private life protected under Article 8 ECHR. The extent of the role of Article 8 ECHR in the dialogue of the national courts with the CJEU regarding the constitutional challenges brought against the implementation of the Directive is then examined in depth. This examination concludes with some reflections on the nature of EU directives as legislative instruments whose normative completion relies upon Member States transposing these EU measures into national law and why that necessarily engages the domestic courts as guardians of the right to private life.[6]

B. Main Provisions of the Directive

1. An instrument that 'complies with the requirements' of Article 8 ECHR?

Article 1(1) of the Data Retention Directive defines its subject matter and broad scope. This principal provision states that data concerning the communications of every natural person and legal entity must be retained and made available for the purpose of 'the investigation, detection and prosecution of serious crime, as defined by each Member State in its national law'. Therefore the Directive imposed a mandatory duty on Member States to require private communication service providers (CSPs) to store and transfer a range of communications data to the competent national authorities for a period between six months to two years.[7]

[4] On the dialogue between the national courts of Member States and the Luxembourg Court via preliminary rulings, see generally Paul Craig and Gráinne de Búrca, *EU Law* (8th edn, OUP 2024) 262–302; Koen Lenaerts and JA Gutierrez-Fons, 'The Constitutional Allocation of Powers and General Principles of EU Law' (2010) 47 Common Market Law Review 1629.

[5] Theodore Konstadinides, 'Destroying Democracy on the Ground of Defending It?' (2011) 36 European Law Review 722, 723; EU Agency for Network and Information Security (ENISA), *Securing Personal Data in the Context of Data Retention* (ENISA 2013) 2. See further Chapter 8.

[6] Analysis of the implementation of Directive 2006/24/EC by each Member State is beyond the scope of this chapter. See generally: European Commission, 'Evaluation of the Directive of the European Parliament and of the Council on the retention of data processed in connection with the provision of public electronic communication services and amending Directive 2002/58/EC', COM(2011) 225 final, 4 April 2011 (Commission Evaluation Report); Marek Zubik, Jan Podkowik, and Robert Rybski (eds), *European Constitutional Courts towards Data Retention Laws* (Springer 2021); Eleni Kosta and Irene Kamara (eds), *Data Retention in Europe and Beyond* (OUP 2025).

[7] Data Retention Directive, Arts 5(2) and 6.

The communications data in question consisted of personal data derived from landline and mobile telephony, Internet access, Internet telephony, and email.[8] Article 5 of Directive 2006/24/EC described this information as 'namely data for identifying' the source, destination, time, duration, type of equipment used, location of the communication, and data concerning unsuccessful call attempts. Any official who fell, as defined by each Member State, under the wide remit of 'competent national authorities' could then seek access to this communications data.[9] These designated public bodies could also have sought access to the communications data of any individual within the EU retained under the Directive given the ongoing growth between Member States in international cooperation and mutual assistance in criminal matters.[10] Consequently, Directive 2006/24/EC provided Member States with significant discretion regarding the scope of access and subsequent processing that could be applied to the communications data retained therein.

The Directive also included several measures concerning data security, oversight mechanisms, and evaluation of the Directive's transposition.[11] This meant that Member States were required to designate a supervisory authority to monitor CSPs to ensure that data protection principles were adhered to in the security of retained data. Under Article 13, Member States were to ensure that the conditions providing for judicial remedies, liability, and sanctions, as set out under the principal Data Protection Directive 95/46/EC, were also fully implemented.[12] Regarding evaluation, Article 10 of Directive 2006/24/EC required each Member State to provide the European Commission with statistical analysis with respect to the impact of the Directive's national implementation annually. These statistics were to include cases in which information was provided to the competent authorities, the time elapsed between the date on which the data was retained and the date on which the competent authorities requested the data, and cases where requests for data could not be met. The Commission was then required to submit to the European Parliament and the Council an evaluation of the implementation of the Directive no later than 15 September 2010.[13] This assessment would consider the statistical information provided by the Member States with a view to determining whether the provisions of the Directive warranted reform. In undertaking the evaluation, the Commission was required to give special regard to the necessity of altering the period of retention or the nature of the data to be retained. The results would then be made public. Like the widely defined scope of access that was left to

[8] ibid Arts 1(2), 3(2), and 5.

[9] ibid Art 4.

[10] Laura Ferola, 'The Fight Against Organised Crime in Europe: Building an Area of Freedom, Security and Justice in the European Union' (2002) 30 International Journal of Legal Information 53.

[11] Data Retention Directive, Arts 7 and 9.

[12] Directive 95/46/EC of the European Parliament and of the Council of 24 October 1995 on the protection of individuals with regard to the processing of personal data and on the free movement of such data [1995] OJ L281/31 (Data Protection Directive).

[13] Data Retention Directive, Art 14(1).

the interpretation of Member States, the data security and oversight provisions of Directive 2006/24/EC were also based on very broad and general standards.

On the one hand, the wide breath of these provisions accorded Member States a considerable level of discretion. On the other hand, this imprecise and vague framework effectively left Member States with little guidance regarding what safeguards to adopt when implementing the Directive into national law. This aspect of the legal regime is curious given its conflict with the notably clear mandate made in the recitals of Directive 2006/24/EC to protect the private lives and personal data of the 500 million EU citizens affected by the Directive.[14] As was expressly provided in recital 9 of the Directive, the 'adoption of an instrument on data retention that complies with the requirements of Article 8 of the ECHR is . . . a necessary measure'. Like the e-Privacy Directive 2002/58/EC,[15] the stated overall aim underpinning the framework of the Data Retention Directive was also to establish a 'European wide harmonization of legislation on retention of traffic data which balances in a proportionate manner the needs of law enforcement, the fundamental rights of the citizens and the interests of the electronic communications industry'.[16] The scope of Directive 2006/24/EC, however, then departed from the e-Privacy Directive in achieving this objective in three major ways.

2. Data Retention Directive diverges from the e-Privacy Directive 2002/58/EC

First, the Data Retention Directive imposed a mandatory obligation on Member States to require private CSPs to retain the communications data of their customers for law enforcement purposes. This mandatory requirement immediately distinguished Directive 2006/24/EC from the *voluntary* communications data retention regime provided for under Article 15 of the e-Privacy Directive.[17] Secondly, the Data Retention Directive specified that the period of retention imposed by each Member States must be no shorter than six month but no longer than two years. In stark contrast, the e-Privacy Directive contains no limitations regarding the duration of data retention that Member States may adopt. Under Article 6 of Directive 2006/24/EC, CSPs were required to retain traffic and location data related to

[14] Eurostat, 'EU27 population 501 million at 1 January 2010', News release, No 110/2010, 27 July 2010.

[15] Directive 2002/58/EC of the European Parliament and of the Council of 12 July 2002 concerning the processing of personal data and the protection of privacy in the electronic communications sector [2002] OJ L201/37 (e-Privacy Directive).

[16] Commission of the EC, 'Annex to the Extended Impact Assessment: Proposal for a Directive of the European Parliament and of the Council on the retention of data processed in connection with the provision of public electronic communication services and amending Directive 2002/58/EC', COM (2005) 438 final, 21 September 2005, 7 (Commission Impact Assessment).

[17] On the background and widespread criticism of Art 15 of Directive 2002/58/EC, see Chapter 6.

telephone calls, online and offline text messaging, Internet access, Internet telephony, and emails for a period of six months to two years, depending on the discretion of the relevant Member State. Furthermore, Member States were permitted to extend the upper maximum period of retention beyond two years 'if facing particular circumstances that warrant an extension'.[18]

Any Member State that availed itself of this extension was then required to notify and explain the necessity for this action to the Commission and other Member States. Thirdly, the scope of purposes for which data could be retained under the 2006 Directive was far more limited than the e-Privacy Directive. The voluntary data retention under the 2002 Directive allows Member States to require CSPs to retain communications data in order 'to safeguard national security (i.e. State security), defence, public security, and the prevention, investigation, detection and prosecution of criminal offences or of unauthorised use of the electronic communication system'.[19] Under Directive 2006/24/EC, these purposes were limited to the investigation, detection, and prosecution of serious crime. This narrower scope was largely the result of one of the few successful amendments proposed by the European Parliament during the rushed drafting process of the Data Retention Directive.[20] Consequently, some views suggested that the Data Retention Directive did not 'embody a total indifference towards individual privacy'[21] and others went so far as to describe it 'as a positive experience' for the protection of EU fundamental rights.[22]

However, like the drafting stage, much concern surrounded the shortcomings of Directive 2006/24/EC with respect to human rights standards following its entry into force, particularly the extent of the Directive's explicit commitment to Article 8 ECHR. First, the ambiguity surrounding the broad scope of categories of communications data and the notion of 'serious crime' provided under the Data Retention Directive prompted questions regarding the exact scope of information to be retained and the particular crimes to which the Directive would be applied. Initially, the private sector was uncertain whether search queries, and detailed logs of personal data generated through Internet search engine usage, fell within the scope of the Directive. Including this type of data would have dramatically expanded the application of the data retention regime and its intrusion into citizens' private lives given that 'an individual's search history contains a footprint of that person's interests, relations, and intentions'.[23]

[18] Data Retention Directive, Art 12(1).

[19] On the broad scope of exemptions to EU data protection rights and obligations permitted under Art 15 of Directive 2002/58/EC, see further Chapter 6.

[20] ibid.

[21] See eg Christiana Markou, 'The Cyprus and Other EU Court Rulings on Data Retention' (2012) 28 Computer Law and Security Review 468, 470.

[22] Francesca Bignami, 'Privacy and Law Enforcement in the European Union' (2007) 8 Chicago Journal of International Law 233, 255.

[23] Article 29 Working Party, 'Opinion 1/2008 on data protection issues related to search engines' (WP 148) 7. See further Chapter 1.

Data protection authorities also contended early on in the transposition stage that the application of the Data Retention Directive did not extend to search queries as the personal data involved constitutes 'content rather than traffic data'.[24] Regarding the concept of serious crime, scholars raised concerns that the lack of any definition would result in very broad interpretations from the Member States and therefore a complete lack of consistency with respect to the implementation of the scope of the Directive throughout the EU.[25] Furthermore, as is the settled case law of the ECtHR, the mere retention of personal data can amount to an interference with the right to respect for private life under Article 8(1) ECHR.[26] In addition, the legality test of Article 8(2) specifically provides that any such interferences must provide protection against arbitrary interference with an individual's rights under Article 8 ECHR and must be sufficiently clear and precise.[27] It was thus already then highly questionable whether the provision of the bald term of serious crime overcame the legality hurdle of Article 8 ECHR.

Secondly, allowing Member States to require that CSPs retain the communications data specified under the Directive for up to two years raised major concerns. Previously, service providers within the EU stored this personal data for six months on average for billing purposes.[28] Exceptions to this approach would only have arisen for reasons of national security or serious crime.[29] This practice complied with one of the key principles mandated under the principal Data Protection Directive that prohibits the collection of data beyond the duration necessary to fulfil the relevant purposes of data collection.[30] Following the enactment of the Data Retention Directive in 2006, retaining this personal data for longer than six months was no longer the exception. Furthermore, no empirical evidence was put forward by any of the EU institutions to justify such a significant departure from the established practice under the voluntary retention regime of the 2002 e-Privacy Directive. Even the Impact Assessment Report prepared by the European Commission in 2005, which served as the basis for proposing the Data Retention Directive, indicated that an upper maximum limit of *one year* would be appropriate.[31]

As observed in the Report, 'a longer retention period would appear to be of little added value for law enforcement authorities while having important financial consequences for operators and [would] infringe disproportionately on citizens'

[24] ibid 12.

[25] Eleni Kosta and Peggy Valcke, 'Retaining the Data Retention Directive' (2006) 22 Computer Law and Security Report 370, 374.

[26] *Amann v Switzerland* [2000] ECHR 87. See further Chapter 3. The CJEU would later adopt the same standard in its data retention case law. See further Chapters 5 and 9.

[27] *Khan v United Kingdom* (2001) 31 EHRR 1016.

[28] Billy Hawkes, 'The Data Retention Directive and Data Protection' (Privacy and Data Retention Directive Conference, Irish Centre for European Law (ICEL), Dublin, 19 July 2006).

[29] ibid.

[30] Data Protection Directive, Art 6(1).

[31] Commission Impact Assessment (n 16).

privacy'.[32] Finally, while Member States were allowed to increase the upper maximum limit of retention to more than two years, they were *not* permitted to reduce the lower limit of the retention period mandated under the Directive. This restriction clearly clashes with the express aim of the Directive to comply with the principle of proportionality. Consequently, Member States were prevented from ensuring that the Directive did not go beyond what was necessary to achieve the harmonization of the retention of certain data by the private sector for the purpose of the investigation, detection, and prosecution of serious crime. As a result, the scope of retention mandated by the Directive unquestionably undermined the express commitment made under the legislation to comply with the condition of proportionality guaranteed by Article 8 ECHR.[33]

Thirdly, uncertainty still surrounded the purpose of the Data Retention Directive even after its entry into force. As provided under Article 1 of the Directive, the application of the data retention regime was concerned with tackling serious crime. This aim could only be fully served through public authorities accessing the data retained pursuant to the Directive. Therefore, the focus of Article 4 of Directive 2006/24/EC concerned competent national authorities and their accessing of communications data. Article 4 explicitly specified that any access to communications data retained under the Directive must have been in compliance with the ECHR. Furthermore, when implementing the procedures governing this data processing, Article 4 mandated that the measures adopted by Member States must have complied with the necessity and proportionality requirements of EU law and 'in particular the ECHR as interpreted by the European Court of Human Rights'. However, as highlighted by the Article 29 Working Party in a critical opinion following the Directive's entry into force in 2006, Article 4 still lacked adequate and specific safeguards with respect to the access and processing of the communications data by public authorities.[34] Subsequently, in a significant judgment upholding the legal validity of the Directive, the CJEU clarified in 2009 that the Directive was 'essentially limited to the activities of service providers and [did] not govern access to data or the use thereof by the police or judicial authorities of the Member States'.[35]

This reasoning may appear curious at first glance. However, limiting the main purpose of the Directive to the imposition of a mandatory duty on Member States in order to harmonize the retention of communications data for internal market reasons enabled the EU legislature to impose a mandatory data retention regime on Member States under the legal framework of a data protection directive.[36] The EU legislature would then have run the risk of jeopardizing the internal market

[32] ibid.
[33] Data Retention Directive, recital 9.
[34] Article 29 Working Party, 'Opinion 3/2006 on the Data Retention Directive' (WP 119) 2.
[35] Case C-301/06 *Ireland v Parliament and Council* [2009] ECR I-00593 [80] (GC).
[36] On the legal basis of the Directive, see further Chapter 4.

justification for the Directive if detailed safeguards governing the access and subsequent processing of the retained data by law enforcement authorities were mandated under the EU framework. Accordingly, the ECJ may instead have upheld the challenge to the legal basis of the Directive in such circumstances.[37] Perhaps unsurprisingly, the dearth of these adequate and specific safeguards provided under the Directive with respect to the access and processing of data and, by extension, within the national laws implementing the Directive, arguably proved to be its 'Achilles heel'.[38] As will be discussed, Article 8 ECHR, and the related case law of the ECtHR, would play a significant role in the response of the national courts towards the question of the Data Retention Directive's compliance with human rights standards.

C. A Troubled Transposition

The implementation of the Data Retention Directive into national legislation across the EU proved difficult for two main reasons. The first hurdle concerned the inconsistent implementation, or complete lack thereof, by Member States that had until 15 September 2007 to implement the Directive,[39] with several Member States making use of the 'considerable leeway' provided under Article 15(3) of the Directive to postpone the application of their implementation legislation to Internet access, Internet telephony, and email until 15 March 2009.[40] Despite the significant scope made available for implementation, the European Commission still had to undertake enforcement action against several Member States that had failed to transpose the Directive following the extended deadline.[41] The second major obstacle in the path of the Directive's implementation was the striking down of the national laws transposing the EU legislation by several national constitutional courts. Most of these judgments were primarily concerned with the constitutionality of the national legal provisions governing the access to, and subsequent processing of, the data retained pursuant to the Data Retention Directive. However, two of these judgments directly criticized the Directive itself. Two constitutional challenges would also result in a joined preliminary reference to the CJEU regarding the compliance of the Directive with EU fundamental rights and Article 8 ECHR.[42]

[37] Konstadinides (n 5) 728.

[38] ibid.

[39] Data Retention Directive, Art 15.

[40] Commission Evaluation Report (n 6) 31.

[41] Case C-211/09 *European Commission v Hellenic Republic* 2009 ECR I-00204*; Case C-202/09 *European Commission v Ireland* [2009] ECR I-00203*; Case C-185/09 *European Commission v Kingdom of Sweden* [2010] ECR I-00014*.

[42] Previously referred to as the ECJ before the entry into force of the Lisbon Treaty on 1 December 2009. In 2024, the European Parliament and Council had approved the adoption of a draft Regulation that would now allow certain preliminary references to go to the General Court (the second-tier

1. Rejection by the national courts and the role of Article 8

Several constitutional challenges across the EU highlighted the lack of compatibility of both the Data Retention Directive and the national laws implementing the Directive with Article 8 ECHR. The first challenge to the implementation stage of the Directive involved the national data retention regime of Bulgaria and Article 8 ECHR. In 2008, the Bulgarian Supreme Administrative Court overturned a lower court judgment and held that certain provisions from the national legislation transposing the Directive were in violation of Article 8 ECHR.[43] The Court referred explicitly to Article 8 ECHR in its assessment and held that the impugned provisions governing the passive access (without judicial authorization) to communications data from Internet-based messaging and telephone calls retained for up to one year by law enforcement purposes and national security contradicted the legality safeguards of Article 8 ECHR due to their lack of limitations and guarantees for the protection of the right to privacy. In particular, the Court stressed that such legislation must comply with the established principles of Article 8 ECHR that require comprehensible and clear grounds to govern both the access to the personal data and the procedures for its subsequent storage. Thus, the transposing measure failed to meet the accessibility and foreseeability tests required under the legality condition of Article 8(2) ECHR. Accordingly, the Court held that this unjustified interference was in violation of the right to respect for private life as guaranteed by Article 8 ECHR, the Data Retention Directive, and Articles 32 and 34 of the Bulgarian Constitution. This judicial review subsequently resulted in a revision of this specific part of the transposing law.[44] A second challenge to the implementation stage of the Directive also arose in 2008 when the Hungarian Civil Liberties Union (HCLU) filed a complaint to the Hungarian Constitutional Court concerning the compatibility of the Hungarian legislation implementing the Data Retention Directive with fundamental rights.[45] By the time that the European Commission's Evaluation Report of the Directive was published in 2011, these court proceedings were still pending.[46]

appeals court of the EU). See Council of the EU, 'Reform of the Statute of the Court of Justice adopted', Press release, 19 March 2024, <https://consilium.europa.eu/en/press/press-releases/2024/03/19/reform-of-the-statute-of-the-court-of-justice-adopted/>.

[43] Bulgarian Supreme Administrative Court, Decision No 13627, 11 December 2008, only available in Bulgarian. The following analysis is based on commentary of the judgment by the Bulgarian privacy NGO (AIP) which filed the complaint, <http://www.aip-bg.org/documents/data_retention_campaign_eng.htm>.

[44] Commission Evaluation Report (n 6) 21.

[45] Constitutional Complaint Filed by HCLU Against Hungarian Telecom Data Retention Regulations, 2 June 2008, <http://tasz.hu/en/data-protection/constitutional-complaint-filed-hclu-against-hungarian-telecom-data-retention>.

[46] Subsequently, however, a new Constitution was adopted in Hungary which entered into force in 2012 and included the abolition of the complaint procedure (*actio popularis*) relied on by the HCLU in bringing this challenge. Consequently, this resulted in the termination of the HCLU complaint.

In 2009, Article 8 ECHR was instrumental again in the mounting number of challenges being brought against the transposition of the Directive, including the Directive itself. The Romanian Constitutional Court was particularly critical of the national legislation implementing the Directive and the general concept of indiscriminate and systematic data retention and clearly relied more on the case law of the ECHR than that of the EU.[47] Both the scope and conditions of Article 8 ECHR were engaged with at length in the examination of the national data retention regime. First, the Court held that the retention of data that determines the 'date, hour and length of the phone call or electronic communication ... the type of phone call ... the device ... the location of the communication device' and the 'related data' necessary to identify the subscriber or registered use of the relevant communication service fell under the protected interest of private life.[48] Therefore the Court concluded that the right to private life, as guaranteed by Article 8 ECHR, applied as the concept 'necessarily implies the secrecy' of correspondence that 'expresses the links a person may establish in different ways of communication, with other members of society, so this includes both telephonic calls and electronic communications'.[49]

Secondly, after observing the 'ambiguous manner of drafting' within the provisions of the national legislation, the court highlighted the importance of the legality test under Article 8(2) ECHR.[50] The court stressed that any legal ambiguity opened up the possibility for abuses in the retention, use, and processing of the data stored by the service providers. In support of this analysis, the court relied on the foreseeability test from the ECtHR judgment of *Rotaru v Romania*.[51] Thirdly, the Court took issue with the indiscriminate nature of the retention regime mandated by the Data Retention Directive in its examination of the proportionality of the national legislation. Specifically, the court observed that the regime transformed 'all users of electronic communication services or public communication networks into people susceptible of committing terrorism crimes or other serious crimes'.[52] On the systematic nature of the data processing, the Court stated

See Katalin Kelemen, 'The Hungarian Constitutional Court in the new constitutional framework' (Conference paper, III Colloquio biennale dei giovani comparatisti, Italian Association of Comparative Law, Aosta, 28–29 June 2012).

[47] Judgment of the Romanian Constitutional Court 1258, 8 October 2009, only available in Romanian. The following analysis is based on a translation of the judgment by Bogdan Manolea and Anca Argesiu, <https://www.eff.org/files/filenode/dataretention/www.legiinternet.ro_fileadmin_editor_folder_pdf_decision-constitutional-court-romania-data-retention.pdf.pdf> (Judgment of the Romanian Constitutional Court). See further Ludovica Benedizione and Eleonora Paris, 'Preliminary Reference and Dialogue Between Courts as Tools for Reflection on the EU System of Multilevel Protection of Rights' (2019) 16 German Law Journal 1727.

[48] Judgment of the Romanian Constitutional Court, 3.

[49] ibid.

[50] ibid 6.

[51] ibid 6.

[52] ibid 9.

that '[t]he legal obligation that foresees the continuous retention of personal data transforms ... the exception from the principle of the effective protection of privacy ... into an absolute rule'.[53]

Furthermore, the Court held that the excessive scope of the national data retention framework and the insufficient legal safeguards to oversee the use of the retained data was 'sufficient to generate' legitimate suspicion regarding respect of private life and the perpetration of abuses.[54] In support of this critical assessment, the Court relied again on the case law of the ECtHR. The Court cited *Klass v Germany*, one of the landmark judgments of the Strasbourg Court on the dangers posed by covert surveillance, and stated 'that taking surveillance measures without adequate and sufficient safeguards can lead to destroying democracy on the ground of defending it'.[55] Although not cited, the stark proportionality assessment of the Romanian Court echoes the condemnation by the Grand Chamber of the ECtHR in the leading judgment of *S and Marper* where the 'blanket and indiscriminate' indefinite retention of DNA materials of all individuals (including juveniles) suspected of criminal conduct was held to have violated Article 8 ECHR.[56] Ultimately, the Court held that the national law was incompatible with both the ECHR and the Romanian Constitution.

Notably, the Romanian Constitutional Court referred to the Data Retention Directive itself in its examination of the national law transposing the Directive. Specifically, the court highlighted the lack of clarity provided under the scope of the Directive regarding the subsequent use by Member States of the data retained pursuant to the Directive. This broad scope, the court observed, consequently provided Member States with a wide margin of discretion on how to interpret and apply the relevant requirement imposed by the EU legislation.[57] However, in its critical assessment of the national framework's proportionality, the reference of the national court to the 'legal obligation that foresees the continuous retention of personal data' also clearly concerns the mandatory duty of data retention that the Directive has imposed on Member States.[58] Furthermore, the implementing law in Romania was struck down despite having the shortest possible retention period permitted by the Data Retention Directive. In other words, the Court effectively indicated that one of the main provisions of the Directive (namely, Art 6 which provides for the mandatory scope of retention) would have to be amended in order to address the Article 8 ECHR concerns raised by the Court.[59] Therefore the judgment goes beyond criticizing the implementation framework and instead

53 ibid 7.
54 ibid 10.
55 ibid 10.
56 *S and Marper v United Kingdom* (2009) 48 EHRR 1169 [119] (GC).
57 Judgment of the Romanian Constitutional Court, 4.
58 ibid 7.
59 Cian Murphy, 'Romanian Constitutional Court, Decision No 1258 of 8 October 2009' (2009) 47 Common Market Law Review 933, 939.

questions the validity of the data retention system mandated by the EU as a whole.[60] A number of commentators interpreted the strong stance of the Romanian Constitutional Court against the blanket and systematic six-month retention of communications data as tantamount to 'a frontal attack' on the Directive.[61]

Finally, in 2009, one of the applicants (the Slovak Republic) seeking to annul the Directive in proceedings before the Grand Chamber of the CJEU, on account of its legal basis, raised the compatibility of the scope of retention mandated by the Directive with the requirements of Article 8 ECHR.[62] The applicants, Ireland and the Slovak Republic, contended that the main purpose of the Directive was to fight serious crimes and therefore constituted a 'third pillar' legislative measure (a framework decision) as opposed to a 'first pillar' measure (a Regulation or Directive). Ultimately, the judgment did not deal with any fundamental rights issues concerning the principle of data retention on the ground that such an assessment was irrelevant to the adoption of the Directive's legal basis, the main issue of the proceedings. The CJEU determined that the predominant aim of the Directive was to harmonize the internal market and not the fight against serious crime.[63] The challenges to the legal basis of the Directive by Ireland and the Slovak Republic were consequently unsuccessful. Nevertheless, a national court would soon thereafter grant a preliminary reference application under Article 267 TFEU requiring the CJEU to review the Directive and its compliance with Article 8 ECHR.

The year 2010 was notable with respect to the Data Retention Directive's ongoing troubled transposition and for the impact of Article 8 ECHR on the future of its existence within the EU legal order. Regarding the former, the Federal Constitutional Court of Germany (Bundesverfassungsgericht) held that the national legislation implementing the Directive was in violation of the German Constitution—this was in response to a constitutional complaint, supported by 30,000 complainants, seeking the immediate suspension of the national law.[64] While its judgment contained no explicit mention of Article 8 ECHR, the Bundesverfassungsgericht's approach to its considerably critical examination of the national legislation implementing the Directive invoked the jurisprudence of the Strasbourg Court.[65]

60 ibid.

61 Katja de Vries and others, 'The German Constitutional Court Judgment on Data Retention' in Serge Gutwirth and others (eds), *Computers, Privacy and Data Protection* (Springer 2011) 15; Markou (n 21) 474.

62 *Parliament and Council* (n 35). See further Ester Herlin-Karnell, 'Case C-301/06, *Ireland* v *Parliament and Council*' (2009) 46 Common Market Law Review 1667.

63 On the significant shift of the CJEU towards a rights-based approach in its data retention case law, see Chapters 5 and 9.

64 German Federal Constitutional Court, Decision of 2 March 2010 (1 BvR 256/08 1 BvR 263/08 1 BvR 286/08). See further Anna-Bettina Kaiser, 'German Federal Constitutional Court: Data Retention Provisions Unconstitutional in their Present Form' (2010) 6 European Constitutional Law Review 503; Christian DeSimone, 'Pitting Karlsruhe Against Luxembourg? German Data Protection and the Contested Implementation of the EU Data Retention Directive' (2010) 11 German Law Journal 291.

65 De Vries and others (n 61) 3. On the relevant case law of the ECtHR, see Chapters 2 and 3.

Like the two-stage examination undertaken by the ECtHR in assessing whether there has been a violation of Article 8 ECHR, the Bundesverfassungsgericht began its analysis with the determination that the retention of data for six months constituted 'a particularly serious encroachment' to the secrecy of telecommunications, protected under Article 10 of the German Constitution (Basic Law for the Federal Republic of Germany). In other words, to use the jurisprudence of the ECtHR regarding Article 8(1) ECHR, the impugned data retention measure amounted to an 'interference' with the 'protected interest' of the secrecy of telecommunications as the retained information in question could be 'used to draw content-related conclusions that extend into the user's private sphere'.[66]

Like the Romanian Constitutional Court, the Bundesverfassungsgericht took particular issue with the threats to privacy posed by the blanket and indiscriminate scope of the national retention regime and the proportionality of the requisite safeguards provided therein. The Bundesverfassungsgericht stressed that the breath of such long-term storage facilitated the creation of 'meaningful personality profiles of virtually all citizens' and the tracking of their movements.[67] This monitoring also increased the risk of citizens being exposed to criminal investigations without themselves having given occasion for this.[68] While the Bundesverfassungsgericht held that six months was an acceptable retention period for enabling effective criminal prosecutions given the 'special significance of telecommunication in the modern world', it held that four other key elements of the national retention regime did not satisfy the principle of proportionality as guaranteed under the Germany Constitution.[69] Of the remaining issues, the Bundesverfassungsgericht primarily criticized the absence of any requirement in the legislation for the private sector to ensure particularly high technical standards regarding data security. These standards should have included a robust system of encryption, separate storage for the relevant data, and audit-proof recordings of data access and deletion.

Furthermore, the national regime provided no balanced system of sanctions for data security violations.[70] The remaining three issues concerned the overly broad provisions governing the purposes for which the national retention regime could be used, the transparency of this processing, and the applicable legal safeguards. One particular provision within the national retention regime greatly exceeded the scope required under the Directive by providing that the retained communications data could be used to investigate any criminal offence that had involved any type of telecommunications. The Bundesverfassungsgericht pointed out the dramatically enlarged scope afforded by such a disproportionate provision: 'in view of the increasing importance of telecommunications in everyday life, the use of these

[66] Judgment of the Bundesverfassungsgericht (n 64) 5.
[67] ibid 6.
[68] ibid 6.
[69] ibid 6.
[70] ibid 13.

data loses its exceptional character'.[71] Subsequently, the Bundesverfassungsgericht held that the national legislation had gone 'far beyond the objective of data storage' specified by the Directive by not ensuring that the relevant communications data would only be used for serious criminal offences.[72] This ultimately resulted, as DeSimone observes, in the Court finding 'a middle path',[73] where the mandated provisions of the Data Retention Directive were left unchallenged but the elements of the German implementation legislation that exceeded the terms of the Directive were annulled until brought in line with German constitutional requirements.[74]

2. *Digital Rights Ireland*: preliminary references made by Ireland and Austria

In contrast to the *Solange II*-driven approach by the Bundesverfassungsgericht where the need to refer to the CJEU regarding the validity of the Data Retention Directive within the EU legal order was considered irrelevant to the proceedings,[75] another national court held otherwise shortly thereafter. In May 2010, the High Court of Ireland granted a preliminary reference application to the CJEU under Article 267 TFEU concerning whether the Data Retention Directive violated Irish citizens' rights to privacy and communications.[76] The CJEU would now finally be required to review the validity of the Directive based on its compliance with fundamental rights standards. The complaint before the Irish High Court alleged that both the Directive and the national legislation transposing the Directive had resulted in illegal processing and data storage contrary to Article 8 ECHR.[77] Like the Romanian Constitutional Court, the judgment of the Irish court included explicit references to Article 8 ECHR and the case law of the ECtHR. First, the Court acknowledged the qualified nature of the right to respect for private life guaranteed

[71] ibid 13.
[72] ibid 13.
[73] It is noteworthy that another national court in Germany, the Administrative Court of Wiesbaden, had already initiated a dialogue with the CJEU on the validity of the Data Retention Directive in a preliminary reference dealing with a very different type of EU legislation concerning the publication of information on beneficiaries of EU agricultural aid. The dialogue was brief and resulted in the CJEU deeming this novel question concerning the Directive to be inadmissible: see Joined Cases C-92/09 and C-93/09 *Volker und Markus Schecke and Eifert*, judgment of 9 November 2010 (ECLI:EU:C:2010:662).
[74] See DeSimone (n 64) 316.
[75] ibid. On the *Solange II* doctrine, see Chapter 4. Streinz attributes the years of avoiding preliminary references on data retention to the CJEU to competition between the Germany Constitutional Court and the CJEU with regard to the former's significant role in shaping Germany's data protection role, particularly the right to self-determination: see Thomas Streinz, 'The Europeanization of Data Protection Law' in Paul Craig and Gráinne de Búrca, *The Evolution of EU Law* (3rd edn, OUP 2021) 911. The national court would eventually directly engage with the CJEU on the matter of data retention law via a preliminary reference in Joined Cases C-793/19 and C-794/19 *SpaceNet and Deutsche Telekom*, judgment of 20 September 2022 (ECLI:EU:C:2022:702) (GC).
[76] *Digital Rights Ireland Ltd v Minister for Communications* (2010) 3 IR 251 [115] (McKechnie J).
[77] ibid [13].

by Article 8 ECHR. Following references to the leading ECtHR judgments regarding Article 8 ECHR and covert monitoring in *Klass v Germany* and *Malone v United Kingdom*, the court then stressed that any interference with this right must satisfy Article 8(2) ECHR.[78] The impugned surveillance measure must therefore be subject to adequate and effective guarantees against abuse.

Again, like the Romanian Constitutional Court, the Irish High Court proceeded by referring to the pertinent passage of *Klass* concerning the danger posed by disproportionate State surveillance powers exercised in secret 'of undermining or even destroying democracy on the ground of defending it'.[79] Notably, the Irish court also relied on *Copland* in determining that the storage of communications data required under the Data Retention Directive constituted an interference with Article 8 ECHR.[80] This was the most relevant judgment of the ECtHR concerning the scope of the Directive given that the focus of *Copland* was the application of Article 8 ECHR to both the use and retention of communications data by public authorities derived from telephone calls and emails. Ultimately, the High Court held that the complaint brought by an Irish privacy NGO (Digital Rights Ireland) concerning the Directive and the national law implementing the Directive had 'raised matters of fundamental public importance' and therefore granted *locus standi* to fully litigate the alleged human rights infringements as part of an *actio popularis*.[81] Furthermore, the Court concluded that the issues identified 'all relate to the validity of Directive 2006/24/EC, in particular with rights under the EU and EC Treaties, the [Charter of Fundamental Rights] and the ECHR'.[82] EU law provides that national courts of Member States are unable to rule on the validity of EU legislation and therefore cannot review a directive.[83] Accordingly, the Irish High Court held that a reference to the CJEU under Article 267 TFEU was required in order for these issues to be addressed.[84]

Two further judgments that highlighted the overall difficult implementation of the Data Retention Directive were delivered before the publication of the Commission's evaluation on the matter in 2011. The first was by the Supreme Court of Cyprus. This judgment only dealt with the measures introduced to transpose the Directive into the national law, not the Directive itself.[85] The Cypriot Supreme

[78] ibid [70].
[79] ibid [70].
[80] ibid [72].
[81] ibid [90]–[93].
[82] ibid [109].
[83] Case C-314/85 *Foto-Frost v Hauptzollamt Lübeck-Ost* [1987] ECR 4199.
[84] The questions from the Irish High Court were referred to the CJEU on 27 January 2012 and joined with a subsequent preliminary reference from the Constitutional Court of Austria. See further Chapter 8.
[85] Supreme Court of Cyprus, Decision of civil applications 65/2009, 78/2009 and 15/2010-22/2010 of 1 February 2011 (only available in Greek) (Judgment of the Supreme Court of Cyprus). A case summary by digital rights NGO EDRI is available at <https://edri.org/edrigramnumber9-3data-retention-un-lawful-cyprus/>.

Court made no reference to the issue of long-term retention and focused solely on the access by law enforcement authorities to the retained communications data.[86] The scope of review involved in this particular national judgment was comparatively quite narrow as it only concerned the possible annulment of four district court orders in very specific circumstances. This distinguished the judgment of the Cypriot court from those by the national courts in other Member States that were required to adjudicate on constitutional complaints with respect to all the national provisions transposing the Directive. The Court here was instead confined to the restricted field of the four *certiorari* orders before it.[87] Three of these applications were held to be unconstitutional on the ground that at the relevant time access to communications data retained under the transposed provisions only applied to the communications of individuals in prison. Accordingly, the Court held that within this limited legal context the specific provisions concerning the transmission and access to the data by law enforcement authorities were in violation of the right to secrecy of communications as guaranteed under Cypriot constitutional law.[88]

In March 2011, the Constitutional Court of the Czech Republic delivered a far more striking judgment that addressed both the national legislation transposing the Data Retention Directive and the Directive itself.[89] Regarding its assessment of the national data retention regime, like several national courts before it, the Constitutional Court engaged at length with the principles and conditions of Article 8 ECHR and the related case law of the Strasbourg Court.[90] In particular, the Court invoked the proportionality jurisprudence from the leading ECtHR judgment of *S and Marper* regarding the minimum safeguards that must underpin any measure of systematic personal data processing to ensure against the misuse and abuse of such information by the State.[91] The necessity to have such guarantees, the Constitutional Court stressed (mirroring the settled Art 8 ECHR case law of the ECtHR), is 'even higher' when the protection of personal data is subject to 'automatic processing, especially when such data is used for police purposes and at a time when available technology becomes more and more sophisticated'.[92] Like the Romanian Constitutional Court and the Bundesverfassungsgericht, while the focus of the instant court's judgment concerned the national legislative framework

[86] Markou (n 21) 472.

[87] ibid 474.

[88] ibid.

[89] Czech Constitutional Court, Decision of 22 March 2011, Pl ÚS 24/10, <www.usoud.cz/en/decisions/2011-03-22-pl-us-24-10-data-retention-in-telecommunications-services>. See Pavel Molek, 'Czech Constitutional Court Unconstitutionality of the Czech Implementation of the Data Retention Directive' (2012) 8 European Constitutional Law Review 338.

[90] Czech Constitutional Court (n 89) [31]–[40] (citing *Klass v Germany* [1978] 2 EHRR 214; *Malone v United Kingdom* (1985) 7 EHRR 14; *Leander v Sweden* (1987) 9 EHRR 433; *Weber and Saravia v Germany* (App No 54934/00) 29 June 2006; *Liberty v United Kingdom* (2009) 48 EHRR 1).

[91] *Marper* (n 56).

[92] Czech Constitutional Court (n 89) [40].

implementing the Directive,[93] the Court was also particularly critical of the threats to private life posed by the long-term retention of communications data. It observed that the contested type of monitoring could lead to the compiling of 'detailed information on social or political profiles, as well as personal preferences, inclinations and weaknesses of individuals'.[94]

The Czech Constitutional Court did not expressly engage with Article 8 ECHR in the final stage of its assessment of the national data retention framework. However, like the two-stage examination undertaken by the ECtHR in determining whether there has been a violation of Article 8 ECHR, the national court held that the retention of communications data represents a serious infringement of the right to respect for private life. In assessing whether this interference was justified, the Court held that its review would have to be subject to the highest standards given that the impugned measure involved the 'universal and preventive collection and retention of data'.[95] The Court also observed the lack of any precise or clear definition identifying which particular public authorities were entitled to access the retained data. Furthermore, the national law was silent regarding the crimes or purposes for which the data could be used. In addition, the Court stressed the absence of any clear and detailed rules providing minimum safeguards for data security. Consequently, the Court stated that the dearth of such guarantees could, in practice, have resulted in the overuse of the retained data by public authorities. The vague and imprecise purposes for the use of the data also made it impossible to judge how far the contested provisions were 'actually necessary'.[96] Therefore the court held that the impugned national legislation transposing the Directive did not contain sufficient safeguards against the risk of data misuse and arbitrariness. Accordingly, the Court stated that the national law had clearly violated the fundamental right to privacy by failing to comply with the principle of proportionality as guaranteed by the Constitution of the Czech Republic.[97]

Finally, while making clear that the following observations were *obiter dicta*, the Czech Constitutional Court concluded its judgment with a detailed critique of the Directive itself. Principally, the national court expressed significant doubt regarding whether the Directive was a 'necessary and appropriate instrument' given its impact on the private lives of an 'enormous number of individuals involved in electronic communication'.[98] Specifically, the Court questioned whether the Directive could even be considered 'an efficient instrument' in the protection against national security threats and serious criminal activity based on two

[93] ibid [41]. These additional types of data included information related to the volume of data downloaded from the Internet and prepaid telephone card identification.
[94] Czech Constitutional Court (n 89) [44].
[95] ibid [45].
[96] ibid [47]–[49].
[97] ibid [53].
[98] ibid [55].

factors.[99] First, the Court noted the absence of data being retained with respect to anonymous SIM cards from the scope of the Directive. According to the law enforcement authorities in the Czech Republic, the Court stressed, these mobile telephony cards were involved in 70 per cent of communications related to engagement in serious crime. Secondly, the court referred to statistics from the Czech Republic and the Federal Criminal Police Office in Germany which concluded that the adoption of the respective data retention regimes in both Member States had had little impact on the reduction of serious crime. In emphasizing that the Court was not alone in its significant reservations towards the Directive, other notable critics were mentioned: 'Within the area of Europe, such opinion is by far not isolated since the Data Retention Directive itself has been heavily criticized from the very beginning of its existence by member states ... as well as legislators in the European Parliament.'[100]

This negative assessment of the Directive by the Czech Constitutional Court is striking for two main reasons. First, the unequivocal opposition of the Court to the 'universal and preventive' retention of communications data runs counter to the earlier assertion of the court that a preliminary reference application to the CJEU under Article 267 TFEU was unnecessary. At the beginning of its judgment, the Court held that the subject matter of the Directive 'leaves the Czech Republic enough possibilities to transpose it into the national law in conformity with the constitution'.[101] Secondly, the undertaking of such a review in and of itself effectively represents an indirect challenge to the supremacy of EU law. The national court appears to acknowledge this fact by explicitly highlighting that the analysis was *obiter dicta* and therefore did not form part of the judgment. Nevertheless, the approach of the Czech Constitutional Court also indicates that it would rather not pursue the matter further with the CJEU by beginning a dialogue through the preliminary reference application under Article 267 TFEU.

3. EU Directives and the national courts as guardians of fundamental rights

The restrictive *locus standi* rules under Article 263(4) TFEU (previously Art 230 EC),[102] which prevent any form of *actio popularis* at the EU level and otherwise make it difficult for natural and legal persons to challenge EU legislative measures,

99 ibid [56].
100 ibid [55].
101 ibid [25].
102 Case C-583/11 P *Inuit Tapiriit Kanatami*, 3 October 2013, nyr (GC). Unheeded calls for change to the restrictive rules established in Case 25/62 *Plaumann* [1963] ECR 95 were made to the ECJ in Opinion of AG Jacobs in Case C-50/00 P *UPA v Council* [2002] ECR I-6677 and in Case T-177/01 *Jégo Quéré v Commission* [2002] ECR II-2365.

have been the subject of much debate and criticism.[103] As a result, the only legal challenge at national level that can be brought in the case of an EU directive is against the domestic law that has implemented the provisions of a directive. However, the national courts can set up a dialogue with the Luxembourg Court *via* a preliminary reference, as provided for under Article 267 TFEU.[104] Moreover, a national court is required under EU law to refer to the CJEU any question concerning the interpretation of EU law unless it reaches the conclusion that the answer is 'so obvious as to leave no scope for any reasonable doubt as to the manner in which the question raised is to be resolved'.[105]

The CJEU has expressed that it considers this dialogue with the national courts of EU Member States to be of the utmost importance. Hence, in a narrow legal sense, preliminary references have had a 'critical impact' on the manner in which the national and EU legal systems communicate and engage with one another.[106] More broadly, the jurisprudential development of the preliminary reference process can be regarded as a 'historical record of legal integration' wherein the Luxembourg Court has delivered key case law that has defined the relationship between the EU and Member States (such as *Van Gend en Loos*, *Costa v ENEL*, *Pupino*).[107] It is therefore perhaps unsurprising that the CJEU has described the Article 267 TFEU procedure as the 'keystone' of the judicial system between the national courts and the CJEU that ensures 'the full application of EU law in all Member States and to ensure judicial protection of an individual's rights under that law'.[108]

The special judicial dialogue that results from this 'sharing of jurisdiction' between the CJEU and the national courts notwithstanding,[109] a generalized problem still prevails in the EU given that the legislative framework derived from directives by this method of implementation may lead to such challenges. In spite of this, the multi-level legal space across the EU created by the legislative cycle of directives (namely their implementation by Member States) results in some

[103] Paul Craig and Gráinne de Búrca, *EU Law* (5th edn, OUP 2011) 502–10. See further Albertina Albors-Llorens, 'The Standing of Private Parties to Challenge Community Measures: Has the European Court Missed the Boat?' (2003) 62 Cambridge Law Journal 72; Anthony Arnull, 'The Principle of Effective Judicial Protection in EU Law: An Unruly Horse?' (2011) 36 European Law Review 51; Niels Baeten and Pieter Van Malleghem, 'Before the Law Stands a Gatekeeper—Or, What is a "Regulatory Act" in Article 263(4) TFEU? *Inuit Tapiriit Kanatami*' (2014) 51 Common Market Law Review 51.

[104] On the preliminary reference process, see further Anthony Arnull, 'The UK Supreme Court and References to the CJEU' (2017) 36 Yearbook of European Law 314; Jasper Krommendijk, *National Courts and Preliminary References to the Court of Justice* (Elgar 2021); Marek Pivoda, 'Constitutional Courts Asking Questions' [2023] Cambridge Yearbook of European Legal Studies 1–20.

[105] Case 283/81 *CILFIT* [1982] ECR 3415 [16].

[106] Thomas de la Mara and Catherine Donnelly, 'Preliminary Rulings and EU Integration' in Craig and de Búrca (n 4) 363.

[107] ibid.

[108] Case C-432/05 *Unibet* [2007] ECR I-2271 [38] (GC); Opinion 1/09 [2011] ECR I-1137 [68]; Opinion 2/13 *Accession to the ECHR*, 18 December 2014, nyr [176].

[109] Francis G Jacobs, 'Judicial Dialogue and the Cross-Fertilization of Legal Systems' (2003) 38 Texas International Law Journal 547, 548.

discretion being left to national courts to apply domestic fundamental right guarantees. Furthermore, there will be instances where the national courts determine that there is no need to engage the CJEU in dialogue via the preliminary reference process due to the clarity of the issue in question. National courts have an important responsibility in ensuring the legal certainty of EU law and maintaining public confidence in EU law within national law while at the same time preventing the CJEU's 'already heavy caseload becoming over-loaded with references, and many more cases where the parties have to face the delay and expense of a reference'.[110] Accordingly, this has led the CJEU[111] and commentators to acknowledge the key role of national courts as guardians of European human rights and of the EU 'constitutional ecosystem'.[112] Notably, the review by national courts that is made possible by the legislative cycle of EU Directives enables the judicial branch of Member States to hold their executives on the EU Council to account for their part in developing EU laws and policies that raise both domestic and EU fundamental rights concerns.[113]

The above analysis shows that the national courts of EU Member States have contributed to a dialogue with the CJEU concerning the compatibility of the Data Retention Directive with fundamental rights within the judgments concerning challenges to the domestic laws at national level. However, more specifically, it shows this dialogue under pressure from national courts opting to exercise the opportunity (in direct conflict with *Foto-Frost*) to voice their criticism of an EU measure when they should have done so via the Article 267 TFEU mechanism. It is interesting to note the different approaches that the constitutional courts adopted in their review of the domestic laws that transposed the Directive. For instance, the Irish High Court chose to open a formal dialogue with the CJEU by referring to it the question of the Data Retention Directive's compatibility with the EU Charter of Fundamental Rights.[114] However, the national courts of two other Member States (Romania and the Czech Republic) opened up an informal dialogue, so to speak, with the CJEU by expressing considerable concerns regarding the Directive's compatibility with Article 8 ECHR and the relevant provisions of their own national constitutions. The reaction of the constitutional courts to the Directive through the indirect (and direct) criticism of the Data Retention Directive placed a strain on the keystone of the EU judicial order that is not conducive to a proper and constructive dialogue. Consequently, the only position left for the CJEU to respond and engage with the concerns expressed by the national courts was through the

[110] *R (HS2 Action Alliance Ltd) v Secretary of State for Transport and another* [2014] UKSC 3 [173]; Lord Reed, 'EU Law and the Supreme Court' (The Sir Thomas More Lecture, 12 November 2014) 12, <www.supremecourt.uk/docs/speech-141114.pdf>.

[111] Opinion 2/13 (n 108).

[112] Konstadinides (n 5) 736.

[113] ibid.

[114] The referral by the Austrian Constitutional Court followed the year after.

preliminary reference judgment it would deliver in response to the constitutional courts of Ireland and Austria. As is examined in detail in Chapter 8, the findings of this judgment convey that the CJEU was keenly aware of the need to respond to the national courts' reservations regarding the fundamental rights issues surrounding the EU Data Retention Directive, particularly its compatibility with Articles 7 and 8 CFR that incorporate the principles, conditions, and safeguards of Article 8 ECHR.

D. Article 8 ECHR and the National Courts

The reliance on Article 8 ECHR in the series of rejections by the national constitutional courts to the transposition stage of the Data Retention Directive, either directly (criticism of the Directive itself) or indirectly (the striking down of national legislation transposing the Directive), raises two significant implications. First, in addition to highlighting the procedural difficulties involved in the implementation of the Directive, these adverse judgments demonstrate the significant role that Article 8 ECHR, and the case law of the ECtHR, played during this challenging time for national courts with respect to the protection of human rights in Europe.[115] With the exception of Germany, all of the judgments that struck down the transposition of the Directive explicitly relied on the human rights standards of Article 8 ECHR regarding the right to respect for private life and the protection of personal data. Most of these national courts also engaged at length with the related case law of the ECtHR in their assessments of the national legislation (particularly Romania, the Czech Republic, and Ireland). Interestingly, although Member States, when implementing EU law, are bound by EU fundamental rights and the related jurisprudence of the ECJ,[116] these national judgments included no engagement with the EU Charter of Fundamental Rights.

The judgment of the Czech Constitutional Court is particularly notable in this regard. As demonstrated in its striking critique of the Directive in *obiter dicta*, the Court would rather align its resistance towards the overall framework of the Directive with the human rights standards of its own constitution and the international human rights standards guaranteed by Article 8 ECHR than entrust such a review to the CJEU. Hence, the stance adopted by the Czech Constitution Court in these circumstances casts considerable doubt over the EU and its protection of human rights. Moreover, the human rights concerns regarding the proportionality of the Directive raised by the national courts of Romania and the Czech Republic represented a threat to the longevity of the *Solange* doctrine (where national courts refrain from reviewing the compatibility of EU law with rights under national

[115] Konstadinides (n 5) 727.
[116] Case 5/88 *Wachauf* [1989] ECR 2609.

constitutions as long as the CJEU continues to protect fundamental rights adequately).[117] Several constitutional courts adhered to the doctrine by only striking down legislative provisions transposing the Directive. However, the courts of Romania and the Czech Republic departed from this approach in that they did not submit preliminary references to the CJEU but nevertheless raised human rights concerns regarding the proportionality of the Directive.

This brings us to the second major implication raised by the reliance of Member States on Article 8 ECHR in their rejection of the national provisions implementing the Directive and, at times, the direct criticism of the Directive itself. The troubled transposition stage of the Directive raises serious questions concerning the capacity of the EU to ensure the protection of human rights. As confirmed by the CJEU in its 2009 judgment on the matter, limiting the scope of the Directive to the imposition of a mandatory duty on Member States in order to harmonize the retention of data enabled the EU legislature to adopt this measure under the legal basis of a data protection Directive.[118] However, in doing so, the EU neglected to deal with the complex task of ensuring that the subsequent access, use, and processing entrenched by the blanket and indiscriminate retention of communications data complied with the principles and conditions of Article 8 ECHR. The responses by national policymakers to this predicament resulted in several constitutional challenges concerning the questionable human rights standards of these frameworks.

These challenges placed considerable pressure on the national constitutional courts in Member States, particularly with respect to growing public concern regarding the compliance of these national measures with the right to respect for private life throughout the EU. Then, in 2010, Article 8 ECHR played a key role in the national court judgment that effectively ensured that the EU could no longer avoid dealing with the glaring gap of human rights protection left within the Data Retention Directive since its inception. Following the granting of a preliminary reference under Article 267 TFEU by the Irish High Court, later joined by the Constitutional Court of Austria in 2012, the CJEU would finally be required to assess the compliance of the Directive with EU fundamental rights.[119]

E. Conclusions

The transposition of the Data Retention Directive was a process fraught with difficulty.[120] Following its entry into force, widespread concern was expressed regarding the shortcomings of the Directive with respect to the right to respect for

[117] On the relevant case law of the ECtHR, see Chapters 2 and 3.
[118] *Parliament and Council* (n 35).
[119] See Chapter 8.
[120] On its evaluation by the European Commission, and subsequent invalidation by the CJEU in the now famous judgment of *Digital Rights Ireland* in 2014, see Chapter 8.

private life and the protection of personal data. Subsequently, in all but one judgment, Article 8 ECHR was involved in the striking down of several national laws transposing the Directive by national constitutional courts. Most of these courts also relied on the jurisprudence of the Strasbourg Court in their critical reviews of these impugned national data retention regimes. Perhaps most importantly, the High Court of Ireland engaged at length with the principles and conditions of Article 8 ECHR, and the related jurisprudence of the ECtHR in its determination that the CJEU be required to assess the validity of the Directive with EU law on human rights grounds. Overall, three notable implications can be drawn from the transposition stage of the Directive. First, Article 8 ECHR played an instrumental role in the direct and indirect criticism of the Directive during its implementation across the EU. Secondly, the Directive's lack of compliance with Article 8 ECHR standards raised significant doubts concerning the capacity of the EU to ensure the protection of human rights within EU law. Thirdly, this case law also highlights the important role that can be played by the national courts as guardians of fundamental rights within the EU legal ecosystem *via* the legislative cycle of EU Directives and the preliminary reference procedure—the keystone of the EU judicial system.

8

Post-Legislative Review of the Data Retention Directive

A. Introduction

Concerns ran rife over the shortcomings of the Data Retention Directive during its difficult drafting and implementation. At the heart of these concerns was the compatibility of this controversial framework with the rights to respect for private life and data protection.[1] Consequently, as the then European Data Protection Supervisor (EDPS) observed,[2] the evaluation of the Directive's progress to date at this time by the European Commission provided the EU with an opportunity to prove that the EU was now operating in a 'fundamental rights culture'[3] in the post-Lisbon era.[4] This review represented no less than a 'moment of truth' for the controversial data retention regime given that the findings would demonstrate its compliance (or lack thereof) with the rights to private life and the protection of personal data.[5] However, this opportune moment would have to wait. Although this highly anticipated evaluation by the Commission was published in 2011, a review of the Directive and its compatibility with EU law, and fundamental rights, did not take place until the long-awaited judgment by the CJEU in 2014. This chapter examines the role of the right to respect for private life under Article 8 ECHR in these *ex post* reviews of the Directive by the Commission and the CJEU. First, the main findings of the Commission are examined. This analysis

[1] Directive 2006/24/EC of the European Parliament and of the Council of 15 March 2006 on the retention of data generated or processed in connection with the provision of publicly available electronic communications services or of public communications networks and amending Directive 2002/58/EC [2006] OJ L105/54. On the drafting and implementation stages of the Directive, see Chapters 6 and 7. All URLs for this chapter were last accessed on 22 April 2024.

[2] European Commission, 'Evaluation of the Directive of the European Parliament and of the Council on the retention of data processed in connection with the provision of public electronic communication services and amending Directive 2002/58/EC', COM(2011) 225 final.

[3] European Commission, 'Strategy for the effective implementation of the Charter of Fundamental Rights by the European Union', COM(2010) 573, 4.

[4] EDPS Peter Hustinx, Opinion of the EDPS on the Evaluation report from the Commission to the Council and the European Parliament on the Data Retention Directive, 31 May 2011, 7; EDPS, 'The "moment of truth" for the Data Retention Directive: EDPS demands clear evidence of necessity' Press Release (10 December 2010), <https://edps.europa.eu/sites/default/files/edpsweb_press_releases/edps-2010-17_data_retention_directive_en.pdf>.

[5] ibid. Indeed, the EDPS went so far as to describe the Data Retention Directive as 'the most privacy invasive instrument ever adopted by the EU in terms of scale and the number of people it affects'.

EU Data Privacy Law and Serious Crime. Nora Ni Loideain, Oxford University Press. © Nora Ni Loideain 2025.
DOI: 10.1093/oso/9780198837169.003.0008

also identifies the procedural and substantive challenges facing the Commission in its undertaking, the role of Article 8 ECHR, and the reasons why this evaluation was never completed. The following section then turns to the striking down of the Directive in *Digital Rights Ireland*, the landmark ruling which became the pivotal starting point from which the CJEU began to position itself as the vanguard EU institution for data retention policymaking and supranational judicial rights scrutiny in Europe.[6] Here the main findings in *Digital Rights Ireland* are explored, including the important roles played by Article 8 ECHR and the Snowden revelations in the influential high standards established by the CJEU in this ground-breaking judgment.

B. Evaluating the Directive's Implementation

The evaluation by the European Commission was undertaken in line with Articles 10 and 14 of the Data Retention Directive. Article 10 required each EU Member State to provide yearly statistics to the Commission on the implementation of the Directive in that Member State. Article 14 stipulated that the focus of the evaluation would be the economic implications of the Directive's implementation. In particular, the Commission was to consider 'the application of the Directive and its impact on economic operators and consumers, taking into account further developments in electronic communications technology'.[7] The Commission was also required to take into account the observations conveyed to it by Member States and the Article 29 Working Data Protection Party (a group that represented the views of data protection authorities from each Member State established under Article 29 of the principal Data Protection Directive (95/46/EC) (Article 29 Working Party).[8] On completion, the results of the evaluation would be made public. This narrow scope of review suggests that the implications of the Directive's provisions for the rights to respect for private life and the protection of personal data formed no part of the evaluation's *raison d'être*. Policy documentation from the drafting stage of the Directive, however, indicates that the European Commission had originally intended otherwise.

[6] Joined Cases C-293/12 and C-594/12 *Digital Rights Ireland and Seitlinger*, judgment of 8 April 2014 (ECLI:EU:C:2014:238) [54]. On the judgment generally, see Orla Lynskey, 'The Data Retention Directive is Incompatible with the Rights to Privacy and Data Protection and is Invalid in Its Entirety' (2014) 51 Common Market Law Review 1789. On the influence of *Digital Rights Ireland* in the subsequent case law of the CJEU, see Chapters 5 and 9.

[7] Data Retention Directive, Art 14(1).

[8] ibid Art 14(2). The Article 29 Working Party has since been replaced by the European Data Protection Board (EDPB) as provided under the EU GDPR: see Christopher Docksey, 'Article 68: European Data Protection Board' in Christopher Kuner and others (eds), *The EU General Data Protection Regulation (GDPR): A Commentary* (OUP 2020) 1041–54.

Prior to the drafting of the Directive, the Article 29 Working Party was an established opponent of the mandatory retention of communications data and had raised concerns that such a regime would unquestionably violate the human rights standards of Article 8 ECHR, particularly the proportionality test of Article 8(2).[9] The Article 29 Working Party maintained that any retention periods of a year or more were clearly disproportionate based on the fact that national law enforcement authorities had not proven a need for retention periods longer than six months.[10] When a draft of the Data Retention Directive was first proposed in 2005, the Commission stressed that the involvement of the Article 29 Working Party in evaluating the transposition of the Directive would ensure that the proposed framework would 'stand the test of compatibility with fundamental rights'.[11] Consequently, the principles and conditions of Article 8 ECHR which had played a key role in the concerns raised by those highlighting the human rights issues surrounding the Directive during its drafting would be relevant again in the assessment of its implementation.

Nevertheless, the narrow parameters of the scope of the evaluation provided under Article 14 of the Data Retention Directive show that an examination of the implications of the Directive for EU fundamental rights was not a priority when it became law. This key policy proposal by the Commission was instead lost during the swift co-decision drafting process between the European Parliament and the Council of the EU.[12] Consequently, the focus of the evaluation under the finalized text of the Directive was limited to economic considerations, namely to determine whether the type of communications data being retained and the retention periods should be revised for the harmonization of the internal market.[13] The scope of the evaluation, however, would later be expanded to examine the impact of the Directive for EU fundamental rights following a wave of human rights concerns raised by national constitutional courts, regulators, and scholars both before and during the Directive's thorny implementation.[14] Following its instrumental role in the critical review of the national measures implementing the Directive, and the Directive itself, Article 8 ECHR would also play a key role in the European Commission's review of the Directive.

[9] Article 29 Working Party, 'Opinion 9/2004 on a draft Framework Decision on the storage of data processed and retained for the purpose of providing electronic public communications services or data available in public communications networks with a view to the prevention, investigation, detection and prosecution of criminal acts, including terrorism' (WP 99) 5.

[10] ibid.

[11] European Commission, 'Extended Impact Assessment: Proposal for a Directive of the European Parliament and of the Council on the retention of data processed in connection with the provision of public electronic communication services and amending Directive 2002/58/EC', COM(2005) 438 final, 21.

[12] See further Chapter 6.

[13] Data Retention Directive, Arts 5 and 6.

[14] See Chapters 6 and 7.

1. Main findings

From the beginning, the European Commission faced several procedural and substantive challenges in its evaluation of the Data Retention Directive. Given the inconsistent and protracted implementation of the Directive across the EU, the detailed collection, analysis, and publication of statistics essential for an effective assessment of this controversial EU law were inevitably delayed and, more importantly, incomplete. In fact, the late publication of the evaluation constituted a breach of Article 14(1) of the Directive by the Commission. It is important to note, however, that the Commission faced many logistical difficulties in satisfying the requirements of Articles 10 and 14 of the Directive. One of these primary obstacles was the complete lack, or significant delay, of key statistical information from Member States regarding their implementation of the Directive. By the time of the evaluation's publication in 2011, twenty-four Member States had transposed the Directive into their national legislation. One Member State (Belgium) had partially transposed the Directive and two (Austria and Sweden) had draft legislation under discussion.[15] Several of these Member States, however, experienced significant delays in their implementation of the Directive as the constitutionality of the national laws transposing the Directive were successfully challenged in the national constitutional courts (Romania, Germany, and the Czech Republic).[16] Consequently, while nineteen Member States provided some form of statistics, delays in transposition resulted in only nine Member States providing the full statistics required under Article 10 of the Directive for either 2008 or 2009.[17]

The coexistence of two overlapping but separate data retention regimes under the EU data protection framework represented another major obstacle to a clear and accurate evaluation of the Data Retention Directive's implementation. Article 11 of Directive 2006/24/EC amended Article 15(1) of the e-Privacy Directive 2002/58/EC to prevent the application of the voluntary, and considerably broader, data retention regime under Directive 2002/58/EC to any communications data retained specifically for the purposes provided for under Article 1 of the Data Retention Directive. However, many Member States failed to comply with establishing a strict distinction between these separate retention regimes due to this legal loophole, the result of which left the Commission with the difficult task of distinguishing between statistics gathered by Member States for the evaluation of national measures implementing the mandatory data retention obligations of Directive 2006/24/EC and the much wider national data retention regimes permitted under the exemptions of the e-Privacy Directive 2002/58.[18]

15 Commission Evaluation Report (n 2) 5.
16 ibid 6. See further Chapter 6.
17 ibid 2.
18 ibid 4.

In addition to the procedural obstacles hindering the Commission's evaluation, the findings showed that the Data Retention Directive had unquestionably failed to harmonize the national data retention regimes across the EU in several major areas. First, the purposes adopted by Member States throughout the EU permitting the access, and use, by public authorities of data retained under the Directive were inconsistent. Only ten Member States specified which serious crimes communications data retained under the Directive could be used for.[19] This means that most Member States allowed access and use of retained data for purposes not covered by the Directive in one of the following two ways. On the one hand, four Member States adopted the approach of referring to the term of 'serious crime' in their national laws without defining its scope.[20] Consequently, this gave their public authorities a very wide discretion when interpreting what specific types of crime fell within this broad and uncertain remit. On the other hand, in a much larger departure that went far beyond the purpose of 'serious crime' permitted under the Directive, eight Member States required communication service providers (CSPs) to retain and provide their public authorities with access to communications data in relation to all criminal offences. Thus, the evaluation identified a hugely controversial finding for the proportionality of the Data Retention Directive that most transposing Member States allowed access and use of retained data 'for purposes going beyond those covered by the Directive'.[21]

Secondly, the evaluation showed that there was no consistent approach across the EU regarding the periods of retention adopted in the implementation of the Directive. Despite evidence that the most frequently requested type of data was related to mobile telephony, fifteen Member States specified a single period for all categories of communications data.[22] Furthermore, while ten Member States implemented the same retention period of one year for communications derived from the use of both traditional telephony and Internet-based communications, only three Member States (Ireland, Italy, and Poland) availed themselves of the maximum period of retention of two years.[23] The Commission observed the 'limited legal certainty and foreseeability' that the lack of harmony in this area provided for citizens whose communications data may have been stored and accessed in different Member States across the EU.[24] With respect to ensuring compliance with the principle of proportionality in future, the European Commission stated that any proposal to reform the Directive would include consideration of whether different periods should be applied to different categories of data with respect to the category of serious crime in question.[25]

19 ibid 6.
20 ibid.
21 ibid 8.
22 ibid 14 and 21.
23 ibid.
24 ibid 15.
25 ibid.

Thirdly, the requirement of Member States to ensure that CSPs complied with four data security principles (as a minimum) when storing, facilitating access to, and deleting data retained under the Data Retention Directive was inconsistently implemented across the EU. These principles stipulated that: (1) the quality of the data retained under the Directive be maintained and protected; (2) that the data be subject to certain 'appropriate technical and organisation measures' to protect against unlawful processing, particularly access; (3) unlawful loss and destruction; and (4) to ensure that the retained data, unless accessed and preserved, is destroyed at the end of the retention period.[26] Only fifteen Member States had implemented these minimum standards by the time of the evaluation's publication in 2011.[27] The Commission acknowledged the need for the adoption of consistent and visible high standards of data protection and data security in order to 'minimize the risk of breaches of privacy', particularly given the 'highly personal and sensitive nature' of the information involved.[28] Additionally, in line with well-established Article 8 ECHR standards,[29] the Commission stressed that these data protection and data security safeguards should be applied at each stage of the data processing cycle, including the retention of the communications data, its transmission to the relevant public authorities, and its subsequent storage and destruction. In its promised future impact assessment of the Data Retention Directive, the Commission stated that 'privacy by design' solutions, and the recommendations of the Article 29 Working Party,[30] would be considered with a view to improving the Directive's data protection and security standards.[31]

In addition to the clear failure of the Directive to harmonize national data retention regimes across the EU, another striking finding by the evaluation concerned the age of retained data accessed by public authorities. In line with the evidence submitted by the Article 29 Working Party against the one-year retention period proposed by the Commission in its draft of the Data Retention Directive in 2005, the evaluation found that *90 per cent* of communications data accessed by public authorities in 2008 were six months old, or less, in nine Member States.[32] The Commission acknowledges that the use of older communications by most Member States is less frequent but still highlights that the longer retention period 'can be crucial', whilst also making the argument that the latter may be useful

26 Data Retention Directive, Art 7.
27 Commission Evaluation Report (n 2) 18.
28 ibid.
29 See Chapter 1.
30 Article 29 Working Party, 'Report 01/2010 on the second joint enforcement action: Compliance at national level of Telecom Providers and ISPs with the obligations required from national traffic data retention legislation on the legal basis of articles 6 and 9 of the e-Privacy Directive 2002/58/EC and the Data Retention Directive 2006/24/EC amending the e-Privacy Directive' (WP 172), <https://resources.law.cam.ac.uk/cipil/documents/eu_data_protection/A29WP_Output_Collated_Document.pdf#page = 3477>.
31 Commission Evaluation Report (n 2) 18.
32 ibid 22.

for the investigating of organized crime, complex financial crimes, and terrorist offences, reflecting the length of time involved in the planning of such serious crimes.[33] Nevertheless, findings from the statistical evidence and other quantitative research (interviews and observations from Member States and the Article 29 Working Party) indicate that the retention period for most data requests by public authorities across the EU at the time of the evaluation in 2011 was six months.

Anything longer, therefore, would have constituted an exceptional type of request. Consequently, for an EU measure to allow Member States to implement an upper maximum data retention period of up to two years is difficult to reconcile with the proportionality test of Article 8 ECHR. This test would only have been satisfied if the scope of the Data Retention Directive was responding to the established Article 8 ECHR standards of 'necessity' and 'proportionality' and the interference with the protected rights to respect for private life was not therefore excessive.[34] Despite the lack of any decisive conclusions on the matter by the Commission, the main findings from the evaluation raised serious doubts regarding the compliance of the Directive, and its implementation, with the rights to respect for private life and the protection of personal data, particularly in light of the legality and proportionality tests under Article 8 ECHR.[35] The Commission referred to both Article 8 ECHR and Articles 7, 8, and 52 CFR in outlining what rights, limitations, and conditions would in future underpin 'the EU's approach to data retention'.[36] However, the analysis by the European Commission fell short of addressing whether the Data Retention Directive had either satisfied or violated these human rights standards.

This general scrutiny approach contrasts starkly with the (albeit qualified)[37] admission by the European Commission that the Directive had failed in its main purpose of harmonizing national data retention regimes across the EU. The statement made by the then European Commissioner for Home Affairs following the evaluation's publication in 2011 that the evaluation itself was not 'a legal assessment' arguably explains the lack of any decisive conclusions regarding the fundamental rights issues raised by the Directive's implementation.[38] There is, of course, an implicit suggestion through this attempt to remove any legal implications from the Commission's findings that the proportionality issues were uncomfortably clear even if not fully acknowledged in the evaluation. Nevertheless, the adoption of this narrow scope of review (or non-legal assessment) is curious as it runs contrary to the express commitment made in the evaluation that it would also examine

33 ibid.
34 On the case law of the ECtHR on Art 8 ECHR and data retention, see Chapter 3.
35 Article 29 Working Party (n 30) 4; EDPS (2011) (n 4) 7.
36 Commission Evaluation Report (n 2) 28.
37 ibid 31: according to the Commission, '[t]he Directive only sought partial harmonisation of approaches to data retention; therefore it is unsurprising that there is no common approach'. The reference to partial harmonization is curious given the absence of this term in the Directive itself.
38 ibid.

'the implications of the Directive for fundamental rights'.[39] It is possible, on the other hand, that the European Commission had fully intended to undertake a detailed review of the Directive's compliance with human rights standards in the second part of its review, particularly since this impact assessment was likely to have contained proposed amendments to the Directive.[40]

However, in 2012, the European Commission announced that the second, and most important, stage of the Commission's assessment of the Directive's implementation would be postponed to a tentative date. The reasoning given for this decision related to the 'complex legal relationship' between the Data Retention Directive and Article 15(1) of the e-Privacy Directive 2002/58/EC.[41] Specifically, the Commission expressed concern regarding how the future reform of the overall EU data protection legislative framework might affect this relationship. The key conclusion being that any reform of the Data Retention Directive would be postponed until '2013 or 2014, depending on the progress of the General Data Protection Regulation'.[42] Following this incomplete evaluation by the European Commission, no 'legal assessment' of the Directive's compatibility with the right to private life as enshrined in the Charter and its validity with EU law would take place until its review by the CJEU in 2014.

2. The role of Article 8 ECHR

Article 8 ECHR played a significant role in the European Commission's often economical examination of the implications posed by the implementation of the Data Retention Directive for EU fundamental rights and human rights standards. For instance, there is no analysis in the evaluation of the key role that the requirements of Article 8 ECHR played in the rejections by national constitutional courts of national measures transposing the Directive or in their criticism of the Directive.[43] Furthermore, the evaluation does not address the significance of these judgments for the reform of the Directive. Instead, as discussed earlier, the Commission stated

[39] ibid 1.

[40] See Cecilia Malmström, Press Conference on the Commission Evaluation Report on the Data Retention Directive (SPEECH/11/280, Brussels, 18 April 2011): 'Building on this evaluation, the Commission will prepare a proposal to amend the Directive. Over the coming months, it will consult law enforcement authorities, the judiciary, data protection authorities, industry and civil society on options for a future legal framework.' This is consistent with a prior commitment by the Commission to amend the Directive following the outcome of its evaluation. See European Commission, 'European Commission plan to deliver justice, freedom and security to citizens (2010–2014)', 20 April 2010: <https://ec.europa.eu/commission/presscorner/detail/en/memo_10_139>.

[41] See Statewatch, 'Revision of Data Retention Directive put on hold with no "precise timetable" for a new proposal' 28 March 2012, <https://statewatch.org/news/2012/august/statewatch-news-online-eu-revision-of-data-retention-directive-put-on-hold-with-quot-no-precise-timetable-quot-for-a-new-proposal/>.

[42] ibid.

[43] See Chapter 7.

that its intention at the time was to 'consider the issues raised by national case law in its future proposal on revising the data retention framework' at a tentative future date, the postponed analysis of which never took place.[44] However, there were two sections of the evaluation where the Commission relied on the rights and conditions under Article 8 ECHR and the case law of the Strasbourg Court when examining the impact of the implementation of the Data Retention Directive for EU fundamental rights and human rights standards.

The European Commission indirectly invokes Article 8 ECHR when responding to the troubling finding that most Member States allowed the access and use of retained data for purposes far beyond those permitted under the scope of the Data Retention Directive.[45] This stark lack of compliance with the Directive across the EU conflicts with the key requirements of accessibility and foreseeability that must be met if the processing of communications data by public authorities is to satisfy the legality test of Article 8(2) ECHR. Specifically, these requirements stipulate that national law must be sufficiently accessible and clear in its terms to give individuals an adequate indication to foresee the circumstances and the conditions in which public authorities are empowered to resort to the measure in question.[46] In order to ensure that the foreseeability requirement would also be met on an EU level, the then EDPS stressed that any future EU data retention measure should provide greater specificity and clarity.[47] In particular, the EDPS proposed that any future revision of the purposes for which the scope of the Data Retention Directive would apply should include the definition of 'serious crime'.[48]

By stipulating for exactly which serious crimes (such as terrorism, organized crime, murder) the communications data retained under the Data Retention Directive could be used, the clarity and scope of discretion conferred on public authorities, and their compliance with the right to respect for private life and the data protection principle of purpose limitation, would be significantly enhanced across the EU.[49] The Commission's response to the human rights concerns raised by the non-compliance of this aspect of the Directive by 2011 was not definitive. However, based on the Court of Justice judgment of *Rundfunk*,[50] the Commission accepted that 'this situation may not provide sufficiently for the foreseeability which is a requirement in any legislative measure which restricts the right to privacy'.[51] By citing *Rundfunk* as supporting legal authority, the European Commission drew from Article 8 ECHR indirectly as the reasoning underpinning

44 Commission Evaluation Report (n 2) 21.
45 ibid 8.
46 On these long-established Art 8 ECHR standards, see Chapters 2 and 3.
47 EDPS (2011) (n 4) 13.
48 ibid.
49 ibid 14.
50 Case C-465/00 *Österreichischer Rundfunk* [2003] ECR I-4989. On the importance of this judgment in the data protection jurisprudence of the CJEU, see Chapter 4.
51 Commission Evaluation Report (n 2) 8–9.

this ECJ judgment relied heavily on the requirements of Article 8 ECHR and the case law of the ECtHR.[52] Secondly, in addition to Articles 7, 8, and 52 CFR, the Commission also engaged with Article 8 ECHR when outlining what rights, limitations, and conditions should form the basis of the EU's approach to data retention.[53] Despite not addressing the Directive's questionable compliance with these human rights standards, the Commission acknowledged that data retention constitutes a limitation of the right to private life and the protection of personal data 'which are fundamental rights in the EU'.[54] The analysis then proceeds to consider case law from both the ECtHR and the CJEU that are notably described as 'judgments ... of relevance for whether the Directive should be amended'.[55]

Based on its examination of this jurisprudence, the European Commission observed that any limits on the right to private life must be precise and enable foreseeability, necessary with minimum safeguards, and 'proportionate to the general interest'.[56] The first identified requirement that the right to privacy 'be precise and foreseeable' drew, albeit indirectly (as previously noted), from Article 8 ECHR as *Rundfunk* is again cited by the Commission as its supporting legal authority for this legal requirement. Notably, the Commission cites the most relevant ECtHR case law to the scope and operation of the Directive when elaborating on the second of its three identified requirements that any limits on the right to private life must be 'necessary with minimum safeguards'. In *Copland*, the first of these two judgments, the ECtHR established that the communications data derived from an individual's telephone calls, emails, and general Internet usage falls under the scope of the right to respect for private life under Article 8(1) ECHR. Any retention, storage, or analysis of this personal data thus amounts to an interference with this right. Similarly with the second cited judgment of *S and Marper*, the ECtHR (sitting as the Grand Chamber) held that the indefinite retention of DNA materials of any individual acquitted of a crime, or whose proceedings are dropped prior to any conviction, also constituted an interference with the right to private life under Article 8(1) ECHR.[57]

The European Commission's subsequent analysis of *Copland* and *Marper* refers interchangeably between the 'minimum safeguards' required by the legality test and the 'appropriate safeguards' that form part of the separate proportionality test under Article 8(2) ECHR.[58] It was therefore identified in the evaluation that certain requirements must be satisfied in order to justify the interference(s) posed by

52 *Österreichischer Rundfunk* (n 50) [73]–[90]. This CJEU judgment includes references to the leading Art 8 ECHR judgments of *Amann v Switzerland* [2000] ECHR 87 (GC) and *Rotaru v Romania* [2000] ECHR 192 (GC). On these latter case law, see Chapter 3.

53 Commission Evaluation Report (n 2) 28.

54 ibid.

55 ibid.

56 ibid.

57 On the importance of these judgments in *S and Marper v United Kingdom* [2008] ECHR 1581 and *Copland v United Kingdom* (2007) 45 EHRR 37, see Chapter 3.

58 Commission Evaluation Report (n 2) 29.

the Data Retention Directive by reference to the conditions of Article 8(2), namely the legality, necessity, and proportionality tests. For its final identified requirement that the right to privacy 'be proportionate to the general interest', the Commission relied on the CJEU judgment of *Volker* as supporting legal authority.[59] Ultimately, this analysis of Article 8 ECHR and the relevant case law of the ECtHR shows that the Commission effectively developed its fundamental rights standards blueprint for the revision of the Data Retention Directive by drawing from the requirements of Article 8 ECHR. This clear reliance on Article 8 ECHR indicates that these standards would have played a key role in any proposals the European Commission would have put forward concerning a revised Data Retention Directive and its compatibility with the right to private life.

C. Striking Down the Data Retention Directive

1. Fate of Directive 'an open question' before Snowden revelations

The Data Retention Directive had been the focus of two judgments before the CJEU prior to the review of its compatibility with EU law, and specifically the Charter, in 2014. Ireland, supported by the Slovak Republic, in 2009 unsuccessfully challenged the adoption of Article 95 EC (now Art 114 TFEU) as the legal basis of the Directive. Both Member States instead contended that the main objective of the controversial law concerned tackling serious crime not the harmonization of the internal market.[60] In stark contrast to the expansive fundamental rights approach of the Court in later cases, the ruling did not deal with any rights issues concerning the principle of data retention on the ground that such an assessment was irrelevant to the adoption of the Directive's legal basis, the main issue of the proceedings.[61] In 2012, Sweden made a preliminary reference to the Court regarding whether the Directive precluded a CSP, as a third party to a civil dispute concerning copyright infringement, from being ordered to disclose subscriber data to a party other than a public authority.[62] Neither of these judgments, however, required the Court to address the compatibility of the Data Retention Directive with EU fundamental rights law. There was also the curious case of the matter being raised in *Volker* by the referring national court in Germany (the Administrative

[59] ibid 29. See Joined Cases C-92/09 and C-93/09 *Volker und Markus Schecke and* Eifert, judgment of 9 November 2010 (ECLI:EU:C:2010:662). See generally Michal Bobek, 'Joined Cases C-92 & 93/09, *Volker und Markus Schecke GbR and Hartmut Eifert*' (2011) 48 Common Market Law Review 2005. On the importance of this judgment in the data protection case law of the CJEU, see Chapter 4.

[60] Case C-301/06 *Ireland v Parliament and Council* [2009] ECR I-00593.

[61] See further Chapter 6.

[62] Case C-461/10 *Bonnier Audio*, judgment of 19 April 2012 (ECLI:EU:C:2012:219).

Court of Wiesbaden). Unsurprisingly, this dialogue was brief.[63] The CJEU deemed this novel question concerning the Data Retention Directive to be inadmissible due to its lack of relevance to the outcome of the main proceedings regarding the publication of information on beneficiaries of EU agricultural aid.[64]

Despite the elevation of the Charter to EU primary law and the historical precedent set in *Volker* that part of an EU law was for the first time struck down due to its incompatibility with the Charter, expectations were not high at this time that the Data Retention Directive would suffer the same fate. Some scholars, such as Bobek, observed rather neutrally that whether the CJEU would invalidate the Directive (in part or in its entirety) based on its incompatibility with EU law following *Volker* remained 'an open question'.[65] Others were more direct with their concerns and cast doubt on the Court taking a robust right-based approach in *Digital Rights Ireland*. Konstadinides, for instance, noted that *Volker* and other recent data protection case law suggested that the Court had a high 'threshold' for allowing data retention and the necessity of the Directive would likely be assessed as simply outweighing 'any proportionality concerns'.[66] Following the evaluation by the European Commission of the Directive's patchy implementation, the striking down of national laws transposing the Directive, and criticisms of the Directive itself by some national courts,[67] it is remarkable that such predictions were made regarding the outcome of the judgment of the CJEU.

Two game-changing developments then took place that undoubtedly shaped the Court's assessment of the Data Retention Directive. In 2012, the European Commission postponed completing its evaluation of the Directive and thus abandoned any immediate plans for its reform. This left a significant gap in the legal assessment at the EU level of an already highly controversial EU law regarding its compatibility with the rights to private life and data protection and the principles of necessity and proportionality as enshrined in the EU Charter. Secondly, the height of the global mass surveillance revelations by Edward Snowden in 2013 coincided with the Court hearings and main arguments presented to the Court in *Digital Rights Ireland*. In addition to prompting ongoing policy debates and legal reforms globally, the Snowden revelations reignited privacy concerns in the EU posed by the extra-territorial reach of US public authorities, further enabled by the global dominance and vast data collection capacity of US-based cloud providers.[68] Both of these developments clearly influenced the CJEU and its robust rights-based assessment in *Digital Rights*

[63] See Bobek (n 59) 2021.
[64] *Volker* (n 59) [42].
[65] Bobek (n 59) 2022.
[66] Theodore Konstadinides, 'Destroying Democracy on the Ground of Defending It?' (2011) 36 European Law Review 722, 735.
[67] See further Chapter 7.
[68] On the Snowden revelations and their legal impact, see Chapter 1.

Ireland and later groundbreaking judgments that have subsequently transformed EU law on data protection.[69]

2. The Data Retention Directive is struck down

Two cases from the national courts of Ireland and Austria resulted in a joined preliminary reference to the CJEU regarding the compatibility of the Directive with EU fundamental rights in *Digital Rights Ireland*. Both proceedings arose from challenges to invalidate the national laws implementing the Data Retention Directive in each Member State. In a notable reflection of the reservations held by EU citizens towards the Directive,[70] the preliminary reference from the Austrian Constitutional Court was the result of a constitutional challenge brought by over 11,000 applicants.[71] Due to the overlap of issues raised, the CJEU joined both references for the purposes of the oral procedure and judgment on 11 June 2013. While numerous questions were referred, the CJEU determined that the focus of its examination would be the 'relevance of Articles 7, 8 and 11 of the Charter with regard to the question of the validity of the Directive'.[72]

Given the otherwise considerable overlap between the judgment of the CJEU (sitting as the Grand Chamber) and the Opinion of the Advocate General, the latter is notably distinguished by its examination of the compatibility of the Directive with both the EU Charter and the proportionality test under Article 5(4) TEU. The second question addressed by the Advocate General (referred by the Irish High Court) concerned whether the Directive was an appropriate measure for attaining its pursued objective but did not go beyond what was necessary to achieve this aim. The Advocate General observed that the test of proportionality under Article 5(4) TEU provides the EU legislature with a broad discretion in complex legal areas of a political, social, and economic nature, thereby leaving the CJEU with limited powers of review. Consequently, Article 5(4) TEU does not require the Court to stringently determine whether the impugned measure was the best option but instead turns on whether its adoption was 'not manifestly inappropriate' to the objective pursued.[73] Following *Ireland v Parliament and Council* regarding the legal basis of the Directive, the Advocate General (albeit reluctantly) conceded that its 'predominant' aim relevant to Article 5(4) TEU was that of ensuring the proper functioning of the internal market.[74]

[69] On the landmark data transfer judgments in *Schrems*, Opinion 1/15, and *Schrems II*, that built on the standards established in *Digital Rights Ireland*, see Chapters 5 and 9.

[70] The successful constitutional challenge to the national legislation implementing the Data Retention Directive in Germany was also supported by 30,000 applicants. See further Chapter 7.

[71] *Digital Rights Ireland* (n 6) [3].

[72] ibid [23].

[73] AG Cruz Villalón, Opinion of 12 December 2013 in Joined Cases C-293/12 and C-594/12 *Digital Rights Ireland and Seitlinger* (ECLI:EU:C:2013:845) [96].

[74] ibid [88].

The Advocate General took no issue with the Directive constituting an appropriate means of achieving its objective of ensuring the functioning of the internal market by harmonizing 'legal and technical differences' between national data retention regimes across the EU.[75] However, the Advocate General contended that the Directive ultimately failed in the final stage of the Article 5(4) TEU proportionality test due to its significant impact on EU fundamental rights. According to the Advocate General, 'the intensity of the intervention in the area of regulation of fundamental rights, constituted by the interference with the right to privacy which, through the implementation of Directive 2006/24 … imposed on Member States [was] manifestly disproportionate to the objective relating to the need to ensure the functioning of the internal market'.[76] The Advocate General then astutely acknowledged the 'paradoxical' result of this assessment whereby the Directive 'would fail the proportionality test for the very reasons which justified its legal basis'.[77] Ultimately, the matter was left unresolved on the ground that its resolution was irrelevant to the cases at issue.

On the compatibility of the Data Retention Directive with the Charter, the examination of the Advocate General focused on the interference with the right to respect for private life under Article 7 CFR and whether that interference could be justified in accordance with the requirements of Article 52 CFR. The Advocate General provided a detailed examination of the Directive's compatibility with Article 7 CFR and Article 52 CFR. Following numerous references to Article 8(1) ECHR and the case law of the ECtHR, the Advocate General stated that the retention and collection of communications data under the Directive constituted 'a particularly serious' interference with the right to privacy.[78] In particular, the robust analysis highlighted the chilling effect created by the 'permanent threat' and 'vague feeling of surveillance' posed throughout the data retention period to the private lives of EU citizens.[79] Furthermore, the Advocate General argued that the intensity of this interference was 'exacerbated' by the possibility of profiling, the risk of unlawful access to the retained data and the lack of any requirement under the Directive that the stored data be retained within the jurisdiction of Member States.[80]

As regards the conditions laid down by Article 52(1) CFR, the Advocate General noted that the interference with Article 7 CFR constituted by the Directive is only permissible to the extent that it is 'provided for by law', meets 'the quality of law' requirements, respects 'the essence of the right to privacy', and satisfies the principle of proportionality.[81] In his detailed examination of the legality test, the Advocate General takes particular issue with the general obligation imposed on Member

75 ibid [97].
76 ibid [100].
77 ibid [102].
78 ibid [70].
79 ibid [72].
80 ibid [74]–[79].
81 ibid [107].

States by the Directive to establish safeguards to govern the access and use of the retained data by competent national law enforcement authorities. Due to the limitation of fundamental rights created by the mandatory framework of the Data Retention Directive (in contrast to the voluntary national data retention regimes permitted under the e-Privacy Directive), the Advocate General persuasively argues that the EU legislature's level of responsibility to ensure compliance with rights changes in kind. In other words, in line with expanding its role into areas that interfere significantly with fundamental rights, the EU must consequently 'play a leading role in defining … the guarantees necessary to ensure that the limitations and their application ("access") comply with all the quality of law requirements and the principle of proportionality'.[82] Otherwise, the Advocate General warned that to leave the task of defining the necessary safeguards capable of justifying such an interference with the Charter to Member States, including the scope of serious crime, would render the provisions of Article 52(1) CFR 'meaningless'.[83]

In addition, the Advocate General proceeds to note that the Data Retention Directive should have been more prescriptive in the regulation of the authorization to access the data (prior judicial review), exceptions to access (communication protected by professional confidentiality), and destruction of accessed data.[84] In concluding his examination of the legality test, the Advocate General determined that the Directive was 'as a whole incompatible' with Article 52(1) CFR.[85] Notwithstanding this result, the Advocate General examined the proportionality test under Article 52(1) CFR. No issue was identified concerning the legitimate objective pursued by the Directive of ensuring the retention of communications data for the purpose of the investigation, detection, and prosecution of serious crime. However, the Advocate General found no justification for the necessity of the data retention period permitted under the Directive 'in the absence of exceptional circumstances' and advised the Court that the maximum retention period of two years was incompatible with Articles 7 and 52(1) CFR.[86]

This brings us to the judgment of the CJEU (sitting as the Grand Chamber). Following *Rundfunk*, the Court established that the obligation imposed by the Data Retention Directive on Member States to ensure the retention of data relating to an individual's private life and communications constituted an interference with the rights guaranteed by Article 7 CFR. The Court made clear, with explicit references to the relevant case law of the ECtHR, that the access by competent national authorities to this communications data also constitutes 'a further interference with that fundamental right'.[87] On the ground that it provided for the processing

[82] ibid [116]–[117].
[83] ibid [120].
[84] ibid [127]–[129].
[85] ibid [130].
[86] ibid [151]–[152].
[87] *Digital Rights Ireland* (n 6) [35].

of data, the Court also held that the Directive constituted an interference with the protection of personal data guaranteed by Article 8 CFR.[88] The Court endorsed the robust view and reasoning of the Advocate General that the interference posed by the Directive to the rights to private life and the protection of personal data was 'wide ranging' and 'particularly serious'.[89] Furthermore, the Court reiterated the Advocate General's warning that the secret retention and use of communications data under the Directive was 'likely to generate in the minds of the persons concerned the feeling that their private lives are the subject of constant surveillance'.[90]

Curiously, in its examination of whether the interference with the rights guaranteed by Articles 7 and 8 CFR could be justified in line with the conditions of Article 52(1) CFR, the CJEU sidestepped any consideration of the legality test. This was a clear departure from the detailed analysis of the Advocate General. Instead, the Court proceeded directly to establishing that the retention of data mandated by the Directive did not constitute an interference with the 'essence' of the right to respect for private life guaranteed by Article 7 CFR as there was no 'acquisition of knowledge of the content of the electronic communications as such'.[91] The Court also determined that the essence of the fundamental right to the protection of personal data, as enshrined in Article 8 CFR, had not been adversely affected due to the requirement under the Directive that CSPs must respect certain principles of data protection and data security. Member States were therefore obligated to ensure that 'appropriate technical and organisational measures were adopted' against accidental or unlawful destruction, accidental loss, or alteration of the data.[92]

The compatibility of the Data Retention Directive with the principle of proportionality, as enshrined in Article 52(1) CFR, was undoubtedly the central question for the CJEU in *Digital Rights Ireland*. Article 52(1) CFR provides that limitations to EU fundamental rights may only occur 'if they are necessary and genuinely meet objectives of general interest recognised' by the EU or 'the need to protect the rights and freedoms of others'. In a deft interpretation separating the main aim of the Directive (harmonization of the internal market) from its 'material objective' (the fight against serious crime), the Court held that the Directive satisfied the 'objective of general interest' test by contributing to 'public security'.[93] In line with its famous judgment in *Kadi*, which established that the fight against international terrorism in order to maintain peace and security constitutes an objective of general interest, the Court held that the 'material objective' of the Data Retention Directive 'to contribute to the fight against serious crime' met an objective of general interest.[94]

[88] ibid [36].
[89] ibid [37].
[90] ibid [37]. The CJEU would expand its assessment of the interferences posed by bulk data retention measures to EU fundamental rights in later case law to include the right to freedom of expression, and the right to non-discrimination, as enshrined in Arts 11 and 21 CFR. See further Chapters 5 and 9.
[91] *Digital Rights Ireland* (n 6) [39].
[92] ibid [40].
[93] ibid [40].
[94] ibid [42]–[44].

For the remaining requirements of the proportionality test, the CJEU noted that the acts of EU institutions must be appropriate for fulfilling the legitimate objectives pursued by the relevant legislation but should 'not exceed the limits of what is appropriate and necessary in order to achieve those objectives'.[95] Drawing from the strict proportionality test of Article 8(2) ECHR in *S and Marper*, the leading data retention judgment of the ECtHR,[96] the Court stated that where interferences with fundamental rights are involved, 'the extent of the EU legislature's discretion may prove to be limited, depending on a number of factors'.[97] In particular, these factors include the area concerned, the nature of the right in question guaranteed by the Charter, the nature and seriousness of the interference, and the object pursued by the interference. Due to the important role played by the protection of personal data in the light of the fundamental right to respect for private life, and the seriousness of the interference constituted by the Directive, the Court held that the discretion of the EU legislature was limited and that the review of such discretion should be strict.[98]

Regarding the final requirement of the proportionality test concerning whether the retention of data was appropriate and necessary for attaining the objective pursued by the Data Retention Directive, the Court took no issue with the first element of this test. Indeed, the Court highlighted the growing importance of electronic communications as 'a valuable tool for criminal investigations' and that the retention of communications data was considered appropriate for attaining the objective pursued by the Directive.[99] In relation to the second element of necessity, however, the Court made clear that while the fight against serious crime was of the 'utmost importance', such an objective 'does not, in itself, justify a retention measure such as that established by Directive 2006/24 being considered to be necessary for the purpose of that fight'.[100] In applying this strict approach to the requirements of the protection of the right to respect for private life, the Court held that 'derogations and limitations in relation to the protection of personal data must apply only in so far as is strictly necessary'.[101]

Drawing openly again from the Article 8(2) ECHR case law of the ECtHR, the CJEU made clear that EU law that places limitations on the protection of personal data 'must lay down clear and precise rules governing the scope and application' of such measures.[102] The Court stipulated that these measures should also impose minimum safeguards in order to ensure that affected individuals 'have sufficient

[95] ibid [46].
[96] See Chapter 3.
[97] *Digital Rights Ireland* (n 6) [47].
[98] ibid [48].
[99] ibid [49].
[100] ibid [51].
[101] ibid [52].
[102] ibid [54]: citing *Liberty v United Kingdom* (2009) 48 EHRR 1; *Rotaru v Romania* [2000] ECHR 192 (GC); *S and Marper v United Kingdom* (2009) 48 EHRR 1169.

guarantees to effectively protect their personal data against the risk of abuse and against any unlawful access and use of that data'.[103] Again invoking the Article 8 ECHR jurisprudence of the ECtHR, the Court stressed that the need for such safeguards carries extra weight where personal data is subject to automatic processing and there is a significant risk of unlawful access to the relevant data.[104] The Court then highlighted numerous areas where the Data Retention Directive had failed to satisfy the necessity element under the final proportionality requirement of Article 52(1) CFR.

First, the Court strongly criticized the blanket and indiscriminate nature of the scope and provisions of the Directive that applied to 'all persons and all means of electronic communication as well as all traffic data without any differentiation, limitation or exception'. This amounted to 'an interference with the fundamental rights of practically the entire European population'.[105] The Court noted that the Directive did not require any relationship between the retained data and threats to public security or in relation to a particular time period, location, or to particular individuals likely to be involved in serious crime.[106] Secondly, the Directive failed to limit access and subsequent use of the data by competent national authorities for the investigation, detection, and prosecution of serious crime. In line with the view of the Advocate General, the Court criticized the lack of any requirement for prior authorization and oversight, the absence of any definition for the concept of 'serious crime', and for 'merely' imposing a general obligation on Member States to define the procedures and conditions to be followed to gain access to retained data in line with necessity and proportionality requirements.[107] Thirdly, the Court noted the lack of any limits placed on the broad retention period under Article 6 of the Directive that allowed Member States to adopt any duration between a minimum of six months to a maximum period of two years. The Court observed that the Directive should have made clear to Member States that the determination of the period of retention should have been based on objective criteria in order to ensure that the scope of the national data retention regime was limited to what was 'strictly necessary'.[108] Consequently, the Court held that the Directive did not provide 'clear and precise rules' governing the extent of the interference with the fundamental rights guaranteed by Articles 7 and 8 CFR.[109]

This robust assessment of the Data Retention Directive then turned to its rules relating to the security and protection of data required, followed by a surprising determination on the question of data localization under Article 8 CFR. Here the

[103] *Digital Rights Ireland* (n 6) [54].
[104] ibid [54]. On the related case law of the ECtHR, see Chapter 3.
[105] *Digital Rights Ireland* (n 6) [56]–[57].
[106] ibid [59].
[107] ibid [61]–[62].
[108] ibid [64].
[109] ibid [65].

Court stated that the Directive did not provide for sufficient safeguards to ensure effective protection of data retained against the risk of abuse and against any unlawful access. No specific obligations were imposed on Member States to establish such rules or to ensure the irreversible destruction of data at the end of the data retention period.[110] In addition, the Court raised the novel issue of where the retained data was stored and linked this to its interpretation of the right to protection of personal data guaranteed by Article 8 CFR. This was not an issue referred for its review by either of the national constitutional courts. Nevertheless, the Court established that the data retained under the Directive should remain within the EU to 'fully' ensure, as required under Article 8(3) CFR, the control 'by an independent authority of compliance with the requirements of protection and security'.[111] Based on the above grounds, the CJEU held that the 'EU legislature had exceeded the limits imposed by compliance with the principle of proportionality' under Articles 7, 8, and 52(1) CFR.[112] By not limiting the temporal effect of its judgment, the Court declared the invalidity of the Directive to take effect *ab initio*, thereby erasing its entire existence from the EU legal order.[113]

3. *Digital Rights Ireland*: the role of Article 8 ECHR

The CJEU relied on Article 8 ECHR, and the related case law of the ECtHR, both directly and indirectly throughout its assessment and scrutiny of the Data Retention Directive and its compatibility with the EU Charter. The first instance of the CJEU 'closing ranks'[114] with the standards of the ECtHR arises when *Volker* is cited as the supporting authority for its determination that the retention of data falls under the scope of private life and protection of personal data under Articles 7 and 8 CFR.[115] By relying on this particular judgment, the Court draws from Article 8 ECHR indirectly as the reasoning underpinning *Volker* was based on the

[110] ibid [67].

[111] ibid [68]. Note that this reasoning echoes similar concerns highlighted in the Opinion of the Advocate General which in turn cites the same concern raised by the German Constitutional Court in its 2010 judgment on the German law transposing the Data Retention Directive. See AG Cruz Villalón (n 73) [78]–[79]: '[N]o provision of Directive 2006/24 lays down the requirement for those service providers themselves to store the data to be retained in the territory of a Member State, under the jurisdiction of a Member State ... That "outsourcing" of data retention admittedly allows the retained data to be distanced from the public authorities of the Member States and thus to be placed beyond their direct grip and any control, but by that very fact it simultaneously increases the risk of use which is incompatible with the requirements resulting from the right to privacy.'

[112] *Digital Rights Ireland* (n 6) [69].

[113] General Secretariat of the Council, 'Judgment of the Court of 8 April 2014 in Joined Cases C-293/12 and C-594/12, 9009/14', 5 May 2014.

[114] Marie-Pierre Granger and Kristina Irion, 'The Court of Justice and the Data Retention Directive in Digital Rights Ireland' (2014) 39 European Law Review 835, 847.

[115] *Digital Rights Ireland* (n 6) [29]. On the assessment by the CJEU of Art 8 ECHR and Arts 7 and 8 CFR in *Volker*, see Chapter 4.

rich jurisprudence of the Strasbourg Court concerning Article 8 ECHR and the protection of personal data. Subsequently, the Court indirectly relies on Article 8 ECHR again in citing the CJEU judgment of *Rundfunk* as its authority for establishing that the retention of communications data imposed by the Directive constitutes an interference with the right to respect for private life guaranteed by Article 7 CFR.[116] The Court then explicitly follows the well-established Article 8 ECHR jurisprudence of the ECtHR by treating the access to the data retained under the Directive by national authorities as 'a further interference' with Article 7 CFR.[117]

In its examination of whether the interference with the rights guaranteed by Articles 7 and 8 CFR could be justified in line with Article 52(1) CFR, the scope and requirements of the strict proportionality test developed by the Court are openly drawn from the leading case law of the ECtHR concerning Article 8(2) ECHR. In assessing the compatibility of EU measures with the proportionality test under Article 52(1) CFR that constitute a serious interference with the fundamental rights to respect for private life and the protection of personal data, the Court relied on *S and Marper*, the leading judgment of the ECtHR concerning the long-term retention of personal data, in establishing that the EU legislature's discretion will be limited.[118] The Court relied yet again on the Article 8 ECHR standards of the ECtHR in requiring that the Directive should have included 'clear and precise rules' governing its scope and application and minimum safeguards to sufficiently protect and ensure against the risk of abuse or misuse of the retained communications data.[119] In addition, the Court closes ranks with the ECtHR once more when highlighting that the requirement for these minimum safeguards carries extra weight where impugned measures (such as the Directive) involve automatic processing and a significant risk of unlawful access is involved.[120]

Following the ECtHR, the CJEU also applied the 'joint analysis' approach in *Digital Rights Ireland* when assessing the legality and proportionality requirements enshrined in Article 52(1) CFR. The specific question of what the 'provided for by law' requirement entails under Article 52(1) CFR was as a result overlooked by the Court in *Digital Rights Ireland*. Instead, the primary focus for the Courts that results from this joint analysis approach is frequently whether a particular data retention regime had complied with the principle of proportionality. This is clearly demonstrated in *Digital Rights Ireland* where the CJEU sidesteps any detailed examination of the legality test and conflates any rule of law considerations within its proportionality analysis. The ECtHR has increasingly adopted a joint

116 *Digital Rights Ireland* (n 6) [33].
117 ibid [35].
118 ibid [47].
119 ibid [54].
120 ibid [55].

analysis approach in its post-Snowden case law dealing with secret surveillance and bulk data retention. This approach departs, however, from previously lauded Strasbourg case law and has been criticized for weakening the substantive protection provided by the right to respect for private life in surveillance and data retention cases.[121]

Nevertheless, it is evident that these Article 8 ECHR standards played a pivotal role in the striking down of the Data Retention Directive by the CJEU given their key contribution to the development of the jurisprudential framework, reasoning, and the high proportionality standards that underpinned the judgment of the Court.[122]

4. *Digital Rights Ireland* and broader implications

By focusing on the compatibility of the Data Retention Directive with the EU Charter, the narrow scope of review adopted by the Grand Chamber of the CJEU in the high-profile case of *Digital Rights Ireland* provided the Court with the opportunity to highlight its role and capacity as a human rights adjudicator. In doing so, the Court delivered a landmark judgment lauded by commentators at the time for confirming that high standards of privacy and data protection apply to the mass processing of personal data within the EU.[123] Although the primacy of EU law is not explicitly addressed in *Digital Rights Ireland*, it is also likely that the judgment reassured national constitutional courts of the EU's commitment to fundamental rights.[124] *Digital Rights Ireland* also reflects the desire of the Court to reinforce the famous *Solange* doctrine,[125] where national courts refrain from reviewing the compatibility of EU law with rights under national constitutions as long as the CJEU continues to protect fundamental rights adequately.[126] A number of national courts, including the German Constitutional Court, adhered to this approach by only striking down legislative provisions transposing the Data Retention Directive. However, the outcome of *Digital Rights Ireland* also addressed the threat to the longevity of the *Solange* doctrine from national courts that did not submit

[121] See Chapters 2 and 3. Given the concerns surrounding this controversial approach, it is welcome that the CJEU has stressed the importance of the 'quality' of law requirements of Art 52(1) in some of its later case law, such as Opinion 1/15 and *Schrems II*: see Chapters 5 and 9.

[122] Indeed, many of these convergences are unsurprising given the constitutional links between the right to private life enshrined in Arts 7 and 52(3) CFR and the benchmark standards set by the rich jurisprudence of the ECtHR concerning its corresponding right in Art 8 ECHR, much of which long predates the Charter. See further Chapter 4.

[123] See eg Steve Peers, 'The data retention judgment: The CJEU prohibits mass surveillance' *EU Law Analysis* (8 April 2014), <https://eulawanalysis.blogspot.com/2014/04/the-data-retention-judgment-cjeu.html>. See further Chapters 5 and 7.

[124] Lynskey (n 6) 1801.

[125] ibid.

[126] See Chapter 6.

preliminary references to the CJEU but nevertheless raised human rights concerns regarding the proportionality of the Directive.[127]

Secondly, the Court made a particularly novel and major contribution to EU data protection law, and for any future EU data retention measures, in its interpretation that the right to the protection of personal data under Article 8 CFR extends to 'data sovereignty'.[128] In other words, data retained under such measures must be stored within the EU. Otherwise, the Court stressed, the control, required under Article 8(3) CFR, by an independent authority of compatibility with the necessary data protection and data security requirements cannot be fully ensured. By engaging so forcefully with an issue not referred by either of the national constitutional courts or decisive to the judgment, the Court's initiative strongly suggests acknowledgement of the Snowden revelations in 2013 which revealed details of numerous US government programmes involving the mass data collection and surveillance of US and EU citizens.[129] This data protection safeguard established in *Digital Rights Ireland* of physical data retention within the EU has subsequently resulted in several landmark data transfer judgments by the CJEU and major reforms of EU data protection law.[130]

Finally, while welcomed by civil society and scholars, the strict requirements and 'minimum safeguards' concerning data retention established in *Digital Rights Ireland* raised several thorny questions for policymakers at the EU and national level. The most significant of these unresolved issues was whether the Court had in fact held in *Digital Rights Ireland* that the very measure of indiscriminate data retention itself was incompatible with the Charter, thereby rendering any enabling national legislation derogating from the e-Privacy Directive invalid under EU law.[131] Furthermore, if these standards under Articles 7, 8, and 52(1) CFR extended to such national legislation by falling within the scope of the e-Privacy Directive, were Member States required to implement all, or some, of the safeguards set out in *Digital Rights Ireland* to comply with EU law. The Court would address these questions by developing its strict standards in later groundbreaking cases and extending their scope to inter alia the e-Privacy Directive 2002/58, data transfers, mass surveillance, passenger name record (PNR) data, and measures adopted for 'safeguarding national security'.[132]

[127] ibid.

[128] Christopher Kuner and others, 'Internet Balkanization Gathers Pace: Is Privacy the Real Driver?' (2015) 5 International Data Privacy Law 1.

[129] See further Chapter 1.

[130] These included major reforms to the pre-legislative drafts of the GDPR, Law Enforcement Directive (EU) 2016/680, and Passenger Name Record (PNR) Data Directive (EU) 2016/681, all of which were finalized after the CJEU judgments in *Digital Rights Ireland* and *Schrems*: see Chapters 5 and 9.

[131] As argued by Peers (n 123): 'The Court has effectively prohibited mass surveillance in the EU and thus taken significant steps to entrench itself as the EU's constitutional court.'

[132] See Chapters 5 and 9.

D. Conclusions

The reviews of the Data Retention Directive by the European Commission and the CJEU represented a moment of truth for the EU and the protection of the rights to private life and data protection as a result on the ongoing data retention saga. The first assessment of the Data Retention Directive's implementation was difficult to undertake and the findings were far from positive. Nevertheless, the Commission concluded that the findings from its evaluation in 2011 demonstrated that 'data retention is a valuable tool for criminal justice systems and law enforcement' in the EU.[133] The Commission accepted, however, that the Directive had clearly failed to achieve its main objective given the limited contribution of the legislation to the harmonization of data retention across the EU. Furthermore, despite the Commission's sidestepping in confirming this key outcome, the main findings of the evaluation raised serious doubts regarding the compatibility of the Directive with the rights to respect for private life and the protection of personal data. The reliance placed on Article 8 ECHR by the Commission in its evaluation of the Directive's implementation shows that this international human rights provision played a key role in influencing the ongoing development and application of the EU fundamental rights to respect for private life and the protection of personal data within EU policymaking in 2011. Nevertheless, in terms of overall human rights compliance, the key finding from the evaluation was that five years after its adoption the operation of the Directive was still grappling with several major procedural and substantive issues.

The Commission's evaluation of the Data Retention Directive was intended to be part of a two-stage review process, the second of which was arguably the most significant. According to the Commission, the conclusions from its evaluation were intended to form the basis of a future impact assessment report in which the Commission would propose amendments to the Directive. In particular, the Commission made clear that the principles and conditions of Article 8 ECHR and the case law of the ECtHR would be relied on for this purpose. Curiously, however, although the then European Commissioner for Home Affairs stated that this impact assessment would be published later in 2011, the second stage of the Commission's evaluation was never undertaken. Following the Commission's incomplete evaluation, no conclusive assessment of the Directive's compatibility with EU law would take place until the CJEU struck down the entire law from legal existence years later in 2014.

Like the European Commission in its evaluation, the CJEU in its landmark judgment of *Digital Rights Ireland* relied on Article 8 ECHR and the related case law of the ECtHR throughout its examination of the Directive's compatibility with

[133] Commission Evaluation Report (n 2) 1.

the Charter. In particular, the pivotal role of Article 8 ECHR in the striking down of the Data Retention Directive cannot be overstated given its key contribution to the development of the jurisprudential framework and strict proportionality test under Article 52(1) CFR that underpinned the judgment of the Court. In its clear attempts to close ranks with Article 8 ECHR and the lauded case law of the ECtHR in *Digital Rights Ireland*,[134] the Court took a step in the right direction towards the development of a more progressive approach in its adjudication of fundamental rights.[135]

From the broader perspective of the Data Retention Directive being a test case on the post-legislative review and mainstreaming of EU fundamental rights as enshrined in the Charter during the post-Lisbon era, the EU scored poorly. As Morijn and others observe, 'in a well-functioning system of fundamental rights protection, dedicated methods and procedures should actually filter out the great majority of potential problems with compliance of legislative and policy measures well before they reach court'.[136] The Commission's incomplete evaluation of an EU instrument, already the subject of major criticism by national courts and regulators, clearly calls into question the existence of a robust fundamental rights culture when the post-legislative scrutiny of the Directive took place between 2010 and 2014. This effectively left the CJEU with the burden of upholding the credibility of the EU fundamental rights agenda in its review of the Data Retention Directive in *Digital Rights Ireland*. It is entirely plausible that this outsourcing contributed to the Court taking a particularly robust approach in its strict scrutiny of data retention and State surveillance, one it has continued, and doubled down on, in later cases.[137]

[134] On the significance of these Art 8 ECHR standards, and especially those established in the landmark judgment in *S and Marper*, see further Chapter 3.

[135] On the clear divergences that have since emerged between the related surveillance and data retention case law of the ECtHR and the CJEU, see Chapters 2–5.

[136] See John Morijn, 'The Charter in EU and Member States' Policy Practice' in Vasiliki Kosta, Nikos Skoutaris, and Vassilis P Tzevelekos (eds), *The EU Accession to the ECHR* (Hart 2014) 137–38.

[137] See further Chapter 5.

9

The EU Passenger Name Record Data Directive and Data Retention

> [T]he Court finds that the retention, during the initial period of six months, of the PNR data of all air passengers subject to the system established by that directive, without any indication as to their involvement in terrorist offences or serious crime does not appear, as a matter of principle, to go beyond what is strictly necessary.
>
> *Ligue des droits humains* (2022)[1]

A. Introduction

The CJEU has delivered a series of landmark rulings on retention measures that allow access by public authorities to various types of electronic communications data initially collected by the private sector for commercial purposes. This rapidly evolving jurisprudence requires that these measures concerning a person's communications and Internet use must have substantive safeguards and be limited to what is 'strictly necessary'.[2] These include clear and precise rules and meeting objective criteria that link the retained data and the aims being pursued by the public authorities. It is essential to note that the level of scrutiny and strict application of these legal requirements by the CJEU will vary depending on two hierarchies. First, the Court has stated that it applies a 'hierarchy' of public interest objectives

[1] Case C-817/19 *Ligue des droits humains*, judgment of 21 June 2022 (ECLI:EU:C:2022:491) [255] (GC). See also AG Pitruzzella, Opinion of 27 January 2022 in Case C-817/19 *Ligue des droits humains* (ECLI:EU:C:2022:65). On the judgment generally, see Marc Rotenberg, 'CJEU PNR Decision Unplugs the "Black Box"' (2022) 3 European Data Protection Law Review 431; Evelien Brouwer, '*Ligue des droits humains* and the Validity of the PNR Directive' (2023) 60 Common Market Law Review 839; Elif Mendos Kuşkonmaz, 'The Grand Gala of PNR Litigations' (2023) 19 European Constitutional Law Review 294; Christian Thönnes, 'A Directive altered beyond recognition' *VerfBlog* (23 June 2022); Kristina Irion, 'Repairing the EU Passenger Name Record Directive' *European Law Blog* (11 October 2022); Christian Thönnes and Niovi Vavoula, 'Automated predictive threat detection after *Ligue des droits humains*' *VerfBlog* (12 May 2023). All URLs for this chapter were last accessed on 22 April 2024.

[2] Joined Cases C-293/12 and C-594/12 *Digital Rights Ireland and Seitlinger*, judgment of 8 April 2014 (ECLI:EU:C:2014:238); Case C-362/14 *Schrems v Data Protection Commissioner*, judgment of 6 October 2015 (ECLI:EU:C:2015:650); Joined Cases C-511/18, C-512/18 and C-520/18 *La Quadrature du Net and Others*, judgment of 6 October 2020 (ECLI:EU:C:2020:791); Case C-140/20 *G.D. v Commissioner of An Garda Síochána*, judgment of 5 April 2022 (ECLI:EU:C:2022:258); Joined Cases C-793/19 and 794/19 *SpaceNet and Telekom Deutschland GmbH*, judgment of 22 September 2022 (ECLI:EU:C:2022:702). See further Chapter 5.

EU Data Privacy Law and Serious Crime. Nora Ni Loideain, Oxford University Press. © Nora Ni Loideain 2025.
DOI: 10.1093/oso/9780198837169.003.0009

in its judgments.[3] Secondly, as identified and examined in Chapter 5, this judicial review is also subject to a 'hierarchy of intrusiveness'. This approach is particularly evident in the Court's leading data retention judgments where different requirements are applied to different types of communications data.[4] For instance, the bulk retention of 'data relating to the civil identity of users' is subject to fewer limits when compared to the stricter rules that apply when public authorities seek access to a person's location data in real time.[5] Indeed, both the CJEU and the ECtHR view the latter as one of the most privacy-invasive types of communications data when accessed and subsequently used by public authorities for monitoring a person's movements. These hierarchies lie at the heart of the CJEU's assessment when it determines the compatibility of these data retention measures with EU law, especially the rights and safeguards enshrined in Articles 7, 8, and 52(1) CFR. The resulting case law has also had significant and far-reaching implications for EU data protection law more broadly. However, it is important to highlight, as examined elsewhere in other chapters, that most of these EU data retention rules and safeguards are not novel. Instead, the case law of the EU's highest court is underpinned by, and continues to build from, standards from another long-established legal system in Europe. The latter is the right to respect for private life as enshrined in Article 8 ECHR and its interpretation and application in the corresponding case law of the ECtHR.[6]

This chapter examines how the CJEU, and consequently other EU bodies, have interpreted and extended these landmark data retention requirements from beyond the realm of communications data to the retention and analysis of air passenger information.[7] The analysis of the legislative cycles of the Advance Passenger Information Directive 2004/82/EC and Passenger Name Record Directive (EU) 2016/681 also considers the impacts for the right to private life within future EU data retention policymaking, human rights protection in practice, and the role of Article 8 ECHR therein.[8] Special consideration is given to the 'mainstreaming' of

[3] *G.D.* (n 2) [56].

[4] On communications data and its use for countering serious crime and safeguarding national security, see Chapter 1.

[5] The Grand Chamber has delivered most of these judgments for which there is no appeal. This is exceptional and at the time of writing further preliminary references are pending. See eg Case C-470/21 *La Quadrature du Net (Hadopi)*; Case C-178/22 *Procura.*

[6] See Chapters 2–5.

[7] These data retention standards have also been applied to other areas of EU law, including international data transfers. On the related judgments of *Schrems* and *Schrems II*, see Chapter 5.

[8] Council Directive 2004/82/EC of 27 April 2016 on the obligation of carriers to communicate passenger data [2004] OJ L261/24 (API Directive); European Parliament and Council Directive 2006/24/EC of 15 March 2006 on the retention of data generated or processed in connection with the provision of publicly available electronic communications services or of public communications networks and amending Directive 2002/58/EC [2006] OJ L105/54 (Data Retention Directive); Directive 2016/681 of the European Parliament and of the Council of 27 April 2016 on the use of passenger name record (PNR) data for the prevention, detection, investigation and prosecution of terrorist offences and serious crimes [2016] OJ L119/132 (PNR Directive).

the right to private life in this area of EU policymaking.[9] Particularly in the pre- and post-legislative stages of the PNR Directive and API Directive and how these compare with the Data Retention Directive 2006/24/EC. The crux of this analysis being that the API Directive and Data Retention Directive became part of the EU legal order before the Lisbon Treaty entered into force in 2009. This was a time before the EU Charter of Fundamental Rights was elevated to the status of being legally binding under EU law.[10] The Lisbon Treaty was intended to represent a milestone in the status and protection of fundamental rights within EU law, including commitments by the European Council and European Parliament to promote EU fundamental rights as a priority for future measures adopted at EU level to counter terrorism and serious crime (area of freedom, security, and justice, AFSJ).[11] Indeed, the European Commission stated that these reforms would promote a 'fundamental rights culture' and that the Charter would serve as a 'compass' for EU policies and their implementation by Member States.[12]

Within the area of EU data retention policymaking and the right to privacy, this book shows where there has been progress towards this more robust fundamental rights culture and where the EU has fallen short. This specific chapter identifies these gaps, how they arose within the context of the API and PNR Directives and the mainstreaming of the right to private life, and how they may be addressed in future. The discussion begins with the legal and political origins that played a crucial role in shaping the measures adopted at EU level permitting the surveillance of air travel to, and later within, the EU—particularly the emergence of the API Directive, its links to the 9/11 attacks in the US, and the early EU–US PNR transfer regimes. Following further political pressure on the EU legislature in the wake of terrorist attacks in Europe, this section examines the patchy scrutiny and fraught mainstreaming of the right to private life during the drafting of the API Directive. Put simply, from the perspective of human rights law and legal certainty, the API Directive is the PNR Directive's lesser-known and problematic older sibling. In a welcome development, however, this chapter shows that the pre-legislative scrutiny of what became the PNR Directive was shaped by a more sophisticated framework of human rights law and data protection in the post-Lisbon era of EU policymaking, within which the case law of the CJEU, Article 8 ECHR, and the relevant case law of the ECtHR all played an important role. Nevertheless, despite this improvement, this chapter also identifies deep flaws in the methodology and

9 Mainstreaming is essentially an attempt by policymakers to ensure that the 'rights review' of law happens throughout the ongoing legislative cycle of a legal instrument. By ensuring this scrutiny occurs across the law's drafting, implementation, and evaluation, it is not then solely a matter for the courts to review. See Chapter 6.

10 On the significance of the Lisbon Treaty for EU fundamental rights and data protection law, see Chapter 4.

11 European Commission, 'Strategy for the effective implementation of the Charter of Fundamental Rights by the European Union', COM(2010) 573 final, 2–4.

12 ibid.

substantive application of the right-based approach in the *ex ante* and *ex post* scrutiny of the PNR Directive.

The next section sets out the main provisions of the PNR Directive, followed by analysis of its post-legislative scrutiny by the European Commission in 2020 and by the CJEU in 2022.[13] In *Ligue des droits humains*, the Court delivered a groundbreaking judgment concerning the retention and use of PNR data as established by the PNR Directive and implemented within Belgian law. This landmark ruling involves a detailed examination of the Directive's compatibility with the EU Charter and the processing of PNR data for countering terrorism and serious crime with a particular focus on its compatibility with the rights to private life and data protection as enshrined in Articles 7 and 8 CFR.[14] However, there are huge divergences between the Commission's positive review of the PNR Directive and the CJEU's highly critical examination in *Ligue des droits humains*. Following a more pragmatic and less rights-based approach, the Commission concluded, following its review, that no changes to the PNR Directive were necessary, ultimately stating that its application after two years was 'overall positive'.[15] It goes without saying that the Court adopted a very different view. One that Thönnes rightly describes as altering the law 'beyond recognition'.[16] Although the Court did not go so far as to strike down the PNR Directive for its invalidity with EU law, PNR systems implemented before this landmark judgment subsequently require major reform by Member States if they are to conform with EU law.

The chapter ends with some reflections on the challenges and deeper implications posed by these complex and diverging reviews of the PNR Directive by these EU institutions, both of which are tasked under EU law in distinct but complementary roles with being guardians of EU fundamental rights law. The importance of enabling the effectiveness of this shared rights scrutiny and oversight will

[13] European Commission, 'Report on the review of Directive 2016/681 on the use of passenger name record (PNR) data for the prevention, detection, investigation and prosecution of terrorist offences and serious crime', COM(2020) 305 final (PNR Directive Review Report); for further detail, see European Commission, 'Staff Working Document accompanying Report on PNR Directive Review', SWD(2020) 128 final.

[14] *Ligue des droits humains* (n 1). Other preliminary references from Germany and Slovenia concerning the compatibility of the PNR Directive with EU law had been submitted to the CJEU but have since been withdrawn. See Joined Cases C-148/20, C-149/20 and C-150/20 *Deutsche Lufthansa* [2020] OJ C279/21 and C-486/20. As discussed later, this judgment was strongly influenced by the standards applied in the CJEU's critical assessment in Opinion 1/15 *Draft agreement between Canada and the European Union on Transfer of Passenger Name Record data*, opinion of 26 July 2017 (ECLI:EU:C:2017:592). See Hielke Hijmans, 'PNR Agreement EU–Canada Scrutinised' (2017) 3 European Data Protection Law Review 406; Christopher Kuner, 'International Agreements, Data Protection, and EU Fundamental Rights on the International Stage: Opinion 1/15, *EU–Canada PNR*' (2018) 55 Common Market Law Review 857; Sara Roda, 'Shortcomings of the Passenger Name Record Directive in Light of Opinion 1/15 of the CJEU' (2020) 6 European Data Protection Law Review 66.

[15] European Commission, PNR Directive Review Report (n 13) 11–12.

[16] Thönnes (n 1); *Ligue des droits humains* (n 1) [86]; EDPB, 'Statement 5/2022 on the implications of the CJEU judgment C-817/19 regarding the implementation of the Directive (EU) 2016/681 on the use of PNR in Member States', 13 December 2022.

only increase given the shift in government surveillance practices from targeted measures to more indiscriminate systems and predictive analytics that monitor the communications and movements of the wider public in an increasingly data-driven world. Such far-reaching capabilities include AI-assisted biometrics recognition (face, gait, emotion), large-scale hacking, and the bulk monitoring of online communications and public places in physical and virtual reality spaces.[17] The 'net-widening' of these measures across Europe strengthens the need to effectively implement and monitor relevant data protection safeguards.[18] These reflections lead to the key finding that the protection of the right to privacy within such systems at the EU level has systematic weaknesses and requires reform.

Some policy recommendations are made regarding how these shortcomings may be addressed. Ultimately, unless the European Commission and the CJEU both fulfil their roles as guardians of EU law, the safeguards enshrined in Articles 7 and 8 CFR will only provide illusory protection for the private lives and personal data of individuals.

B. From Advance Passenger Information to PNR

1. The Advance Passenger Information Directive 2004/82/EC

(a) Legal background

The events of 9/11 were hugely significant in terms of shifting the balance in security-rights policymaking debates and acted as a catalyst for governments worldwide to adopt a data-driven approach for countering both terrorism and serious crime.[19] Indeed, when announcing plans for the EU's AFSJ in 2010, the European Commission acknowledged that the 9/11 terrorist attacks, as well as bombings in Madrid and London in 2004 and 2005, 'had triggered *another*

[17] See eg European Commission, 'Fighting Child Sexual Abuse: Commission proposed new rules to protect children' Press Release (11 May 2022) (CSAM); Lisa O Carroll, 'French court's approval of Olympics AI surveillance plan fuels privacy concerns' *The Guardian* (18 May 2023); European Commission, *Extended Reality: Final Report* (DG for Communications Networks 2023). <https://digital-strategy.ec.europa.eu/en/library/extended-reality-opportunities-success-stories-and-challenges-health-and-education>. See further Chapter 1.

[18] FRA, Annual Report 2023 (June 2023) 182.

[19] Louise Amoore and Marieke de Goede, 'Datawars: Reflections Twenty Years After 9/11' (2021) 14 Critical Studies on Terrorism 425, 426. Plans to establish travel data collection systems to track and profile passengers for counter-terrorism (and commercial) purposes in the US were taking place long before 9/11. Note eg industry collection of airline reservation data in the 1960s and the controversial development and abandonment of the 'Computer Assisted Passenger Pre-screening System' (CAPPS) during the 1990s which would be replaced after 9/11 by CAPPS II. See further Paul de Hert, 'Balancing Security and Liberty Within the European Human Rights Framework' (2005) 1 Utrecht Law Review 68, 87; Maria Tzanou, *The Fundamental Right to Data Protection: Normative Value in the Context of Counter-Terrorism Surveillance* (Hart 2017) 110–115. See generally Chris Wiggins and Matthew L Jones, *How Data Happened* (Norton 2023).

dynamic' in the development of the EU's information management policies.[20] The 9/11 attacks thus accelerated the adoption of information sharing and bulk data collection systems that were already under consideration for uses beyond countering terrorism. This move towards a more data-driven approach of intelligence gathering is evident in a European Council meeting on the creation of the AFSJ years earlier in 1999 which clearly signals a shift away from bilateral agreements between Member States on information exchange.

It was at this time before 9/11 that the adoption of crime prevention measures across EU 'external and internal policy' towards a more integrated EU-level approach was being advocated.[21] Hence, the API Directive 2004/82/EC and (the now invalidated) Data Retention Directive 2006/24/EC would later be categorized as 'information management' instruments, adopted to regulate the retention and exchange of personal data for the aims of 'law enforcement or migration management'.[22] Regarding the specific role (and impact) of the events of 9/11 as a catalyst for this shift in EU governance, the then US President sent the Commission what would become an instrumental letter for EU data retention policymaking in October 2001. This contained no less than forty proposals for US–EU counterterrorism cooperation that stressed the need for proactive and large-scale data collection.[23] The detailed list also urged the EU to establish data-sharing procedures for improving border security, strengthening transit procedures to combat terrorism, and for US–EU efforts to encourage other nations to utilize secure, machine-readable passports and explore further use of biometrics.[24]

In line with these proposals, and following a Member State initiative by Spain, the Council of the EU published a draft of the API Directive in 2003. The draft required Member States to establish an obligation for 'carriers' to transmit passenger

[20] European Commission, 'Overview of information management in area of freedom, security and justice', COM (2010) 385 final, 2 (emphasis added). Following the entry into force of the Lisbon Treaty, the (previously intergovernmental) AFSJ was integrated into the main body of EU Treaty Law. See further Chapter 6.

[21] Presidency Conclusions, Tampere European Council, 15–16 October 1999, para 41. The European Council (not to be confused with the Council of the EU) comprises the heads of State of the twenty-seven EU Member States, the European Council President, and the President of the European Commission. Note also Europol's establishment in 1995: Council Act of 26 July 1995 drawing up the Convention based on Article K.3 of the Treaty on European Union, on the establishment of a European Police Office (Europol Convention) [1995] OJ C316/1; Schengen Convention: Convention implementing the Schengen Agreement of 14 June 1985 between the Governments of the States of the Benelux Economic Union, the Federal Republic of Germany and the French Republic on the gradual abolition of checks at their common borders [2000] OJ L239/19.

[22] European Commission (n 13) 3, 8, 12. On EU information systems within the context of immigration, see generally Niovi Vavoula, *Immigration and Privacy in the Law of the European Union* (Brill 2022).

[23] On the impact of 9/11 and its links to the enactment of the EU Data Retention Directive, see Chapter 7.

[24] US Mission to the President of the European Commission, Letter concerning Proposals for US–EU Counter Terrorism Cooperation, 16 October 2001: <https://statewatch.org/news/2001/nov/06Ausalet.htm>. Also included were proposals for the long-term retention of communications data. See Chapter 6.

data to authorities responsible for carrying out external border checks for the 'sole purpose' of combating illegal immigration.[25] The US also adopted several laws in the aftermath of 9/11 requiring airlines flying to or from US territory to transfer the PNR data of any passengers and crew members, including the Aviation and Transportation Security Act of 2001.[26] However, the Article 29 Working Party, a group representing data protection authorities across the EU (now the EDPB), advised that complying with these US legal requirements ran contrary to EU data protection law.[27] This conflict placed airlines in a stark 'legal dilemma'.[28] They were obliged to observe national legislation on data protection transposing Directive 95/46, the then principal EU data protection law (now the GDPR), and, on the other hand, US laws required airlines to forward data and imposed severe penalties for non-compliance. Thus, alongside the API Directive being proposed in 2003, the EU launched negotiations with the US to reach an agreement providing for the transfer of PNR data. A draft EU–US PNR Agreement was reached in 2004.

The European Parliament raised serious concerns regarding the Draft Agreement's legal basis, scope, and fundamental rights implications, and subsequently brought proceedings against the Council and Commission before the CJEU.[29] Rather than taking the expansive fundamental rights approach that the CJEU is now so well known for in cases dealing with data retention for law enforcement and national security matters,[30] the very opposite occurred in this now infamous ruling. The Court annulled the EU–US PNR Agreement in 2006 solely on the grounds of its legal basis without addressing the specific questions raised by Parliament regarding the Draft Agreement's compliance with the principle of proportionality and fundamental rights.[31] As Docksey aptly notes, this 'jurisdiction approach' involves the Court dealing solely with the legal basis of an impugned measure regardless of its broader consequences and giving little explicit

[25] Council of the EU, 'Initiative of the Kingdom of Spain with a view to adopting a Council Directive on the obligation of carriers to communicate passenger data' [2003] OJ C 82/23, Art 4(1), recital 1. Note that this was not limited to 'air carriers' and thus applied to other transport carriers.

[26] Under the Act of 2001, Congress has authorized the US Transportation Security Administration (TSA) to use 'voice stress analysis, biometric, or other technologies to prevent a person who might pose a danger to air safety or security from boarding the aircraft of an air carrier or foreign air carrier in air transportation or intrastate air transportation'. This power has allowed the TSA to permit air carriers to use facial recognition technology for passengers checking in baggage. See US Government Accountability Office, 'Facial Recognition Technology: Current and Planned Uses by Federal Agencies', GAO-21-526 (GAO 2021) 24–25.

[27] Article 29 Data Protection Working Party, 'Opinion 6/2002 on transmission of Passenger Manifest Information and other data from Airlines to the United States' (WP 66) 24 October 2002.

[28] ibid 4.

[29] Joined Cases C-317/04 and C-318/04 *European Parliament v Council and Commission*, judgment of 30 May 2006 (ECLI:EU:C:2006:346). See also Article 29 Data Protection Working Party, 'Opinion 4/2003 on the Level of Protection ensuring in the US for the Transfer of Passengers' Data' (WP 78) 13 June 2003.

[30] See further Chapter 5.

[31] On the judgment generally, see Gráinne Gilmore and Jorrit Rijpma, 'Joined Cases C-317/04 and C-318/04, *European Parliament* v. *Council and Commission*' (2007) 44 Common Market Law Review 1081.

consideration to any rights issues raised for its scrutiny.[32] The judgment has since been widely criticized on two main grounds. Many considered it a failure of the CJEU not to deliver any fundamental rights analysis on a highly controversial framework with wide-ranging 'repercussions for the civil liberties of EU citizens'.[33] Secondly, Parliament was criticized for securing a Pyrrhic victory which would result in a revised EU–US PNR Agreement that was even more problematic from a fundamental rights standpoint.[34] After the judgment, a provisional replacement in the form of a seven-year EU–US PNR Agreement was concluded in 2007.[35] Parliament then postponed its approval vote of this revised proposal until after the Lisbon Treaty had entered into force in 2009, and subsequent renegotiations had taken place, resulting in another Agreement.[36] After nine years of negotiations (and renegotiations) a revised 'Second Generation' EU–US PNR Agreement was adopted in 2012.[37] This regime would also be criticized for its lack of proportionality, weak provisions on access and judicial redress, and lengthy data retention periods.[38]

Against this fraught background of EU external policymaking, data retention, and PNR transfers,[39] it is unsurprising that the proposed API Directive prompted similar concerns within the sphere of EU internal policy. Particularly given its *raison d'être* to introduce an obligation for air carriers to transmit passenger data to authorities responsible for carrying out external border checks within the EU. However, despite Parliament and the Commission raising serious concerns, the

[32] Christopher Docksey, 'The European Court of Justice and the Decade of Surveillance' in Hielke Hijmans and Herke Kranenborg (eds), *Data Protection Anno 2014: How to Restore Trust?* (Intersentia 2014) 97. The CJEU often adopted this approach in its pre-Lisbon Treaty case law dealing with State surveillance and data retention: see Chapter 6.

[33] Elaine Fahey, 'Of "One Shotters' and "Repeat Hitters": A Retrospective on the Role of the European Parliament in the EU–US PNR Litigation' in Fernanda Nicola and Bill Davies (eds), *EU Law Stories* (CUP 2017) 528. Literature on this topic is extensive. See further Bruno De Witte, 'Too Much Constitutional Law in the European Union's Foreign Relations?' in Bruno De Witte and Marise Cremona (eds), *EU Foreign Relations Law* (Hart 2008); Gilmore and Rijpma (n 31); Valsamis Mitilegas, 'The EU and the Globalisation of Criminal Law' (2010) 12 Cambridge Yearbook of European Legal Studies 337; Docksey (n 32); Sophie in't Veld, 'Transatlantic Relations and Security: Reflections from a Politician, Practitioner and Litigator' in Elaine Fahey and Deirdre Curtin (eds), *A Transatlantic Community of Law* (CUP 2014) 237–54.

[34] ibid.

[35] De Witte (n 33) 11.

[36] European Commission, 'New EU–US Agreements on PNR improves data protection and fights crime and terrorism', IP/11/1368, 17 November 2011.

[37] Agreement between the United States of America and the European Union on the use and transfer of passenger name records to the United States Department of Homeland Security [2012] OJ L215/5.

[38] See Veld (n 33); Tzanou (n 19) 134–38; EDPS, Opinion on the Proposal for a Council Decision on the conclusion of the Agreement between the United States of America and the European Union on the use and transfer of Passenger Name Records to the United States Department of Homeland Security, 9 December 2011.

[39] Negotiations on PNR agreements were also taking place with Australia and Canada: House of Lords EU Committee, 'The Passenger Name Record (PNR) Framework Decision' (HL Paper 106, 2008) 41. The European Parliament would later challenge the legality of the EU–Canada PNR draft agreement in Opinion 1/15 (n 14).

Council of the EU would ultimately rush through and enact a significantly revised draft of the API Directive by May 2004 in response to a terrorist attack in Madrid on 11 March 2004.[40] On 19 March 2004, Parliament, via the Committee on Citizens Freedoms and Rights (LIBE), nevertheless rejected an amended version of the Spanish initiative of the proposed API Directive and called for it to be withdrawn. In doing so, MEPs raised numerous issues. The main criticisms concerned the overall technical viability of the proposal, its general lack of clarity, and outstanding issues surrounding proportionality, subsidiarity, and data protection.[41] These concerns would largely go unaddressed as the final draft of the proposed API Directive, presented by the Council to Parliament in March 2004, would be adopted exceptionally without the opinion of the European Parliament.[42]

The final text also made major amendments which dramatically expanded the scope of the API Directive, extending its use for improving border controls and, more controversially, for the far wider undefined scope of 'law enforcement purposes'. Some references to general compliance with EU data protection law were also added but these are brief and notably vague. The final draft also replaced any reference to 'third country nationals' with the far broader term of 'passengers'.[43] In an attempt to address this effective sidestepping of any final parliamentary oversight, the Commission added a declaration to the final text urging that the Directive be interpreted in line with 'its stated purposes' to combat illegal immigration effectively and to improve border control.[44] The Commission also announced its intention to propose a comprehensive legislative measure on data protection and information transfers between law enforcement authorities by June 2004. In addition, the Commission stressed that it 'would have preferred to await that measure before dealing piecemeal' with the law enforcement issues raised by the revised API Directive.[45] From the perspective of legal certainty and fundamental rights protection, these non-binding commitments by the Commission—though welcome—still fall short of being an adequate substitute for meaningful scrutiny by the Parliament and other relevant EU bodies. Furthermore, this final draft of

[40] API Directive 2004/82/EC, Art 9.

[41] European Parliament, 'Report on the initiative of the Kingdom of Spain with a view to the adoption of a Council directive on the obligation of carriers to communicate passenger data', A5-0211/2004, 19 March 2004, <https://europarl.europa.eu/doceo/document/A-5-2004-0211_EN.html>.

[42] Since 1 May 2004, the Council can no longer act on initiatives from Member States. The 'co-decision procedure' established by the Maastricht Treaty in 1992 was critical to putting Parliament on an equal footing with the Council in EU policymaking. This was extended again under the Amsterdam Treaty in 2004. The Lisbon Treaty would further consolidate the role of Parliament as co-legislature with the Council when it came into effect in 2009, renamed as the 'ordinary legislative procedure' (Art 294 TEU). See Chapter 6.

[43] European Parliament, 'Combating illegal immigration', 2003/0809(CNS), 1 April 2004, <https://oeil.secure.europarl.europa.eu/oeil/popups/summary.do?id=4720&t=e&l=en>.

[44] ibid.

[45] ibid.

the API Directive was significantly more far-reaching in scope than the original version (which was heavily criticized by Parliament).

(b) Main provisions

The API Directive 2004/82/EC was the first EU Directive to require Member States to adopt measures to collect travel data from the private sector (when requested by relevant public authorities) concerning individuals travelling across EU external borders. In addition to EU Member States, the API Directive also regulates the collection and transfer of data to Schengen-associated countries (Norway, Iceland, Liechtenstein, and Switzerland) and thus applies to thirty-one participating countries. The deadline for transposing the API Directive was September 2006.[46]

There are strong links between the API Directive and PNR Directive: the primary aims of the former being border control and the fight against irregular migration and, for the latter, the prevention, detection, investigation, and prosecution of terrorist offences and serious crime. The European Commission has also stressed the growing importance of API data, particularly with regards to the PNR Directive, 'as a key component of the border management and internal security *acquis*'.[47] As Vavoula rightly points out, however, these linked EU instruments still contain many differences which have proved problematic in their implementation and in reviewing their compliance with EU data protection law and fundamental rights.[48]

(i) *Advance passenger information* API data is commonly understood as the information of an air passenger which is collected at check-in at the airport or following online check-in and used by airlines for their own commercial and operational purposes.[49] It mainly covers biographical data contained in the 'machine readable zone' (MRZ) of a passenger's travel document but also includes information concerning the flight.[50] Article 3(2) of the API Directive provides for the following non-exhaustive list of information to be transferred to public authorities across Europe: number and type of travel document; nationality; full names; date of birth; border crossing point into the territory of Member State; code of transport; departure and arrival time of transport; total number of passengers; and initial point of embarkation. The list of API data to be collected under Annex I of the PNR Directive is also non-exhaustive. However, it is important to note that

46 API Directive 2004/82/EC, Art 7(1).

47 European Commission, 'Evaluation of Council Directive 2004/82/EC on the obligation of carriers to communicate passenger data (API Directive)', SWD (2020) 174 final, 53; European Commission, Staff Working Document Impact Assessment Report, SWD/2022/422 final, 8: <https://eur-lex.europa.eu/legal-content/EN/TXT/?uri=CELEX%3A52022SC0422> (Evaluation of API Directive).

48 Niovi Vavoula, 'The future developments regarding Prüm and the API Directive', Study requested by LIBE Committee (European Parliament 2020) 53. On similar complex legislative overlaps between the former Data Retention Directive 2006/24/EC and the e-Privacy Directive 2002/58/EC, see Chapter 6.

49 PNR Directive (EU) 2016/681, recital 8.

50 European Commission, Evaluation of API Directive (n 47) 8.

the CJEU established in 2022 that both lists under the API Directive and the PNR Directive must be interpreted exhaustively, and therefore cover 'only the information expressly referred to' in order to satisfy the proportionality requirements of clarity and precision enshrined in Articles 7, 8, and 52(1) CFR.[51]

Law enforcement authorities have consistently stated that API data is particularly useful for reliable verification of PNR-based analysis and profiling and that this is mainly due to the way in which API is collected.[52] PNR data is provided voluntarily by passengers (or on their behalf by travel operators) and is often subject to spelling mistakes or other errors. API data, in contrast, has traditionally been taken directly from the travel document which avoids manual entries and ensures that specific details (such as dates) are transcribed more accurately.[53] As a result, API data is frequently used for checking against watch lists and for early identification of persons of interest already known to public authorities.[54] Public authorities have been critical more recently, however, of the increasing approach by airlines to require passengers to manually enter API data via self-check-in systems at airports.[55] This manual process of entering API data raises the same issues of unreliable data posed by passengers entering their own PNR data which is often not verified, regularly leading to inaccurate data (including misspelt names and dates) which is later shared with public authorities in bulk. Once such datasets become part of an automated decision-making system (such as machine learning), there are increased risks that this incorrect data will hinder investigations for law enforcement and intelligence services and/or result in unlawful targeting of innocent individuals and miscarriages of justice.[56]

(ii) *Scope and purposes* The API Directive states in several provisions that its aim is to 'improve border controls and combat illegal immigration' via the transfer of API data by carriers to competent national authorities (at their request).[57] Article 3(1) of Directive 2004/82/EC further specifies that the obligation to provide this information to a Member State relates only to flights arriving in that Member State from a third country (extra-EU flights) after passengers have checked in. Public authorities in twenty-nine Member States reported using API data for the purposes of border control and countering illegal immigration. API data was used inter alia for identifying persons/items of interest, including as part of an arrest,

[51] *Ligue des droits humains* (n 1) [139]–[140]. This non-exhaustive list for API data was previously criticized for falling short of international law standards on the transfer of API data. See ICF and Unisys, 'Study on Advance Passenger Information (API)—Evaluation of Council Directive 2004/82/EC on the obligation of carriers to communicate passenger data', Final Report for European Commission (2020) 13.

[52] House of Lords (n 39) 12; Vavoula (n 48) 45; European Commission, Evaluation of API Directive (n 47) 65.

[53] ibid.

[54] ibid.

[55] ICF and Unisys (n 51) 76; European Commission, Evaluation of API Directive (n 47) 56.

[56] See further Chapter 1.

[57] API Directive 2004/82/EC, Arts 1 and 2, recitals 1, 3, 7, 9.

identification of a missing person, or identification of missing or stolen or counterfeit documents.[58] Matches were made with API data against the Schengen Information System (SIS) and the Visa Information System (VIS). However, the overall effectiveness of these provisions was difficult to assess in the 2020 study on the API Directive for three main reasons.

First, Member States provided limited data on the number of persons who were refused entry or apprehended following hits generated by API data processing and, secondly, public authorities often combined the use of API and PNR data.[59] Thirdly, the scope of the API Directive is also subject to a major caveat which has allowed Member States considerable discretion to expand the application of the system established under the API Directive in their national transposition of this EU law. In accordance with their national laws, Article 6(1) of the API Directive explicitly provides that Member States 'may also use' personal data collected under the API system for the broad and undefined aim of 'law enforcement purposes'. All but two Member States consequently extended the scope of their national transposition laws by allowing API data to be used for law enforcement and countering terrorism,[60] purposes that go far beyond the API Directive's original *raison d'être* of combating illegal immigration. Unsurprisingly, this has also led to the scope of each Member State's API system diverging significantly with respect to the different purposes adopted by each Member State, rendering any comparative assessment difficult or indeed moot. This has included Member States applying API data to internal flights for law enforcement purposes.[61]

Finally, there are divergences in the 'uneven' scope and 'disjointed' implementation of the API Directive across the EU.[62] Article 2(a) of the API Directive specifically states that the term 'carrier' concerns the provision of 'passenger transport by air'. Some Member States, however, have made the retention of API data mandatory for other modes of transport.[63] Belgium has, for instance, combined its implementation of the API Directive, PNR Directive, and Directive 2010/65 (passenger data retention for maritime transport) into one national statute.[64] This national law applies to carriers and tour operators and applies the system established by the PNR Directive to all intra-EU flights and transport by train, road, and sea in the EU which depart from, go to, or transit through, Belgium.[65] As noted later, the CJEU provides a critical assessment of this law in *Ligue des droits humains*.

(iii) *Data retention* Following a passenger's arrival, Article 6(1) of the API Directive provides that border authorities may retain API data for 24 hours from

58 ICF and Unisys (n 51) 67–71.
59 ibid 69.
60 ibid 35 (Netherlands and Slovenia).
61 ibid 73.
62 ibid 103; Commission, Evaluation of the API Directive (n 47) 54.
63 ibid 42. Estonia, Finland, France, and the UK reported use of API data concerning train travel.
64 *Ligue des droits humains* (n 1) [42].
65 ibid [287].

transmission. After passengers have entered, and subject to their 'statutory functions', border authorities are required to delete the data within 24 hours after transmission from the air carriers. From the perspective of closely adhering to the data protection principle of storage limitation, and the long-established legal requirements of necessity and proportionality, this retention period could be considered a data protection by design and the default benchmark for EU information management systems. A study for the European Commission in 2020 also reported that most Member States had complied with the 24-hour retention period for API data used for border control purposes.[66] The same study, however, also highlighted that several Member States had changed their laws and data retention requirements regarding the storage of API data following their transposition of PNR Directive.[67] Article 12 of the PNR Directive introduced a far longer retention period of six months, or up to five years, subject to PNR data being 'depersonalised'. Hence, the existence of both EU instruments has led to 'inconsistencies' in the application of the API Directive across Member States, with public authorities retaining API data for longer periods, and for other purposes, as permitted under the PNR Directive.[68]

(iv) ***Data protection safeguards and oversight*** Like the PNR Directive and most large-scale EU information management systems, the API regime operates using a decentralized system of information sharing between private operators and public authorities. The European Commission has previously expressed the strongly held view that this is the most conducive framework for ensuring data protection compliance and enforcement.[69] The API Directive itself, however, lacks any substantive provisions which provide for specific data protection safeguards. Strikingly, there is no explicit requirement for any review, oversight, or *ex post* scrutiny to be undertaken at the EU level with respect to its evaluation, only some cursory references to data protection compliance in Article 6(1) of the API Directive. These require that any retention of API data by public authorities or their use for 'law enforcement purposes' are subject to the 'data protection provisions' under the Data Protection Directive 95/46 (the GDPR's predecessor). Article 6(2) places an equally brief requirement on Member States to oblige carriers to inform passengers of the data collection permitted under the API system in line with their transparency requirements under Directive 95/46. Finally, the API Directive contains

[66] ICF and Unisys (n 51) 162. Eight Member States did not implement this requirement. The UK eg adopted a retention period of up to ten years.

[67] ibid 162.

[68] ibid 17.

[69] European Commission (n 17) 3. The development and management of several centralized EU large-scale systems (eg Eurodac, SIS II, VIS) is the task of 'eu-LISA', a dedicated EU Agency. See Regulation (EU) 2018/1726 of the European Parliament and of the Council of 14 November 2018 on the European Union Agency for the Operational Management of Large-Scale IT Systems in the Area of Freedom, Security and Justice (eu-LISA), and amending Regulation (EC) No 1987/2006 and Council Decision 2007/533/JHA and repealing Regulation (EU) No 1077/2011 [2018] OJ L 295.

no references or requirements to respect or comply with fundamental rights law, as enshrined in the EU or ECHR legal systems. The API Directive is also silent on the rights to private life and non-discrimination as guaranteed under the 'general principles of EC law', the leading EU framework on human rights law prior to the Charter becoming part of EU law.[70]

(c) Pre-legislative scrutiny

The rapid enactment of the final and comparatively short text of the proposed API Directive prevented the opportunity for any detailed pre-legislative scrutiny by the European Commission and other EU institutions at the final drafting stages.[71] Although the final drafting of the Data Retention Directive 2006/24/EC was also subject to strong criticism for its incompatibility with fundamental rights, the final text of the API Directive was adopted exceptionally without the opinion of the European Parliament or any impact assessment. For all the haste and cost to the democratic legitimacy and pre-legislative scrutiny of the API Directive, only nine Member States would meet its transposition deadline in 2006.[72] Thus, from the perspective of the rule of law and fundamental rights, the apparent need to side-step the API Directive's final stage of pre-legislative oversight by the most democratic institution of the EU clearly becomes more questionable in hindsight. It is therefore evident from the scant pre-legislative scrutiny of the API Directive that a robust culture of EU fundamental rights during this pre-Lisbon period of EU policymaking in law enforcement was sorely lacking.[73] Alongside its rushed final drafting stages and general lack of engagement with the rule of law and other relevant human rights, the role of Article 8 ECHR and the right to private life in the shaping and pre-legislative scrutiny of the API Directive was also non-existent.

(d) Post-legislative scrutiny

(i) ***Main findings*** The European Commission published its first evaluation of the API Directive in 2013, eight years after its implementation deadline in 2006. It reported that nineteen Member States had implemented API systems (mostly pilot systems).[74] Consequently, the Commission rightly notes in this review that the effectiveness and added value of the API Directive could not 'be fully realised' with so many Member States having not implemented any API systems.[75]

[70] On EU human rights law before the entry into force of the Lisbon Treaty in 2009, see Chapter 4.

[71] European Commission, Evaluation of API Directive (n 47) 8. The API Directive contains nine articles. The GDPR has ninety-nine articles.

[72] ICF GHK and Milieu, 'Evaluation on the implementation and functioning of the obligation of carriers to communicate passenger data set up by Directive 2004/82', Final Report for European Commission (DG Home Affairs 2013) 77.

[73] On the drafting of the Data Retention Directive and Art 8 ECHR in the pre-Lisbon era, see Chapter 7.

[74] ICF GHK and Milieu (n 72) 4. 'Member States' refers to the EU27, Iceland, Norway, Switzerland, and Liechtenstein.

[75] ibid 116.

When the second evaluation was published in 2020, most Member States (and four Schengen-associated countries) had 'fully functioning' API systems with twenty-nine countries collecting API data for border control and twenty-one for law enforcement purposes.[76] However, this evaluation, and an independent study commissioned by the European Parliament, make clear that three major issues persist concerning the API Directive.[77] First, the wide discretion accorded to Member States to use API data for the undefined scope of 'law enforcement purposes' has made assessing the adequacy of the API Directive's uneven implementation across the EU and its general compliance with EU law practically impossible.[78] This significant carve-out from the API Directive's scope has thus resulted in API data being extended to internal flights for the use of law enforcement purposes despite its explicit scope being 'checks on persons at external borders'.[79] Secondly, the API Directive also lacks any data retention requirements for API data used for law enforcement purposes, leaving any such limits to national law. Thirdly, the overlap and unclear relationship between the API Directive and the PNR Directive has created 'several discrepancies' between both frameworks, causing incoherence with respect to their exact scope, relevant data protection safeguards, and general operation.[80] This has resulted in public authorities retaining API data for longer periods and for additional purposes.[81] All these issues invariably cast doubt on the compliance of Member States' use of API data under the API Directive regime with EU law, particularly the storage limitation principle under the GDPR, the LED, and the data retention case law of the CJEU.[82]

(ii) *Fundamental rights impact and Article 8* The 2020 study undertaken for the Commission's evaluation found 'little evidence' of any oversight or monitoring regarding the specific implementation of the API Directive by Member States and their compliance with data protection standards,[83] Observing that any monitoring of the use of API data as permitted under the regime of the API Directive in Member States has effectively been subsumed within post-legislative scrutiny of the PNR Directive.[84] This ongoing lack of adequate oversight is deeply problematic, particularly given the differences and overall unclear relationship between

[76] European Commission, Evaluation of API Directive (n 47) 13; ICF and Unisys (n 51) 8.
[77] ICF and Unisys (n 51); Vavoula (n 48).
[78] European Commission, Evaluation of API Directive (n 47) 13, 47.
[79] API Directive 2004/82/EC, Art 3(1).
[80] Vavoula (n 48) 53; European Commission, Evaluation of API Directive (n 47) 54.
[81] ICF and Unisys (n 51) 161–62.
[82] Directive (EU) 2016/680 of the European Parliament and of the Council of 27 April 2016 on the protection of natural persons with regard to the processing of personal data by competent authorities for the purposes of the prevention, investigation, detection or prosecution of criminal offences or the execution of criminal penalties, and on the free movement of such data, and repealing Council Framework Decision 2008/977/JHA [2016] OJ L119/89 (Law Enforcement Directive) (LED). See further Chapter 6.
[83] ICF and Unisys (n 51) 50.
[84] ibid.

the API Directive and the PNR Directive, their exact scope, data protection safeguards, and general operation. The Commission acknowledges these issues in its evaluation report of the API Directive in 2020. Indeed, as the Commission itself states, the vague scope and lack of limitations surrounding the use by Member States of API data for law enforcement purposes 'impairs clarity and foreseeability for data subjects and hence their right to the protection of personal data'.[85] The Commission notes the shared concerns expressed by representatives from the EU institutions that the API Directive, as a pre-Lisbon Treaty era instrument, falls short of the data protection requirements in more recently adopted EU instruments.[86] However, the Commission provides no assessment in this evaluation of the API Directive regarding its implications for the right to private life, as enshrined in Article 7 CFR (and Art 8 ECHR). Its legal analysis is notably silent on the compatibility of the API Directive with the leading data retention case law of the CJEU at the time of the report's compilation. There is no engagement with the requirements established in *Digital Rights Ireland*, *Tele2*, or even Opinion 1/15, the latter of which specifically deals with the retention and analysis of API and PNR data and Articles 7 and 8 CFR.[87] Instead, the Commission provides a far more general level of scrutiny, noting that national systems implementing the API Directive fall short of the storage limitation requirements of the LED, namely establishing 'appropriate time limits' for the erasure of personal data or for a periodic review of the need for the storage for personal data.[88]

(iii) *Lacking an evidence-based approach* In line with claims made by Member States, the European Commission concludes that the overall implementation of API systems has been 'effective' for border control, tackling irregular migration, terrorism, and serious crime.[89] However, the Commission later notes that this assessment is based on a scant amount of quantitative and qualitative evidence.[90] The study undertaken for the Commission's evaluation confirms that limited data was received from Member States regarding the number of persons refused entry or apprehended because of API data processing.[91] In other words, the Commission's evaluation of the API Directive's effectiveness and fundamental rights impact is mainly based on anecdotal case studies and lacks the support of

85 European Commission, Evaluation of API Directive (n 47) 47.

86 ibid 69. Indeed, it is observed in the evaluation that leaving such a wide margin of interpretation to Member States regarding the consistent implementation of the API Directive also raises questions regarding the adequacy of border control and security standards across the Schengen area.

87 Opinion 1/15 (n 14) [161].

88 European Commission, Evaluation of API Directive (n 47) 48; LED (n 82) Art 5. On the roles of the GDPR and LED within the context of migration, see Teresa Quintel, *Data Protection, Migration and Border Control* (Hart 2022).

89 European Commission, Evaluation of API Directive (n 47) 48, 54.

90 ibid 22, 52. On why quantitative data plays a key role in the oversight of automated decision-making systems in the public and private sectors since the 1960s, see generally Wiggins and Jones (n 19).

91 ICF and Unisys (n 51) 69.

any independently-verified quantitative statistics concerning the operation of API systems in each Member State. After over a decade of the API Directive's transposition deadline, the limited statistics provided by Member States to the Commission concerning its operation is striking. On the other hand, this limited evidence-gathering from Member States (and associated Schengen countries) was arguably inevitable given the lack of any legal requirement to do so in the API Directive.

2. The proposed PNR framework decision

(a) An 'obsolete' but influential proposal

Moves towards enacting a broader EU framework of data retention for both tracking and profiling passengers travelling within the EU began with a draft Council framework decision in 2007.[92] It is noteworthy that several key elements of the PNR Directive stem from this earlier proposal. Both regimes include: an extensive list of PNR data categories; calls for the decentralized collection of PNR data; and a key role for the national Passenger Information Unit (PIU) as a hub for the transfer, processing, and access of PNR data by public authorities.[93] However, in contrast to the PNR Directive which covers all flights to and from the EU for the aims of countering terrorism and serious crime, the scope of the framework decision was narrower in two key respects. First, it focused on harmonizing legal requirements for air carriers transferring PNR data concerning passengers on flights between the EU and third countries (extra-EU flights), thereby excluding intra-EU flights.[94] An exception to the latter being international flight stopovers within the EU. Secondly, the purposes for transferring such information were initially limited to combating terrorist offences and organized crime.[95] By 2009, its adoption by the Council of the EU was still pending. This transpired to be a critical deadline rendering the proposal 'obsolete' due to the entry into force of the Lisbon Treaty which replaced the previous system of EU lawmaking.[96]

(b) Insufficient safeguarding of rights and data protection

The demise of the proposed PNR framework decision can also be attributed to other key factors. First, doubts were cast over the compatibility of its legal basis

[92] Proposal for a Council Framework Decision on the use of Passenger Name Record (PNR) for law enforcement purposes, COM(2007) 654 final (Proposed PNR Framework Decision). See Evelien Brouwer, 'The EU Passenger Name Record System and Human Rights' (Working Document No 320, Centre for European Policy Studies 2009).

[93] Proposed PNR Framework Decision (n 92) Arts 3–8.

[94] ibid Art 2.

[95] ibid Art 1. The Council later proposed expanding the scope to the wider aims of countering terrorist offences and 'serious crime': Council doc 5618/2/09 REV 2, 29 June 2009, 6.

[96] PNR Directive (EU) 2016/681, recital 1. On the Lisbon Treaty and EU fundamental rights, see Chapter 4.

with EU law. This concerned the adoption of a 'third pillar measure' (a framework decision) despite the far-reaching private sector obligations envisaged for air carriers which then required a 'first pillar measure' (a Directive or Regulation).[97] Secondly, the proposal prompted extensive criticism for its compatibility with EU fundamental rights law from the European Parliament, the EU Fundamental Rights Agency (FRA), data protection authorities, civil society, and scholars. These focused on the proposal's broad scope, a lack of adequate safeguards for the envisaged profiling of passengers, and that the interferences with the rights to private life, data protection, and non-discrimination were simply not justified in terms of their necessity.[98] Member States also expressed reservations in Council negotiations on the framework decision, including the retention of innocent individuals' PNR data and the proposal's overall compliance with 'data protection and constitutional requirements'.[99] In sum, the legality and proportionality of the entire proposal faced widespread criticism. This included a broad list of uses for PNR data deemed incompatible with the rule of law test of foreseeability and a data retention period of thirteen years.[100] Data protection authorities were highly critical of the latter given the far more limited storage periods under similar EU laws.[101] Finally, concerns were raised regarding the proposed ability of governments to 'pull' data directly from air carriers and the lack of clarity surrounding the instrumental tasks played by PIUs in their analysis and transfer of PNR data.[102]

(c) Necessity of EU PNR regime questioned

Underpinning the waves of criticism of the draft PNR framework decision was its '*raison d'être*' and what added value would be gained by adopting this framework at the EU level.[103] The European Parliament, the FRA, and Article 29 Working Party

[97] Article 29 Working Party and Working Party on Police and Justice, 'Joint opinion on the proposal for a Council Framework Decision on the use of Passenger Name Record (PNR) for law enforcement purposes' (WP 145), 5 December 2007, 4.

[98] European Parliament, Resolution on the proposal for a Council framework decision on the use of Passenger Name Record (PNR) for law enforcement purposes, 20 November 2008 [2010] OJ C 16 E 44; Article 29 Working Party (WP 145) (n 97); EDPS, Opinion of 20 December 2007 on the Proposal for a Council Framework Decision on the use of Passenger name record (PNR) data for law enforcement purposes [2008] OJ C110/1; FRA, Opinion on the Proposal for a Council Framework Decision on the use of Passenger Name Record (PNR) data for law enforcement purposes, 28 October 2008; Brouwer (n 92) 18–28; Paul De Hert and Vagelis Papakonstantinou, 'The EU PNR Framework Decision Proposal' (2010) 26 Computer Law & Security Review 368, 374–76; Tzanou (n 19) 156–57; David Lowe, 'The European Union's Passenger Name Record Data Directive 2016/681' (2017) 17 International Criminal Law Review 78, 89.

[99] Council of the EU, 'Proposal for a Council Framework Decision on the use of Passenger Name Record (PNR) for law enforcement purposes', 5618/1/09 REV 1, 17 April 2009, para 5.

[100] Proposed PNR Framework Decision (n 92) Art 9.

[101] Article 29 Working Party (WP 145) (n 97) 9. The API Directive requires deletion of passenger data 24 hours after arrival. The Data Retention Directive required CSPs retain communications data for no more than two years.

[102] See European Parliament Resolution (n 98); EDPS (n 98) 23; Article 29 Working Party (WP 145) (n 97) 8.

[103] De Hert and Papakonstantinou (n 98) 375.

all highlighted the lack of evidence showing the impact to date of existing measures concerning data on individuals travelling to the EU from abroad including the API Directive.[104] The FRA also called for detailed reviews of the adequacy to date of the Visa Information System (VIS) and the then Schengen Information System (now SIS II).[105] These were timely criticisms in 2007 as only nine Member States had implemented the API Directive by 2006.[106] As data protection authorities rightly pointed out, this stark statistic already raised serious questions about the necessity of the API Directive itself and its rushed enactment.[107] The API Directive's lack of implementation by Member States understandably cast some doubt on the pressing need for more related measures, especially the far broader data collection regime proposed under this PNR regime.[108]

C. The PNR Directive (EU) 2016/681

1. Legal background

Despite the unaddressed legal issues surrounding the lapse of the proposed PNR framework decision, plans were announced soon after in 2010 that the European Commission was preparing a new EU PNR proposal. This initiative stemmed from the Stockholm Programme Action Plan to further develop EU data exchange systems for law enforcement purposes, forming part of an overall PNR 'package' which included the renegotiation of PNR transfer agreements with the US, Canada, and Australia.[109] Within the EU, however, the UK was the only Member State with an established PNR system at this time.[110] France, Denmark, Belgium, Sweden, and the Netherlands had either just enacted relevant legislation or were testing the use of PNR data in preparation for setting up PNR systems.[111] Thus, in contrast to the rise in bulk retention of PNR data by third countries, the status quo across most of the EU was the opposite. Member States were using PNR data for

[104] Article 29 Working Party (WP 145) (n 97) 6; European Parliament, Resolution (n 98); Opinion of the European Union Agency for Fundamental Rights on the Proposal for a Council Framework Decision on the Use of Passenger Name Record (PNR) data for law enforcement purposes (2008) 7.

[105] SIS II upgraded the SIS system by allowing border and law enforcement authorities to exchange information in real time across the EU from 2021. From a policing perspective, commentators view the UK's loss of access to SIS II as one of the most significant consequences of its departure from the EU. See Nora Ni Loideain, 'Brexit' in Eleni Kosta and Franziska Boehm (eds), *The Law Enforcement Directive: A Commentary* (OUP 2023).

[106] ICF and Unisys (n 51) 30.

[107] As observed by the WP29 (WP 145) (n 97) 6: 'If not even the value of API data can be proved how can the need for a vast amount of additional data be substantiated?'

[108] The Commission would only publish its first review of API Directive 2004/82/EC several years later in 2012.

[109] European Commission (n 17) 20.

[110] House of Lords (n 39) 21.

[111] European Commission (n 17) 20.

law enforcement on a case-by-case basis.[112] On the need to adopt an EU Directive in 2011, the Commission stressed again the need for harmonization across the EU. Allowing different approaches by Member States to process PNR for countering terrorism and serious crime would otherwise 'lead to inconsistencies, uncertainty and different rights for individuals'.[113] The Commission thus argued that an EU PNR Directive should be urgently adopted on the basis that the resulting harmonization would ensure a more uniform level of protection for individuals' personal data and human rights. It was also suggested that Member States were being disadvantaged by the absence of an expanded EU-level data retention regime of passenger information. And, if adopted, the reciprocity element of PNR transfer regimes with non-EU countries (US, Australia, and Canada) would be 'implemented more thoroughly'.[114]

Consistent with the lapsed PNR framework decision, significant concerns were again raised by the European Parliament, regulators, and scholars.[115] The Parliament's European Economic and Social Committee (EESC) expressed particularly strong reservations, effectively advising that the status quo should be allowed to continue with PNR data only being accessed by public authorities via PIUs on a case-by-case basis. The EESC further criticized provisions which conflicted with the data protection principle of purpose limitation and the absence of any monitoring requirement that would automatically record when public authorities accessed any PNR data or related data obtained from analysis.[116] Consequently, this proposal was put on pause when the Parliament Committee LIBE voted against it in 2013.[117] LIBE also called on other Members of the European Parliament (MEPs) to reject the proposal and for its withdrawal by the Commission.[118] The European Council and Council of the EU pushed back, maintaining that an EU PNR system was a priority throughout 2014 out of concern for threats to the security of the EU posed by 'foreign fighters' in Iraq and Syria.[119] It was not, however, until terrorist

[112] ibid.

[113] European Commission, PNR Directive Impact Assessment (n 47) 38.

[114] ibid 15.

[115] See eg Maria Tzanou, 'The War Against Terror and Transatlantic Information Sharing' (2015) 31 Utrecht Journal of International and European Law 87; FRA, Opinion 1/2011 on the Proposal for a Passenger Name Record (PNR) Directive, 14 June 2011, 4–5. For a contrary view that the PNR Directive is fit for purpose, see Cristina Blasi Casagran, 'The Future EU PNR System' (2015) 23 European Journal of Crime, Criminal Law, and Criminal Justice 241 and Lowe (n 98).

[116] European Parliament (EESC), Opinion on the Proposal for a Directive of the European Parliament and of the Council on the use of Passenger Name Record data for the prevention, detection, investigation and prosecution of terrorist offences and serious crime, COM(2011) 32 final [2011] OJ C 218/107.

[117] Far from a resounding majority, LIBE MEPs rejected the initial proposal thirty votes to twenty-five: European Parliament, 'Civil Liberties Committee rejects EU Passenger Name Record Proposal', 24 April 2013.

[118] European Parliament (LIBE), 'Report on the proposal for a directive of the European Parliament and of the Council on the use of Passenger Name Record data for the prevention, detection, investigation and prosecution of terrorist offences and serious crime', COM(2011) 0032, 29 April 2013.

[119] Council of the EU, 'The Challenge of foreign fighters and the EU's response', 9 October 2014.

attacks in Paris and Copenhagen in 2015 that the debate was reopened on the need to collect PNR data for monitoring travel to and within the EU for ensuring public safety.[120] This renewed impetus across the EU legislature is evident in the commitment made by the Parliament in 2015 to 'the finalisation of an EU PNR Directive by the end of the year'.[121] MEPs across Parliament made many amendments (over 800 by June 2015) to the Commission's initial proposal leading up to the second report presented by the LIBE rapporteur in September 2015.[122]

Major proposed changes included expanding the scope of the revised text to include intra-EU flights, allowing Europol access to the use and exchange of PNR data, and extending data retention obligations to also include 'non-carrier economic operators', such as travel agencies.[123] The Article 29 Working Party (WP29) acknowledged 'some improvements' in the revised text but stressed the necessity and proportionality for the entire measure still lacked evidence and thus justification.[124] The EDPS raised similar concerns, specifically advising that the dearth of available evidence justifying the untargeted and indiscriminate retention for five years of PNR data concerning millions of 'non-suspect passengers' cast doubt on its 'lawfulness and legitimacy'.[125] Nevertheless, the Parliament delivered on its commitment to finalize the revised proposal that year. The LIBE Committee, following further terrorist attacks in Paris in November 2015, also endorsed an agreed draft reached between the Parliament and Council in December 2015.[126] Thus, in a trifecta moment of truly contrasting measures, the PNR Directive was enacted in 2016,[127] the most far-reaching EU data retention law since the Data Retention

[120] BBC, 'Charlie Hebdo Attack' BBC News (14 January 2015); Chris Johnston, 'One dead and three injured in Copenhagen "terrorist attack"' *The Guardian* (14 February 2015).

[121] European Parliament, Resolution of 11 February 2015 on anti-terrorism measures, (2015/2530(RSP)) para 13.

[122] EU Counter-Terrorism Co-ordinator, 'Follow-up to the statement of the Members of the European Council of 12 February 2015 on counter terrorism', Council of the EU, 10 June 2015, <https://data.consilium.europa.eu/doc/document/ST-9422-2015-REV-1/en/pdf>.

[123] European Parliament, 'Second Report on the proposal for a directive of the European Parliament and of the Council on the use of Passenger Name Record data for the prevention, detection, investigation and prosecution of terrorist offences and serious crime', 7 September 2015, <https://europarl.europa.eu/doceo/document/A-8-2015-0248_EN.html>.

[124] Article 29 Working Party, 'Letter to LIBE Committee on EU PNR', 19 March 2015. Note that the Second Report text of the PNR proposal included a sunset clause, as previously called for by the Working Party.

[125] EDPS, Second Opinion on the Proposal for a PNR Directive, Opinion 5/2015, 7; EDPS, 'EDPS supports EU legislature on security but recommends rethinking on EU PNR', 10 December 2015.

[126] European Parliament, 'EU Passenger Name Record (PNR): Civil Liberties Committee backs EP/Council deal', 10 December 2015. The LIBE Committee voted by thirty-eight to nineteen. See Nick Beake, 'Brussels attacks: Trial begins over 2016 attacks that killed 32' BBC News (5 December 2022), <https://bbc.co.uk/news/world-europe-63834777>.

[127] European Parliament, 'Use of passenger name record (PNR) data for the prevention, detection, investigation and prosecution of terrorist offences and serious crime', 14 April 2016. Parliament adopted the final text by a considerable margin with 461 votes to 179 (nine abstentions). Note the latter may have been affected by the ISIS attacks in Brussels in March 2016 which were linked to the previous attacks in Paris.

Directive, alongside the EU data protection reform package of the GDPR and the LED.[128]

2. Main provisions

(a) PNR data

Article 3(5) of Directive 2016/681 describes PNR data as 'a record of each passenger's travel requirements' with Annex I providing that air carriers must collect no less than eighteen types of PNR data. This list includes any API data and further requires air carriers to include 'all historical changes' to the PNR listed in all eighteen sub-categories.[129] The wide-ranging scope of personal data covers a passenger's name; contact details, including email and mobile numbers; all payment information, including billing addresses; details of other passengers; and the general categories of 'frequent flyer information' and 'general remarks'. Based on a literal interpretation of the Directive, the latter categories are potentially very comprehensive. The scope for both is non-exhaustive and the PNR Directive provides no details regarding what constitutes frequent flyer information. Accordingly, there are no limits in the text of the Directive explicitly preventing the inclusion of traffic and location data from online purchases (flights, hotels, car rental) via use of frequent flyer programmes. The category of general remarks may also reveal sensitive personal characteristics, such as special dietary requirements (requesting a halal meal option) and health conditions/status (pregnancy). Their collection and transfer to a PIU thus runs the risk of 'discriminatory profiling' when being transferred from air carriers to public authorities for subsequent use and analysis.[130] The level of interference with the rights to private life, data protection, and non-discrimination posed by the bulk retention, use, and analysis of millions of passengers' PNR data for countering terrorism and serious crime under the PNR Directive is thus far from trivial.

(b) Scope and purposes

The PNR Directive provides for the transfer by air carriers of PNR data of passengers of extra-EU flights to public authorities, specifically a PIU in each Member State.[131] This scope extends to any subsequent processing of this PNR data by Member States, including its collection, use, and retention.[132] Member

[128] Giovanni Buttarelli, 'The EU GDPR as a Clarion Call for a New Global Digital Standard' (2016) 6 International Data Privacy Law 77; EDRi, 'Vote on Data Protection and Passenger Name Record package' Press release, 13 April 2016.

[129] PNR Directive (EU) 2016/681, Annex I.

[130] See FRA, Opinion 1/2011 (n 115) 20.

[131] PNR Directive (EU) 2016/681, Arts 1(1)(a), 4, and 6.

[132] ibid Arts 1(1)(b) and 7.

States via their PIUs may also exchange PNR data or results from their analysis to other Member States and third countries.[133] Any PNR data collected under the Directive may be used by competent authorities designated by each Member State, and Europol, for the aims of countering terrorist offences and serious crime.[134] The Directive also allows Member States to extend its scope to intra-EU flights for which Member States shall provide notification thereof to the Commission.[135] Moreover, subject to complying with EU law, the recitals advise that the Directive does not prevent Member States from establishing PNR systems under their national law which would collect and process PNR data from non-carrier economic operators, including travel agencies or other transportation providers.[136] In the long gestation period between the proposed PNR framework decision in 2007 to the enactment of the PNR Directive in 2016, the scope of this EU regime was significantly expanded. Noteworthy developments include Member States being permitted to apply the PNR system to intra-EU flights, the shift from its use for combating terrorist offences and organized crime to countering terrorism and the far wider area of 'serious crime', and granting Europol access to the PNR data (and analysis) from Member State PNR systems.[137]

By 2020, with one exception, all Member States had notified the Commission of their decision to extend the collection of PNR data to intra-EU flights.[138] Some Member States had also extended the application of the PNR system to other modes of transport on the basis of national law (maritime, rail, and road carriers).[139] Member States thus clearly embraced the discretion provided to them by the EU legislature to further expand the material scope and application of the Directive. Indeed, some Member States urged that the scope of the PNR Directive be expanded further still.[140]

(c) Passenger Information Unit (PIU): role and tasks

PIUs play an important and central role in the operation of the PNR Directive. Articles 6 to 11 of the PNR Directive set out the various purposes and circumstances by which a PIU in each Member State may process PNR data received from air carriers, which they do on behalf on competent national authorities and Europol, other Member States, and third countries, such as the UK. Such processing (mostly automated) includes carrying out general and indiscriminate

[133] ibid Arts 9 and 11.
[134] ibid Arts 1(2), 3, 6(2), and 10. These authorities include police, intelligence services, military, and financial services: European Commission, Staff Working Document (n 13) 12–13.
[135] PNR Directive (EU) 2016/681, Art 2.
[136] ibid recital 33. See further Art 19(3).
[137] ibid Art 10. On the offences falling within the scope of 'serious crime' for the purposes of the PNR Directive, see Art 3(9) and Annex II.
[138] European Commission, Staff Working Document (n 13) 37. See EU (Passenger Name Record Data) Regulations 2018 (SI No 177/2018) (Ireland), reg 3(a).
[139] European Commission, Staff Working Document (n 13).
[140] ibid 40–41.

assessments of millions of passengers in real time prior to their arrival or departure in a Member State to identify persons who 'may be involved' in a terrorist offence or serious crime. Article 6(3) states that PIUs may use databases 'relevant' to countering terrorism and serious crime (such as SIS II) and 'pre-determined criteria' when carrying out this profiling. Recital 7 of the Directive advises that the criteria used should be defined in a way 'which keeps to a minimum the number of innocent people wrongly identified by the system'. After a person's arrival or departure, PIUs may also be requested to provide and analyse PNR data on a case-by-case basis and provide any results to relevant public authorities for the aims of countering terrorism or serious crime. Article 6 provides that PIUs may use PNR data 'proactively' for the purpose of creating or updating any predetermined criteria for the real-time assessment of passengers prior to their arrival of departure from Member States.[141] The Commission notes that these criteria are otherwise known as 'targeting rules' or 'search criteria'.[142] Based on past and ongoing criminal investigations and intelligence, the Commission reported in its 2020 review of the PNR Directive that PIUs use this PNR data to filter out passengers and develop 'abstract profiles', with various factors informing such profiling, such as payment for travel in cash at short notice. The Commission stressed that the creating and updating of such predetermined criteria was 'still at an early stage of implementation in some Member States'.[143]

(d) Data retention and access

Article 12(1) of Directive 2016/681 permits a PIU to retain any PNR data concerning any passenger received from air carriers for up to five years following their transfer to the PIU of the Member State where the flight is arriving or departing. After an initial six months, Article 12(2) requires that the PNR data must be 'depersonalised' through the 'masking out' of certain elements which could directly identify the passenger to whom the PNR data relates. This masking covers: names of passengers; address and contact information; all payment information; frequent flyer information; general remarks that could directly identify passengers; and any API data. Article 12(2) provides, however, that a PIU may share full/repersonalized PNR data to national competent authorities (or Europol) after six months subject to two requirements. First, under Article 12 and Article 6(2), these disclosures are subject to the reasonable belief of PIUs that it is necessary to give these authorities access to the full PNR data in specific cases and where said authorities have submitted a 'duly reasoned request based on sufficient grounds' for the purposes

[141] ibid 11. Subject to the requirements of Art 6 of the Directive, the Commission notes that PNR data may be used 'proactively' for creating and updating predetermined criteria 'in real-time' to assess passengers prior to their arrival or departure, or 'reactively' when a PIU receives a 'duly reasoned request' from a Member State.

[142] ibid 40–41.

[143] ibid 12.

of countering terrorism and serious crime. Secondly, Article 12(3) leaves it to the discretion of Member States to determine whether a judicial authority 'or another national authority' verifies whether the disclosure requirements are satisfied. The Data Protection Officer (DPO) of the PIU must also be informed and is required to undertake a review of the request (after it has been granted). Article 4 provides that PIU staff may be seconded from authorities tasked with countering terrorism or serious crime.

(e) Data protection safeguards and automated decision-making

The PNR Directive, like the API Directive, relies on a decentralized system of data retention and processing. Unlike its older sibling, the PNR Directive also provides that Member States must adopt substantive safeguards that protect the personal data of passengers. Member States are required to ensure that passengers have the same right to data protection as provided under EU law and national law regarding any processing of personal data undertaken pursuant to the PNR Directive.[144] In order to safeguard against unfair discrimination, Article 13(4) also mandates that Member States 'prohibit the processing of PNR data revealing a person's race and ethnic origin, political opinions, religion or philosophical beliefs, trade union membership, health, sexual life or sexual orientation'. PIUs are also required to 'immediately' delete any such data sent to them from industry. In line with a similar provision under Article 22 GDPR concerning automated decision-making,[145] Article 6(5) of Directive 2016/681 provides an additional safeguard for enabling greater transparency and accountability of passenger profiling by PIUs. This requires Member States ensure that any positive match from the automated processing of passengers by a PIU to identify whether 'such persons may be involved in a terrorist offence or serious crime' prior to arrival or departure from a Member State is individually reviewed by a human ('non-automated means'). Article 6(5) states that this is to verify whether any further action by a competent authority is required, such as whether this identification provided by the automated system is accurate.

It should be noted that Article 12(5) allows for these 'negative matches' by any automated systems (as later identified by human oversight) to be stored for up to five years to 'avoid future "false" positive matches'. Thus, the PNR Directive allows Member States to retain and use records of negative matches to reduce the risk of passengers being unnecessarily detained or further monitored because they were incorrectly identified to have been involved in terrorism or serious crime ('a false positive'). Relatedly, Article 13(5) requires PIUs to document all processing.

144 PNR Directive (EU) 2016/681, Art 13(1).

145 On the risks of over-reliance on human oversight as a safeguard for AI-based systems and algorithmic decision-making, see Reuben Binns, 'Human Judgment in Algorithmic Loops' (2022) 16 Regulation & Governance 197; Ben Green, 'The Flaws of Policies Requiring Human Oversight of Government Algorithms' (2022) 45 Computer Law & Security Review.

This should include records of any positive matches by automated systems, the outcome of any subsequent human oversight, and any records of when PNR data, or its analysis, have been transmitted to public authorities, Europol, or a third country. Upon request, PIUs must provide this documentation to the DPA (Art 13(5)). Unfortunately, as discussed later, it is difficult to know how effective these safeguards were in practice as the Commission received limited statistical information from Member States for its 2020 review regarding the implementation into national law of these safeguards.

(f) Oversight and statistics

The PNR Directive requires Member States to establish various oversight mechanisms for their PNR regimes. In another welcome departure from the API Directive, these involve being subject to both internal and external forms of accountability at the EU and national levels. Under Article 15 of the PNR Directive, external and independent monitoring of the PNR system must be provided by a DPA in every Member State. Article 5 also requires that PIUs appoint a DPO. The DPO provides an essential system of internal oversight and is tasked with monitoring the implementation of all relevant safeguards concerning the processing of PNR data by the PIU. DPOs are not involved in determining the purpose of any PNR processing but may also be based within the same public authority of the PIU. Significantly, Article 6(7) provides that the DPO should have access to 'all data processed' by PIUs and may refer any issues of unlawful processing to the independent data protection regulator. DPOs are tasked with being a contact point for data subjects seeking to exercise their right to access and other data protection rights.[146] In line with the oversight standards in the GDPR and the LED, Article 5 of the PNR Directive provides that Member States must ensure that the DPO is adequately resourced to the extent that they operate 'effectively and independently'.[147]

Unlike the API Directive, Articles 19 and 20 of the PNR Directive required that its implementation by Member States was to be reviewed at the EU level. Following this review, the Commission is also to be provided with annual statistical evidence provided by each Member State. These statistics are required to cover 'as a minimum' the number of passengers whose PNR data has been collected and exchanged and the number of passengers identified for further examination.[148] Unfortunately, the Commission received limited statistical data from

[146] PNR Directive (EU) 2016/681, Arts 5(3) and 6(7). See generally Cecilia Alvarez Rigaudias and Alessandro Spina, 'Tasks of the Data Protection Officer' in Christopher Kuner and others (eds), *The EU General Data Protection Regulation: A Commentary* (OUP 2020) 709–15.

[147] GDPR 2016/679, Art 38(2), LED 2016/680, Art 33(2). The requirement to ensure adequate powers and resources is crucial if any oversight bodies are to be sufficient in carrying out their tasks. These 'competence' standards for surveillance oversight were established in Art 8 ECHR case law in the 1970s. See Chapter 2.

[148] Similar statistics were required for the Commission's evaluations of the GDPR, the LED, and the Data Retention Directive 2006/24/EC. See further Chapter 8.

Member States for its 2020 review thereby hindering the impact of this accountability mechanism at the EU level.

3. Pre-legislative scrutiny

(a) Fundamental rights impact and Article 8 ECHR

Debate on the need for a PNR system at the EU level for the aims of countering terrorism and serious crime had been taking place since 2007. This long gestation period did not prevent the PNR Directive during its drafting stages from being free from serious criticism in terms of its interference with the right to private life and other affected rights under EU law. Far from it. Nevertheless, compared with the limited human rights mainstreaming in the drafting of the API Directive, the *ex ante* scrutiny of the PNR Directive clearly shows a more developed culture of EU fundamental rights in the post-Lisbon era of EU policymaking and countering serious crime.[149] Indeed, in the Commission's Impact Assessment, one of the main justifications for adopting the Directive was to ensure the harmonized safeguarding of the 'rights of individuals living in the EU'.[150] The Commission stressed that an EU Directive could provide safeguards ensuring that passengers have access to enforce their rights and human oversight of any data processing, particularly if they are the subject of determinations made by automated decision-making.[151] Thus, the Commission explicitly recognized the importance of complying with the rights to private life and data protection as enshrined in the EU Charter and Article 8 ECHR.[152] Unlike the API Directive (which lacked any *ex ante* impact assessment), the PNR Directive also contains commitments to the rights to private life and other rights in its recitals, specific data protection safeguards, and several oversight mechanisms.[153]

Yet, while improvements in the mainstreaming of the right to private life are evident in the drafting and negotiations between the Parliament and the Council on the PNR Directive, concerns remained regarding its compatibility with the EU Charter and Article 8 ECHR. On the one hand, Article 13 requires that Member States ensure passengers have the same right to the protection of their personal data 'as laid down' in EU law. There is no mention, however, of the Charter or the ECHR in any of the legally binding provisions of the PNR Directive or regarding

[149] European Commission, 'Strategy for the effective implementation of the Charter of Fundamental Rights by the EU', COM (2010)573. On the rise of the Charter and its impact within EU policymaking, see Chapters 4–8.

[150] Commission, PNR Directive Impact Assessment (n 47) 17–18.

[151] ibid 25. On the legal challenges for redress posed by use of automated decision-making in EU laws concerning AFSJ, see generally Simona Demková, *Automated Decision-Making and Effective Remedies* (Elgar 2023).

[152] Commission, PNR Directive Impact Assessment (n 47) 19.

[153] PNR Directive (EU) 2016/681, recitals 15, 20, 28, 31, and 36.

Member States' compliance with the principles of legality and proportionality.[154] Instead, these requirements are limited to the recitals and *ex post* review by the Commission of the PNR Directive's implementation under Article 19. Although useful for understanding the context and aims of EU legislation, it is noteworthy that recitals have no binding legal force.[155] Findings from the Commission's *ex post* review, as noted later, also transpired to be strikingly deferential on fundamental rights scrutiny given the dearth of statistical information received from Member States on the actual implementation and impact of the PNR Directive in practice.

During the pre-legislative scrutiny of the PNR Directive, regulators for EU data protection and fundamental rights law pushed for the EU legislature to provide further clarification concerning three main safeguards.[156] First, that PIUs were not to process any sensitive data. Secondly, that there be an explicit requirement for any positive match from the profiling of passengers to be individually reviewed. Thirdly, regulators stressed that it be clearly understood that the PNR retention regime only provides for the 'masking' of data after six months not its anonymization. The crucial point being that anonymization would have been a more robust data security safeguard. Regulators also welcomed the addition of PIUs being required to appoint a DPO to enhance internal oversight.[157] These were, however, secondary concerns. Ultimately, these oversight bodies, and many in the European Parliament, consistently cast doubt on the overall compliance of the proposed Directive with the right to private life and the case law of the CJEU.[158] Strong reservations were expressed concerning the necessity of its lengthy retention regime. The proportionality of allowing Member States the discretion to expand the scope of the PNR Directive to require air carriers to collect and share with Member States (and Europol) not only PNR data from external flights to the EU but also PNR data concerning flights within the EU was also roundly criticized.[159]

In sum, the EDPS, FRA, and WP29 had consistently questioned the compatibility of the proposed PNR Directive since its inception with the legality and proportionality standards enshrined in Articles 7, 8, and 52(1) CFR and Article

[154] In contrast, Art 4 of the Data Retention Directive 2006/24/EC specifically required public authorities' access to data to comply with EU law and the ECHR. See further Chapter 6.

[155] Koen Lenaerts, Piet Van Nuffel, and Tim Corthaut, *EU Constitutional Law* (OUP 2021) 769. It is worth noting also that the CJEU has used recitals as important tools in its normative and expansive interpretation of EU law especially in its landmark case law on data protection. Thus, rendering certain recitals akin to legal requirements in waiting. See eg *Ligue des droits humains* (n 1) [205]–[207].

[156] EDPS, 'Opinion on the Proposal for a PNR Directive' [2011] OJ C181/24, paras 49–50; Article 29 Working Party, 'Opinion 10/2011 on the Proposal for a PNR Directive' (WP 181) 5 April 2011; FRA, Opinion 1/2011 (n 115); EDPS, Opinion 5/2015 (n 125) paras 62–66; FRA, Twelve operational fundamental rights considerations for law enforcement when processing PNR data' (March 2014) 3–4; FRA, 'Embedding fundamental rights in the security agenda' (01/2015) 11 February 2015; Article 29 Working Party,' Letter on EU PNR to LIBE Committee', 19 March 2015.

[157] EDPS, 'Opinion on the Proposal for a PNR Directive' (n 156).

[158] ibid.

[159] See Article 29 Working Party, 01/2015 (n 156); EDPS, Opinion 5/2015 (n 125); FRA, 01/2015 (n 156) 2.

8 ECHR. From 2014, these concerns focused on whether the proposed Directive complied with the standards established in *Digital Rights Ireland* which draw at length from Article 8 ECHR case law.[160] Before the Court delivered this landmark data retention judgment, the proposed EU PNR regime was being jointly scrutinized in light of its compliance with EU law and Article 8 ECHR.[161] Indeed, even after *Digital Rights Ireland* took centre stage in the rights review of EU data retention policymaking, EU institutions and regulators still cited Article 8 ECHR standards in their *ex ante* scrutiny of the proposed EU PNR regime.[162] Thus, as with the Data Retention Directive,[163] Article 8 ECHR played a clear role in the mainstreaming of the right to private life in the drafting of the PNR Directive, initially stemming from the ECHR legal order and then via the EU legal order, as a corresponding right to Article 7 CFR, and as a floor of minimum standards for EU data retention law as enshrined in Article 52(3) CFR.

(b) Lacking an evidence-based approach

The European Commission's Impact Assessment Board (now the Regulatory Scrutiny Board) advised in 2010 that although the impact assessment for the PNR Directive provided a 'sound basis for action', further clarity was required. More information was requested regarding its scope, the data retention periods, and 'examples' of how PNR data are an effective tool for combating terrorism and serious crime.[164] As the Commission rightly highlights, the five-year retention period put forward in the draft PNR Directive on the one hand marks a tangible departure from the retention period of thirteen years under the proposed PNR Framework Decision in 2007, the latter of which was highly criticized by regulators for its lack of proportionality.[165] On the other hand, the Board's overall support for an EU PNR Directive is surprising given the difficult implementation and incomplete evaluations at that time of two similar EU laws.[166] The Parliament and regulators had also criticized the lack of relevant examples showing that a general and indiscriminate retention regime of PNR data at the EU level would be an effective tool for countering terrorism and serious crime.[167] In particular, the FRA stressed

[160] See further Chapter 8.

[161] EDPS, 'Opinion on the Proposal for a PNR Directive' (n 156) para 10; FRA, Opinion 1/2011 (n 115) 11–14.

[162] See eg European Parliament, 'Second Report on Proposed PNR Directive' (n 123) 132 (citing the ECtHR Grand Chamber judgment of *S and Marper*); EDPS, Opinion 5/2015 (n 125) paras 11, 28, 31.

[163] See Chapter 6.

[164] European Commission, PNR Directive Impact Assessment (n 47) 7. On the Regulatory Scrutiny Board, see Roman Senninger and Jens Blom-Hansen, 'Meet the Critics' (2021) 15 Regulation and Governance 1436.

[165] European Commission, PNR Directive Impact Assessment (n 47) 7.

[166] On the issues with the API Directive, see earlier comments. On the Data Retention Directive, see Chapter 8.

[167] European Parliament, Resolution of 11 February 2011 (n 121); FRA Opinion 1/2011 (n 115) 22; EDPS, Opinion 5/2015 (n 125) 4.

that examples put forward by the Commission to justify the necessity of the PNR system only concerned 'serious transnational crimes'.[168]

The EDPS and FRA consequently advised that use of the proposed PNR Directive—if indeed enacted—should at least be limited to countering terrorism and serious transnational crime. The scope of these purposes should also be clearly defined in the PNR Directive.[169] Considerable concerns were additionally raised regarding the lack of evidence demonstrating the necessity for the five-year retention period and the EU legislature's decision to make the Directive applicable to intra-EU flights at the discretion of Member States. The EDPS further advised the EU legislature to address the prior weaknesses of the EU system of information sharing and data analysis before adopting the PNR Directive.[170] Thus, the PNR Directive's wide scope of application to the flights of millions of passengers, including a five-year retention period, continues an unremitting gap in the mainstreaming of the rights to private life and data protection in EU data retention policymaking. This is the absence of any *ex ante* independent statistical evidence demonstrating, or informing, the necessity and proportionality of adopting such data retention regimes at the EU level. The proportionality issues and lack of rights scrutiny are then left to be resolved in the *ex post* review of these EU laws by the Commission and (invariably) the CJEU.

4. Post-legislative scrutiny by the Commission

(a) A narrower scope of rights review

At first blush, Article 19 of the PNR Directive provides broad parameters for the European Commission's review of the Directive. These cover 'all elements' of the Directive's implementation and even allow the Commission to propose future reforms. Indeed, the Commission states in its two published review documents that it gathered information and feedback via 'a variety of sources'.[171] This additional information included targeted consultations with national law enforcement authorities, the travel industry, field visits to Member States, and a full analysis by an external contractor of the national laws transposing the Directive in twenty-three Member States.[172] The Commission's review also provides some anecdotal

[168] FRA, Opinion 1/2011 (n 115) 16–17.

[169] ibid 3; EDPS, Opinion 5/2015 (n 125) 15–16.

[170] 'EDPS supports EU legislature on security but recommends re-thinking on EU PNR', 10 December 2015.

[171] European Commission, PNR Directive Review Report (n 13) 2.

[172] ibid 5. Twenty-three Member States had notified full transposition by 19 June 2019. A full analysis of these laws was undertaken by an external contractor (Milieu Law and Policy Consulting) in time for the Commission's review. Denmark does not participate in measures proposed pursuant to Title V of Part Three TFEU, including the PNR Directive. Thus, 'Member States' should be understood as all EU Member States except Denmark. The UK was also bound by the PNR Directive until 31 January 2020.

examples from national authorities of when PNR data was used to combat terrorism and serious crime. It further emerges from the review that the Commission played a substantial role in assisting Member States with their implementation of the PNR Directive, providing €70 million for PNR-related activities to ensure PIUs developed the 'capabilities needed' to exchange PNR data and the results of PNR data processing with each other and Europol'.[173]

Article 19(2) of the Directive also required 'special attention' be given to reviewing five certain areas. These were data protection compliance; the necessity and proportionality of PNR data collection and processing for the Directive's purposes; length of the data retention; effectiveness of data exchange between Member States; and the quality of statistical information provided by Member States. Article 19(3) also tasked the Commission with assessing the 'necessity, proportionality, and effectiveness' of the controversial option provided to Member States to expand the scope of the Directive to intra-EU flights. Following this review, Article 19(4) states that the Commission shall 'if appropriate' propose amendments to the Directive as part of a legislative proposal to the European Parliament and the Council. Curiously, however, the information the Commission was required to consider when assessing the effectiveness of the Directive's data protection safeguards in practice was far narrower in scope when compared to its evaluations of similar EU laws. The Commission was specifically required to review the PNR Directive solely 'on the basis of information' from Member States.

Without context, this seems reasonable. As required under Article 20 of the PNR Directive, this included annual sets of statistical information provided from each Member State and the 'experience' of Member States. Indeed, in its evaluation of the Data Retention Directive 2006/24/EC, the Commission was also required to 'take into account' statistics and observations from Member States. However, the evaluation of the Data Retention Directive crucially involved the examination of other sources of information. The Commission was specifically required to examine 'all observations' from data protection regulators and to take account of technological developments.[174] The parameters of the PNR Directive review are also narrower than those for the GDPR and the LED. The Commission is required when reviewing the latter to consider the 'positions' and 'findings' of other EU institutions and bodies, such as the EDPS and FRA. The PNR Directive contains no such requirement.[175] This narrower scope of rights review, and thus more limited

[173] European Commission, PNR Directive Review Report (n 13) 3.

[174] For the evaluation of the Data Retention Directive, the Commission took account of reports from the WP29 in its assessment of Member State compliance with data protection requirements. See Chapter 8.

[175] GDPR, Art 97. LED, Art 62(4) provides: 'In carrying out the evaluations and reviews referred to ... the Commission shall take into account the positions and findings of the European Parliament, of the Council and of other relevant bodies or sources.'

scrutiny, of the PNR Directive is striking as these three EU laws were finalized over the same post-Lisbon Treaty era in 2016.

(b) Main findings

Twenty-four Member States notified the Commission of their full transposition of the PNR Directive into national law by the time of the review. It is not clear, though, from the Commission's review how many Member States met the actual transposition deadline of May 2018.[176] Of the five areas warranting special consideration in the review of the Directive, three received positive evaluations while two were found wanting. First, the Commission states that its review 'points to an overall compliance' with the data protection requirements of the PNR Directive,[177] acknowledging also that some national laws failed to 'fully mirror' the Directive's data protection requirements.[178] More detail is provided regarding examples of non-compliance in both review documents. For instance, contrary to Article 6(7) of the Directive, four Member States do not explicitly recognize in national law the competence of their DPOs to refer cases of unlawful processing to a national supervisory authority.[179]

When discussing the interferences with the rights to privacy and data protection posed by the PNR Directive, the Commission stresses at length that the Directive prohibits the processing of sensitive data.[180] It is welcome from a rule of law and rights perspective that the prohibition of PIUs processing sensitive data was fully transposed by all Member States, with two exceptions. Furthermore, all but one Member State required that any such data be immediately deleted and all Member States transposed the obligation to verify the matches resulting from automated processing. On the other hand, five Member States did not transpose the obligation that decisions of competent authorities must respect the principle of non-discrimination. Four Member States also failed to correctly transpose the prohibition on use of discriminatory predetermined criteria or criteria based on sensitive data. Relatedly, some national authorities explained that their IT systems are designed in a way to make the collection and processing of sensitive data 'technically impossible'.[181] The Commission thus concludes that since this data is not collected in practice this 'excludes the possibility' of predetermined criteria under the PNR regime being based on sensitive categories of personal data.[182]

Secondly, the Commission states that there are 'several elements confirming' the necessity and proportionality of PNR data collection and processing for the

[176] European Commission, PNR Review: Staff Working Document (n 13) 8–9.
[177] European Commission, PNR Directive Review Report (n 13) 5.
[178] ibid.
[179] European Commission, PNR Review: Staff Working Document (n 13) 17.
[180] European Commission, PNR Directive Review Report (n 13) 6–7; European Commission, PNR Review: Staff Working Document (n 13) 20, 27.
[181] European Commission, PNR Review: Staff Working Document (n 13) 20.
[182] ibid.

Directive's purposes and that the Directive 'has proven to be effective in achieving its aims'.[183] The Commission stresses that '[a]ccording to the Member States' the processing of PNR data provided for under the Directive has delivered 'tangible results in the fight against terrorism and crime'.[184] Member States are reported to have provided some qualitative evidence to this effect, which the Commission states 'illustrates how the comparison of PNR data against databases and pre-determined criteria has contributed to the identification of potential terrorists or persons involved in other serious criminal activities'.[185] It is not clear from the Commission's review which, or how many, Member States provided these case studies.

Thirdly, the Commission strongly advances the view that the retention of all passengers' PNR data for five years is necessary to achieve the objectives of the PNR Directive. This view is based on two main justifications. The PNR system relies both on the lengthy retention and indiscriminate and general scope of passenger data due to its nature as an intelligence tool for identifying 'known threats' and 'unknown risks'. The second justification is that the investigation and prosecution of terrorism offences and serious crime often involve years of work. The Commission adds that Member States confirmed the necessity of this five-year retention period based on their 'operational point of view'.[186] However, the review also highlights a number of areas of clear non-compliance by some Member States with the PNR Directive that cast doubt on its finding that the retention regimes in Member States has been proportionate. Four Member States failed to comply with the purpose limitation requirement in their transposition of the PNR Directive by extending its use for national security purposes.[187] Another two Member States did not explicitly limit the use of databases relevant for countering terrorism and serious crime for processing data from the PNR system in their national laws.[188]

Areas the Commission admitted were found wanting in its review of the PNR Directive's implementation concerned data exchanges between Member States and the lack of annual statistical information provided by Member States as required under Article 20. The Commission reports that data exchanges between Member States based on duly reasoned requests are operating effectively. However, the provision in the PNR Directive allowing PIUs to transfer PNR on their own initiative was less successful. Based on information provided by Member States, the Commission's review attributes the reluctance of law enforcement authorities to exchange PNR data without a duly reasoned request to its 'broad and relatively unclear formulation' under the Directive.[189] Article 20 of the Directive was

183 European Commission, PNR Directive Review Report (n 13) 6.
184 ibid.
185 ibid 7.
186 ibid 8.
187 European Commission, PNR Review: Staff Working Document (n 13) 15.
188 ibid.
189 European Commission, PNR Directive Review Report (n 13) 9.

the other special area which was reviewed less positively. It is noteworthy that the Commission does not reveal how many, or which, Member States contributed annual sets of statistics for 2018 and/or 2019.

Consequently, the Commission refers to the statistics received from Member States in a vague and general manner throughout its review.

What the Commission does make clear is that the statistics provided for its review of the PNR Directive were not 'fully standardised' and not 'amenable to hard quantitative analysis'.[190] The Commission explains that to address this gap it collected 'various types of evidence to establish a solid evidence base for the review'.[191] Based on these general statistics gathered for 2019, 0.59 per cent of all passengers whose data was collected were identified through automated processing as requiring further examination and an 'even smaller fraction of 0.11% was transmitted to competent authorities'. Based on statistics collected in 2018, these findings were 0.25 per cent for matches from automated processing and 0.04 per cent transferred to authorities following individual review.[192] Despite clear issues with the limited data collection from Member States, and the lack of transparency surrounding its analysis and the methodology applied by the Commission, the Commission still came to the following key conclusion in its review. Overall, the Commission found that 'PNR systems deliver targeted results which limit the degree of interference with the rights to privacy and the protection of personal data of the vast majority of bona fide travellers.'[193]

(c) A 'once-off review' lacking an evidence-based approach

The Commission states that its review shows 'several elements confirming' the necessity and proportionality of PNR data collection and processing for the PNR Directive's purposes and that the Directive 'has proven to be effective in achieving its aims'.[194] In support of these strong claims, the Commission explains that Member States provided 'qualitative evidence' illustrating how the comparison of PNR data against databases and predetermined criteria 'has contributed to the identification of potential terrorists or persons involved in other serious criminal activities'.[195] The Commission also points to five case studies provided by Member States using historical data in support of its arguments that the Directive's five-year retention period is necessary and proportionate.[196] Another key finding in the Commission's review is that the safeguards in the PNR Directive concerning access by the competent authorities to data stored by PIUs, and concerning the

[190] European Commission, PNR Review: Staff Working Document (n 13) 37.
[191] ibid.
[192] ibid, 28 and 36.
[193] ibid.
[194] European Commission, PNR Directive Review Report (n 13) 6.
[195] ibid 6–7.
[196] European Commission, PNR Review: Staff Working Document (n 13) 32–33.

depersonalization and repersonalization of data, have been 'shown to be sufficiently robust to prevent abuses'.[197] Despite the limited statistical information received by Member States, the Commission collected various types of evidence to establish a solid evidence base for these main findings.

The Commission notes that the lack of quantitative information on the PNR Directive's implementation was 'compounded by the relatively early stage of development' of most national PNR systems and coverage of data collection also varied across Member States.[198] This difficult challenge for the Commission's review inevitably raises key questions. What statistical information was in fact provided to the Commission in 2018 and 2019? How many Member States provided the Commission with any statistical information as required under the PNR Directive? Did most Member States provide the minimum statistical information on the total number of passengers whose PNR data was collected and exchanged and the number of passengers identified for further examination? How many passengers' PNR data were transferred to competent authorities in 2019? 0.11 per cent of what total number of passengers? As the EDPS and Advocate General rightly point out concerning the massive reach of the PNR Directive's 'non-targeted' scope, the EU's office for statistics (Eurostat) reported that over 1 billion passengers travelled by air across the EU in 2018 and 2019.[199] The Commission's review, however, does not provide any context for the real-world impact of the Directive, such as how many millions of passengers would have been subject to the collection of PNR data.

In sum, the Commission's review does not address these important questions.[200] The independent external report which examined the implementation of the PNR Directive by Member States, which would have informed the overall findings of the Commission's review, has also not been published. This external report was completed in September 2019 but has not (yet) been published.[201] Its inaccessibility years later is noteworthy as previous related external reports have been made publicly available alongside the Commission's review documents. This lack of transparency invariably casts doubt and uncertainty over the evidence underpinning the Commission's review of the PNR Directive and, by extension, its key findings. Consistent with its reviews of the API Directive and the Data Retention Directive, the Commission acknowledges again that its findings regarding the PNR Directive were not informed by quantitative evidence of adequate quality. The Commission's review of the PNR Directive's effectiveness

197 European Commission, PNR Directive Review Report (n 13) 8.

198 European Commission, PNR Review: Staff Working Document (n 13) 37.

199 EDPB, 'Letter to the European Commission on PNR Directive Review', 22 January 2021, <https://edpb.europa.eu/sites/default/files/files/file1/edpb_letteronreviewpnrdirective.pdf>; AG Pitruzzella (n 1) [80].

200 European Commission, PNR Review: Staff Working Document (n 13) 36–37.

201 ibid 3.

and fundamental rights impact in practice is instead mainly based on anecdotal case studies and general feedback from Member States, law enforcement, and industry. Thus, a more transparent and appropriate finding from the Commission regarding its assessment of Article 20 of the PNR Directive would have been to simply conclude that its review lacked 'a solid evidence base' due to the lack of statistics from Member States.

Its review, in other words, was effectively inconclusive and should not have been completed until further information from Member States had been provided regarding their implementation of the PNR Directive.[202] The Commission instead makes the confusing observation in its review that as PNR data is just one tool it is often not possible to draw conclusions on its effectiveness 'based solely on quantitative assessments' and it is 'often not possible to isolate the results attributable specifically to the use of PNR alone'.[203] The Commission then pivots away from questioning the importance of these statistics on the Directive's implementation and states that it will work closely with Member States to improve the quality of these statistics in future.[204] From the perspective of legal certainty, and the European Commission's role as guardian of the EU Treaties and the application of EU law,[205] the position ultimately adopted here is welcome. Indeed, subject to the EU legislature determining otherwise in future and amending the PNR Directive to this effect, Member States remain legally required to provide these statistics under Article 20 of the Directive concerning its compliance with proportionality and EU data protection law.

A problem arises, however, with this otherwise welcome commitment to this future *ex post* scrutiny of the PNR Directive at the EU level. Article 19(1) of the Directive only required the Commission to assess the quality of these statistics as part of 'once-off, non-repetitive review'.[206] This again departs from the more stringent *ex post* review clauses in the GDPR (Art 97) and the LED (Art 62) which require the Commission to provide reports by 2020 and 2022 and 'every four years' thereafter. The PNR Directive also included what is considered a 'lighter' review clause for EU legislation due to the short time frame between its transposition deadline in 2018 and its review in 2020 being less than three years.[207]

[202] There is precedent for the Commission to conduct these reviews in two parts. However, the second part of its *ex post* review of the Data Retention Directive was never published. See further Chapter 8.

[203] European Commission, PNR Review: Staff Working Document (n 13) 3.

[204] European Commission, PNR Directive Review Report (n 13) 9–10.

[205] EU, Consolidated Version of the Treaty of the European Union [2010] OJ C83/13 (TEU), Art 17.

[206] European Parliamentary Research Service, 'Review Clauses in EU Legislation adopted during Eighth Parliamentary Term (2014–2019)' (2022) 23.

[207] ibid 18. The European Parliament submitted an amendment to change the Commission's proposed review time frame from two years to 'four years' but this was not successful: Parliament, Second Report (n 123) 55.

(d) Fundamental rights and Article 8 ECHR

Three main issues arise from the Commission's review of the PNR Directive and its impact on the rights to private life and data protection enshrined in Articles 7 and 8 CFR and other affected rights, such as the right to non-discrimination under Article 21 CFR. First, despite contrary advice from the WP29, the Commission only treated certain standards established by the CJEU (sitting as the Grand Chamber) in Opinion 1/15 as relevant to its review of the PNR Directive.[208] The Commission, for instance, shares the Court's view that while PNR data may reveal very specific information regarding a person's private life, this intrusion is 'limited to certain aspects of private life'.[209] The Commission also points out that the Court took no issue with the provision in the Draft EU–Canada PNR Agreement allowing for the general and indiscriminate transfer of all air EU passengers' PNR data to Canadian public authorities for entry to Canada. The Court reasoned that excluding any categories (persons or origins) could prevent the aim of the automated processing of the PNR data to identify 'persons liable to present a risk to public security from amongst all air passengers'.[210] However, the Commission stressed that other standards established in Opinion 1/15, including limits on data retention, were not relevant to the PNR Directive and its aims.[211]

The Commission explains its approach to Opinion 1/15 based on the following grounds. First, in contrast to the Draft EU–Canada Agreement, the 'performance of border controls is not an aim of the PNR Directive' and EU Member States share responsibility for ensuring public security under the PNR Directive.[212] Secondly, the Commission rightly points out that the PNR Directive prohibits the processing of sensitive data. As the CJEU criticized in Opinion 1/15, this safeguard was missing from the Draft EU–Canada Agreement.[213] Thirdly, and perhaps most importantly, the Commission stresses that Opinion 1/15 concerns EU external policy on PNR and data transfers to a third country while the PNR Directive constitutes internal policy on PNR and the collection of passenger data from and to the EU by Member States.[214] Relatedly, the Commission notes that as an EU secondary law, the Directive falls within the EU *acquis*. This means that the PNR Directive is subject to additional guarantees not applicable to international agreements involving data transfers outside the EU. These extra safeguards include judicial oversight from the national courts of Member States and the CJEU. Furthermore, national

208 WP29, 'Letter to European Commission on PNR', 11 April 2018: <https://ec.europa.eu/newsroom/article29/document.cfm?action=display&doc_id=51023>.
209 European Commission, PNR Review: Staff Working Document (n 13) 26.
210 Opinion 1/15 (n 14) [186]–[189].
211 European Commission, PNR Review: Staff Working Document (n 13) 32.
212 ibid 32.
213 ibid 27.
214 ibid.

laws in Member States implementing the LED (and the safeguards therein) also apply to data processing in the EU under the PNR Directive.[215]

Legal challenges from Belgium and Germany concerning the PNR Directive's compatibility with EU law, pending before the CJEU at the time of the Commission's review, are thus briefly mentioned in the review but not examined in the light of Opinion 1/15.[216] Nevertheless, the Commission's inconsistent approach to the EU fundamental rights standards established in Opinion 1/15 is at best confusing and inconsistent. At worst, it could be argued that the Commission has negated its role as guardian of the EU Treaties by limiting its analysis to the more general standards in Opinion 1/15 and opting out of examining the compatibility of the PNR Directive with the more stringent proportionality standards established in Opinion 1/15. The latter being substantive requirements which indicate that the data retention and processing regime under the PNR Directive may not be compatible with the rights to private life and data protection as enshrined in the Charter. This ad hoc application of these standards is also suspect as Opinion 1/15 specifically deals with the retention and use of PNR data for countering terrorism (an aim of the PNR Directive) and when such processing may be incompatible with EU law and Article 8 ECHR.[217] Thus, the Commission's approach would have been more persuasive if none of the standards in Opinion 1/15 had been applied in its review of the PNR Directive, based on the reasoning—as argued by the Commission—that Opinion 1/15 only concerned EU external policy on PNR and not EU internal policy on PNR.

Secondly, the Commission does not address in its review any of the concerns raised by national data protection authorities regarding the implementation of the PNR Directive in Member States and its compatibility with EU law and Article 8 ECHR,[218] especially their doubts concerning the proportionality of using predetermined criteria and pattern matching across different databases for the abstract profiling of passengers.[219] The omission is striking given the Commission's role as guardian of the EU Treaties and thus EU fundamental rights law (Art 17 TEU). Moreover, the Commission states robustly in its review that 'it will not hesitate' to use its powers as guardian of the EU Treaties to launch infringement procedures to ensure Member States fully respect the requirements set out in the PNR Directive 'in particular on the protection of personal data'.[220] This commitment by

[215] ibid.

[216] ibid 6. European Commission, PNR Directive Review Report (n 13) 4. Slovenia also submitted a preliminary reference to the CJEU in 2020: see Case C-486/20.

[217] The European Parliament in its arguments to the CJEU, and the Grand Chamber itself, both cite and draw from Art 8 ECHR case law in this notable PNR ruling. See Opinion 1/15 (n 14) [39], [141].

[218] Federal Commissioner for Data Protection and Freedom of Information, 'BfDI Activity Report 2021 (Germany 2022)', 62–63; WP29, 11 April 2018 (n 208).

[219] Federal Commissioner for Data Protection and Freedom of Information ibid.

[220] European Commission, PNR Directive Review Report (n 13) 5.

the Commission to the protection of EU fundamental rights law in future is welcome. At the time of writing, the Commission had not yet used its powers for the purpose of addressing a Member State's non-compliance with said data protection requirements.[221]

The final issue is the Commission's lack of engagement in its review with the risks posed to the right to private life from the use of Big Data and 'machine learning' (ML) systems for the aims of the PNR Directive, particularly the capacity of these algorithmic systems to *infer* sensitive personal data when processing PNR data for profiling. Indeed, during the Commission's review of the Directive, EU regulators and scholars had clearly established that such inferences are one of the causes of discriminatory AI and require certain legal safeguards to be in place to counter these risks.[222] Without question, effective implementation of the Directive's requirement for PIUs to immediately delete any sensitive data in the vast volumes of PNR data received from airlines will help to reduce the risk of direct discrimination and discriminatory profiling. However, this is no silver bullet solution. ML systems are often leveraged to extract information to find relevant patterns, create profiles, and predict future behaviour of individuals or groups.[223] This is possible even if PIUs do not retain any sensitive data given the capacity of ML systems to infer this from other personal data. Even when protected characteristics 'are removed from the pool of available inputs, algorithms might select apparently unrelated but de facto correlated data points ("proxies") for prediction purposes ... this might still lead to [indirect] discriminatory outcomes'.[224] Most ML systems are designed to act as inference machines filling in the blanks. Thus, PNR data that fall within the scope of 'general remarks' as defined under the PNR Directive and that are processed by such systems may indirectly reveal sensitive personal data, such as a passenger's religion from their dietary requirements (a halal meal) or ethnicity from the postcode included in their payment details. This runs the risk of PNR data processing which should not be taking place, is not limited to what is strictly necessary, and is thereby incompatible with Articles 7 and 52(1) CFR.

221 ibid. Infringement proceedings were launched against a Member State for failing to meet the transposition deadline for the PNR Directive. Spain was referred to the CJEU in July 2020.

222 The review was published in July 2020. See eg Solon Barocas and Andrew D Selbst, 'Big Data's Disparate Impact' (2014) 104 California Law Review 671; EDPS, 'Opinion 7/2015: Meeting the challenges of big data', 19 November 2015; Lilian Edwards and Michael Veale, 'Slave to the Algorithm' (2017) 16 *Duke Law & Technology Review* 18, 27–30; Sandra Wachter and Brent Mittelstadt, 'On the Right to Reasonable Inferences' (2019) 2 Columbia Business Law Review 494.

223 Janneke Gerards and Raphaële Xenidis, *Algorithmic Discrimination in Europe* (Publications Office of EU 2021) 33–34.

224 ibid 51. See Chapter 1.

5. The judgment of the CJEU

(a) Context and main questions

A Belgian NGO, *Ligue des droits humains*, brought a challenge against the national law (Act of 25 December 2016) implementing the PNR Directive, the API Directive, and (partially) the Reporting Formalities for Ships Directive 2010/65. The NGO contested its compliance with EU law, particularly the EU Charter, the GDPR, and Article 8 ECHR, ultimately seeking full or partial annulment of the impugned national law. The Belgian Constitutional Court consequently referred ten questions to the CJEU in 2019 regarding whether this national law implementing the PNR Directive was compatible with EU law, particularly in the light of the standards previously established by the CJEU in Opinion 1/15.[225] Given the many issues addressed in this rich and lengthy judgment, this section examines the Court's analysis of the right to private life and the related requirements Member States must now meet to ensure their implementation of the PNR Directive complies with Articles 7, 8, and 52(1) CFR.[226]

(b) 'Undeniably serious interferences' with Articles 7 and 8 CFR

The Court draws frequently in *Ligue des droits humains* from its earlier jurisprudence in Opinion 1/15 when assessing the interferences with EU fundamental rights law entailed by the PNR Directive and the extent of their seriousness. As PNR data defined under the regime of the PNR Directive includes 'information on identified individuals', the Court makes clear that various forms of processing to which those data may be subject affect the right to respect for private life as enshrined in Article 7 CFR. The processing of this PNR data also falls within the scope of Article 8 CFR because it 'constitutes the processing of personal data within the meaning of that article'.[227] The Court proceeds to state, consistent with its settled case law, that the communication of personal data (in this instance PNR data) to a public authority constitutes an interference with the rights enshrined in Articles 7 and 8 CFR, as does their retention for the purpose of future access and use by public authorities. These interferences do not depend on whether the relevant 'information relating to private life is sensitive or whether the persons concerned have been inconvenienced in any way on account of that interference'.[228] This means that the transfer of PNR data by air carriers to the PIU of a Member State, its subsequent retention and use, and any further transfers to the competent

[225] *Ligue des droits humains* (n 1) [51]–[62]. Most of the referred questions concern Arts 7, 8, and 52(1) CFR.

[226] On the Court's analysis of other EU Charter rights, including non-discrimination, freedom of movement, and effective remedy as enshrined in Arts 21, 45, and 47 CFR, see Brouwer (n 1) and Janneke Gerards, 'Machine learning and profiling in the PNR system' *VerfBlog* (8 May 2023), <https://verfassungsblog.de/ml-pnr/>.

[227] *Ligue des droits humains* (n 1) [94]–[95].

[228] ibid [96].

authorities of that Member State, other Member States, Europol, or third countries, pursuant to the aims of the PNR Directive, constitute interferences with the rights enshrined in Articles 7 and 8 CFR.[229]

Following the analysis of the Advocate General, the Court gives weight to the same five factors in assessing the seriousness of these interferences. First, it is highlighted that the PNR Directive 'provides for the systematic and continuous transfer to the PIUs of PNR data relating to any air passenger on an extra-EU flight' (within the meaning of Art 3(2) of the Directive) operated between third countries and the EU; a transfer that involves general and full access, by the PIUs, to said PNR data 'concerning all the persons using air transport services, irrespective of subsequent use of those data'.[230] Secondly, the Court notes that Articles 2 and 3 of the Directive allow Member States to apply to extend the application of said Directive from extra-EU flights to intra-EU flights.[231] Thirdly, the Court stresses that when 'taken as a whole' the PNR data listed in the Directive 'may, inter alia, reveal a complete travel itinerary, travel habits, relationships existing between one or more persons and the financial situation of air passengers, their dietary habits or state of health, and may even reveal sensitive information about those passengers'.[232] Fourthly, the Court considers at length the provisions for profiling by PIUs permitted under Article 6 of the PNR Directive.

These allow for the processing of data transferred by air carriers to be used for the advance assessment of any passengers prior to their arrival and departure as well as their subsequent assessment. This advance assessment is carried out 'systematically and by automated means ... continuously and regardless of whether there is any indication that there is a risk that the person concerned is involved in terrorist offences or serious crime' and that their PNR data may be compared and processed against 'relevant databases' and 'predetermined criteria'.[233] The Court highlights, as previously held in Opinion 1/15, that the level of the interference entailed by the automated analysis of PNR data in respect of the rights enshrined in Articles 7 and 8 CFR 'essentially depends on the pre-determined models and criteria and on the databases on which that type of data processing is based'.[234] Relatedly, the Court states that the comparison of PNR data against these 'relevant databases' may provide additional information on the private lives of air passengers thereby allowing 'very precise conclusions to be drawn in that regard'.[235] The Court then recognizes that Article 6(4) of the PNR Directive requires that any assessment of PNR data against predetermined criteria when PIUs carry out

[229] ibid [97].
[230] ibid [98].
[231] ibid [99].
[232] ibid [100].
[233] ibid [101]–[102].
[234] ibid [103].
[235] ibid [104].

an assessment of passengers prior to their arrival or departure for the purposes of Article 6(2)(a) must be carried out in a non-discriminatory manner.

It must also be based on criteria that exclude specific types of personal data as set out in Article 6(4) and the criteria used by PIUs must be 'targeted, proportionate and specific'.[236] At the same time, the Court makes clear that as automated analysis of PNR data is carried out for the purposes permitted by Article 6 of the PNR Directive on the basis of 'unverified personal data', and predetermined models and criteria, 'they necessarily present some margin of error'.[237] The Court is keen to stress the reality of such errors, citing the Advocate General's Opinion that it is 'apparent' from the Commission's review of the PNR Directive that a 'fairly substantial' number of positive matches from automated processing proved to be incorrect following human review.[238] Following its approach in Opinion 1/15, the Court clearly considers the need for individual review by non-automated means of these profiling systems as significant, effectively treating the Advocate General's interpretation of the Commission's review of the PNR Directive as proof that this final (human) oversight of the processing operations 'lead to a careful analysis of the PNR data relating to the said persons'.[239] Regarding the subsequent assessment provided for in Articles 6 and 12 of the Directive, the Court notes that PIUs may be subject to requests from competent authorities to provide them with PNR data and analysis thereof in specific cases during the six months after the transfer of PNR data to PIUs. After that six-month period, subject to approval by 'a judicial authority or another [competent] national authority', PIUs may be required to disclose full PNR data that permits the identification of the data subject by the competent authorities in specific cases 'where it is reasonably believed that it is necessary' for the aims set out in Article 6(2) of the Directive.[240]

Fifthly, the Court is particularly critical of the retention limit of five years permitted under the regime of the PNR Directive. It pointedly observes that this element of the Directive makes it possible for information on the private life of air passengers to be available for a period of time already described by the Court as 'particularly long' in Opinion 1/15.[241] Combined with how commonly air transport services are used, the Court reasons that this long retention period under the Directive has the effect of 'a very large part' of the EU's population having their PNR data retained 'repeatedly'. Accordingly, this PNR data is liable to be accessed 'for analyses carried out in the context of advance and subsequent assessments by

[236] ibid [105].
[237] ibid [106].
[238] ibid [106]. As noted earlier, the weight given by the AG and the Grand Chamber to these statistics is unfortunate given the outstanding questions that surround their accuracy, robustness, and the fact that the Commission itself acknowledges that these findings were not the result of 'hard quantitative analysis'.
[239] ibid [106]. See Opinion 1/15 (n 14) [168]–[174].
[240] *Ligue des droits humains* (n 1) [107]–[108].
[241] ibid [109].

the PIU and competent authorities over a considerable—even indefinite—period of time' for those who travel by air more than once every five years.[242] The Court then concludes that the PNR Directive 'entails undeniably serious interferences' with the rights enshrined in Articles 7 and 8 CFR, describing it as a regime that seeks, inter alia, 'to introduce a surveillance regime that is continuous, untargeted and systematic, including the automated assessment of the personal data of everyone using air transport services'.[243] Furthermore, the Court highlights later in its judgment that the seriousness of these interferences stemming from the processing of PNR data from extra-EU and intra-EU flights under the regime of the Directive is 'even greater' when the application of that system covers other means of transport within the EU.[244]

Despite using the same five factors in their assessments of the interferences the PNR Directive entails to the rights to private life and data protection, the final determinations of the Court and the Advocate General diverge. The high threshold of 'undeniably serious' clearly departs from the advice (and main argument) in the Advocate General's detailed Opinion that the interference with private life entailed by the Directive is 'at least serious', on the basis that accessing PNR data is less intrusive than accessing the contents of communications or traffic and location data.[245] Accordingly, the Advocate General advised, at least in respect of the generalized and indiscriminate transfer of PNR data, the Court should continue to distance itself from 'the more rigorous approach' it has taken in relation to the retention of and access communications data.[246] These more robust determinations by the Court in its intrusiveness assessments of Articles 7 and 8 CFR would no doubt have raised different expectations regarding the ultimate fate of the PNR Directive and its validity under EU law.

However, it is evident from the analysis of the PNR Directive and its compatibility with Article 52(1) CFR later in the ruling that the Advocate General's main recommendation clearly resonated with the Court. History did not repeat itself in the form of the PNR Directive being struck down in its entirety as was the outcome for the Data Retention Directive in *Digital Rights Ireland*. The validity of the PNR Directive instead remains intact. Of course, this is subject to Member States making major reforms to their national laws which transposed the Directive by adopting the following standards that essentially amend most of the PNR Directive.

(c) Article 52(1) CFR: legality, essence, and objectives of general interest

Before assessing the requirements of legality, essence, and objectives of general interest, the Court reiterates its settled case law that the rights to private life and

[242] ibid [110].
[243] ibid [111].
[244] ibid [279].
[245] AG (n 1) [81], [205].
[246] ibid [195].

data protection are not absolute and must be considered 'in relation to their function in society'.[247] Article 52(1) CFR nevertheless requires that any limitation on the exercise of these rights 'must be provided for by law' and respect the essence of those rights. Article 52(1) CFR further provides that the principle of proportionality requires that any limitations to these rights must be necessary and genuinely meet objectives of general interest recognized by the EU or protect the rights and freedoms of others. Consistent with its landmark jurisprudence and the recent surveillance case law of the ECtHR, the CJEU's specific examination of the legality principle is brief.[248] This means that the crux and bulk of the Court's Article 52(1) CFR assessment in *Ligue des droits humains* is the PNR Directive's compliance with proportionality. Thus, the Court notes that the Directive is an act of EU law 'which permits interference with those rights, itself defines the scope of the limitation on the exercise of the rights concerned'. This includes a list of PNR data, the framework for the processing of PNR data, and the purposes and detailed rules governing those processing operations. Following its approach in *Schrems II*, the Court determines that as that question is 'largely the same' as that of compliance with the proportionality requirement, it will examine these safeguards as part of that analysis.[249]

In an equally brief assessment, the Court jointly examines the essence of the rights enshrined in Articles 7 and 8 CFR. The Court ultimately concludes, following its approach in Opinion 1/15, that the serious interferences entailed by the PNR Directive 'do not adversely affect the essence of these rights'.[250] This is based on three main grounds. First, the Court considers that the data covered by the PNR Directive 'do not by themselves allow for a full overview of the private life of a person' as the nature of the information revealed is limited to certain aspects of a person's private life, particularly that person's air travel and the Directive expressly prohibits the processing of certain categories of sensitive data by PIUs. Secondly, the Court notes that the Directive's provisions circumscribe the purposes for which PNR data are processed. This includes Annex II which defines what offences fall under the scope of serious crime. Thirdly, the PNR Directive (Arts 4–15) lays down the rules governing the transfer, processing, and retention of those data as well as 'the rules intended to ensure, *inter alia*, the security, confidentiality, and integrity of those data, and to protect them against unlawful access and processing'.[251]

247 *Ligue des droits humains* (n 1) [112].

248 On the surveillance and data retention case law of the ECtHR and the CJEU and their combined assessments of the legality and proportionality requirements, see Chapters 3–5.

249 *Ligue des droits humains* (n 1) [119]. This joint analysis approach follows the corresponding Art 8 ECHR case law of the ECtHR. It has also been criticized by leading human rights scholars. See Chapter 2.

250 *Ligue des droits humains* (n 1) [120]. Note the detailed analysis in the AG's Opinion which examines the essence of each right enshrined in Arts 7 and 8 CFR separately: AG Pitruzzella (n 1) [89]–[99].

251 *Ligue des droits humains* (n 1) [120].

The Court accepts that the objectives of combating terrorism and serious crime pursued by the PNR Directive 'undoubtedly' constitute objectives of general interest of the EU capable of justifying even serious interferences with the rights enshrined in Articles 7 and 8 CFR.[252] Furthermore, the Court establishes that the possibility of the system under the Directive producing 'false negatives' (flagging as irrelevant a person of interest) and even a 'fairly substantial number' of 'false positives' (incorrectly flagging a person to be of interest) 'are not capable ... of rendering the said system inappropriate for the purpose of contributing to the attainment of the objective of combating terrorist offences and serious crime'.[253] The Court arrives at this rather deferential determination on two grounds. First, the Court deems it 'apparent' from the Commission's review of the PNR Directive that automated processing carried out thereunder has 'already made it possible to identify air passengers presenting a risk in the context of the fight against terrorist offences and serious crime'.[254] Secondly, the Court highlights that the appropriateness of the system established under the PNR Directive essentially depends on the proper functioning of the subsequent verification of these automated results by 'non-automated means' by the PIU. It is then concluded that the human review 'provisions laid down to that effect' by the Directive contribute to the attainment of the objectives to combat terrorism and serious crime and thus appears to treat this non-automated review as a sufficient safeguard against inaccuracy and discrimination.[255]

These are significant developments for the CJEU's case law on EU data protection law and automated decision-making. At the same time, some scholars have rightly questioned the CJEU's heavy reliance on human intervention as a safeguard for countering unlawful discrimination within the PNR system. Human beings, of course, also being 'prone to stereotyped thinking'.[256] An additional *ex ante* safeguard, Gerards persuasively argues, would be for the Court to determine in future that ML systems may only be deployed if sound non-discrimination safeguards are built into the programming and training processes.[257]

(d) Article 52(1) CFR: limiting interferences to what is 'strictly necessary'

The Court in *Ligue des droits humains* frequently cites and applies the Article 52(1) CFR standards it established in Opinion 1/15 and its other landmark data retention case law when assessing the proportionality of the Belgian PNR law implementing

[252] ibid [122], [283].
[253] ibid [123].
[254] ibid [123]. Again, the weight given by both the AG and the Court to the Commission's review of the PNR Directive is unfortunate given the lack of any detailed statistical evidence provided by Member States and the lack of transparency underpinning the Commission's research methodology.
[255] *Ligue des droits humains* (n 1) [124]. See also on the review of predetermined criteria at [201].
[256] See eg Gerards (n 226).
[257] ibid.

the PNR Directive.[258] This proportionality requirement can only be satisfied if the following well-established standards are met. First, the relevant legislation entailing the interference 'must lay down clear and precise rules' governing the scope and application of the measures involved and impose 'minimum safeguards'. In particular, the legislation must indicate what circumstances and what conditions may permit such data processing to be adopted. This is to ensure that the persons whose data have been transferred have sufficient guarantees to 'effectively' protect their personal data against the risk of abuse, thereby ensuring that the interference is limited to what is strictly necessary.[259] Secondly, the Court stresses that the need for these safeguards is 'all the greater' where personal data is subject to automated processing. Thirdly, those considerations apply 'especially' where PNR data are liable to reveal 'sensitive passenger data'.[260] In applying these established standards, the Court closely scrutinizes the compatibility of the PNR Directive with the Charter to the extent that the Court's reinterpretation of this EU legislation in the light of Articles 7, 8, and 52(1) CFR renders the Directive beyond recognition. National PNR systems implemented across the EU based on the original text of the PNR Directive now require major reform by Member States if they are to conform with this stricter interpretation of the PNR Directive, and thereby comply with EU law.

(i) ***A more limited scope: PNR data and purposes to be read exhaustively*** The Court held that certain categories of PNR data read in the light of the Charter do not define for air carriers in 'a clear and precise manner' what PNR data they are required to provide to PIUs. This means that Member States are now required to adopt the 'clarifications' established by the Court if the interferences resulting from these categories in the PNR Directive are to be limited to what is strictly necessary.[261] For instance, the Court held that 'Frequent Flyer Information' must be interpreted as referring exclusively to data relating to the status of the passenger concerned in the context of a customer loyalty programme of a given airline, or a given group of airlines, as well as the number identifying that passenger as a 'frequent flyer'. The Court accordingly held that this heading does not require air carriers to provide to Member States the richer 'collection of information relating to transactions through which that status was acquired'.[262]

[258] *Ligue des droits humains* (n 1) [115]–[125], citing *La Quadrature du Net and Others*, Case C-140/20 *G.D.*, and Case C-207/16 *Ministerio Fiscal*. See further Chapter 5.

[259] *Ligue des droits humains* (n 1) [117].

[260] ibid. It is unclear why the Court has limited the heightened need of protection here to only 'sensitive passenger data' as a result of PNR data processing as opposed to the processing of 'sensitive data' in general under the PNR Directive. See Opinion 1/15 (n 14) [141].

[261] *Ligue des droits humains* (n 1) [125]–[140]. Headings 5, 6, 8, 12, and 18 require reform: address and contact information; all forms of payment information; frequent flyer information; general remarks; any API data collected.

[262] ibid [133]; Opinion 1/15 (n 14) [163]. The preliminary reference to the CJEU from Slovenia (C-486/20) also queried the lack of clarity in the PNR Directive surrounding the scope and collection of frequent flyer information and its compatibility with EU law.

Regarding the purposes of combating 'terrorism offences' and 'serious crime' that PNR data may be used for under the PNR Directive, the Court notes that Article 1(2), Article 3, and Annex II of the Directive define these offences in a clear and precise manner.[263] That said, the Court highlights that there are some 'very general' categories of offences in Annex II. The Court observes these may be still be 'regarded as meeting the requirements of clarity and precision' provided that they are interpreted as referring to terrorism offences or serious crime, as defined under the relevant national/EU law.[264] Thus, the Court points out that while serious crime is an aim capable of justifying the serious interference with the rights guaranteed in Articles 7 and 8 CFR which the PNR Directive entails, 'the same is not true of the objective of combating criminality in general'.[265] This means that the Directive must ensure, by means of clear and precise rules, that the application of the system established by the Directive is limited to offences amounting to serious crime.[266] The Court consequently held that Member States must ensure that their application of the PNR Directive 'is effectively limited to combating serious crime and ... does not extend to offences that amount to ordinary crime'.[267]

Relatedly on scope, the Belgian Constitutional Court sought clarification on whether the PNR Directive, read in the light of Articles 7, 8, and 52(1) CFR, must be interpreted as precluding national law which allows PNR data processed in accordance with the PNR Directive to be used for monitoring activities by the intelligence and security agencies. The CJEU responded affirmatively, noting that Article 1(2) of the Directive states that PNR data collected in accordance with that Directive may be processed 'only for the purposes of preventing, detecting, investigating and prosecuting terrorist offences and serious crime'.[268] Thus, the Court stresses that it is clear from the wording in Article 1(2) and Article 6(2) of the Directive that 'the list included therein of the objectives pursued by the processing of PNR data under the PNR Directive is exhaustive'.[269] The Court notes that monitoring activities within the remit of the intelligence and security services is one of the aims for which PNR data may be processed under the contested Belgian law. Consequently, the CJEU warns that this law 'is liable to disregard the exhaustive nature of the list of the objectives pursued by the processing of PNR data under the PNR Directive' and 'is a matter for the referring court to verify'.[270]

(ii) *Terrorist offences and serious crime must have an objective link with carriage of air passengers and limits on intra-EU flights* Despite acknowledging that the text of the PNR Directive 'does not expressly refer to a criterion' capable of

[263] *Ligue des droits humains* (n 1) [141]–[146].
[264] ibid [141]–[147]. This applies to the categories under 7, 8, 10, and 16 of Annex II.
[265] ibid [147].
[266] ibid [148].
[267] ibid [152].
[268] ibid [232].
[269] ibid [233].
[270] ibid [236].

confining its scope solely to offences that may have 'an objective link ... with air travel', the Court deftly advances an interpretation to the contrary.[271] It does so on the basis of reading Article 3 and Annex II of the Directive in the light of the requirements stemming from Articles 7, 8, and 52(1) CFR established in its previous case law. In reaching this determination which drastically limits the scope of the Directive, the Court also relies on observations made by the Advocate General and arguments by the Commission in 2011 on the need for an EU PNR Directive. The Court stresses that certain offences in Annex II of the Directive, such as human trafficking, are 'by their very nature, likely to have a direct link with the carriage of passengers by air' and that the 'same is true of certain terrorist offences, such as causing extensive destruction to a transport system'.[272] The Court then highlights that many of the examples cited by the Commission when justifying the need to adopt the PNR Directive 'concerned offences having a direct link with the carriage of passengers by air in that they were offences targeting the carriage of passengers by air as well as offences committed during or through travel by air'.[273] Thus, Member States must now ensure that the application of their PNR system relies on individual review by non-automated means as per Article 6(5) of the Directive, and is limited to terrorist offences and serious crime 'having an objective link, even if only an indirect one, with the carriage of passengers by air'.[274]

Consistent with Opinion 1/15, the Court found no proportionality issues arose from Member States being required by the PNR Directive to undertake the general and indiscriminate transfer and advance assessment of the PNR data of all air passengers entering or leaving the EU. The reasoning being 'the very nature of the threats to public security that may stem from terrorist offences and serious crime having an objective link, even if only an indirect one, with the carriage of passengers by air' between the EU and third countries (extra-EU flights).[275] However, the Court strongly criticized Article 2(1) of the PNR Directive which allows Member States to extend the application of their PNR systems to passengers flying between different EU Member States (intra-EU flights). The Court takes pains to highlight that the Directive did not make it mandatory for Member States to apply their PNR systems to all intra-EU flights. For instance, the Court stresses that the EU legislature had 'reserved its decision concerning such an extension' on the basis that the Commission was tasked by Article 19 of the Directive with reviewing the proportionality of including within the scope of the Directive the mandatory collection and transfer of PNR data of 'all or selected' intra-EU flights.[276] The Court then

[271] ibid [153].
[272] ibid [154].
[273] ibid [155]. The 9/11 terrorist attacks in the US in 2001 was one of these cases.
[274] ibid [156]–[157]. The Court stated that an indirect link includes when air transport is used as a means of preparing an offence or evading criminal prosecution after committing such offences.
[275] ibid [162].
[276] ibid [165].

clarifies that Member States' power to extend the application of the PNR Directive system to intra-EU flights, to all flights, or just selected flights 'is not exempt' from the requirement to verify that this extension is 'effectively necessary and proportionate' for attaining the objectives in Article 1(2) of the Directive.[277]

Citing various recitals, particularly recital 22, in support of this interpretation, the Court held that Member States must verify that PNR data processing of passengers of intra-EU flights or selected such flights 'is strictly necessary' having regard to the seriousness of the interference with the rights guaranteed in Articles 7 and 8 CFR.[278] The Court proceeds to lay out more prescriptive requirements for Member States. These mirror the detailed safeguards the Court established previously in Opinion 1/15 for the processing of passengers' PNR data by Canadian public authorities. First, any selection by Member States of intra-EU flights must be limited to the transfer and processing of PNR data relating 'inter alia, to certain routes or travel patterns or to certain airports' where there are 'indications' to justify the application of the system established by the PNR Directive in that Member State.[279] This selection must be based on the outcome of the above proportionality assessment Member States must carry out to verify that this processing of PNR data from intra-EU flights is strictly necessary. Member States must also 'review that assessment regularly in accordance with changes in the circumstances that justified their selection' to ensure that this application of the implemented PNR Directive system in that Member State 'continues to be limited to what is strictly necessary'.[280] Furthermore, the Court held that the API Directive (also part of the contested Belgian law) must be interpreted as not applying to intra-EU flights.[281]

It is important to note that the Court has established that exceptions may be made to these requirements with respect to threats related to terrorist offences. One of the key justifications for this carve-out is that 'it is of paramount interest for each Member State to prevent and punish those activities to protect the essential functions of the State and the fundamental interests of society in order to safeguard national security'.[282] Consistent with its data retention case law dealing with national security, the Court highlights why such threats are exceptional, observing that they are 'distinguishable, by their nature, their particular seriousness and the specific nature of the circumstances of which they are constituted, from the general and permanent risk of serious criminal offences being committed'.[283] Any encroachment by the Court in its data retention case law on what limits may be placed on national security matters for Member States remains highly controversial,

[277] ibid [168].
[278] ibid [167]–[169].
[279] ibid [174].
[280] ibid [174].
[281] ibid [269].
[282] ibid [170].
[283] ibid [170].

especially given its explicit prohibition from the scope of EU law in Article 4(2) TEU which states that 'national security remains the sole responsibility of each Member State'.[284] The Court encroaches again on this remit in *Ligue des droits humains*. Subject to certain safeguards, the Court held that the 'indiscriminate application' by a Member State of its implementation of the PNR Directive to all extra-EU flights and all intra-EU flights where that Member State is confronted with 'a genuine and present or foreseeable terrorist threat' falls within the limits of what is strictly necessary.[285]

(iii) *Safeguards and limits on automated processing and 'relevant databases'* The Court stresses the importance of the *ex ante* and *ex post* oversight provisions already within the PNR Directive for the automated processing of PNR data and establishes additional safeguards. Member States must thus ensure their national laws implementing this Directive meet these requirements if their laws are to comply with Articles 7, 8, and 21 CFR, and be within the limits of what is strictly necessary.[286] Regarding the advance assessment of PNR data under Article 6(2)(a) of the Directive, the Court notes that PIUs process this PNR data using automated means by comparing them against databases and predetermined criteria. The Court expresses its concern that this 'automated processing necessarily presents a fairly substantial margin of error, since it is carried out on the basis of unverified personal data and is based on pre-determined criteria'.[287] It 'must be ensured', the Court emphasizes, that any data transfer or decision by PIUs or competent authority that produces an adverse legal effect on a person, or significantly affects them, only happens after individual review by non-automated means.[288]

The Court then states the importance of the oversight powers of the DPO, national supervisory authority (DPA), and the national courts with respect to being able to review the 'lawfulness of all automated processing'.[289] Three new safeguards are then established. First, the DPA, the DPO, and the PIU must be provided with the 'resources necessary' to carry out their reviews under the Directive. It is welcome that the Court highlights the need here to ensure capacity for robust oversight by national DPAs of the PNR Directive as only Article 4(3) of the Directive expressly requires Member States to provide PIUs with adequate resources. Secondly, national legislation transposing the Directive must lay down 'clear and precise rules for the determination of databases and criteria for analysis used' and, thirdly, Member States cannot rely on methods not referred to in Article 6(2) for the purpose of advance assessment.[290] The Court proceeds to strongly criticize the

[284] See further Chapter 5.
[285] *Ligue des droits humains* (n 1) [170]–[173].
[286] ibid [213].
[287] ibid [177]–[178].
[288] ibid [179]. See the earlier discussion on Arts 6 and 7 of the PNR Directive.
[289] *Ligue des droits humains* (n 1) [179].
[290] ibid [180].

broad discretion afforded to Member States by Article 6(3)(a) of the PNR Directive regarding what exact databases could fall within the scope of 'databases relevant' for the advance assessment of passengers.

For instance, the Court explains that Article 6(3)(a) does not expressly indicate the 'nature of the data' in those databases or whether the PNR data must be compared exclusively against databases managed by public authorities or also against databases managed by private individuals.[291] Article 6(3)(a) could therefore lend itself to an interpretation whereby PNR data 'may be used as mere search criteria' for conducting analysis using various databases, including databases 'exploited by the security and intelligence agencies' of Member States to pursue objectives not provided for in the PNR Directive and also for 'data mining'.[292] The Court then states that the fact that such analyses could be conducted 'may give rise in the minds of passengers ... to the feeling that their private life is under a form of surveillance'.[293] Thus, the Court makes clear that this problematic interpretation cannot be adopted if Article 6(3)(a) is to be interpreted in a way that ensures 'full respect' for the rights enshrined in Articles 7 and 8 CFR. To do so would 'lead to a disproportionate use of those data' by providing the means of establishing a detailed profile of individuals solely because they intend to travel by air.[294]

The Court then puts forward an interpretation that effectively amends Article 6(3)(a). In the light of the obligation to comply with the requirements of clarity and precision necessary to ensure the protection of the rights enshrined in Articles 7 and 8 CFR, PIUs must limit the automated processing provided for in Article 6(3)(a) to databases identifiable therein. Accordingly, the 'only databases' against which a PIU may now compare PNR data under Article 6(3)(a) are 'databases on persons or objects sought or under alert, in accordance with [EU], international and national rules applicable to such databases'.[295] Additional safeguards are then established by the Court based on Opinion 1/15 and its retention case law on communications data that effectively amends Article 6(4) of the PNR Directive. Previously, Article 6(4) had only required Member States to ensure that any advance assessment of passengers under Article 6(2)(a) using 'pre-determined criteria' was carried out in 'a non-discriminatory manner' but now these requirements have been extended to apply to the comparison of relevant databases with PNR data. The Court explains that Article 6(4) must be interpreted in this way in the light of Articles 7, 8, and 21 CFR, especially 'since those requirements correspond, in essence, to those adopted by the case-law arising from Opinion 1/15' for the purposes of cross-checking PNR data against databases.[296]

[291] ibid [183].
[292] ibid [184].
[293] ibid [184].
[294] ibid [184]–[185].
[295] ibid [187]–[188].
[296] ibid [189].

In making this link, the Court specifically refers to its data retention judgment in *G.D.* and certain further requirements ('*inter alia*') that should form part of such databases of a non-discriminatory nature. First, any entry into the databases on persons sought or under alert must be 'based on objective and non-discriminatory factors, defined in EU, international and national rules applicable to such databases'.[297] Secondly, in order to satisfy the requirement of predetermined criteria being 'targeted, proportionate and of a specific nature', the relevant databases must be used in relation to the fight against terrorist offences and serious crime having an objective link, even if only an indirect one, with the carriage of passengers by air.[298] Thirdly, these databases must be managed by the competent authorities referred to Article 7 of the PNR Directive. Regarding EU and international databases, these must be exploited by those authorities in the context of 'their mission to combat terrorist offences and serious crime'[299] thereby prohibiting competent authorities from using these databases for other tasks that also fall within their remit, such as research or monitoring activities by intelligence agencies.

(iv) *Safeguards and limits on 'machine learning' and 'pre-determined criteria'* The Court states that processing of PNR data against predetermined criteria is intended 'to identify persons who may be involved in a terrorist offence or serious crime' and the criteria PIUs may use to that end should 'according to the very wording of Article 6(3)(b) ... must be "pre-determined"'.[300] In one of the most far-reaching standards on the use of ML systems and EU law more broadly, the Court then states that this 'precludes the use of artificial intelligence technology in self-learning systems ("machine learning"), capable of modifying without human intervention or review the assessment process'. This also includes 'the assessment criteria on which the result of the application of that process is based as well as the weighting of those criteria'.[301] The Court explains that 'use of such technology would be liable to render redundant the individual review of positive matches and monitoring of lawfulness' required by the PNR Directive. Moreover, the Court states that 'given the opacity which characterises the way in which artificial intelligence technology works, it might be impossible to understand the reason why a given program arrived at a positive match' which may also deprive data subjects of their right to an effective judicial remedy.[302] Based on Article 21 CFR, the Court then establishes that for predetermined criteria, Member States cannot use any criteria based on the characteristics referred to in Article 6(4) of the PNR Directive which could lead to 'direct and indirect discrimination'.[303]

[297] ibid [190].
[298] ibid [191].
[299] ibid [192].
[300] ibid [193]–[194].
[301] ibid [194].
[302] ibid [195].
[303] ibid [197].

On requirements relating to the targeted, proportionate, and specific nature of predetermined criteria, the Court states that criteria used for advance assessment 'must be determined in such a way as to target, specifically, individuals who might be reasonably suspected of involvement in terrorist offences or serious crime covered by that directive'.[304] In other words, the Court states that PIUs and competent authorities when undertaking this process referred to in Article 6(4) 'cannot, generally, rely on those characteristics'.[305] This is a significant amendment to the PNR Directive where it is difficult to understand how Member States will be able to undertake any targeted advance assessment of air passengers without relying on any of many characteristics listed in Article 6(4). Perhaps given these difficulties, the Court then suggests an alternative. Authorities may instead consider 'specific features in the factual conduct of persons when preparing and engaging in air travel which, following the findings of and experience acquired by the competent authorities, might suggest that the persons acting in that way may be involved in terrorist offences or serious crime'.[306] Member States must also ensure that the predetermined criteria 'must be defined in such a way' that takes into consideration '"incriminating" as well as "exonerating" circumstances'.[307] In a further amendment to Article 6(4) that explicitly draws from its data retention case law in *G.D.*, the Court states that the regular review of this criteria 'must be updated in accordance with changes in the circumstances that justified their being taken into consideration for the purposes of advance assessment'.[308] This review must also take into account 'the experience acquired in the context of the application of the predetermined criteria' in order to reduce false positives, thereby contributing to the 'strictly necessary nature' of applying those criteria.[309]

The Court proceeds to determine that all the above requirements for automated processing of PNR data that now form part of Article 6(4) of the PNR Directive also apply 'throughout the process of processing those data'.[310] This encompasses several new requirements under the PNR Directive for PIUs. For instance, PIUs must set the assessment criteria 'which keeps to a minimum the number of innocent people wrongly identified by the system established' by the PNR Directive 'in a non-discrimination manner'.[311] PIUs must also refrain from transferring results from those automated processing operations to relevant competent authorities should either of the following circumstances arise. First, where those results do not have 'anything capable of giving rise, to the requisite legal standard, to a reasonable

[304] ibid [198].
[305] ibid [199]. These concern 'a person's race or ethnic origin, political opinions, religion or philosophical beliefs, trade union membership, health, sexual life, or sexual orientation'.
[306] ibid [199] (citing an example from the German government).
[307] ibid [200].
[308] ibid [201].
[309] ibid [201].
[310] ibid [202].
[311] ibid [203].

suspicion of involvement in terrorist offences or serious crime in respect of the persons identified'. Secondly, the PIUs 'have reason to believe that those processing operations lead to discriminatory results'.[312] Member States must relatedly 'lay down clear and precise rules capable of providing guidance and support for the analysis carried out' by those in charge of the individual review and verification of such results within the PIU. The Court explains that this is necessary for 'ensuring full respect for the fundamental rights enshrined in Articles 7, 8 and 21 CFR, and to guarantee a uniform administrative practice within the PIU that observes the principle of non-discrimination'.[313]

(v) *Ensuring the 'lawfulness' of decisions and automated processing* New safeguards are established in *Ligue des droits humains* in relation to when authorities take decisions concerning a person based on PNR data analysis, as provided for under Article 7(6) of the PNR Directive. This includes the requirement that competent authorities must now 'ensure the lawfulness' of the automated processing, its 'non-discriminatory nature', and that of the individual review.[314] Consequently, the Court stresses that Member States must ensure that the person concerned 'is able to understand how those criteria and those programs work ... so that it is possible for that person to decide with full knowledge of the relevant facts whether or not to exercise his or her right to the judicial redress'.[315] The Court also establishes two important caveats to these new safeguards. The first concerns when the information is being sought. This means that during the 'administrative procedure' itself, the Court states that the authorities must provide this information 'without necessarily allowing that person ... to become aware of the pre-determined assessment criteria and programs applying those criteria'.[316]

In contrast, if seeking redress as provided for under Article 13(1) of the PNR Directive, both the person concerned and the court responsible for reviewing the legality of the decision adopted by the competent authorities must be allowed greater access to the above information. This extends to having the opportunity to examine 'all the grounds and the evidence on the basis of which the decision was taken ... including the pre-determined assessment criteria and the operation of the programs applying those criteria'.[317] Secondly, the CJEU makes clear that these requirements for when a person is exercising their right to seek redress do not apply in cases concerning 'threats to State security'.[318] Furthermore, the Court determines that in order to ensure the monitoring of the lawfulness of this automated processing (including its non-discriminatory nature), both the DPO and

312 ibid [204].
313 ibid [205].
314 ibid [209].
315 ibid [210].
316 ibid [210].
317 ibid [211].
318 ibid [211].

the national supervisory authority must have access to the predetermined criteria and the databases used by the PIU.[319]

Based on Member States meeting all the new requirements established in *Ligue des droits humains*, the CJEU determines that the provisions governing the advance assessment of PNR data under Article 6(2)(a) of the Directive 'lend themselves to an interpretation' that is consistent with Articles 7, 8, and 21 CFR and the limits of what is 'strictly necessary'.[320] It is noteworthy that the Court has established in these new proportionality requirements that the court and the concerned person should both be able to examine 'all the grounds and the evidence' on which the decision was taken under the PNR Directive at the redress stage, including the predetermined assessment criteria and its role in the contested decision. Indeed, as Brouwer rightly highlights, it is welcome that the Court is applying these procedural safeguards from its case law on immigration and thereby addressing the issue of what is effectively opaque decision-making, the latter of which arises when visa applicants are not informed about the precise reasons for a rejected application and where there is a clear parallel with the use of algorithms and automated decision-making systems under the PNR Directive.[321]

Though not acknowledged by the CJEU, there is a clear convergence here between the above standards and caveats and the long-established foreseeability safeguards under the case law of Article 8 ECHR, particularly, the importance of *ex post* oversight by an independent body and judicial review as a remedy where the data processing (or in this instance profiling) by public authorities is covert and involves automated processing.[322] Given the risks of misuse and abuse, these long-established rule of law standards in related Article 8 ECHR case law provide that the law must be sufficiently accessible and clear in its terms to give individuals an adequate indication to foresee the circumstances and the conditions in which authorities are empowered to resort to using a secret measure of surveillance. Of course, there cannot be full transparency due to the nature of law enforcement and border security. The ECtHR in recognition of this has made clear in its Article 8 ECHR case law that the meaning of foreseeability in the 'special context' of secret surveillance (and data processing) is different from many other fields. The level of detail provided cannot mean that individuals should be able to foresee when public authorities are likely to resort to such measures 'to the extent' that they could be rendered ineffective by allowing bad actors to adapt their conduct.[323]

Thus, striking this difficult balance between the above limits set by the CJEU on what factors PIUs may rely on in the use of predetermined criteria and ensuring

[319] ibid [212].
[320] ibid [213].
[321] Brouwer (n 1) 858–59. The CJEU cites various related immigration cases here, including Case C-300/11.
[322] See further Chapters 2 and 3.
[323] *Big Brother Watch and Others v United Kingdom* [2021] ECHR 439 [332]–[335] (GC).

the law is sufficiently foreseeable for individuals (before the redress stage) will be far from straightforward for Member States.[324]

(vi) ***The disclosure and subsequent assessment of PNR data*** Drawing on standards established in Opinion 1/15 and its case law dealing with the retention of communications data, stricter rules now apply to the subsequent disclosure and analysis of PNR data to competent authorities. The Court begins its review of this provision by highlighting that competent authorities may request PIUs in 'specific cases' to disclose PNR data, and its analysis, on a case-by-case basis under Article 6(2)(b) of the PNR Directive. As confirmed by the European Commission in response to a question from the Court on the matter, the Court points out that these requests could in practice be rather broad in scope as they may not be limited to the PNR data of 'a single air passenger' but could concern groups of individuals that 'share a certain number of characteristics'.[325] The Court then proceeds to clarify that such requests must now also reflect the revised and more limited scope of the PNR Directive. This includes the requirement that such PNR data may only be disclosed and analysed under Article 6(2)(b) in order 'to verify whether there are indications that the data subject may be involved in terrorist offences or serious crime having ... an objective link, even if only an indirect one, with the carriage of passengers by air'.[326] Relatedly, the Court specifies that the standard on which this access was previously granted no longer concerns 'a duly reasoned request based on sufficient grounds' from competent authorities to PIUs. Based on the PNR Directive 'being interpreted in the light of Articles 7 and 8 of the Charter', competent authorities must now meet the stricter standard for accessing this PNR data as established by the CJEU in its case law concerning the retention of communications data. Thus, competent authorities must now provide requests based on 'objective evidence capable of giving rise to a reasonable suspicion that the person concerned is involved in one way or another in serious crime having an objective link, even if only an indirect one, with the carriage of passengers by air'.[327]

The CJEU further ratches up the procedural requirements for Article 6(2)(b), stressing that it is 'essential' PNR data disclosure for the purposes of subsequent assessment be subject to a prior review carried out by a court or an independent administrative authority 'as a general rule'.[328] This effectively expands Article 12(3) of the PNR Directive which previously had only applied this requirement to requests for PNR data disclosure under Article 6(2)(b) if the PNR data in question had been retained beyond six months since its initial transfer to the PIU. The Court makes

[324] The ECtHR will also apply different foreseeability standards in cases concerning national security: ibid [370]. See further Chapters 2 and 3.

[325] *Ligue des droits humains* (n 1) [216].

[326] ibid [217].

[327] ibid [220]. Requests concerning terrorist offences are subject to a different standard.

[328] ibid [223]. Citing *G.D.* (n 2) and noting the exception for events of 'duly justified urgency'. The latter being a long-established standard in the related case law of the ECtHR. See Chapter 2.

clear that the requirement for prior review under Article 12(3)(b) 'must also apply, *mutatis mutandis*, where the request for disclosure is introduced before the expiry of that period'.[329] This requirement is particularly important, the Court explains, 'in order to ensure, in practice, fundamental rights are fully observed in the system put in place by the PNR Directive'.[330] These stricter standards represent yet another major realignment of the PNR Directive's provisions with those set previously by the CJEU in Opinion 1/15 and its landmark data retention law.

(vii) ***General and indiscriminate retention of PNR data: limited to six months*** On the referring court's question of whether the PNR Directive, read in the light of Articles 7, 8, and 52(1) CFR, must be interpreted as precluding national law which provides for the retention of PNR data for five years, without drawing any distinction based on whether the passengers concerned present a risk to public safety, the CJEU responds affirmatively. The Court establishes that the five-year retention regime under Article 12(1) of the Directive 'cannot be justified in the absence of an objective connection between that retention and the objectives pursued by that directive, namely the fight against terrorist offences and serious crime having an objective link, even if only an indirect one, with the carriage of passengers by air'.[331] Placing significant weight on recital 25 of the Directive and the intention of the EU legislature,[332] the Court explains that it is 'apparent' that 'a distinction must be drawn between' the initial retention period of six months in Article 12(2) and the later period in Article 12(3) of the Directive.[333] The Court then determines that the retention of the PNR data for six months of 'all air passengers' subject to the system established by the PNR Directive, without any indication as to their involvement in terrorist offences or serious crime, 'does not appear, as a matter of principle, to go beyond what is strictly necessary'.[334]

The Court's strikingly brief reasoning for this important assessment is based on two grounds. First, the 'aims' pursued by the PNR Directive. Secondly, 'the needs of the investigation and prosecution of terrorist offences and serious crime ... in so far as [the retention] allows the necessary searches to be carried out' for identifying those not suspected of involvement in terrorist offences or serious crime.[335]

329 *Ligue des droits humains* (n 1) [223]–[226].
330 ibid [223].
331 ibid [251] (emphasis added).
332 Recital 25 provides: 'The period during which PNR data are to be retained should be as long as is necessary for and proportionate to the purposes of preventing, detecting, investigating and prosecuting terrorist offences and serious crime. Because of the nature of the data and their uses, it is necessary that the PNR data be retained for a sufficiently long period to carry out analysis and for use in investigations. To avoid disproportionate use, after the initial retention period the PNR data should be depersonalised through masking out of data elements. To ensure the highest level of data protection, access to the full PNR data, which enable direct identification of the data subject, should be granted only under very strict and limited conditions after that initial period.'
333 *Ligue des droits humains* (n 1) [252]–[256].
334 ibid [255].
335 ibid [255].

Permitting the general and indiscriminate retention of PNR data by public authorities for six months affirms the earlier assessment of the CJEU in Opinion 1/15. Although it does not rely on the nature of PNR data as one its grounds for this determination, this standard clearly indicates that the CJEU views the bulk retention of PNR data as less intrusive to the rights to private life and data protection, and thus lower down its hierarchy of intrusiveness, than the bulk retention of traffic and location data. As the Court has stated elsewhere in *SpaceNet*, the latter enables more aspects of a person's private life to be revealed than PNR data due to its greater volume and variety. It thereby provides 'the means of establishing a profile of the person or persons concerned, information that is no less sensitive ... than the actual content of communications'.[336]

Building on similar concerns of five years being a 'particularly long' proposed retention period in Opinion 1/15, the Court is unequivocally critical of the five-year regime of general and indiscriminate retention provided for under the PNR Directive,[337] establishing that the continued storage of PNR data 'of all air passengers' after the initial six months is not limited to what is strictly necessary.[338] Drawing from its data retention case law, the Court stresses that this lengthier retention period runs counter to the proportionality requirement in recital 25 and allows for a 'significant quantity of data ... to be retained continuously' which 'entails an inherent risk of disproportionate use and abuse'.[339] The Court makes clear that this prohibition includes passengers who have not been subject to any of the following three situations. First, the advance assessment under Article 6(2)(a) of the PNR Directive. Secondly, any verification carried out during the period of six months referred to in Article 12(2) of the Directive. Thirdly, any other circumstance that has revealed the existence of objective evidence capable of establishing a risk that relates to terrorist offences or serious crime having an objective link, even if only an indirect one, with the carriage of passengers by air.[340] In a notably reluctant tone, the Court provides an example of where it 'seems permissible' for Member States to store a passenger's PNR data beyond this six-month period. This concerns specific cases where 'objective evidence ... is identified from which it may be inferred that certain passengers may present a risk that relates to terrorist offences or serious crime' such as 'the PNR data of passengers which gave rise to a verified positive match'.[341]

[336] *SpaceNet* (n 2) [87]. See further Chapter 5.

[337] Opinion 1/15 (n 14) [132]. The AG also expresses concerns regarding the risks to Arts 7 and 8 CFR posed by 'prolonged general retention' of personal data: AG (n 1) [243].

[338] *Ligue des droits humains* (n 1) [258].

[339] ibid [256], citing *La Quadrature du Net* (n 2).

[340] *Ligue des droits humains* (n 1) [262].

[341] ibid [259].

D. Conclusions and Looking Forward

1. The PNR Directive and landmark standards from the CJEU

It is perhaps unsurprising, given the above issues, that regulators, scholars, and Advocate General Pitruzzella all cast doubt on the European Commission's positive review of the PNR Directive and its compliance with EU law.[342] The CJEU reiterated many of these concerns in its highly critical and detailed assessment of the PNR Directive in *Ligue des droits humains*. This rich judgment established several important and novel standards for EU data retention law and the right to private life in EU policymaking in AFSJ more broadly. From the perspectives of the protection of EU fundamental rights, the rule of law, and evidence-based policymaking, it is welcome that the Court limited the scope of the PNR Directive in the following three ways.

First, establishing that the aims of countering terrorism and serious crime must have an objective link with the carriage of air passengers. Secondly, holding that the general and indiscriminate retention of PNR data for five years is disproportionate. Thirdly, limiting the application of the PNR Directive system to intra-EU flights. These changes closely reflect the evidence first put forward by the European Commission when it initially set out justifying the need to adopt the PNR Directive. Building on its standards from Opinion 1/15, the Court also scrutinizes the PNR regime's capacity for large-scale profiling and the use of automated decision-making and ML systems and the risks for unfair discrimination, as safeguarded against by Articles 7, 8, and 21 CFR. This increasing scrutiny by the Court in its data protection case law of such interferences posed by the automated processing of personal data, and of the rights affected in addition to private life, is welcome.[343] As scholars rightly highlight, these important standards have relevance beyond the PNR Directive and should be considered by the EU and Member States in other related areas of EU policymaking (such as the AI Act and the proposed CSAM Regulation).[344]

[342] EDPB, 22 January 2021 (n 199): Kuşkonmaz (n 1) 300. AG Pitruzzella specifically criticizes the Commission's review of the PNR Directive, particularly its proportionality examination: AG Opinion (n 1) [126].

[343] *Ligue des droits humains* (n 1) [88], [189], [197], [205], [213], [228]. The CJEU had highlighted (albeit briefly) the link between the processing of PNR data by public authorities, sensitive data, and the risks to Art 21 CFR in Opinion 1/15 (n 14) [165]–[167]. See generally Gerards (n 226).

[344] Brouwer (n 1) 861; Rotenberg (n 1) 434; Thönnes and Vavoula (n 1). On the proposed EU AI Act, see EDPB-EDPS Joint Opinion 5/2021; Michael Veale and Frederik Zuiderveen Borgesius, 'Demystifying the Draft EU Artificial Intelligence Act' (2021) 22 Computer Law Review International 97; Meeri Haataja and Joanna Bryson, 'The European Parliament's AI Regulation' (2023) 4 Amicus Curiae 707; Gianclaudio Malgeiri and Frank Pasquale, 'Licensing High-Risk Artificial Intelligence' (2023) 52 Computer Law & Security Review; Marco Almada and Anca Radu, 'The Brussels Side-Effect: How the EU AI Act Can Reduce the Global Reach of EU Policy' (2024) 25 German Law Journal 646. On the proposed controversial EU Regulation that aims to counter online Child Sexual Abuse Material (CSAM), see Chapter 1.

Thirdly, in a dramatic departure from previous related case law which surprised various scholars and commentators,[345] the PNR Directive was not unequivocally struck down for its lack of conformity with EU law. Based on their incompatibility with the EU Charter, the Court had previously struck down various related EU frameworks for arguably far less. These have included the Data Retention Directive in *Digital Rights Ireland*, the two invalidated adequacy agreements on EU–US data transfers in *Schrems I* and *Schrems II*, and the draft agreement on EU–Canada PNR data transfers in Opinion 1/15.[346] In *Ligue des droits humains*, the Court adopted a rather different approach. It did so by effectively identifying shortcomings for Member States to address in order to ensure their regimes implementing the PNR Directive are compatible with EU law. Moving away from the invalidation approach marks a clear departure from the CJEU's prior data retention case law. It also avoids the immediate legal vacuum left in the wake of *Digital Rights Ireland* which the Court, and the EU more widely, are still grappling with over a decade later.[347] Moreover, this jurisprudence shift indicates a move towards a more constructive dialogue with the Commission, Member States, and the national courts in its judgments dealing with EU data retention law and other State surveillance measures. It also brings the CJEU's approach closer in alignment with the more holistic 'shortcomings' approach of the ECtHR in its Article 8 ECHR judgments on data retention and bulk surveillance.[348]

However, a major divergence between the data privacy standards of both legal orders remains. The CJEU nevertheless retains its 'strict scrutiny' standards when examining interferences with the right to privacy unlike the more holistic and deferential approach of the ECtHR in its recent corresponding case law. The overall proportionality assessment in *Ligue des droits humains* raises three further important issues. The first of these concerns the inconsistency between the robust assessment of the seriousness of the interferences with Articles 7 and 8 CFR posed by the PNR Directive, and the later proportionality assessment involving the same under Article 52(1) CFR. The CJEU stresses at length early in its judgment that the different types of PNR data collected under the PNR Directive when 'taken as a whole' may reveal sensitive information about those passengers. In a robust approach that clearly goes beyond its view in Opinion 1/15, the Court then warns that the PNR Directive 'seeks to introduce a surveillance regime that is continuous, untargeted and systematic, including the automated assessment of the personal data of everyone using air transport services' and entails 'undeniably serious interferences' with Articles 7 and 8 CFR.[349] After this initial highly critical assessment

[345] See Rotenberg (n 1) 434.
[346] A third EU–US adequacy agreement under the GDPR (EU–US Data Privacy Framework) was adopted on 10 July 2023 to address the legal concerns raised in *Schrems II*.
[347] Brouwer (n 1) 840. See further Chapters 5 and 8.
[348] *Big Brother Watch v United Kingdom* [2021] ECHR 439 (GC). See further Chapters 2 and 3.
[349] *Ligue des droits humains* (n 1) [100]–[111].

of the Directive's interferences with affected passengers' rights to privacy and data protection, and the many limits imposed thereafter to its scope and profiling provisions, the permitted period of six months for the bulk retention of PNR data is firmly at odds with this robust analysis.

Secondly, the general and indiscriminate retention period of six months strikes a jarring note with the far stricter limits consistently applied by the CJEU concerning the bulk retention of traffic and location data for countering serious crimes. These include investigations of murder and rape for which no period of any duration is permitted for the indiscriminate and general retention of these specific types of communications data.[350] Other than six months being provided for in the text of the PNR Directive, the judgment is silent regarding why the retention of this 'significant quantity of data' suddenly falls within the scope of entailing 'an inherent risk of disproportionate use and abuse' when it goes beyond this initial six months. There is no clear reasoning that explains why this specific period of retention falls within the scope of what is 'strictly necessary' under the EU Charter. If the Court is to continue its quasi-policymaking role, as was the approach in *Ligue des droits humains*, there must be greater clarity and consistency surrounding its reasoning for introducing novel standards that have far-reaching implications in related areas of EU law (such as international data transfers).[351]

Thirdly, it would be welcome if the Court could provide greater clarity on the relationship between what constitutes 'appropriate' processing of personal data for the aims of countering terrorism and serious crime and the proportionality assessment under Article 52(1) CFR. This element of 'appropriateness' used to be part of the overall assessment of the proportionality principle in the Court's early data retention case law.[352] However, in more recent judgments, this requirement has been applied inconsistently. In Opinion 1/15 and *Ligue des droits humains*, 'appropriateness' has been examined separately thereby falling outside the proportionality assessment of Article 52(1) CFR.[353] There has been no explanation for this change which risks watering down the strict scrutiny approach of the Court in its assessment of Articles 7, 8, and 52(1) CFR. This gap is evident in *Ligue des droits humains* where the Court determines that the question of whether the system established by the PNR Directive is producing 'a fairly substantial number' of false positives falls under the assessment of whether this system is appropriate for the purpose of countering terrorism and serious crime. In other words, this could include evidence that a novel ML system (or other type of automated decision-making) is

[350] *G.D.* (n 2) [65]; *SpaceNet* (n 2). See Chapter 5.

[351] On the CJEU in the role of policymaker in its data retention case law, see further Chapter 5.

[352] See eg *Digital Rights Ireland* (n 2) [46]–[50]. This approach to the proportionality principle is also in the first line of Art 15(1) of the e-Privacy Directive 2002/58/EC: 'Member States may adopt legislative measures to restrict the scope of the rights and obligations provided for in ... this Directive when such restriction constitutes a necessary, *appropriate* and proportionate measure within a democratic society' (emphasis added).

[353] Opinion 1/15 (n 14) [152]; *Ligue des droits humains* (n 1) [121]–[124].

incorrectly and systematically identifying the same group(s) of people to be involved in terrorism or other serious crimes.

The Court states that while evidence of an algorithmic system producing many false positives is liable to limit the appropriateness of that system, 'it is not capable ... of rendering the said system inappropriate for the purpose of contributing to the attainment of the objective of combating terrorist offences and serious crime'.[354] It then concludes that the 'appropriateness' of the system established by the PNR 'essentially depends on' on just one safeguard, the verification of incorrect results by human review.[355] This general level of scrutiny is at odds with the long-established proportionality standards applicable to the use of automated processing of personal data under Article 8 ECHR and Article 7 CFR in the relevant case law of the ECtHR and the CJEU.[356] Indeed, as the CJEU has consistently held, the need for proportionality safeguards 'is all the greater where personal data is subjected to automated processing'.[357] Thus, it is submitted that the Court should in future assess—as part of its proportionality assessment in Article 52(1) CFR—whether a fair balance is being struck between the aims of countering terrorism and serious crime and evidence which shows the privacy and data protection rights of a particular group of individuals being disproportionately interfered with as a result of a fairly substantial number of false positives.

2. The API Directive and the right to private life: 'gaps' to be addressed

The API Directive 2004/82/EC, the PNR Directive's older problematic sibling, contains no specific requirements to respect or comply with fundamental rights law, as enshrined in the EU or ECHR legal systems. It is also silent on the right to private life. Alongside its rushed final drafting stages and general lack of engagement with the rule of law and other relevant human rights, the role of Article 8 ECHR and the right to private life in the shaping and pre-legislative scrutiny of the API Directive was non-existent. It is therefore evident from the limited pre-legislative scrutiny of the API Directive that a robust culture of EU fundamental rights during this pre-Lisbon era of EU policymaking in data protection and law enforcement was sorely lacking. Regarding the evaluation of the API Directive in 2020 and the mainstreaming of the right to private life, there is evidence of improved engagement with fundamental rights within the area of EU data protection law and countering serious crime. Passengers' rights to privacy and data

[354] *Ligue des droits humains* (n 1) [123].
[355] ibid [124]. In this instance, the Passenger Information Unit (PIU).
[356] See Chapters 2, 3, and 5.
[357] See eg *Ligue des droits humains* (n 1) [117].

protection are mentioned (albeit briefly) and the Commission shares the concerns expressed by representatives across the EU institutions and related EU bodies that the API Directive, as a pre-Lisbon Treaty era instrument, falls short of data protection requirements in the GDPR and LED. However, the Commission provides no assessment of the Directive's impacts for the right to private life as enshrined in Article 7 CFR. Its legal analysis is also notably silent on the compatibility of the API Directive with the leading data retention case law of the CJEU at the time of the report's compilation, including the Court's scrutiny of the Draft EU–Canada PNR Agreement in Opinion 1/15. This omission was particularly striking given that Opinion 1/15 deals specifically with the retention and analysis of API and PNR data and Articles 7 and 8 CFR. Indeed, the importance of the standards established by the Court in Opinion 1/15 for the protection of passengers' rights to private life and data protection were made resoundingly clear in *Ligue des droits humains*.

Prior to the CJEU's groundbreaking judgment in *Ligue des droits humains*, the European Commission had already acknowledged in its 2020 evaluation report that there are many legal and operational shortcomings within the API Directive. However, the Commission stopped short of making any clear and specific recommendations in terms of what actions the EU legislature should pursue to address these issues. As with the Data Retention Directive 2006/24/EC, the Commission deferred any meaningful assessment of the API Directive and PNR Directive's proportionality and compliance with Articles 7, 8, and 52(1) CFR to the CJEU. No doubt prompted by the then pending judgment by the Court, the Commission announced in May 2022 that it was preparing a 'new legislative initiative' that would address the 'gaps' apparent from its 2020 evaluation of the API Directive.[358] Following the CJEU's judgment on the PNR Directive and API Directive in June 2022, the Commission published not one but two draft Regulations to replace the API Directive, stating that the collection of API data under these proposed laws will apply the requirements and safeguards established in *Ligue des droits humains*.[359] Furthermore, the impact assessment for both proposals considers their impact for various EU fundamental rights including the right to private life, protection of personal data, freedom to conduct a business, and freedom of movement.[360]

Given the absence of any *ex ante* impact assessment for the API Directive 2004/82, these proposals show some welcome progress in the pre-legislative scrutiny of EU fundamental rights in the post-Lisbon Treaty era for EU data retention policymaking. The proposals also set the stage for how closely the requirements

358 European Commission, 'State of Schengen Report 2022', COM(2022) 301 final/2, 19.

359 European Commission, 'EU proposals to increase security and tackle serious crime', 13 December 2022, <https://home-affairs.ec.europa.eu/news/eu-proposals-increase-security-and-tackle-serious-crime-2022-12-13_en>.

360 European Commission, 'Impact Assessment Report', SWD(2022) 422 final, 34–41, <https://home-affairs.ec.europa.eu/proposal-regulation-collection-transfer-advance-passenger-information_en>.

stemming from Articles 7 and 8 CFR in *Ligue des droits humains* will shape the future of EU policymaking and data retention in the field of data protection law and AFSJ. At the time of writing, the proposed API Regulation on the collection and transfer of API for enhancing and facilitating external border controls had advanced to the negotiations stage of the trilogue process.[361]

3. A fundamental rights and evidence-based approach: achievements and challenges

The API Directive 2004/82 was adopted without any *ex ante* impact assessment by the European Commission. Alongside its rushed final drafting stages and general lack of engagement with the rule of law and other relevant human rights, the role of Article 8 ECHR and the right to private life in the shaping and pre-legislative scrutiny of the API Directive was also non-existent. This was not the case for the PNR Directive. The EU Charter, judgments of the CJEU, and Article 8 ECHR all played a role in the pre-legislative scrutiny of the first EU data retention law for countering serious crime enacted since the Data Retention Directive was struck down in *Digital Rights Ireland*. These post-Lisbon developments demonstrate clear and welcome progress in the protection of EU fundamental rights in an area of EU policymaking where the impact of data protection law had previously been lacking. That said, while there has been progress towards a more robust fundamental rights culture and the mainstreaming of the rights to private life and data protection across all stages of the legislative process, there have also been shortcomings. These gaps are particularly evident when it comes to the post-legislative evaluations and reviews of both the API Directive and PNR Directive.

The European Commission's reviews of how adequately and effectively these EU laws were implemented were both based on patchy and often limited amounts of qualitative and quantitative evidence. Despite highlighting many legal and operational gaps, the Commission ultimately concluded that the overall implementation of the API Directive has been effective for border control, tackling irregular migration, terrorism, and serious crime. This review of the PNR Directive's implementation by Member States produced three key problems for the effective mainstreaming of the right to private life, despite being drafted, implemented, and reviewed all in the post-Lisbon era. First, there was a stark lack of statistical evidence from Member States supporting the Commission's overall positive assessment of the PNR Directive. Secondly, the Commission adopted a highly pragmatic approach when examining the PNR Directive's compliance with the rights enshrined in Articles 7 and 8 CFR. Thirdly, Article 19 of the PNR Directive required that it would only be subject to a one-off evaluation and an overall 'lighter' review

[361] See further European Parliament, 'Revision of API Directive', 2022/0424(COD).

process. The limited evidence gathered for the review of the API Directive was arguably inevitable given the lack of any legal requirement for Member States to collect such information. However, even where such transparency and statistics are explicitly required in EU laws for the purpose of post-legislative scrutiny, such as the PNR Directive, it is still a challenge for the European Commission to acquire this evidence in practice.

The fact that this remains an ongoing challenge indicates that EU policymaking in this area is falling short of the Lisbon Treaty's goal for the EU to be operating within a robust fundamental rights culture.[362] Three main issues underpin this challenge. First, there is a general gap in the capacity for evidence-based policing in certain Member States. This comprises various factors, including the nature of specific 'national technology ecosystems' and the ever-growing role of the private sector in acquiring, collecting, and analysing data for law enforcement and intelligence agencies.[363] There is also the factor of delays in the provision of statistics by more 'digitally-advanced' Member States whose public authorities lack the necessary budget and resources for this data-gathering.[364] In addition, there is the systemic inability by many Member States to meet the transposition deadlines of EU laws adopted for the purposes of countering terrorism and serious crime.[365] Furthermore, Member States are only required to provide very basic statistics on the operation and impact of these EU information systems. Even the minimum level of information required under the PNR Directive, for instance, does not mandate Member States to provide statistics on where individuals, or particular groups, have been incorrectly identified and/or subject to unlawful profiling, detention, or arrest.[366] Finally, as Eckes rightly notes, the lack of focus on ensuring more effective information sharing between the EU institutions and Member States is even more entrenched when it comes to EU counter-terrorism measures.[367] The lack of comprehensive and comparable statistics in this specific area of EU law and policymaking is compounded by two further factors. These concerns national agencies' culturally ingrained reluctance to share statistics on

[362] See generally Fay Kartner and Anne Meuwese, 'Responsiveness Towards Fundamental Rights Impacts in the Preparation of EU Legislation' in Janneke Gerards and Eva Brems (eds), *Procedural Review in European Fundamental Rights Cases* (CUP 2017) 95–123.

[363] Anu Bradford, *Digital Empires* (OUP 2023) 142. See further Chapter 1.

[364] ibid. This is also a major issue for the regulation and oversight of policing elsewhere (including the US). See Sarah Brayne, *Predict and Surveil* (OUP 2020) 17–36.

[365] Indeed, as the case studies in this book show, several Member States failed to meet the transposition deadlines for the Data Retention Directive (see Chapter 8) and the PNR Directive. Only nine met the transposition deadline for the API Directive. Another related example is the EU Counter-Terrorism Directive (EU) 2017/541, adopted without an impact assessment on grounds of urgency. However, only seven Member States met its transposition deadline in 2018. See European Commission, 'Report on Directive (EU) 2017/541', COM(2020) 619 final.

[366] See PNR Directive (EU) 2016/681, Art 20(2).

[367] Christina Eckes, *EU Counter-Terrorism Policies and Fundamental Rights* (OUP 2009) 68–71. On the link between the long-term effectiveness of national security measures with international law, see Sophie Duroy, *The Regulation of Intelligence Activities under International Law* (Elgar 2023).

policing, and intelligence on terrorist threats and attacks for beyond internal use, and the fact that Member States often adopt different counter-terrorism policies at the national level.[368]

This ongoing evidence gap is deeply problematic for the protection of EU fundamental rights in this area of EU policymaking. These statistics are vital for assessing not just the effectiveness of adopting these data retention measures at the EU level for protecting public safety but also their fundamental rights impacts. As the FRA points out, this scrutiny is 'crucial' for monitoring and detecting when and why a person has been negatively affected by these systems without justification.[369] While recognizing the limits of quantitative statistics, the lack of *any* detailed robust evidence-gathering clearly hinders the EU legislature's ability to assess the actual effectiveness of these measures' key aims for enhancing the security and fundamental rights protection of individuals across the EU. The combination of this systemic evidence gap, the Commission's general approach to its scrutiny of the rights impacts of these EU laws, and deferral of any proportionality issues for the review of the CJEU all amount to systematic weaknesses in the protection of human rights law within EU data retention policymaking. These gaps in the current system render it impossible to measure the effectiveness of these public safety measures and any non-compliance with the right to private life and other related fundamental rights. Consistent with the *ex post* reviews and legislative fall-outs of the e-Privacy and Data Retention Directives, these findings also show that the European Commission has fallen short in its role as guardian of EU fundamental rights with respect to the API and PNR Directives.

4. Enabling a fundamental rights culture in EU data retention policymaking

Monitoring and thereby enabling the compatibility of EU law with EU fundamental rights is a crucial part of the European Commission's role as guardian of the EU Treaties, a role which thereby clearly applies to the pre- and post-legislative stages of EU data retention law and its implementation by Member States. The Commission's role is distinct but complementary to that of the CJEU, the ultimate arbiter of EU law. Since the elevation of the EU Charter of Fundamental Rights to the status of EU law, the Commission has consistently made clear its commitment to promote a fundamental rights culture across all stages of the legislative

[368] Eckes (n 367) 70. Eg although the UK has collected statistics on the use of counter-terrorism law since the 1970s, publication and consistent collection of this data was paused during a critical period in the use of such powers, namely the post-9/11 era between 2001 and 2008: Grahame Allen, Matthew Burton, and Alison Pratt, *Terrorism in Great Britain* (House of Commons Library 2022) 5.

[369] FRA, Opinion 1/2011 (n 115) 21.

process and provide 'a truly mainstreamed approach to fundamental rights'.[370] The EU legislature (Council and Parliament) have also promised that they would promote EU fundamental rights as a 'priority' for future measures adopted at the EU level to counter terrorism and serious crime (AFSJ).[371] By ensuring that this rights scrutiny occurs across the drafting, implementation, and evaluation of these laws, such as the Data Retention Directive and PNR Directive, it is not then solely a matter for the CJEU to review. However, this chapter and others have shown that there are systematic weaknesses in the mainstreaming of the fundamental rights to private life and data protection, as enshrined in Articles 7 and 8 CFR, within EU data retention policymaking, shortcomings which have directly contributed to the CJEU adopting a role of de facto lawmaker.[372] Some of these issues could be addressed by the EU legislature and European Commission through the following recommendations.

The European Commission has placed considerable focus in its policy strategies for strengthening a fundamental rights culture within the EU on its role in the mainstreaming of the EU Charter at the pre-legislative stages of AFSJ proposals and their compliance with fundamental rights. Less attention has been given in these policies, however, to addressing the systemic challenges that have arisen as a result of the evidence gaps, and the limited engagement with relevant rights standards from CJEU case law, in the evaluations of these EU laws regarding their adequate and effective implementation by Member States. In order to address the ongoing evidence gap and lack of rights scrutiny, as noted earlier, the FRA should be given a greater role in assisting and supporting the Commission with the pre- and post-legislative scrutiny of any current and future AFSJ proposals involving any digital or data-driven technologies, including data retention measures. Indeed, as the Commission has itself highlighted, the FRA 'has developed into a trusted EU body providing comparable data and analysis on fundamental rights to support the work of the EU institutions and the Member States'.[373] The FRA already as part of its mandate collects and analyses comparable, objective, and reliable information relevant to developing and implementing policies on fundamental rights and provides independent evidence-based advice to policymakers. Moreover, Members of the European Commission have commended the FRA on the opinions it has provided concerning EU criminal justice proposals that have highlighted key rights issues and for the support it provides the Commission in its evidence-based policymaking on rights.[374]

[370] European Commission (n 11); European Commission, 'Strategy to strengthen the application of the Charter of Fundamental Rights in the EU', COM(2020) 711 final, 15–16.

[371] ibid.

[372] On the role of the CJEU and its jurisprudence on Art 7 CFR and EU data retention law, see Chapter 5.

[373] European Commission (n 370) 1–2.

[374] See Salla Saastamoinen, 'FRA's Policy Impact and Future Posture' in Rosemary Byrne and Han Entzinger (eds), *Human Rights Law and Evidence-Based Policy* (Routledge 2019) ch 4. Specific examples include the FRA opinions on: the draft Directive for a European Investigation Order (EIO) in

In providing a greater role in assisting and supporting the Commission with the pre- and post-legislative scrutiny of any current and future AFSJ proposals in highly sensitive rights areas, including data retention, the FRA should be tasked with two key responsibilities. First, the FRA could lead and undertake a Fundamental Rights Impact Assessment (FRIA) of any such proposals.[375] The FRA would undertake this FRIA at both the proposal stage and later at the review and evaluation stage following the implementation of the relevant EU law by Member States. These FRIAs would inform the Commission's overall impact assessment process at both the *ex ante* and *ex post* legislative stages. Secondly, again in line with their existing mandate, the FRIA could lead and coordinate the collection and analysis of statistical information gathered by Member States concerning their implementation of any relevant EU law.[376] Adequate funding and resources would be required for these new responsibilities and the FRA would also be in a much clearer and better position than previously to fulfil its dual mandate as an advisory and monitoring body for EU fundamental rights. The FRA is already primarily tasked with providing 'assistance and expertise' to the EU legislature and Member States relating to fully respect fundamental rights when they implement EU law.[377] However, scholars have raised serious concerns that its lack of resources, restricted mandate, and the ambiguity surrounding its dual functions as an advisory and monitoring body hinder its ability to carry out this role in practice.[378] This proposed change is in line with the intention of the EU legislature that following the entry into force of the Treaty of Lisbon, 'the Agency's scope should also cover police cooperation and judicial cooperation in criminal matters, areas which are particularly sensitive with regard to fundamental rights'.[379]

2011; the proposal to establish a European Public Prosecutor's Office in 2014; and on the exchange of information on third country nationals under a possible system to complement the European Criminal Records Information System in 2015.

[375] On the scope of definitions of FRIAs, see Regulation (EU) 2024/1689 of the European Parliament and of the Council of 13 June 2024 laying down harmonised rules on artificial intelligence and amending Regulations (EC) No 300/2008, (EU) No 167/2013, (EU) No 168/2013, (EU) 2018/858, (EU) 2018/1139 and (EU) 2019/2144 and Directives 2014/90/EU, (EU) 2016/797 and (EU) 2020/1828 (Artificial Intelligence Act) [2024] OJ L1/144, Art 27.

[376] In line with the FRA's scope to collect data provided directly from Member States, there is no issue of compatibility with Art 258 TFEU as the European Commission is ultimately tasked with reviewing the data and analysis provided by the FRA concerning the implementation by a Member State of any EU data retention law. See Council Regulation (EC) No 168/2007, Arts 3–4, as amended by Council Regulation (EU) 2022/555 of 5 April 2022 amending Regulation (EC) No 168/2007 establishing a European Union Agency for Fundamental Rights [2022] OJ L108/1, Art 1.

[377] Council Regulation (EU) 2022/555, Art 1.

[378] See Jan Wouters and Michal Ovádek, *EU Law and Human Rights* (OUP 2021) 44–53; Gráinne de Búrca, 'The Evolution of EU Human Rights Law' in Paul Craig and Gráinne de Búrca, *The Evolution of EU Law* (3rd edn, OUP 2021) 494–95. On the origins and mandate of the FRA, see generally Byrne and Entzinger (n 374).

[379] Council Regulation (EU) 2022/555, recital 3. The independent evaluation of the FRA also made the recommendation that its legal framework should be amended to explicitly state that the Agency's remit should cover the area of police and judicial cooperation in criminal matters 'in order to meet the

Two further changes would also address the above weaknesses in the mainstreaming of the right to private life in this area of EU data retention policymaking. First, specific funding, guidance, and training should be provided to Member States to develop and support their capacity for evidence-gathering. This is essential to clearly explain and justify the necessity and proportionality of measures being adopted at the EU level. Making EU fundamental rights a meaningful priority with respect to the effective implementation of AFSJ measures invariably means providing financial support or related resources. The sum of €70 million was provided for PNR-related activities to ensure PIUs developed the 'capabilities needed' to exchange PNR data and the results of PNR data processing with each other and Europol. The same level of support should be provided to Member States for the capacity building that is needed for demonstrating their compliance of these implemented EU systems with EU fundamental rights. Finally, there should be greater consistency regarding the *ex post* scrutiny requirements of these laws in EU legislation with respect to their review and evaluation. It is unclear, for instance, why such a controversial legislative proposal like the PNR Directive was only subject to a once-off and comparatively lighter review when compared with the far more stringent *ex post* review clauses in the GDPR and the LED.

These above measures would help to address the EU legislature's current lack of capacity to assess the actual necessity and effectiveness of these measures' key aims for enhancing the security and fundamental rights protection of individuals across the EU. Indeed, without being able to evaluate the impact of similar EU laws to date, it is difficult to understand how the EU can measure the extent to which these measures are countering terrorism and serious crime and where reforms may be necessary, while at the same time ensuring full respect of EU fundamental rights. As the European Commission notes, failing the latter may 'undermine the sense of security without which persons cannot exercise their freedom and individual rights effectively'.[380] In any event, retention, access, and analysis of passengers' travel data for the aims of countering terrorism and serious crime is likely to remain one of the most dynamic and technically complex areas of privacy and data protection law within EU law.

needs of stakeholders at the national and EU level'. See 2nd Independent Evaluation of the European Union Agency for Fundamental Rights (31 October 2017) 7, <https://fra.europa.eu/sites/default/files/fra_uploads/2nd-fra-external-evaluation-october-2017_en.pdf>.

[380] European Commission, 'Impact Assessment: Proposal for a European Parliament and Council Directive on the use of Passenger Name Record data for the prevention, detection, investigation, and prosecution of terrorist offences and serious crime', SEC(2011) 132 final, 8.

Index

For the benefit of digital users, indexed terms that span two pages (e.g., 52–53) may, on occasion, appear on only one of those pages.